NYMPHS

NYMPHS

by ERNEST SCHWIEBERT

A Complete Guide to Naturals and Their Imitations

Illustrated by the Author

WINCHESTER PRESS
An Imprint of *NEW WIN PUBLISHING, INC.*

All illustrations are four times life size, except as noted

Printing code
12 13
Library of Congress Catalog Number: 82-62597

ISBN 0-8329-0340-X
Printed in the United States

Introduction

THIS book has grown slowly over several years. Its painstaking period of gestation has triggered countless jokes among friends, since it has been evolving for about a decade. The painting and writing have occupied only thirty months but, in a sense, its roots are the same as those which started *Matching the Hatch*—the boyhood summers on the jackpine creeks and storied rivers of lower Michigan thirty years ago.

It has been twenty years since Jack Case sought me out on a college campus to inquire about an unpublished manuscript on fly-hatches. Case had detoured from his duties as a college textbook editor to pursue rumors about my work on trout-stream entomology, and we agreed to meet at the Faculty Club. Case was a scholarly man with steel-rimmed glasses and worn tweeds. His thin face was deeply lined and grave, but behind his usual gravity was a wry sense of humor; there was an austere sense of quality and craftsmanship too. His mood could have a biting edge when he felt a writer was working below his capability, and Case was the kind of man who demanded impossible standards of the people he loved. His rumpled appearance and erudition had its roots at Williams College in Massachusetts; years of editing in a cluttered office a few blocks above Washington Square had added both insight and a patina of absent-mindedness that echoed his care-and-feeding of college professors. His chain-smoking and a strong liking for a fine cognac revealed facets in his character more suited to the city room of a major newspaper. Case loved trout fishing too, and returned each summer on a pilgrimage to boyhood rivers near his cottage in northern Michigan.

We met in the foyer of the Faculty Club, and I was struck at once with both his warmth and his frailty. We shook hands and went inside, and he sat over a brandy and soda studying me.

You're younger than I thought, he said finally.

Yes. It was the winter of my sophomore year. *But I've had the chance to fish a lot the last ten years.*

Case lit another cigarette. *Where?* He asked.

Michigan and Wisconsin, I said. *Colorado and Wyoming and Montana out West, Catskills and Adirondacks—and in Europe too.*

Case smiled owlishly. *You still seem young,* he said.

Maybe I'm not ready to write this book, I began suddenly. *Maybe I should wait a few years.*

Case spent a few minutes riffling the draft manuscript, pausing here and there to read various passages. He smoked a half-dozen Camels while he worked through the roughly-typed pages, holding the cigarettes deep in the corner of his mouth. His frown was almost hidden in the drifting smoke, and finally he looked up.

Write it now, he said.

It was a warm and friendly lunch. Case rummaged through a weathered briefcase for a box of elegantly dressed dry flies with parachute hackles and extended bodies.

What do you think of them? he asked.

You tied them? It was obvious from the animation in his tired face and twinkling eyes. *They're beautifully done!*

But we need the color plates in your book, he smiled. *We don't have all these hatches available in other places.*

What color plates? I blurted.

The color plates you're going to paint, he continued paternally, *when you finish this book for me.*

You're going to publish it? It seemed impossible.

Yes, he said softly.

Jack Case made it come true, arguing back in his Manhattan offices for publishing a book from an unknown author who was still a college sophomore, and even flying me to visit him and talk with various staff members.

There are always nitpickers, he explained gently.

Case shepherded the book through its two-year process, arranging a generous advance that made it possible to work an entire summer on the manuscript. His enthusiasm was infectious, spreading to his editorial colleagues in the trade department.

It will last twenty years, he insisted.

Finally, the book was born. Case juggled his budgets to fly me back to Manhattan for a formal party in the darkly-paneled dining room, where he again offered his twenty-year prediction over raised glasses of sherry. Nobody in the room believed him, but it has proved true.

Jack Case was a serious fisherman who understood the need for *Matching the Hatch* after other publishers had rejected it, but it took courage to commit his reputation and resources to such a book from a totally unknown writer. The book has sold steadily for eighteen years, and its impetus has made it possible to fish extensively. Its reputation grew slowly among fishermen, until another writer who loves trout fishing argued that *Matching the Hatch* and its youthful author had the makings of a picture essay.

Paul O'Neil toiled for years as a principal writer at *Life*, working over a battered typewriter and wearing the same moth-eaten sweater in his cubicle high above Rockefeller Center. O'Neil argued that *Matching the Hatch* had developed a considerable underground in its first four years, and that its author was still less than thirty—while most trout-fishing experts were gray-haired patriarchs with years astream.

His enthusiasm resulted in a *Life* picture essay with George Silk as its photographer. Their coverage resulted in both book sales and considerable magazine work in the past twelve years. Magazine assignments have allowed me to travel and fish widely, constantly adding to the specimens and notebooks that had formed the basic research for *Matching the Hatch*. Literally hundreds of fish-stomach autopsies and collected insects form the basis of this new manuscript on nymphs and nymph-fishing.

American stream entomology is a problem in observing and imitating the diet-forms of an entire continent, instead of the relatively limited spectrum of fly-hatches that has been studied and matched in the British Isles. Its lessons are extensive, and as the lexicon of insects in my collection grew, it became obvious that our waters pose problems not found in Europe—Skues and Sawyer and Kite have written exhaustively of the slow-water nymphs of their chalkstreams, but our catalogue of fly-hatches is a galaxy of trout-stream insects compared with their brief roster of naturals—and our American writers on nymph fishing have focused on tactics, rather than a disciplined study of the nymphs themselves.

Nymphs attempts to provide a foundation for nymph-fishing techniques on American waters, firmly based upon the living subaquatic naturals. The experience of the years since *Matching the Hatch* has made me realize that trout are as selective in their nymph feeding as in their rises to floating insects. However, fishing nymphs is not only a problem of dressing flies that imitate the naturals in terms of color, size and configuration, but also understanding how the natural nymphs behave and move in various depths of water. Knowledge of their preferences in water types, their behavior in their normal subaquatic cycle, and the character of the nymphs during a hatch is critical—their movements at the bottom, the intermediate depths of water, the few inches under the surface, and the final hatching movements in the film itself.

It is hoped that *Nymphs* will help American trout fishermen to catalog the subaquatic life of their favorite rivers. Its chapters and illustrations will make precise imitation and presentation possible, keying their manipulation of the flies to the behavior of the natural nymphs.

Since even the catalogue of flies outlined in *Nymphs* is not a complete treatise of American aquatic hatches, it is also hoped that these chapters will encourage other anglers to investigate the diet-forms found on their rivers. There is still more to learn about trout, and our matchless sport of seeking them, than is found in the sum of our knowledge about their character and their habits.

Many readers will undoubtedly balk at the complexity of American fly-hatches emerging in these pages, but like a Chinese puzzle, the fish are always revealing new secrets and fresh enigmas. Fly-fishing companions have watched me collecting insects and painting them and writing for years, with an amused tolerance reserved for eccentric family members and friends.

You have to be crazy to write a book like that, they laughed, *but we're glad somebody took the time!*

ERNEST SCHWIEBERT
Princeton, New Jersey

JOHN GAYLORD CASE
1907–1970

Faithful son of Michigan and her rivers, disciple of Walton
and Halford in working the slender rod and the fragile flies,
skilled and creative dresser of dry flies, loyal graduate of
Williams College, scholar of English literature and the
humanities, sympathetic editor, companion and friend.

Persephone, fulfill my wish,
And grant that in the shades below
Thy ghost may seek the ghosts of fish!

Contents

The Origins of Nymph Fishing

THE COBBLESTONE ROAD winds south into the pastoral Vils Basin below Amberg, passing through narrow streets among the half-timbered villages. Their churchtowers have the graceful onion-shaped domes found sometimes in Bavaria. Ducks and geese forage in their millraces, waddling through the marketplaces in the rain. Storks build intricate nests of sticks in the chimneypots. It is a lovely region.

April winds stir the alders along the rivers, smelling of freshly plowed fields. The winds are perfumed with orchards then. There are new hops frames on the hillsides, and later the fly hatches are heavy in the water meadows at Schmidsmühlen.

The Lauterach is a classic little river. Its winding meadows and willow-lined pools were the laboratory where I first learned to fish nymphs well. More than twenty seasons have passed since those April mornings above Regensburg, although it seems as fresh as yesterday.

Before that first season in Europe, and the opportunity to polish eager boyhood skills on the difficult fish of German rivers, nymphs seemed like a half-understood variation on conventional wet-fly themes. The nymphs in our fly books were strange creations. Some had been tied in England and looked good, but we had little real faith in them. American nymphs were fanciful patterns that usually had no counterparts in aquatic entomology.

Except for the odd fish on some dark British pattern and a few small nymphs I had copied in the flat-bodied Hewitt style of dressing, most of my nymph fishing had proved relatively unproductive.

Bergman was my first instructor in nymph-fishing theory and technique. His book *Trout* introduced an entire generation to nymphs, although American writers had not really studied the naturals and their behavior like the British fishing experts. Still, the lessons in Bergman were sound, even if they were incomplete. Sometimes his slow hand-twist retrieves produced impressive baskets of fish, but the so-called nymphs pictured in *Trout* were more feathered lures than viable nymph imitations.

There were many times when wet flies seemed to work on nymphing trout. Sometimes we caught fish easily on a worn hackle pattern or March Brown when they were working in the surface film. Weathered wet flies like the Hare's Ear or Greenwell's Glory also took fish well when they were porpoising softly to a hatch. It never occurred to us that such patterned wet flies worked as well as they did because they imitated emerging nymphs and pupae.

Bergman outlined simple tactics in his writings on nymph fishing. His methods were merely extensions of wet-fly tactics. They included the dead-drift presentations, downstream wet-fly swings with a teasing rhythm of the rod, and the slow hand-twist retrieve in quiet waters. These techniques often worked, and I took my first fish with a nymph on the swift Taylor in Colorado. It porpoised softly to the upstream dead-drift cast, lying tight against the grass, and the pale line tightened as it was hooked.

During my boyhood summers in Michigan and Colorado, the painstaking collection of insects for my book *Matching the Hatch* had already begun. The unexplained success of the nonimitative Bergman patterns puzzled me, since it seemed a complete accident. Its patterns of cause-and-effect had little resemblance to the obvious relationships between fly hatches and our dry-fly imitations. The absence of such rational topologies disturbed me in those early years.

It was the old riverkeeper at Schmidsmühlen on the Lauterach who cured my confusion. His patient tutelage solved the puzzle. We met him at lunch in the half-timbered *Gästhaus* near the river. There were fresh sausages and a thick potato soup and red cabbage; and we finished over coffee with talk about his river and his flies.

His boxes were filled with delicate little uprights and sedges and drakes, but the old man was especially proud of his nymphs. His favorite pattern had a pale fox dubbing ribbed with brown crewel, and had wing cases and legs of partridge. It looked much like the modern March Brown Nymph on Catskill rivers.

This nymph is best now. The old man picked up his rough partridge-legged pattern.

Are they hatching? I asked.

Ja, the old riverkeeper answered. *The nymphs migrate into the shallows and fly off quickly when they hatch.* He filled his intricately carved pipe. *The flies are hard to catch, so the fish take mostly nymphs.*

Let's try them, said my father.

We walked upriver through the water meadows above the village. There was a long reach of river where the mayflies were coming off. Two fish were working where the riffles shelved off into a dark undercut bank.

They're rising over there! I pointed.

Nein. The old man shook his head. *They're taking the nymphs just under the surface.*

How do we fish them?

The riverkeeper pointed to the riffles upstream. *The nymphs are there,* he explained. *They drift down, wriggling and working in the current.*

Shall I move the fly? I asked.

Ja! The old man answered. *These nymphs can swim, and you should work them with the rod.*

The first cast went fishless. The second dropped the nymph tight against the grass, where the swift riffle deepened into an undercut bank, and I teased its swing with the rod. Its sweep worked deep where the trout had been showing. Suddenly there was a strong pull and the fish hooked itself.

They seem to like your nymph, I laughed.

We took fish easily that afternoon, killing a brace of fat two-pounders for supper and breakfast. Stomach autopsies verified their diet of big *Siphlonurus* nymphs, and the naturals were perfectly matched with the nymphs dressed by the riverkeeper. It was a fine lesson in nymph technique.

That weekend was my baptism in the method.

The old man patiently taught me what kinds of nymphs lived in the different types of water. Although his flies were roughly tied and unprofessional, he attempted to suggest the color and configuration and size of the naturals, and he insisted that his nymphs be fished to duplicate their movements in the river. Tactics keyed to the behavior of both the nymphs and the trout were a revelation after a diet of Hewitt and Bergman.

Their somewhat casual approach to imitation of the natural nymphs and their emphasis on only dead-drift and slow hand-twist manipulation of their flies had not always worked. Many times obviously nymphing trout ignored such methods. Yet we had taken fish after fish from the Lauterach meadows that afternoon, moving each working trout with the clockwork regularity that comes when you have really solved the equation. That degree of effectiveness is the measure of success. It had eluded me in the fumbling experiments with the Hewitt and Bergman patterns.

It is no accident that many American fly-fishermen are still relatively uninformed about nymphs. Our books have not examined the naturals and their behavior systematically, and have limited fishing nymphs to dead-drift and hand-twist techniques of presentation. Some books have also discussed fishing them with the timeless chuck-and-chance-it methods, but our angling writers have provided only fragments of the puzzle. Most secrets are still missing. Many fishermen already expert with dry flies readily admit their lack of success with the nymph, particularly with fish in the film

They're working steadily, they shrug unhappily. *Tried nymphs and they didn't take them.*

It is a familiar refrain on trout water. Fishermen seem to think that trout are not selective when they are nymphing, and that any nymph pattern will work. It is like the old story of the Broadway showgirl who read her first book, found it boring, and never tried another.

Using just any nymph pattern when fish are taking nymphal forms cannot work. The flies must be accurate imitations of the naturals. It is surprising to find that men who fully understand selectivity in its context of dry-fly imitations and adult insects are often unaware of selectivity to wet flies and nymphs. Trout can examine subsurface foods readily, without the distortions of the surface film and broken current patterns, and see them better than diet-forms on the surface; and therefore trout are perhaps more selective to nymphs in terms of color, configuration, and size than they are to dry flies fished in the mirrorlike meniscus.

Our preoccupation with the dry-fly method has resulted in our relative ignorance about nymph fishing. The considerable influence of Halford on subsequent American writers like Theodore Gordon and George La Branche has led us into two surprisingly common errors. The first is the mistaken attitude that the dry-fly method is more difficult, and somehow morally superior to wet flies and nymphs. Knowledgeable anglers all enjoy the surface rise to a floating imitation immensely, but no one can build a case that the dry-fly method is more difficult than the full spectrum of nymph tactics. Since about ninety percent of trout diet is focused on subaquatic foods, floating insect forms play a minor role in their activity, although Halford ultimately convinced himself that the dry fly was not only the moral superior of other methods, but also the most effective.

The second error commonly made by contemporary fly-fishermen, in their preoccupation with the dry-fly method, is the assumption that a visible rise automatically means a surface-feeding trout. Fish often porpoise and swirl to nymphs and pupae riding just under or in the surface film. These insect forms are nymphs in the process of hatching, pupae struggling to escape their pupal skins, and other ecotypes that breathe in the meniscus of the water. Each of these stages is still lying under the surface, yet when a trout takes them, his movements are betrayed by a showy surface rise. Such rises are to nymphs and pupae, and must be fished with nymphs and pupal imitations fished just under or in the film. Other rises, particularly in lakes and slow-flowing streams, are indicative of feeding on Diptera pupae hanging motionless with their minute gill structures entrained in the surface film of water.

Although many anglers are confused about nymphs, the methods of fishing them are surprisingly ancient. Such methods include each of the conventional wet-fly techniques, depending upon how the nymphs and pupae themselves move in the water, and have their origins deep in prehistory. Most of the early fly patterns, and even many with their roots in the past three centuries, were fished wet and could be taken for emerging mayflies and hatching pupal forms of the Trichoptera. Serious fishermen have apparently imitated fly hatches since long before Aelianus recorded the existence of fly-fishing on the rivers of Macedonia in the second century. His book *Animalium natura* described both fishing and fly-dressing for the trout and grayling in the Astraeus, and his passages seem to picture caddis flies fluttering and ovipositing on the current.

Aelianus is not the father of nymph fishing, although the relatively simple flies he described could easily be taken for a hatching mayfly or sedge. The roots of nymph fishing are also missing from the poetry of Richard de Fournival, who described fly-fishing in the thirteenth century. Although the half-legendary Dame Juliana Berners, the Prioress of Sopewell Nunnery outside London, did not specifically describe nymph fishing in her *Treatyse of Fysshynge wyth an Angle* two centuries later, some of her fly patterns are unmistakably nymphlike. Such patterns as the March Donne Flye, Blacke Louper, and the Shelle Flye could easily be taken for emerging mayflies or caddis. Mascall made no mention of nymphs in his *Booke of Fishing* published in 1590, a century after Berners. His fly patterns were obviously pirated from her *Treatyse*, and little innovation occurred between Mascall and the fly-dressing innovations that Charles Cotton added to *The Compleat Angler* in 1676. Several of his patterns sound likely as nymph imitations, particularly the hackle types Cotton recommends in February and March, and the Whirling Dun found in April on the Dove.

Although Cotton is certainly the father of modern fly-fishing, it was the British writer John Taverner who first described the relationship between subaquatic nymphal forms and the aquatic insects that fishermen had observed and imitated since Aelianus. His observations are found in his little book *Certaine Experiments Concerning Fish and Fruite*, which was published in 1600.

> I have seene a younge flie swimme in the water too and fro, and in the ende, come to the upper cruste of the river, and assay to flie up: howbeit, not being perfitely ripe or fledged, hath twice or thrice fallen downe againe into the bottome: howbeit, in the ende receiving perfection by the heate of the sunne, and the pleasant fat water, hath in the ende within some halfe houre after taken her flyte, and flied quite awaye into the ayre, and of such younge flies before they are able to flie away, do fish feede exceedingly.

Cotton and Walton had obviously failed to digest these passages in Taverner, since his clear grasp of hatching nymphs and adult aquatic flies was somehow lost in the century of angling books that followed. Taverner sounds very much like a modern entomologist describing the restlessness of *Leptophlebia* flies, migrating several times between the bottom and the surface in anticipation of their emergence.

The parade of angling authors who apparently failed to read Taverner is extensive. John Dennys fails to mention the nymph in his *Secrets of Angling* of 1613. The following year, Gervase Markham proved himself a stranger to Taverner too, since his *Discourse on the General Arte of Fishing* did not consider nymphs in its preoccupation with fluttering aquatic insects. William Lawson followed with his *Discourses* in 1620, the year that the successful Massachusetts Colony was established in America, without clarifying the connection between nymphs, pupae, and fly hatches.

Barker came next with his *Art of Angling* in 1651, and although it contains the first written descriptions of gaffs and fly reels, it does not explore nymph fishing. Barker was a Cromwellian from Shropshire, with a half century of fly-fishing knowledge. His unpretentious little volume also gives the first real instructions in fly-dressing techniques, and although Barker is apparently unaware of nymphs, some of his fly patterns are reasonable imitations of emerging aquatic insects. Barker was also a light-tackle man, arguing that a single horsehair tippet fished the fly more subtly, and would raise and capture more trout in skilled hands.

Walton published his first edition of *The Compleat Angler* two years after *The Art of Angling* in 1653. There was little on fly-fishing in the early printings of Walton, and Barker was reprinted in 1657. Richard Franck appeared with his *Northern Memoirs* the following year, although his manuscript was not published until 1694. Walton was loyal to the British Crown in these years, unlike Barker and his fellow Cromwellian Colonel Robert Venables. That officer published his *Experienced Angler* in 1662, and although each of these works has considerable importance in the history of angling, none is a factor in the evolution of nymph tactics.

However, there are some beginnings in the lyric *Being Instructions How to Angle for Trout and Grayling in a Clear Stream* that Charles Cotton added to the Walton classic in 1676. His list of flies included sixty-five patterns. Several are surprisingly nymphlike in character, as discussed earlier in this introductory chapter, and the Great Blue Dun that Cotton recommended for late February sounds like a prototype for the relatively modern Hare's Ear—the most effective hatching-nymph pattern ever dressed.

James Chetham followed Cotton with his *Angler's Vade Mecum* in 1681. Although Chetham borrowed fly patterns shamelessly from Cotton, he also included an original list of flies developed for the swift rivers of Lancashire. Many of his original patterns, particularly the dub-flies he recommended throughout the fishing year, are excellent hatching-nymph imitations. Chetham is also the author of the venerable Blue Dun, a fly pattern dressed without hackles that is the prototype of the popular modern dressing.

Although Cotton richly deserves his historical rank as the father of fly-fishing, it is certainly the work of Richard and Charles Bowlker that begins the age of modern fly-dressing. Numerous angling books appeared during the eighteenth century, and none was distinguished in any literary sense. However, the Bowlkers assembled several editions of *The Art of Angling*, and their work dominated both the century and several generations of British anglers. Richard Bowlker was the father, and like Barker came from the pastoral landscapes of Shropshire. There is some question about the first publication of his book, but the Bodleian Library at Oxford dates the Richard Bowlker manuscript to 1747. Charles Bowlker was a son who followed and ultimately surpassed the skills of his father, until it is generally acknowledged by both contemporaries and subsequent generations that he was the finest fly-fisherman of his century. Charles Bowlker was the author of *The Art of Angling* as it was republished in 1780, and it became a popular work that easily dominated discussions of fly-dressing and streamcraft for more than fifty years.

Bowlker is simple and direct in its style. Its importance lies in a posture of clearing away the myth and debris of earlier patterns and its knowledge of aquatic entomology. Bowlker has no hesitation in disposing of earlier fly-dressing practice from Berners through Cotton and Chetham, listing many of their patterns as flies of limited use, and then describing his own catalogue of thirty-odd imitations.

His flies include surprisingly modern versions of standard patterns like the Blue Dun, which Chetham first described in a no-hackle version, and the Iron Blue. Other favorites that apparently began with Bowlker were the Cowdung, Willow Fly, Grannom, Yellow Sally, Green and Grey Drakes, Black Gnat, March Brown, Whirling Blue Dun, Little Pale Blue, and Welshman's Button. Authorship of so many patterns that have survived for almost two centuries is an impressive feat. The following passages from *The Art of Angling* are surprisingly modern:

> When you make an artificial fly, you must, in the first place, make choice of a hook of a size proportionable to the fly you intend to copy, which must be whipped on to your gut or hair in the same manner you would whip on a worm-hook; only with this difference, that instead of fastening near the bend of the hook, you must fasten your silk near the top of the shank, and let your silk remain; then, taking as much feather as is necessary for the wings, lay it even as you can upon the upper side of the shank, with the butt of the

feathers downward, towards the bend of the hook, and tye it fast three or four times with the silk, and fasten it; then, with a needle or pin, divide the wings as equal as you can; then, take your silk and cross it three or four times between the wings, bringing the silk still downwards, towards the bend of the hook, then taking your hackle feather, tye it fast at the bend with the point of the hackle upwards; next, your fur or dubbing being ready, which is to make the body of the fly, take a little bit of it and twist it gently round your silk, and work it upwards to the butt of the wings, and there fasten it; then take your hackle and rib it neatly over your dubbing, and fasten it; then, bending the wings and putting them in the form you desire, bring on the butt end of your hackle towards the head, and there fasten it firmly; then, taking a bit of dubbing or fur, as near to the colour of the head of the live fly as you can, whip it twice round with your silk, and then fasten it just above the wings; so your fly is completed.

Bowlker still used the reverse-wing dressing evolved in earlier centuries. His bodies were slim and graceful in true north-country style of dressing, sometimes ribbed with a twist of silk or a hackle feather. His theories advocated the use of hackles to suggest legs, but such delicately palmered fur bodies are also excellent imitations of nymphs having well-defined gill structures. John Waller Hills tells us in his charming book *A Summer on the Test* that he served his apprenticeship with a copy of Bowlker, much as generations of Americans have learned to fish trout reading Bergman.

Certainly there are still echoes of Bowlker found in fly-dressing practice throughout the United Kingdom, and in the sparse dressings of the Catskill school. The emphasis on size, color, and configuration is surprisingly modern, and although no specific reference to nymphs is found in *The Art of Angling*, many of the patterns suggest emerging naturals. The success and influence of the Bowlker flies were wide. Patterns dressed at Kilbreda in Ireland about 1789 are similarly tied with dubbed bodies and split wings, and sparsely hackled. Similar flies were fashionable in Hampshire as late as 1825. Yorkshire is renowned for its slender-bodied flies in modern times, and several local styles in both Scotland and England commonly displayed sparse emerging-nymph construction only fifty-odd years ago, particularly on the Tweed and the Clyde—and especially on the swift-flowing Usk, not too distant from Ludlow and the Shropshire rivers of the Bowlkers.

The fishing books of the eighteenth century were largely so undistinguished that Richard and Charles Bowlker utterly dominated the century following 1750. The nineteenth century, however, proved a renaissance in fly-fishing literature. That revolution began at its very threshold.

George Scotcher appeared with his little *Fly-Fisher's Legacy,* published at Chepstow in 1800. It is memorable chiefly because it was first to depict aquatic fly-hatches in color, and although there is mention of a floating fly, there is no reference to the nymph. Sixteen years later, George Bainbridge published his *Fly-Fisher's Guide* at Liverpool. Bainbridge was a sound little manual containing five comparatively good color plates of aquatic hatches. William Carroll wrote his *Angler's Vade Mecum,* which appeared at Edinburgh in 1818. It included many color plates of flies, but their draftsmanship was so poor that the book is of only marginal value. However, Alfred Ronalds arrived with his *Fly Fisher's Entomology* in 1836, the first disciplined work on matching the hatch.

Ronalds is one of the major milestones in the entire literature of fly-fishing, and with his *Entomology* the scientific method had reached angling in full flower. Ronalds was completely original in its content and research, setting the yardstick for all subsequent discussion and illustration of aquatic fly hatches. The graphic work is beautifully executed, and the copper plates remain equal to most modern lithography. Ronalds is the prototypical mixture of angler and biologist that would appear again later in the nineteenth century, and continues to play a major role in contemporary thought.

Richard and Charles Bowlker so completely dominated their period, in terms of the full spectrum of fly-fishing theory, that little new appeared concerning tackle and tactics until the publication of *River Angling* by John Younger in 1840. Ronalds made no mention of nymphs, but Younger wrote convincingly of their role in the trout diet. His technique of fishing the hackle-flies of partridge and grouse, superb imitations of emerging caddis flies, is simple and effective. Younger believed in casting directly across or even slightly upstream, depending on the current speed, and allowing his flies to swing motionless on the tension of the fly-line. Although Younger did not develop imitative nymphs, he was certainly the first writer since John Taverner to speculate on their importance.

Both Hewitt Wheatley and John Beever published their books in London in 1849. Four years later, Michael Theakston published his *List of Natural Flies,* an outstanding contribution to knowledge of fly hatches and techniques of imitating them. George Pulman first described fishing the dry-fly method in those same years on the Axe in Dorsetshire, and his *Vade Mecum of Fly-Fishing for Trout* became a seminal book in the evolution of angling. The development of oiled-silk lines, eyed light-wire hooks, precise knowledge of the British fly hatches, upstream presentation, and the techniques of dressing the floating flies all followed each other in the final half of the nineteenth century. Knowledgeable anglers are familiar with the high points of this development, since the dry-fly method virtually owned the century after 1851, when Pulman published his book and its introduction of the dry fly.

However, there was a parallel evolution in the technique of wet-fly fishing that was moving toward the innovation of the imitative nymph. W. C. Stewart was an attorney from Edinburgh who advocated fishing his wet-flies upstream, a keystone in the arch of both dry-fly and nymph tactics. Stewart published his theories in *The Practical Angler* in 1857, and his little book has since become a classic in angling history. Its importance is evident in the fact that it remains in print more than a century later. Stewart filled his fly books with dour patterns like the Woodcock and Brown, Grouse and Green, and Bluewing Hare's Ear, but he often favored even simpler patterns like his Golden Plover Spider, Grouse Spider, Starling Spider, Partridge Spider, Dotterel Spider and Woodcock Spider. These flies were often fished by Stewart and his companions on the Scottish border rivers, along with rolled-wings like the Corncrake and Orange, Woodcock and Red, and Starling and Brown. Such soft-hackled wet flies in a subdued palette of colors had considerable influence on Skues in England, and on Leisenring in America a half-century later. Such brown-mottled flies are superb imitations of emerging aquatic insects in swift-flowing streams everywhere.

Stewart discusses the life cycle of the large Ephemeroptera found in the United Kingdom. Along with using their burrowing nymphs as bait, his chapters also recommend the use of caddis larvae and stonefly nymphs in bait-fishing, clearly recognizing their importance in the trout diet. However, Stewart did not consciously attempt to imitate such insect forms, or work out fly-fishing methods for the artificial nymph.

There were other wet-fly fishermen who wrote compellingly about their craft after Stewart in 1857. David Webster published his classic *The Angler and the Loop-Rod* that same year, and his techniques of dressing the wet-fly with rolled wings and delicate fur bodies were adopted by Skues fifty-odd years later for restoring the subsurface techniques to the Hampshire chalkstreams. Canon Charles Kingsley stubbornly refused to abandon the wet-fly technique, and in his little *Chalkstream Studies* of 1858 demonstrated both a thorough knowledge of fly life and the continuing viability of the method in the stronghold of the dry fly. H. C. Cutcliffe wrote his *Trout Fishing in Rapid Streams* in 1863, a cogent and practical little book based on years of experience with the trout of the west-country streams of Devonshire. Cutcliffe offers a clear account of west-country flies and the techniques of fishing them in swift water. His tactics include stalking the fish carefully, and fishing the upstream wet fly to keep out of sight. Cutcliffe thoroughly understood fishing pocket water and the small-stream behavior of the trout, distinguishing clearly between reaches of water where exact imitation is necessary, and swift currents where the fish must take quickly or remain hungry. Cutcliffe also thoroughly grasped the life cycle of the aquatic insects, and in his book we find the following observation:

> I find so much spoken about the natural fly and its imitation, but little about the insect before arrived at maturity. How seldom does one imitate the larva or pupa of the several insects.

Four years after Cutcliffe, Francis Francis published his *Book of Angling* in 1867. While Kingsley refused to adopt the evolving dry-fly methods in his devotion to the classic wet-fly techniques, Francis was thoroughly versed in both schools of thought on the chalkstreams. Francis was perhaps the most open-minded fishing writer of the period, refusing to take sides in the quarrels between the traditional wet-fly fishermen and the dry-fly disciples forming around George Selwyn Marryat. Francis believed that the accomplished angler had to master all methods, and his perspective of moderation served to dampen the arguments of the dry-fly school in the years that followed.

George Marryat and Henry Hall were the conceptual thinkers who worked out the dry-fly method, while Frederick Halford added his knowledge of aquatic hatches and writing skills to codify the technique. Their studies were thoroughly catalogued in such Halford books as *Floating Flies and How to Dress Them*, which was published in 1886, and *Dry-Fly Fishing in Theory and Practice*, completed three years later. The comprehensive volume entitled *Dry-Fly Entomology* appeared in 1897, and *Modern Devel-*

opment of the Dry-Fly came four years before his death in 1914.

Such books had immense impact on fly-fishing theory and technique in both Europe and the United States. Theodore Gordon became fascinated with the work of Halford, and the two writers began a correspondence concerning the potential of the dry-fly method on American waters. Their letters culminated in the now-famous set of Halford dry flies, dressed by the master himself, which was sent to Gordon in 1889. The legendary folio of Halford patterns survives intact in the collection of the Angler's Club of New York, and its flies are the progenitors of American dry-fly practice.

However, the validity and fashionable success of the dry-fly method did not eclipse the older wet-fly techniques entirely, even on the smooth-flowing chalkstreams, where its acolytes actually tried to restrict the fishing to dry-fly only. Halford was about to publish his *Floating Flies and How to Dress Them* when another Yorkshire author, following in the footsteps of Michael Theakston and John Jackson, wrote a brilliant little book on wet-fly tactics for the north-country rivers.

T. E. Pritt was a fishing writer for the *Yorkshire Post,* and secretary of the Yorkshire Angling Association. His little book was entitled *Yorkshire Trout Flies,* and contained eleven handpainted plates of sixty-odd wet flies. The patterns fished and recommended by Pritt are a simple collection of relatively plain wet flies, hackled without wings and with soft feathers of pheasant, plover, grouse, woodcock, jackdaw, and snipe. Some winged patterns were included, slim and sparsely dressed in the elegant Yorkshire style. Pritt used the full palette of fly presentation available to the wet-fly man, casting upstream, across the current, and quartering downstream. Depending upon the fly hatches and the mood of the fish, he fished his flies dead-drift, allowed them to swing in the current on the tension of the line, or teased their drift with the tip of his rod. The hand-twist retrieve in quiet pools was useful on his Yorkshire rivers, and sometimes Pritt skittered his flies in the surface film to suggest the erratic egg-laying of the Trichoptera flies. Although Pritt did not consciously imitate and fish nymphs, his soft-hackles and sparse-winged patterns are perfect suggestions of hatching mayflies and caddis-fly pupae. The writings of Pritt also had considerable influence on Leisenring, the solitary wet-fly expert on the Brodheads, just as the books of Halford were the catalyst for the earlier dry-fly work of Theodore Gordon.

Pritt and the scientific posture created in the work of Ronalds and Halford were the prelude to the nymph technique. George Edward Mackenzie Skues was the genius who would fit the pieces together on the threshold of the new century, and both the theory and technique of nymph-fishing would quickly evolve toward maturity. Skues was a solitary bachelor who fished and loved the Itchen for many years, and was certainly the conscious forefather of modern nymph techniques.

It was this setting that produced the dry-fly method, which some angling historians credit to William of Wykeham, who fished the Itchen at Winchester. The shy trout in the silken currents of the chalkstreams were such a challenge, and both the dry-fly and the nymph were born on the Itchen. Such fish were the catalysts of modern fly-fishing.

The Evolution of Modern Nymph Tactics

Hampshire is a richly pastoral landscape of villages and chalkdowns and country churchyards. It is a setting worthy of both fly-fishers and poets. There are millraces and water meadows and fields of fat dairy cattle. Medieval inns with richly half-timbered gables house both anglers and travelers. The chalkstreams flow smooth and crystalline through their rich beds of chara, pondweed, watercress, celery, ribbon weed, and starwort. There are water buttercups and dropwort too, rooting deep into the cretaceous silt of the bottom, the source of the ecosystemic richness of these rivers.

The countryside is filled with a sense of history. Salisbury Cathedral rises across its Wiltshire river bottoms, its single tower slender and richly Gothic above the roofs of the town. Several miles farther east lies the somber cathedral at Winchester, the brooding patina of time in its Romanesque stonework. Its chapels and chambers are clumsy and dark beside the soaring stained-glass spaces of Salisbury.

Izaak Walton lies buried under its stone floor.

There are rich fly hatches in the rivers; the weeds and chalky silt harbor countless nymphs and pupae. The trout are fat and healthy, and rise steadily to a diet of sedges and Diptera and mayflies. It is the region of the Caperer, the Iron Blue, the Pale Watery, and the Bluewinged Olive.

The fish were challenging and difficult. It was this setting, pastoral and contemplative in its mood, that provided each of the principal developments of modern fly-fishing. These south-country rivers shaped fishermen like Pulman, Marryat, Hall, Halford, and Sir Edward Grey of Fallodon. Walton spent his final years in the water meadows of the Itchen, the same river that deeply influenced Skues.

George Edward Mackenzie Skues was a distinguished attorney in London who divided his talents between the courts and his fishing. Skues was a bachelor, like his colleague Leisenring on the Brodheads, and he had ample time to devote to his streamside studies. His intelligence refused to admit that the skills and knowledge of wet-fly tradition should be jettisoned in favor of the new dry-fly dogmatics, and although he remained primarily a chalkstream angler all his life, Skues continued to explore alternatives to the dry-fly method on those waters.

His studies were finally published in the book *Minor Tactics of the Chalk Stream,* which appeared in 1910. The book was based upon a penetrating reason, a deep-seated dislike of dogma, a thorough knowledge and understanding of angling tradition, and much original thought. It made a case for retaining wet fly tactics on the chalkstreams, and although it aroused a chorus of vocal opposition, its arguments were so subtly and convincingly laid that it has never been successfully refuted. *Minor Tactics* remains a classic of fly-fishing literature, with its subtle and pleasant brief for wet-fly fishing on the chalkstreams, and it began the trend away from the dry-fly purism of the Halford school to the more broadly based philosophy of modern angling. It is from this first Skues book that the conceptual evolution of nymph fishing can be traced in the history of the sport.

Skues continually faced strong opposition to his evolving theories from fellow chalkstream anglers. His viewpoint challenges the *ex cathedra* arguments voiced by Halford and his disciples, that dry flies alone were the method worthy of the British chalkstreams. It was a foolish argument that Skues easily parried, since even chalkstream fish take eighty to ninety percent of their diet in nymphal and pupal forms. Skues refused to feel guilty for fishing his delicate nymphs in waters the Halford school had consecrated to the dry-fly method. The feud reached its climax in a famous encounter at the Flyfisher's in London, when the aging Halford and his curia of disciples cornered Skues in the foyer.

Young man! Halford said testily. *You cannot fish the Itchen in the manner you describe!*

But I've done it, Skues replied softly.

Although his book *Minor Tactics of the Chalk Streams* did not appear until 1910, Skues had fished the Itchen regularly for almost thirty years when it was published. His interest in fishing and imitating nymphal forms had been generated in those summers, and angling historians believe that the genesis of the nymph closely followed the development of the dry-fly method. Unlike the mere speculation of writers like Younger and Cutcliffe, who observed that nymphs and larvae deserved more attention from anglers and fly-tiers, the work of Skues was a patient and dedicated search for precise imitation of the nymphal life found in the Itchen.

Skues began his work in an attitude of complementing the dry-fly method, but his writings in various British journals attracted such negative response that he found himself outside the pale of accepted doctrine, not unlike the religious reformers of the sixteenth century. Angling historians might speculate on Skues' research that followed, and whether its single-minded intensity was a response to the wrath of Halford and his disciples. Perhaps otherwise Skues would have pursued his nymph studies in more leisurely style, mixing his new methods with the dry fly during periods of surface feeding activity, and even working a conventional wet fly at times. His success with chalkstream fish made him a legend among Hampshire anglers in his own time, and his willingness to adapt his techniques to the moods and rhythms of the trout made him consistently more successful than his dry-fly rivals on the hallowed Test.

The studies recorded first in *Minor Tactics* were expanded in 1921, with publication of *The Way of a Trout with a Fly,* and in this classic Skues outlined a fully polished doctrine of imitating and fishing the nymph. Sufficient time has elapsed since the books of Skues were published to permit us a sound perspective of their worth. Skues was deeply grounded in fly-dressing theory and technique from Berners through Halford, with particular emphasis on such well-known north-country writers as Cutcliffe, Webster, and Pritt. The books of Skues are among the best in the entire literature of angling, ranking him surely with Berners, Walton, Cotton, Stewart, and Halford in historical importance. His work has the discipline of a legal mind, an intelligence trained to reason and define, and the ability of the scholar to sift and weigh both the evidence of the past and his own powers of observation. Such impressive gifts enabled Skues to succeed where lesser men would have failed, yet there is also a charm and humor in his work, found in such overtones as these brief verses:

> Oh, thrilling the rise to the lure that is dry,
> When the shy fish comes up to his slaughter,
> Yet rather would I have
> The turn to my fly,
> With a cunning brown wink under water.
> The bright little wink under water!
> Mysterious wink under water!
> Delightful to ply
> The subaqueous fly,
> And watch for the wink under water!

The books of Skues are absolutely essential in the library of the modern angler, and his work was ultimately codified in the little book *Nymph Fishing for Chalk Stream Trout*, which he published in 1939. Skues was in his eighties, with the world about to plunge into a catastrophic war, when his last technical fishing book was published. The book is somewhat flawed with a detailed and critical analysis of the fallacies in Halford, sustaining an argument won thirty-odd years before with a theoretical adversary who had died twenty-five years earlier. The book also includes a lifetime of observations on the behavior of both the nymphs and the trout, fishing the nymph, and methods and materials best suited for imitating them. It also compiles a list of patterns imitating fifteen nymphs that Skues had found important in his many years on the Hampshire chalkstreams.

It should be understood that Skues fully grasped the limitations of fishing theories evolved on the chalkstreams, and his books always included evidence of that ecological awareness. The spectrum of fly hatches on these south-country rivers is clearly limited, just as the heavy hatches on the limestone rivers of the eastern states and the western spring creeks are restricted to relatively few species. Most stillwater insects are swimming flies, and move in the current both during their normal subaquatic lives and the brief period of hatching. There are many more types of insects and small crustaceans found in other aquatic biosystems, such as the swifter rivers of Shropshire and Yorkshire, and the tumbling rivers of America. Such exceptions to the Skues philosophy in no way weaken its importance, since the conditions endemic to the chalkstreams are also found on slow-flowing alkaline rivers, still reaches within most watercourses, and lakes and impoundments everywhere. Skues is still the father of nymph fishing, and his chalkstream studies are the benchmark of our subsequent investigations, even if his conclusions miss the full scope of nymph tactics.

There were other fine British writers working in these same years, both on the chalkstreams and on the swift-flowing rivers farther north. Such fishermen fully recognized that the chalkstreams were largely limited to the slow-water species of sedges and mayflies, and that species requiring considerable alkalinity were most prevalent. Stomach autopsies continually revealed that nymphs, larvae, and pupal forms are certainly the principal components of trout diet. Small crustaceans, aquatic beetles, and terrestrial insects such as leafhoppers and ants all play a major role in fly-fishing. Adult mayflies, caddis flies, and stoneflies are also important in their symbiotic relationship to the dry-fly method, although the Plecoptera are more important in swift-running waters.

Leonard West outlined this enlarged catalogue of trout foods in *The Natural Trout Fly and its Imitation*, which was published privately in 1912. West illustrated his book copiously to describe more than a hundred flies, including the materials required in their dressings. J. C. Mottram was a skillful and famous surgeon who also focused his intelligence on the problems of trout fishing with insight and creativity. His interesting little book entitled *Fly Fishing: Some New Arts and Mysteries* was published in 1914, and in addition to some revolutionary concepts about dry-fly imitations, Mottram also speculated on nymphs and nymph fishing. The genesis of the fly-dressing theories found in the writings of fishermen like Marinaro, Swisher, and Richards can be traced to the work of Mottram. Martin Moseley was a first-rate entomologist whose interest in fishing came from his uncle, Frederic Halford, and his little book *The Dry-Fly Fisherman's Entomology* was a hand-colored volume designed for the pocket of a fishing coat; its cover was folded into a slotted binding. It was an attempt to codify the Halford studies and enlarge their entomological base. Unfortunately, Moseley made no attempt to imitate the insects described and illustrated in his streamside manual. The speculations offered in the studies of Mottram continued to germinate in fly-fishing circles, until the equally brilliant J. W. Dunne expanded them in *Sunshine and the Dry Fly* in 1924. Structure, silhouette, and light pattern made by various insects in the surface film were all carefully considered, in addition to the color emphasized in Halford. The work of West, Mottram, and Dunne reached a climax in *The Flyfisher and the Trout's Point of View* published by Colonel E. W. Harding in 1931. It is a particularly noteworthy book, singular in its considerations of turbidity, light transmission, optics, light patterns in the meniscus, and a labyrinth of factors affecting the vision of the trout with respect to both their natural foods and our fly patterns. Harding added to the theories of Mottram and Dunne on the floating imitation and the nymph. Colonel Harding had considerable influence on many subsequent fishing writers, and books like *A Modern Dry-Fly Code* and *Selective Trout* as well as my own *Matching the Hatch* owe a considerable debt to this contemplative officer who loved to exercise an almost military discipline in his studies of fly-fishing. It is unfortunate that his untimely death robbed us of his later insights and observations.

Skues had enlisted several important disciples in these years between the world wars. Mottram was experimenting with nymphs in the period that produced *Some New Arts and Mysteries*, and Eric Taverner included both fly patterns and tactics for nymph fishing in *Trout Fishing from All Angles,* which was published in 1929. Major John Waller Hills also embraced the nymph technique in his lyric *Summer on the Test,* published in the following year. Colonel Harding was a singularly important convert, and Roger Wooley added his prestige to the nymph-fishing method in his *Modern Trout-Fly Dressing* in 1932, which included both patterns and tactics.

That same year, Skues published his little *Sidelines, Sidelights and Reflections,* which included an original checklist of eleven imitative nymph-patterns. It was a brilliant collection of articles contributed over the years to various British journals, and their scope revealed the comprehensive spectrum of his experience and wisdom. Skues possessed an immense store of knowledge, both scholarly and practical in its application to trout-fishing problems. There were no facets of fly-fishing which he could not penetratingly discuss, dissect knowingly, and evaluate with objectivity and fairness. His later book *Nymph Fishing for Chalk Stream Trout* expanded the original fly list to fifteen patterns. The little *Silk, Fur and Feathers* was published posthumously in 1950, gathering his observations on fly-dressing into a single volume, and *Itchen Memories* recorded a rich assemblage of memories gathered in a lifetime on his favorite chalkstream.

The singular character of those waters provides both a unique and carefully defined ecology. Fly hatches are limited to slow-water species. Swift watercourses, lakes, and impoundments are subject to totally different environmental frameworks, presenting completely different problems. Such waters harbor completely different ecotypes of food for the trout, in terms of color, configuration, and movement. Skues himself was completely aware that his nymph patterns and techniques of presentation could not solve the problems posed on such waters. His writings in *The Journal of the Flyfisher's Club* of London, which appeared just after the First World War, argued that the problems of swift-flowing rivers and lakes and impoundments required creative investigators like Marryat, Halford, and Moseley to work out their entomological details. Skues condemned the empirical trial-and-error approach to fishing as undisciplined and lazy-minded—deploring, along with Harding, that most fishermen deserve that censure.

Since his death there have been a number of Skues disciples among the roster of British fishing writers. Perhaps the best known of these nymph experts, probably through Charles Ritz and his charming book *A Flyfisher's Life,* is the legendary Frank Sawyer, riverkeeper on the pastoral Avon above Salisbury. Sawyer is renowned in both Europe and the United Kingdom for his skills with the nymph. It is Wilson Stephens, the former editor of *The Field* in the United Kingdom, who has made it possible for us to investigate Sawyer and his techniques. Both men collaborated on *Nymphs and the Trout,* which Stephens gleaned and polished from the notebooks and manuscripts of Sawyer. Skues argued that casting nymphs to rising fish was rather like dry-fly fishing, but Sawyer believes it is completely different, more difficult in some ways, and in no manner inferior to the dry-fly method. Sawyer has had a half-century of practical experience as riverkeeper on the Avon near Stonehenge. Stephens and Sawyer had collaborated on the charming book *Keeper of the Stream* in 1952, which revealed in Sawyer both a striking knowledge of river ecology and a considerable touch of the poet. It has been said that Sawyer sees deeply into the river, not just into its physical secrets of the trout and the fly-hatches and the grayling, but into the soul of its gentle weed-trailing currents.

Sawyer wrote *Nymphs and the Trout* about twenty years after Skues published his last technical book, the classic *Nymph Fishing for Chalk Stream Trout,* and his work is a valuable addition to the beginnings outlined in the three books written by Skues. The men who wish to become expert in fishing the nymph, particularly for trout that are visibly working to natural nymphs, must read Sawyer. There are other modern British writers whose works are equally important to the well-versed angler. W. H. Lawrie contributed *The Book of the Rough-Stream Nymph* with its insights into nymph fishing on tumbling currents in the north-country rivers, completing the speculations begun in the writings of Bowlker, Cutcliffe, Stewart, and Pritt. Harold Plunket-Greene described his experiments with nymphs in *Where the Bright Waters Meet,* which has caught perfectly the character of the lyric little Bourne. Its rich, weed-filled currents have a special poetry, especially the reach of river below Hurstbourne Priory and the churchyard where Plunket-Greene lies buried among the moss-covered headstones.

The entomological studies of lake fly hatches suggested originally in the articles of Skues were started in books like *Loch Fishing in Theory and Practice,* which R. C. Bridgett published in 1924. Many British fly-fishermen consider it still the best general work on the subject. Although Bridgett was no skilled entomologist, in the sense that he had studied each of the principal fly-hatches on his home waters, he possessed a sound working knowledge of the principal insect groupings and the methods of imitating them. His work covers all conceivable aspects of lake fishing except a detailed study of still-water entomology, and it is clear from *Loch Fishing* that Bridgett himself realized that omission:

> It is somewhat difficult to decide to what extent the angler should be versed in the entomology of the loch, but I think that most will agree that a little knowledge at least of the subject is essential. My own opinion is that the slow advance in the art and science of loch-fishing is largely accounted for by the lack of interest displayed in the food of loch-trout.

Sidney Spencer contributed his brilliant little *The Art of Lake Fishing with the Sunk Fly* in 1934, a book filled with important insights. His arguments are especially important for those anglers who have assumed, perhaps in blind obedience to the dry-fly dogmatics found in Halford, that selectivity is not a primary factor in fishing wet-flies and nymphs. Spencer believed that matching the hatch was equally important in dry flies and imitations fished below the surface. Our expanding knowledge of stillwater entomology, and the selectivity of lake fish exposed to significant angling pressure, certainly confirm his insights expressed forty years ago.

H. P. Henzell followed Spencer with his *Art and Craft of Loch Fishing,* which appeared in 1937. It is a delightful little book that captures perfectly the character of loch fishing. Henzell did not believe that lake fish were unsophisticated, and argued that a knowledge of entomology is the keystone to consistent success in stillwater fishing. His book argues that fishless days are less indicative of inactivity among the fish than of our ignorance about their feeding. The chapters of *The Art and Craft of Loch Fishing* include the following paragraph which indicates that Henzell understood completely:

> It is a reasonable assumption that trout, like other fish and animals, feed sometime during each day, and the fact that no fish are breaking the surface is much more likely to mean that they are feeding on subaqueous forms of life than that they are not feeding at all. The face of the loch may remain as undisturbed as a mirror, and all our wiles fail to induce one solitary trout to take the fly. We can imitate very well, by the use of nymphs and wet flies, the various larvae of flies and freshwater shrimps, and that if we study the entomology and learn to fish these imitations properly, there will be few blank days on the loch, and interest in our fishing will tremendously increase.

J. R. Harris published his singular and definitive *Angler's Entomology* in 1952, adding considerable knowledge to the catalogue of fly hatches found in the books of Ronalds, Halford, Moseley, and Skues. The Harris book is a modern masterpiece in its comprehensive treatment of fly hatches and other trout foods. It covers the principal river and loch hatches throughout Ireland and the United Kingdom, with details on their morphology and imitative fly patterns, and maps pinpointing their distribution and range. However, in addition to the principal mayflies, stoneflies, and sedges treated in past books, Harris also covered the Odonata, crustaceans, craneflies and midges, damselflies, two-winged flies, Hymenoptera, and reed-smuts. It is a seminal work which formed a scientific basis for much fly-fishing speculation, particularly in the British Isles.

Colonel Jocelyn Lane was the first British writer to work with the *Angler's Entomology* at his elbow, and his *Lake and Loch Fishing for Trout* was published in 1954. The influence of Harris is readily apparent. However, it must be admitted that Lane has not merely relied on Harris and his research, but has consistently enriched our knowledge of stillwater fly hatches from his own observations. Lane made extensive use of aquariums to observe the ecotypes found in the diet of fish in the lochs. There are two chapters on the fly hatches and other foods common in such waters, and Colonel Lane professes the conviction that imitative flies are critical to success—admitting that the fancy loch-fishing patterns he had once recommended were on the wane.

Perhaps the best book on the entomology of the lakes and reservoirs of the United Kingdom is *Lake Flies and Their Imitations*, published by Commander C. F. Walker in 1960. Walker has augmented our knowledge of trout diet-forms in lochs and impoundments. His book includes a relatively thorough coverage of mayflies, sedges, midges, and other two-winged flies, water beetles, dragonflies and damselflies, alderflies, stoneflies and freshwater crustacea. Other chapters outline fly-tying theory for imitating the subaquatic stages of these insects and crustacea, and appropriate fly patterns are described. Walker is unquestionably in favor of imitation, and clearly understands the importance of nymphs in lake fishing. The knowledgeable modern nymph fisherman and fly-dresser must include *Lake Flies and Their Imitations* in his library, whether he fishes waters in Europe or the United States.

Oliver Kite is the most recent British fishing writer to explore nymph fishing, and his book *Nymph Fishing in Practice* was published in 1963. Major Kite includes an extensive investigation of the south-country nymphs, wth observations on their life cycles, habits, and character. His chapters correlate the imitative flies developed for the chalkstreams with practical manipulation of the nymphs intended to match their subaquatic movements. Studies in the natural species, artificial nymph imitations, fishing nymphs in lakes and impoundments, basic solutions for typical nymph-fishing problems, and nymphing tackle are combined with portraits of fishing days on such south-country rivers as the Torridge, Avon, Bourne, Wylye, and Test. The relative simplicity of his fly books and presentation is evidence of the limited palette of fly hatches that must be matched on the chalkstreams of the Salisbury Plain. Kite clearly acknowledges his intellectual debt to Skues and his writings, and in his preface he offers gratitude to Frank Sawyer of Netheravon—the man who introduced him to nymph fishing.

Oliver Kite completes the circle of nymph development that began with Skues about seventy-five years ago, and is the last writer to explore the technique which began on the chalkstreams of the United Kingdom. Its heritage has its genesis in the landscape of thatch-roofed cottages and water meadows and parish churchyards, sharing this pastoral countryside with the development of the dry-fly method.

The evolution of the dry-fly technique on American waters was a process of studying our fly hatches, working out imitations that matched the naturals indigenous to our varied watersheds, and expanding on British tactics to meet the complex spectrum of an entire continent. American nymph fishing has also begun to develop its own directions since men like Leisenring and Hewitt and Jennings started to adapt British theories to American trout streams, and those beginnings were found on the classic rivers of our eastern mountains—from the tumbling little Brodheads in Pennsylvania to the half-legendary rivers of the Catskills.

American Studies in Nymph Fishing

THE RIVERS WIND down their pastoral valleys, tumbling through simple towns, long-abandoned colonial farms, and white-clapboard houses. There are slender belltowers above the country churches, and in late summer the hot wind eddies in the trees. Locusts buzz noisily in the elms and syca- mores. The mountains rise in a surprisingly small region on both sides of the Delaware, rolling ridges covered with second-growth forests and smoke- colored in the distance.

It is still a wild and beautiful region behind a tragic façade of roadside diners and elaborate summer colonies and honeymoon motels. The high ridges are a series of somber outcroppings, wounded with the grinding scars of the glaciers that shaped them. Hawks and eagles soar on the winds that sigh through these hemlock ridges. There are beavers working in the feeder streams. Kingfishers are active along the rivers, and swallows catch mayflies during a hatch. Bears and wildcats are killed each season, and sometimes there is even the report of a cougar. There are still thousands of deer in the dense second-growth forests of hardwoods, hemlocks, and pines, whitetails that wax fat on the apples of colonial orchards long abandoned and overgrown.

Wild turkeys are coming back slowly. Grouse and woodcock are plenti- ful enough for those who know the covers. Sometimes there is a horned owl flushed from a hemlock thicket, and an angler working a bend away from the road may see a pileated woodpecker threading among the trees.

American fly-fishing literature has its genesis in the little rivers of these eastern mountains. Fishermen like Theodore Gordon, Edward Ringwood Hewitt, George La Branche, and Preston Jennings wrote their books about such rivers as the Neversink, Beaverkill, Willowemoc, and the Brodheads. These rivers are still beautiful, although some of their solitude has been sur- rendered to gas stations and automobile graveyards and drive-in movies, and there are still trout rising to their fly hatches.

Nymph fishing arrived on these rivers about thirty-odd years after Hal- ford sent his folio of dry flies to Theodore Gordon at a simple farmhouse near the Neversink. Gordon became interested in Skues, in spite of his early debt to the dry-fly methods perfected by Halford, and he fished nymphlike patterns when the fish were taking subaquatic forms. George La Branche speculated about nymphs in his classic book *The Dry Fly and Fast Water*, which appeared four years after Skues published his original *Minor Tactics of the Chalk Stream*, the book that introduced nymph fishing in the United Kingdom. La Branche outlined his frustrations with rising fish that were clearly nymphing, ignoring the adult mayflies riding and fluttering down the current.

La Branche is perhaps most famous for modifying British dry-fly theory to fit the swift little rivers of the Catskills and Appalachians. His little *Dry Fly and Fast Water* was primarily shaped on the Beaverkill, Brodheads, and Willowemoc. Although his reputation among fly-fishermen is focused on the dry-fly method, La Branche also had a practical knowledge of nymphs and nymph-fishing tactics. His dry-fly purism is more a legend in the minds of his disciples than a narrow dogma constricting his own vision, and La Branche was never blindly committed to the dry-fly method. His writings suggest fishing a sparsely dressed wet fly to nymphing trout, selecting a color and configuration suggesting the naturals, and working it past the fish like a hatching nymph.

Guy Jenkins is a man who fished with both Gordon and La Branche, and furnished much of the material in *The Notes and Letters of Theodore Gordon,* which John MacDonald collected and edited in 1947. Jenkins and his father knew Gordon well, and both regularly purchased the exquisite dry flies that came from his workbench.

Gordon and La Branche were not the dry-fly purists everybody thinks they were. Jenkins smiles puckishly. *They fished wet flies and nymphs fairly often—and even a Scripture bucktail or two when they found a good fish minnowing!*

Edward Ringwood Hewitt was the first American fishing writer to explore the subject of nymphs and nymph tactics consciously. His soft-cover pamphlet entitled *Nymph Fly Fishing* was published in 1935, and although it introduced several fresh ideas to a transplanted British doctrine, it was constrained in its scope by the character of his fishery on the Neversink. His mileage of that famous river is now buried under the Neversink Reservoir, except for a few cribbing pools presently included in the holdings of the Big Bend Club. The Hewitt water was famous for its log-cribbing pools, with relatively quiet impoundments above and deep, slow-flowing water below. Big trout loved the foaming, well-oxygenated water under the cribbing. Without such dams, the Neversink is a surprisingly cold ecosystem for its size, with sweeping riffles and strong chutes and empty-looking ledge-rock pools. It was incredibly clear and slightly acid, holding fine fastwater hatches of mayflies and Plecoptera and sedges. Its chemistry and temperature favor several fly hatches that are more common farther north, insects like the exaggeratedly flat *Rhithrogena* nymphs and the strikingly triangular-shaped nymphs of the *Baetisca* mayflies. The cribbing dams raised the temperature of the Hewitt mileage, and the creation of slow-water zones tended to favor insect forms that had existed in minimal populations before Hewitt added his stream improvements.

Such ecosystemic changes made the swimming nymphs and pupae more important to the Neversink fishery than they originally had been. The unchanged riffles and chutes still held the clinging flat-bodied mayfly nymphs and the tent-shaped nymphs of the *Baetisca* genus. Rising temperatures also favored the swimming slow-water nymphal forms.

These natural and man-made factors played a major role in both the innovations and limitations of *Nymph Fly Fishing*, although it was written with the typical Hewitt posture of complete expertise in all facets of the subject. The unusually large populations of flat-bodied and triangular nymphs led to the development, in concert with John Alden Knight at the Hewitt camp on the Neversink, of shaping lacquer-soaked dubbing with a pair of needle-nosed pliers. Their jaws had been filed to make the nymphs flat and elliptical, or sharply triangular in cross section. Although saturation in lacquer reduced the lifelike character of the dubbed-fur bodies, Hewitt clearly recognized that the nymphs of his river included configurations not found among the round-bodied species imitated by Skues. The slow currents above and below his cribbing dams increased the population of swimming nymphs, and led Hewitt to resurrect the slow hand-twist retrieve to fish his nymphs with a swimming motion along the bottom. It is an ancient wet-fly method in which a sunk fly is retrieved at various speeds, from the fast, almost erratic movements of the *Callibaetis* mayflies to the laborious travels of some clambering species. The speed of the retrieve varies, although the teasing motion imparted to the nymph is governed by winding the incoming fly line on the left hand, with a steady rolling movement of the wrist. Hewitt found the hand-twist retrieve essential on his impoundments and cribbing pools, and Bergman emphasized the technique in *Trout,* believing it the key to successful nymph tactics. The comprehensive study of subaquatic entomology, which interested neither Hewitt nor Bergman, puts the hand-twist method in better perspective. However, it is a critical factor in fishing quiet waters with nymphs.

Both Hewitt and his fishing camp are gone now, like Bergman and John Atherton as well, men whose fishing was strongly influenced by the old master and his river. The ancient Buick with the rod holes cut in its roof no longer traverses the rough twin-rut trails along the Neversink. Change is still inevitably erasing the pastoral beauty of the region, although its sense of the past still survives in the white clapboard church at Claryville, with its wooden trout weathervane.

Preston Jennings devoted an entire chapter to fishing his imitative nymphs in *A Book of Trout Flies,* which the famous Derrydale Press published in 1935. It was the genesis of the disciplined studies in American fishing entomology that Gordon had suggested in his notes fifty-odd years before. The precise taxonometric identification of the hatches and the illustrations of the insects themselves equaled the British books of Ronalds, Halford, and Moseley. Jennings ranged widely along the eastern rivers, collecting fly hatches from the Raritan and Brodheads in the south through all the famous Catskill rivers to the Ausable and Battenkill in northern New York. His imitations of the fast-water American nymphs were a marked improvement over the earlier lacquered patterns developed by Hewitt and Knight on the Neversink. The Jennings series included several imitations of the principal *Ephemerellas* and *Stenonema* nymphs so important to our fly-fishermen. Jennings was a frequent visitor to the charming West Kill Tavern, fishing the tumbling West Kill and the pastoral Schoharie. The proprietor was Arthur Flick, and Jennings and Chip Stauffer taught Flick the secrets of dressing and fishing the elegant flies of the Catskill school.

Flick became fascinated with the entomological studies of Jennings and Leslie Thompson, ultimately tied flies that equaled the best efforts of his teachers in their slender perfection, and began the systematic collection of fly hatches on his beloved Schoharie. Thompson and Raymond Camp, then fishing editor for *The New York Times,* constantly badgered Flick into writing his excellent little *Streamside Guide.* It has become a classic portrait of the Schoharie and its fly hatches, and an essential book in any working collection on trout fishing. Flick still ties his exquisite flies and fishes the river, but the charming West Kill Tavern is gone. It was lost in a winter fire that engulfed its rambling clapboard frame, licking at the tiger-maple chairs and antimacassar couches, smoldering in the worn oriental runners and colonial hooked rugs, and melting the nineteenth-century glass cases of woodcock and grouse.

Except for the scholarly work of Jennings, with the proper taxonometric definition and illustration of the insects found in his *Book of Trout Flies,* most American work on nymphs and nymph fishing was primitive and incomplete when compared with the British work of the preceding fifty years. Charles Wetzel is the recognized Dean Emeritus of the Weikert water on Penns Creek in Pennsylvania, and although he added to our knowledge of American flies and nymphs in his *Practical Fly Fishing,* its pen drawings were inaccurate and lacked information about the precise coloring of the natural insects. Wetzel published his little book in 1943, four years before Flick appeared with his *Streamside Guide to Naturals and Their Imitations.* The first printings of Flick were tarnished by erratic color reproductions of the naturals, but this failing has been corrected in the modern edition issued in recent years.

However, the muses of history are fickle, and the most important American studies in nymph fishing went virtually unnoticed in this period. Those investigations were the work of a simple Pennsylvania toolmaker who fished the Analomink water on the Brodheads. Jim Leisenring spoke in the broken rhythms that betrayed his ancestry in the German Palatinate, but his mind was disciplined and thorough. Leisenring was not really a writer, but like Gordon and his almost legendary correspondence with Halford fifty years earlier, Leisenring had exchanged letters with Skues.

Our myopic preoccupation with the dry-fly method, mixed with blind reverence for the trinity of Gordon and La Branche and Hewitt, led most American anglers to neglect Leisenring and his wet-fly theories in favor of the more glamorous myth-heroes of American fly-fishing. Yet it was Leisenring who quietly adapted the techniques of Cutcliffe and Stewart and Skues to the character and fly-life of American rivers, just as Gordon and George La Branche modified the British dry-fly theories for the swift little rivers of the Catskills.

Leisenring worked primarily on the Brodheads, and its difficult fishing had considerable influence on both his tactics and his fly patterns. The little river has a rich and storied past, its history detailed in my book *Remembrances of Rivers Past,* and it was famous a half-century before the genesis of the Catskill tradition. Such a sense of history had its effect on Leisenring and his subaquatic studies. The river had attracted all of the famous American anglers from George Washington Bethune to Edward Ringwood Hewitt. It was the favorite of La Branche when he was at work on *The Dry Fly and Fast Water,* and it was home water for Leisenring and his circle of disciples—wryly called the twelve apostles whenever they gathered at supper in the little hotel at Analomink.

Such disciples included skilled fishermen like Chip Stauffer and Pete Hidy and Richard Clark, all famous anglers and fly-dressers in subsequent years. It was these men who talked Leisenring into organizing his notebooks into *The Art of Tying the Wet Fly* in 1941, and Hidy helped him polish the manuscript in its final form. The outbreak of war caused its audience to miss the book and dilute its importance, and it has survived as a collector's item among knowledgeable anglers. There was a new commemorative edition of Leisenring published twenty years after his death in 1971, with some annotations and additions by Pete Hidy, and another generation is finding new wisdom in *The Art of Tying the Wet Fly.*

There was a portrait of Leisenring behind the bar in the little hotel at Analomink. Both the little hotel and most of its fly-fishing regulars are gone now, like the Spruce Cabin Inn and the Lighthouse Tavern and the family-operated hotel at Henryville which sheltered six generations of fishermen before it was finally sold and its river holdings leased to a private fly-fishing club. The little river is still there. The public water that Leisenring loved at Analomink and the Stokes Mill has been tragically changed by floods. His notebooks on its fly hatches, and the precise coloring required to match them, still survive as they were assembled along the river. Leisenring insisted that such judgments be resolved *in situ* with the singular quality of the light along the Brodheads, with its dark ledges and rhododendron and somber hemlock thickets. Brodheads regulars still fish the dancing riffles below Canadensis, the tumbling runs and flats on the century-old club water at the Brodheads Forest and Stream property, and the smooth-flowing pools under the spreading oaks and buttonwoods at Henryville. April rain trickles down the windows of the Haase farmhouse, the home water of the Brodheads Flyfishers, and the portraits of the famous watch silently from the sitting-room walls. Leisenring knew them all in his tenure on the river, and there are still days when his lessons are as bright as freshly minted coins, when the regulars on the river are fully aware of their debt to the father of American nymph-fishing.

Other fishing writers have followed his example. Two books appeared in 1951, the year that Leisenring died, and each added fresh material to our nymph techniques. Edward Sens was another expert fly-dresser who studied the nymphs of the Catskill rivers in considerable depth. The result was a superb series of imitative flies, keyed to nymph dressings for the better known dry-fly patterns. It included the best-known modern nymphs on our eastern rivers. Although they are effective, most of these mayfly nymphs are rather directly evolved from the theories of Skues. Sens, however, added two caddis-fly pupal imitations that were extremely effective and completely original concepts. Edward Sens did not write about his nymph fishing, leaving that work to Ray Ovington and his *How to Catch Trout on Wet Flies and Nymphs,* which largely codified studies made by Sens.

John Atherton wrote the second book that included new data on American nymph fishing. His little volume *The Fly and the Fish* was also published in 1951, and both its innovative thinking and its lyric mood have made it an American classic. The pervasive influence of Hewitt is found in some of the fly-tying techniques recommended by Atherton, but the series of nymph patterns is completely original. Atherton was both a skilled fisherman and a superb artist with a mind delicately balanced between creativity and a sense of tradition. His death while fighting a salmon on the Miramichi has robbed us of the sequel to *The Fly and the Fish*.

A. J. McClane published his fine book *The Practical Fly Fisherman* in 1953, and it included an excellent chapter on fishing the nymph. McClane is thoroughly versed in nymph fishing, suggesting imitation of the tiny pupae that trigger a smutting rise in still waters, as well as more conventional nymphs and tactics. McClane also speculated on emerging nymphs and their imitative requirements, a subject tentatively explored two years later in my book *Matching the Hatch,* which also included a series of conventional nymph patterns.

Sid Gordon was a knowledgeable limnologist and angler who understood the relationships between fly fishing and stream entomology. His observations on nymphs in Michigan, Minnesota, and Wisconsin are found in *How to Fish from Top to Bottom,* which was also published in 1955. It was a book that had a wealth of wisdom and fresh information concealed in its random, disarmingly anecdotal style. Jim Quick published an introductory book called *Fishing the Nymph* five years later, in 1960. It is a loosely organized primer on the nymph method, but explored a wide range of nymphs from the imitative patterns of Flick and Sens to a series of fancy patterns without any entomological basis. Ted Rogowski introduced his series of hatching nymphs in a contribution to *American Trout Fishing,* the anthology compiled to commemorate Theodore Gordon by members of the prestigious Theodore Gordon Flyfishers. It is a major addition to American nymph-fishing theory. The fine little book entitled *Tying and Fishing the Fuzzy Nymphs* was written by E. H. Rosborough in 1969. It outlines the patterns and tying methods evolved over the past thirty-odd years on western rivers by one of the best professional tiers in America. Its flies include not only the common mayflies, stoneflies, and Trichoptera imitations, but also caddis larvae, crustaceans, caddis pupae, damselfly and dragonfly nymphs, and midge patterns. Although its catalogue of imitations is based on insects and crustaceans found on rivers of the Pacific Northwest, both its flies and its fishing methods have application on trout streams everywhere. Rosborough and his original research are perhaps the first major contribution to the theory and techniques of American nymph fishing since Leisenring.

The second major innovation occurred only two years later when Douglas Swisher and Carl Richards completed their book *Selective Trout,* a sizable volume remarkable for its original studies in entomology, its experiments in fly design and construction, its studies of nymph behavior, and its emphasis on imitating emerging nymphs. Most fishermen have been fascinated with their no-hackle and parachute dry flies, believing that these demonstrate a unique innovation in the fly-dressing art. Such critical judgments could come only from anglers who are not fly-tiers themselves, or from fly-tiers who are unfamiliar with the history of fly-making. No-hackle flies have been fished in the film since Cotton and Bowlker and Pritt, and the original twelve patterns described in the *Treatyse on Fysshynge with an Angle* were similar no-hackle patterns in common use during the fifteenth century. It is not the structure of their dry flies that is unique, but their understanding that a no-hackle design offered some advantages in fooling selective trout with imitations of the smaller mayflies, particularly in smooth currents. Parachute hackles, extended-body imitations, and hackle-wing spinners have also been tied and fished for many years in both Europe and the United States. Extended-body mayfly imitations and nymphs have also been used by several tiers. Nevertheless, such criticism is intended not for the content of *Selective Trout* but for those who believed these concepts were completely new. Yet the book is a cornucopia of original contributions to American trout-fishing theory and technique.

Its innovations lie in the areas of identifying and imitating a whole phalanx of new aquatic insects, fresh observations about their behavior before and during emergence, insights into the flight patterns of egg laying, the attempt to devise a whole series of imitations in precise imitation of the various stages in a hatch, experiments in imitating the hatching mayflies and sedges in the film, and a whole series of exploratory ideas in imitating nymphs and pupae. Perhaps the most unusual nymph-theory concept is a modification of the extended-body nymphs explored by others, a hinged body-extension that moves freely in the current, suggesting the writhing body movements of a nymph en route from the bottom to the surface of the water. The major importance of these concepts has sometimes been missed in our preoccupation with its dry-fly innovations and extensive color photographs of living insects, but their fresh thinking in terms of emerging nymphs, pupal forms, and larvae place them in a class with the other creative thinkers of fly dressing in this century—Skues, Dunne, Harding, Mottram, and Marinaro—and our fly-fishing theory needs additional work in these directions.

Such innovation will certainly continue in the future, and it is hoped that *Nymphs* will place our investigations in imitating and fishing the subaquatic insect forms on a sound entomological basis. It must not be assumed that the nymphs, larvae, and pupae described and portrayed in this book include all of the subaquatic insects important to American anglers. Other fishermen will undoubtedly add to this catalogue of nymphal forms in the future, just as *Selective Trout* has greatly expanded our knowledge of American fly hatches since *Matching the Hatch* was completed twenty years ago. There will always be missing pieces in our puzzle.

Nymphs, larvae, and pupal forms constitute between seventy-five and ninety-five percent of the trout diet. The flies and tactics outlined in *Nymphs* are intended to suggest the principal underwater diet available to the trout in various regions of the United States. These studies include all types of immature aquatic insects between their subsurface lives and their hatching, including the brief transistory moments that lie between the emerging nymph and its adult. The principal American nymphs, larval forms, and pupae of the various insect orders and genera are covered in these pages, along with the tiny scuds, freshwater shrimps, and sowbugs.

Proper imitation of these many diet forms is not only a problem of fly-dressing color and configuration, with the single problem of a drag-free float, but also a whole spectrum of presentation designed to simulate different nymphal forms at varying depths of water. Each order and genus has different patterns of movement and behavior, and there are subvariations in these patterns along the bottom, in the intermediate depths of water, working immediately under the surface, hanging in the surface as breathing pupal forms, and actually emerging in the meniscus film.

Therefore the primary key to success with nymphs is both precise imitation and techniques of fishing those imitations to suggest the underwater behavior of the naturals. The following chapters will attempt to outline my preferences in nymph-fishing tackle, experience with selectivity to subaquatic diet forms, the collection of nymphal forms and experiments in fly-dressing since *Matching the Hatch,* and observations of nymph behavior that affects the methods of fishing them. These chapters will perhaps outline a more comprehensive matrix of American nymphs—their precise coloring and configuration, their hatching cycles and distribution, and the relationships between their behavior and fishing their imitations, to suggest their singular patterns of movement.

Some Notes on Nymph-Fishing Tackle

Since the father of our modern nymph-fishing tactics was the British writer George Edward MacKenzie Skues, perhaps his tackle preferences are worth studying. Skues abandoned traditional British tackle rather early in his career and almost casually recorded that minor heresy in his *Nymph Fishing for Chalk Stream Trout*. The catalyst for his conversion was an American-made rod from the skilled hands of Hiram Leonard. Skues acquired it through an American friend in 1903. It measured ten feet, but Skues was soon intrigued with even smaller rods.

Edward Ringwood Hewitt and his young friend Edward Mills traveled to the Crystal Palace in 1904, participating in the International Fly-Casting Tournament in London. Hewitt demonstrated a classic nine-foot Leonard to Skues at the tournament, and Edward Mills represented the New York agents for the Leonard shop.

The following winter, Skues completed a particularly successful case for his clients, and in gratitude for his legal services Skues was offered the finest fly rod that British sterling could purchase.

The master nymph fisherman chose a nine-foot Leonard. Skues observed that its smooth, fluid action was a marked contrast to the relatively stiff dry-fly actions that had become fashionable under the influence of Halford and Marryat. Such rods were conceived to switch-cast the moisture from a floating fly before it was cast again. Skues observed that such equipment seemed like weaver's beams once he had fished the Leonard. Its smooth action permitted him to false-cast without drying his nymphs. The wet nymphs sank with precision when they touched the current above a working fish. Skues tells us, in *Nymph Fishing for Chalk Stream Trout,* that its precise character was a major factor in his Itchen experiments, and he fished the Leonard happily for a half-century.

Such conclusions were at odds with the accepted tackle recommended by Stewart in his *Practical Angler,* fifty years before Skues acquired his second Leonard. Stewart preferred relatively light, stiff-action rods, although he was writing about the long, three-piece designs fashionable early in the nineteenth century.

Stewart did argue for rod tapers that flexed into the grip, and discussed construction in ash, hickory, yew, lancewood, logwood, greenheart, and bamboo. His favorite rod had its butt and middle joints of cane, with a three-strip tip section assembled with its power-fibers outside. His preference for a stiff rod is understandable when one examines the soft, willowy equipment usually fished in his time, and the clumsy, hollow-butt rods used to store extra tips were so unresponsive that Stewart turned gratefully to lighter gear that flexed well into the butt section.

Frank Sawyer is a riverkeeper at Salisbury in the pastoral chalk-downs of Wiltshire, and is the present heir to the Skues nymph-fishing tradition. His thoughts on nymphing rods are found in the book *Nymphs and the Trout,* and are a logical evolution from the nine-foot Leonard that Skues discovered at the Crystal Palace Exposition in 1904.

Sawyer likes a rod that works its slow power deep into the butt section, is relatively stiff in its middle tapers, and finishes radically in a rather delicate tip. Such compound tapers are usually called parabolic or semi-parabolic actions. The concept evolved in a number of parallel experiments performed by anglers like Hewitt, Payne, Young, Garrison, Knight, and Ritz. Sawyer fishes a semi-parabolic designed and built in France for his techniques by Charles Ritz.

It is described in *Nymphs and the Trout* and was made by Pezon and Michel at Amboise. Ritz has christened it his Sawyer Nymph, and it measures eight feet, ten inches, with an action similar to his other parabolic type tapers.

Ritz prefers a rod with a smooth, progressive power that works deep into the butt section. His best designs can be felt flexing below the cork grips under the load of casting. Like most parabolic-type actions, the middle section of the rod is relatively stiff and the tip calibrations are rather delicate. Such designs will accommodate heavier line loads and longer casts, and strike more delicate tippets relative to their weight, once an angler has mastered their timing. Most polished fishermen prefer such rods for all-around fishing, and their compound fine-tip actions are ideally suited to presenting the nymph.

Skues, Stewart, and Sawyer were all correct in their preference for supple, powerful rods with delicate tips and tapers that stressed deep into the butt section. These writers were not advocating the soft wet-fly actions fashionable for brook trout in the nineteenth century, supple ring-and-keeper rods designed for the relatively short casts and small *fontinalis* of eastern streams, but for the modern compound tapers refined by craftsmen like Young and Garrison. Similar compound tapers have been worked out by the artisans at Pezon and Michel under the nervous eyes of Charles Ritz. Everett Garrison and Paul Young have built many small rods of such compound design. But they never argued that only the tiny rods weighing less than three ounces were truly sporting.

Nymph fishing also demands sufficient length to manipulate a drifting fly-swing properly, mending line upstream or down to dampen or accelerate fly speed. Such rods must also have sufficient power to strike a fish against the current load on a sinking line, or the slack drift of a long leader fished greased-line at the surface. They must also avoid shearing a fine tippet. Rod length is often key to manipulating the nymph on rising fly swings or surface drifts that suggest the struggles of an emerging insect.

Nevertheless, it is difficult to discuss rods and other tackle in completely abstract terms. Perhaps it would be best to investigate the equipment that I fish regularly. There are a number of fine rods in my collection that fish the nymph beautifully under many conditions, and perhaps discussing each is the best vehicle for expressing my attitudes.

Perhaps the best all-purpose nymph rod in my tackle closet is a fine eight-foot Parabolic Fifteen built with an extra-slow butt taper by the late Paul Young. This particular rod has two tip sections. There is one designed for distance or relatively large flies or a sinking line. It is fitted with a five-sixty-fourths tip guide, and will punch out a weighted size-two nymph a considerable distance on a big western river. The fine tip is tapered for more delicate work. It has a four-sixty-fourths tip guide and will still cast eighty feet cleanly. Working closer, its tip calibrations are delicate enough to handle a fine 6X tippet of the modern limp nylons. The ferrule is a fifteen-sixty-fourths, hand-machined friction type of German silver, and its size gives the Parabolic Fifteen its name. Its cane has surprisingly little change in taper between the single ferrule and its grip. The middle calibrations provide power and control under the stress of long line-loading and the double-haul. Its most radical tapers lie in the final eighteen inches below its tip guide on both the distance and fine-tackle tips. This custom Parabolic Fifteen has performed flawlessly over sixteen seasons, fishing huge pools on the Yellowstone as perfectly as tiny nymphs on the little Brodheads.

Such rods work in slow, rather powerful rhythms in spite of weighing only four ounces. Their timing is difficult to master when an angler has fished his entire life with so-called dry-fly actions, with their stiff butt sections and soft tips, or extremely fast tapers that matched the philosophy of rod-makers like Dickerson. These fast-action rods are the legacy of writers like Halford and Hewitt, who argued that a fast action was best suited to the rapier flick-flick rhythm of false casts needed to work the moisture from a dry fly.

Hewitt apparently abandoned his fast-action theories in the last years of his life, for he wrote, in *Trout and Salmon Fisherman for Seventy-five Years,* that he no longer preferred the stiff butt sections and soft tip actions he had advocated years before. There are films of the old master in his twilight years, fishing slow-action rods that look relatively stiff in the tip-section tapers. Hewitt advocated smooth power instead of softness, much like the tapers that Paul Young evolved later in designs like the Parabolic Fifteen; the evolution of such actions is not yet complete.

Hewitt and other experts of his generation preferred three-piece rods because the shorter sections were more conveniently transported. Hewitt also agreed that the single ferrule in a two-piece design imposed only one dead point in the flow of its action, but argued that a single midpoint ferrule occurred at a critical nodal point in its flexing under stress.

Since his books have become less influential in the years past midcentury, modern rod-makers have virtually all turned to two-piece rods. The trend represents both a desire to shave weight in the light modern rods, and a search for optimal power-flow.

Most anglers believe that two-piece designs are superior rods. It is certainly true that a single ferrule reduces the weight of a delicate fly rod, and that it means slightly more power in ratio to that weight. Such concepts are more applicable in light rods under eight feet in length, and in most designs they are more theoretical than practical considerations. Fly fishermen are almost universally committed to two-piece designs under nine feet. However, the practical superiority of two-piece rods over the older three-piece designs is perhaps more critical in the minds of modern anglers than it is in demonstrable fly-rod dynamics.

Hewitt pioneered a number of modern concepts in rod fittings too. His sense of craftsmanship is still evident in the exquisitely machined reel seats found on rods built by Leonard and Payne. Larger guides more closely spaced were another Hewitt specification, along with oversized butt guides placed well out from the grip to facilitate shooting the line. Such butt-guide spacing also helps with line work in driving a double haul. Closely spaced guides distribute both casting and fish-playing stress more evenly across a delicate rod. Their spacing is a balance between eliminating line-slap between guides and cumulative guide friction. Each of these factors is related to precise casting and presentation and each has its virtues in nymph fishing too, since smooth line work handles the flies more gently and entrains more moisture in their bodies and hackles.

However, Hewitt did not anticipate our postwar revolution in fly lines. His generation fished the supple English lines of silk, and used exquisite leaders of Spanish silkworm gut. There was a poetry in such materials. The lines and leaders were organic and almost alive. Woven silk lines and silkworm gut leaders functioned in absolute harmony, turning over beautifully when perfectly balanced, and a well-soaked leader sank delicately through the surface film.

Yet there were flaws in such poetics. The silk lines rotted easily and developed tacky finishes when not in use. Constant cycles of dressing and drying lines required that a well-equipped angler have two of each type he was fishing. The undressed silk fly line sank moderately and provided a medium-depth presentation of the wet fly more effectively than a modern sink-tip taper, but it had a short lifespan fished entirely wet. Silkworm gut leaders were equally short-lived, required soaking in glycerin and water in special cases to achieve their full breaking strain, and were relatively fragile even in the heavy diameters. Our modern lines and leaders are a great improvement, although there are fishermen who are still addicted to gut and silk.

Modern fly lines offer us a wholly new spectrum of fly-fishing tactics that did not exist twenty-odd years ago. Nylon floating fly lines really float well with a modicum of cleaning and maintenance, and they last for years. Composite synthetic fibers and plastic finishes are the reason. The nymph-fisherman who works the surface film or presents his imitations just under the surface would benefit from the modern double-tapers, fishing small rivers over shy trout, or using the floating weight-forward types on bigger water where distance is the criterion. My reels carry mahogany floating lines for difficult fish, and white lines for big water, where line color helps keep track of the fly-swing.

Sinking fly lines offer a remarkably precise palette of wet-fly tactics. There are the original Dacron types with plastic finishes that are roughly equivalent to the present standard sinking lines. There are also slow-sinking lines that roughly approximate the behavior of the undressed silk designs fished in earlier times and, like the sink-tip lines, they are intended for fishing at moderate depths. Sink-tip designs offer the benefit of a running line behind the sinking tapers which floats, providing both faster pick-up and better shooting qualities on a long cast. Fast-sinking lines permit us to fish wet flies and nymphs at depths totally impossible in the past, and to fish swift, heavily broken current that would quickly ride a fly-swing to the surface on normal lines. My reels are fitted with dark-green sinking lines, since such tapers swing deep among the fish and are too visible in pale colors. Although I am thoroughly converted to the modern lines, and the broad range of tactics they make possible, a sense of tradition and esthetics causes me to have doubts about the garish greens and blues and oranges we see from some manufacturers. Anyone who began his fishing with the rich green, chocolate, yellow, and amber fly lines of the past, and remembers the smell and feel of a fine King Eider in those years before the Second World War, is inevitably offended at such lapses in taste. Our manufacturers should offer a better example to the buying public.

Many anglers are unhappy with the difficulty they have in picking up a sinking-type line to make a fresh cast. It is surprising how many do not realize that these lines are not designed for a long-line pickup, and that they must be fished out or retrieved at the end of a cast until relatively little line remains in the water. Then the entire cast must begin again. Since these modern lines have caught me many nymphing trout that could not have been taken on a silk or nylon floating line, I cannot agree with the attitude that sinking fly lines are an unsporting kind of bottom fishing, and that any fish not willing to rise to a shallow fly-swing is not worth taking. On the contrary, the sinking lines have extended fly-fishing into types of water and and cold-weather conditions which were formerly the domain of trolling, bait-fishing, and spinning gear. Such trends should not be discouraged in the future, out of an exaggerated sense of purism or tradition.

Several recent books have exhaustively covered the field of line-to-leader knots and leader tapers, and I shall not duplicate their material here. However, some comments on my preferences in knots and leader design might prove useful in your nymph fishing. The demands of relatively small rivers, quiet currents, and shy trout cause me to fish almost entirely with long, delicate leaders of the modern limp nylons. Such leaders are from ten to fifteen feet, depending on current speed and the depth of the water. Their butts are matched to line weights of four, five, and six since heavier lines drop too harshly under such conditions. The tippets are never stronger than 4X, should the imitation fished be rather large or wind-resistant in casting, and I usually fish 5X or 6X nylon points. Sometimes finer European nylons, between .003 and .0045, are useful, but I find them difficult to fish without breaking off when fished on sinking lines. Such tackle is well suited to still ponds, chalkstream-like flats, and sophisticated trout that see many anglers. Double-taper lines land softly and are best suited to such conditions. Heavier water and big lakes are less demanding, although still currents and windless days can sometimes be a problem on larger waters too. However, wind and distance casting usually dictate compound leaders with butts of stiff nylon and tippets of limp material. Extreme winds can sometimes require leaders tapered entirely of stiff nylon. Depending on fly size, I fish such nymph waters with tippets between 0X and 3X limp nylon. Floating lines are useful and should be fitted with leaders of ten to fifteen feet, depending on tippet size. The use of sinking tip and full sinking lines requires somewhat shorter leaders, since the fine nylon tends to float and ride relatively high in the water because of its specific gravity, making the deeper line-swing less effective. The line-belly is the section riding deepest in the water, and too long a leader will only cancel its depth capabilities. Therefore, I usually fish ten-foot leaders on sink-tip lines, dropping back to nine feet on full sinking types.

Fly knots are a simple problem, and I use the standard nylon clinch knot for all but the biggest nymphs. Really large imitations of the burrowing mayflies, beetle larvae, dragonfly nymphs, or the large Plecoptera are best fastened with the regular Turle knot described in most books. Well-tied nail knots coated with Pliobond to smooth their contours are superb joints between lines and leaders. Dave Whitlock is a brilliantly innovative fly-dresser and tackle man who has experimented extensively with leader butts seated inside the fly-line core with epoxy. Certainly, in the delicate leaders such a knot is less visible and creates less disturbance in the water. Whitlock has also pioneered the use of small fluorescent markers, both with tubes of hot orange line slipped along the leader, and with hot fluorescent paints to smooth the contours of a nail-knot. His innovations are a great improvement on the old method of watching the floating line pause with a nymphing take or using a dry fly as a bobber. The dry-fly bobber was always clumsy to cast and difficult to keep floating, and the ordinary line was sometimes lost in the light or tumbling current. The bright spot of orange or yellow fluorescent is better, since it is visible both shallow and deep in the water, requires no attention like a dry-fly bobber, and casts and fishes normally.

But enough about lines and leaders for nymph fishing. We were talking about rods and reels designed to work the line easily in both short and long casts, teasing the fly-swing gently and holding as much moisture as possible in the flies during false-casting.

The Parabolic Fifteen in my collection is perfect for such work on most water with a wide range of nymph sizes. It weighs just under four ounces with a skeleton reel seat. The grip and reel seat are of my own design, concealing the hooded reel cap under the handle with the sliding ring below the reel. Such a system is self-tightening with the weight of the reel working down into the ring, much like the head of an axe or hammer seated with its own inertia.

The rod is perfectly matched with a Hardy Princess, measuring 3½ inches in diameter and weighing 4¾ ounces. Its action is complemented perfectly with six-weight lines of both floating and sinking types. Either three reels, or a reel with two extra spools, will permit a fisherman to carry a floating double-taper, sink-tip torpedo taper, and weight-forward line on each. Such equipment will cover the full spectrum of nymph techniques.

Greased-line tactics to emerging nymphs and pupae in or near the surface film require a floating line, and rods like the Parabolic Fifteen are perfect for fishing difficult conditions on fairly big water with a mahogany DT-6-F Aircel Supreme. Such lines are surprisingly close to the supple handling of the silk HDH English line I first used when Paul Young made the rod years ago.

Fishing intermediate depths to simulate swimming or hatching species is best accomplished with a modern sink-tip line. The type I have been using this past season with good success is an Orvis weight-forward line with a longer front taper and line-belly than are found on most designs of this character. Such tapers permit a relatively delicate delivery, rather untypical of weight-forward lines, and even cooperate for reasonably good roll-casts. The Orvis sinking lines have a brown forward-taper and sinking belly, with a pale tannish running line. Although my traditional sense is a little unsettled when confronted with two-color lines, the pale floating section is easily followed in conflicting currents.

The Wetcel WF-6-S or DT-6-S sinking lines are ideal for fishing the deeper reaches of a river, or working a freshwater shrimp just above the weeds in an inlet channel or beaver pond. Nymphs are often active along the bottom several hours before they actually hatch, exposing themselves to both the light and the fish rather recklessly. Many nymphal forms seldom stray far from the bottom until they emerge, like the clambering stoneflies and Ephemeroptera and caddis-fly larvae, and imitations must be fished there if the fish are taking them. Sinking lines and weighted nymphs are critical in imitating such forms.

The different tip sections of the Parabolic Fifteen give it a wide-ranging capability, working relatively still water with fine tippets, and big western riffles and flats with the heavier tip. Covering such water, and the shelving areas of impoundments and lakes, requires at least the density of six-weight lines to sink quickly enough to fishing depths.

There are several other fly rods in my collection that have similar actions and tapers. Some are slightly more powerful. Such equipment is best on huge western rivers, sprawling boat-rivers like the MacKenzie in Oregon or the Calcurrupe in Chile. Some climates are famous for wind, and rivers from the Laxamyri in Iceland to the Collón Curá and Chimehuin in Patagonia are big-rod water.

My collection includes the Orvis 8½-foot Battenkill at 4¾ ounces, the superb Young Parabolic Seventeen, and a matchless 8½-foot three-piece Garrison. These rods are perfectly suited to big water, fish the bigger nymphs, and will punch out a hundred-foot cast when required.

The Battenkill is excellent. It is a relatively new taper from Orvis, with somewhat finer tip calibrations and a softer action deep into the butt section. Its power is matched with eight-weight lines, ideally suited to sweeping western rivers like the Deschutes in Oregon or the Big Hole in Montana. Most often I fish them with WF-8-S and WF-8-S fast-sinking lines, using a Hardy Saint Aidan or Scientific Anglers System 8 reel. Such reels measure about 3¾ inches in diameter and weigh just under six ounces. This past summer I have been using the Orvis weight-forward WF-8-F with a long-taper that permits roll casting and a relatively soft presentation.

Such lines work big water with emerging nymph tactics, following flies in the film or a teasing fly-swing just under the surface to suggest hatching insects that drift some distance in their pupal and nymphal shucks. Eight-weight sinking, fast-sinking, and sink-tip lines add a full dimension to this superb Battenkill.

Similiar lines and reels match the experimental Young Parabolic Seventeen in my arsenal. It was originally built and owned by the late Paul Young and has an extra-slow butt. It has almost no taper between the butt guide and the grip. Its extreme compound taper is somewhat complex in its rhythms under stress, but its timing combines an ability to handle long casts easily, as well as protect a 4X tippet. The rod is fitted with three tips. One delicate taper is designed for light leaders, another is for most all-around tactics, and the third is a power taper for long casts, large flies, and winds. The power taper will load and deliver a nine-weight WF-9-S sinking line more than 100 feet under fishing conditions.

Most customers considered this remarkable rod too radical in its calibrations and timing, but Paul Young loved its qualities. It has been fished with both commitment and care, and he had expected to use it during the big *Hexagenia* hatch on the Au Sable the summer of his last illness. His widow sent the rod to me on the eve of my first trip to Argentina, more than twelve years ago.

Paul always wanted to fish Patagonia, Martha Young explained in the brief note that accompanied the rod. *You should fish it for him on those rivers down there.*

The final big-nymph rod in my collection is a seasoned 8½-foot three-piece Garrison, with the workmanship and patina of a fine violin. It is superbly matched with the same eight-weight lines and reels. Everett Garrison is a genius, the rare mixture of technician and poet, who builds a six-strip section in natural yellow cane so perfect that it almost lacks a high side. One rolls them in vain to find the stiff and soft bending planes to seat the guides. His skeleton reel seats and grips are almost ascetic in their lack of affectation. The chocolate silk wrappings at the ferrules and cork are a counterpoint for the translucent cream-silk wrappings at the guides. The exquisitely machined hard-alloy aluminum ring that secures the reel is tapered, another unique Garrison refinement in a rod whose visual character is a simple complement to the perfection of its craftsmanship. Like all truly great artisans, Everett Garrison insists on an almost monastic understatement in his work, refusing extra weight and ornamental embellishments and wrappings. His fly rods speak only through the functional perfection of their construction.

There are a number of lighter rods which I sometimes find well suited to nymph tactics. Their character is ideally suited to the easily spooked trout of eastern rivers, American chalkstreams like Letort Spring Run in central Pennsylvania, and western spring creeks from Sun Valley to Montana. They include Orvis Battenkills of recent eight-foot and 7½-foot models, one particularly delicate seven-foot Leonard, and another experimental compound-taper design from Paul Young.

Perhaps the best all-around rod in this group is the new eight-foot Orvis Battenkill designed for six-weight lines. It is a modern slow-action taper, less radical than the Young designs and somewhat easier to cast. It will fish a relatively wide range of line types and fly sizes, and I have found it unusually versatile, from my home rivers near New York to Montana and the tumbling Nantahala in North Carolina. It has the delicacy to fish a tiny nymph on a 6X tippet. It also has considerable power, and this past season I used one to take seventeen salmon in a single day on the Grimsá in Iceland. The wind was down and a delicate presentation was important in the Laxabakki meadows, and the best fish was a hook-jawed male of almost twenty pounds.

The rod weighs about four ounces, and is perfectly balanced with a Hardy Princess, using either the Orvis WF-6-F long-belly floating line or a WF-6-S Wetcel. The Princess measures 3½ inches and weighs 4¾ ounces. The fittings and walnut reel seat are typical of Battenkill craftsmanship, and it is one of the best rods in the Orvis line. Its eight-foot length is perfect for mending line and manipulating a nymph at varying depths and in conflicting currents.

Orvis has also experimented in recent years with a special eight-foot 3¾-ounce nymph rod designed for difficult fish with a light four-weight line. Unlike the four-ounce, eight-foot Battenkill, it will fish emerging nymphal and pupal imitations in the film on cobweb-sized nylons as fine as .0031. Such refinements are sometimes useful on very shy trout that are gorging on minute forms like *Chironomus* pupae. The tapers are clearly unsuited for windy days and distance casting, and they lack the muscle to fish a sinking line with real control, but the rod is capable of exquisite work. Mine is perfectly balanced with the Hardy Lightweight at 3 3/16 inches and 3½ ounces. It is best with a delicate DT-4-F floating line. Nymph-fishing with tiny imitations is its forte, and anglers having chalkstream-type conditions on their home waters should consider its unique properties—the eight-foot length permits ready manipulation of the nymph in quiet currents, and the four-weight line is well suited to fish selective trout.

Another fine rod manufactured by Orvis is its 7½-foot Battenkill Midge. Its action and length are also adapted to nymphing. The calibrations are not so radical as those found in the tapers designed by Paul Young, Everett Garrison, and Charles Ritz, but the action is certainly related to the relatively fine-tip and slow-butt school of thought. The rod will fish nylon as fine as .004, but will also cast eighty to ninety feet. It is balanced with the Hardy Lightweight and a floating line like the old HEH silks. The modern DT-4-F floating and DT-4-S sinking lines are perfect. Such capability matched with the delicacy for 7X tippets is valuable.

Paul Young built and owned a second experimental parabolic that has found its way into my hands. Like the longer Parabolic Seventeen, it has extremely delicate tip calibrations and a radical slow-butt taper between its grip and the stripping guide. Unlike the production Perfectionist, at 7½ feet and 2⅝ ounces, this rod weighs 2½ ounces with its light tip section and 2¾ ounces with its sinking-line tip. The finer tip takes a four-sixty-fourths tip-guide, and the heavier tip is mounted with a 4½-sixty-fourths fitting. The standard Young Perfectionist is a relatively stiff-butt design with both tips calibrated for four-sixty-fourths tops. With its somewhat slower butt-tapers and two tip-sections, it is an extremely versatile rod for small-stream work on shy fish.

The Hardy Featherweight at 2⅞ inches and three ounces is an excellent match for this little Young. However, this season I have been fishing it with the prototype of a new fly-reel design. It utilizes the ultralight alloys evolved from aerospace metallurgy, and is built for Orvis in Britain.

Its most striking feature is the complete absence of the enclosing reel frame found in most designs. There is an elegantly machined backplate. The spool is perforated in both faces, both to dry the line and reduce weight. The standard frame is eliminated to further cut weight, and in its place are simply the flange which supports the seat plate and a simple T-shaped pillar. The inner face of the reel spool is machined to receive the top edges of the T-shaped pillar and the flange. The reel slot must be kept well lubricated to function properly, and the prototype I have been testing measures three inches and weighs only three ounces, half an ounce less than the comparable Hardy. The reel will be named in honor of Charles Orvis, whose single-action ventilated-spool design patented in 1874 was the father of modern fly-reels. My prototype is utterly without trademark or engraving. Its workmanship speaks for itself, needing no such identification, and one hopes the future production models will show similar judgment. The weight, precision, and equilibrium between elegance and function make it a worthy heir to the original Orvis designs.

John Waller Hills observed in his contemplative book *A Summer on the Test* that each fly-fisher in his life encounters a rod that so matches his temperament and physical skills that it becomes part of him. The Young Perfectionist at 7½ feet and 2½ ounces, with its experimental butt-tapers and fitted with this delicate Orvis reel, passed on to me from the collection of its maker, is that rod in my fishing odyssey thus far—that perfect poetic balance of delicacy and power that feels alive in the hands.

The lightest and shortest rod I use for nymph fishing is a delicate little seven-foot Leonard. It is a delightful variation on the Leonard ACM-38 Catskill Fairy, weighing about 2¼ ounces. Although it is clearly possible to fish the nymph on shorter rods built by several manufacturers, including the classic Young Midge and Orvis Flea, many years of nymph-fishing experience lead to me believe that at least seven-foot rods are needed to control fly-swing properly. The little Leonard is one ferrule size larger than comparable Catskill Fairy models, but retains standard calibrations at the grip. The tip-guide is an extremely fine four-sixty-fourths and the rod takes a delicate DT-4-F floating line. It is matched with a Hardy Featherweight at 2⅞ inches and three ounces. Leonard originally built the rod to fish terrestrials on nylon as fine as .0031 and .0036. It has since proved itself in extremely difficult nymph-fishing, with minute imitations fished in the film. During late summer, when the riffles and runs of an eastern river become silk-smooth flats, such delicate gear is necessary on selective fish.

There are other fine rods built in the shops of other artisans, but I have attempted to limit this discussion to equipment I own and fish regularly. Superb split-cane rods have a unique quality. However, over the years I have seen and fished a number of superb fly rods ideally suited to modern fly tactics and nymphing in particular.

Such rods have usually been the work of craftsmen evolved in the family tree of skills that began with Hiram Leonard in 1871. Those original apprentices included men like Fred Thomas, Edward Payne, Eustis Edwards, and the Hawes brothers. Each of these artisans later made exquisite rods in his own shop.

Their work in turn inspired a fresh cycle of split-cane craftsmen. The roster includes names like Halstead, Gillum, Garrison, and the late Jim Payne, whose father had been one of the original Leonard apprentices. Gradually the magic of working bamboo emigrated west into the shops of makers like Powell and Stoner on the Pacific coast, Young and Dickerson in Detroit, and Granger and Philippson in Denver. Sewell Dunton left Montague when that company abandoned cane rods, and set up a new shop in western Massachusetts. Crompton began experimenting with five-strip rod theory in Minnesota, and his concepts were carried farther in the shop run by Nathaniel Uslan in New York. Cross worked wth twelve-strip double-built rods, adding two circumferential layers of bamboo power fibers. Such structures also multiplied the deadening effects of extra adhesives. However, Cross also trained Wes Jordan, the artisan who has controlled the craftmanship and calibrations at Orvis for several decades.

The angler fortunate enough to own such a masterpiece has a priceless piece of equipment, since the making of split-cane rods is a dying art. Various fishing friends own many fine examples of their work, and sometimes I have had the pleasure of fishing them, just as a concert master will sometimes let another violinist sample his Stradivarius.

There is the classic Payne that Bob Abbett let me fish on the home pool of the Beaverkill Trout Club, and I remember clearly the Thomas that a boyhood mentor let me fish on the Au Sable in Michigan. Jack Case was the editor who encouraged *Matching the Hatch*, and I once fished a delicate Halstead that he loved for years. Philip Nash and Martin Bovey have shared their Garrisons with me on the Brodheads in Pennsylvania and the Ruby in Montana. There was a Winston that belonged to Colin Pittendrigh, and Philip Wright has a favorite three-piece Leonard with the patina of years on the Roaring Fork. Gerry Queen owned a matched brace of Dickersons that he shared with me on a poetic reach of the Pere Marquette, and Leroy Whitney had a favorite four-strip Edwards Quadrate that he often carried to the Neversink and Willowemoc.

These rods were all perfectly suited to nymph fishing. Each offered the slow rhythms of a semi-parabolic action, relatively delicate tip-calibrations, and oversize guides. Such rods are capable of false-casting nymphs without costing them moisture, laying them softly on still currents, and fishing a fine leader without breaking off on good fish.

The first really good nymph rod I owned was a fine eight-foot Granger. It was the birthday rod my father gave me when I was seven years old. Granger built three-piece rods in those years, precisely wrapped in olive silk under a perfect finish of hand-rubbed varnish. The ferrules were exquisitely machined with elegant angular welts, and it had the hooded German-silver reel seat that ultimately became the Granger trademark. Its action was slow and smooth, perfectly matched with an HDH King Eider.

It was years later that I came to appreciate fully its ability to fish a nymph, on the Grundbach in southern Germany.

It is a pastoral reach of water. Mists shroud the mountains of the Allgäu in the mornings, and there were fine hatches. The little Grundbach is man made, gathering several alpine brooks into a half-mile millpond at Fischen-im-Allgäu. Its entire length measures about two miles from those duckpond beginnings to the bigger glacier-melt river below Oberstdorf.

We fished it regularly after the war, finding good fly hatches of dark claret-bodied *Leptophlebias* almost every morning. The overcast mornings were best, with a light misting rain that hung in the valley. The trout rose steadily to these little mayflies, but one rainy weekend in September the fly-hatches were unusually heavy. Good browns porpoised softly in the rain, working steadily in the weedy channels. The current was covered with mayflies, but we fished dry-fly imitations for several hours. Finally I tried a small nymph and took a fish promptly on the first cast.

They're nymphing! I called to my father.

Like most fly-fishermen these past few years, we were intrigued with ultra-small tackle, and I was fishing a two-ounce rod of six feet. It worked reasonably well on the trout working close along the bank, and those swirling to emerging nymphs along the weeds from forty to sixty feet out. We took fish after fish that morning on nymphs, until I located a really large brown working in midchannel below the town. It was a cast of almost ninety feet, virtually beyond the little rod when I was waist-deep in the trailing weeds. There were conflicting currents between my position that required mending the fly-swing both up and down. It was a difficult problem.

Cast after cast worked out into the rain and either fell short or dragged slightly just under the surface. The fish ignored me, porpoising every few seconds. Finally I walked back to the car and put up the eight-foot Granger, stringing its undressed silk line and selecting a ten-foot leader tapered to about .005. The worn little nymph that had taken fish steadily that morning was added to the tippet, and I waded back out toward the trout.

The fish was still working. *Let it soak*, I thought, pressing the coiled leader into a layered bed of silt.

Finally, I was ready and the leader sank readily in the current. The nymph worked out and settled above the trout. The rod delivered the cast without drying the fly, and it sank cleanly into a swing across the slow current above the fish. Raising the tip, I mended line and held the rod high as the fly reached its feeding station.

It porpoised lazily and I tightened.

He's on! I shouted.

The trout finally surrendered, weighing almost five pounds and measuring twenty-four inches. The rod was perfect for reaching the bigger fish, and I continued to fish it when they were nymphing. Its length worked the fly-swing perfectly in the crosscurrents among the weeds, its smooth action kept the nymphs wet, and its power was sufficient to reach fish beyond eighty feet easily. The little Granger was a superb rod, and although it was stolen a year after our return from Europe, there are times, twenty years later when I fish it happily in my mind.

Fishing the

THE RIVER is sm..lo-grass
meadows and swa..riffles a
half mile in length..aders of
city fisherman wh..ng in its
pools are a familia...g weeds.
Sometimes there....................................tails and
greenhead mallar..ountains
are cloaked in forests, and the river meadows....................se stands
of spruce and lodgepole pine.

The river is rich with fly life. Although it seldom produces heavy hatches and dry-fly fishing conditions, except for the big *Ephemera* and *Pteronarcys* flies that follow the spring snow-melt, it is a superb fly-fishing river. Its weeds are filled with scuds, freshwater shrimps, and mayfly nymphs, its riffling shallows with heavy populations of giant stoneflies. The man who can cast long and cover its sweeping currents with big nymphs can always catch his share of fish.

These are the headwaters of the Madison in the Yellowstone country. Its rich alkalinity and teeming life are born in the hot-spring meadows and geyser basins that feed its principal tributaries, the little Gibbon and the more famous Firehole that drains the area below Old Faithful. It is one of the most challenging reaches of fly water anywhere in the world. Its broad, weed-filled currents are a gargantuan copy of the weedy rivers in Hampshire—making it perhaps the largest chalkstream on earth.

It has been restricted to fly-fishing in recent years. The result is a river so good that its sport is better now than when I fished it in boyhood. Few rivers have improved in these decades of wanton bait-fishing and spinning, and its fish have never been easy. It is perfect for fly-fishing only.

The character of the river, with its extensive population of relatively small insects and smooth surface currents, has always made its trout selective. There are sometimes fishless days, with a raw wind storming down across the border or the first clinging snowfall in September. It was once primarily a rainbow fishery, and anglers who know its secrets can usually count on several two-pounders per day. But the heavy tourist pressure of the past thirty years has gradually decimated the rainbows, while its canny population of brown trout has survived and multiplied.

Fishermen who know the rainbow places, like the mile of swift water about ten miles above West Yellowstone or the pools behind the maintenance barns, can always find the odd rainbow between three to six pounds. But such big fish are usually browns.

There is a moderate spring run of fat rainbows coming into the upper Madison from Hebgen Reservoir, and anglers who like the raw spring weather and the heavy snow-melt currents can always find good sport. Although the early summer hatches of big *Pteronarcys* flies are not as impressive as the salmon-fly flights on other rivers, like the Big Hole and the Gunnison and the lower reaches of the Madison at Varney Bridge, it is still the best time to catch big fish with dry-fly imitations in its headwaters.

But its regulars prefer October fishing. The tourist crowds are gone then, and a man can find a modicum of solitude. The river is low and perfectly clear, accessible to anglers of average size and strength. Nights are cold and bright with stars, and the daylight hours are windless and warm after the false-winter squalls of early September. There is a good fall spawning run of brown trout from the Hebgen Reservoir, with a few camp-following rainbows after freshly spawned eggs. Migrating browns arrive steadily after the first hard frost, and fishing the straw-colored meadows then has a special poetry.

The rutting season has started too. Elk are gathering their harems in September, grazing in the bunch-grass bottoms and crossing the swift shallows of the river single file, their coats sleek with summer, antlers polished and glittering in the sun. The river and its marshy shallows and the lodgepole meadows teem with life in prelude to the bitter sleep of winter.

The principal fly hatches of the season on such rivers consist of the giant stoneflies, with two- and three-year life cycles. Therefore not only the giant, full-grown nymphs measuring two inches in length are available to the trout, but also the intermediate stages of growth, which vary between a half inch and the full-grown sizes. Nymphs of the giant *Acroneuria* and *Pteronarcys* flies are readily available in good numbers throughout the seasons. Although the well-known Montana nymphs were originally tied to simulate the *Acroneuria nigrita* species with its yellowish-orange thorax and thoracic gills, its configuration and black materials make it a consistent fish-taker on most western rivers—even though its yellow-chenille thorax makes it a poor imitation of the bigger *Pteronarcys* nymphs.

Although the giant stoneflies are represented by species on both eastern and western rivers, these genera are not found in heavy populations on waters east of the Rocky Mountains. The nymphs of the big *Perla* and *Pteronarcys* flies on eastern rivers emerge sporadically for several weeks, with hatches that never equal the blizzardlike stonefly flights typical of early summer in the west. However, the big eastern species are readily recognized and accepted by the trout, and imitations of their nymphs consistently produce large fish.

The Madison is a special case, and when the big autumn browns are running and in a taking mood, it is like a run at the tables of some elegant casino. The last time I fished it it was too early, in the middle of September, and the sport was only fair until the first autumn squall left the Yellowstone country covered with six inches of fresh snow. The mood of the river changed with the hard-frost nights that followed.

Gene Anderegg and I were fishing the Madison and Firehole that week, and each morning found more migratory browns moving up from the Hebgen Reservoir. Fishing improved on both rivers with the cool weather, but our last morning we decided to fish the upper meadows of the Madison.

Try the fast water at the rock slides, suggested Bud Lilly in his tackle shop at West Yellowstone. *It's the water below the road about ten miles above town.*

The morning was clear and cold. The bunchgrass meadows were pale with new frost, and steam rose in clouds from the hot springs along the river. There were several elk in the basin above West Yellowstone, and a small flock of geese were resting on a still reach of the river. We parked the station wagon above the stretch that Lilly recommended, where a jackstraw tangle of deadfalls lines the current.

Looks good, said Gene.

It was too cold for hatches, and no fish were working in the quarter mile of water below the car. Gene put up his powerful nine-foot Winston, and I strung the fly-line through a five-ounce parabolic. It is big water.

It's a good flat downstream, Gene observed. *You want to try the heavier rips along the logs?*

Fine, I agreed. *It all looks like good water.*

Gene waved and walked down the road, while I picked my way down the rockfall to the river. The swift current danced in the sunlight, sucking at the pale spruce logs lying in the river along the opposite bank. Gene is sales manager of a major camera manufacturer, and is a superb photographer. We were both hung with Leicas that morning, and had been shooting pictures of each other all week.

Yell if you hook one! he shouted.

The river looked alive and I waded out eagerly into its strong currents. The line worked out in a tight loop, gathering speed with a left-hand haul, and the big *Pteronarcys* imitation dropped tight against the deadfalls. The nymph settled into the current, there was a heavy swirl as a big brown turned from behind the logs and seized it, and the reel sang shrilly above the wind.

Gene! I shouted happily. *Gene!*

Anderegg was still walking along the road, and he came dogtrotting back with his cameras. The fish fought stubbornly in the swift current, but finally I forced it into the shallows toward the net. It thrashed angrily in the meshes, a deep-bellied brown of five pounds.

Okay. He finished shooting pictures and started back up the rock slide toward the road.

The river flowed smooth and deep along the drowned lodgepole. It was a perfect holding-lie, its current slow and emerald-green with weeds, and I dropped the nymph to drift enticingly along the run. The line tightened in the current, swinging the nymph lazily across the dark holding water, and I teased it with the rod tip. There was a heavy strike.

Fish! I shouted. *Fish on!*

Gene stopped in disbelief, laughed and shook his head in mock dismay, and started laboriously back down along the rock slide. It was a smaller fish, and its wild cartwheeling fight down the current spelled rainbow. It weighed about three pounds and we released it like the first fish, while Gene worked rapidly with his camera.

He was changing film in the shallows when I waded back into midstream. There was another likely run thirty feet below the holding lie that produced the rainbow. The first cast worked through the run, the nymph probing deep along the deadfalls, and nothing happened.

Looks like a good place. I shook my head.

Gene looked up from his camera. *Should be good,* he agreed. *Try another cast against the logs.*

The nymph settled into a deep swing, and I teased it seductively with a steady rhythm of the rod. There was no swirl, but a strong pull signalled a fish. *Another one!* I laughed happily. *Feels like a heavy fish!*

Damn! Anderegg laughed. *I don't mind playing photographer on this trip, but I'd like to get in a cast or two between your trout.*

Sorry, I grinned. *They're in the mood.*

It was a mood that lasted until twilight, when the cold night air raised a dense fog along the river, but during that day it wantonly surrendered its riches. We fished steadily back downstream toward West Yellowstone, leapfrogging from place to place in the station wagon. It was easy fishing, and we released thirty-odd fish between us that went from two to six pounds, all on the giant stonefly nymphs.

These big Plecoptera nymphs are unique among the stoneflies of American waters. Although some stoneflies are found in the outlets and inlets of lakes and impoundments, and along rocky shorelines where the wave action generates sufficient oxygen, the relatively high oxygen requirements of the Plecoptera find them in greater abundance on swift rivers and streams with bottoms of coarse gravel and rubble. Stoneflies play a considerably smaller role in the diet of trout in the limestone streams and western spring creeks, but on big swift-flowing rivers of our western mountains, the giant Plecoptera are so numerous that they are the principal component of the insect forms available to the fish.

The big stoneflies are unique in the sense that an imitation of the Plecoptera is perhaps the oldest fly pattern to reach us virtually unchanged in both dressing and name. Dame Juliana Berners included a stonefly in her legendary dozen patterns, when her *Treatyse of Fysshynge wyth an Angle* appeared almost five centuries ago. There were no sedges or mayflies identified in her list, although some of her dressings match common British hatches of those insect orders.

Flights of stoneflies are rather sporadic on eastern rivers, although small genera like *Taeniopteryx* and *Isoperla* sometimes emerge in sufficient numbers to cause a decent rise of trout. The large eastern stoneflies sometimes emerge in good numbers just after daylight, causing the fish to prowl the shallows in search of *Perla* and *Pteronarcys* nymphs, but such activity rarely produces a dry-fly hatch. Since the larger species have life cycles of more than a year, the big nymphs are available all season in various sizes and stages of development.

Stoneflies differ from mayflies and sedges in a number of obvious structural ways. Their wings are relatively shiny and brittle, resembling the better known Odonata in texture. When not in flight, the wings are folded flat and lie quite close over the abdominal segments. Their wing tips protrude well past the end of the body. There are two antennae at the head and two conspicuous tails almost as long as the abdomen.

Big stoneflies look rather flat with their wings folded, although the smaller genera wrap themselves in their wings to a larger degree. The genus *Leuctra* rolls its wings so tightly that it has been called the Needle fly since Charles Cotton described it in the seventeenth century. Stoneflies are relatively subdued and insignificant-looking when at rest, although they scuttle and run with surprising agility to avoid capture. The same flies look huge in flight, their bodies hung somewhat vertically under the expanse of four relatively large wings. Their flight is clumsy and lumbering, like an aircraft almost at stalling speed, and the wing spread makes such insects look much larger than they actually are.

The Plecoptera consist structurally of a head, thorax, and abdomen. The three subsections of the thorax and the head taken together are approximately the same length as the body. There are ten body segments, although only nine are easily discernible. The tails are joined with the posterior laterals of the last abdominal segment, and trail toward the rear. Each of the thoracic sections supports legs, and the wings are rooted in the second and third segments of the thorax. The legs are powerful and well developed, having rather stout claws. The first two joints of each leg, the coxa and trochanter respectively, are rather knucklelike and small. The tarsal feet consist of three segments. The major segments of the legs consist of the femur, which is rather like the shoulder and upper arm in human morphology, and the tibia, or forearm structure. The nymphal forms closely resemble the adults, except that the undeveloped wings lie under the wing cases that cover the posterior thoracic segments. The obvious differences between the stonefly nymphs and mayfly nymphs of the two-tailed genera lie in the character and location of their breathing apparatus. Such gills are always located at the sides or back surfaces of the abdominal segments in the mayflies. Most stoneflies have filamentlike gills attached to the under surfaces of the thoracic segments, like hairy growths at the roots of the legs. Some few species have trace gill-systems at the abdominal posterior, and many have no tracheal gills in their structures.

The life-cycle of the Plecoptera between the oviposition of the eggs in the river and hatching of the adults is typically one year, although larger genera such as *Acroneuria, Perla,* and *Pteronarcys* have three-year cycles. Some individual specimens of the *Isoperla* and *Chloroperla* flies have two-year cycles. The cycle of egg, nymph, and adult is incomplete in entomological terms, since there are no pupal and larval stages. The mayflies have a similar incomplete life cycle.

The eggs are laid in the river. Incubation ranges from a few hours to more than three and four months, depending on altitude and temperatures. The most rapid incubation apparently occurs in the *Capnia* stoneflies, which emerge in late winter. Most species reach eclosion and hatch in three to five weeks. Giant stoneflies incubate as long as three to four months.

The nymphs which eclode from the eggs are essentially subaquatic insects that crawl rather than swim, although they can swim rather clumsily through limited leg action and undulation of their bodies. Therefore stonefly nymphs are best imitated with a mixture of upstream dead-drift presentation, and casting across or slightly downstream, sometimes using a slow, teasing rhythm from the rod. They are extremely agile in the bed of the river, moving in all directions with equal dexterity. Large stonefly nymphs are well known to bait fishermen, who call them water crickets on eastern and European rivers. Western fishermen incorrectly call them hellgrammites, since the true hellgrammite is a member of the completely different *Corydalis* genus and hatches into the giant Dobsonfly. Catching the giant stonefly nymphs in large numbers for commercial sale to bait fishermen has long been common on large western rivers. It is an unfortunate practice, since imitations of these nymphs fish superbly, and such human impact on the principal diet-form of our western rivers should probably be banned to protect the ecosystemic equilibrium of such watersheds.

Nymphs of the smaller stoneflies are similar in their morphological structures, although their proportions are slender and more delicate. They can be distinguished from nymphs of the two-tailed mayflies by the absence of gills on their bodies. The stonefly nymphs are both vegetarian and carnivorous organisms, depending on their size, and the character of their available food chains. All of the Plecoptera eat plant matter, but the meat-eating behavior is most typically found among proto-adult nymphs of the giant stoneflies. Animal organisms typically consumed by the Plecoptera are smaller nymphs and larvae of the other orders, and there is even some cannibalism. Herbivorous stoneflies typically eat mosses and higher plant forms in the river, and some species of algal life.

The presence of giant stonefly nymphs in large populations is a mixed blessing on even the western rivers. Most caddis flies are protected by stone and fibrous cases in their larval stages, and in tough cocoons during pupation, so the impact of the big stonefly nymphs on the Trichoptera is rather limited. However, the relatively sparse mayfly hatches on rivers having major populations of the giant Plecoptera stems directly from the decimation of their nymphs by the larger stoneflies.

Like other immature aquatic insect forms, the stonefly nymphs molt many times as they grow. Full details of the precise number of moltings and instar stages in all species are not known, although studies of the large *Perla* genus have revealed thirty-three separate moltings in its three-year cycle. When such nymphs are fully grown, they crawl and swim short distances along the bottom to the shallows, ultimately crawling to the water line on stones and bridge abutments and ledges to emerge. Their empty nymphal skins are found in large numbers on certain rocks and other places. Few shucks are found in the rest of the river. The concentration of hatching in certain sites indicates that the nymphs have distinct preferences in selecting places to emerge. Such considerations are not fully understood. Perhaps they are a combination of subtle factors, including proximity to optimal river-bottom habitat, availability of relatively safe migratory routes between that habitat and the emergence points, and the character of the current extant in these places. The actual final molting is relatively slow, with the

adult stonefly emerging through a split extending along each segment of
the thorax, and along the epicranial suture of the head. Most knowledgeable anglers have seen certain rocks covered with the empty nymphal skins
of the larger stoneflies, and I know a bridge on the Brodheads that has one
abutment almost encrusted with the tiny shucks of the *Taeniopteryx*
hatches. The position of the cast skins on the concrete reveals the April
water levels when the flies emerged. There are virtually none on the opposite abutment, indicating some mysterious preference in hatching sites
for the nymphs.

Although there are many species of giant stoneflies across the full spectrum of American waters, there are about eight ecotypes generally representative of the full range of important nymphal forms. These eight species
are outlined in this chapter.

1. Giant Salmon Fly Nymph (*Pteronarcys californica*)

The nymphs of this species constitute the most numerous insect form on our
major western rivers, and are typically called hellgrammites among bait-
fishermen from the Gunnison and Rio Grande in Colorado to the Madison
and Big Hole in Montana. Since the full-grown nymphs measure as much
as two inches in length, and their three-year life cycle makes them available
to the fish in many stages of growth, their imitations are the staple western
patterns throughout the entire fly-fishing season. The hatches occur in late
April on the Pacific coast streams, and in early summer in the higher eleva-
tions from Colorado to Montana.

The species is most numerous in swift, relatively alkaline rivers at moderate altitudes. It is present in good numbers in the swift-flowing riffles of
the Madison and Firehole at altitudes of about seven thousand feet, because
these rivers are warmed by geothermal flowages in their headwaters.

The colder Big Hole is another ecosystem. There are fine *Pteronarcys*
hatches on its lower reaches, from Twin Bridges to the watercress spring
below Wise River. The river is colder above the Jerry Creek Bridge in midsummer. It receives spring creek seepages from several ranches in the Wise
river basin, which lies at about seven thousand feet. Although these flowages keep the river warmer and relatively ice-free in midwinter, its summer
temperatures are a little too cold to support the big stoneflies in good
numbers. Salmon fly hatches are sparse above the Wise River, and virtually
nonexistent above Fishtrap Creek. The Big Hole simply becomes too cold
for the giant stoneflies above seven thousand feet.

The full-grown nymphs are a dark chocolate color, measuring about one
and a half inches at full growth. The species *Pteronarcys princeps* is a similar, although somewhat smaller black stonefly nymph that is common on
Pacific coast streams.

The nymph is touched with a deep orangish brown in its body and
thoracic joints, its antennae and tails, its legs and its undersurfaces. The
naturals are perfectly imitated by the Giant Salmon Fly Nymph in sizes
eight through four. Dressing these patterns during most of the season, I
usually weight the bodies with brass pins or soft lead wire in the method
developed by George Grant, a famous western tier from Butte. Grant also

developed my favorite dressing technique for the bodies of the giant stone-fly imitations. Grant winds a small three-quarter-inch brass pleating pin on either side of the hook shank with nylon, and fixes it in lacquer cement to create a flat foundation suggestive of the nymphs. It is also possible to use two pieces of heavy brass or copper wire. This flat base is wrapped in soft lead wire, which is then wound with a smooth foundation of black rayon floss. The tails are seated conventionally, and the belly of the nymph lacquered a dull reddish orange. The body is then wound tightly in brown-dyed flat nylon, forming a perfect segmented body, gleaming dully above its dark and orange-bellied core. The remainder of the nymph is dressed conventionally.

Tails: Medium brown, ⅝ inch
Tergites: Slate brown, ⅞ inch
Thorax: Slate brown, ½ inch
Sternum: Orangish brown, ½ inch
Wing cases: Slate brown, ⅜ inch
Legs: Slate brown, marked with orange, ¾ inch
Antennae: Medium brown, ⅜ inch
Head: Slate brown, 3/16 inch

Hook: Sizes 1-8 Mustad 79580 4X long
Nylon: Dark-brown 6/0 nylon
Tails: Dark-brown condor quill fibers
Body: Brown-dyed flat nylon mono-filaments over a black floss founda-tion with an orange-lacquered belly
Thorax: Same as body above
Wing cases: Dark-brown goose-quill sections
Legs: Chocolate-dyed pheasant body hackle
Antennae: Dark-brown condor quill fibers
Head: Dark brown nylon

These imitations are perhaps the best all-around nymph for fishing the big western rivers. Sometimes I dress such flies on a flat nylon core without the fuse-wire, intending to fish the big nymphs in the shallows when they are hatching. The best fish that has fallen to these flies for me was a hook-jawed brown of almost eight pounds on the Emigrant Flats of the Yellow-stone, while fishing with the late Joe Brooks.

2. Golden Stonefly Nymph (*Acroneuria californica*)

These big insects are almost as important as the larger *Pteronarcys* flies on western rivers. Many bait-fishermen are familiar with these nymphs, which they call water crickets, and there are good populations on some streams. Fully grown specimens measure one and a quarter inches. These flies typi-cally emerge in early June in the Pacific Northwest, and a month later in the Rocky Mountain region. E. H. Rosborough, the famous Oregon profes-sional tier from Chiloquin, rates this *Acroneuria* species one of the most important insects on his rivers. Depending on the weather, the hatching activity can range from ten days to four weeks. The importance of these stoneflies varies widely from river to river, depending on their temperature and physical character and chemistry.

This species is a beautiful, rich amber color, with a ringed brown body and strong brown markings on the head, thorax, and wing cases. Polly Rosborough ties a good fur-bodied imitation of these *Acroneuria* nymphs, but in recent seasons I have been experimenting with a flat nylon dressing derived from the experiments of Grant, using the same three-quarter-inch brass pleating pins and lead wire foundation, and wrapping the underbody in a rich amber-yellow floss. The distinct ringing of the tergites is simulated with chocolate-colored lacquer, and the entire body length ribbed with undyed flat nylon to form a hard, sharply segmented overbody. It is a perfect suggestion of the natural, its body glistening dully with its darker markings visible through its translucency.

Tails: Pale amber, ½ inch
Tergites: Amber ringed with brown, ⅝ inch
Sternites: Pale amber, ⅝ inch
Thorax: Amber mottled with brown, ⅝ inch
Sternum: Pale amber, ⅝ inch
Wing cases: Amber mottled with brown, ⅜ inch
Legs: Amber mottled with brown, ½ inch
Antennae: Pale amber, ⅜ inch
Head: Amber mottled with brown, 3/16 inch

Hook: Sizes 4-10 Mustad 79580 4X long
Nylon: Pale-yellow 6/0 nylon
Tails: Pale-amber goose quill fibers
Body: Natural flat nylon monofilament over a pale-amber core with brown lacquer sternite rings
Thorax: Same as body above
Wing cases: Darkly mottled brown turkey sections
Legs: Pale mottled pheasant body hackles
Antennae: Pale-amber goose quill fibers
Head: Pale yellow nylon

These big nymphs are found among the rocks and bottom rubble of swift western rivers. During emergence, they release their hold on the stones in the riverbed and are swept away in the current. Writhing and working to reach the shallows, the nymphs desperately search for a foothold where they can catch their breath and split their nymphal skins. Such heavy currents mean a slack cross-stream cast, lowering the rod to permit a ten-foot drift while the nymph has time to sink. Then the rod is held low, between twenty and thirty degrees above the surface, following the swing of the nymph in the current. Big western fish in heavy water are a lot like Atlantic salmon, and I like to keep the line clamped firmly under my index finger at the grip, with a few feet of slack hanging from the reel. Such slack allows a few seconds of grace when a heavy fish rips off line at the strike, a move that can overspin even the best reel, tangle the line, and break off. The natural nymphs are tumbling and wriggling in the current and the nymph should be worked rhythmically in its full drift and swing. Just as most fish come to the wet fly at the forty-five-degree point in the drift, most rises to the stonefly nymphs come at this critical focal point. It is not accidental since the artificial has reached the deepest position of its swing and has started toward the surface like a hatching fly.

3. Brown Willow Fly Nymph (*Acroneuria pacifica*)

The adult stoneflies that hatch from these nymphs superficially resemble the larger Salmon Flies, with their rich orange sternites and smoke-gray wings. However, these *Acroneuria* flies are somewhat smaller, and their full-grown nymphs measure approximately one inch in length. Sometimes these flies are mixed with the larger *Pteronarcys* flies on rivers like the Gunnison, and the Willow Flies are an important hatch in their own right. The Upper Yellowstone and the headwaters of the Snake have long been famous for good, early-season hatches of *Acroneuria pacifica*.

The fully mature nymphs are brown and richly mottled on the head and thoracic segments and wing cases. The dark patterns on the thorax are quite striking, and the adult naturals are rather beautiful insects.

These are handsome, strongly colored nymphs, fully an inch in length and almost irresistible to the fish. There are good populations at relatively high altitudes, in the cold headwaters of alkaline streams like the Frying Pan in Colorado and the Encampment and Gros Ventre in Wyoming. The *Acroneuria* nymphs are big enough that the flat-body foundations of brass pins and fuse wire are still effective. The floss-wrapped foundations are amber, lacquered black to suggest the ring markings on the back, and lacquered orangish on the belly surfaces. Such a base is then wrapped with flat nylon monofilament dyed chocolate brown.

The dressing that I have evolved over the years to imitate *Acroneuria pacifica* uses the indicated materials, and since it is called the Willow Fly on many western rivers, we have come to call it the Brown Willow Fly Nymph.

Tails: Orangish-brown, ½ inch
Tergites: Rich brown ringed with amber, ½ inch
Sternites: Orangish brown, ½ inch
Thorax: Richly mottled brown, ½ inch
Sternum: Orangish brown, ½ inch
Wing cases: Richly mottled brown, ⅜ inch
Legs: Mottled orangish brown, ½ inch
Antennae: Orangish brown, ¼ inch
Head: Mottled brown, ⅛ inch

Hook: Sizes 6-10 Mustad 79580 4X long
Nylon: Pale-tan 6/0 nylon
Tails: Medium-brown condor quill fibers
Body: Chocolate-dyed flat nylon monofilament over a base of amber floss lacquered black and orange
Thorax: Same as body above
Wing cases: Dark mottled turkey quill sections
Legs: Brown-dyed pheasant body hackle
Antennae: Medium-brown condor quill fibers
Head: Dark-brown lacquer on top of tan 6/0 nylon

Studying samples of these nymphs brings back thoughts of a memorable three hours on the Frying Pan, about twenty-five years ago, on the meadow water between Meredith and Ruedi. It was an exceptional reach of pocket water, with some beautiful runs below a stand of slender Engelmann spruce.

Two days earlier I had collected a half-dozen specimens of *Acroneuria pacifica* from the Footbridge Pool at Ruedi. Working with a coal-oil lamp at the ranch, since fishing was too good during the daylight hours to waste time making flies, I had dressed several attempts at imitation. Several were disappointingly clumsy, but one pattern seemed promising. The next morning it took fish after fish from the pockets, good browns and deep-bellied rainbows shaped like smallmouth bass. The sun was high when I reached a strong run where the current slowed into deep eddies above the rust-colored bottom. It was apparently empty of fish, but it looked so inviting that I tried it anyway. The experimental nymph dropped into the swirling currents above the place, and I watched it swing deep across the crystalline pocket in the bright sunlight. Suddenly the seemingly empty run came alive with fish, milling in a half-wild cloud around the fly. Some looked big, and when the line paused in its swing I struck. It was a fat three-pound brown, and I coaxed it gently away from its lie before it really began to fight. Four times the same thing happened, with fish churning curiously under the fly-swing, before the run settled back to normal. It was strange to find a school of browns behaving like a pool of Labrador brook trout, and I have never seen it since.

4. Black Willow Fly Nymph (*Acroneuria nigrita*)

This medium-sized, dark species is found in limited numbers on most swift northern streams of the United States, but its most significant populations are found in the northern Rocky Mountains. Its yellowish thorax and gill filaments at the root of the legs undoubtedly make this black-and-yellow *Acroneuria* nymph the prototype of the popular Montana Nymphs. The fully grown nymphs measure about seven-eighths inch in length and are strikingly colored, appearing almost totally black until one notices the orangish-yellow sternum, gills, jaw structure, and posterior body segment. Hatching on the northeast rivers occurs late in June, with hatches four to six weeks later farther west. The widespread success of the Montana Nymphs would seem to indicate that the species does not produce hatches of dry-fly densities, although it is a familiar subaquatic diet-form to the trout from North Carolina to Vancouver.

Although there are better imitations of these yellow-thorax *Acroneuria* nymphs, their success cannot be ignored. My pattern is constructed on the weighted, flat-base underbody developed with half-inch brass dressmaker pins and fuse wire, but it employs fur dubbing to simulate the unique body markings of this nymph.

Tails: Orangish brown, ⅜ inch
Tergites: Blackish brown with orange tip, 7/16 inch
Sternites: Blackish brown ringed with amber, 7/16 inch
Thorax: Pale amber heavily marked in black, ½ inch
Sternum: Orangish yellow with pale gills, ½ inch
Wing cases: Amber heavily marked in black, 9/16 inch
Legs: Black with orange joints, ⅜ inch
Antennae: Orangish brown, ¼ inch
Head: Amber marked with black, 3/16 inch

Hook: Sizes 8-10 Mustad 79580 4X long
Nylon: Brown 6/0 nylon
Tails: Brown condor quill fibers
Body: Rich brown-dyed flat nylon over a black floss core ribbed with medium-gold tinsel and orange tip
Thorax: Orangish-yellow fur dubbing
Wing cases: Richly mottled turkey quill section
Legs: Pheasant body hackle dyed black
Antennae: Brown condor quill fibers
Head: Black lacquer on top of working nylon, with orange lacquer at face

The Black Willow Fly Nymph is a superb asset to any flybook on waters from Long Island to the Pacific coast. Although I have never witnessed a fly hatch of these *Acroneuria* stoneflies, there have been times when an imitation would be taken by fish after fish. The species is always recognized by a hungry trout, and working it is always good for a few fish.

The nymph is an ace in the hole on some pools. Arnold Gingrich was fishing the Bridge Flat on the Henryville water of the Brodheads the first day he ever fished there. It was hot and still. There were no hatches and no trout were working openly, although there are always a few fish dimpling surreptitiously under the bridge, their rise-forms tight against the concrete. Gingrich was fishing a big skater, and had only coaxed a few splashy rolls.

How're you doing? I asked.

It's too hot. Arnold wiped his face with a handkerchief wetted in the river. *They're pretty lazy.*

Have you tried a nymph above the bridge?

No, he answered.

We moved upstream through the trees to the head of the tumbling Bridge Run stretch, circling well back from the river so the fish could not see us. During the morning I had collected an occasional adult *Acroneuria nigrita,* and I was reasonably sure the fish had been seeing them. Arnold accepted one of my nymphs and waded carefully into the current.

The run works strong and full down through its boulders, sliding past the trunk and branches of a fallen elm. The swift current eddies and slows along the shadowy tangle of branches. The boulders and rubble bottom and the rich oxygenation of the tumbling currents make it prime stonefly water. It is a fine holding-lie.

Gingrich dropped the nymph perfectly and I watched it settle deep into the deadfall shadows, swinging against the teasing line. *Look out,* I said softly. *It's a good place.*

There was a bright-yellow flash deep in the current, and the rod dipped under the angry head-shaking of a sixteen-inch brown. *You make a pretty good ghillie,* Arnold laughed.

He's an old friend, I said.

5. Orange Stonefly Nymph (*Perla immarginata*)

This is another medium-sized stonefly that is well distributed in the trout streams of America. It is beautifully mottled with brown over an amber color touched with orange. The full-grown nymphs are about seven-eighths inch in length and are among the most handsome of our aquatic insects.

This is another nymph that is perfectly imitated by the Grant tying techniques, shaping a foundation of orangish amber-colored floss over two brass half-inch dressmaker pins set on either side of the hook shank. Fuse-wire should be wrapped over this flat base if the nymph is for fishing heavy water, and omitted over a foundation of heavy nylon seated along the shank with 6/0 nylon, if the imitation is for shallow fishing in a hatch.

Tails: Amber, 7/16 inch
Tergites: Orangish yellow with dark-brown mottlings, ½ inch
Sternites: Amber ringed with pale yellow, ½ inch
Thorax: Orangish yellow with dark-brown mottlings, ½ inch
Sternum: Amber with pale gills, ½ inch
Wing cases: Orangish yellow with dark mottlings, 5/16 inch
Legs: Orangish yellow mottled with brown, ⅜ inch
Antennae: Amber, ¼ inch
Head: Orangish mottled with brown, ⅛ inch

Hook: Sizes 8-12 Mustad 79580 4X long
Nylon: Pale-tan 6/0 nylon
Tails: Amber goose quill fibers
Body: Amber-dyed flat nylon monofilament over a base of brown lacquer mottlings on a pale-amber floss base
Thorax: Same as body above
Wing cases: Dark mottled turkey quill sections dyed orange
Legs: Pale pheasant body dyed orangish yellow
Antennae: Amber goose quill fibers
Head: Orange and brown lacquer mottling over pale-tan nylon

There is a minor western species classified as *Perla expansa* that is virtually identical in its coloring and configuration, and is well matched with the imitation above.

6. Great Stonefly Nymph (*Perla capitata*)

These are the familiar stonefly creepers that most eastern trout fishermen used as bait during their boyhoods. The population of the *Perla* nymphs is never extensive enough to produce a viable dry-fly hatch, but trout seldom bypass the opportunity to take one of the nymphs should it drift or swim into their taking-lies.

Nymphs of the *Perla capitata* species are the prototypes of several popular eastern patterns. Perhaps the best known are the stonefly imitations dressed by celebrated Catskill tiers like Harry Darbee on the Willowemoc and Art Flick on the Schoharie. Such flies are excellent for fishing the water on days without a hatch; I have used them many years with consistent success on the Ausable. The fully grown nymph is a big, succulent insect that will usually coax a large trout into rising even during his indifferent moods.

The flat-shaped foundation and coloring system worked out by George Grant on the Big Hole is also perfect for imitating the nymphs of *Perla capitata* on eastern rivers. The base should consist of two brass half-inch dressmaker pins set at either side of the hook shank with pale-amber working nylon. Soft lead wire can be used to wrap the entire body for fishing deep, or omitted for working shallow during the hatching periods in June and July. The underbody should then be shaped smoothly in amber synthetic floss, with a final wrapping of natural flat nylon. Before wrapping the nylon, the amber underbody should be marked with longitudinal stripes of brown lacquer, darkening both lateral edges and the dorsal centerline, suggesting the tergite markings of the naturals.

The Great Stonefly Nymph is a superb addition to any fly book, and it has taken several trophy fish in the past:

Tails: Amber, 7/16 inch
Tergites: Amber with brown dorsal and lateral markings, ½ inch
Sternites: Amber with pale joints, ½ inch
Thorax: Amber with brown markings, ½ inch
Sternum: Amber with pale joints, ½ inch
Wing cases: Amber with brown mottling, ¾ inch
Legs: Amber with brown markings, ½ inch
Antennae: Amber, 9/16 inch
Head: Amber with brown markings, 5/16 inch

Hook: Sizes 6-12 Mustad 79580 4X long
Nylon: Pale-tan 6/0 nylon
Tails: Amber goose-quill fibers
Body: Natural flat nylon over striped amber underbody
Thorax: Same as body above
Wing cases: Mottled turkey quill sections
Legs: Pale pheasant body hackle
Antennae: Amber goose-quill fibers
Head: Pale-tan nylon

This pattern has produced some impressive catches. Twenty years ago I was fishing the Boulder Pool on the Upper Ausable not far from Lake Placid. It had rained heavily during the night, the storm breaking the heat of early July in a violent hour of thunderclaps and lightning just before daylight. The wind and driving rain had forced me from my sleeping bag in the meadows above Upper Jay, and I spent the rest of the night in the car. The East Branch was milky and chocolate-colored at breakfast, and I drove across the mountain at Keene.

The West Branch was a little high, but its stretch below the Olympic ski jump was still clear. There were sporadic hatches of big *Perla* flies in the gathering early light, although I saw no fish working as I organized my tackle and waded into the current.

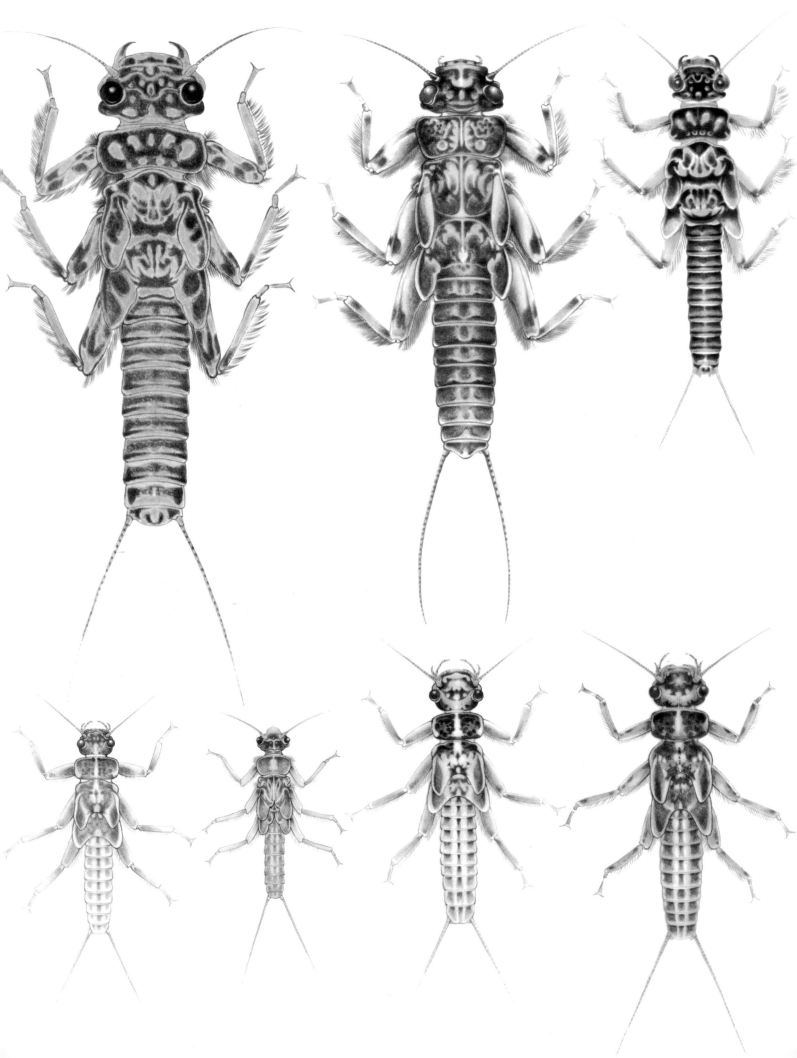

Let's try it, Mac agreed.

It was almost cold when we worked into our waders on the porch at Henryville House and shouldered stiffly into our wading jackets. There was mist layered against the hemlock ridges. We drove down below the iron bridge to the spring holes.

How shall we fish it? Mac asked.

Let's stay together, I suggested. *We can alternate fishing it pocket-by-pocket or fish-by-fish in the pools.*

Mac started first, working a size-ten *Pteronarcys* nymph in the spring seepages under the hemlocks upstream. There was a swirl on the second cast and he was into a fat thirteen-inch brook trout. The cold-water shallows above produced two more good browns lying tight under the bank. It was easy fishing, with a short upstream cast to each likely holding-lie, and most of these carefully placed casts moved a trout.

Amazing! Mac laughed when a fifteen-inch brown slipped out from a boulder in an open riffle and intercepted his nymph with a vicious swirl. *They're hooking themselves!*

They're hungry, I said.

You mean it's too hot to eat during the afternoon, and the river doesn't cool off in the evening?

Exactly, I said. *They're hungry.*

We moved good trout in every small pocket, undercut grassy bank, and shallow riffle. Pools and smooth runs often surrendered two or three fat browns, and we had taken a dozen fish between us in only the first hundred yards.

Top, left to right: *Acroneuria californica, Perla capitata, Acroneuria ruralis*
Below, left to right: *Isoperla bilineata, Alloperla imbecilla, Isoperla marmona, Isoperla signata*

The first waist-deep run along a big deadfall usually shelters some heavy trout. It was my turn, since Talley had just lost a good fish that came off after a spirited fight in the swift riffle downstream. Sometimes I had taken a big brown under the boulder halfway up the run, and when no fish rose along the deadfall, I dropped the nymph upstream beside the rock. The cast had scarcely settled when the leader twitched hard upstream, and I tightened into a heavy fish. There was a huge splash that sent waves down the current. The trout bored deep up the bottom gravel, flushing several other fish past us in panic. It was a deep-bellied brown of three pounds, and we released it in the small pool downstream.

Talley hooked a fine fourteen-inch brown in the next boulder-strewn pocket above, and it was already getting hot when I rose a final one-pound fish in the Elbow Pool. It was an anticlimax to a morning of fast sport.

How long do these nymphs hatch? Mac asked.

There are a few all summer, I explained, *but most of the nymphs emerge this week in June—and on a morning like this every fish in the river is looking for them.*

It's a good thing they don't last longer, Mac laughed. *You could clean the fish out this way!*

You're right, I said.

Notes on the Smaller Plecoptera

THERE ARE swift sun-washed riffles on the headwaters of the Pere Marquette, where I fished in those early Michigan summers. The still Little South flows down its final mile of tree-sheltered flats and forms the bigger Pere Marquette at its confluence with the Middle Branch in the Forks Pool. The smaller Middle Branch is clear and cold. The Little South is dark and tea-colored with rotting logs and leaves in its sluggish currents. The swift little Middle Branch is much colder, its flowage born in the rich marl swamps southeast of Baldwin.

Its alkalinity and colder temperatures make the upper Pere Marquette a fine reach of water in midsummer. Below the Forks Pool, there is a sweeping riffle that works into the wide S-shaped bend downstream. The deep run of the Forks Pool holds against the right bank and then slides across the river, spreading and working against the roots and deadfalls along the left. Kingfishers used the overhanging branches to watch the river for unwary trout. Squirrels chattered in the trees, and sometimes I was startled by a chipmunk scuttling busily in the dry winter leaves.

It was still cool just after breakfast. There were no fish working when I slipped into the river just below the Forks Bridge. I decided to fish the water with a wet Cahill, and quickly moved a good fish in the shallows. There was a deep flash downstream when the sunlight caught a trout turning to capture something.

It took the pale little Cahill on the first swing of the wet fly through its holding-lie. The fishing was surprisingly fast. There were a few stoneflies in the air, fluttering clumsily in the sunlight, but there were still no rises. Fish after fish took the little Cahill. Most were medium-sized trout of eight to twelve inches, but one brown of fifteen inches drifted out from the shadows of a hickory deadfall, chased the Cahill into the open sun, and hooked itself solidly. Finally, downstream where a huge kingfisher snag rose throbbing from the swift currents, there was a heavy pull and a bulldogging surge under the log jam that spelled size. The big fish sheared the leader, taking my only wet Cahill. No other fly pattern seemed to work, although I fished a productive riffle for another hour before wading back to our camp on the Little South.

It had been a curious morning.

There were only a few stoneflies hatching, I explained to my father while he laid our lunch cookfire, *and there were no rises anywhere—but the fish went crazy for my Cahill.*

Did other wet flies work? he asked.

No, I answered thoughtfully. *They acted like selective trout taking a fly they really wanted.*

It was probably an accident, he observed. *Why don't you check their stomachs and find out why?*

Good idea, I agreed.

The fish were quickly dressed, and I collected their stomachs in the grass. My father brought me a white soup plate, and my field supply of alcohol mixed with a touch of glycerin. *Study them in this,* he suggested. *Their food should show up clearly.*

I sliced the first stomach. *Look at this!*

It was stuffed tight as a sausage with pale-brownish nymphs, and I squeezed them out like toothpaste into the alcohol. There were almost a hundred in the first three fish alone. *What are they?* asked my father. The stomach contents of the fourth fish was the same.

Stoneflies, I answered. *Filled with their nymphs.*

The little nymphs were pale-brown, with slightly darker markings on their tergites, thoracic segments, and wing cases. My dozen fish contained almost seven hundred of the nymphs.

They look a little like the Cahill I used, I said. *That certainly explains why the fish liked my fly.*

Probably, agreed my father.

The specimens were culled for a dozen perfect little nymphs which were sealed in a collection vial. Later these nymphs were identified as *Isoperla signata,* and during the next few days our experimental imitations took a number of good catches.

This chapter includes descriptions of nine species that have been depicted in color plates, as well as eleven other small Plecoptera important to American fishermen. Although these minor stoneflies seldom trigger consistent dry-fly hatches, there are times when they become important. Although stoneflies thrive in swift rivers all across the continent, the large, relatively unpolluted rivers of our western mountains support especially large populations of Plecoptera nymphs. Some of the most strikingly beautiful nymphs found in American trout streams are the pale, richly patterned insects of these smaller stoneflies. Their coloration varies from pale yellow, olive, delicate green, light brown, reddish brown, and pinkish brown to black and chocolate-brown.

Like the larger species, these smaller nymphs have relatively long, slender tails and no gill structures on their bodies. Their filamentaceous gills are located at the thorax, lying around the bases of the legs. These small Plecoptera range from three-quarters inch to slightly less than one-quarter inch in length. Obvious gill-filaments are lacking in the smallest species.

The small Plecoptera are more slender and less flat-bodied than the bigger species of the *Acroneuria* and *Pteronarcys* types. These little nymphs are seldom carnivorous; their diet is limited mostly to subaquatic vegetable matter and algae.

Their adults fly more gracefully than their larger cousins among the Plecoptera order, and the tiny green and pale-yellow ecotypes have swift and erratic flight-behavior above the water. There are the almost black little *Capnia* and dark-brown *Leuctra* stoneflies, and the brown-and-pink-bodied species of the early hatching *Taeniopteryx* genus. There are the strongly colored amber and dark-brown *Acroneuria* nymphs, and the light-brown and bright-ocherous nymphs of the genera *Alloperla* and *Isoperla*. Finally, there are the intense greens of the genus *Chloroperla* over midsummer streams.

Adult stoneflies oviposit their eggs in sporadic masses directly into the current in most genera. These ova incubate from a few hours in rivers of relatively high temperatures, particularly those having the consistent thermal character of full-grown spring creeks, to a period of as much as four months in the icy high-altitude waters of our western mountains. Following eclosion from the egg-stage, these smaller species have a nymphal life cycle of one to two years. Generally speaking, these little stoneflies of our swift mountain streams are interesting insects, from the dark little *Capnias* on the snowbanks of late winter to the pale yellow *Alloperlas* of midsummer and the brown *Taeniopteryx* flies of spring.

Most hatching occurs at the waterline of certain rocks, smooth ledges, and deadfalls polished by the current. The Plecoptera almost never emerge free in the surface film, like the caddis-fly pupae and the mayfly nymphs. There is a bridge abutment on the Brodheads in Pennsylvania, my home river these past twelve seasons, which is literally encrusted with delicate little *Taeniopteryx* shucks every season before late April. Some years when we have unseasonably warm weather in February and March, our hatches of the winter *Capnia* and *Taeniopteryx* flies generate surface-feeding activity long before our legal season begins. Sometimes these hatches are completely over before opening day in April.

1. Yellow-Legged Stonefly (*Acroneuria ruralis*)

This colorful little nymph, measuring about thirteen-sixteenths inch in length at full growth, is perhaps the most striking of the subaquatic stoneflies. Unlike its small cousins, these little *Acroneuria* are surprisingly predatory for their size, eating both vegetation and smaller animal organisms. Although well distributed in American waters, these brightly marked little nymphs are extremely numerous in cold mountain streams.

Tails: Pale amber distinctly mottled with light brown
Tergites: Amber distinctly ringed with dark brown, 7/16 inch
Sternites: Pale amber ringed with light brown, 7/16 inch
Thorax: Amber marked with strong brown patterns, 3/8 inch
Sternum: Pale amber, 3/8 inch
Wing cases: Amber marked with elegant dark brown markings, 3/8 inch
Legs: Pale amber pheasant hackle or woodcock breast hackle, 5/16 inch
Antennae: Pale amber, 1/4 inch
Head: Amber heavily mottled with brown, 1/8 inch

Hook: Sizes 8-10 Mustad 9671 2X long
Nylon: Pale-amber 6/0 nylon
Tails: Pale-amber goose-quill fibers
Body: Natural flat nylon over an amber floss core with brown lacquer back ringing
Thorax: Pale-amber fur dubbing
Wing cases: Dark mottled turkey wing-quill sections
Legs: Amber woodcock body hackle
Antennae: Pale-amber goose-quill fibers
Head: Amber nylon with brown lacquer top markings

The Yellow-Legged Stonefly Nymph is an aggressive little species, and it should be fished across and downstream, with a gentle half-teasing rhythm of the rod. During hatching activity, the imitations should be worked into the shallower currents just outside the heavier water, where the naturals are migrating to emerge in midsummer.

2. Little Green Stonefly (*Alloperla imbecilla*)

This pale little nymph emerges during the summer months and is found like bright-green embers in the sunlight, fluttering above the swift riffles. Fully grown nymphs measure approximately seven-sixteenths inch in length, and inhabit crevices among the stones in the swiftest riffles. This species is principally indigenous to rivers in the eastern and north central states.

The Little Green Stonefly is a vegetable-eater. It is not a strong swimmer, and imitations should be fished dead-drift in both riffles and shallows. It is sometimes useful in summer.

Tails: Pale yellowish green, 3/16 inch
Tergites: Pale yellowish green, 3/16 inch
Sternites: Pale yellowish, 3/16 inch
Thorax: Pale yellowish green delicately mottled with olive, 3/16 inch
Sternum: Pale yellowish, 3/16 inch
Wing cases: Pale yellowish green lightly mottled with olive, 1/8 inch
Legs: Pale yellowish green, 3/16 inch
Antennae: Pale yellowish green, 1/8 inch
Head: Pale yellowish green, 1/16 inch

Hook: Sizes 14-16 Mustad 9671 2X long
Nylon: Pale yellow 6/0 nylon
Tails: Pale yellowish olive
Body: Fine flat monofilament wound over hot yellow nylon underbody
Thorax: Same as body construction
Wing cases: Pale mottled feather sections dyed yellowish olive
Legs: Pale olive-dyed hen hackle
Antennae: Pale yellowish olive
Head: Pale yellow nylon

There are two similar western species which have occasional importance on western rivers, and are virtually identical in coloring and size. They are the bright-greenish-yellow *Alloperla borealis*, which measures about one-half inch and is especially common on the rivers of Montana. It hatches in the evenings in July and August. The related species *Alloperla pacifica* is a little more yellowish, and is found on streams of the Pacific mountains. It measures about five-eighths inch at full growth.

3. Early Black Stonefly (*Capnia vernalis*)

These dark little stoneflies sometimes emerge in late winter, not unlike the February Red of British fishing literature, since the time of Cotton and Bowlker. The adults can be observed on bright winter afternoons, scurrying actively on streamside snowbanks. Sometimes on warm days there are even enough of these flies hatching to coax the fish into a surface rise. It is a common occurrence on eastern rivers like the Brodheads in Pennsylvania and the Musconetcong in New Jersey. The adult nymphs measure approximately five-eighths inch.

The Early Black Stonefly Nymph is a handsome pattern, and its body should be dressed with rather slender proportions to suggest the configuration of the naturals. It should be fished in the swift riffles and their downstream pools in bright spring weather, and the cold temperatures often mean their movements in the current are rather deliberate. Imitations should be fished to suggest such behavior. The species *Capnia vernalis* is principally found in our northern and northeastern rivers.

Tails: Dark slate gray, ¼ inch
Tergites: Dark slate gray distinctly ringed, 5/16 inch
Sternites: Dark slate gray distinctly ringed, 5/16 inch
Thorax: Dark slate gray mottled with black, ¼ inch
Sternum: Dark slate gray, ¼ inch
Wing cases: Dark slate gray mottled with black, ¼ inch
Legs: Dark slate gray, ¼ inch
Antennae: Dark slate gray, ¼ inch
Head: Dark slate gray, ¼ inch

Hook: Sizes 10-12 Mustad 9671 2X long
Nylon: Black 6/0 nylon
Tails: Iron-blue dun hen hackle fibers
Body: Flat monofilament dyed dark brown wrapped over a black floss underbody
Thorax: Same construction as body
Wing cases: Mottled iron-blue feather sections
Legs: Iron-blue dun hen hackle
Antennae: Iron-blue dun fibers
Head: Black nylon

Three similar species are found on western streams. The relatively small *Capnia minuta* is a species which hatches in late winter on the rivers of Montana, and although its fully grown nymph measures about three-eighths inch in length, the imitation is excellent. Pacific coast rivers have the five-eighths inch *Capnia elongata,* and the somewhat larger *Capnia grandis* measures almost three-quarters inch in length. Both insects are matched with the Early Black Stonefly Nymph.

4.   Little Olive Stonefly (*Chloroperla coloradensis*)

Although this pale little western species is quite similar to the eastern *Alloperla imbecilla,* its nymphs are somewhat larger and more olivaceous. The fully developed nymphal forms measure approximately five-sixteenths inch in length.

These little stoneflies are particularly common on the rivers of the Rocky Mountains, hatching primarily in July and August.

Tails: Pale olive green, ¼ inch
Tergites: Pale olive green with a pale median and lateral coloring, ¼ inch
Sternites: Pale olive green, ⅛ inch
Thorax: Pale olive green delicately marked and mottled at the anterior margins with a white median marking, ⅛ inch
Sternum: Pale olive green, 3/16 inch
Wing cases: Pale olive green with delicate anterior mottlings, 3/16 inch
Legs: Pale olive green, 3/16 inch
Antennae: Pale olive green, ⅛ inch
Head: Pale olive green, 1/16 inch

Hook: Sizes 12-14 Mustad 9671 2X long
Nylon: Pale olive green 6/0 nylon
Tails: Pale olive green hen hackle fibers
Body: Flat monofilament wrapped over a pale olive green underbody
Thorax: Dressed of same construction as body
Wing cases: Pale olive green feather sections
Legs: Pale olive green hen hackle
Antennae: Pale olive green
Head: Pale olive green nylon

Pacific coastal and mountain rivers have the similar species *Chloroperla pallidula* in relatively large numbers.

5.   Little Yellow Stonefly (*Isoperla bilineata*)

This is one of the classic eastern species, surprisingly similar to the pale little Yellow Sally which made its debut in the writings of Richard Bowlker, with his descriptions of fly hatches on Shropshire rivers. The full-grown nymph is about one-half inch in length.

Tails: Pale yellowish, ¼ inch
Tergites: Pale yellowish with an olive
    flush of median and lateral
    coloring, 5/16 inch
Sternites: Pale yellowish, 5/16 inch
Thorax: Pale yellowish delicately
    mottled with olive, and having a
    paler median line, 3/16 inch
Sternum: Pale yellowish, 3/16 inch
Wing cases: Pale yellowish olive,
    delicately mottled, ⅛ inch
Legs: Pale yellowish, ¼ inch
Antennae: Pale yellowish, ⅛ inch
Head: Pale yellowish mottled with
    olive, 1/16 inch

Hook: Sizes 12-14 Mustad 9671 2X
    long
Nylon: Pale yellow 6/0 nylon
Tails: Pale yellow hen hackle fibers
Body: Pale yellow with a median
    dorsal stripe and delicately mottled
    lateral margins
Thorax: Dressed like the body
Wing cases: Pale yellow with olive
    mottled anterior surfaces
Legs: Pale yellow hen hackle
Antennae: Pale yellow fibers
Head: Pale yellow nylon mottled with
    olive

These stoneflies emerge on most swift eastern rivers, fluttering in good numbers over the riffles at twilight. Most hatching commences in July and continues through August into September on some waters. These bright-yellow stoneflies are typically found mixed with the pale-green *Alloperla* flies. The delicate Little Yellow Stonefly Nymph is a superb imitation.

6. Western Yellow Stonefly (*Isoperla marmona*)

This is a similar pale-yellow Plecoptera, not unlike its eastern and British counterparts, that measures a slightly larger five-eighths inch in length. It emerges in July and August and is particularly plentiful on the swift rivers of Wyoming and Montana.

Tails: Pale yellowish, ¼ inch
Tergites: Pale yellowish with an olive
    median line and lateral margins
    flushed with olive, ⅜ inch
Sternites: Pale yellowish, ⅜ inch
Thorax: Pale yellowish darkly
    mottled with olive, and a pale
    median stripe, ¼ inch
Sternum: Pale yellowish, ¼ inch
Wing cases: Pale yellowish, 3/16
    inch
Legs: Pale yellowish, ¼ inch
Antennae: Pale yellowish, 3/16 inch
Head: Pale yellowish mottled with
    olive, ⅛ inch

Hook: Sizes 10-12 Mustad 9671 2X
    long
Nylon: Pale yellow 6/0 nylon
Tails: Pale yellowish hen hackle
    fibers
Body: Flat monofilament wrapped
    over pale yellowish nylon under-
    body
Thorax: Same construction as body
Wing cases: Pale yellowish mottled
    feather section with pale median
    stripe
Legs: Pale yellowish
Antennae: Pale yellowish
Head: Pale yellow nylon

Like the other pale summer stoneflies, these insects emerge primarily at twilight on warm evenings. Sometimes *Isoperla marmona* flights are mixed with the *Chloroperla* species. The nymphs have relatively dramatic head, shoulder, and thoracic markings. The Western Yellow Stonefly Nymph is a fine imitation.

7. Light Brown Stonefly (*Isoperla signata*)

This insect emerges rather early in the eastern season, hatching early in May, not long after the last of the dark *Taeniopteryx* flies. Sporadic flights can be observed all month. The fully developed nymphs measure about eleven-sixteenths to three-quarters inch in length. These *Isoperla* nymphs favor swift, tumbling currents in our eastern mountain streams, and peak emergence lasts for about ten days.

The delicate little imitation of this insect, the Light Brown Stonefly

Nymph, is a superb pattern. It once produced more than thirty trout in a single morning of fishing, high in the brushy headwaters of the Little Manistee in Michigan. It was difficult fishing, casting a short line and working the nymph deep under the alders and log jams. It has been more than twenty-five years since that morning, but I remember it as clearly as the borrowed waders that accordioned down my legs.

Tails: Pale amber mottled with brown, 5/16 inch
Tergites: Pale amber with a dark median stripe and mottled lateral margins, 5/16 inch
Sternites: Pale amber, 5/16 inch
Thorax: Pale amber mottled with brown, 5/16 inch
Sternum: Pale amber, 5/16 inch
Wing cases: Pale amber mottled with brown, 1/4 inch
Legs: Pale amber delicately mottled with brown, 1/4 inch
Antennae: Pale amber, 7/16 inch
Head: Pale amber mottled with brown, 3/32 inch

Hook: Sizes 10-12 Mustad 9671 2X long
Nylon: Light brown 6/0 nylon
Tails: Lemon woodduck fibers
Body: Pale brown flat monofilament over an amber underbody with median and lateral stripes
Thorax: Dressed like body above
Wing cases: Light brown mottled feather sections with pale median stripes
Legs: Light brown woodcock hackle
Antennae: Lemon woodduck fibers
Head: Light brown nylon

8. Needle Fly (*Leuctra grandis*)

These dark little stoneflies are never numerous, either in their nymph or adult populations, but fish seem to take them eagerly at times. Unlike the Little Black Stoneflies and *Taeniopteryx* hatches, these little Needle flies are insects of late summer and fall. Their name comes from the uniquely rolled configuration of their wings, tightly wrapped into a slim tapered point when the flies are resting in the alders. It has been a pattern since Bowlker and Pritt imitated its British counterpart, and nineteenth-century writers like Ronalds identified the European species as *Leuctra geniculata*.

Tails: Dark brown, 1/8 inch
Tergites: Darkly ringed with gray and brown and touched with a faint purplish cast, 1/8 inch
Sternites: Darkly ringed with gray, 1/8 inch
Thorax: Dark grayish mottled brown, 1/8 inch
Sternum: Dark grayish, 1/8 inch
Wing cases: Dark brownish-mottled, 3/32 inch
Legs: Dark mottled brown, 1/8 inch
Antennae: Dark brown, 1/8 inch
Head: Dark brown, 1/16 inch

Hook: Size 16 Mustad 9671 2X long
Nylon: Dark brown 6/0 nylon
Tails: Brown mallard fibers
Body: Bleached peacock quill wrapped over an underbody of purple floss
Thorax: Dressed like body above
Wing cases: Dark mottled brown feather sections
Legs: Dark mottled partridge hackle
Antennae: Brown mallard fibers
Head: Dark brown nylon

Unlike most stoneflies, nymphs of this genus are at home in a wide spectrum of water character and chemistry. Good populations are found in both the limestone streams of Pennsylvania and the more acid waters of the Appalachians. The nymphs are found in surprisingly deep and slow-flowing water, and can inhabit fairly soft bottoms mixed with stones. They are also sometimes found in lakes having moderate wave action to generate sufficient oxygen in the shallows. Some biologists have recorded *Leuctra* nymphs burrowing deep into soft bottom materials, sheltering themselves on the surfaces of buried rocks. However, the utilization of such micro-habitat is infrequent, and most nymphs are found in open bottom areas. The fully grown nymphs of *Leuctra grandis* measure about three-eighths inch in length. They are delicate little insects.

There are two related western species. The chocolate-colored little *Leuctra occidentalis* is a virtually identical nymph common on Rocky Mountain waters, and the diminutive *Leuctra sara* is indigenous to watersheds of our Pacific mountains.

9.   Little Sepia Stonefly (*Nemoura cinctipes*)

These are small sepia-colored Plecoptera that hatch sporadically from April until September. They are widely distributed, and although scattered, are relatively abundant. The nymphs live in stony reaches of river with a stable bottom of rubble and boulders. Adults are medium brown to dark brown, with gray to slate-colored wings. Some individual species of this genus are found in habitats much closer to those of the *Leuctra* flies.

Tails: Dark brown, ⅛ inch
Tergites: Dark brown ringed with black, ⅛ inch
Sternites: Medium brown ringed with black, ⅛ inch
Thorax: Dark mottled brown, ⅛ inch
Sternum: Medium brown, ⅛ inch
Wing cases: Dark mottled brown, 3/32 inch
Legs: Dark mottled brown, ⅛ inch
Antennae: Dark brown, ⅛ inch
Head: Dark brown, 1/16 inch

Hook: Size 16 Mustad 9671 2X long
Nylon: Dark brown 6/0 nylon
Tails: Dark brown mallard fibers
Body: Fiery brown dyed flat monofilament
Thorax: Fiery brown dyed flat monofilament
Wing cases: Dark mottled brown feather section
Legs: Dark mottled partridge hackle
Antennae: Dark brown mallard fibers
Head: Dark brown nylon

Fully grown nymphs measure about three-eighths inch in length. The Little Sepia Stonefly Nymph is a first-rate pattern.

10.   Little Western Stonefly (*Nemoura californica*)

Although this minor *Nemoura* is quite similar to the widely distributed species described above, its nymphal forms prefer relatively slow-flowing water and subaquatic vegetation. Its nymphs measure about seven-sixteenths to one-half inch in length. Consequently, species of this genus are often found in lakes, impoundments, and still reaches of rivers. They are present in both acid and alkaline river chemistry.

Tails: Medium brown, ¼ inch
Tergites: Medium brown with pale ringing, ¼ inch
Sternites: Slightly paler than tergites, ¼ inch
Thorax: Mottled medium brown, ¼ inch
Sternum: Slightly paler brown, ¼ inch
Wing cases: Dark brown-mottled with pale median, 3/16 inch
Legs: Dark brown-mottled, ¼ inch
Antennae: Dark brown, ¼ inch
Head: Dark brown, 1/16 inch

Hook: Sizes 12-14 Mustad 9671 2X long
Nylon: Medium brown 6/0 nylon
Tails: Medium brown hen fibers
Body: Pale brown-dyed flat monofilament wrapped over a medium brown underbody
Thorax: Dressed like body
Wing cases: Medium brownish mottled feather sections
Legs: Dark woodcock hackle
Antennae: Medium brown hen fibers
Head: Medium brown nylon

The Little Western Stonefly Nymph is a useful imitation on our Pacific and Rocky Mountain rivers, particularly in late summer and early autumn. It is capable of swimming movements.

There are two other western *Nemoura* flies of importance. They are the relatively large species classified as *Nemoura oregonensis,* found in the Pacific mountains, measuring approximately nine-sixteenths inch in length. The tiny *Nemoura sinuata* has fully grown nymphs of approximately one-quarter inch and is a species of our northern Rocky Mountains.

11. Early Brown Stonefly (*Taeniopteryx nivalis*)

These are the fluttering little early brown Plecoptera common on many eastern rivers. Sometimes during a false spring these little stoneflies hatch well before the trout season legally opens. The fully developed nymphs are about five-eighths inch. Although the best-known species of this genus in Britain, the bright little February Red of Derbyshire and Yorkshire rivers, is not widely distributed there, the Early Brown Stoneflies are common in American waters.

Tails: Medium brown, 5/16 inch
Tergites: Dull reddish brown, 5/16 inch
Sternites: Slightly paler than tergites, 5/16 inch
Thorax: Dull reddish brown, slightly mottled with a pale anterior stripe, ¼ inch
Sternum: Slightly paler brown, ¼ inch
Wing cases: Dull reddish brown, slightly mottled, ¼ inch
Legs: Medium brownish, ¼ inch
Antennae: Medium brownish, 3/16 inch
Head: Mottled brown, 1/16 inch

Hook: Sizes 10-12 Mustad 9671 2X long
Nylon: Brown 6/0 nylon
Tails: Medium brown hen fibers
Body: Flat monofilament wound over a brown nylon underbody slightly darkened on the back
Thorax: Tied like body
Wing cases: Medium brown-mottled feather sections
Legs: Medium brown hen hackle
Antennae: Medium brown fibers
Head: Brown nylon

Since a similar species, taxonometrically designated *Taeniopteryx occidentalis,* is common on Rocky Mountain streams, the Early Brown Stonefly Nymph is useful there. It has given me good sport as early as late May in the high-basin headwaters of the South Platte, and in the nine-thousand-foot meadows of the Upper Arkansas.

12. Little Red Stonefly (*Taeniopteryx fasciata*)

This is a major early-season fly hatch on some eastern rivers like the Beaverkill, Brodheads, and the Paulinskill in New Jersey. It is important enough on the Schoharie in the Catskills that Art Flick included an imitation in his *Streamside Guide.* Preston Jennings recorded it on several eastern rivers, and Edward Ringwood Hewitt even dressed an imitation for his difficult water on the Neversink.

Its habitat is diverse in character, and its fully grown little nymphs are about one-half inch in length. Although it is found in fast currents typical of most Plecoptera, it is also quite common in surprisingly sluggish water. Pools having some vegetation and a relatively silty bottom are also acceptable habitat. Emergence can occur at almost any time from January to April, although the heaviest hatches typically occur in the spring. E. H. Rosborough, the famous Oregon fly-maker based at Chiloquin, ties an imitation of a similar insect which is probably the *Taeniopteryx pacifica* common on rivers of the Pacific northwest.

Although the adults are often an interesting dry-fly hatch, particularly in good April weather, on streams in Pennsylvania and New Jersey the nymphs are occasionally better. The insects are numerous on relatively still pools of the classic little Brodheads, which typically has dry-fly sport two weeks earlier than its Catskill neighbors farther north. The Little Red Stonefly Nymph is also useful.

Tails: Rusty brown, 5/16 inch	*Hook:* Sizes 12-14 Mustad 9671 2X long
Tergites: Dark reddish brown, darkening toward the lateral margins, 5/16 inch	*Nylon:* Rusty brown 6/0 nylon
Sternites: Dark reddish brown, 5/16 inch	*Tails:* Rusty brown hen fibers
Thorax: Similar to tergites, ¼ inch	*Body:* Fiery brown dyed flat monofilament wound over a reddish underbody lacquered black at lateral margins
Sternum: Similar to sternite coloring, ¼ inch	*Thorax:* Tied like body
Wing cases: Dark brownish with pale median stripe, ⅛ inch	*Wing cases:* Rusty brown feather sections
Legs: Rusty brown, ¼ inch	*Legs:* Rusty brown hen hackle
Antennae: Rusty brown, ¼ inch	*Antennae:* Rusty brown fibers
Head: Dark brownish, 1/16 inch	*Head:* Rusty brown nylon

Sometimes *Taeniopteryx fasciata* is more important than the highly touted mayflies of early season. Although the milder days of April are usually associated with the first good fly-fishing on eastern rivers, the hatches can come in surprisingly raw weather. Wetzel observed in his book *Practical Fly Fishing* that these little red-bodied stoneflies seemed to favor cold days on his favorite Allegheny streams, and that hatching tapered off in better weather. I have even seen them in a sporadic Catskill blizzard of clinging April snowflakes.

It was cold at breakfast in the West Kill Tavern. The raw wind sighed at the eaves and roof-slates. Winter leaves still scuttled in the road outside the inn, and Art Flick was adding a log to the main fireplace when we finally came downstairs.

Cold! Jim Rikhoff shivered.

Art Flick stoked the fire expertly. *Well,* he smiled, *the nice thing about these April hatches is they're not too early!*

Thank God! Rikhoff shuddered melodramatically.

What should come off? I asked.

Provided anything hatches at all! Rikhoff interjected. *Bugs that come out in weather like this have a death-wish!*

Art laughed. *You should see some Gordon Quills.*

But they come just after lunch, I said.

Usually, Art agreed.

We drove unenthusiastically down to Lexington, crossed the Bridge Flat over a river covered with whitecaps, and stopped in the shelter of the Lexington Inn. Sleet rattled on the windshield.

This is ridiculous, I laughed.

Rikhoff watched the hailstones unhappily. *It's time to regroup and think this out over some Irish coffee.*

We ducked our heads into the squall and dashed clumsily into the Lexington Inn. The dining room was empty, and the proprietor was busily tending his fireplace too.

Irish coffee, Rikhoff announced grandly.

The proprietor laughed and wiped his hands. *That's the first intelligent thing anybody's said all morning.*

The bar was empty too. The proprietor warmed the glasses with a little flaming whisky in the bottom, twisting them expertly as they heated. Then he doused the flame with hot coffee, mixed in sugar, and added another generous dollop of Irish.

No whipped cream, he announced sadly.

No problem, Rikhoff consoled him enthusiastically. *All the important ingredients are there!*

We decided to drive upriver to Hunter, checking for water that was not being fished and watching the weather for a break. There are fine pools and swift runs above Hunter where the Schoharie dances along banks of birches and hardwoods, with an occasional pine standing tall and somber above the river. There are swift runs along the ledgerock, beautiful pocket-water among the boulders, a waist-deep flat well away from the road, and a deep white-water pool behind the summer camp at Jeanette.

We drove upstream through Hunter and turned toward the mountains and the river. There were no other fishermen anywhere along the valley. Rikhoff had fished the stretch before. We decided that I would fish down from the bridge, while he drove around the back road past the summer camp to leave the car.

It was an unproductive two hours. It is a particularly beautiful reach of water, but my stream thermometer read forty-four and the current felt icy around my legs. There were no hatches and the wind was colder than the river. It dropped slightly and the sun filtered weakly through the overcast. Rikhoff was fishing about two hundred yards downstream. Suddenly there were a half-dozen tiny Plecoptera flies rising across the current. Although I watched the river carefully for several minutes, no more flies emerged and the current seemed lifeless under the pale April sun.

This flat should warm the river, I thought.

Finally I decided to wade downstream, disappointed that two o'clock had arrived without a sign of the *Epeorus* mayflies, and suddenly I realized that Rikhoff was playing a fish. Before I reached him at the Camp Pool, he had caught another.

How've you done? he yelled.

Nothing. I shook my head unhappily. *What are you getting them with down there—Gordon Quill?*

No, he said. *I'm fishing wet.*

There were a few stoneflies coming off again. The Camp Pool begins in a long, tumbling run of broken water that chutes into the deeper water below the tributary brook. There is a deep eddying-zone of water before the current gathers again, spreading along the tail-shallows into a swift little run against the rocks; downstream I saw the flash of a nymphing trout.

What are you using? I asked curiously.

Don't know what you call it, he laughed, *but it's got a reddish body and a woodduck wing—it's taken four already.*

Probably a wet Red Quill, I said.

It made sense with the little *Taeniopteryx* flies. Another nymphing fish porpoised deep in the gathering tail-shallows, like a salmon lying at the lip of the pool. Quickly I knotted a Little Red Stonefly Nymph to the leader and covered the first fish with a teasing swing of the fly. It took eagerly and I worked it gently out of the shallows, while the second fish rolled again. Two casts later I had the porpoising trout too.

Suddenly a squall lashed along the river, gusting a blizzard of wet snowflakes on the wind. The banks and trees were quickly blanketed, and the hatch stopped. It was almost impossible to see the river through the driving snow, and we climbed back up the embankment to our car.

Ridiculous! I brushed snow off my hat.

It's worse than duck shooting, Rikhoff laughed, *and I thought only duck shooters liked to be miserable.*

Where's the thermos? I shivered.

How many fish did you get there at the last? He reached for the thermos. *Was it two or three?*

You know damn well it was only two! I grinned at him.

Well, Rikhoff shrugged, *you should be proud of your pupils when they match the hatch!*

Thermos! I laughed.

Matching the Emerging Trichoptera

I<small>T IS OLD</small> and hallowed water. The river is smaller here, tumbling musically down its pastoral valley in a series of pianissimo moods that are a prelude to the big water below its meeting with the Willowemoc. The current is clear over pale-yellow gravel. There is a timber-cribbing dam near the bottom of the old Hardenburgh farm. The other breaks in its gentle currents are also manmade, casual lines of thoughtfully placed stones that are a subtle counterpoint to the natural character of the river. It is the classic Little Beaverkill.

The log-frame clubhouse is unpainted, bleaching silver and aging gracefully after almost three-quarters of a century. Its timbers are racked and twisted with time. The members still insist on outdoor plumbing and no electricity, lighting their social rituals with an ancient coal-oil lamp. It is a sanctuary with a sense of time.

The group had its beginnings·on the Brodheads at Henryville House, and when its brook-trout fishery played out in 1897, they emigrated north to the Hardenburgh farm on the Beaverkill. Sparse Grey Hackle has made them immortal in his little classic *Fishless Days*, catching perfectly the character of their fishing house and its rambling porch in the sunny orchard above the river. The founders were a group of wealthy brewers and businessmen, and included Ernest Palmer, Abraham Snedecor, James Rice, R. J. Sayre, Lodie Smith, C. B. Boynton, Chancellor Levison, H. B. Marshall, R. M. Coleman, J. L. Snedecor, F. S. Howard, Ralph Burnett, J. E. Bullwinkle, C. H. Fitzgerald, and Charles Bryan. Their history began on the opening weekend in 1895, and is recorded in a time-stained hotel register from Henryville House. The founding ceremony was sealed with a full-page scroll, executed in gracefully flowing nineteenth-century penmanship. Several of these men were part of the nucleus which ultimately became the Anglers' Club of New York, and this historic group of dedicated men, with its genesis on both the Beaverkill and the Brodheads, first banded together as the Brooklyn Flyfishers.

Their club water is lovely. It has been protected and stocked and painstakingly restored over the past seventy-five years, releasing its trout and fishing only flies. Several times the members have had to rebuild their banks and log-cribbing, binding up the wounds of hurricane flooding. The quality of the fishing on their brief mileage is eloquent testimony to enlightened stream management, just as the fly-fishing-only water on the lower Beaverkill clearly demonstrates the only viable method of providing good sport over decent-sized trout on our heavily fished rivers. It is not a matter of snobbish fly-fishermen attempting to reserve mileage for themselves—it is simply the only way to preserve good public fishing.

The last evening I fished the Brooklyn Flyfishers water, I drew the upper riffles with a deep run against the county road. It was a soft evening with a warm wind moving up the valley. Normally I would have expected a hatch of pale *Stenonemas*, and began fishing upstream under the willows with a little mayfly nymph. There were two fish that took the nymph lightly and came off after a brief struggle. One brown porpoised to the nymph like it was taking a dry fly, and I hooked it solidly in the corner of its jaws.

The next fifty yards proved unproductive. There were no trout rising anywhere, and then suddenly the river came alive. It was the miracle of a heavy *Psilotreta* hatch, coming shortly past five o'clock. There were a few of the little slate-colored caddis flies rising from the current. Swallows and phoebes began working, with the swallows wheeling high above the river and the smaller, fly-catching phoebes darting back and forth from the bankside alders.

There were dozens of flies now. Trout were working, too, and the birds were highly agitated. Hundreds of caddis were hatching in just minutes, and there were soon thousands of naturals riding the gentle upstream wind. Some were sixty-odd feet above the current, judging from the chimney swifts and swallows. Others were scudding clumsily on the surface.

The fish literally went crazy. Trout were rolling and porpoising in the current. The flat was alive with rises. Fish sipped and splashed along the rocks, fed eagerly in their backwaters, and held and rose greedily in their cushion of upstream currents. Many of the rise-forms were eager and slashing, and I concluded that such energy indicated the difficulty of capturing the fluttering caddis.

The little Trichoptera were difficult to catch. When the browns refused a dozen dry-fly patterns, I spent fifteen minutes before I finally caught one of the little slate-colored naturals. It had a dark-brown abdomen, darkly mottled legs, pale antennae, light-grayish rear wings, and darkly speckled forewings the color of slate.

These sedges should have worked, I puzzled.

Carefully watching the fish, I soon discovered that the rise-forms were vigorous and greedy, but that they were seldom focused upon a struggling adult. There was an occasional caddis fly that disappeared unhappily into an obvious surface rise.

What are they taking? I thought.

The fish were rolling and splashing eagerly, expending the kind of energy usually involved in surface rises to a fluttering adult. It had to indicate some type of nymphal form, and an ecotype capable of swimming. Its ability to move underwater would explain the energetic rise-forms to an escaping insect, and I searched my fly books for a soft-hackled wet with a dark body dubbing. For a few seasons on the Brodheads, I had been experimenting with partridge and woodcock hackle flies, in the tradition of Stewart and Pritt, during caddis hatches, and I selected a dark little pattern with a hare's-mask body.

There was a good fish porpoising above a flat rock in the gathering currents at the tail of the pool beside the road. I cast the wet fly upstream to the rising trout, just like a typical dry-fly presentation. There was a quick rise and the fish was hooked.

It was easy then, and trout that had consistently refused my earlier dry-fly patterns took the soft-hackled wet readily. It was a good lesson in reading rise-forms for all kinds of fly hatches, but it is especially true of the Trichoptera. There was no question about having matched the hatch. Thirty-six fish were caught and carefully released while the caddis flies lasted, and when they stopped emerging and disappeared from the river, it flowed dark and silent in the gathering darkness.

It was an evening that remains in the mind.

The Beaverkill experiences the miracle of two immense caddis hatches each season. The first is the blizzardlike emergence of shadflies in May. These little *Brachycentrus* caddis begin emerging on the lower Beaverkill first, hatching a little farther upriver each evening. The hatches are literally clouds of dark green-bodied little insects, dwarfing all of the earlier mayfly hatches together in the sheer weight of their numbers. The second hatch of little slate-colored Trichoptera is almost as numerous. These *Psilotreta* were the insects that puzzled me that long-ago twilight on the Beaverkill, and were first described in the work of Preston Jennings. However, Jennings attempted a dry-fly imitation, and among his fishing companions he was usually skeptical about the successful imitation of such caddis hatches. Jennings was right in terms of a dry-fly prototype, but imitating the sub-aquatic pupal stages during a hatch is obviously another matter.

Louis Rhead made a similar observation in his relatively early *American Trout-Stream Insects,* an undisciplined and rather primitive little book published in 1920. The solitary Rhead was a regular Beaverkill fisherman, and he was writing about its shadflies.

> The shadfly is the most abundant trout insect-food that appears on our eastern, and some middle and far western, streams. Trout are ravenous for it. When the shadfly is on the water you will never fail to see trout rising.
> However, when the great rise appears it is hardly possible to catch a trout with any prevailing artificial now tied.

Both Rhead and Jennings were right about dry-fly imitations of the caddis flies, but they were clearly wrong in not recognizing that most sedge-hatch feeding is subsurface in character.

The logic behind this phenomenon is clear. It is much easier for a trout to capture the swimming pupae enroute to the surface, or pupal forms pinioned and actually emerging in the film, than it is for them to slash and leap for the fluttering adults.

Unlike caddis larvae, which are virtually impossible to imitate effectively in their case-building species, all pupal ecotypes of the Trichoptera are available to the fish. The free-ranging campodeiform larvae do not build such sheltering cases of tiny stones and vegetable matter, and their imitations are fishable. But the case-builders are firmly attached to the bottom stones or encrusted along deadfalls like the stick-case *Stenophylax,* and they are difficult to simulate with a free swinging fly.

Trout exist in a delicate equilibrium between calories ingested and calories expended. Since the pupal stages of the caddis flies represent the only period in which all species of Trichoptera are both vulnerable and easily imitated by fly-fishing tactics, it is easy to understand their interest for fish and fishermen. Such factors seem increasingly significant, since the caddis flies are perhaps better equipped to survive the impact of pollution and pesticides than the more fragile stoneflies and mayflies. The selection of a particular diet-form over other available food-types, and the consistent concentration on such foods by feeding trout, is explained in a simple pattern of relationships. These interrelationships are between the relative availability of the food-types, their calorie content and weight, and their difficulty of capture. Assuming optimal and constant feeding-and-digestion temperatures are present, these topologies are expressed in the following equation:

$$\text{Energy expended per calorie ingested} = \frac{\text{Availability of ecotype} \times \text{its caloric content}}{\text{Factor of capture}}$$

The caddis flies or sedges are perhaps the most numerous of the aquatic insects extant in American trout waters, making their availability factor relatively high. There are literally hundreds and hundreds of caddis-fly species. These insects differ from the stoneflies and mayflies in one singular respect. The Plecoptera and Ephemeroptera traverse a life cycle from egg through the nymphal stages to the winged adult. The mayflies have two winged stages: the subimago duns that exist upon hatching, and the fully adult imago spinners that emerge from a final molt in the streamside vegetation. However, the caddis flies have a complete life cycle, encompassing ova, larvae, pupal stages, and winged adults.

Adult sedges resemble moths, especially in attitudes of flight, but a cursory inspection highlights a number of significant differences. Their wings lack the powdery residues found on moths, residues which in fact result from innumerable minuscule scales covering their upper surfaces. Caddis-fly wings are covered with diminutive hairs. Such textures are more densely distributed in some caddis-fly species than others.

These hairs are difficult to see without magnification, although on some species their dense distribution makes them quite readily visible without a glass. Caddis flies are also somewhat more slender in their structural physiology, as well as more slender in appearance, since they fold their tent-shaped wings tightly. Such tent-shaped attitudes completely cover the abdominal anatomy of the Trichoptera, while the moths hold their wings rather flatly. The trout can readily distinguish between moths and caddis flies, and very few moths play a role in the diet of the fish.

The caddis-fly head carries a pair of moderately sized compound eyes, and as many as three simple eye ocelli. The mouthparts are situated at the ventral surfaces, with readily visible palps. Antennae are sometimes almost two to three times wing length. The thoracic structure consists of three segments. Each of these carries a pair of legs. The anterior forewings are rooted in the middle thoracic segment, and the secondary wings come from the posterior segment. The bodies are considerably shorter than the wings, are structured of nine abdominal segments, and completely lack tails.

The larvae of the Trichoptera are discussed in detail in the following chapter. Such larvae feed omnivorously, taking vegetable matter, animal organisms, and large numbers of insect eggs. Incubation and eclosion of the ova vary with temperature and altitude. The species can be separated into two distinct groups, in terms of their larval behavior. There are both the case-building species and the campodeiform ecotypes which live free among the stones. Species inhabiting swift currents build their cases of sand, stones and tiny bits of shell, seeking a specific gravity in their cases that will help them hold their position securely. Slow-water species utilize fragments of wood or leaves which create relatively buoyant shells that permit easy movement. The caseless species inhabit crevices in the bottom, or construct tiny food-catching nets and enclosures among the stones.

Fully grown larvae construct a silklike pupal cocoon in the stones among the campodeiform species, forming an enclosure of tiny pebbles around its base. The case-bearing species seal the ends of their shelters with a web of sufficient porosity to allow the entry of oxygenated water.

The transformation from larva to pupa is not unlike the metamorphosis from caterpillar to chrysalis among moths and butterflies. The process includes molting, when the larva sheds its skin and evolves its pupal stage. Pupal forms vary considerably from the larvae, stop eating, and enter a brief cycle somewhat like hibernation. Pupation can take from a few weeks to as much as the entire winter period.

When the pupal cycle is complete, the emerging caddis penetrates its cocoon with its sharp mandibles. The morphological structure of the pupa bears a considerable resemblance to its adult development. The thorax and abdomen are distinctly formed. The evolving wings are readily visible inside their pupal skin, and both the antennae and the legs lie parallel to the body; the legs and antennae trail past the posterior abdominal segment. The legs are heavily fringed at this stage of development, permitting the pupa to swim readily toward the surface. Such pupae emerge in two ways: some species emerge in open water, using the tensile character of the surface film to split their pupal skins, while others creep out of the water on plant stems or rocks or deadfalls to hatch.

The Trichoptera are therefore readily available to the trout in the pupal stages of each genus. Some swim readily toward the surface film and emerge almost immediately, while others drift some distance with the current. Those which migrate to rocks, plant stems, and deadfalls are vulnerable during their movements from the site of pupation to the place of hatching. The trout feed eagerly on such extensive and easy prey.

Caddis flies are widely distributed in unpolluted waters throughout the United States. They occur in streams, reservoirs, lakes, beaver ponds, rivers, and small tributaries. Their tolerance of pollution, wide ranges of temperatures, pesticides, and variations in water chemistry is good. They are found in both acid and alkaline environments. Although most species are extremely adaptable to a wide range of habitats, some are found only in seriously constrained environments.

Fly-fishermen have too often ignored the caddis, and my earlier *Matching the Hatch* was also guilty of this omission. Although many species are important enough to cause rises of fish themselves, the Trichoptera are also important collectively. Several species are often present together, and in spite of each emerging in relatively small numbers, their aggregate populations are large enough to trigger a rise of fish. The presence of several species at once seems to result in general non-selective feeding. Concentration on a single species often results in selectivity. The trout feed on each of its several stages. Most readily take the pupae swimming to the surface of the shallows to hatch. Others capture the freshly hatched flies in the surface film, drying their wings or resting on the current, and scuttling across the water toward shore. Trout also rise eagerly to egg-laying females, and to both males and females lying spent after mating. But most caddis are captured in their pupal stages.

Although there are literally hundreds of species, most are remarkably similar, and for our purposes here we have chosen to illustrate fifteen pupal forms in color. These typical species will provide effective prototypes for a series of imitative flies covering most fly hatches found on American waters.

1. American Grannom (*Brachycentrus fuliginosus*)

This is a major species on our rivers, with its sister species *Brachycentrus subnubilus* rich in the tradition of British fly-fishing, and its pupal imitation is important to American anglers. Its larvae live in the swift riffles, building tapered little cases of plant fibers that are square in cross-section. They live on vegetable matter and minute organisms carried to their clustered colonies among the rocks. Pupation usually occurs in weedy shallows or attached to sticks and deadfalls. Following this stage of growth, the pupae migrate to the surface and emerge. The species is widely distributed on eastern rivers, emerging in heavy hatches late in May. The pupal forms measure approximately five-eighths inch in length at full growth.

No well-stocked wading vest can be without this imitation, which I have adapted from the north-country flies developed by such British writers as Stewart and Pritt and Scrope a century ago. Based upon my studies in entomology, and the correlative behavior of the fish to certain caddis-fly pupae and imitative types of flies, I am convinced that such soft-hackled border dressings primarily owe their effectiveness to the heavy populations of caddis-flies in the north-country rivers.

Tergites: Dark brown with paler ringing, 7/16 inch
Sternites: Slightly paler brown, 7/16 inch
Thorax: Deep brownish black, 3/16 inch
Wing cases: Dark slate gray, 5/16 inch
Legs: Dark mottled brown, ½ inch
Antennae: Mottled brown, ⅞ inch
Head: Dark brownish black, 3/32 inch

Hooks: Sizes 10 through 14 Mustad 3906 sproat
Nylon: Dark-brown 6/0 nylon
Body: Dark-brown dubbing ribbed with fine oval tinsel
Thorax: Deep-chocolate-colored dubbing
Wing cases: Slate-colored duck quill sections tied at the sides
Legs: Darkly mottled partridge body hackle
Antennae: Brown mallard fibers
Head: Dark-brown nylon

The Grannom Pupa is a singularly effective pattern dressed in sizes ten to fourteen, fished in the shallows and eddies of relatively swift currents.

There are a number of related American species. The eastern Grannom hatch described above has a parallel in the *Brachycentrus numerosus,* which on some waters is mixed with other insects. Western variations of the Grannom exist too. Particularly interesting is the ecotype *Brachycentrus simulis* found on Rocky Mountain watersheds, and Pacific coast fly-fishermen have both *Brachycentrus americanus* and *Brachycentrus occidentalis.* The Grannom Pupa pattern is also useful there, imitating the subaquatic migrations of the insects before a hatch.

2. Little Western Sedge (*Cheumatopsyche gracilus*)

This ubiquitous little species hatches on our Rocky Mountain rivers early in July, riding the evening wind by the thousands. It is a net-spinning genus closely related to the *Hydropsyche* flies. Sometimes the fish respond with a surface rise that sets dry-fly fishermen muttering with frustration. The flies look straw-colored in the late evening sun, and fishermen are always searching their fly boxes for pale Cahill-colored patterns. It is a fruitless and impossible choice, doomed to failure of rejection after rejection from the rising fish. All of the caddis flies, and most insects of other orders, look much paler in flight than they actually are on the water. It was a lesson learned with this hatch almost twenty-five years ago on the Frying Pan, in an incident recorded in *Matching the Hatch.* However, it was later that I fully began to realize that the most convincing secret of a Trichoptera hatch lies in imitating its pupal stages.

The pupa of *Cheumatopsyche gracilus* measures approximately seven-sixteenths inch at full development.

These pupae hatch into the winged adults in the surface film of open water, both in and downstream from relatively swift reaches of river, where the *Cheumatopsyche* flies live and pupate. The pupal forms of this species are a major diet-form on Rocky Mountain streams, and I have come to prefer a delicate little soft-hackled pattern dressed in the style of Theakston and Pritt. It is derived from the Brown Partridge Quill

Tergites: Darkly ringed brownish gray, ⅜ inch
Sternites: Ringed brownish gray, ⅜ inch
Thorax: Dark chocolate brown, 3/32 inch
Wing cases: Medium gray, ¼ inch
Legs: Mottled brown, ⅜ inch
Antennae: Pale amber mottled at joints, ½ inch
Head: Dark brown, 7/16 inch

Hook: Sizes 14-16 Mustad 3906 sproat
Nylon: Dark-brown 6/0 nylon
Body: Bleached peacock quill over brown nylon underbody
Thorax: Dark-brown dubbing
Wing cases: Medium-gray duck quill sections tied at sides
Legs: Dark mottled partridge hackle
Antennae: Lemon woodduck fibers
Head: Dark-brown nylon

3. Medium Brown Sedge (*Ganonema americana*)

This is a well-distributed eastern species which measures approximately eleven-sixteenths inch at full development of its pupal stages. The larvae build their cases of hollowed-out sticks and stems. Its adults are rather similar to the energetic little *Halesus radiatus,* the scuttling Caperer sedge so familiar from the studies of riverkeeper William Lunn, on the British Test at Stockbridge.

Imitations of such pupal forms should be weighted slightly and dressed rather sparsely for a deep presentation. Such tactics should use sink-tip and sinking lines, depending on the depth and speed of the current. The two well-known pupal imitations developed by Edward Sens, and described in *How to Catch Trout on Wet Flies and Nymphs*, which Ray Ovington published in 1951, are typical of dressings designed for intermediate depths. Flies tied to imitate a hatching pupa should be dressed with more hackle fibers and rather rough dubbing to suggest a loosening pupal skin in the surface film. Light-wire hooks are an advantage in such dressings. Ribbing a hatching pupa with fine oval tinsel—gold with brown fur dubbing and silver with gray—to simulate the tiny bubbles of gas entrapped inside such a splitting pupal shuck is a useful refinement on selective fish.

The pattern I dress to imitate *Ganonema americana* is a modern variation on one of the historic Pritt flies, the classic Brown Partridge of the Yorkshire rivers.

Tergites: Medium brown with pale ringing, ½ inch
Sternites: Slightly paler than tergites, with pale ringing, ½ inch
Thorax: Dark brown, 3/16 inch
Wing cases: Dark slate-gray, ⅜ inch
Legs: Dark brown, ⅝ inch
Antennae: Dark speckled brown, ¾ inch
Head: Dark brown, 3/32 inch

Hook: Sizes 8-10 Mustad 3906 sproat
Nylon: Dark-brown 6/0 nylon
Body: Medium-brown dubbing ribbed with fine oval tinsel
Thorax: Dark-brown fur dubbing
Wing cases: Dark mallard quill sections tied short at the sides
Legs: Dark brownish-gray partridge hackle
Antennae: Brown mallard fibers
Head: Dark-brown nylon

4. Little Sepia Sedge (*Glossosoma califica*)

This is a well-distributed little western species, particularly on the rivers of our Pacific mountains, where their need for cold, well-oxygenated water is easily fulfilled on mile after mile of streams. Its cases and pupal shelters are constructed of tiny pebbles, resembling little igloos attached to the stones. These little caddis live singly in their tiny, turtle-shaped cases until time for pupation. Then they congregate on the stones in tightly bunched colonies, their cases placed side by side in the current. Larvae, pupal forms, and adults are available all summer, measuring about nine-sixteenths inch at full pupal development. These Trichoptera are not large, but their sporadic hatching activity over the entire season makes them important.

Tergites: Medium brown distinctly ringed with darker color, 5/16 inch
Sternites: Slightly paler than tergites, 5/16 inch
Thorax: Deep brownish black, 1/16 inch
Wing cases: Dark brownish gray, ¼ inch
Legs: Dark brown with blackish mottlings, ⅜ inch
Antennae: Dark mottled brown, 7/16 inch
Head: Blackish brown, 1/16 inch

Hook: Size 16 Mustad 3906 sproat
Nylon: Dark-brown 6/0 nylon
Body: Medium-brown dubbing ribbed with darker fun spun on a light-chocolate-colored ribbing-thread
Thorax: Brownish-black dubbing
Wing cases: Dark-brownish-gray duck quill sections tied at sides
Legs: Darkly mottled partridge hackle
Antennae: Brown mallard fibers
Head: Dark-brown nylon

The imitation is a fine general pattern in the small sizes. The eastern species *Glossosoma americana* is quite similar, and the Rocky Mountain species found at relatively high altitudes is *Glossosoma intermedium*. There is a somewhat paler ecotype found on the rivers of Montana. Its taxonometric designation is *Glossosoma alacense,* and the same imitation is useful with a paler dubbed body. The ancient border pattern developed in the studies of Blacker, which he called the Medium Grouse and Brown, is the basis of this pupal imitation of the Little Sepia Sedge.

5. Little Sand Sedge (*Goera americana*)

The little larval cases of these *Goera* flies are found on smooth, current-polished stones from the late summer until the following spring. The cases are constructed of tiny pebbles arched into miniature barrel vault, with larger stones as buttresses on either side. Pupation occurs during late March on eastern waters, and somewhat later on western streams. The adults hatch between April and May on eastern and north central rivers, and emergence can occur as late as midsummer farther west. Full-grown *Goera* pupae measure about nine-sixteenths inch in length.

The little Scottish pattern called the Corncrake and Yellow was the basis for the accompanying pupal imitation of the Little Sand Sedge.

Tergites: Light brown distinctly ringed with medium brown, 5/16 inch
Sternites: Slightly paler than tergites, 5/16 inch
Thorax: Dark brownish, 1/16 inch
Wing cases: Medium grayish, ¼ inch
Legs: Pale mottled brown, ⅜ inch
Antennae: Pale mottled amber, 7/16 inch
Head: Light brown, 7/16 inch

Hook: Sizes 12-14 Mustad 3906 sproat
Nylon: Tan 6/0 nylon
Body: Pale dirty-yellowish dubbing
Thorax: Light brown dubbing
Wing cases: Light gray duck quill sections tied at sides
Legs: Light grayish brown fibers
Antennae: Lemon woodduck fibers
Head: Tan nylon

6. Medium Speckled Sedge (*Helicopsyche borealis*)

These medium-sized caddis flies have uniquely spiral-shaped cases fabricated of pebbles and tiny fragments of shells. They are most common in sandy-bottomed still waters or the quiet eddies of slow-flowing streams, and creep along the bottom in search of feeding zones. These larvae lead solitary lives until the pupal phase approaches, when they gather in large communities among the stones. Sealing their cases to the rocks, they weave silken coverings to close their pupal shelters. The full-grown *Helicopysche* pupae measure about three-fourths inch in length, and on eastern waters they emerge in June and July.

Tergites: Light brown distinctly ringed with darker brown, ½ inch
Sternites: Slightly paler brown ringed with darker coloring, ½ inch
Thorax: Dark brown, 3/16 inch
Wing cases: Medium gray, 3/8 inch
Legs: Medium mottled brownish, ½ inch
Antennae: Pale mottled brown, 11/16 inch
Head: Dark brown, 3/32 inch

Hook: Sizes 10-12 Mustad 3906 sproat
Nylon: Dark-brown 6/0 nylon
Body: Light-brown dubbing ringed with darker-brown fur on an orange ribbing core
Thorax: Dark-brown dubbing
Wing cases: Medium-gray duck quill sections tied at sides
Legs: Medium brownish mottled dotterel hackle
Antennae: Lemon woodduck fibers
Head: Dark-brown nylon

These adults are not unlike the British sedge called the Speckled Peter, and there is a parallel species of considerable significance to western anglers.

It is the *Helicopsyche californica* found in the trout waters of the Pacific mountains. Pritt dressed a pattern he called the Dotterel and Orange, and a variation of his fly is the origin of my *Helicopsyche* pupal imitation.

7. Small Spotted Sedge (*Hydropsyche alternans*)

This is a small grayish-brown caddis typical of several related American species. Specimens average about one-half inch. The genus is perhaps the best known of the net-spinning Trichoptera on this continent. Its campodeiform larvae do not construct the sheltering cases typical of the other immature caddis, and are therefore available to the fish in both larval and pupal stages.

There are several closely associated species of considerable importance to American fly-fishers. Wetzel first discussed *Hydropsyche alternans* in his *Practical Fly Fishing*, along with its sister eastern species *Hydropsyche slossonae*. Both are important on eastern streams.

Western anglers who know their caddis flies are familiar with species like the profusely distributed *Hydropsyche simulans*, *Hydropsyche occidentalis*, *Hydropsyche bifida*, and other related ecotypes found in Rocky Mountain waters. Pacific coast watersheds support similar species. Limnologists making studies of the trout diet on several east-flowing streams of the Sierra Nevada discovered that *Hydropysche oslari*, *Hydropsyche californica*, and *Hydropsyche grandis* played a principal role in the food chain sustaining their fish populations.

The adults of these species are largely small, grayish-mottled sedges with yellowish or yellowish-green bodies. Eastern rivers typically have twilight hatches in June and July, while our western species come later in the summer. The eastern *Hydropsyche alternans* pupa measures a half-inch in length at full development.

The genus *Hydropsyche* is important in British waters, too, where the best-known species is the little *Hydropsyche pellucidula*, which Moseley has called the Grey Sedge. There are other British species identified in his definitive book on British caddis flies which are important in the catalogue of a fly-fisher.

The larvae of this genus are found in relatively swift water and require stones and bottom rubble for optimal habitat. They collect their food from the current with little nets constructed in crevices among the rocks. Such webbings are tightly woven, facing upstream to strain the current, catching various organisms. The larvae conceal themselves in a protective silken tent, virtually an extension of the food-collecting net.

Adult *Hydropsyche* flies hatch in open currents, dropping slightly with the flow to emerge in the quieter water downstream from their larval and pupal habitat. The genus is of exceptional value to fishermen because, unlike most nocturnal Trichoptera flies, its species are daytime insects. Males can be observed hovering in the sunshine throughout the daylight hours. The female sedges join them in mating swarms in late afternoon, laying their eggs at evening. The period of emergence, when the pupal forms are migrating toward the surface and using the tensile character of the meniscus to split the nymphal skins, is critical to nymphing tactics—

and happily this hatching is a sporadic day-long cycle, beginning in early morning and lasting until dark, mixed with the mating and oviposition.

These past few seasons I have been using a delicate little variation on the classic Woodcock and Yellow, the century-old pattern that has its roots on the Yorkshire border. It is extremely effective on fast pocket-water streams having good *Hydropsyche* hatches.

Tergites: Light brown ringed with medium brown, ⅜ inch
Sternites: Similar to tergites, ⅜ inch
Thorax: Medium brown, ⅛ inch
Wing cases: Pale grayish brown, ¼ inch
Legs: Pale mottled brown, ½ inch
Antennae: Pale mottled yellowish, ⅝ inch
Head: Medium brown, 3/32 inch

Hook: Sizes 12-14 Mustad 3906 sproat
Nylon: Medium-brown 6/0 nylon
Body: Pale-brownish dubbing ribbed with medium-brown fur dubbed on a brown ribbing core
Thorax: Medium-brown dubbing
Wing cases: Pale-grayish-brown duck quill sections tied at sides
Legs: Pale mottled brown woodcock hackle
Antennae: Lemon woodcock fibers
Head: Medium-brown nylon

8. Medium Cinnamon Sedge (*Limnephilus americanus*)

These relatively large caddis flies are found principally in slow-flowing streams, lakes, and impoundments. The famed Cinnamon Sedges of British waters, the *Limnephilus lunatus* and *Limnephilus flavicornis* found in the Hampshire chalkstreams, are prototypical of the genus. The adults are delicately mottled insects measuring approximately three-fourths inch in length at maturity.

The young larvae quickly construct stick-cases of a ragged, almost hedgehog texture shortly following their eclosion from the eggs. However, as they develop farther, their case structures change. The larvae migrate away from the weedy shallows, gathering their materials from the bottom in deeper water. When tiny mollusks are available, the *Limnephilus* larvae build their cases almost entirely of them. Sometimes these intricate little tubes are constructed primarily of *Planorbis* and spectacular little *Sphaerium* shells, even with their original inhabitants intact and thriving.

The pupal forms of these insects often have a dark brownish-orange cast to their abdominal segments, and on emergence they swiftly swim toward the surface in a series of pulsing movements. Such migrations are perfectly simulated with a hand-twist retrieve.

T. E. Pritt liked a border pattern called the Grouse and Orange and a variation has proved effective for me over the years. There is a western species commonly distributed in lakes and streams at about ten thousand feet, the orange-bodied *Limnephilus coloradensis*.

Tergites: Dark orangish brown slightly mottled, ⅝ inch
Sternites: Slightly paler than tergites, ⅝ inch
Thorax: Dark mottled brown, 3/16 inch
Wing cases: Dark brownish gray, ½ inch
Legs: Dark mottled brown, ¾ inch
Antennae: Pale mottled brown, ⅞ inch
Head: Dark mottled brown, ⅛ inch

Hook: Sizes 8-10 Mustad 3906 sproat
Nylon: Dark-brown 6/10 nylon
Body: Dark-orangish fur dubbing
Thorax: Dark-brown fur
Wing cases: Dark-brownish-gray duck quill sections tied at sides
Legs: Darkly mottled grouse hackle
Antennae: Lemon woodduck fibers
Head: Dark-brown nylon

9. Medium Dark-Olive Sedge (*Macronema aspila*)

These are relatively large caddis flies, important to fly-fishermen because they belong to the campodeiform genera of Trichoptera that do not build case-shelters. The larvae are easily recognized by their dark green dorsal tergites and the vivid green of the ventral segments, with their silvery little belly-gill filaments. The pupae have similar body coloring and are about three-fourths inch in length. It is locally common in rapid, shallow streams.

W. C. Stewart used an ancient Scottish border pattern to imitate similar caddis flies on his beloved Whitadder, Teviot, and Tweed. It is the Grouse and Green, and I have modified its traditional dressing to imitate these olive-bodied *Macronema* flies.

Tergites: Dark blackish green, ⅝ inch
Sternites: Bright olive green, ⅝ inch
Thorax: Dark blackish green, 3/16 inch
Wing cases: Dark bluish gray, ½ inch
Legs: Dark mottled brown, ¾ inch
Antennae: Dark mottled brown, ⅞ inch
Head: Dark blackish green, ⅞ inch

Hook: Sizes 8-10 Mustad 3906 sproat
Nylon: Dark-olive 6/0 nylon
Body: Bright-green fur or crewel dubbing marked very dark blackish on back with indelible felt-tipped pen, ribbed with fine oval tinsel
Thorax: Blackish-olive dubbing
Wing cases: Bluish-gray duck quill sections
Legs: Dark mottled grouse hackle
Antennae: Lemon woodduck fibers
Head: Dark-olive nylon with a drop of black lacquer on head

The western species *Macronema zebatum* is also found in swift-flowing rivers of the Rocky Mountains. Pupation of these caddis occurs in a silken shelter, enclosed in an oval of anchoring pebbles.

10. Great Dark-Brown Sedge (*Neuronia lapponica*)

This is a slow-water caddis that builds its case of leaf fragments, wrapping them like thin, slightly curved little cigars. These cases often measure as much as one and a quarter inches, delicate and textured with the tiny venation of the leaves. Pupation involves migration into the shallows, where the insects worm into deadfalls or creep under rotting layers of bark.

Tergites: Dark mottled brown distinctly marked with paler ringing, ¾ inch
Sternites: Dark mottled brown and palely ringed, ¾ inch
Thorax: Blackish brown, ⅜ inch
Wing cases: Slate gray, ½ inch
Legs: Dark mottled grouse hackle, ¾ inch
Antennae: Pale mottled brown, ⅞ inch
Head: Dark brown, ⅛ inch

Hook: Sizes 6-8 Mustad 3906 sproat
Nylon: Dark-brown 6/0 nylon
Body: Dark-brown dubbing ribbed with fine oval tinsel
Thorax: Dark blackish brown dubbing
Wing cases: Dark slate-colored duck quill sections tied at sides
Legs: Dark grouse hackle
Antennae: Brown mallard fibers
Head: Dark-brown nylon

Fully developed pupae measure about one and an eighth inches and hatch by swimming or clambering to the surface in the shoreline shallows. The Dark Grouse and Brown is a good basis for imitating the relatively large pupae of the *Neuronia* flies.

11. Great Western Caperer (*Phryganea coloradense*)

This is a superb hatch that comes off on Rocky Mountain lakes at about ten thousand feet in late August. It is most easily recognized by its erratic, spiraling patterns in the surface film after hatching. Although the fish often take such scuttling adults with savage rises, most of the swirls are subsurface rises to emerging pupae. Sometimes the lakes and reservoirs of Colorado generate heavy hatches of these insects and their surfaces are literally alive with fish. Such a hatch once produced a hook-jawed brown of six pounds for me on the shallow waters of Granite Lake in Colorado.

The larvae of the *Phryganea* genus build cases of vegetation and live submerged in the weeds of lakes and ponds. They are seldom found on the bottom. The leafy fragments are arranged in a rather coarsely fashioned spiral. These larvae measure about one inch in length and are quite carnivorous and fierce. Sometimes even tiny fish are captured and eaten. During pupation, these larvae burrow into submerged logs and detritus on the bottom with only a tiny breathing-end of their cases exposed.

Hatching occurs in open water with a rather swift approach to the surface. It is certainly this agile swimming of the pupae that triggers such vicious swirls from the rising fish. The freshly hatched sedges then gyrate and scuttle toward the shoreline; most emergence activity occurs in late afternoon and early evening.

The fly pattern I echo to imitate this big *Phryganea* on the Colorado lakes is a large Pheasant and Olive, not unlike the big green-bodied wets dressed by George Grant on the Big Hole. His body techniques are perfect for suggesting the bright-green core of forming egg masses living inside the translucent olive outerbody.

Tergites: Medium olive lightly mottled, ⅝ inch
Sternites: Slightly paler and translucent with bright-greenish core, ⅝ inch
Thorax: Dark mottled brown, 3/16 inch
Wing cases: Slate-colored gray, ½ inch
Legs: Brownish mottled, ¾ inch
Antennae: Pale mottled brown, ⅞ inch
Head: Medium brown, ⅛ inch

Hook: Sizes 8-10 Mustad 3906 sproat
Nylon: Medium-brown 6/0 nylon
Body: Bright-green core ribbed with gold tinsel and wound with flat monofilament overbody
Thorax: Dark-brown dubbing
Wing cases: Slate-colored duck quill sections tied at sides
Legs: Brownish mottled pheasant fibers
Antennae: Lemon woodduck fibers
Head: Medium-brown nylon

There are several related hatches. The eastern *Phryganea vestita* is a similar insect that emerges from our lakes in late June. The brownish species *Phryganea cinerea* is a dark-brownish hatch found in Rocky Mountain waters, and the hatch *Phryganea californica* is a brown olive-bodied species of the Pacific coast. These are the flies that are related to *Phryganea striata* and *Phryganea grandis*, the Great Red Sedges so storied in the writings on Britain and Ireland.

12.   Dark Blue Sedge (*Psilotreta frontalis*)

This is the prolific slate-colored caddis fly described in the opening paragraphs of this chapter. It is a handsome little sedge of considerable importance to American fishermen. The *Psilotreta* sedges are found in the riffles of swift, stony-bottomed streams. Watersheds having optimal habitats often support remarkable populations of these insects and experience hatches like pewter-colored blizzards.

During the winter months, these larvae range boldly over the bottom of the river, carrying their cornucopia pebble-cases with them. However, just before pupation begins in the early spring they congregate together in complex encrustations at the sides of stones. Many are fastened on top of each other, forming a crude beehive of caddis flies. These cases are piled with the heads upstream, lying parallel in the current. The cases measure a half-inch, but the larvae are somewhat shorter at full growth. These clustered colonies are a singular quality, since few Trichoptera exhibit such gregarious tendencies. Before pupation, the larva seals its case with a tiny pebble, both keeping out its enemies and permitting the oxygenated water to reach its cocoon.

Tergites: Dark brownish, ½ inch
Sternites: Dark brownish, ½ inch
Thorax: Blackish brown, 3/16 inch
Wing cases: Slate-grayish, ⅜ inch
Legs: Dark mottled brown, ⅝ inch
Antennae: Pale mottled brown, ¾ inch
Head: Dark brown, 3/32 inch

Hook: Sizes 10-12 Mustad 3906 sproat
Nylon: Dark-brown 0/0 nylon
Body: Dark-chocolate dubbing
Thorax: Blackish-brown fur dubbing
Wing cases: Slate-gray duck quill sections tied at sides
Legs: Dark woodcock hackle
Antennae: Lemon woodduck fibers
Head: Dark-brown nylon

The delicate little adults of this hatch are similar to the lovely little slate-gray caddis called the Grey Silverhorns in Britain, named for its pale and slender antennae. The imitation I have used with exceptional success is like the Woodcock and Brown, a dressing also derived from the Yorkshire writings of Pritt in northern England.

13. Western Olive Sedge (*Rhyacophila grandis*)

This is the major western species. Its bright-green larvae and pupae of the campodeiform type live caseless and free in the stones of a swift-running current. The ecotype is extremely abundant in streams suited to its requirements. Unlike the net-spinning species, *Rhyacophila* does not build a tiny corral-like structure with a silken food-net and shelter. Its food consists of minute organisms, smaller nymphs and larvae, and filamentaceous algae. Such larvae range freely along the bottom in search of food, a quality that makes them important to anglers since their boldness also exposes them to a foraging trout.

Tergites: Bright olive green, 7/16 inch
Sternites: Slightly paler than tergites, 7/16 inch
Thorax: Dark olive brown, ⅞ inch
Wing cases: Dark slate gray, 5/16 inch
Legs: Dark mottled brown, ½ inch
Antennae: Pale mottled amber, ⅝ inch
Head: Dark brown, 3/32 inch

Hook: Sizes 12-14 Mustad 3906 sproat
Nylon: Dark-brown 6/0 nylon
Body: Pale-olive cellulite or rayon floss picked apart and dubbed over intense green nylon underbody
Thorax: Dark-olive-brown dubbing
Wing cases: Dark-slate-gray duck quill sections tied at sides
Legs: Dark-brown woodcock hackle
Antennae: Lemon woodduck fibers
Head: Dark brown

Just before pupation the larvae patiently select a rock to construct the tiny enclosure of pebbles. Within the enclosure they spin a delicate little ovoid cocoon that covers the bright-green pupae like flat little sleeping bags. The cocoon is transparent enough that the vivid green little pupa is visible inside, its chroma affecting the coloring of the entire pupal cocoon.

The fully developed pupa migrating toward the surface measures about five-eighths inch. There are a number of related western species that provide fly hatches throughout the season.

The Dark Woodcock and Green is another old Blacker pattern from the hills of Yorkshire, and it has provided a personal variation that is an excellent imitation of this *Rhyacophila* hatch.

Related Rocky Mountain and Pacific coast species include *Rhyacophila hyalinata, Rhyacophila pacifica, Rhyacophila bifila,* and *Rhyacophila coloradensis.* These several species emerge rather sporadically, starting in early summer and lasting into October. This past season I witnessed a superb hatch of *Rhyacophila coloradensis* coming off the chutes below the Seven Castles pool of the Frying Pan, while fishing with Jonathan Wright of Aspen, and my old friend Prescott Tolman of New York. It was an evening of fine sport that ended with a three-pound Colorado rainbow.

14. Giant Red Sedge (*Stenophylax scabripennis*)

There are several related genera of these large nocturnal caddis flies on American waters. Their hatching pupae are often the reason for the success of night fishing with big wet flies. They are somewhat larger than the Fetid Browns and Great Red Sedges commonly found in the waters of Ireland and the United Kingdom.

These are the builders of the large stick-cases so commonly found in spring holes and cold headwater streams. Their cases are a complex linear alignment of sticks and leaf fragments, and when they are not foraging for food, only the legs protrude from the shelter of the case. They are quite common in the mountain tributaries of eastern rivers that still support wild brook trout and in those larger rivers that are slightly acid and remain quite cold through the summer. Wild rivers like the Upper Neversink and the Allagash are good examples of such habitat, along with the acid streams of northern Michigan—the rivers made famous in books like *Trout Madness* and the *Anatomy of a Fisherman* in which John Voelker has confessed his piscatorial aberrations.

Perhaps the most impressive populations of *Stenophylax* larvae I have seen were on the Pinchot water of the Upper Sawkill in Pennsylvania, where I once spent a pleasant weekend of fishing with the British angler Lawrence Beck. There are cold brook-trout beaver ponds on its headwaters, with deadfalls of hemlock and pines in its icy currents. The cleared walls marking the boundaries between colonial fields are still there, lost in the thick second-growth timber that has erased their colonial farmsteads. There were bear tracks in the silty shallows and there were so many *Stenophylax* cases on the deadfalls they looked like rough layers of bark.

The pupal forms of these giant sedges measure as much as one-and-a-quarter inches in length at full development and swim rather strongly toward the shallows to emerge. Emergence usually takes place on a half-submerged boulder or deadfall and the fish cruise in the shallows after dark, hoping to intercept these pupae.

The imitation that I like is a large, pheasant-hackled pattern that I have derived from British prototypes in the style of Theakston and Pritt. The mottled, rust-colored bodies of the naturals are perfectly matched with a roughly dubbed brown fur body on orange silk, taking care to leave the rusty guard hairs showing. The modified Pheasant and Brown has taken a lot of big fish for me over the years.

Tergites: Darkly mottled brown with paler ringing, ⅞ inch
Sternites: Slightly paler mottled brown, ⅞ inch
Thorax: Dark blackish brown, ¼ inch
Wing cases: Dark slate-colored gray, ½ inch
Legs: Amber heavily mottled with brown, 1 inch
Antennae: Pale mottled brown, 1⅛ inch
Head: Dark brown, 3/16 inch

Hook: Size 4-6 Mustad 3906 sproat
Nylon: Dark-brown 6/0 nylon
Body: Dark-brown fur dubbing marked with almost black indelible felt-tipped pen, and ribbed with medium oval tinsel
Thorax: Blackish-brown dubbing
Wing cases: Slate-gray duck quill sections tied at sides
Legs: Mottled pheasant hackles dyed dark brown
Antennae: Lemon woodduck fibers
Head: Dark-brown nylon

15. Little Olive Sedge (*Rhyacophila basalis*)

This is one of the most important fly hatches on eastern rivers. Since pesticides and floods have virtually decimated the classic mayfly species in recent years—eliminating entirely the once-famous Green Drake hatches of late spring—these Little Olive Sedges have become virtually the most important single hatch on the Brodheads.

Like the other *Rhyacophila* larvae, this species does not build a sheltering case and forages openly on the river bottom for its food. Its pupal behavior parallels that of the Western Olive Sedge described earlier, except that its pupal color has less intense chroma. Migration to the surface is surprisingly rapid, considering the relatively tiny size of the pupae, and rises to an emerging sedge can be savage.

The fully grown pupa measures about seven-sixteenths inch and its hatching begins early in May. The most extensive hatches last for almost forty-five days, but there are occasional flurries of these sedges all summer. Anglers who live along the Brodheads report the odd *Rhyacophila* flight as late as October.

There are other eastern species that are similar in size, color, and configuration in their pupal stages. The *Rhyacophila fenestra* is a significant fly hatch on our north-central rivers, and the swift mountain rivers of the Allegheny tier counties of Pennsylvania have important hatches of the slightly larger *Rhyacophila lobifera*—a hatch mentioned prominently in the writings of Charles Wetzel and the late John Alden Knight.

Tergites: Pale olive gray, ⅜ inch
Sternites: Pale olive with a bright-green core, ⅜ inch
Thorax: Dark brown, ⅛ inch
Legs: Mottled brownish, ⅝ inch
Antennae: Pale mottled brown, ¾ inch
Head: Dark brown, 1/16 inch

Hook: Sizes 12-14 Mustad 3906 sproat
Nylon: Dark-brown 6/0 nylon
Body: Pale-olive cellulite or rayon floss picked apart and dubbed over a medium-olive core
Thorax: Dark-brown dubbing
Wing cases: Medium-gray duck quill sections tied at sides
Legs: Medium mottled partridge hackle
Antennae: Lemon woodduck fibers
Head: Dark-brown nylon

Both men jealously guarded the dressings of their imitations, flies that used bodies of two types of materials. Although their choice of materials was different, the basic principles were identical. Neither man ever revealed his secret, although Richard Alden Knight hinted at his father's experimental solutions in a conversation with me a few months before his own tragically premature death. The accompanying pattern, modeled on the Partridge and Olive of the Scottish border rivers, embodies just such a compound-body theory as the secret of its deadly qualities.

Wetzel described the egg-laying habits of the species *Rhyacophila lobifera* in both of his books on fly hatches. Its behavior is practically identical to the Brodheads hatch. His observations are of some interest here since their habit of venturing beneath the surface to lay their ova in the river led Wetzel to conclude that perhaps such subaquatic egg-laying habits of the *Trichoptera* might be the ecological basis of wet-fly tactics, along with drowned adult flies and those species which reach a proto-winged state just before hatching. It is a conjecture of penetrating logic.

Rhyacophila basalis has produced so many exciting days on eastern rivers that my mind is rich with memories of these green-bodied little sedges. They are both a fine dry-fly species and a pupal form that can generate some exceptional nymphing during a hatch. Sometimes the trout work eagerly to the fluttering adults, and at other times they ignore the freshly hatched sedges to feed exclusively on the hatching pupae. The reason is never quite clear.

Perhaps my most memorable afternoon with these little olive pupae occurred some years ago on the Brodheads. Colin Pittendrigh called me late one Tuesday night. *What about some fishing on the Brodheads tomorrow?*

Fine, I agreed. *It should be good.*

What's hatching now?

Well, I thought back across the prior ten days, *the Hendricksons and Gordon Quills should be about finished—and we're just about due for those little olive caddis flies.*

Sounds good, he said.

Pittendrigh was the Dean of the Graduate School at Princeton in those days when I was completing five years of writing and research for my doctorate. We agreed to meet at breakfast and drove north into the forested ridges of western New Jersey, toward the Delaware Water Gap and the little valley of the Brodheads that lies in the mountains beyond. The shadbush was blooming, but the morning was overcast with a light, misting rain. We reached the Henryville water and drove down along the river to the Twin pools. There was no sign of rising trout anywhere in either run.

Still think the caddis will work? Colin asked.

They're overdue.

He laughed and strung his little Winston. *It's a good time to test your powers of prediction.*

It's only a guess, I insisted.

What are you planning to fish? he continued.

The river flowed moody and slightly discolored in the rain. *Maybe a little green-bodied wet fly,* I said.

Okay, he said. *I'll fish something different.*

Good luck! I shook my head.

Pittendrigh insisted that I fish down the fast-water run at the head of Upper Twin pool while he watched. The river felt cold against my waders and I was sorry that I had forgotten my Norwegian mesh underwear. The fast-water chutes and eddies deep along the rocks at the top flow swiftly along a chest-deep backwater and slide past a pyramid-shaped rock. The spine of the pool flows forty yards below this stone, its smooth current sliding past two smaller boulders. It then spreads out into a rocky tail-shallows famous for its selective fish.

The river looked dead, but it felt like the trout might be working unseen along the bottom. Such premonitions are impossible to explain, but most experienced fishermen have them.

The first cast dropped my pupal imitation across the main current tongue behind the first boulder. The fly-swing had scarcely started when there was a sudden pull and a sixteen-inch brown showered water high in the shallows.

That's some beginning! Colin laughed.

It was one of those mornings. Every few casts another trout intercepted the deep-swinging little pupa and hooked itself in its eagerness. Although we released them all, several fish had their throats and gill-structures crammed with tiny green-bodied naturals. It suggested that a major *Rhyacophila* hatch was coming soon and the fish were seeing a lot of the pre-hatch pupal activity. Sixteen browns between ten inches and about two pounds were hooked, landed, and slipped back into the river.

Okay, Colin surrendered wryly, *I'm sold!*

Dean Pittendrigh, I began with mock gravity, *these premature results are hardly a full test of my theory!*

Colin waded unceremoniously into the river. *How about a few of those little green-bodied flies?* He began fishing through my tackle vest like a jovial Scottish burglar. *It's still not to late to call another faculty meeting on doctoral candidates!*

You mean you'd actually revoke my degree? I laughed.

Campus politics! he said puckishly.

Fishing Larval Imitations of the Caddisflies

IT WAS haying time in the Tomichi bottoms above Gunnison. There were pintails and cinnamon teal in the shallows, and a hawk was stalking a ground squirrel where a herd of whiteface cattle was grazing. The mowing crews had finished cutting several fields along the river, and the high ground was stacked with hay bales.

It was already late August. Deer hunters were thinking about the coming season, carrying binoculars along on their trips into high country and oiling their rifles absently in the evenings. The rivers were low and clear, their intricate channels tracing a shallow lacework of currents across the valley floor. The nights were getting colder now, and there was frost on the hay-fields in the mornings. The willows and cottonwoods that lined the river stirred and moved restlessly in the rising wind. The cold nights would begin to change their color soon.

The gravel road to Tincup climbed slowly through the rail-fence pastures and weathered ranch buildings into the lodgepole foothills at the bottom of the pass. The road wound higher into the Engelmann spruce and pine, and the pastoral-meadow character of the creek gradually changed to a plunging mountain stream among its bedrock and boulders. Tailings from long-abandoned mines scarred the timberline, and the narrow road wound through fifty-odd switchbacks before we reached the barren summit of the pass.

Beautiful, I thought. *It's beautiful up here.*

The pass lies above twelve thousand feet, its half-melted snow fields lying in the sheltered places. The wind sighed through the twisted pines below the road.

The high peaks of the Collegiate Range rose toward the east, the summit of Mount Princeton clearly visible, and ahead lay the sprawling meadows of the Taylor basin. The high mountains of the wilderness behind Aspen were our horizon toward the north, and clinging to the barren shoulder of the pass were the skeletal remains of the houses and mine-tipples and stores that had once been the thriving silver camp of Tincup.

The road wound slowly down the sagebrush and piñon foothills into the Taylor basin, and we rented one of the cabins on the low moraine above the reservoir. There was a family from Pueblo in the other cabin.

There were brook-trout beaver ponds and winding meadow headwaters in those years, with an August run of brown trout into the tributaries feeding the Taylor Reservoir. We took a fair number of fish with the standard Colorado patterns that first evening, but when we returned to our cabin, we

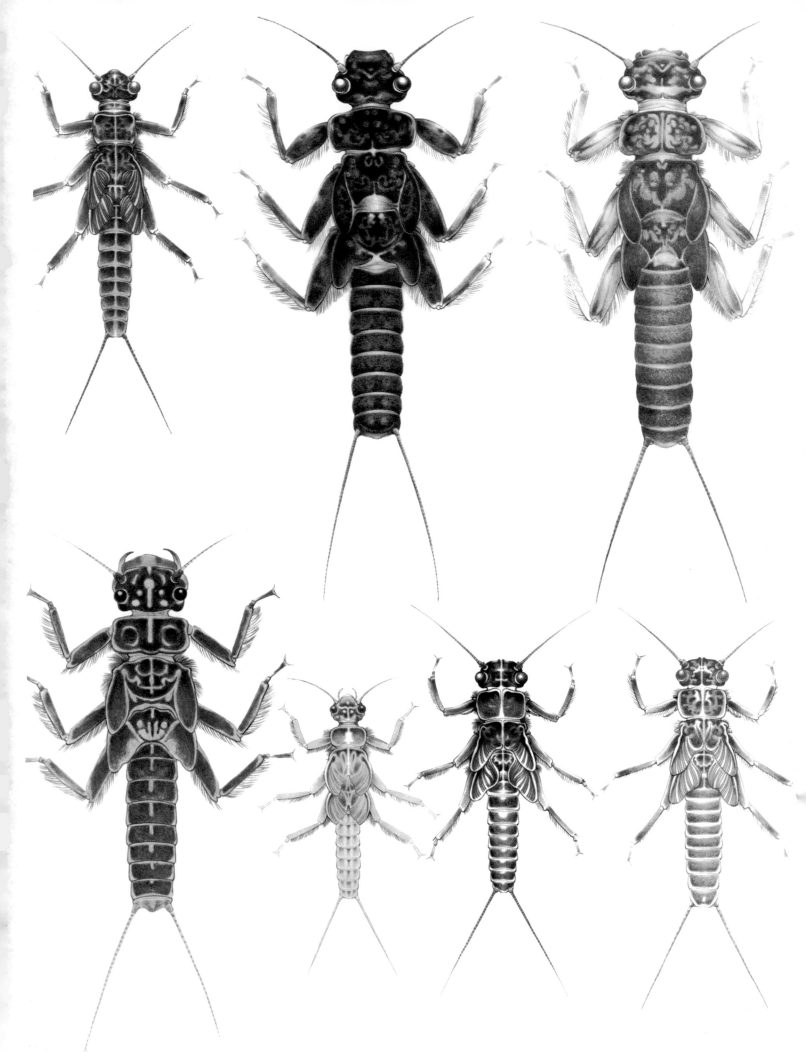

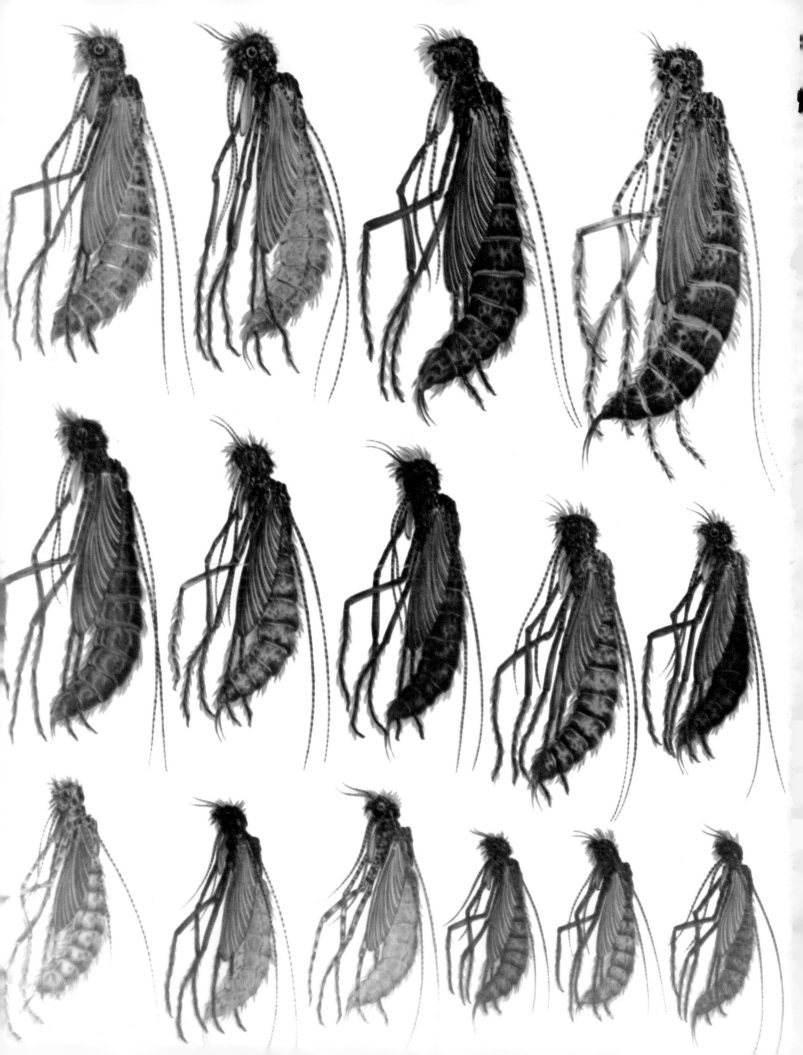

found the Pueblo fisherman dressing an impressive creelful of heavy trout.

That's some catch! I said admiringly.

Yes, said the fisherman casually. *Took them from Texas Creek about a half-mile above the lake.*

Fall spawners? Frank Klune asked.

Probably, said the fisherman. *They're fatter than the stream fish at this altitude—and look at the pink meat.*

Get them on bait? I asked.

The man stopped halfway through gutting the last fish. *Bait?* He shook his head. *Bait?*

You mean you took these trout with flies?

Sure. He finished dressing the fish and cleaned the knife.

Klune and I exchanged glances.

What kind of flies did you use? he asked. *We fished everything in the book and we didn't move anything much.*

My own pattern.

Something unusual? Klune pressed.

Yes, he explained. *It imitates a green worm I've found in the trout around here—don't know what they are.*

The fisherman sliced open a trout stomach and squeezed a half-dozen bright-green *Rhyacophila* larvae into the wooden pump trough.

They're caddis worms, I said.

Whatever they are, he laughed, *the fish like them.*

We'll tie some too, I said. *Thanks!*

That night I dressed a dozen bright-green larval imitations, weighting them with fuse-wire, and we took fish after fish with them the next few days. It was more than twenty-five years ago, in those euphoric summers that followed the war, and it was the first time I fully realized the need for effective imitations of the Trichoptera in their larval stages.

Caddis-fly larvae are separated into two distinct groups. The best known are the case-builders, which shape their protective shelters of tiny pebbles, fragments of leaves and shells, and various plant materials. These case-making larvae attach themselves to the stones, bedrock ledges, deadfalls, and weeds. Some species clamber about on the bottom in search of forage, but the case-sheltered species are seldom found moving freely in the water at depths that can be imitated with flies. In recent years some tiers have begun to use actual caddis cases, with their larvae removed, slipping them on crewel-wool foundations and fixing them with Pliobond. The heads and legs are then imitated, giving a perfect likeness of the various cased caddis-flies that will produce some fish. Less well known than the case-builders, which are readily visible in the water, are the Trichoptera larvae that live free of protective cases along the bottom. It is these so-called campodeiform caddis worms that are important to the fly-fisher, since their freewheeling behavior along the bottom can be simulated easily with fly-fishing tactics.

However, before discussing the campodeiform caddis larvae and their imitations, we should perhaps explore the spectrum of the case-building species for American anglers. There are a number of primary ecotypes

Top, left to right: *Phryganea coloradense, Limnephilus americanus, Neuronia lapponica, Stenophylax scabripennis*
Middle, left to right: *Macronema aspila, Ganonema americana, Brachycentrus fuliginosus, Helicopsyche borealis, Psilotreta frontalis*
Bottom, left to right: *Hydropsyche alternans, Rhyacophila grandis, Rhyacophila basalis, Glossosoma califica, Goera americana, Cheumatopsyche gracilus*

that a knowledgeable fisherman can readily recognize from his days astream. His ability to identify such species can provide him with important tactical insights for his fishing.

Arctoecia caddis-flies hatch from the so-called leafcase caddis worms, and are common in cold-temperature ecosystems on both eastern and western waters. Their cases measure about one inch to approximately an inch and a half. Such shelters are triangular in cross section, and are constructed of vegetable matter and tiny pieces of leaves all cemented together with silken secretions. The genus is widely distributed and many of its adults emerge in early summer.

The larvae of the *Brachycentrus* flies are most common in the cold headwaters of our trout streams, and in those larger rivers that have not been excessively warmed by lumbering and agriculture in their watersheds. Their cases are formed of minute fragments of wood placed in a square cross section, tapering from its upstream opening to a smaller dimension at its posterior. Such cases measure from one-half to three-fourths inch in length. While these larvae are young, they are solitary feeders living in the shallows. Later they move toward the principal current tongues, encrusting the bottom stones with gregarious colonies of their precisely tapered cases. Most adults of the *Brachycentrus* emerge in May, June, and July.

Chilostigma flies build heterogeneous case-shelters of sand, tiny pebbles, and some plant fibers. The shelter is roughly cylindrical in cross section, with a gently cornucopia-shaped length. *Chilostigma* is also a cold-water species that gathers in large colonies on the deadfalls and stones, and its adults hatch all summer.

The relatively small *Goera* caddis is quite common. Its larvae cleverly attach themselves to the bottom stones, using larger pebbles as ballast enclosing their sand-grain cases of smaller materials. It is often found in biosystems favoring caddis larvae of the *Psilotreta* and *Glossosoma* genera, where they fasten themselves to the rocks in the swiftest riffles during the pupal stages. The larva closes both ends of its case with a tiny pebble. Most adults emerge during late spring and early summer, and their larval shelters are quite common on the rocks throughout the year.

Glossosoma larvae build their cases of minute pebbles and tiny grains of sand securely cemented together. The larval forms move them freely in search of food. However, in the pupal stages the larvae fasten their cases firmly to the bottom. They are quite common in American trout streams, and literally hundreds of their cases are clustered on the bottom. Hatching is distributed across the entire summer and early fall, and all three stages of development are available to the fish throughout the entire season. Trout eat them regularly, ingesting both cases and worms.

The unique, spiral-shaped *Helicopsyche* caddis-fly cases are snail-like in their configuration. Their cases are so much like tiny snails that our early limnologists actually classified these small sedge larvae with the *Planorbis* or *Trivolvis* genera, believing the *Helicopsyche* genus an unusual fast-water species of these pond snails. Such tiny snails, incidentally, play a considerable winter role in the diet of trout. There are shallow lakes in Colorado where all-season fishing is legal, and I have taken January trout so full of snails that their stomachs bulged and actually rattled when handled in the net. The *Helicopsyche* worms are found in surprisingly fast water, ranging freely in heavy bottom flows in search of food. During their pupation the larval cases are closed with a little silken webbing. The fish literally force the larval and pupal cases from the bottom, not only the *Helicopsyche* cases but those of the other caddis flies. During periods of extensive feeding on these bottom-forms the trout actually rub their noses raw, and their digestive tracts are filled with sand and vegetable matter and tiny stones. Such things are seldom accidental, but are the residues of various Trichoptera cases.

Leptocerus flies build true cornucopia-shaped cases made of fine stream-bottom sand. They are relatively communal species and gather together in large numbers on the bottom. The larvae forage rather freely, clambering among the crevices in the rocks. Their pupal colonies are seated firmly on the bottom, their cases sealed with a fine webbing of silken fibers.

The cases of the *Limnephilus* sedges are constructed of various materials. Some species build their relatively rough cases of sand, tiny pebbles, and minute bits of shell. Others have extremely heterogeneous cases constructed of shredded bark, seeds, tiny stones, toothpick-sized sticks, and pine needles. Most larvae of this genus are quiet-water forms, most commonly found in ponds, but also present in cold, slow-moving currents. There are common *Limnephilus* types in ponds that build extremely rough hedgehoglike cases of tiny stick and plant stems. The popular Strawman Nymph tied by the late Paul Young was an imitation of these larvae. One group builds these coarse little stick cases in its early, shallow-water stages, and later wraps its larvae in vegetable matter like tiny little cigar coverings. *Ganonema* larvae build their cases of actual twig fragments, the cores hollowed out. These larvae forage extensively in the pond weed.

Molanna larvae are found in great abundance in habitat suited to their particular needs. They prefer quiet currents where their flat cases of sand particles are lost in the protective coloration of their bottoms. The cases are slightly hooded to shelter the head of the larvae and conceal it from view. The fine sand-bottomed rivers of our northern states, great trout streams like the Brule and Namekagon in Wisconsin, and the Manistee and Au Sable in Michigan, are exceptional biosystems for *Molanna* larvae.

Neuronia larvae build their cases of leaf fragments wrapped like a tiny cigar into a slender, slightly curving tube. They measure approximately one inch in length, and clamber about in the weeds of ponds and slow-moving streams. The *Phryganea* genus has similar habits, rarely venturing from its aquatic weed beds to forage on the bottom. The adults of both genera are summer-hatching insects.

The caddis-fly genus *Platyphylax* includes the largest American sedges in its number. Its species are most numerous in very cold streams and spring holes, particularly flowages that seldom freeze in winter. Their cases are cylindrical in cross section, tapering slightly toward the rear of the larvae. Species such as *Platyphylax designatus* can measure as much as two inches in length at full larval development. Their cases are a composite of sand, tiny pebbles, minute fragments of shell, little sticks and slivers of wood, and pieces of bark and leaves. Their adults are largely nocturnal in both habits and hatching, and are found in the largest numbers in spring and early summer.

Psilotreta cases are rather elegant. Their larvae are quite numerous in our swift northern rivers and in cold-water habitats as far south as the mountain trout streams of Georgia, Tennessee, and North Carolina. Their cases are little curved tubes, tapering only slightly toward their posterior body segments. They are constructed of minute pebbles and tiny, stream-polished sand particles. During their first months following eclosion from their ova stage, the larvae forage rather openly over the bottom. However, just before their pupal cycle starts in the spring, the *Psilotreta* larvae gather in colonies among the rocks of the bottom. These communal instincts are matched only by the sedge larvae of the *Brachycentrus, Leptocerus, Sericostoma,* and *Chilostigma* flies. Before pupation, each larva seals its case with a tiny flat pebble at both ends, and then spins a watertight silken cocoon around itself.

The *Sericostoma* larvae are well distributed in the swift mountain streams throughout the United States. The famous Welshman's Button sedges found on British streams are of this fast-water genus. Although they favor swift-water streams, their larval colonies are usually found in eddies and backwaters. During spates, large numbers of these larvae and their cases are washed downstream. Such conditions of high water are optimal for fishing imitations of the cased caddis worms, using the actual cases slipped and cemented on the hook shank. The larval cases are as much as one inch in length. They are shaped of very fine-grained sand held in a delicate and surprisingly strong matrix of silk. Like the other caddis-fly species, these larvae often subsist on the decaying bodies of dead fish and other aquatic organisms. When stripped of their cases, these larval forms are pale yellow to bright green, with V-shaped markings on their heads.

The big, cinnamon-colored nocturnal sedges found on most American rivers are of the *Stenophylax* genus. Their larvae often measure as much as one and one-quarter inches in length, and are distinguished by their stick cases. The tiny sticks and pieces of wood are assembled in a rough cylindrical tube, its sticks and toothpicklike slivers aligned lengthwise to form the case. The related genus *Neophylax* builds similar shelters. Both species like cold-water habitats, particularly small feeder brooks and the headwaters of major watersheds. The adults emerge in the summer.

Triaenodes larvae prefer slow-moving streams and weedy ponds. Their cases are between three-quarters inch and an inch in length, and are built of leaves that are cut and lapped in a spiral-shaped little tube of remarkable precision. This species is unique in the sense that its cased larvae are not fixed to the bottom, or clambering among the water plants and stones. Its larvae swim freely, moving with surprising agility generated by their relatively long fringed legs. The color of these cases varies, depending upon the plant materials available to the larvae. Since they are free-swimming, these larvae are useful prototypes for artificial flies, and it is their presence that can account for the occasional effectiveness of a wet fly so shredded by the fish that only a slender body and a few hackle fibers remain. The adults hatch in late spring and summer.

The so-called campodeiform caddis do not build sheltering cases and are more often available to the trout. Therefore, it is these species which are most easily imitated by the fly-tier, and most important to the fly-fisherman. There are six principal larval forms, numbering literally thousands of species in American waters, and for that reason I have not attempted to match specific insects. Since the naturals never venture freely into open currents, the imitations should be weighted and fished almost dead-drift along the bottom. The imitative larval patterns that I prefer are designed to cover the full range of coloring found among the *Trichoptera* larvae.

The smallest of these caddis flies that do not build cases are the sedges of the *Chimarrha* genus. These are tiny net-spinning caddis with pale-yellowish and orangish larvae which measure approximately one-quarter inch in length. Their nets are usually a parallel series of little test-tube-shaped tunnels, firmly cemented to the stones. These tiny little tubes both shelter and collect food for the slender little larvae. *Chimarrha atterima* is a well-known eastern species, while the orange-bodied *Chimarrha augustipennis* is more widely distributed in American trout waters. There are two delicate little caddis-worm imitations I have used successfully over the years.

LITTLE YELLOW CADDIS LARVA
Hook: Sizes 16-18 Mustad 9672 3X long
Nylon: Dark brown 6/0 nylon
Body: Dirty yellowish fur dubbing
Ribbing: Fine oval tinsel or gold wire
Legs: Dark partridge hackle fibers
Thorax: Dark brown dubbing
Head: Dark brown nylon

LITTLE ORANGE CADDIS LARVA
Hook: Sizes 16-18 Mustad 9672 3X long
Nylon: Dark brown 6/0 nylon
Body: Dirty orange fur dubbing
Ribbing: Fine oval tinsel or gold wire
Legs: Dark partridge hackle fibers
Thorax: Dark brown dubbing
Head: Dark brown nylon

The *Macronema* caddis flies, considered all together, are relatively large insects, measuring between a half and three-quarters of an inch. These campodeiform genera have dark-green dorsal surfaces, and extremely bright-green bellies. Their habitat is largely composed of swift pocket-water and rapid shallows. Species like *Macronema americana* and *Macronema zebatum* are typical.

The most numerous of the American sedges are probably the flies of the *Hydropsyche* larvae. These are a small, net-spinning species that inhabit the riffles by the thousands. They are also found in lakes having sufficient wave action at the shoreline to oxygenate the larvae and carry food into their collecting nets. These nets are funnel-shaped and look like miniature bag-nets suspended in the crevices between the stones. The larvae construct a tiny semicircular enclosure sited at the apex of the net structure, and they feed on minute organisms and plant materials trapped in the net by the currents. When frightened or resting the larvae retreat into the pebble shelter at the rear of the net. Such combination net-shelters measure only about three-quarters inch across their outer margins, but they are so numerous that they are easily located by an observant angler. The sites for these net shelters are typically found in the swift currents between stones, the irregularities in stream-polished ledges, and in the gathering currents at the bottom of a pool. The larvae have a delicate fringe of gills along their belly segments, and their several species measure from one-quarter inch to a full inch in length. The trout are fond of these larvae, and are often observed rooting them out of the crevices in the stones, their sides catching the sunlight and their tails disturbing the current.

There are a number of important *Hydropsyche* species indigenous to American waters. Perhaps the best-known eastern species are flies like *Hydropsyche alternans* and *Hydropsyche slossonae*. Other important American species are western hatches like *Hydropsyche bifilis*, *Hydropsyche occidentalis*, and *Hydropsyche californica*. The full spectrum of species includes a wide range of sizes and colors.

The Dark Green Caddis Larva is a fine imitation of the several *Macronema* larvae. There have been various white caddis-worm patterns around for years, like the pattern that Ray Bergman included in his classic book *Trout*. However, its use of peacock antennae and a black head at both ends of its body has always puzzled me, since the naturals are completely different.

DARK GREEN CADDIS LARVA
Hook: Sizes 10-14 Mustad 9672 3X long
Nylon: Dark brown 6/0 nylon
Body: Bright-green dubbing darkened with dark brown felt pen
Ribbing: Fine oval tinsel or gold wire
Legs: Dark partridge hackle fibers
Thorax: Dark brownish black fur dubbing
Head: Dark brown nylon

WHITE CADDIS LARVA
Hook: Sizes 8-18 Mustad 9672 3X long
Nylon: Dark brown 6/0 nylon
Body: Dirty white dubbing
Ribbing: Fine oval tinsel or silver wire
Legs: Medium brown partridge hackle fibers
Thorax: Dark brown fur dubbing
Head: Dark brown nylon

The Yellow Caddis Larva is useful in the smaller sizes. The Gray Caddis Larva is an extremely versatile pattern in all sizes, and both are fine imitations of the *Hydropsyche* flies.

YELLOW CADDIS LARVA
Hook: Sizes 8-16 Mustad 9672 3X long
Nylon: Dark brown 6/0 nylon
Body: Dirty yellowish dubbing
Ribbing: Fine oval tinsel or gold wire
Legs: Medium brown partridge hackle fibers
Thorax: Dark brown fur dubbing
Head: Dark brown nylon

GRAY CADDIS LARVA
Hook: Sizes 8-16 Mustad 9672 3X long
Nylon: Dark brown 6/0 nylon
Body: Dark grayish muskrat fur dubbing
Ribbing: Fine oval tinsel or wire
Legs: Dark partridge hackle fibers
Thorax: Dark brown fur dubbing
Head: Dark brown nylon

The *Polycentropus* larvae are unique net-spinners. These insects spin paraboloidal little tubes of silken mesh, and in turn suspend the tubes in alignment with the current, using hundreds of silken threads to hold them between the rocks in a remarkably intricate tensile-structure of subaquatic cobwebs. These systems both collect food and shelter the larvae. *Polycentropus radiatus* and *Polycentropus halidus* are perhaps the most common American species.

Since their larvae neither build nets nor construct sheltering cases of various materials, but forage openly over the bottom rubble in search of their food, the *Rhyacophila* flies are probably the most important subaquatic sedges to both the fish and the fisherman. These little worms are extremely abundant. Their spectrum of color varies from pale olive through a rich olive to an intense green rich with chroma. The genus is widely distributed. *Rhycophila lobifera* and *Rhyacophila basalis* are important species on eastern rivers, and these species are found with *Rhyacophila grandis* on some watersheds in Michigan and Wisconsin. The genus is represented by many western species. Perhaps the best-known species are *Rhyacophila pacifica, Rhyacophila bifila, Rhyacophila wyaynata,* and *Rhyacophila coloradensis.*

The Dark Gray Caddis Larva is a good general pattern as well as an imitation of the *Polycentropus* larvae. The Pale Olive Caddis Larva is also a general larval imitation, and its importance is also related to the *Rhyacophila* species.

DARK GRAY CADDIS LARVA
Hook: Sizes 8-18 Mustad 9672 3X long
Nylon: Black 6/0 nylon
Body: Dark hare's mask dubbing
Ribbing: Fine oval tinsel
Legs: Dark mottled partridge hackle
Thorax: Dark hare's mask dubbing
Head: Black nylon

PALE OLIVE CADDIS LARVA
Hook: Sizes 12-18 Mustad 9672 3X long
Nylon: Dark brown 6/0 nylon
Body: Pale olive dubbing
Ribbing: Fine oval tinsel or wire
Legs: Light partridge hackle fibers
Thorax: Dark brown dubbing
Head: Dark brown nylon

The Olive Caddis Larva is particularly good for imitating the *Rhyacophila* larvae on Western rivers like the Roaring Fork in Colorado. The Green Caddis Larva is my current dressing for the bright green little worms that the Pueblo fly-fisherman showed me in the pump trough that long-ago summer in Colorado. Both have served me well.

OLIVE CADDIS LARVA
Hook: Sizes 12-18 Mustad 9672 3X long
Nylon: Black 6/0 nylon
Body: Rich olive dubbing
Ribbing: Fine oval tinsel or wire
Legs: Dark partridge hackle fibers
Thorax: Dark brownish black dubbing
Head: Black nylon

GREEN CADDIS LARVA
Hook: Sizes 12-18 Mustad 9672 3X long
Nylon: Black 6/0 nylon
Body: Bright-green fur dubbing
Ribbing: Fine oval tinsel or wire
Legs: Dark partridge hackle fibers
Thorax: Black fur dubbing
Head: Black nylon

Some Notes on Fishing the Microcaddis

I$_T$ IS a unique little river winding through buffalo-grass meadows and dense stands of lodgepole pine. Steam rises high in the cold September mornings; its ghostly sulphur-smelling fog drifts soundlessly across the river bottoms. Skeletal trees rise like tombstones from the mist of smoking geysers and hot springs. The river riffles and eddies in its lava ledges, flowing smooth and swimming-pool green into mile-long reaches of pale gravel shallows rich with weeds.

Tumbling chutes of white-hot water spill across multi-colored outcroppings of lava, searing the cold river in clouds of hissing steam. The fish porpoise softly to hatches of tiny flies, rising only inches away from scalding currents that could cook them in seconds. Hot springs bubble in the shallows, and there is even a miniature geyser in one riffle, its tiny volcano pulsing steam with the *putt-putt* rhythm of one-lung engine.

The river is the storied Firehole, which flows west from the geyser basins of the Yellowstone. It is unique among the trout streams of the world. Its smooth, weed-trailing currents are like the famed chalkstreams of Hampshire, except that the Firehole is warmed by thousands of hot springs and the geyser at Old Faithful.

Since its praises were written at considerable length almost forty years ago in *Trout*, Bergman has been its patron saint, and his book emphasized its superb dry-fly sport with tiny patterns. It is also a superb nymph-fishing river, both for its mayflies and Plecoptera hatches, and for its pupa fishing to midges and caddis flies. Its selective trout in the Nez Percé meadows were the masters who first taught me about the microcaddis flies.

These are tiny Trichoptera with pupal forms measuring between an eighth and a quarter inch in length. The subfamilies Philopotamidae and Hydroptilidae are tiny net-spinning and case-building caddis flies distributed throughout the trout rivers of North America. There are times when a tiny pupal imitation of these microcaddis is the key to a heavy rise of dimpling trout that refuse every midge-sized dry fly in the box.

There was an evening ten years ago on the Firehole with John Young and Milt Resnick when its trout checkmated us completely. The fish rolled and porpoised and sipped for three hours in the smooth currents, while we failed to fool a single trout.

It was a frustrating night. Rises disturbed the twilight stillness of the river, covering its currents everywhere. We cast to fish after fish, using everything from jassids to midge pupae and ants. The trout humiliated us, rejecting everything fished above and below the surface on the most delicate tippets. There were a considerable number of diminutive, mothlike

Trichoptera coming off in the darkness, but the trout refused dry-fly imitations of them too.

What're they doing? yelled John.

Another good fish refused my tiny Adams again. *God knows,* I shouted back in the darkness. *I sure as hell don't.*

It was another September on the Firehole that the pieces of the puzzle fell into place. History repeated itself with a huge rise of fish dimpling the smooth currents below Fairy Creek, and in my fly book were a half-dozen delicate little wet flies dressed for eastern fishing on eighteen hooks with grouse hackles and olive bodies.

The difficult fish became surprisingly easy with these tiny wets fished on a cross-stream swing of the fly. Dozens and dozens of selective trout were possible in a single evening on the Firehole, yet the fish refused anything other than the little partridge patterns. Difficult browns became incredibly gullible, and the usually difficult Firehole surrendered a cornucopia of fish to four pounds. The river has been a favorite of mine for more than twenty years, and it has been restricted to fly-fishing all that time. Through twenty-odd years of fishing, I had not killed one of its fish, including a six-pound brown caught in Biscuit Basin a dozen years ago.

But I killed one free-rising trout when I realized that the fish were selective to the tiny partridge flies. *There has to be a reason,* I thought. *Got to check his stomach and find out why they're taking them!*

The secret was tiny caddis pupae with olive-colored bodies, hatching Trichoptera so small they looked almost like little brown ants. The fish had taken several hundred of these microcaddis. Several dozen were transferred to my field specimen bottle.

I've got to find out about these, I vowed.

My subsequent research proved intriguing, since it opened a whole line of thought about selective fish that had previously been unknown to my circle of friends. The subfamily Philopotamidae included several tiny, net-spinning genera even smaller than the size eighteen and twenty *Chimarrha* caddis described in the preceding chapter. Caddis larvae of genera like *Oligophleboides* and *Wormaldia* and *Dolophiloides* are net-spinners that secure parallel little tubes of silken mesh to the stones, like a colony of tiny fabric quonset huts.

The larval cases of the subfamily Hydroptilidae are flat little parchment-like shelters, shaped like silken coins attached firmly to the rocks. The pupal stages of these subfamilies are passed in their flat little cases.

The pupae of the Philopotamidae simply seal their silken tubes. During their time of pupal development, the Hydroptilidae seal the tiny openings in the upstream sides of their adhesive, potato-shaped larval cases to pupate without fear of their enemies. Both subfamilies are extensively found in both swift and slow-flowing streams, and the flies of the *Chimarrha* genus are their largest species.

Since that breakthrough on the Firehole, I have continued to experiment with tiny, soft-hackled pupal imitations. Their prototypes lie in the tradition of British wet-fly experts like Theakston and Blacker and Pritt, Scottish fishermen like Stewart and Webster, and Americans like Leisenring.

There are literally hundreds of microcaddis ecotypes in our American rivers, and systematic imitation of them, like our work in the larger aquatic insects, is virtually impossible. Therefore ten prototypical species are included here, with imitations that suggest a wide range of microcaddis flies. The Hydroptilidae include genera like *Oxytheira* and *Agraylea* and *Hydroptila*. The subfamily Philopotamidae includes the genera *Oligophleboides* and *Wormaldia* and *Dolophiloides*, discussed in the following hatches:

1.   Olive Microcaddis Pupa (*Oligophleboides minuta*)

Oligophleboides minuta

This species is typical of several microcaddis measuring between one quarter and one eighth inch in length. The tiny dark Partridge and Olive originally attributed to the Yorkshire rivers of Pritt is a fine imitation.

Body: Medium olive
Wing cases: Dark slate-gray
Thorax: Dark chocolate brown
Legs: Dark mottled brown
Antennae: Pale amber mottled at the joints
Head: Dark chocolate brown

Hook: Sizes 18-22 Mustad 6948A
Nylon: Dark brown 6/0 nylon
Body: Medium olive rayon floss
Wing cases: None
Legs: Dark partridge hackle fibers
Antennae: None
Head: Dark brown nylon

2.   Pale Microcaddis Pupa (*Wormaldia gabriella*)

The Snipe and Yellow dressed on the Brodheads by Leisenring is an excellent imitation of such tiny pupae.

Body: Dirty yellowish gray
Wing cases: Pale grayish
Thorax: Medium brown
Legs: Light gray
Antennae: Grayish mottled at the joints
Head: Dark brown

Hook: Sizes 18-22 Mustad 7948A
Nylon: Medium brown 6/0 nylon
Body: Dirty yellowish gray dubbing
Wing cases: None
Legs: Light mottled gray snipe hackle fibers
Antennae: None
Head: Medium brown nylon

3.   Green Microcaddis Pupa (*Dolophiloides pacifica*)

The traditional Yorkshire pattern called the Grouse and Green is used here as an imitation:

Body: Bright green
Wing cases: Dark slate-grayish
Thorax: Dark blackish brown
Legs: Dark mottled brown
Antennae: Pale amber mottled at the joints
Head: Dark blackish olive

Hook: Sizes 18-22 Mustad 7948A
Nylon: Dark olive 6/0 nylon
Body: Bright green
Wing cases: None
Legs: Dark mottled grouse hackle fibers
Antennae: None
Head: Dark olive nylon

4.   Black Microcaddis Pupa (*Dolophiloides nigrita*)

The traditional border pattern called the Jackdaw and Brown was a soft-hackled fly recommended by Stewart.

Body: Dark brownish black
Wing cases: Dark leadwing brown
Thorax: Blackish
Legs: Dark iron-blue hackle fibers
Antennae: Dark mottled brown
Head: Blackish

Hook: Sizes 18-22 Mustad 7948A
Nylon: Black 6/0 nylon
Body: Dark blackish brown dubbing
Wing cases: None
Legs: Dark jackdaw hackle fibers
Antennae: None
Head: Black nylon

5. Golden Microcaddis Pupa (*Wormaldia occidentalis*)

Theakston liked the delicate Plover and Yellow.

Body: Golden yellowish
Wing cases: Light brownish gray
Thorax: Medium brown
Legs: Light mottled brown
Antennae: Pale mottled amber
Head: Medium brown

Hook: Sizes 18-22 Mustad 7948A
Nylon: Medium brown 6/0 nylon
Body: Golden yellow rayon floss
Wing cases: None
Legs: Golden mottled plover hackle
fibers
Antennae: None
Head: Medium brown nylon

6. Pale Olive Microcaddis Pupa (*Agraylea bifila*)

The Light Partridge and Olive found in the Yorkshire flybooks of Pritt is dressed according to the accompanying instructions.

Body: Pale olive gray
Wing cases: Pale brownish gray
Thorax: Dark olive brown
Legs: Light mottled brownish
Antennae: Pale mottled amber
Head: Dark olive

Hook: Sizes 18-22 Mustad 7948A
Nylon: Medium brown 6/0 nylon
Body: Pale olive rayon floss
Wing cases: None
Legs: Light partridge hackle fibers
Antennae: None
Head: Medium brown nylon

7. Light Brown Microcaddis Pupa (*Agraylea diminuta*)

The Light Partridge and Brown was preferred by Blacker.

Body: Light brown
Wing cases: Light grayish brown
Thorax: Medium brown
Legs: Light mottled brown
Antennae: Pale mottled amber
Head: Medium brown

Hook: Sizes 18-22 Mustad 7948A
Nylon: Medium brown 6/0 nylon
Body: Light brown dubbing
Wing cases: None
Legs: Light mottled brown partridge
fibers
Antennae: None
Head: Medium brown nylon

Hydroptila rono

8. Brown Microcaddis Pupa (*Hydroptila rono*)

The Partridge and Brown as dressed by Pritt is indicated here.

Body: Dark brown
Wing cases: Dark brownish gray
Thorax: Dark brownish
Legs: Dark mottled brown
Antennae: Pale mottled brown
Head: Dark brown

Hook: Sizes 16-22 Mustad 7948A
Nylon: Dark brown 6/0 nylon
Body: Dark brown dubbing
Wing cases: None
Legs: Dark mottled partridge fibers
Antennae: None
Head: Dark brown nylon

9. Orange Microcaddis Pupa (*Hydroptila hamata*)

The Theakston pattern called the Partridge and Orange is an excellent imitation of these minutae.

Body: Dirty orange
Wing cases: Dark brownish gray
Thorax: Dark brown
Legs: Dark mottled brown
Antennae: Pale amber mottled at the joints
Head: Dark brown

Hook: Sizes 18-22 Mustad 7948A
Nylon: Dark brown 6/0 nylon
Body: Dirty orange rayon floss
Wing cases: None
Legs: Light mottled partridge hackle fibers
Antennae: None
Head: Dark brown nylon

10. Dun Microcaddis Pupa (*Hydroptila americana*)

The Dark Snipe and Hare's Ear is recommended in the writings of Blacker.

Body: Dark brownish gray
Wing cases: Dark slate-colored brown
Thorax: Dark brownish gray
Legs: Dark mottled brownish gray
Antennae: Dark mottled brown
Head: Dark brownish

Hook: Sizes 18-22 Mustad 7948A
Nylon: Dark brown 6/0 nylon
Body: Dark brownish gray hare's mask dubbing
Wing cases: None
Legs: Dark mottled snipe hackle fibers
Antennae: None
Head: Dark brown nylon

Oxytheira coloradensis

11. Dark Microcaddis Pupa (*Oxytheira coloradensis*)

The Woodcock and Hare's Ear pattern is described in Blacker and Theakston.

Body: Dark brownish gray
Wing cases: Dark slate-colored brown
Thorax: Dark brownish gray
Legs: Dark mottled brownish
Antennae: Dark mottled brown
Head: Dark brown

Hook: Sizes 18-22 Mustad 7948A
Nylon: Dark brown 6/0 nylon
Body: Dark brownish gray hare's mask dubbing
Wing cases: None
Legs: Brown mottled woodcock hackle fibers
Antennae: None
Head: Dark brown nylon

12. Red Microcaddis Pupa (*Oxytheira needhami*)

The Stewart soft-hackled pattern for this pupa is called the Landrail and Brown.

Body: Rusty brownish
Wing cases: Slate-grayish brown
Thorax: Rusty brownish
Legs: Dark brownish gray
Antennae: Mottled brown
Head: Dark brown

Hook: Sizes 18-22 Mustad 7948A
Nylon: Dark brown 6/0 nylon
Body: Dark rusty brown dubbing
Wing cases: None
Legs: Dark brownish gray landrail hackle fibers
Antennae: None
Head: Dark brown nylon

Larvae and Pupae of the Larger Two-Winged Diptera

T HE RIVER has its birthplace in the high timberline ridges above Fairplay, and the vast buffalo grass bottoms of the South Park. Its feeders are born in the high meadows above Buffalo Creek and Kenosha Pass, the Hoosier Pass summits north of Fairplay, and the barren shoulder between Buffalo Mountain and the Mosquito Range.

South Park itself is a sprawling wilderness of grass, controlled only by a few vast ranches, and slightly scarred by the irrigation ditches and the eroding trestles and roadbed of the historic Colorado Midland Railroad. There are also the ugly placer and dredge tailings of the gold mining below Fairplay, and the dredge itself is still there, like the rotting skeleton of some mechanical dinosaur.

Yet the scars have healed in the past half-century, until the sprawling hundred miles of grasslands must look much as they did when the first trappers reached the summits of Wilkerson Pass and looked west toward the high peaks of the Continental Divide.

The watercress bogs and lime-rich bottoms in the sprawling valley floor combine with the hot springs found at various sites to produce the rich little tributaries. The cities lying east of the foothills, with the parched high plains of Colorado reaching out toward the horizon, have tapped their water resources with a series of reservoirs. The impoundments at Antero and Eleven Mile Canyon collect the spring runoff from Buffalo Mountain and the Mosquito Range. Tarryall Creek begins on the shoulders of Bald Mountain and the Hoosier Pass, its flow dammed at Bison Peak, and it joins the river before it enters the Cheeseman Dam above Deckers. It flows smoothly through the Deckers Canyon, and winds out into the foothills toward a rendezvous with Denver and its sprawling suburbs.

The river is the challenging South Platte in Colorado. Its flow varies radically with the exaggerated storage and release of water in these reservoirs. Such ebbing and flowing have damaged the fly hatches, and sometimes make the river almost unfishable. But it has its benefits too. The storage of snow melt in the reservoirs, and their effect as man-made settling basins, combine to produce clear, relatively low water in the South Platte below Antero and Tarryall, when other rivers are chocolate-colored with the spring thaw. These clear, early-spring currents have a run of strong steelhead-like rainbows from Cheeseman and Eleven Mile.

Both the reservoirs and the serpentine, slow-flowing character of the river support huge larval and pupal populations of the two-winged Diptera flies. The marl bogs and geothermal springs contribute the fertile alkalinity of the river and its extremely rich population of aquatic insects. Many of its hatches are composed of tiny flies, and the trout are hard-fished and difficult. These selective trout are the challenge that shaped expert Colorado fly-makers and fishermen like James Poor and Charles Fothergill, who are famous for minute flies and skilled nymph tactics.

Bait dealers in the region sell something other than the usual worms and nightcrawlers and minnows. Their suppliers also muck through bogs and backwaters, sluicing the silt and bottom trash with a screen to extract the crane fly larvae. These fat, dirty-olive larvae are greatly prized by both fishermen and fish.

Fish-wigglers, one old-timer always called them. *Forget them flies and use fish-wigglers—you'll see!*

Such skilled bait-fishermen are common on the South Platte, fishing the larvae with tiny hooks and dead-drift presentation on delicate weighted nylon. These larval forms and pupae are not capable of agile swimming movements, and should be presented either dead-drift or with a patient hand-twist retrieve on the bottom.

Since the tiny midge larvae and pupae form such an important group of insect forms in themselves, this chapter on the immature stages of the two-winged Diptera is devoted to other genera and species of the order, while the midges and other minute forms are discussed in a chapter focused entirely on the smutting rise.

The two-winged flies of the Diptera order are precisely that, insect sub-orders and families and genera that have only two wings. They have a complete metamorphosis consisting of larval, pupal, and adult forms. Unlike the mayflies, caddisflies, and stoneflies, which have two pairs of wings, the Diptera have a pair of atrophied second wings called halteres. There are scalelike calypteres above these knoblike appendages, and some species have a small, lobe-shaped alula at the root of the wings. There are more than ten thousand American species, although very few of these ecotypes are found in a subaquatic environment. The subaquatic forms are those of some importance to the American nymph fisherman.

These aquatic families of interest to the fly-fisher include the crane flies, soldier flies, midges, Dixa flies, dance flies, net-veined midges, March flies black flies, and *Ceratopogon* flies. The Tipulidae encompass the crane flies, the suborder Stratiomyidae includes the soldier-fly larvae, and the snipe flies are among the Rhagionidae.

Comprehensive imitation of such a vast order is clearly impossible, since the fly-tier is confronted with literally thousands and thousands of larval and pupal forms. Therefore, it is useful to sort through this galaxy of species to isolate a few of the most common types, with a coloring, size, and configuration typical of the others.

Perhaps the most common genus of the Tipulidae is the group taxonometrically designated as the *Tipula* crane flies. Most crane flies are only semi-aquatic, living in wet forests and damp moss and decaying deadfalls in marshy places. There are more than three thousand species. This genus also includes a large number of crane flies that are rather widely distributed in American waters. Pupation is passed in the damp soil near the water.

Their larvae vary between one-half inch and two inches in length. Such larvae are abundant in the silty bottoms of quiet-flowing streams and ponds, foraging in the water-saturated, decaying plant materials for their food. These larvae are rather translucent, their coiled respiratory tubes sometimes clearly visible from the outside. Such insects are perfectly suited to imitation with wet, roughly dubbed bodies. The *Tipula* larvae are herbivorous, feeding on diatomaceous algae and decayed vegetable tissues. There are a number of prototypical species.

1.   Orange Crane Fly Larva (*Tipula bicornis*)

This dirty-orangish-brown crane-fly larva is predominantly found in waters from New England to Minnesota, and south to the Carolinas. Fully grown larvae measure five-eighths to seven-eighths inch.

Gills: Dirty brownish, 1/16 inch
Body: Dirty brownish orange, ½ inch
Thorax: Dirty brownish, ⅛ inch
Head: Dark brownish black, 1/16 inch
Antennae: Dirty brownish, 1/16 inch

Hook: Sizes 10-14 Mustad 79580 4X long
Nylon: Dark brown 6/0 nylon
Gills: Short dark brown fibers tied short
Body: Medium brown dubbing roughly spun on orange silk core rib-
Ribbing: Fine oval tinsel
Thorax: Dark brown dubbing spun on working nylon
Antennae: Short dark brown fibers
Head: Dark brown nylon

Tipula bicornis

2.   Whirling Crane Fly Larva (*Tipula furca*)

This species is slightly larger than its sister species *Tipula bicornis*, and is brownish and olivaceous in coloring. It is widely distributed from Maine to Montana, and its maturing larvae range between five-eighths inch and slightly more than one inch.

Gills: Dirty olive brown, 1/16 inch
Body: Dirty olive brown, ⅝ inch
Thorax: Dark olive brown, ¼ inch
Antennae: Dirty olive brown, 1/16 inch
Head: Dark blackish brown, ⅛ inch

Hook: Sizes 6 through 10 Mustad 79580 4X long
Nylon: Dark olive 6/0 nylon
Gills: Dark brownish fibers tied short
Body: Dark brownish dubbing roughly spun on medium olive silk
Ribbing: Fine oval tinsel
Thorax: Dark brownish dubbing on working nylon
Antennae: Short brownish fibers
Head: Dark olive nylon

3.   Summer Crane Fly Larva (*Tipula augustipennis*)

The pale species is found in cold western ponds and streams, and its larvae measure one-half to seven-eighths inch.

Gills: Pale grayish, 1/16 inch
Body: Pale grayish cream, 7/16 inch
Thorax: Pale grayish, ⅝ inch
Antennae: Pale grayish, 1/16 inch
Head: Dark grayish brown, 1/16 inch

Hook: Sizes 12-14 Mustad 79580 4X long
Nylon: Pale grayish brown 6/0 nylon
Gills: Pale grayish dun fibers tied short
Body: Pale grayish red fox dubbing
Ribbing: Fine oval tinsel
Thorax: Slightly darker muskrat dubbing
Antennae: Short pale grayish dun fibers
Head: Pale grayish brown nylon

Tipula furca

Pedicia larva

4.   Western Crane Fly Larva (*Tipula pendulifera*)

This species is quite common in Rocky Mountain waters, and is a grayish larva of three-quarters inch to one inch in length.

Gills: Dark bluish gray, 1/16 inch
Body: Dark bluish gray, 7/8 inch
Thorax: Dark brownish dun, ⅛ inch
Antennae: Dark bluish gray, 1/16 inch
Head: Dark brownish, 1/16 inch

Hook: Sizes 10-12 Mustad 79580 4X long
Nylon: Gray 6/0 nylon
Gills: Dark bluish gray fibers tied short
Body: Dark bluish gray muskrat dubbing
Ribbing: Fine oval tinsel
Thorax: Dark bluish gray
Antennae: Dark bluish gray fibers
Head: Gray nylon

5.   Giant Crane Fly Larva (*Tipula abdominalis*)

This common species is widely distributed in American waters, and is perhaps the largest of the Tipulidae in our trout streams. Its larvae are dull green, averaging one to two inches.

Tipula mono is a similar western species.

Gills: Brownish olive, 3/16 inch
Body: Dull brownish green, 1 to 1¾ inches
Thorax: Dull brownish, ¼ to ⅜ inches
Antennae: Brownish olive, ⅛ inch
Head: Dark brownish olive, ⅛ inch

Hook: Sizes 4 through 8 Mustad 79580 4X long
Nylon: Dark olive 6/0 nylon
Gills: Brownish olive fibers tied short
Body: Dull green dubbing on bright green core
Ribbing: Fine olive tinsel
Thorax: Brownish olive dubbing on brown
Antennae: Brownish olive fibers
Head: Dark olive nylon

6.   White Spring-Hole Crane Fly Larva (*Pedicia albivitta*)

This cold-water crane-fly species is commonly found in spring holes and spring-fed ponds in the northeastern states.

Pedicia dorsolineata is a related species found in our Pacific mountain streams.

Helius larva

Gills: None
Body: Dirty grayish white, 1⅛ inch
Thorax: Dark grayish, ¼ inch
Antennae: Dark bluish gray, 1/16 inch
Head: Dark grayish, ⅛ inch

Hook: Sizes 6 through 10 Mustad 79580 4X long
Nylon: Dark gray 6/0 nylon
Gills: None
Body: Dirty grayish white dubbing
Ribbing: Fine oval tinsel
Thorax: Dirty grayish dubbing
Antennae: Dark grayish fibers
Head: Dark gray nylon

7.   Little Olive Crane Fly Larva (*Helius americanus*)

These small larvae are found in the reeds and weedbeds of trout ponds and quiet streams, and average about one-half to three-quarters inch in length.

Gills: None
Body: Bluish gray, ⅜ inch
Thorax: Dark bluish gray, 1/16 inch
Antennae: Bluish gray, ⅛ inch
Head: Dark bluish gray, 1/16 inch

Hook: Sizes 12-14 Mustad 79580 4X long
Nylon: Dark gray 6/0 nylon
Gills: None
Body: Bluish gray muskrat dubbing
Ribbing: Fine oval tinsel
Thorax: Dark bluish gray dubbing
Antennae: Dark bluish gray fibers
Head: Dark gray nylon

8. Riffle Crane Fly Larva (*Epiphragma bella*)

This medium-sized species is well distributed, and is typically found in the leaf drift and detritus that gathers between the stones in the riffles. Its larva measure three-quarters inch to one inch in length.

Gills: Dark iron-blue, 1/16 inch
Body: Dark brownish gray, ¾ inch
Thorax: Dark brownish gray, ⅛ inch
Antennae: None
Head: Dark blackish brown, 1/16 inch

Hook: Sizes 10-12 Mustad 79580 4X long
Nylon: Dark brown 6/0 nylon
Gills: Dark iron-blue fibers
Body: Dark brownish black hare's mask dubbing
Ribbing: Fine oval tinsel
Thorax: Dark brownish black dubbing
Antennae: None
Head: Dark brown nylon

9. Burrowing Crane Fly Larva (*Limnophila occidentalis*)

These little western larvae are agile and voracious, living in the silt at midday and foraging boldly in the hours just after daylight, and just before dark. They are highly carnivorous, often resorting to their fellow larvae as prey. These larvae are about one-half to three-quarters inch long.

Gills: Dark olive, ⅛ inch
Body: Dark blackish olive, ⅜ inch
Thorax: Dark blackish olive, 3/32 inch
Antennae: None
Head: Dark olive, 1/16 inch

Hook: Sizes 12-14 Mustad 79580 4X long
Nylon: Dark olive 6/0 nylon
Gills: Dark olive grayish fibers
Body: Dark olive rayon floss picked apart and dubbed
Ribbing: Fine oval tinsel
Thorax: Dark olive rayon floss dubbing
Antennae: None
Head: Dark olive nylon

10. Yellow Riffle Crane Fly Larva (*Antocha saxicola*)

This little species thrives in fast water and tumbling riffles, and has a pair of highly developed anal gills to extract oxygen from the current. The larvae live in the crevices between the stones, building little silken seines like the net-spinning caddis. The tracheae are in two caudal lobes, and the western species *Antocha monticola* is a closely related western species.

The Yellow Riffle Crane Flies are imitated with the indicated larval pattern. They average three-eighths to three-quarters inch in length at full development.

Gills: Pale yellowish gray, ⅛-¼ inch
Body: Pale yellowish gray, ⅜-⅝ inch
Thorax: Pale yellowish gray, 1-16-⅛ inch
Antennae: None
Head: Pale yellowish, ⅛-¼ inch

Hook: Sizes 12-16 Mustad 9672 3X long
Nylon: Pale yellow 6/0 nylon
Gills: Two pale yellow duck quill fibers
Body: Pale yellowish gray dubbing
Ribbing: Fine oval tinsel
Thorax: Pale yellowish gray
Antennae: None
Head: Pale yellow nylon

Although some biologists include the Tabanidae larvae, and the larval forms of *Syrphus* flies, among common aquatic foods available to trout, these insect families typically inhabit stagnant or semi-aquatic environments unsuitable for the maintenance of a viable Salmonidae ecosystem. However,

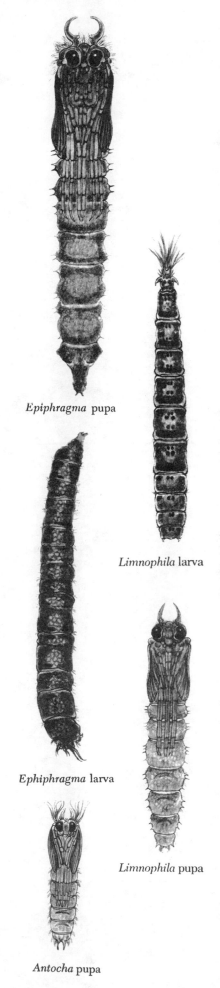

Epiphragma pupa

Limnophila larva

Ephiphragma larva

Limnophila pupa

Antocha pupa

Antocha larva

the solder flies and snipe flies do hatch from waters inhabited by trout, and their larvae are worth imitating.

The soldier flies are members of the Stratiomyidae, and only a few species are truly aquatic. They are not exceptionally abundant, but trout seem to take them readily, and the aquatic forms are easily recognized. These larvae are spindle-shaped, with a fine series of plumelike bristles that protect the breathing spiracles. The larvae are carnivorous, and forage with a surprising agility at times. There are two principal genera, the *Stratiomys* larvae and the *Odontomyia* flies. Pupation occurs in the wet soils near the water, using the larval skin.

Snipe flies frequent faster currents, loving the coarse gravel and bottom stones of trout streams. The larvae creep awkwardly along the riffle bottoms, using their leglike protuberances to move. The head is slender, shaped to the currents, and the posterior culminates in a pair of fringed gills. Snipe flies are classified in the genus *Atherix*, and are important trout foods in some waters during their larval cycles.

11.   Soldier Fly Larva (*Stratiomys discalis*)

These larvae are approximately one inch in length, and like the sister species *Odontomyia cincta*, they are well distributed throughout American trout waters.

Gills: Pale grayish dun, 1/32 inch
Body: Pale yellowish gray, ¾ inch
Thorax: Pale yellowish gray, 3/32 inch
Legs: None
Head: Pale yellowish gray, 1/16 inch

Hook: Sizes 10-14 Mustad 79580 4X long
Nylon: Pale yellowish 6/0 nylon
Gills: Pale grayish dun fibers tied short
Body: Pale yellowish gray dubbing tied very thin along initial 20 percent of body at gills
Ribbing: Fine oval tinsel
Thorax: Pale yellowish gray dubbing
Legs: None
Head: Pale yellow nylon

Stratiomys larva

12.   Snipe Fly Larva (*Atherix laterans*)

These little fast-water larvae are widely distributed in our trout streams, and average about three-eighths inch.

Gills: Dirty grayish, 1/32 inch
Body: Dirty grayish, ¼ inch
Thorax: Dirty grayish, 1/16 inch
Legs: Dirty grayish, 1/32 inch
Head: Dirty grayish, 1/16 inch

Hook: Sizes 14-16 Mustad 9672 3X long
Nylon: Pale gray 6/0 nylon
Gills: Pale grayish fibers
Body: Pale grayish dubbing tapered at both tail gills and head to suggest naturals
Thorax: Pale grayish dubbing
Legs: Pale gray hackle trimmed short and Palmered full length of body, trimming all fibers off back and sides when nymph is complete
Head: Pale gray nylon

Atherix larva

Tiny Two-Winged Diptera and the Smutting Rise

It was a still reach of river above the millrace. Its bottom was rich with chara and *Dichelyma* mosses, streaming and waving lazily in the quiet currents. There was a soft wind from the south, smelling faintly of freshly plowed earth. Dairy cattle were grazing in the meadows above the village, and a timber honey wagon rattled emptily as it passed. The mill was silent, its huge water wheel creaking absently as it touched the river. Smoke rose from the chimneys of the thatched-roof cottages and ducks were nesting under the bridge. The current flowed smooth and tea-colored through its trailing weeds. The ruined castle stood high above the valley floor, where the cobblestone road wound toward the grist mills at Forcheim.

Trout were porpoising softly in the surface film. Their rises dimpled the smooth current above the millrace with a steady feeding rhythm. *I've tried fifteen or twenty patterns*, I explained to the old riverkeeper. *The fish keep rising but they won't take dry flies!*

Jawohl! The old man nodded. *They're like that.*

Can't see anything hatching, I said.

The old man filled his pipe slowly. *There is nothing hatching yet*, he observed softly. *They're rising but they're not feeding on the surface.*

But look at all the rising fish! I pointed.

It's a smutting rise, he smiled.

The old riverkeeper explained that the fish were taking reed smuts, the emerging pupae of the *Simulium* flies. These tiny pupae were migrating from their cocoons in the gently undulating weeds, working toward the surface from the chara and pale-green water moss. Thousands of minute smuts were rising from the bottom, drifting with the current as they struggled to escape their pupal skins, and the fish gorged themselves lazily on the abundance.

The old man gave me a tiny pupal imitation. It was tied with a dark dubbing of hare's mask, brightly ribbed with fine silver tinsel to suggest the gaseous bubbles of the rising pupal sac. It had a few soft leglike fibers.

It's minuscule! I shook my head in disbelief.

The tiny little pupa worked.

Fish that had rejected a boxful of minute dry flies were suddenly transformed into easy prey, and I cast the little pupa upstream to each rising trout. It drifted back on a leader rubbed with mucilin, and when the fish took them softly, the nylon paused and tightened almost imperceptibly as the tiny hook caught and held.

It was an unforgettable lesson. Since that early summer evening years ago, I have remembered that the smutting rise is almost always a problem of tiny larval and pupal imitations fished just in or under the surface film. These insect forms consist of various families of the minute Diptera, and such midge feeding is seldom focused on the adults.

The old riverkeeper had not discovered the secret. *There was an Englishman who regularly came to fish my river before the war,* he explained. *He taught me about smutting.*

Skues? It was a wild guess.

The old man frowned thoughtfully. *Skues.* He tasted the name momentarily. *It was Skues!*

Several years later, I learned that Skues had sometimes fished this little river in Franconia, and that its selective trout had both charmed and challenged the master nymph fisherman of the chalkstreams.

His lessons about the smutting rise preoccupied me over the intervening years, and I have found a number of larval and pupal Diptera that can trigger such feeding behavior. The trout are interested in many other types of tiny insects, and smutting rises are not confined to the pupal migrations of the *Simulium* smuts that gave rise to that terminology. This chapter covers minutae involved in smutting-rise behavior on American waters.

The minute Diptera prototypical of American smutting-rise imitations include the dance flies, tiny net-veined midges, sand gnats, riffle smuts, *Ceratopogon* midges, dark little Dixa flies, Tanypus flies, and the mosquito-like subaquatic stages of the Chironomidae.

1. Black Dance Flies (*Hilara femorata*)

The species *Hilara femorata* is typical of the American dance flies, and the parallel *Hilara occidentalis* is indigenous to our western trout waters. Such minute dance flies are considerably more important in the trout diet, particularly on lakes and slow-moving streams, than fishermen have believed in the past. Their prolific numbers virtually rival the ants, and their distribution is extensive.

BLACK DANCE FLY LARVA

Hook: Sizes 18-24 Orvis Premium 1X long
Nylon: Black 6/0 nylon
Gills: None
Body: Black or dark grayish dubbing tied sparse and thin
Ribbing: Fine silver white
Thorax: Black or dark grayish dubbing tied thin
Legs: None
Head: Black nylon

BLACK DANCE FLY PUPA

Hook: Sizes 18-26 Mustad 94840 1X fine
Nylon: Black 6/0 nylon
Gills: Black or dark iron-blue fibers tied short at hook bend
Body: Sparse black or dark gray dubbing ribbed with fine silver wire
Thorax: Roughly dubbed black or gray fur
Wing cases: Dark gray teal wing quill sections or omit
Legs: Black or iron-blue fibers
Head: Black nylon

The larval forms inhabit the silty roots of elodea and other aquatic weeds, particularly in the quiet shallows of the stream. Our preoccupation with mayflies and caddisflies and the Plecoptera has led us to ignore the importance of these minute larval forms. During periods of emergence, which occur cyclically across the season, the trout follow the evolving pupae from their weed-bed cocoons toward the surface. This final prehatching stage of the *Hilara* pupae lasts as long as several minutes, depending on weather conditions and water temperatures, with the little pupae hanging with their breathing gills in the surface film. Such pupal forms fill the surface currents by the thousands and thousands, and although they are minuscule in size, they are available in such quantities that even large trout can fill their stomachs while expending a minimal amount of calories.

2. Net-Veined Midges (*Blepharocera americana*)

Although their larval forms are clinging types, and are not readily available to the trout, there are still specimens found in most of my early-season stomach autopsies. Since they are an entirely swift-water genus, they are part of our cold-water ecosystems.

The larvae cling firmly to the bottom stones, looking like a roughly shaped row of tiny beads. Most measure between one-quarter and three-eighths inch in length, with the head and thoracic structure forming the first segment, and the other five segments comprising the abdomen. It completely lacks feet, but its ventral median consists of six little suction points. They breathe through the tufted tracheal gills on each body segment.

Blepharocera larva

The pupae are also clinging ecotypes, egg-shaped, with a pair of earlike breathing appendages. Pupation and subsequent hatching into the adult net-veined midges occurs in late spring and early summer. Since both larval and pupal forms are clinging insects attached to the bottom stones, the trout ingest most of them while foraging there, scraping them from their footholds, and these are eagerly taken by the fish. Such hapless insects are carried in the bottom currents, and their imitations should perhaps be weighted with lead wire.

NET-VEINED MIDGE LARVA
Hook: Sizes 16-18 Orvis Premium 1X long
Nylon: Dark brown 6/0 nylon
Body: Dark brownish black hare's mask dubbing tied full
Ribbing: Rich brownish 2/0 silk wound tight to produce strong body segments
Thorax: Dark brownish black hare's mask
Prolegs: None
Head: Dark brown nylon

Simulium larva

NET-VEINED MIDGE PUPA
Hook: Size 16-18 Mustad 7948A
Nylon: Dark brown 6/0 nylon
Body: Dark brownish black hare's mask dubbing wound over flat oval base of dubbing soaked with lacquer and flattened to form fat, ovoid shape
Thorax: None
Gills: Two short dark brown pheasant tail-fiber points about 1/32 inch in length
Head: Dark brown nylon

These little imitations should be weighted and fished dead-drift in the riffles, and in the quiet currents immediately downstream from the fast-water pockets.

3. Riffle Smuts (*Simulium hirtipes*)

These insects include the infamous biting black flies found in our northern latitudes, and the nonbiting *Simulium* gnats as well. The smut larvae are black and dirty-gray, measuring about three-eighths inch at full development. There are often so many of these little larvae that the riffle stones appear literally black with these tiny clinging insects undulating like minute filaments of moss in the flow. The larvae cling to the bottom with tiny suction-cup appendages at their abdominal posteriors, with the mouths free to take the diatomaceous foods collected on their fan-shaped brushes. The

Simulium pupa

larvae maneuver from one suction appendage to the other, duck-walking clumsily on the bottom. When they lose their footing, the larvae remain attached to a delicate silken thread suspended from their lost footholds. These salivary threads are used not only as anchors, but also as a means of traveling downstream from stone to stone in swift water. Respiration is accomplished with retractile blood-gills located between the suction-plate appendages.

The pupal cocoons form brownish, mosslike blankets on the stones. They breathe through delicate tracheal gills that trail downstream in the current, like tiny little filaments projecting from the sheltering pupal membranes. Pupation takes place in a cone-shaped cocoon. It is attached to the weeds or stones with its apex upstream and its wider opening downstream, trailing the delicate gills. Shortly before hatching the pupae generate gases inside their pupal sacs. These gases form a sheltering bubble around the emerging *Simulium* flies, and their pressures both split the pupal skins and buoy them toward the surface. Such gaseous bubbles sparkle in the water, making a bright touch of tinsel important in a pupa imitation. Emergence occurs quite close under the surface film, and the adults fly off almost at once. These pupae are typically black or dirty-grayish, often displaying tiny speckled legs. Hatching occurs sporadically throughout the season, with peak emergence coming mostly in spring and early summer.

There are a great many species on American waters. The northern eco-type *Simulium arcticus* has plagued anglers with their biting swarms, and swift little western rivers have good populations of *Simulium piperi* and *Simulium tuberosum*.

Trout feed extensively on these *Simulium* in their larval, pupal, and fully developed stages. Their importance is out of all proportion to their diminutive size, and their most extensive populations are in swift little rivers with some riffle weed.

Culicoides larva

RIFFLE SMUT LARVA
Hook: Sizes 16-20 Mustad 7948A
Nylon: Black 6/0 nylon
Clingers: Two peacock herl tips tied short
Body: Dark blackish olive rayon floss shaped to suggest natural
Thorax: Dark blackish olive rayon floss tied to suggest natural
Ribbing: Fine silver wire
Prolegs: None
Head: Black nylon

RIFFLE SMUT PUPA
Hook: Sizes 18-26 Mustad 94840 1X fine
Nylon: Black 6/0 nylon
Body: Black or medium gray dubbing tied full
Ribbing: Fine oval tinsel
Thorax: Black or medium gray dubbing tied full
Wing cases: Dark slate-colored duck quill sections or omit
Legs: Black or dark blue dun fibers
Antennae: Barred teal fibers
Head: Black nylon

4. Sand Gnats (*Culicoides minutes*)

These tiny little insects measure between one-sixteenth and one-eighth inch in adulthood. However, the larval forms are agile, swimming types frequently taken by smutting trout. The pale larvae and pupae are similar to those of the better-known Chironomidae, in both configuration and habits.

Their imitations should be fished dead-drift in the film with a silicone-oiled tippet and leader.

SAND GNAT LARVA	SAND GNAT PUPA
Hook: Sizes 16-24 Orvis Premium 1X long	*Hook*: Sizes 16-26 Mustad 94840 1X fine
Nylon: 6/0 nylon matching body color	*Nylon*: 6/0 nylon matching body color
Gills: Pale grayish dun fibers tied short	*Gills*: Pale grayish dun fibers tied short
Body: Gray, brown, black, olive, tan, yellow or green rayon floss tied delicate and thin	*Body*: Gray, brown, black, olive, tan, yellow or green rayon floss, dressed thin
Ribbing: Fine silver or gold wire	*Thorax*: Dubbing of same colors
Thorax: Above colors without ribbing	*Wing cases*: Dark gray teal wing quill sections or omit
Prolegs: None	*Legs*: Pale grayish dun fibers
Head: Nylon matching body color	*Antennae*: None
	Head: Nylon matching body color

Palpomyia larva

5. Ceratopogon Midge (*Palpomyia americana*)

These are tiny biting flies that are quite similar in configuration to the better-known Chronomidae, which look like mosquitoes but are nonbiting insects. These larvae inhabit the bottom detritus and trash in mountain lakes and streams. They are slender and almost needle-shaped, averaging three-eighths to slightly more than a quarter inch. Pupal forms are similar to the *Simulium* flies.

CERATOPOGON MIDGE LARVA	CERATOPOGON PUPA
Hook: Sizes 16-20 Orvis Premium 1X long	*Hook*: Sizes 18-26 Mustad 94840 1X fine
Nylon: 6/0 nylon matching body color	*Nylon*: 6/0 nylon matching body color
Body: Black, gray, brown, olive, tan, yellow or green rayon floss tied slim along hook shank	*Body*: Black, gray, brown, olive, tan, yellow or green rayon floss
Thorax: None	*Ribbing*: Fine gold or silver wire
Ribbing: Fine gold or silver wire	*Thorax*: Same colors used above and dressed slightly more full
Head: Nylon matching body color	*Wing cases*: Duck wing quill sections or omit
Gills: Tiny short fibers slightly darker than body and no longer than 1/16 inch	*Legs*: Soft fibers matching body colors
	Antennae: Woodduck fibers or omit
	Head: Nylon matching body color

Dixa larva

6. Dixa Flies (*Dixa minuta*)

This family of little two-winged flies is not represented by a large number of indigenous American species, but they are relatively abundant where they are found. Streams flowing through moist forest bottoms are particularly suited to the species. Dixidae are distinguished by strongly arched apical wings, with their basal cells reaching beyond the middle of the adult wing structure. The joints in the antennal flagellum are indistinctly separated and formed.

Dixa pupa

DIXA FLY LARVA
Hook: Sizes 16-24 Mustad 9523 5X short turned-up eye
Nylon: Black 6/0 nylon
Tail-gills: Iron-blue dun fibers tied short, deep around bend of hook toward the barb
Body: Black, brown, olive, or green rayon floss
Ribbing: Fine gold or silver wire
Thorax: Same colors as body floss
Antennae: Iron-blue dun fibers tied short like throat hackle
Head: Black nylon

The larva of these diminutive two-winged flies are usually bent double, swimming with the curved middle of their bodies foremost in the current. Pupation usually occurs in such shallow waters, or even in the moist bank soils themselves, and the fish apparently do not take them in large numbers. For that reason a pupal imitation has not been designed.

7. Tanypus Flies (*Tanypus arcticus*)

These insects are superficially similar in the larval stages to the Dixidae, although they are slightly larger. Their larvae also swim in a bent-over attitude, their curving bodies held forward into the water. Pupation also occurs in bank silts.

Tanypus larva

TANYPUS FLY LARVA
Hook: Sizes 14-20 Mustad 9523 5X
    short turned-up eye
Nylon: Brown 6/0 Nylon
Tail-gills: Dark blue dun fibers tied
    short and deep around bend of
    hook toward barb
Body: Brown, olive, green or tan
    rayon floss
Ribbing: Fine gold or silver wire
Thorax: Same colors as body floss
Antennae: Dark blue dun fibers tied
    short like throat hackle
Head: Brown nylon

8. Two-Winged Midges (*Chironomus lobiferus*)

There are so many American species of these elegant little Chironomidae midges that I have given the above species only as a prototypical example of the subfamily rather than as a specific insect for imitation. These midges hatch sporadically from early spring to deep autumn, and on some rivers there are extensive winter cycles of emergence.

Although their most impressive populations are found in lakes and impoundments, the Chironomidae are also a primary component of the trout diet in large, slow-flowing streams. The adults are rather long-legged flies with bodies slightly longer than their wings. Their thoracic shoulders are somewhat humpbacked. Size ranges from one-eighth inch to one-half inch in length. The wings are pale-grayish or white, and in some species are held tightly along the body, while others spread them wide. Some writers have called them short-winged gnats.

Since they are the most important subfamily of the huge Diptera order, it is impossible to place too much emphasis on their somewhat unnoticed role in fly-fishing. Our neglect of the midge forms is understandable, given our preoccupation with the bigger and better-known aquatic hatches.

Ronalds called them midges in his *Flyfisher's Entomology*, and most anglers still use his terminology. However, various popular names are also employed on waters in Ireland and the United Kingdom. Scotland has long referred to its midges with names like the Blae and Black, while on the lakes of the Irish moors they are sometimes known as Buzzers and Duck Flies. British anglers call them midges and gnats.

During their transformation from the larval stage to the point of pupal emergence, the Chironomidae are available to the fish in almost astronomical numbers.

Emergence occurs when vast quantities of these minuscule pupal insects migrate toward the surface, where they remain suspended for a few minutes, their thoracic gills breathing in the surface film. During this brief period of lying under the meniscus, the pupal sac is split and gradually escaped by the hatching midges. Schools of fish sometimes cruise the lake-sized flats of the Delaware, the smooth, deep-water tailings of the Ozark reservoirs, smooth reaches of our big western rivers, and reservoirs from Eleven Mile in Colorado to the weed-filled shallows of Wickiup in Oregon, taking midges by the millions in gentle porpoising rises.

Adult midges have small heads which virtually merge with the thoracic shoulders. The dorsal surface of the thorax is clearly humped. The mesothoracic segment is exaggerated, supporting the single pair of wings. These wings are relatively small when compared with the legs and the overall length of the abdomen. British species and some ecotypes present in American waters hold their wings back along the body, and the delicate *Anisomera* midges typical of this configuration are primary hatches in northern Europe, Iceland, and the waters of the United Kingdom. Many American midges hold their wings at right angles to their thoracic roots, like tiny spent-wing mayflies without tails. The abdominal structure consists of nine segments, completely devoid of even atrophied cerci.

Males are distinguished from females by several anatomical points. They have conspicuous plumelike antennae completely lacking in the females. The male abdomen is quite slender. Its last body segment has the sexual forceps. Females have a slightly fatter and delicately tapered abdominal configuration, and are somewhat larger in size.

The Chironomidae have a complete metamorphosis of larva, pupa, and adult insect, typical of endopterygotid genera. They change little between hatching and egglaying except for a slight darkening in color.

The larval forms are rather active, swimming in open water and inhabiting the surface waters of the deepest parts of lakes and impoundments. They exist in numberless colonies in the shallows too, reaching optimal abundance in alkaline environments. The distribution of the pupae is somewhat dependent on weather, wind conditions, direction of current flow, and water temperature. Weather and water temperature determine the length of time spent escaping the pupal skin at the surface, and both winds and currents affect their lines of drift during that hatching period.

Chironomidae occur in all types of water. Specimens have been recovered from ditches, ponds, marshes and bogs, lakes, reservoirs, canals, rivers, streams, and tiny brooks. Emergence in their diurnal hatching cycles varies with species and season of the year. During the spring, the dark-colored midges come off at midday and into the afternoon. The females return to join the mating swarms and oviposit their eggs in the evening, and most midday flights are male flies. Such male swarms are often found well inland from their aquatic habitats. Further into the year emergence occurs later and later during the day, until in late summer they hatch in early evening. Some species are thought to emerge at dusk, continuing into the darkness. Other summer species hatch just after daylight, and I once witnessed an immense rise of fish to this pupal activity just at first light on the Beaverkill. Winter hatches occur on most western rivers too, and it is strange to watch trout rising to Chironomidae and other midges on the Roaring Fork in Colorado—at the apogee of the ski season in Aspen.

It has been observed that the chemistry of the water can play a role in midge species and coloring. Perhaps the most common color spectrum in the myriad species of Chironomidae consists of black, ruby, purple, reddish brown, brown, dark olive, medium olive, green, pale olive, light brown, dirty grayish, amber, dirty yellow, yellowish cream, and white.

Generally speaking, the black and dirty dun-colored species are widely distributed in most types of water. However, there are also some curious relationships between color and water chemistry. Olivaceous and brown-colored species predominate in waters having high alkalinity and concentrations of dissolved oxygen, often through photosynthesis. The bright-reddish and purplish species are common on acid waters with relatively little oxygenation. Larvae are found almost everywhere, including the depths and silt-bottomed shallows of lakes and reservoirs. They are also common in riverine environments, loving the rich detritus of still currents and searching out quiet bottom cushions between the weeds and stones of very fast currents.

British entomologists have observed that the ruby-colored larvae are common in the bottom silt of surprisingly deep water. Some years ago, during the planning and construction of the United States Air Force Academy, we lived in Colorado Springs at the foot of the Rocky Mountains. It gave me the opportunity to spend many evenings and weekends on the watershed of the South Platte, and the reservoirs in the foothills and mountains. During that time I witnessed many periods of dramatic feeding on the Chironomidae, from the minute black pupae that took fish after fish on the South Platte, to the large, purplish larvae found in vast numbers at Tarryall Reservoir in October.

Little is known about the larval and pupal behavior on a species-by-species basis. Lake ecotypes inhabit bottom silt and detritus and sand. Most of these quiet-water forms are fond of algal mosses and mud and the silty root structures of aquatic vegetation. Midge larvae thrive in the shallow littoral acreages, sublittoral zones of moderate depths, and in the pelagic deeps as well. All species are environmentally selective, some tolerating a considerable range of conditions, others having precise ecosystemic needs. Sometimes those which are found in the primary depths of lakes are rare in their littoral and sublittoral zones.

Similar differences occur between lakes, in terms of their singular palettes of Chironomidae species, and some ecologists have recognized the interesting relationship between the limnological character of a lake and the visible symptoms of its indigenous midge species.

Common speces in the trout waters east of the Mississippi are hatches like *Chironomus lobifera*, *Chironomus modestus*, and *Chironomus plumosus*. Western habitats exhibit widely distributed populations of species like *Chironomus utahensis*, *Chironomus nigritus*, and *Chironomus stigmaterus*. There are thousands and thousands of American species.

The larvae vary between three-eighths and three-quarters inch in length.

They are slender and wormlike. Their movements are accomplished by sinuous undulations and bottom-crawling like the terrestrial inchworms. Their diet consists primarily of algae and decaying plant materals, forming a major benchmark in the aquatic food chain between the trout and the more microscopic forms of diatomaceous life.

The well-stocked flyfisher should carry a representative assortment of colors and sizes, until stomach autopsies can determine the coloring most common in his home waters. Collection of larvae and pupal forms will also establish the colors required to match his regional Diptera.

CHIRONOMUS LARVA

Hook: Sizes 14-24 Orvis Premium 1X long
Nylon: 6/0 Matching body color
Gills: Short fibers matching body color
Body: Black, ruby, purple, reddish brown, brown, dark olive, medium olive, green, pale olive, light brown, dirty grayish, amber, dirty yellow, yellowish cream and white rayon floss ribbed with fine silver wire
Thorax: None
Prolegs: Short fibers matching body color
Head: Nylon matching body color

CHIRONOMUS PUPA

Hook: Sizes 14-24 Orvis Supreme 4X fine turned-up eye
Nylon: 6/0 nylon matching body color
Gills: Short blue dun fibers tied in at midpoint of hook bend
Body: Black, ruby, purple, reddish brown, brown, dark olive, medium olive, green, pale olive, light brown, dirty grayish, amber, dirty yellow, yellowish cream and white rayon floss ribbed with fine silver wire
Thorax: Polypropolene dyed to match body and dubbed in fat little thorax
Wing cases: Duck quill sections or omit in tiny sizes
Legs: Soft hackle fibers slightly darker than body colors
Antennae: Woodduck, brown mallard or grey mallard fibers
Head: Nylon matching body color

Chironomus larva (l.) and pupa (r.)

There is another aspect of the smutting-rise problem that I discovered totally by accident. Several years ago, I was fishing the main Au Sable in Michigan with Art Neumann and George Griffith, two early pioneers in the movement that ultimately evolved into Trout Unlimited.

It was the opening weekend of the season, but in spite of the raw weather, there were some fishable hatches of *Ephemerella* and tiny *Paraleptophlebia* flies. However, our talk in the evenings covered the full range of the season, and for smutting rises both men were high on a pattern unfamiliar to me at that time. George Griffith gave me a half-dozen.

It's called Griffith's Gnat, Art laughed.

George flushed slightly with embarrassment. *It is called Griffith's Gnat,* he admitted, *but it works!*

During the midge activity? I asked thoughtfully.

Exactly! said Art. *It's really good.*

It was puzzling, since the tiny flies were simple grizzly palmers dressed on size-twenty hooks with a body of thin peacock herl. The silhouette bore no resemblance to the configuration of the Chironomidae, and it made no sense in terms of imitation.

You fish them dry? I frowned.

Barely, Art crawfished slightly, *but we do fish them awash and drifting in the surface film.*

I'll give them a try, I said.

The half-dozen midge flies were forgotten in the corner of a Wheatley fly box for more than a year, until one evening on the lower Musconetcong with Arthur Morgan. The river seemed lifeless during the afternoon, and we caught a few hapless sunfish and rock bass, but at twilight in the flats below the meadow the trout began feeding everywhere.

The rises were soft, dimpling swirls typical of feeding to minute insects, but nothing in my special box of minute dry flies moved a single fish. We tried jassids, tiny beetles, ants, midge larvae and pupae, and tiny conventional dry-fly patterns. Nothing seemed to work until I tried one of the tiny Griffith's Gnats, and suddenly I was catching fish after fish.

Why this pattern? It was puzzling.

Finally I stopped fishing to study the river and see if it concealed the answer. The collecting screen interrupted the quiet backwater currents while the solution to the puzzle gathered in a translucent little scum against its meshes—hundreds of delicate little pupal shucks and sometimes there were blackish little pupae still entangled in their skins.

It was quite simple. The tiny halo of pale grizzly hackle, awash in the surface film with its body core of dark peacock herl, looked different to the fish. The conventional dry-fly midge offered another light pattern indenting the surface and a totally different silhouette to them. The little black pupa fished in the film represented the midge before its pupal skin began to split and loosen. The grizzly hackle and its dark body core imitated a subtle stage of the hatch between the migrating pupa and the adult—the *Chironomus* pupa before its complete escape from its pupal skin.

There are always a few in my fly boxes now. The tiny little palmers are dressed on delicate fine-wire hooks from sizes eighteen to twenty-four. The body cores are ruby-colored, rusty brown, chocolate, olive, green, pale olive, muskrat, black seal, and yellow synthetic floss, all palmered with tiny grizzly hackles. The box still has a few peacock-herl dressings too, in deference to the original Griffith's Gnat.

It has worked many times in recent years, from the still twilight flats of the Catskills to the Frying Pan in Colorado and the smooth grayling headwaters of the Big Hole. It has also fooled selective smutting fish on the Malleo in Argentina, and the weedy little Cumilahue in Chile.

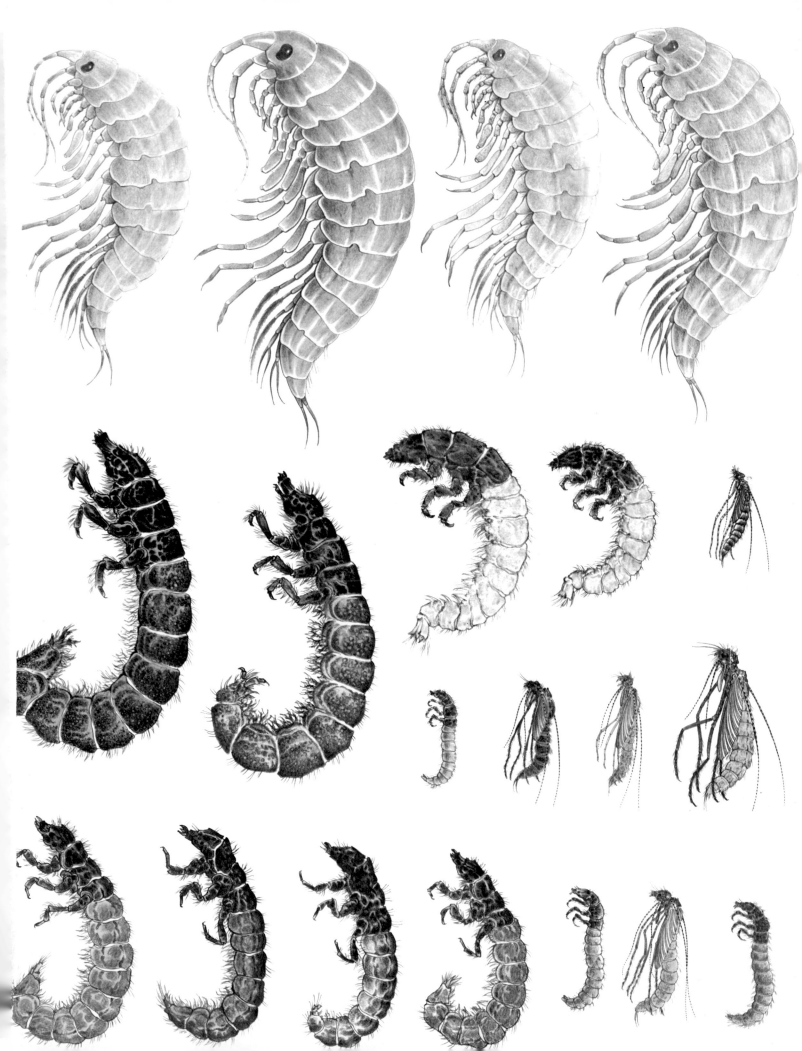

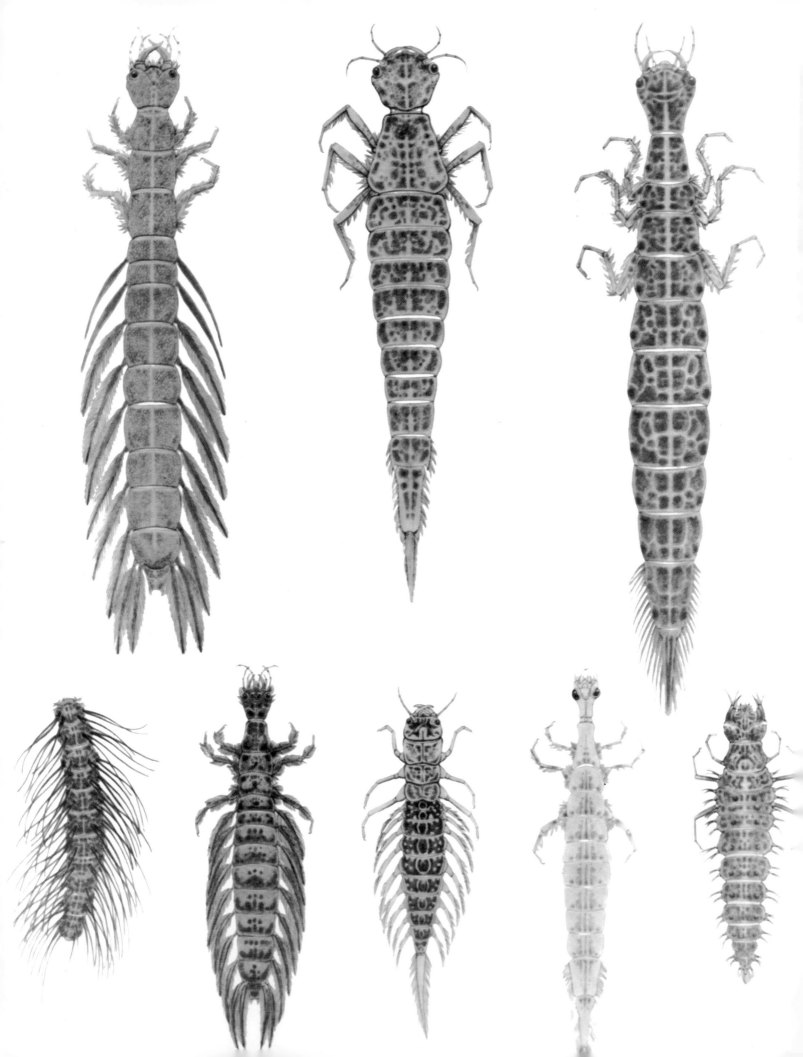

Hemiptera frequent sheltered waters, with thickly grown aquatic plants and dead vegetation, and in quiet little streams and backwaters. There they forage widely for other insects and feed upon dead organisms. They are typically active as soon as the winter ice is gone, and some species lay their eggs in early April. Their intense metabolism requires a vigorous activity that lasts well into winter, when most adult forms hibernate. Their hibernation usually occurs in sluggish little colonies hiding in the chara and eelgrass beds, with other groups skulking in the silt and bottom trash. Most live longer than a single year.

Their diet consists of any organism they can successfully defeat and devour. Larger prey includes young baitfish, snails, and tadpoles, but their diet also requires large numbers of small crustaceans, midge and mosquito larvae, and other unlucky subaquatic forms. The Corixidae are less predatory and voracious, concentrating primarily on vegetable foods, although they feed extensively in the diatomaceous ooze of the bottom. Since they are less aggressive, these little water boatmen sometimes provide food for their more voracious cousins.

1. Corixa Bug (*Arctocorixa alternata*)

Like many species of the Hemiptera, these little *Corixa* bugs are active almost the entire year. Sometimes they are called water boatmen. Most species are dark grayish, somewhat mottled with brown and black. Their rear legs are flattened to facilitate swimming, extending out like the back-swimmers, and the Corixidae swim with their dorsal surfaces up.

Water boatmen dive down with great agility, their bodies wrapped in a cloak of glittering bubbles. Their buoyancy is such that they cannot remain submerged without attaching themselves to a plant stem. Their slender middle legs terminate in very slender claws, and it is these appendages that are used to cling in the weeds. It is extremely difficult to distinguish one species from another, according to H. B. Hungerford in his definitive *Biology and Ecology of Aquatic and Semi-Aquatic Hemiptera,* and the species identified in this chapter is merely prototypical. Its adults average about three-sixteenths to one-quarter inch in length.

Gills: Dark brown, 1/16 inch
Body: Dark blackish brown, 3/16 inch
Thorax: Dark blackish brown, ⅛ inch
Wing cases: Dark mottled brownish, ¼ inch
Swimmer-legs: Light brownish, ¼ inch
Legs: Light brownish, 3/16 inch
Head: Amber at anterior surfaces with brown face

Hook: Sizes 14-16 Orvis Premium 1X long
Nylon: Dark brown 6/0 nylon
Gills: Two short pheasant-tail fibers
Body: Dark brownish gray hare's mask dubbing tied full
Ribbing: Fine oval silver tinsel
Thorax: Dark hare's mask dubbing tied full, mixed roughly with guard hairs
Wing cases: Mottled brown turkey wing section tied in at hook bend and pulled up over entire body like wing case
Swimmer-legs: Two pheasant-tail fibers extended like oars, tied in between body and thorax
Legs: Thorax dubbing guard hairs suggest legs
Head: Dark brown nylon with amber lacquer at back of head

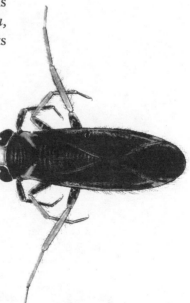

Corixa alternata

118

The *Corixa* imitation closely parallels the fly pattern worked out in the United Kingdom by the British fishing writer Commander C. F. Walker. His fine book *Lake Flies and Their Imitation* is a pioneering study in still-water problems in trout fishing.

2. Creeping Pigmy Bug (*Plea striola*)

These tiny little pigmy water bugs live in tangled beds of eelgrass and candelabra weed, and are carnivorous in their feeding habits. They measure about three-sixteenths inch.

Body: Dark brownish gray, ⅛ inch
Wing-shells: Dark olive gray, 3/16 inch
Thorax: Dark brownish gray, ⅛ inch
Legs: Dark olive gray, 3/16 inch
Head: Dark olive gray

Hook: Sizes 16-20 Mustad 9523 5X short turned-up eye
Nylon: Dark olive 6/0 nylon
Body: Dark brownish hare's mask roughly dubbed on olive silk tied in at midpoint of hook bend
Wing shells: Mallard wing quill sections dyed dark olive dun tied in at either side to cover entire body on back and sides
Thorax: Dark brownish hare's mask dubbed on olive silk
Legs: Dark olive dun hen hackle palmer-tied on forward half of body and thorax
Head: Dark olive nylon

Top, left to right: *Eucrangonyx gracilus, Gammarus fasciatus, Gammarus minus, Gammarus limnaeus* Upper middle, left to right: *Macronema zebatum, Macronema aspila, Hydropsyche gracilus, Hydropsyche bifilis, Hydroptila americana* Lower middle, left to right: *Chimarrha atterima* larva and pupa, *Oxytheira occidentalis, Sericostoma montana* Bottom, left to right: *Rhyacophila grandis, Rhyacophila coloradensis, Rhyacophila pacifica, Rhyacophila lobifera, Chimarrha augustipennis* larva and pupa, *Chimarrha immarginata*

There are several species of backswimmers which are classified in the Notonectidae family, and they are distinguished by the habit of swimming upside down on their boat-shaped backs. Their rear swimmer-legs are extended widely.

The backswimmers hang head down from the surface film with their bodies breathing in the meniscus, their rear legs dangling like trailing oars. When disturbed or hunting, they dive toward the bottom wth surprising agility, enveloped in a sheath of translucent air bubbles. Like the Corixidae, they can remain submerged by grasping plant stems. Backswimmers are extremely prolific, and Hungerford found more than two hundred and fifty eggs in a single female. Egglaying lasts from March until early summer, and the adults live more than a year.

3. Gray-Winged Backswimmer (*Notonecta irrorata*)

These tiny little water bugs are widely distributed, averaging about one-quarter to three-eighths inch.

Gills: Brownish gray, 1/32 inch
Body: Dark brownish gray with an olive cast, ¼ inch
Thorax: Brownish gray with olive cast, ⅛ inch
Wing cases: Dark grayish ⅜ inch
Swimmer-legs: Dark grayish, ⅜ inch
Legs: Dark grayish, 3/16 inch
Head: Dark brown, 1/16 inch

Hook: Sizes 16-18 Orvis Premium 1X long
Nylon: Dark brown 6/0 nylon
Gills: Two pheasant tail fiber points tied very short
Body: Dark brownish gray hare's mask dubbed on olive silk
Thorax: Dark brownish hare's mask on olive silk mixed with guard hairs
Wing cases: Dark slate-colored duck quill section tied in at hook bend pulled over body like wing case
Swimmer-legs: Two pheasant-tail fibers extended like oars between body and thorax
Legs: suggested by guard hairs in thorax dubbing
Head: Dark brown nylon

4.   Grouse-Winged Backswimmer (*Notonecta undulata*)

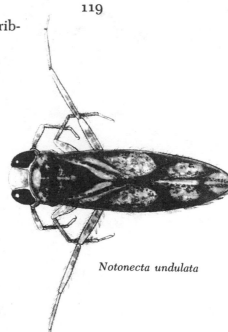

These active half-inch backswimmers are perhaps the most widely distributed American species, recorded from Quebec to California.

Gills: Dark brownish, 3/32 inch
Body: Dark brownish olive, ⅜ inch
Thorax: Light brownish olive, ⅛ inch
Wing cases: Dark mottled brown with distinct light and dark markings, ⅜ inch
Swimmer-legs: Light brownish gray, ⅝ inch
Legs: Light brownish gray, ¼ inch
Head: Dark brownish, 1/16 inch

Hook: Sizes 12-16 Orvis Premium 1X long
Nylon: Dark brown 6/0 Nylon
Gills: Two pheasant-tail fibers tied short
Body: Dark hare's mask dubbing on olive silk
Thorax: Dark hare's mask roughly dubbed with guard hairs on olive silk
Wing cases: Brown mottled feather tied in at hook bend and pulled over entire body like a wing case with light brown lacquer markings to suggest naturals
Swimmer-legs: Two pheasant-tail fibers extended like oars and tied in between body and thorax
Legs: Suggested by thorax guard hairs
Head: Dark brown nylon

Notonecta undulata

5.   Pale Moon-Wing Backswimmer (*Buenoa margaritacea*)

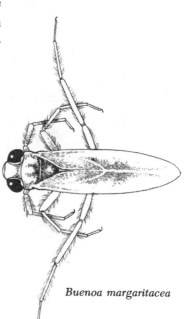

This elegant little species is representative of its slender moon-winged genus. Its behavior is atypical, in the sense that these backswimmers occasionally swim and hang resting in middle depths of water. The wings are pale white, with a pinkish thorax and a dark rust-colored abdomen. Unlike the other backswimmers, these delicate little moon-wings lay their eggs in the stems of water plants. Adults measure about three-sixteenths to one-quarter inch in length.

Gills: Pale olive, 1/32 inch
Body: Pale olive with a pink sternite area, 3/16 inch
Thorax: Pale olive with a pink dorsal spot, 3/32 inch
Wing cases: Pale grayish white, 3/16 inch
Swimmer-legs: Pale bluish gray, 5/16 inch
Legs: Pale olive dun, ⅛ inch
Head: Pale olive, ⅛ inch

Hook: Sizes 18-20 Orvis Premium 1X long
Nylon: Pale olive 6/0 nylon
Gills: Pale olive duck quill fiber points
Body: Pale olive floss with a ventral line of pink lacquer or silk
Thorax: Pale olive floss with a dorsal pink spot
Wing cases: Pale grayish white duck quill section tied in a hook bend and pulled over entire body like a wing case
Swimmer-legs: Pale bluish gray duck quill fibers
Legs: Pale olive dun hackle fibers
Head: Pale olive nylon with pink spot

Buenoa margaritacea

Top, left to right: *Dineutes vittatus, Dysticus verticalus, Cybister fimbriolatus*
Bottom, left to right: *Peltodytes americanus, Gyrinus americanus, Sialis infumata, Acilius occidentalis, Berosus americanus*

Some Secrets of the Subaquatic Coleoptera

It has been twenty-five years since that first Leadville summer. The haying was finished, and the little streams that work in willowlined lacework patterns across the Arkansas bottoms were low and clear. It was clearing just after daylight, and the peaks of the barren Mosquito Range were purplish against the rising sun.

My tackle hung on a series of finishing nails I had placed in the bunkhouse walls. The rain that had rattled on its corrugated roof just before dawn had stopped, but water still dripped rhythmically from the gutters. The fire I had built in the early-morning darkness had warmed the bunkhouse. It was dying now and its coals shifted, collapsing and cooling in the pot bellied stove. The mice had stopped their midnight scuttling behind the wainscoting.

Breakfast in the main house was typical of Colorado ranch life, with its eggs and fried potatoes and steak. *You've got some chores this morning,* my aunt reminded me tartly.

Yes. It interfered with fishing. *Clean the stables.*

Don't sound so unhappy, my uncle laughed. *When you finish I thought we might take the weapo up the mountain.*

Fish the cutthroat ponds on Massive? I grinned.

Sure. He smiled and took a second steak.

My uncle had purchased a surplus weapons carrier after the war, and we used it as an all-purpose vehicle on the ranch, but the best trips were our mountain expeditions in four-wheel drive. Twice we took it high above timberline into the wild-flower lap of Mount Massive, climbing from there to the highest of its three summits through the August snowfields and mountain buttercups and harebells. Sometimes we drove high along the old railroad grade above Turquoise to the abandoned Frying Pan tunnel, hiking to Busk Lake and over the ridge to fish Ivanhoe. But my uncle had always promised a trip in the weapons carrier to the marshy little timberline lakes in the headwaters of Rock Creek, high on the northeast shoulder of Mount Massive.

The prospect of clearing manure from the stable seemed happier now with the thoughts of fishing the Massive ponds. It was hard work, shoveling the stalls into a wheelbarrow and trundeling it to the compost heap outside the corral. Finally the shovel scraped ringingly on the stonework, and the gutters ran fresh and clear again with water from the irrigation ditch.

My uncle fished a dripping can of Coors from the icy, spring-fed cattle trough. *Finished with the barn?*

Yes, I sighed happily.

The weapons carrier growled and leaned precariously, rocking and clawing in four-wheel drive along the steep logging road. Marmots and ground squirrels scurried up the rock slides toward their burrows, terrified of the grinding engine and gear box.

The snowfields on Mount Massive were closer now, and a red-tailed hawk circled high above a beaver pond. Finally the road climbed into dense stands of pines and Engelmann spruce and fir, and ahead was the bright glitter of the ponds.

It was still and warm in the sun while we ate lunch in the boulders, sharing some of the sandwich bread with a whiskey-jack. The ponds were like a mirror. There were no rises anywhere.

Want to fish some? said my uncle.

I'll rig my gear. I watched the smooth water. *But I think I'll wait for the trout to start working.*

Okay, he said. *Feel like taking a nap?*

My fly rod leaned against the boulders, and I clinched a small grayish Woolly Worm to the tippet. It was an impulse that caused me to select it among the patterns in my fly book. Perhaps it was a premonition.

Clouds built gradually through the morning, gathering on the thermals that carry the moisture of the valleys into the cold, dryer air at higher altitudes. The sun was weaker now, filtered through the overcast that was forming over Massive, and finally I watched a misting rain begin in the meadows above timberline. The summer squall drifted slowly toward the lakes, sliding down the shoulder of the mountain until its raindrops pattered gently in the water.

Suddenly the quiet water along the reeds and thickly matted beds of *Dichelyma* and fountain-moss was alive with rising fish. They were working steadily while the gentle rain both aerated the water and offered them concealment. The fish were apparently prowling, feeding in a sequential chain of rises along the sheltered weeds.

Working carefully into position, wading in the beaver sticks and interlaced weeds, it was a little precarious, and twice my foot plunged through into a muskrat channel. There was a trout cruising just off the weeds, threading four rises together in a necklacelike series, and I dropped the cast where the fifth rise was coming. It is the secret of presentation to a cruising fish in quiet waters.

The fifth rise came in the feeding rhythm established by the trout and the leader twitched softly. I tightened and the fat cutthroat bored deep into the lake, stripping line from the reel. It went fifteen inches, and there were a dozen more before the misting rain passed and the bright sun forced the trout back into deeper water. The rises stopped abruptly.

What made them do that? asked my uncle.

Don't know. I waded ashore thoughtfully and reeled in my line. *You catch anything on bait?*

No, he said. *You sure took fish on flies!*

Wonder why they liked the Woolly so much? I wondered aloud. *Maybe I should check their stomachs.*

The stomachs were sausage-tight with a strange little larva, its rough, brownish-mottled body covered with hairy little gill filaments. No wonder the peacock-bodied little Woolly Worm took fish with such regularity. It looked just like the larvae in their stomachs. It was a fine lesson the trout have taught me many times over the past twenty-five years—nothing in their behavior is accidental once we can discover its reasons.

It would be several years before I would recognize these larvae as the immature forms of *Peltodytes* beetles, but it was my introduction to their importance in the trout diet. Beetles are all classified as members of the Coleoptera, and there are almost two hundred thousand American species in approximately eighty-odd families and subfamilies. However, only a few of these families are aquatic beetles.

Both the adults and pupae of these aquatic beetles are air-breathing organisms. Some of the most intriguing behavior and physiology of the larvae lie in their methods of breathing in the water. There are a few with tracheal gills that permit breathing under water. The Gyrinidae and a few of the Hydrophilidae have filamentous gills along their abdomens. The larvae of the Dytiscidae breathe through the spiracles at the rear of their bodies. The *Berosus* larvae breathe through lateral gill structures, and the immature forms of the *Tropisternus* beetles must hold their abdominal gill filaments in contact with the surface of the water to effect respiration.

Nearly all aquatic Coleoptera live in quiet waters, thickly grown with plants on which they stalk their prey and oviposit their eggs. They love quietly flowing water and comparatively still backwaters littered with detritus and decaying plant materials and bottom trash. Their habitat is often rich in algal matter, and is heavily populated with other insect eco-types. The water pennies, the larvae of the Psephenidae, are the only form that is confined to fast water. They have fringed gills under their coin-shaped bodies, but since they are firmly attached to the bottom stones, they are not useful as prototypes for flies.

Unlike the other aquatic orders, the water forms of the Coleoptera spend their summer months as larvae and pupae, and winter as adults. The Psephenidae are the only exception. The adult beetles hibernate in the silt and bottom trash. Water-penny larvae forage over the winter bottom for diatomaceous foods.

The larvae of the diving Dytiscidae and the whirligig Gyrinidae are predacious carnivores. The smaller Haliplidae are vegetarians, like the water pennies. The Hydrophilidae are carnivorous in their larval stages, but confine themselves to plant materials once they have become adults. The larvae of the Dytiscidae, Gyrinidae, and Haliplidae ingest their food through mandibles that are shaped to transfer fluids. The other larvae chew their foods.

Their predatory character notwithstanding, these beetle larvae are not without enemies. The larvae are fierce cannibals from their eclosion, attacking each other almost immediately on emerging from the eggs. The dragon-fly larva is another predator that feeds on the beetle larvae extensively. Turtles and waterfowl and birds also consume large quantities of Coleoptera, and these predatory hunters are also among the hunted.

The cocoonlike pupal sacs are typically suspended in the weeds, concealed in the bottom trash, or wedged among the stones. *Dineutes* passes pupation in the moist bank soils. Therefore, such Coleoptera pupae are not available to the trout and are of little interest to the angler.

1. Brown Crawling Beetle Larva (*Haliplus ruficollis*)

This is a crawling water-beetle larva typical of the forty-odd American species. It feeds primarily on algal matter, and is a dark-brownish-gray larva often mistaken for small sticks or plant stems. The larvae breathe through spiracles in the breathing tube at the posterior of their abdomens, and measure about three-quarters inch.

Gills: Dark grayish single tail-gill system, ⅛ inch
Abdomen: Brownish gray distinctly ringed, ½ inch
Thorax: Brownish gray distinctly ringed, ¼ inch
Legs: Dark grayish, ¼ inch
Head: Dark brown. 1/16 inch

Hook: Sizes 12-16 Mustad 79580 4X long
Nylon: Dark brown 6/0 nylon
Gills: Single dark gray feather point
Abdomen: Grayish fur dubbing ringed with dark rusty dubbing wound on olive silk
Thorax: Grayish fur dubbing roughly mixed with guard hairs
Legs: Dark blue dun hen hackle palmer-tied along thorax
Head: Dark brown nylon

Haliplus larva

2. Gray Crawling Beetle Larva (*Peltodytes americanus*)

This is the slender-gilled beetle larva that I found in the fish we caught that rainy afternoon on Mount Massive. It also feeds on algae and plant materials. The females oviposit their eggs on the stems of aquatic weedbeds and grasses. *Peltodytes* larvae breathe through the slender tracheae that cover the full length of their bodies. They measure about three-eighths to five-eighths inch at full larval growth.

Gills: Mottled grayish filaments along entire larva, ¼ inch
Body: Dark brownish olive, ½ inch
Thorax: Dark brownish olive, 1/16 inch
Legs: Dark olive
Head: Dark brownish, 1/16 inch

Hook: Sizes 12-16 Mustad 9672 3X long
Nylon: Dark brown 6/0 nylon
Gills: Dark grizzly hackle tied palmer-style along full length of body and thorax
Body: Fully dressed peacock herl
Thorax: Fully dressed peacock herl
Legs: None
Head: Dark brown nylon

3. Brown Diving Beetle Larva (*Dysticus fasciventris*)

This diving beetle larva averages about one inch in length, and is an extremely predatory form. These species are the most dominant of the aquatic Coleoptera, and their larvae are known as water tigers. They lie in wait for their prey, with their breathing system in the surface film, and then attack with agility. Fishing the *Dysticus* imitations should suggest this behavior.

Gills: Pale grayish olive, 1/8 inch
Body: Pale grayish olive, 3/4 inch
Thorax: Pale grayish olive, 1/4 inch
Legs: Pale grayish blue dun, 1/4 inch
Head: Pale grayish olive, 1/8 inch

Hook: Sizes 10-14 Mustad 79580 4X long
Nylon: Pale olive 6/0 nylon
Gills: Two pale olive dyed hackle points
Body: Pale olive fur mixed with muskrat
Ribbing: Fine oval tinsel
Thorax: Pale olive fur mixed with muskrat, with a pale olive gray goose quill section tied down over the thorax like a wing case
Legs: Pale grayish dun hen hackle tied palmer-style along thorax
Head: Pale olive nylon

4. Black Diving Beetle Larva (*Dysticus hybridus*)

This is an extremely dark iron-blue beetle larva, averaging about seven-eighths inch in length.

Gills: Iron-blue dun, 3/32 inch
Body: Dark brownish black, 5/8 inch
Thorax: Dark brownish black, 3/16 inch
Legs: Dark iron-blue dun, 3/16 inch
Head: Black, 3/32 inch

Hook: Sizes 12-16 Mustad 9672 3X long
Nylon: Black 6/0 nylon
Gills: Two iron-blue dun hackle points
Body: Dark brownish black hare's mask dubbing
Ribbing: Fine oval tinsel
Thorax: Dark brownish black hare's mask dubbing with a slate-colored goose quill section tied over the thorax like a wing case
Legs: Iron-blue dun hen hackle palmered along thorax
Head: Black nylon

5. Olive Diving Beetle Larva (*Dysticus verticalis*)

This mottled, brownish-olive larva averages slightly more than one inch in length, and is a voracious carnivore.

Gills: Dirty olive gray, 3/16 inch
Body: Mottled brownish olive, 7/8 inch
Thorax: Mottled brownish olive, 1/4 inch
Legs: Dirty olive gray, 1/4 inch
Head: Mottled brownish olive, 3/16 inch

Hook: Sizes 12-14 Mustad 9672 3X long
Nylon: Dark olive 6/0 nylon
Gills: Two dirty olive gray hackle points
Body: Dirty olive gray dubbing on olive silk, ribbed with a roughly dubbed wrapping of hare's mask guard hairs
Thorax: Dubbed like body with a brown mottled turkey quill section dyed olive tied over the thorax like a wing case
Legs: Dirty olive gray hen hackle palmer-tied along thorax
Head: Dark olive nylon

6. Pale-Olive Beetle Larva (*Acilius occidentalis*)

This medium-sized diving-beetle larva is a western species typical of the American species. Fully developed larvae average approximately five-eighths inch in length. These larvae are gracefully agile swimmers, and imitations should be fished accordingly. Resting just under the surface film, their bodies are gracefully curved. Sometimes they attach themselves to the weeds, hiding themselves from their prey. However, the air entrained in their posterior gill tubes is quite buoyant, forcing them back toward the surface when they release their hold on a plant stem. Their most common attitude is hanging head down, their gill systems breathing rapidly in the oxygen-filled meniscus.

Gills: Pale olive gray filaments at posterior of body, 1/32 inch
Body: Pale olive gray with faint brown dorsal markings, ⅝ inch
Thorax: Pale olive gray, ¼ inch
Legs: Pale olive mottled, ⅛ inch
Head: Pale olive gray, 1/16 inch

Hook: Sizes 12-16 Mustad 9672 3X long
Nylon: Pale olive 6/0 nylon
Gills: Roughly dubbed dirty olive fur untrimmed on last third of body
Body: Dirty olive dubbing ribbed with fine oval tinsel
Thorax: Dirty olive dubbing with olive-dyed duck quill section tied down like a wing case
Legs: Olive-dyed grizzly hen hackle dressed palmer-style along thorax
Head: Pale olive nylon

7. Gray-Gilled Beetle Larva (*Coptotomus interrogatus*)

Unlike the *Dysticus* and *Acilius* larvae, these medium-sized forms are not dependent upon direct contact with the oxygenated surface film of the water for respiration. The larvae average about a half-inch in length, and are bottom-crawlers that swim only brief distances while foraging for their food. Imitations should be fished deep and slow.

Gills: Blue dun, ⅛ inch
Body: Dark brownish mottled gray, ¼ inch
Body Gills: Blue dun filaments, ⅜ inch
Thorax: Dark brownish mottled, 3/16 inch
Legs: Dark brownish mottled, 3/16 inch
Head: Dark brownish, ⅛ inch

Hook: Size 14-16 Mustad 9671 2X long
Nylon: Brown 6/0 nylon
Gills: Two blue dun hackle points
Body: Dark hare's mask dubbing well mixed with guard hairs
Body Gills: Blue dun hackle palmer-tied along the body
Thorax: Dark hare's mask dubbing with a mottled brownish turkey quill section tied down like a wing case
Legs: Darkly mottled brown multi-color hackle fibers
Head: Brown nylon

Coptotomus larva

8. Great Olive Beetle Larva (*Cybister fimbriolatus*)

These relatively large diving beetle larvae average as much as an inch and one-half in length, and some species of *Cybister* larvae are even larger. These larvae are voracious and extremely predatory, often feeding heavily on freshly hatched tadpoles and fingerling baitfish.

Unlike the water-tiger larvae of the *Acilius* and *Dysticus* genera, these huge larval forms do not hang head down from the surface while breathing. They hold their heads and thoracic sections in the meniscus for respiration. Like the *Acilius* larvae, these insects are distinguished by their narrow, delicately tapered neck segments.

When not breathing at the surface, these larvae clamber and swim in the weedy shallows, searching for food. Like the aggressive dragonfly nymph, they typically seize a tadpole or minnow in its soft belly and suck its flesh until only the shriveled skin remains. These larvae are the shrews of the subaquatic world, seldom hesitating to attack much larger organisms.

Gills: Brownish olive, ¼ inch
Body: Mottled brownish olive, 1 inch
Thorax: Mottled brownish olive, 5/16 inch
Legs: Mottled brownish olive, ¼ inch
Head: Mottled brownish olive, 3/16 inch

Hook: Sizes 4-8 Mustad 79580 4X long
Nylon: Olive 6/0 nylon
Gills: Medium olive hackle palmer-tied along posterior quarter of the body
Body: Mottled hare's mask mixed with guard hairs and olive dyed seal fur
Thorax: Mottled hare's mask mixed with olive, and an olive-dyed feather section over back
Legs: Grizzly hackle dyed medium olive trimmed off on the back
Head: Mottled hare's mask mixed with olive

9. Olive Whirligig Beetle Larva (*Gyrinus americanus*)

These centipedelike larvae are pale, rather delicate creatures which clamber over the bottom trash and detritus. Sometimes they swim in search of their prey, moving sinuously in the water, using their heavily fringed gills and tails. The larvae move forward and backward with equal agility. The larvae average about three-quarters inch in length. Their posterior gills include minute sickle-shaped hooks that are used to clasp weeds and grasses while they wait for an unsuspecting *Callibaetis* nymph.

Gills: Dark brownish olive, 3/16 inch
Body: Dark mottled brownish olive, ⅝ inch
Thorax: Dark mottled brownish olive, ⅛ inch
Legs: Dark brownish olive, 3/16 inch
Head: Dark brownish olive, 1/32 inch

Hook: Sizes 12-14 Mustad 79580 4X long
Nylon: Medium olive 6/0 nylon
Gills: Dark brown-olive hackle stripped on one side and trimmed to ¼-inch length, palmer-tied along body
Body: Dark hare's mask dubbing mixed with guard hairs, spun on olive silk
Thorax: Dark hare's mask dubbing mixed with guard hairs on olive silk, with dark olive feather section over back
Legs: Dark brown-olive hen hackle trimmed off on back
Head: Dark hare's mask dubbed on olive silk

10. Gray Whirligig Beetle Larva (*Gyrinus occidentalis*)

These small whirligig larvae average about one-half inch in length, and are found in weedy western streams and ponds.

Gills: Dark grayish, 3/16 inch
Body: Dark brownish gray, ⅜ inch
Thorax: Dark brownish gray, ¼ inch
Legs: Dark grayish, ¼ inch
Head: Dark brownish, 1/16 inch

Hook: Sizes 14-16 Mustad 9672 3X long
Nylon: Dark brown 6/0 nylon
Gills: Dark grayish hackle palmered along body
Body: Dark muskrat dubbing
Thorax: Dark muskrat dubbing
Legs: Dark grayish hackle palmered along thorax
Head: Dark brown nylon

11. Black Whirligig Beetle Larva (*Gyrinus nigritus*)

These dark little larvae average about three-eighths inch in length and are agile swimmers, feeding on Diptera larvae and tiny nymphs.

Gills: Black, ⅛ inch
Body: Dark brownish black, ¼ inch
Thorax: Dark brownish black, ⅛ inch
Legs: Black, ⅛ inch
Head: Black, 1/16 inch

Hook: Size 16 Mustad 9672 3X long
Nylon: Black 6/0 nylon
Gills: Black hackle stripped on one side and trimmed to ⅛-inch length on the other, palmer-tied along body
Body: Brownish black hare's mask dubbing
Thorax: Brownish black hare's mask dubbing
Legs: Black hen hackle
Head: Black nylon

12. Great Olive Whirligig Beetle Larva (*Dineutes vittatus*)

This is the largest of the fringe-gilled whirligig-beetle larvae, averaging about one and one-quarter inches at full growth. These larvae differ from the closely related *Gyrinus* forms through the fringeless gills on their first two body segments.

Gills: Medium olive, ¼ inch
Body: Brownish olive with pale olive median stripe, ⅞ inch
Thorax: Brownish olive with pale median stripe, 5/16 inch
Legs: Medium olive, 3/16 inch
Head: Medium olive, ⅛ inch

Hook: Sizes 6-10 Mustad 79580 4X long
Nylon: Olive 6/0 nylon
Gills: Brown-olive dyed hackles stripped on one side and trimmed to length to simulate tracheal gills
Body: Olive-dyed rabbit fur dubbing roughly spun with guard hairs, with single strand of flat monofilament tied in at hook bend, secured under palmered hackle, and tied off at head
Thorax: Olive-dyed rabbit mixed with guard hairs
Legs: Brown olive-dyed hen hackle
Head: Olive-dyed dubbing

13. Dark Whirligig Beetle Larva (*Dineutes discolor*)

This little blackish-brown species averages seven-eighths inch in length, and is particularly agile in its movements.

Gills: Dark brownish, ¼ inch
Body: Dark brownish black, 9/16 inch
Thorax: Dark brownish black, ¼ inch
Legs: Dark brownish, ¼ inch
Head: Dark brownish black, ⅛ inch

Hook: Sizes 10-14 Mustad 9672 3X long
Nylon: Dark brown 6/0 nylon
Gills: Dark fiery brown hackle stripped off on one side and trimmed on the other to simulate gills
Body: Dark brownish black hare's mask dubbing
Thorax: Dark brownish black hare's mask dubbing
Legs: Dark fiery brown hen hackle
Head: Dark brown nylon

14. Yellow Whirligig Beetle Larva (*Dineutes emarginatus*)

This pale little species is common in quiet, sunny backwaters where it swims and clambers along the bottom.

Gills: Pale grayish dun, ⅛ inch
Body: Pale olive yellow, ¼ inch
Thorax: Pale olive yellow, 3/16 inch
Legs: Pale grayish dun, 3/16 inch
Head: Pale olive, 1/16 inch

Hook: Sizes 14-16 Mustad 9672 3X long
Nylon: Pale olive 6/0 nylon
Gills: Pale grayish dun hackle stripped on one side and trimmed to simulate gills palmered along the body
Body: Pale olive grayish dubbing
Thorax: Pale olive grayish dubbing
Legs: Pale grayish dun hen hackle
Head: Pale olive nylon

15. Gray Scavenger Beetle Larva (*Hydrophilus obtusatus*)

The same shallow-water habitat that shelters the *Dysticus* and *Cybister* larvae offers a favorable environment to the smaller but equally aggressive scavenger beetle larvae. These little half-inch larvae feed on decaying matter, but they also eat plant material and living organisms. The *Hydrophilus* larvae hold their heads and thoracic segments in the surface film to breathe. They are equipped with powerful mandibles, club-shaped antennae, and slender palpi that are sometimes mistaken for antennae.

Body: Dark grayish, 5/16 inch
Gills: Dark iron-blue dun colored, ⅛ inch
Thorax: Dark grayish, 3/16 inch
Legs: Dark iron-blue dun, ⅛ inch
Head: Dark grayish, 1/16 inch

Hook: Sizes 14-16 Mustad 9671 2X long
Nylon: Dark gray 6/0 nylon
Body: Dark hare's mask dubbing
Gills: Dark iron-blue dun hackle stripped off on one side and trimmed off to simulate gills, palmer-tied along body
Thorax: Dark hare's mask dubbing
Legs: Dark iron-blue dun hen hackle
Head: Dark gray nylon

16. Black Scavenger Beetle Larva (*Hydrophilus triangularis*)

This relatively large scavenger larva is virtually black, and measures approximately three-quarters inch in length.

Body: Dark brownish black, ⅜ inch
Gills: Dark iron-blue dun, ⅛ inch
Thorax: Dark brownish black, 3/16 inch
Legs: Dark iron-blue dun, ¼ inch
Head: Dark brownish black, 3/16 inch

Hook: Sizes 10-12 Mustad 9672 3X long
Nylon: Black 6/0 nylon
Body: Dark brownish black hare's mask dubbing
Gills: Dark iron-blue hackle stripped on one side and trimmed to simulate gills, palmer-tied along body
Thorax: Dark brownish black hare's mask dubbing
Legs: Dark iron-blue hen hackle
Head: Dark hare's mask dubbing

17. Brown Scavenger Beetle Larva (*Tropisternus lateralis*)

These larvae usually measure from one-half to three-quarters inch in length, and abound in most habitat suitable for the aquatic species of the Coleoptera. These medium-sized larvae are perhaps the most common of the American species. They are virtually omnivorous, eating plant materials as voraciously as they kill living subaquatic prey. Extremely agile, these larvae exert themselves so much in hunting that they demand a constant supply of oxygen. Therefore they usually swim to the nearest water plant or stick after seizing their prey. The larva then backs up toward the surface, its struggling food still locked in its strong mandibles, until its body filaments can breathe in the meniscus and sustain its metabolic needs. The voracity and gluttony of these larvae are virtually unmatched, even among the bigger water tigers of the *Cybister* and *Dysticus* groups.

Body: Dark brownish gray, ½ inch
Gills: Dark brownish, 1/16 inch
Thorax: Dark brownish gray, 3/16 inch
Legs: Dark brownish, ⅛ inch
Head: Dark brownish, ⅛ inch

Hook: Sizes 10-14 Mustad 79580 4X long
Nylon: Dark brown 6/0 nylon
Body: Dark gray hare's mask dubbing mixed with guard hairs
Gills: Dark brown hackle stripped on one side and trimmed short to simulate gills, **palmer**-tied along body
Thorax: Dark gray hare's mask mixed with guard hairs
Legs: Dark brown hen hackle
Head: Dark brown nylon

18. Brown Algae Larva (*Berosus americanus*)

These are extremely hardy little beetle larvae, measuring about three-eighths inch in length. Their food is primarily green algae, in both the larval and adult stages. Their movements are quite sluggish along the bottom, and since their respiratory system relies on tracheal gill-spines along their bodies, these *Berosus* larvae need not leave the bottom chara and nitella weed to breathe. Such small fringed-gilled larvae undoubtedly explain the success of weighted palmer-tied wet flies fished slow and deep.

Berosus larva

Body: Dark brownish gray, ¼ inch
Gills: Dark brown, 3/16 inch
Thorax: Dark brownish gray, ⅛ inch
Legs: Dark brown, 1/16 inch
Head: Dark brown, 1/16 inch

Hook: Sizes 14-16 Mustad 9671 2X long
Nylon: Dark brown 6/0 nylon
Body: Dark muskrat dubbing
Gills: Dark brown Palmer-tied hackle along body
Thorax: Dark muskrat dubbing
Legs: Small brown hackle tied **palmer**-style, since legs are smaller than gill-length
Head: Dark brown nylon

19. Gray Riffle Beetle Larva (*Elmis sculptius*)

These are the only riffle beetle ecotypes that are clambering and swimming species. They resemble caddis fly larvae of the campodeiform type, the Trichoptera that do not build larval cases, instead of the water pennies of the beetle *Psephenus*.

Body: Pale grayish with darker dorsal surfaces and posterior segments, ½ inch
Thorax: Dark grayish with darker dorsal surface, ¼ inch
Legs: Dark grayish brown, 3/16 inch
Head: Dark brownish, 1/16 inch

Hook: Sizes 10-14 Mustad 79580 4X long
Nylon: Dark brown 6/0 nylon
Body: Dark grayish muskrat dubbing tightly ribbed with fine flat monofilament, after darkening the dorsal surfaces with a dark brown felt-tipped pen
Thorax: Dark grayish muskrat dubbing marked with felt-tipped pen
Legs: Dark brown hen hackle palmer-tied at thorax
Head: Dark brown nylon

Elmis larva

20. Yellow Riffle Beetle Larva (*Elmis occidentalis*)

Encountering these cream-colored larvae in the stomachs of Colorado brook trout, we were first convinced that they were immature caddis flies. The species was quite numerous that spring in the inlet of Hermit Lake, and the fish fed on them ravenously. However, the relative absence of gills on the belly segments of the larvae, and the distinct angularity of the dorsal margins, are clear points separating these subaquatic beetle larvae from the caddis worms.

Body: Dirty yellowish cream with brownish dorsal surfaces, ½ inch
Thorax: Dirty yellowish gray with dark sepia dorsal surfaces, ¼ inch
Legs: Medium brown, 3/16 inch
Head: Medium brown, 1/16 inch

Hook: Sizes 10-14 Mustad 79580 4X long
Nylon: Medium brown 6/0 nylon
Body: Dirty yellowish cream dubbing tightly ribbed with flat monofilament after dorsal surfaces are darkened with brown felt pen
Thorax: Dirty yellowish dubbing darkened with felt-tipped pen
Legs: Medium brown hen hackle
Head: Medium brown nylon

Studies of these several aquatic beetle larvae are a revelation in nymphal configurations unfamiliar to most anglers, and the sizable tracheal gill systems in such genera as *Peltodytes* and *Dineutes* and *Gyrinus* are the answer to a puzzle. There are a number of familiar wet flies with thickly dressed bodies and palmer-tied hackles that are regularly successful, without any apparent prototypes in subaquatic entomology.

Well, many anglers have asked over the years, *you believe in matching the hatch and the concept that an effective pattern can be traced to some counterpart in nature—but what about flies like the Grubs and Peacock Palmers and Woolly Worms?*

It is a question I once found difficult to answer, although I was convinced that the consistent success of such dressings had an ecotypical explanation in nature. The larvae of the subaquatic Coleoptera completed the missing pieces of that puzzle.

Fishing the Freshwater Crustaceans

It is a deep, spring-fed pond lined with oaks and hickory trees. Fat green-head mallards forage in its shallows. There are extensive chalk-colored marl beds and deep holes in the weeds, where the bottom is swimming-pool green with algae. Thick beds of chara and nitella are rooted in the rich silt of the bottom. Below the swamp maples at the outlet channel, these candelabra-shaped stoneworts are a dense underwater forest.

The stones that line the outlet are covered with pale *Spirogyra*, its interlacing hair-fine strands undulating almost imperceptibly in the flow. The concrete abutments of the outlet weir are brown with the gelatinous growths of microscopic *Rivularia* algae. These beds of algae are thick with dense colonies of tiny desmids; the leaf-drift and deadfalls in the shallows are covered with minute single-celled diatomaceous life. These delicate little diatoms and desmids are the microscopic food-chain beginnings of insect life in the pond, a fragile pyramid of subaquatic communities.

There are arrowhead and pickerelweed in the backwaters. The jackstraw tangle of dead trees lines the shallows of the upper pond, where the surface is thick with frog spittle. *Utricularia* beds shelter a rich ecosystem of life there, from the plantlike organisms which depend on photosynthesis, and in turn feed the tiny nymphs and larvae, to the larger predatory beetle larvae and dragonfly nymphs and crustaceans which prey on them. Ultimately, this intricate chain of life leads to the fat, sleek-bodied trout themselves—graceful and richly spotted and shy, cruising the pale-green weeds in search of their breakfast.

The morning sun is already high above the pond. Its sheltering weeds and pale-marl sinks and gravelly shallows are revealed in the naked light. Earlier the trout were rising, ranging just under the surface at daylight in search of mayfly nymphs and freshly hatched flies, but now the brightness has forced them deep over the moss. The sunlight exposed them to their enemies, and this cool forest-lined pond attracts its share of fish ducks and sharp-billed kingfishers and herons.

It also has a good population of rainbow trout. There is an occasional survivor of the original brook-trout population mixed with the introduced species. The pond is especially rich in tiny scuds and freshwater shrimps and sowbugs. This diet of minute crustaceans conditions the trout beautifully; their flesh is firm and almost salmon-colored. The spotted flanks of the rainbows are richly patterned, and their gill covers and sides are a bright carmine. The brookies are strongly vermiculated on their backs, and heavily spotted with scarlet and olive. Their lower fins are bright orange, boldly edged with black and white. Fishing pressure has made these fish shy and selective. Although they witness a parade of flies every week, these are conventional dry flies and winged wet flies and streamers, and are seldom imitative patterns. Such offerings work sometimes, but imitations of the small crustaceans that throng the weeds are a better choice.

Tony Coe and I were fishing it a few years ago on such a bright spring morning. Good rainbows were cruising in twos and threes over the pale-green *Spirogyra* beds. Several times a fat two-pound trout passed in the bright sunlight, foraging over the bottom in about six to eight feet of water. Three times I watched the rainbow open and close its jaws, taking some thing deep with a white flash of its mouth.

They're feeding! I yelled.

Where? Tony answered. *There aren't any rises.*

Right over the moss, I said. *I'm watching them take something just above the weeds—probably scuds and shrimps.*

What will they take?

Weighted shrimp on a sinking line, I shouted back.

That sinking-line stuff's not my speed, Tony said. *They'll have to take this dry fly or go hungry!*

Purist! I shouted.

There were only two surface rises all morning, both deep in the shade of a swamp maple along the path. The fish stayed down over the algae and candelabra-weed, cruising in plain view as they passed. Catching them with a weighted shrimp proved surprisingly easy, although it lacked the delicacy of the dry-fly method.

The technique was simple enough. However, it did require concentration and sharp powers of observation. Like a salt water fly-fisherman, I waited with coils of line, and a shooting head stripped beyond the tip guide. The rest was watching and timing. It involved waiting for several trout to cruise within range, observing their pattern of feeding, and casting well ahead of them to give the line and weighted shrimp enough time to sink to their feeding level. It took a few casts to get the timing right. Finally, I got the sink rate of the line correct, and deduced what windage was required to place the cast far enough ahead of the fish for the weighted shrimp to reach their level just before they reached it. The rest was simply a matter of watching a trout turn as the starting retrieve caught its attention, and striking as its jaws closed.

The score for the morning was twenty-three trout, the best a strong four-pound rainbow that took the hand-twist retrieve in plain view above the weeds. There was a moment of suspense while it approached the sinking shrimp fly, its broad stripe and rose-colored gill covers clearly visible.

The hand-twist retrieve started slowly, and the big rainbow turned curiously. *Take it!* I whispered.

Its jaws opened and the sunlight flashed as it turned with the shrimp securely hooked in its tongue. Fish hooked there usually fight with a dash of wildness, and this trout was no exception. Twice it ran across the pond, the delicate little Hardy protesting shrilly, and three times it cartwheeled into the sun. It was the climax of a fine morning, fishing the weighted little shrimp on a delicate 6X tippet. There was no surface feeding.

The freshwater crustaceans are widely distributed in American waters, particularly those with high alkalinity and good oxygenation through photosynthesis. Some of the most famous trout streams and mountain lakes are rich with these small Amphipoda and fairy shrimps and sowbugs. The checklist of famous lakes would have to include remote brook trout fisheries like Ashuanipi and Assinica, sprawling Yellowstone and Henry's Lake in the Rocky Mountains, famous fly-fishing lakes like Davis and Hosmer in Oregon, the score of British Columbia lakes half-legendary for their Kamloops rainbows, and thousands of lesser-known waters rich in weeds and crustaceans. Streams famous for their scuds and shrimps and sowbugs include the weedy limestone rivers of Pennsylvania—particularly the Little Lehigh and Big Spring and storied Letort Spring Run. The South Platte in Colorado, the several spring creeks of Jackson Hole, the Firehole and Gibbon and Madison in the Yellowstone, the spring creeks of Montana, Silver Creek and the Teton in Idaho, and Hot Creek in the Sierras are all fisheries rich in crustaceans. These little organisms are worth our study, since they form an important part of the trout diet.

Freshwater crustaceans form a somewhat more limited spectrum of organisms than their saltwater cousins. Marine forms include a galaxy of lobsters, crayfish, crabs, shrimps, and prawns. Freshwater ecotypes include the true *Paleamonetes* prawns, the crayfish, fairy shrimps, scuds, and sowbugs. There are also a multitude of minute crustaceans like water fleas, copepods, and ostracods in freshwater ponds and lakes, forms so microscopic and transparent that they are virtually impossible to imitate. The *Daphnia* water fleas are typical of these organisms.

Superficially, crustaceans resemble insects in their jointed appendages, although in the crustacea there are many more of these joints. Unlike the insects, these little shrimplike organisms have heads that are broadly jointed, and a definite neck structure is lacking. They breathe with a system of abdominal gills. Their bodies are enclosed in a hard exoskeleton secreted by a layer of cells just under its surfaces. That shell can be firm and lime-hard, which accounts for their abundance in alkaline waters, or virtually transparent like the tiny *Daphnia*. Lime and calcium entrained in the water form the material of these shells. During their growth, the crustaceans change shells just as insect forms molt between instar stages.

The crustaceans have intricately jointed bodies, antennae, legs, and even mouth parts. The larger forms like the crayfish visibly demonstrate these multijointed anatomies. Such jointed appendages are both the most diverse and the most characteristic quality of all crustaceans. These structures clearly demonstrate their functions of breathing, swimming, eating, and reproduction.

Nearly all of the crustaceans breathe through gills. Crayfish have their gill systems on each side of the thorax, protected by the shell-like carapace which covers the thoracic structure and head. Water continually flows past and between these gills. The fairy shrimps and scuds have ventrally located gill structures.

Crustaceans are divided into two principal groups. The larger ecotypes

134

are classified under the Malacostraca, while the smaller forms are the Entomostraca. The crayfish, freshwater shrimps, scuds, and sowbugs are taxonometrically included in the former group, while the fairy shrimps, water fleas, and copepods are placed in the latter. Since the copepods and water fleas are too tiny and transparent for imitation, the only member of the Entomostraca of interest to the fly-fisher is the fairy shrimp.

1. Fairy Shrimp (*Eubranchipus vernalis*)

Eubranchipus vernalis

The fairy shrimps are classified in the suborder Branchiopoda, and measure between five-eighths inch and an inch in length. Common colors are amber, olive, and pale bronze. They are the largest of their order, distinguished by the leaflike appendages of their feet. These leaflike systems are really both feet and gills combined, carried on the body segments behind their heads. Fairy shrimps always swim on their backs, waving the gill-plumes of their feet above them. Therefore, the imitations should be weighted so the hook shanks ride down like a keel. These little crustaceans are so transparent that it is possible to observe the beating of the slender coils of their cardio-vascular systems.

Female fairy shrimps are infinitely more abundant than males, which accounts for the remarkable fecundity of these little crustaceans. Mating occurs when the males and females swim together, the male clasping the female to his ventral surfaces. Just behind the gills, located on segment eleven of the body of the fairy shrimp, are the tubelike penes which transfer the sperm cells to the females. The females of the *Eubranchipus* shrimps carry the fertilized eggs in conspicuous brood pouches until the young actually hatch.

Fairy shrimps live in small cold-water habitats, and are widely distributed in American waters. They cavort actively on their backs, and while they are most active in the months of late winter and early spring, they oviposit their ova into the bottom silt and trash.

Their food consists of microscopic organisms, protozoans and diatomaceous life, and other algae which share their shallow spring-fed ponds. These foods are gathered in a foot-trough formed between the gill feet and transferred to the mouth.

Uropods: Tan, amber or olive, 1/16 inch
Bodies: Tan, amber or olive, ⅜ inch
Thorax: Tan, amber or olive, ⅝ inch
Gills: Tan, amber or olive, ⅛ inch
Legs: Tan, amber or olive, ¼ inch
Head: Tan, amber or olive, 1/16 inch

Hook: Sizes 8-14 Mustad 38941 sproat 3X long
Nylon: Tan, amber or olive 6/0 nylon
Uropods: Tan, amber or olive fibers tied short
Bodies: Tan, amber or olive dubbing mixed with hare's mask, ribbed with fine monofilament
Thorax: Tan, amber or olive dubbing guard hairs ribbed with fine gold wire
Gills: Tan, amber or olive marabou fibers tightly bunched under the thorax
Legs: Legs and gills are identical
Head: Tan, amber or olive nylon

The Malacostraca are perhaps best known for the crayfish, the common crustaceans classified in the genus *Cambarus*. Crayfish are often found in quiet waters of our streams, and under the stones in the swifter currents. Crayfish much prefer the hard-water chemistry of our alkaline watersheds, scuttling about to scavenge food from decaying organisms and tiny fishes. The genus is omnivorous, eating insects and plant life as well.

The eggs and young are carried beneath the short swimmers, under the abdomen. The gills are along the sides, between the roots of the legs and sheltered under the overhanging carapace of the thoracic shell.

Crayfish have five pairs of legs, the first pair armed with conspicuous lobsterlike claws. Some species mate in the autumn and spawn the following spring, while others mate and oviposit their eggs throughout the entire year. The eggs hatch after seven to eight weeks. The tiny crayfish larvae ride the legs and swimmers of their mothers as long as a week.

These crayfish are three to four inches in length at full growth, too large to serve as prototypes for flies, but the smaller suborders of the Malacostraca are important both as trout foods and the source of imitative fly patterns. These are the true freshwater shrimps of the *Palaemonetes* genus, the scuds, and the sowbugs. Scuds are a rather large and widely distributed group, classified under the suborder Amphipoda. The sowbugs are flat little crustaceans designated among the suborder Isopoda, and are widely distributed in American waters.

2. Freshwater Shrimp (*Palaemonetes paludosa*)

These are the true miniature prawns or freshwater shrimps, and are alkaline-loving organisms. Full-grown freshwater prawns measure about an inch in length.

Uropods: Dark olive grayish, 3/16 inch
Bodies: Dark olive grayish, ⅜ inch
Thorax: Dark olive grayish, ⅝ inch
Gills: Dark olive grayish, ⅛ inch
Legs: Dark olive grayish, ½ inch
Head: Dark olive grayish, ⅛ inch

Hook: Sizes 8-12 Mustad 3906B Sproat 1X long
Nylon: Olive 6/0 nylon
Uropods: Olive fibers tied short
Body: Olive dubbing mixed with hare's mask guard hairs
Overbody: Matte vinyl over dorsal surfaces, secured with fine monofilament
Springers: Dark olive-dyed pheasant hackle fibers
Thorax: Olive dubbing mixed with hare's mask
Legs: Olive-dyed pheasant hackle fibers
Antennae: Olive-dyed pheasant fibers
Head: Olive nylon

The suborder Amphipoda consists of the shrimplike scuds that have long been mistakenly called freshwater shrimps, perhaps because they were originally called Caledonia shrimps. That popular name came from Seth Green, who designed the prototypical trout hatcheries using water from the famous Caledonia Springs in New York. The watercress that grew profusely at Caledonia sheltered *Gammarus limnaeus* in incredible numbers, and these prolific little scuds became known as Caledonia shrimp. There are many other species found in our American trout waters.

Freshwater scuds are much smaller than the crayfish, and have quite a different configuration. These Amphipoda are excitingly agile acrobats, climbing and jumping and darting rhythmically through the water. Their configuration is relatively flealike, with a curved body shell. There are climbing legs at the thorax, under the narrow, arch-backed bodies, with swimming and jumping appendages under their bellies. The coloring of the freshwater scuds is typically yellowish gray, olive, tan, gray, or pale brown. They love the weedy growth of quiet ponds and slow-flowing currents, clambering and darting among the interlacing stems. They are voracious scavengers, cleaning the bottom of dead fish and other carrion.

The *Gammarus* scuds are the largest of the American species in the suborder Amphipoda, and its fully developed crustaceans measure three-quarters inch to an inch in length. They are present throughout the year in both streams and ponds. Their period of fertility lasts from April through November, and their fertility is so high that a single female can produce more than twenty eggs every two weeks. It has been established that a single pair of the species *Gammarus fasciatus* might spawn over twenty thousand progeny per year. The genus is particularly fond of hard water, demonstrated by its relative absence from habitats lacking as much as seventy-five parts per million calcium. It loves streams with watercress and chara, and in western spring creeks displaying rich alkalinity, more than five thousand scuds have been harvested from a cubic foot of elodea weed. Scuds are widely distributed in American waters and apparently prefer cold springfed habitats of relatively constant flowage. The ability to thrive is apparently related to relatively low water temperatures, alkalinity, and the sustenance and shelter provided by luxuriant aquatic weed.

The genus is clearly identifiable through its first antennae, which are longer than the second pair, and its possession of secondary flagella. There are hairy filaments on the dorsal surfaces of the last three abdominal segments. There are small posterior appendages on the abdomen.

3. Gray Freshwater Scud (*Gammarus fasciatus*)

This species is widely distributed in American waters, its grayish specimens ranging from five-eighths inch to an inch in length.

Uropods: Dark grayish, 1/16 inch
Body: Dark grayish, ½ inch
Springers: Dark grayish, ⅝ inch
Thorax: Dark grayish, ½ inch
Legs: Dark grayish, ⅜ inch
Antennae: Dark grayish, ⅜ inch
Head: Dark grayish, ⅛ inch

Hook: Sizes 6-10 Mustad 3906B sproat 1X long
Nylon: Dark gray 6/0 nylon
Uropods: Dark grayish fibers tied short
Body: Dark grayish dubbing mixed with hare's mask
Overbody: Matte vinyl over dorsal surfaces, secured with fine monofilament
Springers: Dark grayish pheasant hackle fibers
Thorax: Dark grayish dubbing mixed with hare's mask
Legs: Grayish mottled pheasant hackle fibers
Antennae: Grayish pheasant hackle fibers
Head: Gray nylon

4.   Olive Freshwater Scud (*Gammarus limnaeus*)

These agile little crustaceans are the ecotype found in rich populations at Caledonia, when Seth Green designed and constructed the first American trout hatchery in New York. Adult scuds of this species are between one-half and seven-eighths inch in length.

Uropods: Olive grayish, 1/16 inch
Body: Olive grayish, 7/16 inch
Springers: Olive grayish, ½ inch
Thorax: Olive grayish, 7/16 inch
Legs: Olive grayish, 5/16 inch
Antennae: Olive grayish, 5/16 inch
Head: Olive grayish, 3/32 inch

Hook: Sizes 6-12 Mustad 38941 sproat 3X long
Nylon: Dark olive 6/0 nylon
Uropods: Dark olive grayish fibers tied in halfway around hook bend
Bodies: Dark olive grayish dubbing with matte vinyl dorsal overlay secured with fine monofilament ribbing.
Thorax: Dark olive grayish dubbing with matte vinyl dorsal overlay secured with fine gold wire ribbing
Gills: Dark grayish guard hairs mixed with thorax
Legs: Dark olive-dyed gray partridge hackle fibers
Head: Dark olive nylon

5.   Yellow Freshwater Scud (*Gammarus minus*)

These pale little crustaceans are common in the watercress currents of the eastern limestone streams, hiding in the elodea and stonewort and milfoil. It is identified from ecotypes collected in the spring creeks around Bellefonte in Pennsylvania, and its specimens are between three-eighths and one-half inch in length.

Uropods: Pale yellowish olive, 1/32 inch
Body: Pale yellowish olive, ¼ inch
Springers: Pale yellowish olive, ⅜ inch
Thorax: Pale yellowish olive, ¼ inch
Legs: Pale yellowish olive, 3/16 inch
Antennae: Pale yellowish olive, 3/16 inch
Head: Pale yellowish olive, 1/16 inch

Hook: Sizes 10-14 Mustad 3906B Sproat 1X long
Nylon: Pale olive 6/0 nylon
Uropods: Pale yellowish olive fibers tied short
Body: Pale yellowish olive dubbing mixed with hare's mask
Overbody: Matte vinyl over dorsal surfaces, secured with fine monofilament
Springers: Pale yellowish olive-dyed pheasant fibers
Thorax: Pale yellowish olive mixed with hare's mask
Legs: Pale yellowish olive-dyed pheasant fibers
Antennae: Pale yellowish olive fibers
Head: Pale olive nylon

The freshwater scuds of the genus *Eucrangonyx* are widely distributed in swampy, spring-fed waters of limited alkalinity. They are quite similar to *Gammarus* taxonometrically, but are not nearly as numerous in population. The genus can be distinguished through its lack of hairy filaments on its dorsal posterior segments. The rather small posterior appendages on the abdomen are rudimentary.

6.   Tan Freshwater Scud (*Eucrangonyx gracilus*)

These medium-sized scuds love waters of low alkalinity, and are approximately three-eighths to one-half inch in length.

Uropods: Tannish gray, 1/32 inch
Body: Tannish gray, ¼ inch
Springers: Tannish gray, ⅜ inch
Thorax: Tannish gray, ¼ inch
Legs: Tannish gray, 3/16 inch
Antennae: Tannish gray, 3/16 inch
Head: Tannish gray, 1/16 inch

Hook: Sizes 10-14 Mustad 3906B
Sproat 1X long
Nylon: Tan 6/0 nylon
Uropods: Tannish gray fibers tied short
Body: Tannish dubbing mixed with hare's mask
Overbody: Matte vinyl secured with fine monofilament
Springers: Tannish pheasant fibers
Thorax: Tannish dubbing mixed with hare's mask
Legs: Tannish pheasant fibers
Antennae: Tannish pheasant fibers
Head: Tan nylon

Freshwater scuds of the genus *Hyalella* are the smallest of these prolific little crustaceans. They are extremely common. During the weeks of early spring, these tiny scuds are thick in the undulating *Spirogyra*, feeding on decaying plant materials. Later, the scuds are omnivorous, eating dead organisms like snails and tadpoles and fish. Some biologists have observed these scuds devouring drowned animals and avifauna, and they are equally fond of decaying stonewort and elodea and pondweed.

During their mating, the males clasp the females with their grasping legs, and swim in animated fashion, holding them beneath their bodies for several days. Females carry their newly hatched young for a time in their thoracic pouches, often still sheltering a prior brood during a new mating swim. The fecundity of a single pair of *Hyalella* is such that they can spawn a clutch of fifteen to twenty eggs every ten days, over a period as long as five months.

Although smaller than either *Gammarus* or *Eucrangonyx*, these little scuds are more widely distributed. They are far more tolerant of varied water chemistry, thriving in both alkaline and acid environments. They are found in both warm and cold waters. Silt bottoms or weedy growths are equally acceptable, as well as both lakes and streams. *Hyalella* is distinguished by its two projecting spinules on the dorsal surfaces of the posterior abdominal segments. Its first antennae are typically shorter than its second pair, and the dorsal hairs of *Gammarus* are also lacking. Paul Needham records a survey of trout available in more than seventy Oregon lakes in his book *Trout Streams*. Scuds were identified from more than half of those lakes, primarily of the *Hyalella* genus. It was found from relatively low-altitude lakes of five thousand feet, and in lakes as high as ten thousand feet. It has been collected at still higher altitudes in Colorado, and I have specimens of *Gammarus* from spring-fed bogs in the Rocky Mountains at altitudes as high as nine thousand feet.

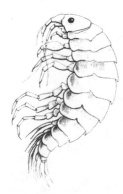

Hyalella americana

7. Tiny Yellow Scud (*Hyalella americana*)

This species averages about one-eighth to one-quarter inch in length at full development.

Uropods: Dirty yellowish olive, 1/32 inch
Body: Dirty yellowish olive, 1/16 inch
Springers: Dirty yellowish olive, 1/16 inch
Thorax: Dirty yellowish olive, 1/16 inch
Legs: Dirty yellowish olive, 1/32 inch
Antennae: Dirty yellowish olive, 1/16 inch
Head: Dirty yellowish olive, 1/32 inch

Hook: Sizes 16-18 Mustad 3906 sproat
Nylon: Yellow olive 6/0 nylon
Uropods: Short yellowish olive fibers
Body: Yellowish olive dubbing mixed with guard hairs
Overbody: Matte vinyl secured with fine gold wire
Springers: Omit
Thorax: Yellowish olive dubbing mixed with guard hairs
Legs: Yellowish olive marabou fibers
Antennae: Yellowish olive fibers
Head: Yellow olive nylon

8.   Tiny Gray Scud (*Hyalella knickerbockeri*)

This prolific little freshwater scud averages one-eighth to one-quarter inch in length.

Uropods: Dark grayish, 1/32 inch
Body: Dark grayish, 1/16 inch
Springers: Dark grayish, 1/16 inch
Thorax: Dark grayish, 1/16 inch
Legs: Dark grayish, 1/32 inch
Antennae: Dark grayish, 1/16 inch
Head: Dark grayish, 1/32 inch

Hook: Sizes 16-18 Mustad 3906 sproat
Nylon: Light gray 6/0 nylon
Uropods: Short grayish fibers
Body: Medium grayish dubbing mixed with guard hairs
Overbody: Matte vinyl secured with fine gold wire
Springers: Omit
Thorax: Medium grayish dubbing mixed with guard hairs
Legs: Medium gray marabou fibers
Antennae: Medium gray fibers
Head: Yellow olive nylon

9.   Tiny Olive Scud (*Hyalella azteca*)

This is a widely distributed American species, particularly in the lakes and watersheds of our western mountains, and it averages approximately one-eighth to one-quarter inch.

Uropods: Medium olive gray, 1/32 inch
Body: Medium olive gray, 1/16 inch
Springers: Medium olive gray, 1/16 inch
Thorax: Medium olive gray, 1/16 inch
Legs: Medium olive gray, 1/32 inch
Antennae: Medium olive gray, 1/16 inch
Head: Medium olive gray, 1/32 inch

Hook: Sizes 16-18 Mustad 3906 sproat
Nylon: Olive 6/0 nylon
Uropods: Short olive fibers
Body: Medium olive dubbing mixed with guard hairs
Overbody: Matte vinyl secured with fine gold wire
Springers: Omit
Thorax: Medium olive dubbing mixed with guard hairs
Legs: Medium olive marabou fibers
Antennae: Medium olive fibers
Head: Olive nylon

The sowbugs are tiny, broad-backed little crustaceans classified in the suborder Isopoda. Their optimal habitat is found in quiet currents of watercress and leaf-drifts and pondweed. They are a remarkable fourteen-legged crustacean, with their legs held quite flat toward the sides. They are a relatively omnivorous scavenger form, but decaying vegetation is their principal staple. Sowbugs are readily taken by trout and are surprisingly agile in their weedbed foraging for food and shelter. Their mating begins in early spring and continues throughout the summer months, producing a fresh brood of fifteen to twenty eggs every five to six weeks. Females are typically sheltering the past brood of tiny sowbugs when they begin a fresh mating cycle.

Some biologists have described them as a minute armadillo-like little crustacean, and the sowbugs are so very numerous in alkaline waters that several thousand are not unusual in a cubic foot of elodea or watercress.

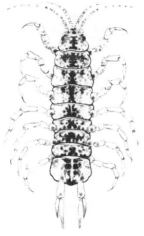

Asellus communis

10.   American Sowbug (*Asellus communis*)

These widely distributed little crustaceans measure about seven-eighths inch at maximum growth, but most specimens average from three-eighths to five-eighths inch in size.

Uropods: Dark grayish, ⅛ inch
Body: Dark grayish, 5/16 inch
Swimmers: Dark grayish, ⅜ inch
Thorax: Dark grayish, ⅜ inch
Legs: Dark grayish, ¼ inch
Antennae: Dark grayish, ⅜ inch
Head: Dark grayish, 1/16 inch

Hook: Sizes 14-16 Mustad 3906 sproat
Nylon: Dark gray 6/0 nylon
Uropods: Dark grayish
Body: Dark grayish muskrat dubbing on flat base
Swimmers: Dark grayish pheasant fibers
Thorax: Dark grayish muskrat dubbing on flat base
Legs: Dark grayish pheasant fiibers
Antennae: Dark grayish fibers
Head: Dark gray

These several suborders of crustaceans and the myriad little freshwater prawns, scuds, and sowbugs their group encompasses are a major part of the trout diet across the United States. The description of fishing their imitations in that rich little spring-fed pond on Long Island is typical of tactics with the tiny crustaceans where the fish are visible. Since all of these crustaceans swim backwards, their imitations should be tied in reverse, with their heads seated halfway around the hook-bend. Dave Whitlock bends the shanks of his books sharply upward 25 percent of the length behind the eyes. His theory argues that this crimped shank suggests the curvilinear tails of the scuds. There are also places where such weighted shrimp flies must be fished deep in the channels above the unseen weeds.

Perhaps the best places to find trout, particularly the larger trout in lakes and reservoirs and ponds, are the outlets of lakes and the inlets of all three types of water. Their foods are primarily found in relatively shallow water, both because photosynthesis is dependent upon the penetration of sunlight into the aquatic ecosystem, and because insects and crustaceans and tiny fish find both food and shelter in the shallows. Most lakes and ponds are inhabited entirely by the stillwater forms of life, except in windy regions where the continuous wave action on a reef or rocky shore produces oxygenation rivaling the dissolved oxygen of a tumbling stream. However, the currents of inlets and outlets also shelter organisms requiring the higher concentrations of oxygen implicit in certain nymphs and larvae, and such channels shelter a more diverse spectrum of life than the rest of the lake or pond. The fish simply forage where food is readily available.

The countdown method of fishing a freshwater shrimp or scud imitation at Henry's Lake in Idaho is a matter of discipline and patience. Bergman described it years ago in his book *Trout,* with an anecdote about twilight fishing with wet flies in the inlet channels of Cranberry Lake, the logging impoundment on the Oswegatchie in the Adirondacks. It is doubtful if Bergman realized that his three-fly cast of conventional wet flies was probably taken because his presentation suggested the tiny freshwater crustaceans deep in the channel.

However, the method involves selecting an inlet channel in the weeds, whether in a remote Maine pond or a weedy reservoir in the foothills of Oregon. The weighted shrimp should be fished on a sinking line. It should be cast well across the channel and allowed to sink without retrieving, while the fisherman counts, perhaps to ten or twenty, depending on the estimated depth. The object of this initial reconnaissance is establishing the length of time required for his cast to sink.

Should the first few casts fish back without touching the moss, the angler must keep adding seconds to his countdown until he finds the level of the weeds. That depth is defined when the retrieve is actually felt ticking along the bottom growth. With that depth established, he should shorten his count so the fly fishes back in the zone just above the beds, where the naturals are found.

The rest is patience, counting each time while the cast sinks. The angler should cover the inlet with a clockwise, fan-shaped pattern of casts, each placed about two feet farther around an imaginary clockface. Such a pattern should intercept any cruising fish, and the countdown will place the nymph at the proper depth. Hooking a fish against the drag of a sinking line fished at such depths is not difficult if a few brief points are mastered. The line should be held under the index finger against the cork grip, the rod tip should be pointed directly at the retrieving fly, the rod should be held low along the water, and the strike on feeling the tugging pull of a fish should be firm enough to tighten the deep belly of sinking line.

The Larval Forms of the Sialidae

Sugar Creek winds sluggishly through farmlands until it reaches the limestone country below Crawfordsville. Its currents enter a steep-walled channel near Turkey Run, with pale limestone ledges rising above the river. Its still pools are milky with the silt of the farm country upstream, but there are reaches of swift water too, where the river is shallow and relatively clear. It has been more than thirty years, but I remember one morning on a swift bedrock riffle on the Sugar that produced a four-pound smallmouth on my wriggling, live-minnow bait.

Sometimes we learn something about trout fishing in our experiences with other species, and this summer morning on Sugar Creek in southern Indiana introduced me to the Sialidae. The four-pound bass struggled with a stubborn power that almost frightened me, since I was only ten that summer, and another fisherman walked upstream to help.

Finally the big smallmouth surrendered, and I beached him eagerly on a gravel bar. The fish was exhausted and my arms were shaking, and we sat admiring his barred, bronze-green coloring in the bright sunlight.

The old bass fisherman was using shiners too, fishing them deep in the silken, foam-flecked pool downstream. His catch included two saugers, five smallmouth bass, and a fine three-pound channel cat. *Use shiners in them pools,* he explained, *but in them shallow places I use hellgrammites.*

What are hellgrammites?

They're big wigglers that live under the stones, he replied. *Come with me and I'll show you.*

The old man waded out into the swift shallows, motioned for me to follow him, and turned over several rocks. Suddenly his hand darted into the riffle and came up with an ugly two-inch larva. It wriggled fiercely and obviously tried to sink its impressive mandibles into his fingers.

Have to be careful, he laughed. *They bite!*

They're pretty mean-looking. I shuddered. *You sure the smallmouths really like them?*

He hooked the hellgrammite under the collar, and dropped it upstream from a glassy run below some rocks. It began to swing back, and he stripped off line to get it much deeper on a dead-drift along the bottom.

Suddenly the drift stopped, the line bellying downstream as a bass mouthed the bait. The old fisherman stripped in line imperceptibly until it throbbed with the weight of the fish. It moved a little upstream and finally the old man struck.

You've got one! I yelled.

142

The fish exploded in a shower of water. The old fisherman lowered his rod skillfully to parry the jump, and worked the bass patiently until it no longer had the strength to hold in the main current. Then he coaxed it to his simple aluminum-frame net and waded ashore.

You catch some hellgrammites. He unhooked the bass and clipped it to my stringer. *And you try in them fast pockets—hear?*

The old fisherman walked back downstream to the deep channel, and I fished hellgrammites in the broken water. This was an introduction to the Sialidae larvae that has proved unforgettable, and in the weeks that followed I studied several books on entomology to learn more about these ugly larvae that lived in fast water.

There are three members of the Sialidae family that are of interest to American trout fishermen. The alderflies, fishflies, and Dobsonflies are all important insects of the order Neuroptera that inhabit our rivers. Their adults are all four-winged flies, and have complex patterns of veins running throughout their wing structures. Their metamorphosis is complete, moving from larva to pupa and adult. Pupation always takes place in the moist soil of the stream bank.

Sialidae larvae live in extremely swift water, where they conceal themselves under the stones. They are frequently found in shallow riffles throughout the winter, and are rather omnivorous in their feeding. The larvae of the fishflies and Dobsonflies, the ugly pincered hellgrammites, are extremely predatory as well as plant-feeders.

1. American Alderfly Larva (*Sialis infumata*)

These little caddis fly-like insects are the American counterparts of *Sialis lutaria*, the British alderfly that has enriched the literature of angling since Charles Kingsley lovingly described it in his book *Chalkstream Studies* in 1858. It was his favorite fly pattern that became the well-known British alderfly imitation.

British anglers called them alderflies because large swarms filled the streamside bushes. These insects are clumsy in flight and easily captured, and will often run rather than fly when threatened. The American species is rather widely distributed, with specimens recorded from Quebec to Minnesota. It emerges in the first week in May on most waters, and insects hatch sporadically for several weeks.

The alderflies are extremely active in the bright spring sunshine, often laying their eggs at midday. These fertile ova are deposited in flat pancakes of two hundred to five hundred eggs. Oviposition usually occurs on a leaf, board, deadfall, or bridge abutment above the current. The ecloding larvae fall directly into the water.

Sialis larvae live in the sandy, silt-mixed bottoms and detritus of both streams and ponds. Sometimes they forage openly in the bottom trash, but in waters rich with more voracious predators, the larvae sometimes burrow into the silt. The related hellgrammites are often a mortal enemy.

The larvae are thick-skinned, with a pair of jointed tracheal gills fringed with hairlike filaments on each body segment. The abdominal posterior has a single fringed tail gill. They are quite predacious, even cannibalistic.

Pupation occurs in stream banks; full-grown, they average about an inch.

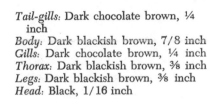

Tail-gill: Yellowish olive, 3/16 inch
Body: Mottled brownish, ⅝ inch
Gills: Yellowish olive, ⅛ inch
Thorax: Dirty mottled yellowish olive, ⅛ inch
Legs: Dirty yellowish olive, ⅛ inch
Head: Dirty mottled olive, 1/16 inch

Hook: Sizes 12-14 Mustad 79580 4X long
Nylon: Medium olive 6/0 nylon
Tail-gill: Dirty yellowish olive fibers
Body: Dark brownish hare's mask dubbing on pale yellow silk
Gills: Dirty yellowish olive hackle stripped on one side and trimmed short, winding it palmer-style the length of the body, trimming off fibers on dorsal and ventral surfaces
Thorax: Dirty yellowish olive dubbing
Legs: Dirty yellowish olive hen hackle fibers
Head: Medium olive nylon

2. Black Fishfly Larva (*Chauliodes pectinicornis*)

The medium-sized larvae of the *Chauliodes* flies superficially resemble the much larger hellgrammites. However, they lack the powerful mandibles and fringed gills of the *Corydalis* larvae. Unlike the hellgrammites, fishfly larvae are not limited to fast water alone, but are found inhabiting the bottom trash of eddies and backwaters.

Larval growth apparently lasts a year, and hatching is sporadic from late May until August. The larvae range from an inch to one and one-half inches at pre-hatch maturity. Both the larvae and the adults are never extremely abundant, but the trout take them eagerly.

The lateral tracheal gills of these flies are slender and spinelike.

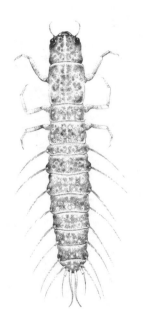

Chauliodes larva   (twice life size)

Tail-gills: Dark chocolate brown, ¼ inch
Body: Dark blackish brown, 7/8 inch
Gills: Dark chocolate brown, ¼ inch
Thorax: Dark blackish brown, ⅜ inch
Legs: Dark blackish brown, ⅜ inch
Head: Black, 1/16 inch

Hook: Sizes 6-10 Mustad 79580 4X long
Nylon: Black 6/0 nylon
Tail-gills: Dark chocolate brown fibers
Body: Dark brownish black dubbing wound over flattened core of two brass pins set at either side of hook shank
Gills: Dark chocolate brown hackle stripped on one side and trimmed to ¼ inch length on the other, palmer-tied the length of the body
Thorax: Dark brownish black dubbing covered with iron-blue dyed duck quill section over hackle legs
Legs: Dark chocolate brown hackles palmer-tied at thorax
Head: Black nylon

3. Hellgrammite Larva (*Corydalis cornuta*)

The larvae of the Dobsonflies are the hellgrammites, and were the bait used years ago by the old bass fisherman on Sugar Creek in southern Indiana. Their habitat is usually the swiftest part of the stream, where they conceal themselves under the stones. They are omnivorous, although the bulk of their diet is living organisms; they eat other nymphs and larvae.

When full-grown they can vary from two to three inches in length, depending upon the ecosystemic character of their habitat. They are aggressive and will use their powerful mandibles at the slightest irritation. Their bodies are powerful and relatively flat, and there are tufts of white, hairlike gills at the base of the lateral appendages on each of the first seven abdominal segments.

Caudal gills: Dark chocolate brown, ¼ inch
Body: Dark brownish black, 1½ inch
Tracheal gills: Dark chocolate brown, ⅜ inch
Thorax: Dark brownish black, ½ inch
Legs: Dark chocolate brown, ⅜ inch
Head: Dark brownish black, ¼ inch
Mandibles: Dark brownish black, 3/16 inch

Hook: Sizes 4-8 Mustad 79580 4X long
Nylon: Dark brown 6/0 nylon
Caudal gills: Two dark chocolate-dyed pheasant-tail fiber points
Body: Dark brownish-black dubbing tied in ten distinct sections over an exaggeratedly flat body using two aluminum finish nails at either side of shank.
Tracheal gills: Two chocolate-dyed pheasant-tail fiber points tied in on each side of the flattened body, at the start of each dubbed segment. Set a tiny drop of white lacquer at base of each pair of gills.
Thorax: Dark brownish black dubbing with black-dyed goose-wing quill section tied down over thorax hackle
Legs: Soft black hackles trimmed and bent to shape
Head: Brownish black dubbing with black-dyed goose section pulled over its back like a wing case
Mandibles: Two dark chocolate-dyed condor quill points

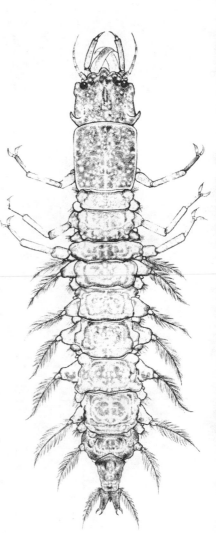

Corydalis larva   (twice life size)

The larvae are furtive and carefully shun the light. They are seldom seen except in the stomach autopsy of a fish, or when a stone is suddenly extracted from a riffle. They crawl by rapidly hitching themselves backward with their abdominal grappling hooks. The full cycle is about three years, so the hellgrammites are available to the fish in a wide range of sizes, from half-inch wrigglers to the giant three-inch dinosaurs found in some waters. Pupation takes place out of the stream, usually under logs or stones or high-water accumulations of leaf-drift and sticks. The period of terrestrial pupation lasts about ten days.

Since these larvae are virtually flat in cross section, I have found that the flat foundation method of tying nymphs developed by George Grant on the Big Hole is useful in imitating *Corydalis* larvae. The flat base can be created by wrapping pieces of soft brass wire or aluminum-finish nails on either side of the hook shank with black working nylon, soaking the entire base in fly-head cement. This creates a rigid core with the two pieces of wire lying side by side with the hook shank at the center. Then black floss is used to smooth the entire base into the tapered shape suggestive of the actual larvae. Since a three-inch nymph is too large to take fish readily, perhaps because, unlike a streamer or bucktail, the trout get too good a look at a dead-drift nymph, I seldom tie the hellgrammite imitations larger than an inch and three-quarters in length. The life cycle of the larvae lasts three years, making imitations in a range of hook sizes feasible.

The Fat-Bodied Nymphs of the Anisoptera

It was getting colder when we reached Tarryall and climbed into the open basin under the foothill ridges of Bison Mountain. The season was only a few days old. Spring weather is unpredictable above eight thousand feet. Angry clouds darkened the summits beyond the ten-thousand-foot Kenosha Pass, and their ink-blue color seemed to promise snow. Soon the clouds obscured the mountains.

We reached the Tarryall Dam and climbed the steep road that leads to the south shoreline of the reservoir. *Looks like a blizzard coming*, Dick Coffee grumbled. *Just our luck!*

The snow was still fifteen miles away. *Well*, I agreed unhappily, *we might as well stay and try it.*

Guess you're right. He set the handbrake.

Must be forty degrees! I shivered.

There were several bait-fishermen working nightcrawlers and canned corn on the bottom. Two had several hatchery rainbows on a bass stringer, with one good two-pound brown.

Wonder what fly'll work in a blizzard?

There's a way to find out, I said. *Maybe they'll let me check the stomach of that two-pound brown.*

Might tell something at that, said Coffee.

We walked down to the bait-fishermen with the stringer. *You will probably think I'm crazy*, my awkward preamble started, *but I would like to clean your big fish for you.*

He's crazy, one laughed.

Why would you want to clean our fish? The other fisherman eyed me warily. *What's in it for you?*

Simple, I explained. *I'll find out what they're eating.*

They looked at each other and shrugged. *Okay*, one said, *but we still think you're crazy.*

Completely, laughed the other.

The knife sliced easily from the ventral fin toward the gills of the big fish, and I stripped the entrails free, cutting away the pectorals and gill-systems. Carefully incising the membrane of the stomach, I squeezed its contents into my palm.

What's he been eating? Coffee asked.

Dragonfly nymphs, I said. *Don't have anything like them in my fly books—have to make some!*

You can tie flies! Coffee laughed. *I'm going fishing!*

Good luck! I opened the tying box.

It was darker when I finished the last nymph, and the basin above the reservoir was black with the advancing snow squall. The fat, muskrat-bodied nymphs lay on the seat. The big flies were weighted with soft lead wire and my rod was equipped with a fast sinking line. The first big snow-flakes hit the windshield as I left the station wagon and started shivering down toward the water.

It was snowing hard in barely minutes, and the opposite shoreline was lost in the swirling flakes. Dick Coffee became a shadowy figure standing in the water. The thick flakes quickly covered the ground, hitting us wetly in the face and encrusting my shooting glasses.

You want one of these nymphs? I asked.

Coffee laughed through the falling snow. *You really think it makes a difference?* he said.

Might. I waded out into the shallows.

They're not going to take anything in this blizzard, he grumbled. *They won't take what I'm using either.*

Their fish was full of nymphs. The other fishermen were leaving, their coats covered with fresh snow.

Winter takes a spring vacation! Coffee growled.

It's not snowing where the fish are, I said.

That's real comforting! Coffee shot a long cast angrily into the swirling snowflakes. *Maybe we should join 'em!*

My first cast worked out and disappeared into the snow, and I let it sink twenty counts before retrieving. The hook came back clean, and I cast again, counting to twenty-five while the weighted nymphs sank toward the bottom. The retrieve ticked into the gravel twice, and there was moss on the hook.

Let it sink twenty-three, I thought.

The laborious hand-twist retrieve worked back along the bottom only six or seven turns when there was a sullen pull, and I was into a good rainbow. It bolted out into the lake and jumped, falling heavily in the swirling snowflakes.

Can hear him, Coffee laughed, *can't see him!*

It was a sleek eighteen-inch rainbow, and I took several more around a pound while the snow covered us with its wet clinging flakes. When the snow stopped, the fish stopped too.

Well, Coffee said, *that was pretty strange.*

The sun came out behind the Mosquito Range and the fresh snow was terribly bright. *They sure wanted dragonflies,* I laughed. *And right in the worst of the squalls.*

Let's get back before we're snowbound.

Although not as densely populated as other subaquatic insects, the dragonfly nymphs are large enough to interest even the largest fish, and I have taken more really big fish on their imitations than almost any other type except the big stoneflies. Many trout caught with the ubiquitous Muddler minnow, when it is fished slow and deep along the bottom, have been taking fat dragonfly nymphs instead of sculpins.

They're fat enough, Dick Coffee had observed that wintry morning in the mountains. *They're a real mouthful!*

Like the more delicate damselflies, the dragonflies are members of the Odonata order. The suborder Zygoptera designates the damselflies, referring to their habit of folding their delicate wings back parallel to their bodies when at rest. The dragonflies are classified in the suborder Anisoptera, describing their outstretched wings both at rest and in flight. They are the swift flying snake-doctors, devil's darning-needles and horse-stingers of frontier folklore.

Dragonflies are wholly aquatic until they hatch into the winged stages. They are highly predacious from eclosion into the nymphal form until termination of the imago stage. Their nymphs capture their food in a completely different fashion from that of the adults in flight. The nymphs catch other subaquatic organisms by lying motionless like a muskellunge in the weeds. Although they are capable of rapid movements, they usually trap their victims with a lower labium that snaps out like the tongue of a frog, its hooks pinioning them securely. The adults hunt while in flight, darting back and forth in swift, perfectly controlled movements, and snaring their prey in a basket between the forelegs and the thoracic sternum.

The dragonflies have an incomplete metamorphosis, consisting of ova, nymphs, and adults, like the other Odonata. The nymphal form has wing cases, but otherwise bears little resemblance to the adult, with its many-veined wings and slender body. Nymphal life lasts more than a year. When fully developed these nymphs crawl from the water on a deadfall, boulder, or reed, climbing slightly above the surface to split the nymphal skin and emerge into the winged imago.

The nymphs have a unique swimming system. The lower intestine is thin-walled and functions as a gill, absorbing oxygen from water drawn in and expelled by the anal orifice. The nymphs are stout and thick-set when compared with the nymphal forms of the damselflies. These Zygoptera swim using their caudal gills as sculling oars, but the dragonflies bolt forward by contracting their rectal muscles and expelling the respiratory water in a hard little stream. The adults are the strongest fliers in the insect world. Their eggs are dropped into the water, attached to the leaves of aquatic plants, or injected into their stems through a stingerlike ovipositor.

Dragonflies are classified into two suborders, the Aeschnidae and the Libellulidae. The distinction lies in their wing venation. There is a triangular vein structure in the basal portion of all dragonfly wings. Still nearer the wing roots is an arcular cross-vein, reaching from about the middle in two primary veins toward the tip of the wings. The roots of these cross-veins touch the main triangular vein structure.

With the Aeschnidae, the distance between this triangle of veins and the arcular venation is about the same in both forewings and rear wings. The Libellulidae have this triangular venation at different distances from the arcular veins in each pair of wings.

The nymphs of the Aeschnidae have a flattened labium, with two prominent canines. The labial structure of the Libellulidae is a somewhat spoon-shaped mask at the ventral surfaces of the head. The teeth are absent in these forms. Other distinctions in the separation of the ocelli distinguish the subfamilies of these two suborders.

1. Whitetail Dragonfly Nymph (*Plathemis trimaculatum*)

These are quite common, widely distributed dragonflies which typically hatch sporadically from May until September. Their nymphs are rather corpulent insects, measuring about seven-eighths inch at their full development. These nymphs are most common on eastern waters, while *Erythemis favida* and *Celithemis ornata* are similar western species. The nymphs are most common in ponds and slow-flowing currents. Their name comes from the chalk-colored bodies of the adult males.

These imitations are all dressed with soft-wire outriggers anchored at the thorax and the bend of the hook. This oval template can be formed of wire heavy enough to weight the nymph, and it should be wrapped in plastic floss set in acetone, building a rigid foundation imitative of the naturals.

Tracheal spinules: Dark grayish, 1/16 inch
Abdomen: Dark brownish mottled gray, ⅝ inch
Wing cases: Dark grayish, ¼ inch
Thorax: Dark brownish mottled gray, ¼ inch
Legs: Dark mottled brownish gray, ¼ inch
Head: Dark brownish gray, ⅛ inch

Hook: Sizes 8-10 Mustad 9672 3X long
Nylon: Dark gray 6/0 nylon
Tracheal spinules: Dark brownish gray fibers tied short
Body: Dark brownish gray mixed dubbing tied over flat foundation of wire outriggers
Wing cases: Short dark brownish gray pheasant fibers in a thickly tied cluster back from the thorax
Thorax: Dark brownish gray mixed dubbing
Legs: Dark brownish gray pheasant body hackle
Head: Dark brownish gray dubbing

2. Red-Bodied Dragonfly Nymph (*Sympetrum ribicundulum*)

These are a species of bright, red-bodied dragonflies which also inhabit ponds and quiet streams. They emerge in late summer, and adults have been observed well into November. This species is distributed from New Brunswick to Minnesota and Wisconsin. *Sympetrum semicinctum* is a closely related species that is found on western waters. The nymphs average five-eighths inch at full growth.

The wire outriggers should be used to shape an ovoid foundation for these nymphs, using a chocolate-colored floss.

Trachael spinules: Reddish brown, 1/16 inch
Abdomen: Dark mottled reddish brown, ⅜ inch
Wing cases: Dark mottled brown, ⅛ inch
Thorax: Dark mottled brown, ⅛ inch
Legs: Dark mottled brownish, ¼ inch
Head: Dark brownish, ⅛ inch

Hook: Sizes 10-12 Mustad 9672 3X long
Nylon: Dark brown 6/0 nylon
Tracheal spinules: Dark reddish brown fibers tied short
Body: Dark reddish brown dubbing mixed with guard hairs from a hare's mask
Wing cases: Dark reddish brown pheasant fibers tied in a thickly bunched cluster back from the thorax
Thorax: Dark reddish brown mixed with hare's mask
Legs: Dark reddish mottled dyed pheasant hackles
Head: Dark reddish brown dubbing

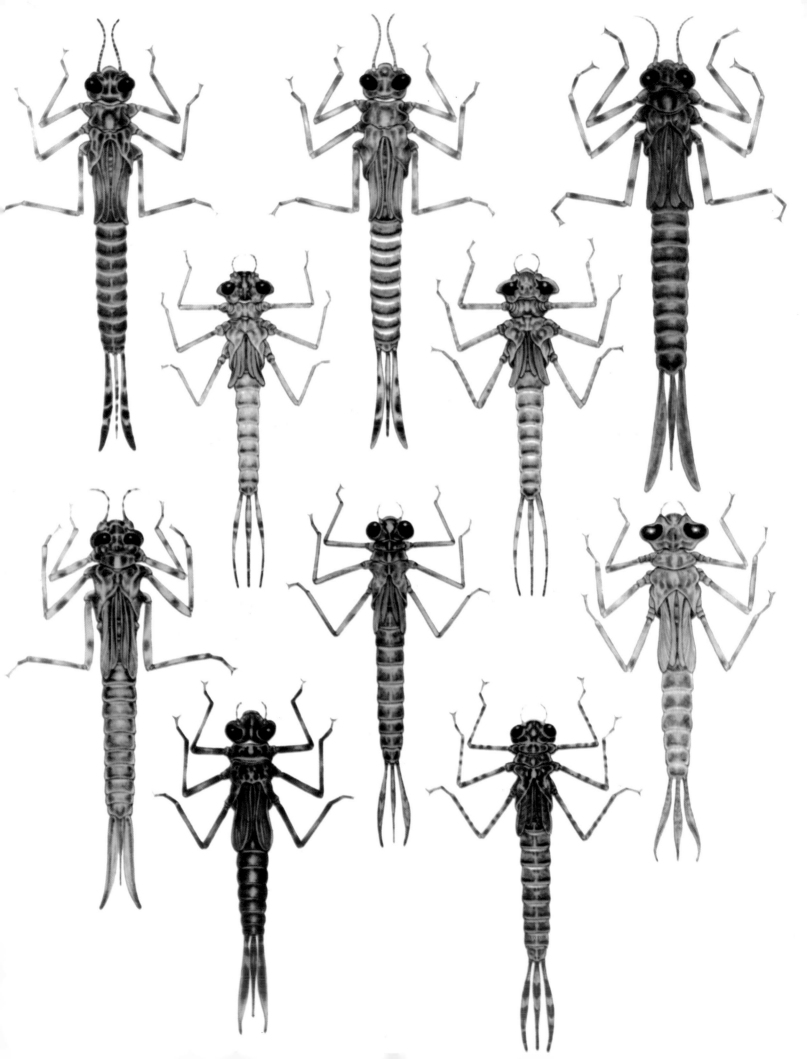

collect fine *Rivularia* algae and coverings of silt. They average about seven-eighths inch in length.

Tracheal spinules: Mottled brownish, 1/16 inch
Abdomen: Mottled brownish distinctly ringed, ⅝ inch
Wing cases: Medium brownish, ¼ inch
Thorax: Medium mottled brownish, ¼ inch
Legs: Medium mottled brownish, ½ inch
Head: Medium mottled brown, ⅛ inch

Hook: Sizes 8-12 Mustad 9672 3X long
Nylon: Dark brown 6/0 nylon
Tracheal spinules: Dark brownish fibers tied short
Body: Dark brownish dubbing mixed with hare's mask guard hairs
Wing cases: Dark brownish pheasant fibers tied in a thickly bunched cluster back from the thorax
Thorax: Dark brownish dubbing mixed with hare's mask
Legs: Dark brown-dyed pheasant body hackle
Head: Dark brownish dubbing

6. Riffle-Burrowing Dragonfly Nymph (*Gomphus stygiatus*)

Gomphus and *Octogomphus* are dragonfly nymphs that are numerous in our western mountains, and are typically found burrowing into the soft beds and bottom trash of cold, swift-flowing streams. They have flat, chisel-shaped heads, and stout, four-jointed antennae. Emergence typically occurs on the stones along the water. The eastern genus *Lanthus* exhibits similar behavior, and the nymphs average three-quarters to seven-eighths inch in length at maturity.

The imitative pattern should begin with a flat wire foundation shaped to simulate the elliptical abdomen of the naturals.

Top five, left to right: *Agrion maculatum, Ischnura barberi, Calopteryx yakima, Ischnura verticalis, Hetaerina brunneicolor*
Bottom five, left to right: *Hetaerina americana, Argia violocea, Lestes inaequalis, Lestes disjunctus, Enallagma civile*

Tracheal spinules: Dark brownish gray, 1/16 inch
Abdomen: Dark mottled brownish, gray with ovoid lateral markings, ⅝ inch
Wing cases: Dark mottled brownish, 3/16 inch
Thorax: Dark mottled brownish gray, 3/16 inch
Legs: Dark mottled brownish gray, ½ inch
Head: Dark mottled brownish gray, ⅛ inch

Hook: Sizes 6-10 Mustad 9672 3X long
Nylon: Dark brown 6/0 nylon
Tracheal spinules: Dark brownish fibers tied short
Body: Dark mottled brownish dubbing mixed with hare's mask
Wing cases: Dark brownish pheasant fibers tied in a thick cluster from the thorax
Thorax: Dark mottled brown dubbing mixed with hare's mask
Legs: Dark mottled brownish pheasant hackle
Head: Dark brownish dubbing

7. Giant Dragonfly Nymph (*Aeschna constricta*)

This dragonfly and the closely related *Epiaeschna heros* species are among our largest insects, with nymphs ranging from slightly more than one inch to as much as two and one-half inches in length. They have T-shaped markings on the heads of the adults, and the nymphs are primarily found in larger lakes and reservoirs.

Tracheal spines: Dark olive grayish, ⅛ inch
Abdomen: Dark mottled olive brown, ¾ inch
Wing cases: Dark olive brown, 3/16 inch
Thorax: Dark mottled olive brown, ⅛ inch
Legs: Dark mottled olive, ¾ inch
Head: Dark mottled olive brown, 3/16 inch

Hook: Sizes 2-8 Mustad 9672 3X long
Nylon: Dark olive 6/0 nylon
Tracheal spinules: Dark olive fibers tied short
Body: Dark olive dubbing mixed with the guard hairs of a hare's mask
Wing cases: Dark olive pheasant fibers tied in thick cluster at thorax thorax
Thorax: Dark olive dubbing mixed with hare's mask
Legs: Dark olive-dyed pheasant body hackle
Head: Dark olive dubbing

Adult dragonflies capture numberless quantities of mosquitoes and flies, which they take in midflight. However, their beneficial aerial diet is balanced with their fierce predatory behavior in the nymphal state. The Anisoptera nymphs compete directly with the trout for insect foods, and fish culturists argue that they are responsible for enormous losses in hatchery-reared fish and baby stream-bred trout.

Most of their movements along the bottom are quite sluggish, and imitations should be fished slow and deep. However, expelling water through their elaborately folded lacework of respiratory tubes transforms their breathing system into a propulsion method. Utilizing this system of jet propulsion, the dragonfly nymphs are capable of swimming with great agility in a series of staccato pulses. Sometimes a fly fisherman should fish them in the middle depths of water, with a retrieve suggestive of their agile and erratic swimming.

Once this method produced a four-pound rainbow at shallow Palmer Lake in Colorado. It took my olive-colored nymph just at dark, and fought me for twenty minutes in the gathering darkness. Such trophy-size fish are not common in a small reservoir that improbably lies between two freight switchyards—but it once gave me several months of fine sport, followed at nightfall by chicken *cacciatore* at the fine little Italian bar across the tracks.

The Slender-Bodied Nymphs of the Zygoptera

THE DIRT COUNTY road climbs toward the south, from the dry scrub-oak ridges above the Arkansas past the abandoned collieries and coke kilns at Florence. It winds and switchbacks lazily toward the sagebrush foothills, working into a sandy *arroyo* of pale, chalk-colored bluffs. The hills are honeycombed and scarred with the sulphur-colored tailings of abandoned mines, and there are smooth rock chimneys polished by the wind.

Twenty-five miles later, the dusty foothills drop behind and the country road reaches straight as a plumb line across the valley floor. Its prairie of pale bunchgrass extends almost fifty miles from Cotopaxi on the Arkansas to the headwaters of the Huerfano. Its emptiness is strangely beautiful.

The rotting skeleton of the mining pit-head structure is silhouetted against the morning light. There are houses clustered in the valley. Past the fir-slab headstones of the cemetery, its wrought-iron fencework choked with weeds, lies the half-deserted mining camp at Silvercliff.

It's a fascinating place, said Beno Walker.

We passed the first outbuildings of the town. Its streets and houses are solitary echoes of the silver boom in this empty, wind-swept valley. The county road reaches west toward the high peaks of the Sangre de Cristo Mountains. Their barren summits were almost ruby-colored with the glow of the rising sun.

They deserve their name, I said.

Beno Walker was starting absently at the empty streets. *What's that?* he asked. *What deserves what name?*

Sangre de Cristo, I replied. *The Blood of Christ.*

The blood-colored sunrise on the mountains faded as quickly as it had begun. The morning wind was cool, rising and stirring across the prairie bottoms. Two mallards exploded from an irrigation canal. Several magpies were quarreling over a dead jackrabbit in the road, and they rose sullen and flapping awkwardly into the wind. They settled again when we passed.

The simple houses and abandoned false-front stores are like gravestones. The courthouse and school are solemn benchmarks of the past, and the adobe-walled saloons are empty too. The dusty boardwalks and hitching rails are weathered silver in the wind. The streetscape looks like a moody Burchfield canvas, empty of people and filled with melancholy.

Lonely, I thought. *Lonely country.*

Two cowboys were walking their ponies in the dusty street, their sweat-stained hats turned low into the wind. It is a long, cold ride that starts before daylight from the outlying ranches, even in mid-summer.

Beno waved and one cowboy nodded in reply.

Beyond the town, willows line the meandering channel of Grape Creek, and the road starts climbing toward the mountains. The creek willows and cottonwoods on the valley floor gradually change to ponderosa on the lower slopes. The jeep road switchbacks steeply along the shoulder of the mountain, climbing through the aspens into the first stands of slender lodgepole pines. Hermit Creek tumbles far below the road, and where it plunges and falls down a steep outcropping of granite, the jeep trail finally becomes impassable for vehicles.

Last stop! I laughed. *Everybody out!*

It is a steep hike to Hermit Lake, the first of a three-lake chain that stair-steps up the timberline basins. The trail climbs the first escarpment into a mountain park thick with aspens and pines, where the mule deer drift down to drink.

The trail is gentle there. It finally winds higher into the second bench, through narrow pathways in the rock, until it reaches firs and Engelmann spruce, their barren deadfalls weathered the color of pewter in the winds and high-country winters.

Beno stopped to catch his wind. *You bring up the rear and collect the tents and pots I drop,* he grinned.

Great! I sighed. *Who picks up behind me?*

It's a problem, he laughed.

It sure is, I agreed. *The way my legs feel now we could starve and freeze to death on what we're still carrying when we finally get to Hermit.* My mouth tasted like old pennies.

Well, Beno sighed. *Let's saddle up.*

Steep rockslides lie across the valley, still echoing the earthquake slides that probably formed the lake milleniums ago. It was ahead now through the trees, glittering in the sun. Chipmunks and marmots scurried among the rocks to reach their hiding places, and a red-tailed hawk circled lazily on the warming wind that rose from the valley floor.

The sun was getting high now.

It is best to make your camp first in the high country and fish later. It is a simple matter of discipline. When you know your weaknesses, you know that the fishing will occupy you into the twilight hours, until it is too dark to make the camp and gather wood for a cookfire.

We staked out the tension-tent in a sheltering grove of tall spruce, where the creek gathered and spilled from the lake through a jackstraw tangle of deadfalls. There was a large snowbank lying among the trees, and I shaped a cooling-hole with my knife. We gathered two nights worth of firewood and stacked it between two trees beside the tent. Beno dug a firepit and lined it with stones, picking a site that would carry the smoke away from our tent—both on the morning winds that rose from the valley floor and the cool evening winds that eddied softly down the mountain.

The afternoon wind dropped down until the lake was still and smooth. *Look there along the dead trees,* Beno pointed. *They're rising over there.*

Dozens of fish were working along the shore.

No rises out in the lake, I thought aloud.

You're right, Beno agreed. *The rises are all right there in the logs along the shoreline. Wonder what they're doing?*

Let's find out, I said.

We walked down to the shallows, where a tangle of dead trees lay in the water. Two fish bolted into deep water when our shadows touched the surface of the lake, and I squatted on my heels to study the logs. Their smooth trunks were covered with pale-green algae, and it was almost five minutes before the clear shallows revealed the secret.

Look at the logs, I said suddenly.

Mixed with the pale-green moss were hundreds of olive damselfly nymphs, climbing imperceptibly toward the waterline or simply waiting for their hatching time. The nymphs hung so motionless that only their working gills betrayed their presence. Their protective coloring was so perfect that only a hatching nymph that crawled into the surface film and hatched revealed their presence.

What is it? asked Beno.

Green damselfly nymphs on the logs, I said. *Hundreds of them getting ready to hatch!*

No wonder the fish are in shallows!

It was a simple matter to catch the fish that afternoon, and we took fat richly spotted brookies until our nymphs were literally shredded from the hooks. It is not always like that, but damselfly nymphs are important in our fly boxes, particularly on the lakes and reservoirs and beaver ponds of our western mountains.

Damselflies are taxonometrically included among the Odonata order, in its extensive Zygoptera subfamily. The adults are the swift-winged dragonflies and delicate damselflies familiar to anyone who has ever fished a farm pond for bluegills and bass. Children are often frightened of them, having been told the old wives' tales about flying darning-needles that sew up their ears, or their role in ministering to the needs of reptiles.

Snake-doctors, the old perch fishermen teased me on the Michigan piers each August. *Watch out or them snake-doctors will get you!*

Damselfly nymphs are agile and restless swimmers, using their posterior gills as sculling oars. Some species are capable of producing several broods of flies in a single season. Both dragonflies and damselflies pass the winter as nymphs in the bottom silt and the detritus caught among the stones. Emergence begins late in spring, and the cast-off nymphal skins can be found clinging to reeds and deadfalls and sticks protruding from the water. The damselflies and dragonflies are the most voracious and predatory of the subaquatic nymphs, devouring each other and any smaller organism. Although both suborders are agile swimmers capable of swift movements, they usually use patience and stealth to capture their prey. The nymphs capture their food with a lightning-quick labium, used to clutch it swiftly and retrieve it toward the waiting jaws. Their appetites are fierce.

The Zygoptera are slender and equipped with three leaf-shaped gills at the posterior. Their heads and eyes are rather widely spaced in contrast to their delicate bodies. The legs are relatively long and thin, and are used for clambering swiftly in the weeds. Most species are abundant in silt-bottomed lakes and ponds with rich aquatic vegetation, although some eco-types inhabit slow-flowing streams and swifter currents. Since the insects are many-brooded, emergence can occur in several periods between April and November.

1. Blackwing Damselfly Nymph (*Agrion maculatum*)

This eastern species is widely distributed. Its adults are the familiar black-winged species with slender bright-green or metallic-blue bodies. Their nervous, almost continuous flight is familiar to anyone who frequents the waterside. Full-grown nymphs vary between three-quarters inch and one inch, and are found in weedy shallows all year.

Agrion aequabile is primarily a western species, found in concert with the more widely known *Agrion maculatum* on the waters of the Rocky Mountains.

Tails: Mottled medium brown, ¼ inch
Body: Mottled brown, distinctly ringed, ½ inch
Wing cases: Medium brownish, ¼ inch
Thorax: Mottled medium brown, ⅛ inch
Legs: Dark mottled brown, ⅜ inch
Head: Mottled medium brown, 3/32 inch
Eyes: Dark blackish brown, 1/32 inch diameter

Hook: Sizes 8-12 Mustad 79580 4X long
Nylon: Brown 6/0 nylon
Tails: Three brown mottled pheasant-tail fibers
Body: Dark brown rayon floss underbody ribbed with medium gold flat tinsel, and flat monofilament overbody dyed medium brown
Wing cases: Several brown mottled pheasant-tail fibers
Thorax: Medium brown dubbing
Legs: Medium brown partridge hackle fibers
Head: Large head shaped from brown 6/0 nylon
Eyes: Two drops of black lacquer

2. Green Damselfly Nymph (*Calopteryx yakima*)

This is a western species found along the Pacific Coast, and reported from Colorado to Montana in the Rocky Mountains. Its fully developed nymphs average about three-quarters inch to one inch in length. *Calopteryx maculata* is closely related.

Tails: Bright green mottled with brown, ¼ inch
Body: Bright green, distinctly ringed, ½ inch
Wing cases: Bright green, ¼ inch
Thorax: Bright mottled green, ⅛ inch
Legs: Bright mottled green, ½ inch
Head: Bright green, 3/32 inch
Eyes: Black, 1/32 inch diameter

Hook: Sizes 8-12 Mustad 79580 4X long
Nylon: Bright green 6/0 nylon
Tails: Three mottled pheasant fibers dyed bright green
Body: Bright green nylon underbody ribbed with flat silver tinsel, wound with an olive-dyed flat monofilament
Wing cases: Bright green-dyed pheasant-tail fibers
Thorax: Bright green-dyed dubbing
Legs: Gray mottled partridge dyed bright green
Head: Large head shaped with bright green 6/0 nylon
Eyes: Two drops of black lacquer

3. Sepia Damselfly Nymph (*Hetaerina brunneicolor*)

This relatively large western species averages about seven-eighths inch to one inch in length.

Tails: Medium brown, 5/16 inch
Body: Medium brown, distinctly ringed, ½ inch
Wing cases: Dark brown, ¼ inch
Thorax: Medium brown, ⅛ inch
Legs: Pale mottled brown, ⅝ inch
Head: Medium brown, 3/32 inch
Eyes: Blackish brown, 1/32 inch diameter

Hook: Sizes 6-10 Mustad 79580 4X long
Nylon: Brown 6/0 nylon
Tails: Medium brown pheasant fibers
Body: Dark brown rayon floss underbody ribbed with flat gold tinsel, and wound with a brown-dyed overbody of flat monofilament
Wing cases: Brown pheasant-tail fibers
Thorax: Medium brown dubbing
Legs: Gray partridge hackle dyed brown
Head: Head shaped of brown 6/0 nylon
Eyes: Two drops of black lacquer

4. Pale Olive Fork-Tailed Nymph (*Ischnura barberi*)

This western species and the closely related Rocky Mountain *Ischnura cervula* are nine-sixteenths to three-quarters inch in length.

Tails: Mottled yellowish tan, ¼ inch
Body: Yellowish tan, faintly ringed, ⅜ inch
Wing cases: Yellowish tan, ¼ inch
Thorax: Yellowish tan, 3/32 inch
Legs: Mottled yellowish tan, ⅜ inch
Head: Yellowish tan, 3/32 inch
Eyes: Dark brown, 1/32 inch diameter

Hook: Sizes 12-14 Mustad 79580 4X long
Nylon: Pale yellow 6/0 nylon
Tails: Pale mottled pheasant-tail fibers dyed yellow
Body: Pale yellow rayon floss underbody, wound with clear flat nylon monofilament
Wing cases: Pale mottled pheasant-tail fibers dyed yellow
Thorax: Pale yellowish dubbing
Legs: Pale yellow-dyed gray partridge fibers
Head: Head shaped of yellow 6/0 nylon
Eyes: Two drops dark brown lacquer

5. Medium Olive Fork-Tailed Nymph (*Ischnura verticalis*)

This eastern species is also of the so-called fork-tailed nymphs, resembling nymphal forms of the *Enallagma* flies except for their sharply tapering tail gills. They are particularly fond of weedy ponds, and are among the earliest damselflies to hatch in the spring. The nymphs measure about one-half inch at maturity.

Tails: Mottled amber, ¼ inch
Body: Amber, faintly ringer, ⅜ inch
Wing cases: Light brown, 3/16 inch
Thorax: Amber mottled with light brown, 3/32 inch
Legs: Mottled amber, ⅜ inch
Head: Mottled amber, 3/32 inch
Eyes: Dark brown, 1/32 inch diameter

Hook: Sizes 12-14 Mustad 79580 4X long
Nylon: Light tan 6/0 nylon
Tails: Mottled pheasant-tail fibers dyed light brown
Body: Light amber rayon floss underbody
Wing cases: Light brown pheasant-tail fibers
Thorax: Light amber dubbing
Legs: Gray partridge fibers dyed light brown
Head: Light tan 6/0 nylon
Eyes: Two drops of dark brown lacquer

6. Great Olive Damselfly Nymph (*Hetaerina americana*)

The adults of this genus are distinguished by their large, delicately tapered wings, unlike the fan-shaped wings of the *Agrion* flies. Their thoracic structure is somewhat larger. The nymphs are relatively large, measuring as much as one and three-eighths inches.

Tail: Medium olive, ¼ inch
Body: Medium olive, ½ inch
Wing cases: Medium olive, ¼ inch
Thorax: Medium olive, ⅛ inch
Legs: Medium olive, ½ inch
Head: Medium olive, ⅛ inch
Eyes: Black, 1/32 inch diameter

Hook: Sizes 6-10 Mustad 79580 4X long
Nylon: Medium olive 6/0 nylon
Tails: Medium olive dyed pheasant-tail fibers
Body: Bright green underbody with a flat nylon monofilament overbody
Wing cases: Medium olive dyed pheasant-tail fibers
Thorax: Medium olive dubbing
Legs: Gray partridge dyed medium olive
Head: Head shaped of medium olive 6/0 nylon
Eyes: Two drops of black lacquer

7. Dark Olive Damselfly Nymph (*Lestes inaequalis*)

The *Lestes* nymphs inhabit ponds and small lakes, where they clamber and hunt in the eelgrass and pondweeds. Their slender bodies are well camouflaged with bandings of green and brown. The nymphs vary from one-half to three-quarters inch.

Tails: Dark olive mottled, 5/32 inch
Body: Dark olive distinctly ringed, ⅜ inch
Wing cases: Dark olive, ¼ inch
Thorax: Dark mottled olive, 3/32 inch
Legs: Dark olive, ⅜ inch
Head: Dark olive, 1/16 inch
Eyes: Black, 1/32 inch diameter

Hook: Sizes 12-14 Mustad 79580 4X long
Nylon: Dark olive 6/0 nylon
Tails: Dark olive mottled pheasant-tail fibers
Body: Bright green rayon underbody ribbed with flat silver tinsel, and wound with clear flat monofilament overbody
Wing cases: Dark olive dyed pheasant-tail fibers
Thorax: Dark olive dubbing
Legs: Dark olive-dyed hackle fibers
Head: Head shaped of dark olive 6/0 nylon
Eyes: Two drops of black lacquer

8. Speckled Olive Damselfly Nymph (*Lestes disjunctus*)

This western species and its similar Rocky Mountain ecotype *Lestes dryas* have mottled legs and strongly ringed body coloring. The nymphs average five-eighths to three-quarters inch in length.

Tails: Dark brown-olive mottled, ¼ inch
Body: Dark brown-olive, distinctly ringed, ⅜ inch
Wing cases: Dark brown-olive pheasant-tail fibers, 5/32 inch
Thorax: Dark mottled olive-brown, 3/32 inch
Legs: Dark olive-brown mottled, ⅜ inch
Head: Dark mottled brown-olive, 1/16 inch
Eyes: Black, 1/32 inch diameter

Hook: Sizes 10-12 Mustad 79580 4X long
Nylon: Dark olive 6/0 nylon
Tails: Dark mottled pheasant-tail fibers dyed olive
Nylon: Dark olive 6/0 nylon
Tails: Dark mottled pheasant-tail fibers dyed olive
Body: Bright olive rayon floss underbody, marked on dorsal surfaces with black lacquer and ribbed with gold tinsel, wound with flat monofilament overbody
Wing cases: Pheasant-tail fibers dyed olive
Thorax: Dark brownish-olive dubbing
Legs: Dark partridge hackle dyed olive
Head: Dark olive 6/0 nylon
Eyes: Two drops of black lacquer

9. Bright Olive Damselfly Nymph (*Enallagma civile*)

This western species closely resembles its eastern counterpart *Enallagma exulsans*, its nymphs averaging about one-half inch. The genus is extensive, having a large number of American species. The nymphs inhabit ponds or slow-flowing streams, where they prowl the dense aquatic vegetation. They are aggressive and predatory. Their labia are slender with a prominent median lobe. Their heads are clearly wider across the relatively large ocelli, and they average about one-half inch at maturity.

Enallagma hageni is a related Rocky Mountain species.

Tails: Pale mottled olive, 5/32 inch
Body: Pale olive, ⅜ inch
Wing cases: Pale olive, ¼ inch
Thorax: Pale mottled olive, ¼ inch
Legs: Pale mottled olive, ⅜ inch
Head: Pale mottled olive, 3/32 inch
Eyes: Black, 1/32 inch diameter

Hook: Sizes 12-14 Mustad 79580 4X long
Nylon: Pale olive 6/0 nylon
Tails: Mottled pale olive-dyed pheasant fibers
Body: Pale olive rayon underbody wrapped with overbody of flat nylon monofilament
Wing cases: Pale olive-dyed pheasant-tail fibers
Thorax: Pale olive dubbing
Legs: Pale olive-dyed hackle fibers
Head: Head shaped of pale olive 6/0 nylon
Eyes: Two drops of black lacquer

10. Purple Damselfly Nymph (*Argia violacea*)

This eastern species is perhaps the most widely distributed member of its genus on American waters. The nymphal forms are found in almost every type of water, although the heaviest populations are found in slow-flowing currents and backwaters. The nymphs are sepia-colored, with some specimens exhibiting a purplish cast that anticipates the bright-violet abdomen of the adult males. The nymphs measure almost one-half inch.

160

Tails: Purple mottled, ¼ inch
Body: Purple, distinctly ringed, 5/16 inch
Wing cases: Purplish brown, 3/16 inch
Thorax: Purplish mottled brown, 3/32 inch
Legs: Purplish mottled brown, ⅜ inch
Head: Purplish mottled brown, 3/32 inch
Eyes: Black, 1/32 inch diameter

Hook: Size 12-14 Mustad 79580 4X long
Nylon: Dark purple 6/0 nylon
Tails: Mottled pheasant-tail fibers dyed purple
Body: Bright purple rayon floss ribbed with flat gold tinsel, with purple-dyed flat monofilament overbody
Wing cases: Purple-dyed pheasant-tail fibers
Thorax: Purple-dyed dubbing
Legs: Gray partridge hackle dyed purple
Head: Dark purple 6/0 nylon
Eyes: Two black drops of lacquer

[1]In a magazine article about a dozen years back, which was devoted to experimental flies, I proposed tying damselfly nymph imitations with extended bodies on stainless-wire cores. The article demonstrated the steps in dressing such flies, stretching .008 stainless music wire between a pair of fly vises and prefabricating several tails and bodies along this taut core. Then I trimmed the wire at the base of the tails and ahead of the body, leaving approximately a quarter inch of bare wire exposed beyond the dubbing. This exposed wire was then tied in, wrapping it quite firmly on a short-shank hook. The wire core is then completely anchored by folding back the stainless wire toward the body, winding this flattened loop of wire tightly under the working nylon. The wing cases, thorax, legs, head, and eyes are finally dressed conventionally on the short-shank hook itself.

This technique creates a delicately curved body that closely resembles the naturals, perhaps more effectively than a rigidly tied body shaped conventionally on a long-shanked hook. Such extended or detached-body nymphs also fish rather erratically, with a fluttering quality that suggests the swimming behavior of the nymphs quite well.

[1]Schwiebert, Ernest. "One Step Ahead of the Trout," *True Fishing Yearbook*, Fawcett Magazines, 1962.

The Gravel-Burrowing Ephemera Nymphs

Franconia is an ancient countryside. Its soft limestone hills and castles and gristmill villages are obvious echoes of its medieval past. There are old, tile-roofed villages like Königsfeld and Behringersmühle south of Bamberg, and the Baroque pilgrimage church of the *Vierzehnheiligen,* where we hunted roe deer in the summers. Later we shot hares and partridges in the fall. Those were happy seasons of living in thatched-roofed farmsteads, with the scars of war beginning to heal. We lived with the farmers and their families, eating the thick cabbage soups and freshly made sausages and drinking home-brewed beer.

Both life and sport were good. There are large populations of deer and *Wildschwein* and red stag in the hills, and north below the forests of the Thuringian border there are the wariest of game birds—the magnificent black *Auerhahn,* so rare that a hunter is permitted to kill only one during his lifetime in a hunting ritual as old as chivalry itself.

The trout fishing is excellent too. There are major trout rivers like the moody Pegnitz, its plateau headwaters in the country above Nürnberg. Field Marshal Hermann Goering had a shooting castle there. The pastoral little Wiesandt winds down its steep-walled limestone valley above Forcheim, where Charlemagne constructed a small castle of slate roofs and timbered gables. It was used for royal hunts at the apogee of the Holy Roman Empire. There are many ruined castles on the precipices, but not all of the castles are empty, their builders forgotten. There is a tributary of the Wiesandt with a sprawling fortress on a towering escarpment. It is the ancient family seat of Count Klaus von Stauffenburg, the brilliant young Wehrmacht colonel who helped engineer the last plot against Adolf Hitler. Stauffenburg actually placed the bomb that nearly killed the dictator and was subsequently executed for his role.

Such overtones of history lend a rich patina of time to fishing these rivers in past years. Since my boyhood experience was focused on the rivers of Michigan, Wisconsin, and the Rocky Mountains, it was odd that it should be the Wiesandt and Pegnitz that introduced me to my first *Ephemera* hatches.

Like the big *Hexagenia* flies, these hatches were so impressive and so many fish were rising that it always seemed like a dry-fly problem. The twilight was filled with mayflies. Fish boiled and porpoised everywhere, and although many evenings found the dry fly workable, there were puzzling failures too.

The farmers were haying in the fields below Behringersmühle, their four-horse teams straining to pull the hay wagons out to the road from the water-meadows below the castle. The late afternoon sun had left the valley floor, and long before I reached the timber bridge across the Wiesandt and saw the mayflies hovering over the river I could see the chimney swifts and swallows working.

The hay-wagon bridge bisects a quarter mile of smooth water, with a sheltering clump of alders along the far side, where the current was steady and deep. Rich beds of weeds trace their undulating rhythms in the currents along the hayfields, and upstream there are many channels in the flowering ranunculus and chara. Bright-green growths of algae feathered and flowed on the bottom stones, and in the channels there were shallows of pale gravel.

Big fish were rolling and swirling everywhere. Their gluttony caused me to miss the stripping guide while I was stringing my rod and I was forced to start again. The deep flat above the bridge was filled with fish slashing at the hatching drakes in a Bacchanalian orgy of feeding. The fisherman seldom witnesses such a hatch and rise of fish. My excitement soon turned to despair, however. My fly boxes were filled with big mayfly imitations dressed from the descriptions of Halford in anticipation of such hatches during my time in Germany. But the fish ignored them.

What's wrong? I thought frantically.

There was a heavy fish porpoise-rolling along the alders, and I placed cast after cast above his feeding station. The big drakes continued to hatch. My fly dropped softly above the fish, floated drag-free through its position, and was refused. Sometimes the trout would boil just before my dry fly reached his lie, permit the artificial to drift through untouched, and then swirl savagely again just as it had passed. Several times fish inspected the fly, but so briefly that it was obviously of little interest. The intensity of feeding continued to increase, along with my frustration. Several fish were swirling and porpoising and slashing, sometimes gently and sometimes lunging like the players in a hard-fought match of water polo. Finally, I gave up on the biggest trout in the flat, admitting my defeat unhappily, and went in search of easier game in the swift channels upstream.

My father had suggested that the fish might be taking the *Ephemera* nymphs, and we tried every nymph pattern in the box. Everything I had read about the Green Drake hatches suggested that the nymphs were pale cream or white, but the large, Wetzel-type imitations that I fished over these trout were totally ignored.

I'm going to fish upstream, I yelled to my father.

What're they taking? he shouted back. *Can't seem to get them to look at anything!* His casting rhythms looked desperate too.

Nymphing! I answered.

Well, he waved, *when you get one let's check his stomach and see what he's doing—there must be one stupid one!*

Upstream along a sweeping bed of ranunculus there was a strong bulge in the shallows. The meadows had just been mowed, giving me scant cover in my infantry-style approach, and I made the cast crouched low on my knees. The fish porpoised and took my fly.

What happened? I thought.

My father came walking upstream through the windrows of freshly cut hay. *You located the stupid one!* He laughed.

The fish fought clumsily, although it felt heavy and strong, and I began to think it did not seem like a trout. Finally it turned toward me, threshing weakly in the riffles. *It's a grayling,* I said.

We should have known. He smiled.

It was a big grayling, sleek and about three pounds with its spreading dorsal fin, smelling faintly of thyme. They are marvelous when broiled *meunière,* dripping in butter and sliced lemons and mushrooms, and I rapped it sharply on the head.

Autopsy? I suggested.

The big grayling had a few adult mayflies scattered among more than a hundred big *Ephemera* nymphs. We were not surprised by the quantity of nymphal forms, but their color was quite dark, totally unlike the descriptions found in Wetzel and Morgan.

The hatch stopped as quickly as it had started. The swallows completed their feeding, and the river flowed smooth and silent again. Its current was undisturbed by rising fish. It was another lesson in the importance of nymphs under conditions that seemed optimal for fishing dry flies, and a striking example of the selectivity of people-wise trout to both surface and subaquatic insect forms. There are only three species of *Ephemera* mayflies on European rivers, but American waters support six species of this important genus of the Ephemeroptera.

The burrowing nymphs of the *Ephemera* live primarily in alkaline environments having extensive beds of fine gravel and sand, although some relatively acid streams like the Brodheads, Beaverkill, and the West Branch of the Ausable have historically supported good hatches. Fine silty mixtures of limestone marl and micro-aggregates seem to provide optimal environments, and in past years perhaps the heaviest populations of these species have been found in Pennsylvania limestone streams like Penns Creek and the famous Spring Creek at Bellefonte.

Unlike the burrowing mayflies of the similar *Hexagenia,* these smaller species are both lotic forms indigenous to running water, and lenitic forms found in quieter currents. They are quite slender and relatively flat-bodied and have plumose gills along their upper abdomens. The nymphs of the *Ephemera* genus are also equipped with the narrow heads and sharp mandibles typical of the *Hexagenia* flies. Their forelegs, however, are not as powerfully shaped. Both genera fold their legs back underneath the thoracic structure while swimming. They are equally shy, and burrow like moles to escape the light if dislodged from their holes. Like the *Hexagenia,* these nymphs feed on diatomaceous material. Their hairy, plumose gill-systems consist of two rows of filamentaceous structures. Their respiratory patterns occur in pulsing movements, the waves of motion rippling along their abdomens from the first abdominal segments at the wing cases to the last segments at the tails. Like the other burrowing forms, these *Ephemera* nymphs breathe with these movements.

Although pollution, extensive use of pesticides to protect our eastern forests, and the scouring of river bottoms by seasonal flooding have seriously depleted our eastern populations of the *Ephemera* mayflies, there are still impressive hatches on some waters. Western and midwestern species remain present in substantial numbers, particularly the *Ephemera simulans* hatches found from New England to Idaho and Montana. Since these are relatively large mayflies and still hatch in large numbers on many rivers, the trout accept them eagerly.

1. American Green Drake (*Ephemera guttulata*)

This is the largest of our *Ephemera* flies, its fully developed nymphs measuring approximately seven-eighths inch to one inch in length. The largest ecotypes are found on the limestone rivers of Pennsylvania, particularly the chalkstream-like environment of Spring Creek.

Distribution of the species is sometimes puzzling. Pennsylvania rivers like Spring Creek, Big Fishing Creek, and Penns Creek still have heavy hatches, along with Honey Creek and Spruce Creek farther west. There are less alkaline watersheds in Pennsylvania, however, that also have good hatches. Kettle Creek and the First Fork of the Sinnemahoning are such rivers. The Brodheads is a slightly acid stream that also had excellent Green Drakes in the past. Its once heavy population of *Ephemera* flies is virtually gone. Strangely, the extremely rich little Pennsylvania chalkstreams of the Cumberland Valley—the Yellow Breeches and Big Spring and the lovely Letort Spring Run—do not have important hatches of the Green Drake.

Tails: Olive brown, ¼ inch
Tergites: Pale amber heavily mottled with dark brown markings, ½ inch
Sternites: Pale amber with light brown markings, ½ inch
Gills: Pale brownish gray, 5/32 inch
Thorax: Amber heavily mottled with brown, 3/16 inch
Sternum: Pale amber, 3/16 inch
Wing cases: Medium mottled brown, 5/32 inch
Legs: Amber with brown mottlings, ¼ inch
Head: Medium mottled brown, 1/16 inch

Hook: Sizes 6-10 Mustad 79580 4X long
Nylon: Tan 6/0 nylon
Tails: Pale grayish olive pheasant fibers
Foundation: Brass pins or wire at sides of hook
Tergites: Amber rayon floss underbody with black lacquer markings at dorsal and lateral surfaces
Sternites: Amber rayon floss underbody with pale brown markings along ventral median
Overbody: Natural flat monofilament
Gills: Pale grayish brown marabou bunched thickly along sides of body and picked out after securing with fine gold wire ribbing
Thorax: Pale amber underbody wrapped with flat monofilament
Wing cases: Dark brownish-mottled feather section tied down over thorax
Legs: Brownish mottled pheasant hackle
Head: Tan nylon

Similar paradoxes exist on the rivers of New York. The Beaverkill still has fine *Ephemera* hatches, along with the West Branch of the Ausable in the Adirondacks. The East Branch has only marginal fly-hatches. Schoharie Creek has sporadic hatches, while its sister river in the adjacent Esopus Valley has only sparse populations. There are few flies on the cold headwaters of the Neversink, yet in the old days before the reservoir irrevocably changed the temperatures and silt-character of the lower river, it had good hatches. The South Raritan in New Jersey and the tumbling Nantahala in North Carolina are famous *Ephemera* rivers too.

Hatches on the Raritan and Nantahala come in late May. Similar emergence dates obtain on the famous limestone streams of central Pennsylvania, but most of the Allegheny and Catskill waters have their hatches starting during the first week in June. Adirondack rivers like the Ausable and Great Chazy and Saranac come a few days later. However, each season can provide weather variables that find the flies coming off a week early, dribbling off in such scattered patterns that no really concentrated hatch appears, or emerging as much as ten days to two weeks late. This past season I traveled to the Nantahala to fish the *Ephemera guttulata* hatch with Hugh Chatham, but the flies failed to appear on schedule—and my baptism with its famous blizzardlike flights must wait another year.

The subimagoes emerge sporadically all day, escaping from the water immediately unless a misting rain retards the drying of their wings. Once in the trees, thousands cluster in a single tree at the height of emergence, hanging under the leaves and branches. The shallow backwaters after such a hatch are often filled with a delicate scum of empty nymphal shucks, pale echoes of the fat nymphs they had housed.

Many American fishing writers have despaired at the ineffectiveness of the nymphs they have tied to simulate *Ephemera guttulata* on their home rivers. Preston Jennings had so little faith in imitations of this species that his *Book of Trout Flies* omits any fly pattern designed to suggest it. Arthur Flick admitted his failure with such flies, but believed that the trouble lay in the large size and a relatively quiet-water habitat that gave the fish too close a look at any imitation.

It was Flick, however, who first succeeded in capturing one of the naturals and discovered that it was brownish, with darker mottlings and gill systems. The fish sometimes capture them when they are dislodged by high water. During a hatch they dart rather swiftly to the surface, and rises to them are usually a decisive swirl. Often the largest fish feeding during the hatch are never seen working near the surface. They are content to take the nymphs deep, just as they abandon their burrows to make the trip to the surface. Artificials dressed to imitate this species should be conceived in terms of spates and hatching, weighted to fish deep along the bottom and tied on light-wire hooks for a fast bucktail-type retrieve to suggest emergence just at the surface.

2. Western Brown Drake (*Ephemera compar*)

This is a relatively large western species, with mature nymphs measuring three-fourths inch in length. Although the original prototypes of the traditional March Brown flies in Britain were mayflies of the *Rhithrogena* and *Ecdyonurus* genera, this western species was given this popular name about twenty-five years ago on the Frying Pan in Colorado. The success of our American March Brown dry-fly pattern during its July hatches led my friends to give its name to the hatch.

The stillwater reaches of the Frying Pan, and its marshy former channels in the alkaline valley floor at Ruedi, were an ideal habitat for such burrowing nymphs. The hatches there are gone now, drowned under the waters of a recently filled reservoir.

These medium-sized *Ephemera* flies always hatched just at dark. I first discovered their presence in the evening rise through a series of stomach-checks on trout. There were good hatches of the equally large *Ephemerella hecuba* species in late afternoon, and an imitation usually worked well until dark. Then the trout began refusing the quill-bodied *Ephemerella* flies, although we were not aware that the hatch had changed until my stomach autopsies showed the dark-brownish mayflies that began hatching later.

Tails: Pale olive gray, 5/32 inch
Tergites: Pale amber very heavily mottled with brown, ⅜ inch
Sternites: Pale amber lightly mottled with brown, ⅜ inch
Gills: Pale olive gray, ⅛ inch
Thorax: Amber mottled with brown, ⅛ inch
Sternum: Pale amber, ⅛ inch
Wing cases: Mottled brownish, 5/32 inch
Legs: Amber with brown mottlings, 5/32 inch
Head: Mottled brownish, 1/16 inch

Hook: Sizes 8-10 Mustad 79580 4X long
Nylon: Tan 6/0 nylon
Tails: Pale grayish olive pheasant fibers
Foundation: Brass pins or wire at sides of hook
Tergites: Amber rayon floss underbody with very dense black lacquer markings at dorsal and lateral surfaces
Sternites: Amber rayon floss with brown markings along median
Overbody: Natural flat nylon monofilament
Gills: Pale grayish olive marabou bunched thickly along sides of body, and picked out after securing with fine gold wire ribbing
Thorax: Pale amber underbody wrapped with flat nylon monofilament
Wing cases: Dark brownish feather section tied over thorax
Legs: Brownish mottled pheasant hackle
Head: Tan nylon

The imitation of this *Ephemera compar* nymph should be fished in the same manner as recommended for the other burrowing mayflies. Needham outlines the distribution of the species in his *Biology of Mayflies* as being limited to Colorado, but there are reports of hatches on suitable waters in Idaho, Utah, Wyoming, and New Mexico.

3. Medium Brown-Olive Drake (*Ephemera simulans*)

This is a major American species. It is perhaps the most widely distributed of our larger mayflies, with specimens reported in all of the trout states from New England to Montana. Canadian provinces sustaining populations of *Ephemera simulans* range from New Brunswick westward to Manitoba, with one remarkable hatch recorded at Moose Factory on Hudson Bay.

The nymphs are quite similar to those of the related larger species, *Ephemera guttulata* and *Ephemera compar*, with their pale olivaceous gills and dark-brown tergite markings. The principal hatches occur in Michigan, Wisconsin, and upper New York during the first two weeks in June, and are recorded a few days later in waters both farther north and in the Rocky

Mountains. The nymphal colonies are found in relatively cold biosystems, particularly those having stream and lake bottoms composed of sand and coarser aggregates. They are seldom found in the silts, detritus, and marl favored by the larger *Ephemera* and *Hexagenia* nymphs, although good hatches are reported from the Firehole, Yellowstone, and the headwaters of the Madison.

Michigan and Wisconsin rivers have superb hatches. I have seen exceptional rises of fish on the Namekagon and Brule, and there are good hatches on other rivers like the Sturgeon and the Pigeon and the Fox. Peak hatching typically occurs about ten days before the bigger *Hexagenia* drakes, although the two genera do not find optimal habitat for their nymphal stages in all rivers.

Hatching usually occurs during the twilight hours, although sporadic emergence does obtain on overcast days. The final molt to the spinner stage takes about twenty-four hours, sometimes being completed during the first night after hatching. Full-grown *Ephemera simulans* nymphs measure approximately five-eighths inch in length.

Like the other burrowing nymphs, *Ephemera simulans* swims quite swiftly upon hatching, and its imitation should be retrieved quickly.

Tails: Light brown, 3/16 inch
Tergites: Light brown heavily mottled with darker brownish markings, ⅜ inch
Sternites: Light brown moderately mottled with darker markings, ⅜ inch
Gills: Light brownish olive, ⅛ inch
Thorax: Light brown heavily mottled with darker brown, ⅛ inch
Sternum: Light brown, ⅛ inch
Wing cases: Light brown heavily mottled with brown, 3/16 inch
Legs: Brownish mottled, 3/16 inch
Head: Light brownish mottled, 1/16 inch

Hook: Sizes 10-12 Mustad 79580 4X long
Nylon: Light brown 6/0 nylon
Tails: Light brown pheasant fibers
Foundation: Brass pins or wire at sides of body
Tergites: Light brown rayon floss, under body heavily marked with black lacquer at dorsal and lateral surfaces
Sternites: Light brown rayon floss, underbody marked with brown lacquer on ventral surfaces
Overbody: Natural flat monofilament
Gills: Light brownish gray marabou bunched thickly at the sides of body and picked out after securing with fine gold wire
Wing cases: Dark mottled brown feather tied down over thorax
Legs: Brownish mottled pheasant hackle
Head: Light brown nylon

4. Medium Pale Sulphur Drake (*Ephemera blanda*)

This is a medium-sized species principally recorded from the swift southeastern rivers of the Smoky Mountains. Specimens in the Cornell Collections catalogued under Needham were taken from trout waters in Georgia, West Virginia, and North Carolina. The adults have pale sulphur-yellow bodies, with relatively unmottled grayish-brown wings. The mature nymphs are slightly smaller than the Green Drakes that are sometimes mixed with their hatching, measuring about five-eighths inch in length.

There is a related southern species, the comparatively small *Ephemera triplex*, which is recorded primarily from the swift trout rivers of West Virginia. The specimens in the Needham collection are from rivers like the Pigeon and the Greenbrier and the Cheat. The gill structures of these ecotypes are pale, yellowish olive, unlike the brownish and pale-gray gills of the other species.

Tails: Medium olive, 3/16 inch
Tergites: Pale amber with faint brown markings, ⅜ inch
Sternites: Pale amber, ⅜ inch
Gills: Medium olive, ⅛ inch
Thorax: Pale amber with faint brown markings, ⅛ inch
Sternum: Pale amber, ⅛ inch
Wing cases: Medium brownish olive, ⅛ inch
Legs: Pale amber, 3/16 inch
Head: Pale amber, 1/16 inch

Hook: Size 14 Mustad 79580 4X long
Nylon: Tan 6/0 nylon
Tails: Medium olive pheasant fibers
Foundation: Brass pins or wire
Tergites: Pale amber rayon floss lightly marked with brown
Sternites: Pale amber rayon floss
Overbody: Natural flat monofilament
Gills: Medium olive marabou bunched thickly along sides of body and picked out after securing with fine gold wire rib
Thorax: Pale amber underbody wound with flat nylon monofilament
Wing cases: Medium brown feather section tied over thorax
Legs: Pale amber pheasant hackle
Head: Tan nylon

5. Pale Yellow Drake (*Ephemera varia*)

This is another important hatch, well distributed across northern waters, from New England to the rivers of Michigan and Wisconsin. Although its populations are not as extensive as those of the larger *Ephemera* mayflies, the species still generates good rises of fish. The nymphs are quite translucent and pale, with delicate light-amber markings, and gill structures and tails of pale bluish gray. These pale ecotypes have often been mistaken for the nymphs of *Ephemera guttulata,* leading a generation of fly-fishers to waste their efforts on cream-colored imitations.

Tails: Pale bluish gray, 3/16 inch
Tergites: Pale amber faintly mottled with brown, ⅜ inch
Sternites: Pale amber, ⅜ inch
Gills: Pale bluish gray, ⅛ inch
Thorax: Pale amber faintly mottled, ⅛ inch
Sternum: Pale amber, ⅛ inch
Wing cases: Pale amber mottled with brown, ⅛ inch
Legs: Pale amber, 3/16 inch
Heads: Pale amber mottled, 1/16 inch

Hook: Size 14 Mustad 79580 4X long
Nylon: Tan 6/0 nylon
Tails: Pale bluish gray pheasant fibers
Foundation: Brass pins or wire
Tergites: Pale amber with brown markings
Sternites: Pale amber floss
Overbody: Natural flat nylon monofilament
Gills: Pale bluish gray marabou thickly bunched and picked out after securing with fine gold wire ribbing
Thorax: Pale amber floss
Wing cases: Pale brownish feather tied down over thorax
Legs: Pale amber pheasant hackle
Head: Tan nylon

Ephemera varia is a relatively warm-water species found in big trout rivers like the Beaverkill and Big Pine Creek and the Lackawaxen in our eastern mountains. According to the studies performed by Justin Leonard, in his superb little book *Mayflies of Michigan Trout Streams,* the distribution of the Yellow Drake there is limited to the warmer trout waters of lower Michigan. There are good hatches on the White, Muskegon, Big Manistee, Big South Pere Marquette, and lower Au Sable. Full-grown nymphs measure about nine-sixteenths inch in length.

These imitations are extremely important to anglers whose home rivers experience good hatches of *Ephemera* flies. There is considerable variation in exact coloring and body markings from river to river, not only among these big mayfly nymphs, but among virtually all subaquatic species. The serious angler should use these descriptions and color plates merely as a catalogue and guide, always alert for his local variations in color, chroma, and markings.

Knowledge of these nymphs and their role in the trout diet is often critical to success during the blizzardlike hatches of these big mayflies. Most fishermen become preoccupied with a twilight full of large fluttering drakes, failing to grasp that fishing a nymph imitation is better than a more obvious dry fly. The trout have demonstrated this truth again and again, in both Europe and the United States. Our myopic commitment to the dry-fly Halford tradition too often causes us to waste a fine *Ephemera* hatch, flailing the current with pattern after pattern. It is a lesson about the big mayflies worth remembering—from the pastoral Gäcka in Yugoslavia, throughout central Europe to the classic Dove that Charles Cotton fished with Izaak Walton.

American anglers can profit too. Although our Green Drake hatches are limited to eastern rivers, from the Great Chazy on the Canadian border to the swift Nantahala in North Carolina, our other *Ephemera* species are widespread—and their nymphs are deadly from Maine to Montana.

The Silt-Burrowing Hexagenia Nymphs

WHIPPOORWILLS WERE calling softly on the sandy ridges above the darkening river, their melancholia muted in the dense thickets of hemlocks and pines. It was warm and still. The late-evening hatches of big *Hexagenia* drakes that come off the Michigan rivers in the last weeks of June had not started. There had been a few flies hatching in late afternoon, but no real evening rise had begun. Some of the big mayflies were still hatching, and finally I heard a good fish work along the deadfalls across the river.

It was not really a rise. The usual response of a big brown to these nocturnal *Hexagenia* flies is a savage splash, especially when they are fluttering on the surface or laying their eggs. But this was a strong, sucking roll that unmistakably spelled a heavy fish in spite of the rippling current sounds among the logs.

It was the lower Pere Marquette in Michigan. It is heavy water even in midsummer, and I leaned into its strong current in the darkness. We were fishing the big dry flies originated in Baldwin for imitating the big *Hexagenia* hatches, the pattern tied by the late Harry Duffing between customers in his Main Street barber shop.

His imitations were big flies. Their tails were long pheasant-tail fibers; the bodies were thickly fashioned of muskrat dubbing. Their wings were dark goose-quill sections, and the hackles were brown both at the wings and palmered the length of the hook.

These big floaters usually worked, but this trout continued to roll in the darkness along the tangled log jam, ignoring cast after cast to the sound of his rises. *There's a good fish here,* I yelled to my father, *but he's not taking my fly so far.*

Stay with him! my father answered.

The trout rose twenty or thirty times, and I must have put a hundred casts over him with increasing desperation. His rises sounded powerful. The night was filled with the frantic *swish-swish* rhythm of my casting, but the trout still refused to take the fly.

Suddenly there was no sound of a rise, but the rod snapped down in a vicious strike. The fish had hooked itself and bulldogged sullenly along the tangled logs. It felt powerful in the heavy current. There was a strong run that bolted upstream, slicing the surface with a shrill humming sound of the line, and somewhere, half-seen in the twilight, the great fish jumped. The splash was almost frightening, magnified by the darkness and my apprehension. We had held a campfire party a few days earlier to celebrate my sixteenth birthday. The fish was still strong, and fear that it might break off in the logs or throw my fly in some angry jump welled up in my chest. My arms were shaking now, half with adrenalin and half in youthful fear, and then the great trout circled weakly just beyond the net.

Finally it surrendered, threshing sullenly in the meshes while I waded ashore in the darkness. *How big is he?* My father had come downstream.

Big, I said wearily. *He's got me tired too.*

We were finished for the night. Turning on a flashlight will spook a wild trout, but it did not matter if we were quitting.

What about some light?

Okay, I said.

It was a heavy male brown trout, nearly six pounds, with dime-sized scarlet spots on its sides. The fly was hooked deep in its throat, and when I freed it there was something strange. Its dubbing was torn apart in a crudely wrapped tangle of fur. The hackles had unwound and broken off at the wings, leaving only a few bunched fibers, and the wings were only a thin echo of the original fly.

It's completely shredded! I said. *The fly couldn't have been floating like this—he must have taken it wet!*

Perhaps he did, said my father.

It was a puzzle. Everyone fished dry flies during the big *Hexagenia* hatches in those days, yet this fish had apparently been feeding below the surface. Its rise-forms had been audible swirls instead of the usual towering splashes. Its take had been a sullen pull, more like a salmon rising to a wet fly than a brown trout rising to a fluttering drake. We killed the fish with a merciful blow from the priest-knife.

Check his stomach, my father suggested.

The knife slipped easily along the ventral surfaces toward the gill structure, and I carefully held the point away from its entrails. The stomach and throat canal were stuffed with emerging nymphs, some still tangled in their shredded and splitting nymphal skins.

Look at them! I said. *Not an adult among this mess!*

The half-hatched nymphs continued to squeeze out from its alimentary tract like the contents of a tightly stuffed sausage. *He's taken nothing but nymphs all evening!* my father said.

It was a valuable lesson in imitating the big *Hexagenia* flies that I have never forgotten. Nymphal imitations have often produced some very big trout for me during these hatches, even when most of the fish were wildly rising to the adults.

The *Hexagenia* nymphs are lenitic or slow-water forms that burrow into the silt, detritus, and soft-bottom materials of lakes, ponds, slow-flowing rivers, and the backwaters of fast-current streams. These burrowing nymphs are rather slender and slightly flat-bodied. They are distinguished by their rather extensive, hairy gill-systems. The nymphs are equipped with narrow heads, tusked mandibles, and powerful front legs perfectly suited for burrowing into the bottom materials. The forefeet are flattened like scrapers, and the head is slightly chisel-shaped. The second and third pairs of legs are held close under the thorax, like the stabilizing legs of a modern earth-moving backhoe. Perhaps most unusual, in the morphological perfection so typical of nature, are the strongly tapered, hornlike mandibles. These mandibles are as long as or longer than the head and are used to support the roof of the burrow as the nymph buries itself. These are the largest of the American Ephemeroptera, measuring as much as one and a half inches in the female nymphs of the *Hexagenia recurvata* species.

These nymphs are virtually as shy as the trout themselves, and are alarmed when displaced and exposed to the light. Such exposed nymphs eagerly attempt to burrow back into their protective silt. The late James Needham compared their persistence, in his definitive *The Biology of Mayflies,* to the dogged subterranean efforts of moles. Needham described the methods of digging in this paragraph:

> It thrusts its shovel-like feet forward, close together, edges upward into the mud and then spreads them apart, removing the mud to right and left. Into the cleft thus opened, it then thrusts its head and gives it an upward toss, lifting the earth far forward on the tops of its long mandibular tusks. Then, lowering its head, it lunges forward into the opening, pushing with its legs and propelling itself also by means of undulations of its long abdomen.

These nymphs subsist on the rich diatomaceous ooze in which they burrow and conceal themselves. They are most commonly found in the muddy shallows of lakes and rivers, sometimes burrowing into the banks of marshy streams. The plumose gill-systems found in these burrowing nymphal forms are unique. These gills consist of dense internal filaments, surprisingly flexible, rising upward in two rows from the lateral back segments. Their respiratory movements may swing them inward, almost meeting along the dorsal centerline, and widely separated when extended outward. They are waved in pulsing movements, together and apart in pairs, with waves of motion rippling along the abdomen toward the posterior segments. These cycles create water currents and supply oxygen to the gills.

These big *Hexagenia* nymphs exist in extensive populations on both lakes and rivers, and their emergence without question produces the most impressive fly hatches found on American waters. Hatching of the several species ranges from May until September, starting with the rivers of North Carolina and finally emerging on the rivers of Canada in late August and September. The trout love them, and their size and numbers attract even the largest fish to concentrate on these nymphs. Since their nymphal life cycle lasts three years, these subaquatic forms are available at several stages of growth.

1. Great Sulphur Drake (*Hexagenia carolina*)

This species is the smallest of its genus to have any importance on American trout waters. Its fully developed nymphs measure about thirteen-sixteenths inch in length upon hatching. It is found primarily in the many trout rivers of our southeastern mountains, from Virginia to the many beautiful rivers that drain the Great Smokies.

Some specimens of these nymphs have a distinct lavender or rose cast on their dorsal and ventral body surfaces. They swim quite swiftly to the surface during a hatch, like all of the *Hexagenias* on emergence, and are quite similar to the somewhat paler species *Hexagenia marlicanda*. This species is also found in the same waters as the related *Hexagenia carolina*, although its hatches are not as heavy.

Tails: Fringed olive gray, 5/16 inch

Tergites: Rose tinted amber darkly tinged and marked with olive and brown, and a pale dorsal stripe, ¾ inches

Sternites: Rose-tinted amber tinged and marked with dusky olive, ¾ inch

Gills: Dusky olive gray, 3/16 inch

Thorax: Amber darkly mottled with brown and olive on its dorsal surfaces, 3/16 inch

Sternum: Amber, 3/16 inch

Wing cases: Dark olive brown, 3/16 inch

Legs: Amber delicately marked with brown, 3/16 inch

Head: Amber darkly mottled with brown, 3/16 inch

Hook: Sizes 10-12 Mustad 79580 4X long

Nylon: Tan 6/0 nylon

Tails: Olive gray pheasant fibers

Tergites: Amber floss underbody marked with dark brown

Sternites: Amber floss underbody marked with brown

Overbody: Natural flat monofilament

Gills: Dusky olive gray marabou thickly bunched at the sides, and secured with fine gold wire

Thorax: Amber floss underbody wrapped with flat monofilament

Wing cases: Dark olive brown feather section tied down over the thorax

Legs: Amber mottled pheasant hackle

Head: Tan nylon with brown lacquer on dorsal surfaces

2. Great Pale-Yellow Drake (*Hexagenia marlicanda*)

This large *Hexagenia* mayfly is quite similar to its related species from the southern watersheds of the Great Smokies. Its heaviest populations are found in rivers like the Conococheague and Falling Spring Run in the limestone valleys of southern Pennsylvania; good hatches are also found in Big Hunting Creek and the Antietam in Maryland.

These nymphs measure approximately fifteen-sixteenths inch at full development, and they are particularly pale and beautiful ecotypes. Some specimens have a pinkish cast in their dorsal surfaces.

Tails: Fringed light olive gray, ⅜ inch

Tergites: Pale yellowish cream delicately marked with light olive gray and dusky brown, and a pale median zone, ½ inch

Sternites: Pale yellowish cream lightly marked with brown, ½ inch

Gills: Pale grayish purple, 3/16 inch

Thorax: Pale yellowish cream delicately marked with brown, 5/32 inch

Sternum: Pale yellowish cream, 5/32 inch

Wing cases: Dusky medium brown, 5/32 inch

Legs: Pale yellowish cream lightly mottled with brown, 3/16 inch

Head: Pale yellowish cream mottled with brown, 3/32 inch

Hook: Sizes 8-10 Mustad 79580 4X long

Nylon: Pale yellow 6/0 nylon

Tails: Pale olive pheasant fibers

Tergites: Pale yellowish cream underbody marked with dark brown lacquer

Sternites: Pale yellowish cream underbody with brown markings

Overbody: Natural flat monofilament

Gills: Pale grayish purple marabou thickly bunched at the sides and secured with fine gold wire

Thorax: Pale yellowish cream with flat monofilament overbody

Wing cases: Medium brown feather section tied down over thorax

Legs: Pale mottled pheasant hackle

Head: Pale yellow nylon with light brown lacquer on the dorsal surfaces

3. Great Brown Drake (*Hexagenia bilineata*)

This is a large, darkly mottled species widely distributed in American waters. James Needham catalogues specimens in his *Biology of Mayflies* that were collected in such disparate regions as Texas, Iowa, Tennessee, Kentucky, Minnesota, Michigan, Illinois, and Wisconsin. Its fully grown nymphs measure about one inch in length, and there are good populations in our north-central trout waters.

These are hatches of late June and early July, and I have frequently collected specimens from cottage screens in Wisconsin and upper Michigan in long-ago boyhood summers.

Tails: Fringed brownish olive, 3/8 inch

Tergites: Medium brown mottled with darker markings, 1/2 inch

Sternites: Medium brown delicately mottled, 1/2 inch

Gills: Dark brownish olive, 3/16 inch

Thorax: Dark mottlings on medium brown, 3/16 inch

Sternum: Medium brown, 3/16 inch

Wing cases: Dark brownish, 3/16 inch

Legs: Medium brown darkly mottled, 1/4 inch

Head: Dark mottled brown, 3/32 inch

Hook: Sizes 6-8 Mustad 79580 4X long

Nylon: Brown 6/0 nylon

Tails: Dark brownish olive pheasant fibers

Tergites: Medium brown underbody with black lacquer markings

Sternites: Medium brown underbody with dark brown ventral markings.

Overbody: Brown-dyed flat monofilament

Gills: Dark brownish olive marabou thickly bunched at the sides and secured with fine gold wire

Thorax: Medium brown underbody wrapped with flat monofilament

Wing cases: Dark brown feather tied over thorax

Legs: Pheasant body hackle dyed dark brown

Head: Brown nylon with dark brown lacquer on its dorsal surfaces

4. Great Leadwing Drake (*Hexagenia atrocaudata*)

This species is a large, slate-colored mayfly that is also widely distributed in American trout streams and lakes. Although it is similar in its configuration and color to the larger Michigan species, the incredibly abundant *Hexagenia limbata*, it is not as numerous in our north-central rivers. Specimens have been recorded from Ontario, New York, West Virginia, Michigan, Pennsylvania, Virginia, North Carolina, Georgia, Minnesota, and Wisconsin. Although it does not generate blizzardlike hatches, it is an important fly-fishing species which is especially partial to marshy streams and beaver ponds having consistently cold temperatures. The icy, spring-fed marl swamps of Michigan are optimal habitats for this species and the larger *Hexagenia recurvata*.

Tails: Fringed dark olive brownish, 5/16 inch

Tergites: Dark brownish amber with pale dorsal stripe and chocolate crescent-shaped markings, 5/8 inch

Sternites: Dark grayish amber with dark median markings, 5/8 inch

Gills: Dark olive brownish, 1/4 inch

Thorax: Dark grayish amber heavily mottled, 5/32 inch

Sternum: Dark grayish amber, 5/32 inch

Wing cases: Dark grayish olive, 3/16 inch

Legs: Dark amber mottled with brown, 1/4 inch

Head: Dark grayish mottled with brown, 1/8 inch

Hook: Sizes 6-8 Mustad 79580 4X long

Nylon: Brown 6/0 nylon

Tails: Dark olive brownish pheasant fibers

Tergites: Dark amber underbody with a pale dorsal stripe and dark brown crescent-shaped markings in lacquer

Sternites: Dark amber underbody with brown lacquer ventral markings

Overbody: Natural flat nylon monofilament

Gills: Dark olive brown marabou thickly bunched at the sides and secured with fine gold wire

Thorax: Dark amber underbody with flat nylon overbody

Wing cases: Dark grayish olive feather section tied down over thorax

Legs: Dark amber mottled pheasant hackle

Head: Brown nylon

The fully grown nymphs measure approximately one-and-one-sixteenth inches in length. Emergence is relatively late in the summer, coming between the middle of July and early August in Michigan and Wisconsin.

5.   Great Olive Drake (*Hexagenia rigida*)

This is a major species particularly numerous on large relatively warm rivers like the Big South Pere Marquette and Muskegon in lower Michigan, but its major hatches are found on lakes. It is primarily a northern *Hexagenia* of considerable importance to fly-fishers. Specimens are recorded from Quebec, Pennsylvania, Ontario, Manitoba, Vermont, New York, Michigan, and Wisconsin. Although its dorsal coloration is somewhat different, and its size slightly smaller, these big nymphs are almost indistinguishable from those of *Hexagenia limbata*. The adults are impressive insects. Their wings are pale grayish olive, the thorax and abdomen are yellowish olive with dark-brown markings, and their tails are amber with woodduck-like markings. They are elegant mayflies. Their fully grown nymphs measure about one and a quarter inches.

These big drakes emerge during the month of July on the rivers of Michigan and Wisconsin, with some sporadic hatches lasting as late as the middle of August. Their nymphs like silty backwaters, but largely avoid the cold, spring-fed headwaters and marl swamps that feed many of our principal rivers in the Middle West.

Tails: Fringed dark grayish dun, 7/16 inch

Tergites: Dark amber with a dusky olive cast and brown markings bordering pale median zone and at lateral margins, ¼ inch

Sternites: Dark amber marked with brown, ¾ inch

Gills: Dark grayish dun, ¼ inch

Thorax: Dark amber with heavy brown and olive markings, ¼ inch

Sternum: Dark amber, ¼ inch

Wing cases: Dark brownish olive, 3/16 inch

Legs: Dark grayish amber with brown markings, ⅜ inch

Head: Dark grayish amber with brown markings, ⅛ inch

Hook: Sizes 4-6 Mustad 79580 4X long

Nylon: Dark tan 6/0 nylon

Tails: Dark grayish dun pheasant fibers

Tergites: Dark amber underbody lacquered with dark brown markings defining a pale median zone

Sternites: Dark amber underbody with brown ventral markings

Overbody: Natural flat monofilament

Gills: Dark grayish dun thickly bunched at the sides and secured with fine gold wire

Thorax: Dark amber underbody wrapped with natural flat monofilament

Wing cases: Dark brownish olive feather section tied down over thorax

Legs: Dark amber mottled pheasant fibers

Head: Dark tan nylon with brown dorsal lacquer

6.   Great Dark-Green Drake (*Hexagenia recurvata*)

This is the largest mayfly found in American waters. Its fully grown nymphs reach a length of as much as one and three-eighths inches, and are found in cold-water habitats. The range of *Hexagenia recurvata* is principally northern, and specimens are recorded from Maine to Michigan. Pennsylvania and West Virginia populations also exist. Although they are larger and considerably darker, these nymphs are quite similar to those of *Hexagenia limbata*. This nymph is distinguishable through its truncated, cone-shaped frontal lobes, and the single gills on the first segment of the abdomen—unlike the double gill-structures of its sister nymphs—are a singular feature of its anatomy.

These big drakes emerge on Michigan and Wisconsin rivers from late May until the last week in June.

Tails: Fringed grayish dun with a dark center, ⅝ inch

Tergites: Dark grayish amber heavily flushed with olive and heavy brown markings, 1 inch

Sternites: Dark grayish amber marked with brown along the ventral median, 1 inch

Gills: Dark purplish gray, 5/16 inch

Thorax: Dark purplish mottled brown, ⅜ inch

Sternum: Dark grayish amber, ⅜ inch

Wing cases: Dark purplish brown, ¼ inch

Legs: Dark amber mottled with brown, ⅜ inch

Head: Dark purplish brown, ⅛ inch

Hook: Sizes 2-4 Mustad 79580 4X long

Nylon: Dark tan 6/0 nylon

Tails: Dark grayish dun pheasant fibers

Tergites: Dark grayish amber underbody with dark brown dorsal markings

Sternites: Dark grayish amber underbody with brown ventral markings

Overbody: Natural flat monofilament

Gills: Dark purplish gray marabou thickly bunched at the sides and secured with fine gold wire

Thorax: Dark amber underbody

Wing cases: Dark purplish brown feather tied down over thorax

Legs: Dark brownish mottled pheasant hackle

Head: Dark tan nylon with brown dorsal lacquer

7. Great Olive-Winged Drake (*Hexagenia limbata*)

Although this is not the largest of its species, it is perhaps the most important to American fly-fishermen. It has been described from such disparate sites as Quebec, Ontario, Manitoba, and British Columbia, in addition to its principal range in Minnesota, Michigan, and Wisconsin.

The heaviest populations are concentrated in optimum habitats, relatively cold lakes and streams with rather firm bottom-silts. Their unusual U-shaped burrows are structurally unsound, except in marls and mud banks firm enough to support such delicate tunneling. These burrows penetrate as deeply as six inches into the bottom. Marl swamps provide such habitat in almost unlimited acreages, and the marl-bottomed lakes of Michigan and Wisconsin are equally rich. Large backwaters and stream banks can also provide such suitable environmental conditions. The fully developed nymphs of *Hexagenia limbata* measure one and a quarter inches.

Although hatching adults have been recorded from the second week in June through the summer to the middle of September, the most concentrated period of emergence lies in the two-week period beginning shortly before the end of June. The nymphs are most readily available to the fish during cycles of emergence, like all of the *Hexagenia* mayflies, but spates and periods of high water also dislodge many of them into the current at other times as well. Stomach autopsies performed in Michigan clearly indicate that these nymphal forms, at several stages in their two-year growth cycle, are a major part of the trout diet all year—and research conducted by Justin Leonard revealed their presence in trout stomachs in surprisingly large numbers throughout the fall and winter months.

Dry-fly fishing is often superb when *Hexagenia limbata* is hatching, but there are times when only the smaller fish are working on top, and the big nymphs take the trophies. Fishing a nymphal imitation in anticipation of a hatch is also productive, even though there are no flies hatching or fish rising yet.

Tails: Fringed grayish dun with a dark purple center, ½ inch

Tergites: Dusky amber flushed with olive and strong purplish crescent-shaped markings, ¾ inch

Sternites: Dusky amber with dark markings along the ventral median, ¾ inch

Gills: Medium purplish dun with dark gill-cores, ¼ inch

Thorax: Dusky amber flushed with purple and mottled with brown, ⅜ inch

Sternum: Dusky amber, ⅜ inch

Wing cases: Medium purplish brown, ¼ inch

Legs: Pale amber mottled with brown, ⅜ inch

Head: Dusky amber mottled with purplish brown, ⅛ inch

Hook: Sizes 4-6 Mustad 79580 4X long

Nylon: Tan 6/0 nylon

Tails: Dark grayish dun pheasant fibers

Tergites: Dark amber underbody with dark purple lacquer crescent-shaped markings

Sternites: Dark amber underbody with dark brown ventral markings

Overbody: Natural flat nylon monofilament

Gills: Medium purplish dun marabou thickly bunched at sides and secured with fine gold wire

Thorax: Dark amber underbody with flat monofilament overbody

Wing cases: Medium purplish brown feather tied down over the thorax

Legs: Pale amber mottled pheasant hackle

Head: Tan nylon with brown dorsal lacquer

It is curious that a relict population of this mayfly species is known from the richly alkaline rivers of northern California, yet the hatch is not recorded in our other western states. There are heavy populations on the Fall River, with excellent dry-fly and nymph fishing when the big drakes are coming off.

The fly-fisherman who has not witnessed these hatches of *Hexagenia limbata* has missed one of the most explosive and dramatic orgies of feeding imaginable. Optimal habitats for the species characteristically support as many as five hundred nymphs per square foot of bottom marl. Such densities of population obviously generate incredible hatches of giant mayflies, their fluttering wingspread as much as two inches. Particularly good hatches literally fill the darkness with flies, obscuring the vision and striking the face of an angler. It is an unsettling experience.

Hatching usually starts at twilight, but peak emergence is usually about nine o'clock. The hatch can last well beyond midnight, but most go on only about three hours. The nymphs swim erratically and rather swiftly to the surface, writhing in their skins for ten to fifty feet before fully hatching through the meniscus. Sometimes I have watched a big subimago ride the current as much as a hundred feet before leaving the water. During such a hatch there are thousands and thousands of flies migrating from the bottom to the surface, and the fish go wild.

The Fringe-Gilled Nymphs of the Potamanthus

The road climbs steadily into the thickly forested foothills above Elkin, where the white-clapboard houses of Blowing Rock lie in the first summits of the Blue Ridge. The midsummer heat of the coastal plain is weaker there. Hawks and ospreys circle patiently on the foothill thermals. The road climbs higher toward Altamont, and behind the barrier of these haze-colored mountains lie the winding currents of the French Broad.

Asheville has changed like everything else in these past thirty years, but underneath the corrosive patina of change—the drive-in diners and the rotting automobile graveyards and the cheaply winking spaghetti of neon—the old echoes of Asheville survive.

Its past is still there. The time of summer houses built to escape the oppressive heat of Raleigh and Fayetteville and Charleston is still visible in its side steets. There were even some families that came from Atlanta and Savannah. Others came to the drier altitudes for their health, in a time when tuberculosis was as feared as cancer, and the fierce humidity of tidewater country was like a sentence of death.

There are still high-ceilinged brick houses and clapboard houses in the steep streets above the town. There are wedding-cake Victorian mansions, with stained-glass lights above their entrances, and the flickering leafwork patterns of the elms sheltering their neweled scrollwork porches. It is easy to imagine the impact of such streets on a budding writer like Thomas Wolfe, and there are echoes of *Look Homeward, Angel* in its old cemeteries, with their moss-covered headstones and classical mausoleums—and winged figures carved in weathering marble.

Beyond Asheville and its winding river the road climbs toward the threshold of the Great Smokies. Its signs point toward hill towns like Cherokee, Tuckasegee, and Shooting Creek. Scaly Mountain lies in these foothills. It is a hard country of mountain people, fighting its hardscrabble poverty with fruit-jar whiskey, and a tight-lipped unwillingness to accept the ultimate defeats of life.

It is surprisingly rich in trout water too. The Nantahala is perhaps the best, draining the high ridges above Shooting Creek, where Georgia and the Carolinas meet. That junction lies high on the shoulder of Persimmon Mountain, in the headwaters of the Chattooga.

The Nantahala spills and tumbles down its pine and dogwood gorge beginnings. It winds briefly in a thin-soiled bottom of poor fields and mountain farmsteads, and then drops swiftly into a ten-mile reach of heavy water that spells big trout

However, it is private water. The dirt road that winds along the shoulder of its shadbush ridges branches back toward the river, under the elms toward the fishing house and its screened tackle porch and the manicured lawn that reaches down to the Home Pool.

Welcome! Hugh Chatham met us in the gathering darkness. *Welcome to the Nantahala and Rainbow Springs!*

We shook hands warmly. *It's been too long.*

Come inside. His tidewater accent was soft as the twilight. *Supper's 'bout ready and there's some sourmash waiting!*

Perfect! I laughed.

There were *Potamanthus* flies on the porch screens. There are many other rivers where I have fished this hatch, and the memory drifts to summer evenings on the lower Beaverkill at Cook's Falls and Peakville, the sprawling flats of the Delaware between Margaretville and Shinhopple before the completion of the Peapacton Reservoir, and the challenging waist-deep runs of the Schoharie below Lexington. These are exceptionally fine *Potamanthus* rivers, but when the bright yellow-winged drakes are hatching in the memory, my thoughts always return to those Olympian evenings on the Nantahala—particularly the four-pound rainbow that took my nymph in a deep ledgerock pool.

Louis Rhead wrote about the *Potamanthus* mayflies in his *American Trout-Stream Insects*, describing their hatching on the Beaverkill more than forty years ago and calling them Golden Drakes. Fifteen years later, Preston Jennings described these hatches in his *Book of Trout Flies*, but observed that the hatches he witnessed had emerged with such warm river temperatures that few rises were seen.

Needham lists eight American species, although not all of these *Potamanthus* flies are found in cold-water habitats associated with trout. Their nymphs are sprawling and swimming forms, inhabiting mud-flat bottoms like the burrowing *Ephemeras* and *Hexagenias,* but without burrowing into the silt. They live just out of the primary current-tongues, even frequenting the bottom eddies of fast water. Fully developed nymphs measure about one-half to three-quarters inch in length. They are unique in their fringe-gilled configuration.

The frontal margin of the head is somewhat rounded. The mandibular tusks are variable in length, depending upon the individual species, and taper toward the apex. Short spinules occur on their dorsal surfaces, and also along each lateral margin. There are fringed hairs on the enlarged basal portions, while the remaining tusk is bare.

The anterolateral surfaces of the pronotum are relatively wide, and it is narrower at its posterior margin. The anterior border is immarginate on each side of the median line. The maxillary and labial palps are three-jointed. The labrum is wider than its length. The femora of the legs are flattened, while their tibiae and tarsi are slender. There is a rather long, curved apical spine on the fore tibia. The foreleg is longest in some species, but in others, the middle leg exceeds it in length. The fringed gills are lateral, dramatically extended from the abdominal segments in perhaps the most unique element in the morphology of the *Potamanthus* nymphs.

These unique gills are rudimentary on the first segment of the body. The gills are paired on segments two through seven, with each primary trachea slender and pointed, fringed on its margins with long hairs. There are three tails, with the center tail somewhat shorter than the outside pair. Each tail is heavily fringed with hairs along its lateral margins.

1.   Pale Cream Drake (*Potamanthus diaphanus*)

This is a pale, almost chalky nymph that many biologists and fishing writers have attributed to *Ephemera guttulata* in the past. Perhaps because of its pale coloring, it tends to conceal itself more thoroughly in the bottom trash and detritus, leading such observers to classify it as a burrowing species. The species is recorded from Pennsylvania and New York, although its range may be wider. It hatches just at twilight from late June until well past the middle of July.

Potamanthus inequalis is a slightly larger but quite similar northeastern species. These nymphs swim rather rapidly on hatching, and the following imitation should be fished with a teasing suggestion of their swimming imparted by the rod tip. They measure about a half-inch at maturity.

Tails: Pale grayish marked at midpoints, ¼ inch
Body: Pale grayish cream, with faint dorsal markings, ⅜ inch
Gills: Pale grayish, ⅛ inch
Thorax: Pale grayish cream with faint dorsal markings, ⅛ inch inch
Legs: Pale mottled grayish, ¼ inch
Head: Pale grayish cream, 1/16 inch

Hook: Sizes 14-16 Mustad 9672 3X long
Nylon: Pale cream 6/0 nylon
Tails: Pale grayish pheasant-tail fibers
Body: Pale grayish cream dubbing
Gills: Pale grayish dun pheasant fiber points tied in at each body segment
Thorax: Pale grayish cream dubbing
Wing cases: Pale grayish brown feather section tied over thorax
Legs: Pale barred mallard fibers
Head: Pale cream nylon

2.   Pale Golden Drake (*Potamanthus distinctus*)

This generally distributed eastern species is recorded on rivers from New England to North Carolina, and is easily recognized from its bright golden-yellow wings to the orangish lateral margins of its body tergites, which appear almost striped. The nymphs hatch from late June until August, and measure about nine-sixteenths inch.

Tails: Pale olive brown with dark markings, ¼ inch
Body: Light brown heavily mottled with dark brown to create a pale median stripe, ⅜ inch
Gills: Mottled brownish olive, ⅛ inch
Thorax: Light brown heavily mottled, ⅛ inch
Wing cases: Medium brown, ⅛ inch
Legs: Pale yellowish brown with medium brown markings, ¼ inch
Head: Medium mottled brown, 1/16 inch

Hook: Sizes 12-14 Mustad 9672 3X long
Nylon: Tan 6/0 nylon
Tails: Olive gray pheasant fibers
Body: Light brown hare's poll dubbing mixed with guard hairs on orange silk core
Gills: Brown mottled pheasant fiber points tied in at each body segment
Thorax: Light brown dubbing mixed with guard hairs and spun on an orange silk core
Wing cases: Medium brownish gray feather section tied down over thorax
Legs: Light brownish mottled woodduck hackle
Head: Tan nylon

3. Little Golden Drake (*Potamanthus neglectus*)

This species is distributed from New York to Maryland, and is similar to *Potamanthus distinctus*, although its nymphs measure only three-eighths inch in length. It hatches at dark during June and July.

Tails: Pale olive brown with dark markings: 3/16 inch
Body: Medium brown heavily mottled with dark markings that define a median stripe, 5/32 inch
Gills: Mottled brownish, 3/32 inch
Thorax: Medium brown heavily mottled, 3/32 inch
Wing cases: Dark brownish, 3/32 inch
Legs: Medium brown mottled, 3/16 inch
Head: Medium brown mottled, 1/16 inch

Hook: Size 16 Mustad 9672 3X long
Nylon: Brown 6/0 nylon
Tails: Pale olive brown pheasant fibers
Body: Dark brownish hare's ear dubbing mixed with guard hairs on orange silk
Gills: Dark olive-dyed brown pheasant fiber points tied in at each body segment
Thorax: Dark hare's ear dubbed on orange silk
Wing cases: Dark brownish feather section tied over thorax
Legs: Mottled woodduck hackle dyed olive
Head: Brown nylon

4. Dark Golden Drake (*Potamanthus rufus*)

This darkly mottled species is the largest of the *Potamanthus* nymphs, measuring about seven-eighths inch at full development. It is this dramatic-looking mayfly that comes off all summer on the Delaware and Esopus, leading fly-tiers like Walt Dette and Harry Darbee to dress big orange-bodied Cahills for their customers. Since their water temperatures have been scrambled ecologically through the erratic flow-level of their reservoir tailings, these rivers can produce good daytime hatches of the *Potamanthus* flies across the entire June to September period.

Potamanthus verticus is a similar species with fully grown nymphs that measure only three-eighths inch. It is distributed from New York to North Carolina and Tennessee.

Tails: Dark olive brown with dark markings at midpoints, ¼ inch
Body: Dark mottled brown with a distinct orangeish cast, ⅜ inch
Gills: Dark brownish olive, 5/32 inch
Thorax: Dark mottled brown with a distinct orangish cast, 5/32 inch
Wing cases: Reddish brown, 5/32 inch
Legs: Pale amber mottled with brown, 5/32 inch
Head: Dark reddish mottled brown, 1/16 inch

Hook: Sizes 10-12 Mustad 9672 3X long
Nylon: Dark brown 6/0 nylon
Tails: Dark olive brown pheasant fibers
Body: Dark reddish brown dubbing mixed with hare's ear guard hairs on orange silk
Gills: Dark olive pheasant fiber points tied in at each body segment
Thorax: Dark reddish brown hare's ear dubbing on orange silk
Wing cases: Reddish brown feather section tied over thorax
Legs: Brown mottled woodduck hackle
Head: Dark brown nylon

Several years ago on the Lower Beaverkill, a good hatch of *Potamanthus* flies caused an amusing incident along the river. The current was covered with the big yellow-winged drakes, and the trout worked on them eagerly. Early in the hatch I took a number of good trout on the nymph imitations, and as the fish began to concentrate more and more on the drifting adults, finally I switched to the dry fly just at dark. It produced a heavy three-pound brown that fought well after nightfall.

There was a wet-fly fisherman working the fast water at the head of the flat, and he was taking fish regularly too. The old man was about seventy-five, and from his dark workshirt and battered hat, it seemed he lived on the river. Just after I released the twenty-inch brown, the old man approached in the darkness. The current whispered softly.

Good fish, he observed laconically.

Yes, I agreed, and reeled my leader into the guides. *Best one I've had this summer in the Catskills.*

You're that matching-the-hatch feller. It was not a question and its tone was faintly belligerent. *Right?*

Yes, I said guardedly.

The old man stood stubbornly in the darkness. *Well,* he continued in a moment, *just come down here to tell you I caught all them fish with a wet Cahill that don't look nothing like them yellow flies hatching.*

Good. I hoped the conversation was over.

Don't believe them matching-the-hatch theories. It was a sermon now and I waited patiently. *This big Cahill catching all them fish proves you wrong—it don't match no yellow flies!*

Let me see the fly, I said.

It was poorly tied, its roughly dubbed body mixed with brownish guard hairs. The tails were soft brown hackle fibers, and the legs were a dark hen hackle. The wings were not woodduck, but a barred mallard feather dyed yellowish-orange.

Tied it myself, said the old man. *It works.*

It should work, I hooked the flashlight on my wading vest. *It's a pretty good imitation of a hatching Potamanthus nymph.*

That one of them yellow flies?

Yes, I continued, *they swim like minnows when they hatch—you work the Cahill with the rod?*

Always work the fly some, he admitted.

Come here. My flashlight scanned the shallows where the empty fringe-gilled shucks of the mayflies covered the surface film. *Look at these dark little skins—imagine them full of hatching nymphs with their yellowish wings beginning to pop out.*

You mean my Cahill looks like them nymphs?

Exactly, I continued. *Just like a hatching nymph.*

Goddam! he said.

Top, left to right: *Hexagenia carolina, Hexagenia marlicanda, Hexagenia atrocaudata, Hexagenia bilineata* Bottom, left to right: *Ephemera guttulata, Ephemera compar, Ephemera simulans, Ephemera varia, Ephemera blanda*

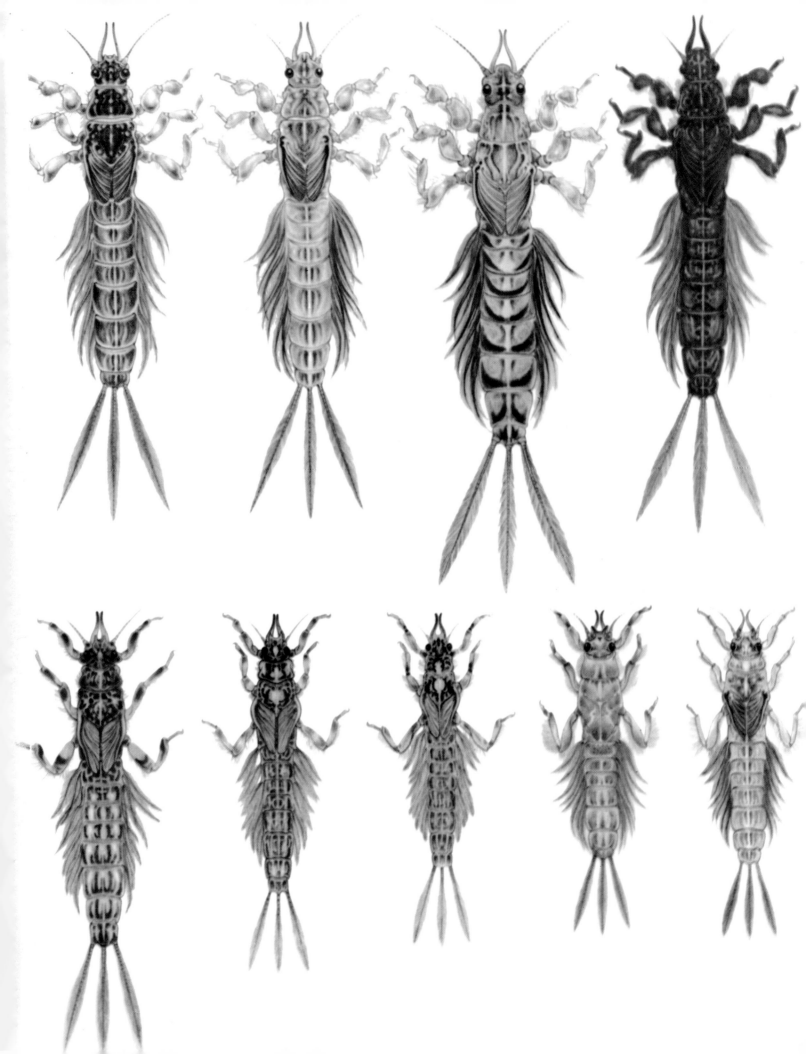

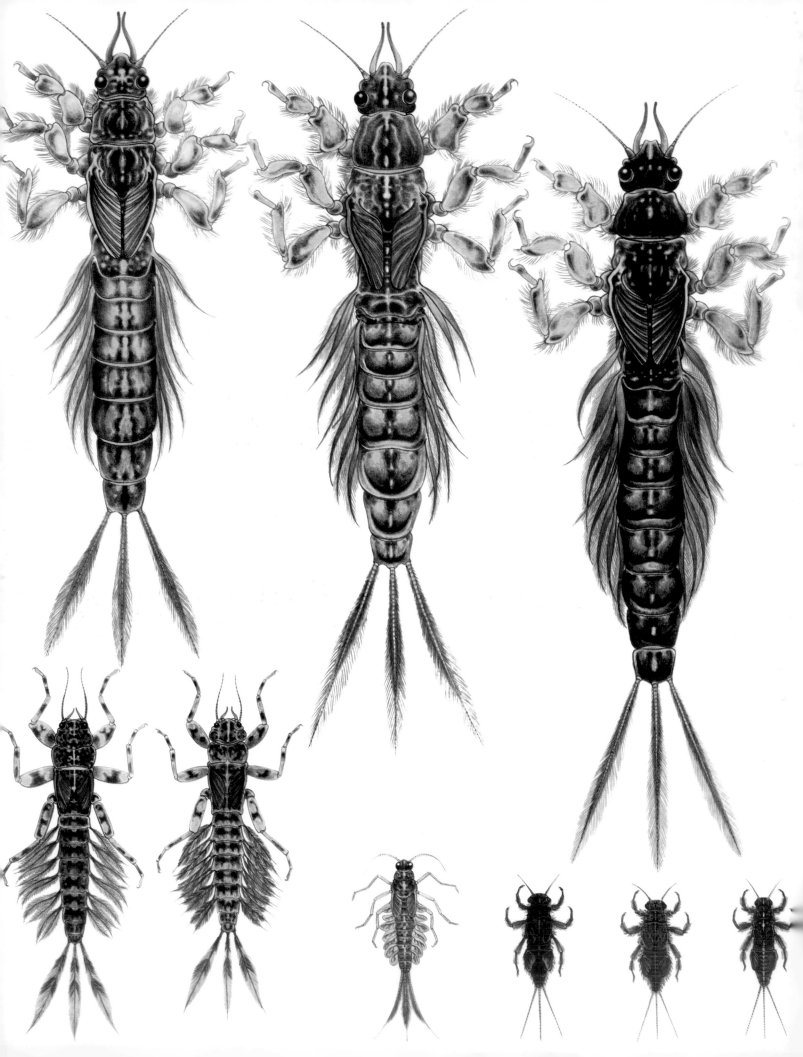

The Swimming Nymphs of Siphlonurus and Siphloplecton

The RIVER DRAINS the immense clearwater lake, its amphitheater of mountains smoke-colored in the distance. Boiling springs bubble and steam on the shoreline. There are dense forests of spruce and lodgepole pine surrounding the lake, and their pewter-colored deadfalls lie bleached and rotting in the shallows. Gulls and pelicans work the outlet shallows of the lake where the current gathers and slides into the huge cutthroat flats of the Yellowstone.

It is impossible water in the summer months. The famous timber truss-work of the Fishing Bridge spans the outlet of the lake and is lined with tourists in garish shirts, like a party-boat chartered out of Sausalito or Perth Amboy. The fish are always there, some dutifully surrendering to the flailing lures and salmon eggs and cheese, but most have reached the final stages of sophistication described in the chalkstream observations of Skues a half-century ago—that trout are at first frightened by clumsy fishermen, but ultimately they came to ignore their clumsiness, feeding disdainfully as though such fishermen did not exist.

Top three, left to right: *Hexagenia rigida, Hexagenia limbata, Hexagenia recurvata*

Bottom, left to right: *Potamanthus rufus, Potamanthus distinctus, Neocloëon almance, Tricorythodes stygiatus, Tricorythodes texanus, Tricorythodes fallax*

The headwaters of the Yellowstone are like that. There are huge flats that look more like extensions of the lake than the genesis of a major river. Giant islands of weeds undulate in the still currents. Whistling swans and herons frequent the river, and the fisherman must sometimes compete with a moose rooting in the shallows.

There are almost constant fly hatches. Millions of midge pupae drift on the gathering currents, born in the volcanic-marl richness of the lake. There are stillwater caddis flies riding the upstream wind in the evenings, and hundreds of tiny mayfly species emerge in vast regattas of delicate little duns. Millions of scuds and shrimps inhabit the dense weeds along with the slender damselflies and the predatory Anisoptera and diving-beetle larvae. But the most dramatic hatches are perhaps the big swimming mayflies that emerge in late summer, reaching a crescendo of hatching *Siphlonurus* drakes in September.

The fly life on this river is so rich that some fish are almost always working in these flats. It is one of the finest cutthroat fisheries left in the world, protected both by its glassy meadow currents and the inevitable selective feeding they cause and by the strict regulations imposed in the management of Yellowstone Park.

It has been twenty years since I last witnessed a major hatch of big *Siphlonurus* drakes on this water, but I have never forgotten either the current covered with mayflies or the greedy rises of the fish. It was a cold and rainy morning in September. The night before I had skirmished with a hungry bear over my carefully prepared stew at the Tower Falls campground, and I had spent the night in the car. It was a restless night, and I was so tired that I stopped along the Yellowstone for a midday nap. Sometimes we can sleep through thunderstorms and fire engines, but sometimes we seem to waken at the most insignificant sounds. Rain squalls had drummed intermittently on the windshield while I was sleeping, and I had dozed off again. But this was a different sound.

Fish! I thought sleepily. *It's rising fish!*

There were a dozen heavy fish working within sixty-odd feet, trout of three to five pounds, and I waded into position carefully. Several big grayish nymphs were in my fly book, and I selected one that matched the size of the hatching flies. The third cast I hooked a big cutthroat that bored past me angrily in the deepening current. It sullenly stripped line from the reel, threatening to erase the backing that remained behind the light fly line, and I turned to follow.

It was a mistake. There are lava outcroppings in the deceptively even bottom-gravel of the Yellowstone that are icy-slick with algae, and as I tried to pursue the big cutthroat, my left foot slipped. There was a desperate moment when I almost recovered my balance and then I was down. The icy current forced me into deeper water, and I was caught and carried downstream. It was too deep to wade. There is no point in fighting a river, and I simply rode the current, touching bottom now and then to keep my head above water.

Finally my wading brogues touched gravel and held, and I worked my way soddenly ashore. It was icy cold and my soaked clothing felt heavy. There was a fly box missing and my dignity was drowned, but the fish was still hooked. I stripped my drenched wading vest and Scandinavian sweater, forcing the big cutthroat into the shallows. It fought stubbornly, with brook trout bulldogging deep along the bottom, and finally drifted head down into the net.

Six pounds, read the pocket-scale.

My car heater was not working that summer, and the wind was getting raw. It had stopped raining. There were some big boulders near the river and in a sheltered place between them was a pile of dry driftwood. Stripping off my wet clothes and getting into a lightweight raincoat to break the wind, I patiently built a fire.

Its heat was welcome. The waders and wading vest and sweater were draped across the rocks and I rubbed my hands and feet. Life and feeling were slowly ebbing back. Suddenly there was the voice of a park ranger.

No fires here, he said.

Yes, I admitted, *I'm outside of a campfire area—but my car heater's not working and I'm freezing!*

Take a spill in the river? he asked.

Yes, I said. *I was fighting a big trout and slipped on one of those algae ledges out there.*

Get the fish? He grinned sympathetically.

Yes. I laughed ruefully. *Six pounds.*

Well, that's something anyway. We shook hands. *Put out the fire carefully when you're warmed up again.*

My teeth chattered slightly. *Thanks,* I said.

The nymphs of the slow-water swimming mayflies, nymphs of the *Siphlonurus* and *Siphloplecton* genera, are big enough that very large trout will take them in habitats where they are found in good numbers. These slender nymphs are distinguished by their smooth hydrodynamic configuration, and a series of prominent gill plates capable of extremely rapid movement. The legs are delicate and strong. The thoracic structures and wing cases are rather strongly humped, being somewhat higher than their width. The heads are small and relatively round. There are dense lateral fringes on both edges of the center tail, and on the inner edges of the two outer tails. This structure is a complex combination of lateral and vertical stabilization, with the additional capability of a sculling oar. The posterior lateral angles of the final abdominal segments have the effect of widening those segments with sharp appendages. This combination of features is singular with these nymphal forms.

These nymphs are widely distributed in both lakes and slow-flowing rivers. They seem to have an affinity for alkaline waters like the Yellowstone, some of the larger limestone rivers of Pennsylvania, and the rich watersheds of the Pacific coast. Many western reservoirs provide such habitat, along with extremely fertile waters like Henry's Lake in Idaho, Wade Lake in Montana, and the geothermal basin of Yellowstone Lake itself.

The *Siphlonurus* and *Siphloplecton* nymphs are extremely agile, capable of rapid swimming movements. Imitations should be fished to suggest their behavior. Such swimming motions are effected by swift, vertical undulations of the abdomen, the sculling movements of the fringed tails, and their relatively large gill plates. Their swimming patterns are extremely erratic, involving swift little pulsing movements and abrupt pauses. Both the legs and gill structures are used in starting and stopping these irregular, subaquatic migrations.

The primary function of the gills, however, is to fan a current of water to supply its breathing system with oxygen. When the nymphs are resting in the weeds or hanging stationary in the water the gills are still moving. This respiration pattern moves the gills from the tail segments along the body toward the wing cases. These nymphs are primarily a species of relatively open water, and are readily available to the fish. They seldom venture deeply into the weeds. Emergence can occur both in open water, using the tension of the surface film to split the nymphal skins, and in the weedy shallows, climbing stems and reeds and deadfalls to hatch at their existing water line. Some specimens hatch on the gravel banks and rocky shores.

1. Medium Summer Olive (*Siphlonurus alternatus*)

This is a pale brownish-olive species of *Siphlonurus* nymph that measures approximately one-half inch at full development. The species is primarily northeastern in its distribution, with collections recorded from Nova Scotia to Wisconsin. It is a handsome insect.

The rivers of northern Michigan, New York, and New England have especially good hatches in their slow-moving reaches. It emerges on the lower mileages of the Au Sable in Michigan from the last week in June until the end of July, with its heaviest hatches typically recorded just after the celebration of Independence Day. Its parallel hatches on the Ausable in the Adirondacks come a few days later, just as they come off the boggy meadows of the Otter in Vermont. The somewhat colder, slow-flowing Battenkill has *Siphlonurus* hatches lasting well into August.

Tails: Medium brown with dark banding at midpoints, ¼ inch
Tergites: Medium mottled brownish, ⅜ inch
Sternites: Pale brown with dark ventral markings, ⅜ inch
Gills: Pale brownish yellow, 1/32 inch
Thorax: Medium mottled brownish, ⅛ inch
Wing cases: Medium brown, ⅛ inch
Legs: Pale mottled brownish, 3/16 inch
Head: Medium brownish, 1/16 inch

Hook: Sizes 12-14 Orvis Premium 1X long
Nylon: Brown 6/0 nylon
Tails: Dark partridge fibers
Body: Flat monofilament over a pale brown base with dark lacquer dorsal and ventral markings
Gills: Pale brownish yellow secured at sides with fine gold wire
Thorax: Flat monofilament over pale brown base
Wing cases: Medium brown feather section tied down over thorax
Legs: Medium mottled partridge
Head: Brown nylon

Since these nymphs are highly active in the water, I have found light-wire, unweighted designs most effective. The highly original hinged nymph dressings developed by Doug Swisher and Carl Richards, described as wiggle-nymphs in their book *Selective Trout*, could have exciting implications for imitating these nymphs.

2.   Little Medium Olive (*Siphlonurus barbarus*)

This is a relatively small member of the *Siphlonurus* genus, its full-grown nymphs measuring only seven-sixteenths inch. Its distribution is largely northeastern, with specimens from Quebec, New England, and the rivers of the Catskills in New York. It is also a summer hatch.

Tails: Medium brown with dark markings at midpoints, 3/16 inch
Tergites: Dark mottled brownish, 5/16 inch
Sternites: Pale brown with dark ventral markings, 5/16 inch
Gills: Pale grayish, 1/32 inch
Thorax: Dark mottled brownish with a paler sternum, 3/32 inch
Wing cases: Dark brownish, 3/32 inch
Legs: Dark mottled brownish, 3/16 inch
Head: Dark brownish, 1/32 inch

Hook: Sizes 14-16 Orvis Premium 1X long
Nylon: Brown 6/0 nylon
Tails: Dark mottled partridge fibers
Body: Pale brown dubbing heavily mixed with hare's mask guard hairs
Gills: Pale grayish marabou secured at sides with fine gold wire
Thorax: Pale brown dubbing heavily mixed with hare's mask guard hairs
Wing cases: Dark brown feather section tied down over thorax
Legs: Dark brown partridge fibers
Head: Brown nylon

3.   Large Summer Olive (*Siphlonurus mirus*)

This is a relatively large mayfly, slightly larger than better known hatches like the Hendricksons and Gordon Quills. Its fully developed nymphs measure eleven-sixteenths inch in length. Emergence has been recorded from New England to North Carolina, and it is a summer hatch, appearing from June until September in its range of distribution.

Tails: Pale brownish with olive mottlings, ¼ inch
Tergites: Dark mottled brownish distinctly ringed, 7/16 inch
Sternites: Dark mottled brownish, 7/16 inch
Gills: Pale olive gray, 1/32 inch
Thorax: Dark mottled brownish, ⅛ inch
Wing cases: Dark slate-colored brown, 5/32 inch
Legs: Dark amber mottled with brown, ¼ inch
Head: Dark mottled brown with a slight median stripe, 1/16 inch

Hook: Sizes 10-12 Orvis Premium 1X long
Nylon: Dark brown 6/0 nylon
Tails: Medium brown partridge fibers
Body: Dark brown dubbing roughly spun with hare's mask guard hairs
Gills: Pale olive gray marabou secured at sides with fine gold wire
Thorax: Dark brown dubbing mixed with hare's mask
Wing cases: Dark slate-brown feather section tied down over thorax
Legs: Dark mottled partridge hackle
Head: Dark brown nylon

4. Great Summer Drake (*Siphlonurus occidentalis*)

This is the largest of the *Siphlonurus* hatches, the insects that I described during that classic rise of fish on the Yellowstone a few years ago. It is the biggest mayfly found on our western trout waters. Its full-grown nymphs measure thirteen-sixteenths inch. Its double gills on the first and second segments are a unique element of its nymphs, and its sternites have dull U-shaped markings.

Hatches are typically found from late July into early October. The best rises of fish and the heaviest hatches of drakes that appear in my notebooks have occurred on the alkaline watersheds of northeastern Idaho and Jackson Hole, and in the Yellowstone country.

The species is widely distributed. The Cornell collection assembled under the direction of James Needham and briefly catalogued in his *Biology of Mayflies* includes specimens gathered from New Mexico to British Columbia. Hatches from Utah, Oregon, Washington, Montana, Idaho, Colorado, and Wyoming are known. There are also good hatches on the South Platte and its several watershed reservoirs in Colorado.

Tails: Pale olive gray with darker mottlings, ⅜ inch
Tergites: Dark grayish brown heavily mottled with a pale median zone, ½ inch
Sternites: Pale grayish with brown ventral markings, ½ inch
Gills: Pale yellowish gray, 1/32 inch
Thorax: Dark grayish brown heavily mottled with a paler sternum, 3/16 inch
Wing cases: Dark grayish brown, 3/16 inch
Legs: Pale amber delicately mottled, 5/16 inch
Head: Dark grayish brown, 3/32 inch

Hook: Sizes 8-10 Orvis Premium 1X long
Nylon: Dark gray 6/0 nylon
Tails: Gray partridge dyed pale olive
Body: Flat nylon monofilament over a brownish gray underbody with brown dorsal mottlings and linear sternite markings on each side of the ventral median
Gills: Pale yellowish brown marabou secured at sides with fine gold wire
Thorax: Flat monofilament over a brownish gray base
Wing cases: Dark brownish feather section tied down over thorax
Legs: Pale amber mottled partridge hackle
Head: Dark gray nylon

My imitation of the Great Summer Drake Nymph, a pattern that has produced a number of trophy fish for me, is dressed with the materials outlined. It is the pattern I once gave to Martin Bovey on a reed-lined pond in Colorado, and it took him a powerful six-and-a-half pound brown that still graces his mantel in Massachusetts.

5. Western Brown Quill (*Siphlonurus phyllis*)

This is a large species of nymph, unique in its double gill plates on each gill-bearing segment of the body. It has uniquely dark tail-banding, and its legs are strongly banded as well. The full-grown specimens measure eleven-sixteenths inch in length. The species is recorded from our Pacific Northwest, Montana, Idaho, and the Canadian Provinces of British Columbia and Alberta. It is a summer hatch.

Tails: Dark olive gray with darker mottlings, ¼ inch
Tergites: Dark olive gray heavily mottled with brown, ⅜ inch
Sternites: Dark olive with brown ventral markings, ⅜ inch
Gills: Dark brownish gray, 1/32 inch
Thorax: Dark olive mottled with brown and an olive sternum, ⅛ inch
Wing cases: Dark brownish gray, ⅛ inch
Legs: Dark amber strongly mottled with brown, ¼ inch
Head: Dark brownish olive, 1/16 inch

Hook: Sizes 10-12 Orvis Premium 1X long
Nylon: Dark olive 6/0 nylon
Tails: Dark partridge dyed olive
Body: Flat monofilament over medium olive underbody, with brown lacquer dorsal and ventral markings
Gills: Dark brownish gray marabou secured with fine gold wire
Thorax: Flat monofilament over medium olive base
Wing cases: Dark brownish gray feather section tied down over thorax
Legs: Dark brown partridge
Head: Dark olive nylon

6. Eastern Brown Quill (*Siphlonurus quebecensis*)

This is perhaps the best-known mayfly of this slow-water genus, although in his classic *Book of Trout Flies* Preston Jennings classified the *Siphlonurus* flies among his species of limited importance. Its full-grown nymphs measure five-eighths inch and its coloring is distinguished by a pale median stripe along its mottled dorsal surfaces.

Tails: Dark olive gray with heavy brown markings, ¼ inch
Tergites: Dark chocolate mottling with a pale median stripe, ⅜ inch
Sternites: Medium brown with dark ventral mottlings, ⅜ inch
Gills: Dark brownish olive, 1/32 inch
Thorax: Dark chocolate mottlings with a median stripe, ⅛ inch
Wing cases: Dark leadwing brownish with a median stripe, ⅛ inch
Legs: Dark olive heavily mottled in brown, ¼ inch
Head: Dark olive brown with median stripe, 1/16 inch

Hook: Sizes 10-12 Orvis Premium 1X long
Nylon: Dark brown 6/0 nylon
Tails: Dark partridge dyed olive
Body: Flat monofilament over a medium brown base with black lacquer dorsal and ventral markings, and pale median
Gills: Dark brownish olive marabou secured at sides with fine gold wire
Thorax: Flat monofilament over a medium brown base
Wing cases: Dark leadwing-colored feather section tied down over thorax, with suggestion of pale median
Legs: Dark partridge dyed olive
Head: Dark brown nylon with pale median stripe

Charles Wetzel described this species as a major hatch on his favorite Pennsylvania rivers, although his *Practical Fly-Fishing* placed its emphasis on the spinner mating flights with their bright-green egg sacs. Alvin Grove included the *Siphlonurus* genus in his catalogue of major fly hatches, which is a singular contribution in his *Lure and Lore of Trout Fishing*. Its hatches in early summer are extremely important on the central Pennsylvania rivers that both men frequent, rivers such as the famous Spring Creek and Big Fishing Creek and the chalkstream-like Spruce Creek. During recent years I experienced a fine hatch with Clyde Carpenter and Charles Fox on the sink-hole headwaters of a classic limestone stream—the alkaline flats of Antes Creek below Williamsport.

Justin Leonard considers it a mayfly of some importance in his entomological studies titled *Mayflies of Michigan Trout Streams*, observing that it seemed to frequent colder biotic habitats than its sister *Siphlonurus* nymphs. It has been recorded on rivers from Quebec to North Carolina, and westward to Michigan and Wisconsin. It typically emerges from late May until the first week in July across this range of distribution.

7.   Little Dark Olive (*Siphlonurus rapidus*)

This is one of the smaller flies of the genus, its nymphs measuring about seven-sixteenths inch. It is quite similar to the related *Siphlonurus* flies, but its nymphs are slightly darker and more extensive in their gill structure. Its distribution has been recorded from Quebec to Michigan, although Leonard, in his comprehensive *Mayflies of Michigan Trout Streams,* asserts that no specimens have been recorded from the rivers of its Upper Peninsula. It hatches in late May and June.

Tails: Medium olive marked with brown, 3/16 inch
Tergites: Dark mottled brownish with an olive cast, 5/16 inch
Sternites: Medium mottled brownish with an olive cast, 5/16 inch
Gills: Olive gray, 1/32 inch
Thorax: Medium mottled brownish with an olive cast, 3/32 inch
Wing cases: Medium brownish, 3/32 inch
Legs: Dark amber mottled with brown, 3/16 inch
Head: Dark brownish olive, 1/32 inch

Hook: Sizes 14-16 Orvis Premium 1X long
Nylon: Dark brown 6/0 nylon
Tails: Dark partridge dyed olive
Body: Dark brownish dubbing spun on olive silk with hare's mask guard hairs
Gills: Olive gray marabou secured at sides with fine gold wire
Thorax: Dark brownish dubbing spun with hare's mask on olive silk
Wing cases: Medium brown feather section tied down over thorax
Legs: Dark partridge hackle
Head: Dark brown nylon

8.   Western Yellow Drake (*Siphlonurus spectabilis*)

This is a unique and rather large western species. Its adults are pale drakes with orangish-gray speckled wings and yellowish bodies with light-brown markings on both the tergites and sternites.

Tails: Pale grayish marked with brown, ¼ inch
Tergites: Pale yellowish brown mottled with olive, ⅜ inch
Sternites: Pale yellowish brown with olive ventral markings, ⅜ inch
Gills: Pale yellowish gray, 1/32 inch
Thorax: Pale yellowish brown with olive sternum, 3/16 inch
Wing cases: Pale yellowish brown, ⅛ inch
Legs: Pale yellowish brown with darker markings, ¼ inch
Head: Pale yellowish brown, 1/16 inch

Hook: Sizes 10-12 Orvis Premium 1X long
Nylon: Pale tan 6/0 nylon
Tails: Pale mottled pheasant fibers
Body: Pale yellowish underbody lightly mottled with brown, leaving a pale median showing under the clear flat monofilament overbody
Gills: Pale yellowish gray marabou secured with fine gold wire
Thorax: Pale yellow underbody cover with flat monofilament
Wing cases: Pale yellowish brown feather section tied down over thorax with delicate white quill over feather to simulate pale median stripe
Legs: Pale brown partridge hackle
Head: Pale tan nylon

This nymph species can readily be identified from the unique type of double gills on its first two abdominal segments. Some specimens exhibit a pinkish cast toward the posterior tergites of the body. The typical dark markings across the fringed tails are faint, and the caudal setae themselves are pale orangish-brown. The fully grown nymphs measure about five-eighths inch in·length, and according to entomological monographs their range is limited to the Pacific mountains.

E. H. Rosborough dresses a pattern designed to match this hatch, which emerges on Oregon streams from the middle of May until July.

The mayflies of the genus *Siphloplecton* are relatively large, usually brownish olive with paler mottlings. The nymphs have slender bodies, resembling the *Siphlonurus* flies, with a somewhat· flattened abdominal structure. Their gills are borne on the first seven body segments, with double gills on the first three. The gills are ovoid in shape. The post-lateral segments terminate in sharp lateral spines. The three tails are approximately equal in length, and each is fringed, although only the center tail is fringed on both margins.

The eyes of the *Siphloplecton* nymphs are oriented laterally rather than vertically like the immature forms of *Metretropus,* a related species of mayflies. The claws of the middle and posterior legs are nearly as long as the tarsus, while the claws of the forelegs are shorter and forked.

Adults are readily distingushed by their heavily mottled wings and vigorous patterns of flight. Emergence on midwestern rivers appears to peak in the last two weeks of May. Males in the mating swarms hover about twenty to thirty feet above the river. Females entering the swarms are quickly mated, rising in a towering flight high above the trees. Finally, the females return to the stream in a dropping glide that ends with oviposition of the eggs, extruded from four to six feet above the current. The heaviest populations of *Siphloplecton* are found in fairly large rivers, especially in deep, relatively strong currents.

The nymphs are such swift and agile swimmers that collection is impossible by dislodging them into a simple screen downstream. *Siphloplecton* nymphs escape upstream into the current; extremely fine-mesh minnow seines are the only feasible devices for capture. Therefore imitations should be fished across the current and worked teasingly like streamers. The nymphs migrate into the shallows to split and escape their nymphal shucks.

9.   Medium Speckled Lake Olive (*Siphloplecton signatum*)

This is a relatively medium-sized species indigenous to the southeastern trout streams of Virginia, West Virginia, and North Carolina. Specimens measure about one-half inch at full growth. It typically emerges on those waters in May and June. The nymphs have a generally paler color than those of the larger *Siphloplecton basale,* and have a single ventral median pattern on their sternites instead of the tripartite markings found on the bigger species.

Tails: Pale grayish marked with brown, ¼ inch
Tergites: Pale amber mottled with brown markings that enclose ovoid patterns, ⅜ inch
Sternites: Pale amber with brown ventral median stripe and margins, ⅜ inch
Gills: Pale brownish gray, 1/32 inch
Thorax: Pale amber with brown mottlings, ⅛ inch
Wing cases: Pale yellowish brown, ⅛ inch
Legs: Pale yellowish mottled with brown, 3/16 inch
Head: Pale yellowish brown, 1/16 inch

Hook: Sizes 12-14 Orvis Premium 1X long
Nylon: Pale tan 6/0 nylon
Tails: Pale gray pheasant fibers
Body: Natural flat monofilament over pale yellow floss underbody, marked with brown on dorsal surfaces, and ventral surfaces as described
Gills: Pale brownish gray marabou secured at sides with fine gold wire
Thorax: Pale yellow floss with flat monofilament overbody
Wing cases: Pale yellowish brown feather section tied over thorax
Legs: Gray partridge dyed olive yellow·
Head: Pale tan nylon

10. Great Speckled Lake Olive (*Siphloplecton basale*)

This is the largest of the *Siphloplecton* flies, and it is rather widely distributed in American waters. Its principal populations are found in coldwater lakes, but good hatches are also found in our larger rivers. Its nymphs are relatively large, measuring about seven-eighths inch in length at full development. The nymphs are strong swimmers.

The flat-foundation techniques of tying pioneered by George Grant of the Big Hole country in Montana are excellent for simulating both the flatness of these nymphal forms and the singular mottled backs and striped belly surfaces that they display to the fish. The bodies should be light in weight, using two pieces of nylon monofilament seated tightly on either side of the hook shank. Then a smooth foundation of light-olive floss should be used to shape the underbody. Dark markings of black can be used to suggest the back mottlings, and dark sepia lacquer can imitate the continuous stripes on the sternite segments of the belly. The gills can be suggested with olive-dyed marabou layered thickly along either edge of the body and tightly seated with fine gold-wire ribbing.

These nymphs have three distinct brownish stripes along their belly surfaces. The median markings are a continuous series of rather bold arrowhead-shaped markings, while the stripes along either edge of the belly are thin and rather linear in character.

Tails: Dark olive gray, 5/16 inch
Tergites: Medium olive mottled in ovoid brown patterns, with a dull median stripe and distinct ringing, ½ inch
Sternites: Medium olive with a brown ventral median and dark margins, ½ inch
Gills: Medium olive, 1/16 inch
Thorax: Medium olive mottled with brown and a pale dorsal median, 3/16 inch
Wing cases: Medium olive brown, 5/32 inch
Legs: Olive heavily mottled with brown, ¼ inch
Head: Medium olive with a pale dorsal median, 3/32 inch

Hook: Sizes 8-10 Orvis Premium 1X long
Nylon: Pale grayish 6/0 nylon
Tails: Pheasant fibers dyed olive gray
Body: Medium olive underbody with ovoid dorsal markings in brown lacquer, and a strong ventral median and later margin markings, all under flat mono
Gills: Medium olive marabou secured at sides with fine gold wire
Thorax: Medium olive underbody below flat monofilament
Wing cases: Dark brownish olive feather section tied over thorax with pale quill to suggest median stripe
Legs: Dark brown partridge dyed olive
Head: Dark grayish nylon with pale dorsal median

The Tiny Swimming Nymphs of the Baetis Flies

THE WHITEWASHED fences and gentle hillsides on the old Chambersburg Pike revealed nothing of the little river where the sign marked the gravel county road to Newville. Holstein cattle filled the steep pastures below the white clapboard farmhouse and its well-kept outbuildings. The limestone outcroppings are a prelude, hinting at the subterranean riches hidden in the water-caves below the fields.

The dirt road winds down from the open hillsides into a mile of elms and maples and oaks. Its coolness is a prologue to the spring that literally spews water from a fissure in the limestone at the base of a densely forested ridge.

It produces thousands of gallons per minute. Its surprising volume of flow fills an icy-cold millpond of spring water with a deep channel in its thick beds of elodea. The weeds are choked with crawling shrimps and sowbugs. The bottom of the channel is rich with aquamarine algae undulating slowly in the imperceptible currents of the pond. It is a mysterious place of green water and shadowy channels, its upper reaches almost devoid of oxygen until photosynthesis in the algae and elodea changes its ecology sufficiently to support its trout.

It has produced some trophy fish over the years. The best is probably the famous sixteen-pound brown that Don Martin took on a big nymph from the Blue Hole in the millpond in 1945. It is still the largest public-water trout ever caught in Pennsylvania waters, and its trophy hangs in the Office of the Fish Commissioner of the Commonwealth.

The overflow of the millpond is divided between the timber spillway and the stonework vault of the mill itself. Its pale masonry has the craftsmanship found in the Pennsylvania barns farther down the valley, its second floor framed in heavy timbers and planking. The stream has its genesis in the meeting of these spillway channels below the mill. Its incredibly clear headwater currents flow over pale gravel there, eddying in the watercress and fountain mosses.

Big Spring has its genesis at this mill. Downstream it winds through the willows into a second millpond a mile below, and then meanders into the gravel flats at McCollough's farm. Its wild brook trout are a selective, free-rising strain that mock the conventional fly fishing wisdom about *Salvelinus fontinalis*—that our native eastern fish are indifferent surface feeders with limited intelligence.

White ducks feed along with the trout. Egrets trap salamanders and frogs in the elodea marshes, and kingfishers plunge into a cornucopia of baitfish species mixed with native brook trout. The fish feed on fine populations of minute nymphs on its gravel bottom, and its riffling currents are perfect for the tiny *Baetis* mayflies.

Big Spring fish often surface-feed, and are famous for their dry-fly sport, but there are times when they prove obstinate. Their rises dimple and porpoise and sip in the surface, but floating flies from jassids to ants and no-hackle midges are refused so completely they are not even honored with curious inspection rises, with a hyperselective trout following a dry fly before rejecting it.

Failure remains persistently in the mind, perhaps more stubbornly than days when things go well. There was such an evening several years ago, when Jeff Norton and I were fishing the gravelly shallows at McCullough's Farm. There was a soft wind blowing in the Cumberland Valley, and the fish were working steadily. The current was covered with tiny *Baetis* mayflies, but little olive-bodied dry flies were ignored by fish after fish for more than an hour.

Finally, I tried a dark little nymph and a fish took it immediately on the first cast. Difficult fishing was suddenly easy. It became simply a matter of locating a good fish, clearly visible as it dimpled the surface, and presenting it with the tiny nymph.

What'd he take? yelled Jeff Norton.

Nymph! I answered happily. *They're not taking the little mayflies on the surface—they're taking the nymphs.*

It's the same hatch we get on the Delaware, he shouted, *but these fish don't want a Blue-Winged Olive!*

They're taking the nymphs of those little Olives!

How about a few nymphs? he laughed.

We took a great many brook trout that evening, the best fish going almost two pounds. It was an unforgettable lesson in the importance of both the tiny *Baetis* mayflies, and also of their minute hatching nymphs. Needham lists more than forty American species in his *Biology of Mayflies*, and several new species have been identified by entomologists since its publication in 1935. Therefore, imitation of the entire *Baetis* group on a species-by-species basis is impractical, and I have attempted to identify ten major species that are prototypical of the nymphs as a whole.

The nymphs of the *Baetis* mayflies are extremely abundant in swift, relatively shallow streams with a clean bottom of small stones, hiding in the trailing beds of algae and chara weed. Although a few *Baetis* nymphs are most common at the edges of the stream, in plants and submerged bottom trash, all of these nymphal forms demand a measurable current.

Baetis nymphs are rather small, ranging from the five-thirty-seconds-inch *Baetis levitans* to the larger species *Baetis heimalis*, with nymphs measuring three-eighths inch at hatching time.

The nymphs are quite streamlined, and move in the current with surprising agility. Their heads are held in a downward-looking attitude. Legs are relatively long and slender. Their claws have numerous fine denticles on their inner margins. There is a slight but readily evident median notch on the apical margin of the labrum. The mandibles are triangular, and the canines are relatively large and blunt. Their maxillary palps are two- or three-jointed, depending on species, and seldom extend beyond the tip of the galea-lacinia. The labial palps are three-jointed. Distal joints are slightly rounded, and seldom truncated on the apical margins. Gills are present on abdominal segments one through seven, and are relatively small. Some species display narrow and lanceolate gills on segments six and seven. All species have three tails, delicately fringed, with the center tail slightly shorter than the outer pair.

Preston Jennings observed in his *Book of Trout Flies* that these tiny mayflies were an early-season group of minimal importance to anglers, using their archaic taxonometric name *Acentrella*. It is one of the few questionable judgments found in the work of Jennings. These little *Baetis* flies are available in incredible numbers, and their emergence is not limited to a single period in each season. Biologists have found the *Baetis* species to have multiple broods in a single season, with a first series of hatches typically coming off from April through June. The second series is a brood lasting from July to the following September. The third brood emerges until November. This multi-brooded behavior means that *Baetis* can hatch sporadically at any time in the season.

1. Pale Gray-Winged Olive (*Baetis adonis*)

This delicate yellowish-olive species is found in our Pacific coastal rivers from California to British Columbia, and its nymphs measure three-sixteenths inch at maturity. It is a hatch of late summer and early fall.

Colorado and the central Rocky Mountain rivers have a parallel species in the slightly larger *Baetis moffati*, with the nymphs measuring five-sixteenths inch.

Tails: Pale olive dun marked with brown, 3/16 inch
Body: Light olive brownish, ¼ inch
Gills: Light olive grayish, 1/64 inch
Thorax: Light olive brownish, 1/16 inch
Wing cases: Medium olive grayish,
Legs: Light olive mottled, 3/16 inch
Head: Light olive brown, 1/32 inch

Hook: Sizes 18-20 Orvis Premium 1X long
Nylon: Tan 6/0 nylon
Tails: Light olive-dyed gray partridge fibers
Body: Light brownish olive dubbing
Gills: Pale olive gray goose quill ribbing
Thorax: Light brownish olive dubbing
Wing cases: Medium olive grayish feather section tied down over the thorax
Legs: Light olive-dyed gray partridge fibers
Head: Tan nylon

2. Little Blue-Winged Rusty Dun (*Baetis brunneicolor*)

This rusty little blue-winged mayfly has nymphs averaging about five-sixteenths inch. Its distribution ranges from Minnesota to New England and North Carolina. The slightly smaller *Baetis intermedius* is a Rocky Mountain species with nymphs of about nine-thirty-seconds inch.

Baetis brunneicolor has its initial hatching cycle from the last of June until early September.

Tails: Brown with dark mottlings, ⅛ inch
Body: Dark brown with a pale median stripe, 3/16 inch
Gills: Pale yellowish brown, 1/64 inch
Thorax: Dark brown with a median stripe, 1/16 inch
Wing cases: Dark brownish, 3/32 inch
Legs: Dark mottled brownish, ⅛ inch
Head: Dark brownish, 1/32 inch

Hook: Sizes 20-22 Orvis Premium 1X long
Nylon: Dark brown 6/0 nylon
Tails: Brown partridge fibers
Body: Dark brown dubbing with a delicate silver wire tied in at the tails and laid along the dorsal median
Gills: Pale yellowish brown goose quill ribbing
Thorax: Dark brownish dubbing
Wing cases: Dark brown feather tied over thorax with a silver median wire
Legs: Dark brown partridge fibers
Head: Dark brown nylon

3.   Dark Blue-Winged Olive (*Baetis cingulatus*)

This delicate little mayfly is a dark olive-bodied insect with smoky bluish-gray wings. It is found in the rivers of Michigan and Wisconsin. Its nymphs average nine-thirty-seconds inch, with pale-whitish gills on an olive ground color. It hatches from May through August. The slightly bigger *Baetis tricaudatus* is a similar Colorado species, that has also been recorded from Wyoming and Montana.

Tails: Pale brown with olive markings, 3/32 inch
Body: Pale yellowish olive, 3/16 inch
Gills: Pale whitish gray, 1/64 inch
Thorax: Medium brownish, 1/16 inch
Wing cases: Medium grayish brown, 1/16 inch
Legs: Medium olive brown, 1/16 inch
Head: Medium brown, 1/64 inch

Hook: Sizes 20-22 Orvis Premium 1X long
Nylon: Light brown 6/0 nylon
Tails: Pale brown partridge fibers
Body: Pale yellowish olive dubbing
Gills: Pale whitish gray goose quill ribbing
Thorax: Pale yellowish brown dubbing
Wing cases: Grayish brown feather section tied over wing
Legs: Medium olive brown fibers
Head: Light brown nylon

4.   Little Slate-Winged Brown Quill (*Baetis heimalis*)

These mayfly nymphs are the largest of the genus, measuring about three-eighths inch at full growth. The western species *Baetis intermedius* is smaller and is found from Colorado to British Columbia.

Baetis heimalis is primarily a midwestern species, reported from Michigan and Wisconsin. It hatches in September and October.

Tails: Dark olive, 3/16 inch
Body: Dark brownish olive distinctly ringed, 5/16 inch
Gills: Medium olive, 1/32 inch
Thorax: Dark mottled olive, 3/32 inch
Wing cases: Dark olive grayish, ⅛ inch
Legs: Dark mottled olive, 3/16 inch
Head: Dark mottled olive, 1/32 inch

Hook: Sizes 16-18 Orvis Premium 1X long
Nylon: Dark olive 6/0 nylon
Tails: Gray partridge dyed olive
Body: Dark brownish olive dubbing
Gills: Medium olive goose quill ribbing
Thorax: Dark brownish olive dubbing
Wing cases: Dark slate-grayish olive feather section tied down over thorax
Legs: Gray partridge dyed olive
Head: Dark olive nylon

5.   Little Gray-Winged Brown Quill (*Baetis intercalaris*)

These tiny little mayflies are found from New England to Michigan and North Carolina. The nymphs are nine-thirty-seconds inch. The initial hatches of the three-brood cycle usually come off from late May until the last week in June.

Tails: Olive with darker mottlings, 3/32 inch
Body: Dark olive distinctly ringed and with a pale median stripe, 3/16 inch
Gills: Pale olive, 1/64 inch
Thorax: Dark mottled olive with a pale stripe, 1/32 inch
Wing cases: Dark olive gray, 1/16 inch
Legs: Dark mottled olive, 3/32 inch
Head: Dark olive, 1/64 inch

Hook: Sizes 20-22 Orvis Premium 1X long
Nylon: Dark olive 6/0 nylon
Tails: Brown partridge dyed olive
Body: Dark olive dubbing with a fine gold wire tied in at tails and laid along body as a median stripe
Gills: Pale olive-dyed goose quill ribbing
Thorax: Dark olive dubbing
Wing cases: Dark olive gray feather section tied down over thorax
Legs: Brown partridge dyed olive
Head: Dark olive nylon

6.   Minute Blue-Winged Olive (*Baetis levitans*)

This is another species distributed from Michigan to New England, and south along the eastern seaboard to North Carolina. Its primary hatching occurs from the last week in May until July, and its nymphs average about five-thirty-seconds inch in length.

The western species *Baetis insignificans* is closely related in both color and size.

Tails: Dark olive heavily mottled, 1/16 inch
Body: Dark mottled brown distinctly ringed, ⅛ inch
Gills: Pale olive brown, 1/64 inch
Thorax: Dark mottled brownish, 1/32 inch
Wing cases: Dark brownish, 1/16 inch
Legs: Dark mottled brownish, 1/16 inch
Head: Dark mottled brown, 1/64 inch

Hook: Sizes 22-24 Orvis Premium 1X long 1/16 inch
Nylon: Brown 6/0 nylon
Tails: Dark brown partridge dyed olive
Body: Dark chocolate brown dubbing
Gills: Pale olive brown goose quill ribbing
Thorax: Dark chocolate brown dubbing
Wing cases: Dark brownish feather tied down over thorax
Legs: Dark brown partridge
Head: Brown nylon

7.   Dark Gray-Winged Olive (*Baetis phoebus*)

These little mayflies hatch from the middle of May until early June, and their nymphs average three-sixteenths inch. Their range distribution is apparently from Michigan to New England, and south to Pennsylvania, Maryland and New Jersey.

The western species *Baetis piscatoris* is slightly larger, and is found from New Mexico to Montana.

Tails: Light olive with dark markings, 3/32 inch
Body: Pale olive yellow with darker olive in last segments, 5/32 inch
Gills: Pale whitish gray, 1/64 inch
Thorax: Medium mottled brownish with a pale median stripe, 1/16 inch
Wing cases: Medium grayish brown, 1/16 inch
Legs: Medium mottled olive, 3/32 inch
Head: Medium brownish, 1/64 inch

Hook: Sizes 20-22 Orvis Premium 1X long
Nylon: Pale olive yellow 6/0 nylon
Tails: Gray partridge dyed pale olive
Body: Pale olive yellow dubbing mixed with light brown at foot of tails
Gills: Pale whitish goose quill ribbing
Thorax: Pale olive yellow dubbing
Wing cases: Medium grayish brown tied down over thorax
Legs: Gray partridge dyed olive
Head: Pale olive nylon with brown dorsal lacquer

8. Little Medium-Olive Dun (*Baetis pygmaeus*)

Baetis pygmaeus is a small three-sixteenths-inch mayfly which primarily emerges from early August until the middle of September.

There is a similar Pacific Coast species, called *Baetis devinctus.*

Tails: Medium olive, 3/32 inch
Body: Dark olive brown distinctly ringed with a pale olive median stripe, ⅛ inch
Gills: Medium olive, 1/64 inch
Thorax: Dark mottled olive with a pale median stripe, 1/16 inch
Wing cases: Dark brownish gray, 1/16 inch
Legs: Dark mottled olive, 3/32 inch
Head: Dark olive, 1/64 inch

Hook: Sizes 20-22 Orvis Premium 1X long
Nylon: Medium olive 6/0 nylon
Tails: Gray partridge dyed medium olive
Body: Dark olive brown dubbing with fine gold wire tied in at the tails and laid along the body as a median stripe
Gills: Medium olive goose quill ribbing
Thorax: Dark olive brown dubbing
Wing cases: Dark brownish gray feather section tied down over thorax
Legs: Dark gray partridge dyed olive
Head: Medium olive nylon

9. Little Slate-Winged Olive Quill (*Baetis spinosus*)

This tiny little dark-olive hatch is perhaps the most widely distributed *Baetis* species, since it is recorded from New Brunswick to California and North Carolina. Its principal hatching in our northern streams occurs in late July and August.

The nymphs average approximately three-sixteenths inch in length. *Baetis parvus* is a similar western species found in the rivers of the Pacific Northwest.

Tails: Medium olive with brown markings, 3/32 inch
Body: Medium olive distinctly ringed, 5/64 inch
Gills: Pale olive yellowish, 1/64 inch
Thorax: Medium olive, 1/32 inch
Wing cases: Dark slate-colored olive, 1/16 inch
Legs: Medium olive, 3/32 inch
Head: Medium olive, 1/64 inch

Hook: Sizes 20-22 Orvis Premium 1X long
Nylon: Medium olive 6/0 nylon
Tails: Gray partridge dyed medium olive
Body: Medium olive dubbing
Gills: Pale yellowish olive goose quill ribbing
Thorax: Medium olive dubbing
Wing cases: Dark slate-gray feather section tied down over thorax
Legs: Medium olive fibers
Head: Medium olive nylon

10. Little Iron-Blue Quill (*Baetis vagans*)

This is a well-known eastern hatch, distributed from Wisconsin to New England, and south as far as North Carolina. It is this early species that

Preston Jennings wrote about in his *Book of Trout Flies,* since its first emergence cycle begins in the middle of April. However, there are sporadic hatches lasting until the last week of September.

Baetis vagans is a fairly large species of its genus, its nymphs measuring approximately one-quarter inch.

Tails: Dark grayish olive, 5/32 inch

Body: Dark mottled grayish olive with a median stripe, ¼ inch

Gills: Medium olive grayish, 1/64 inch

Thorax: Dark mottled grayish olive with a pale median stripe, 1/16 inch

Wing cases: Dark olive grayish, 1/16 inch

Legs: Dark mottled olive, 5/32 inch

Head: Dark mottled olive, 1/32 inch

Hook: Sizes 18-20 Orvis Premium 1X long

Nylon: Dark olive 6/0 nylon

Tails: Dark gray partridge dyed olive

Body: Dark olive mixed with hare's mask guard hairs, with a fine gold wire as median stripe

Gills: Medium olive goose quill ribbing

Thorax: Dark olive mixed with hare's mask

Wing cases: Dark olive-dyed feather section tied down over thorax, with a fine gold wire as median stripe

Legs: Dark gray partridge dyed olive

Head: Dark olive nylon

The Clambering Slow-Water Callibaetis Nymphs

SPRING COMES suddenly to the scrub-oak foothills. It has its unseen harbingers in the April wind, its bitter edge softening almost without warning, until the smooth bunchgrass hills lose their barren winter look in the fresh surprise of spring. Its pale grass has a delicate velvet-soft quality in the lengthening afternoons. The earth awakens slowly in the rich progression of warming days, until finally the prairie draws and creek bottoms are bright with larkspur and harebells and Indian paintbrush.

Springtime in the foothills of the Rockies is a special season, gathering its sweetness imperceptibly until even the north winds lose the raw winter bite of the Wyoming prairies. The twilight wind from the mountains carries the smell of snow melt in the high country.

The creek willows are first to bud. Their rattling winter branches turn pale yellow along the winding creek bottoms, and the brittle pewter-colored groves of aspen follow, their olive leaves bright against the lodgepole pines. Milky snow melt fills the creeks and rivers, spreading into the water meadows. Migrating pintails gather in these grassy shallows. Spring lambs hide in the sheltered places. High in the timberline ridges, and beside the melting ice fields there are snow buttercups and avalanche lilies.

The spring spate makes the rivers unfishable, and the fly fisherman is forced to explore the lakes and impoundments and beaver ponds at lower altitudes. The really high lakes remain ice-locked until the last weeks in July, but the rivers begin to clear much earlier.

There are good *Callibaetis* hatches on most American trout waters, but the genus is considerably more important in the quiet ponds and reservoirs of our western mountains. Its slender swimming nymphs and pale speckle-winged duns are many-brooded, taking only five to six months between eclosion and emergence in summer. That means as many as three separate hatches during a single season. There can be *Callibaetis* flies in the last days of May, with a second emergence at the middle of the summer, and a third hatch in September and October. Both their abundance and their many-brooded availability makes them important to anglers.

The mottled little *Callibaetis* nymphs are among the most agile and elegant inhabitants of our lakes and ponds, especially in alkaline waters with rich aquatic vegetation. They are great favorites of both the fish and other carnivorous forms of nymphs. The fully developed nymphs range from one-quarter to five-sixteenths inch in length.

The maxillary palp of the nymphs are two-jointed forms, with a three-jointed labial, its distal joint rather short and conical. The mandible canines are rather long and slender. The claws are delicate and denticulate. The gills are rather large and ovoid, double on segments one through six on most species, and one through seven in some. The ventral portion of the gills on the first two segments is rather well developed, sometimes exhibiting a small secondary flap. Tracheation of the gills is pinnate. There are three fringed tails of approximately equal length and thickness.

Eastern species typically display their first period of emergence in the middle of May, coming off sporadically for three to four weeks. My notes record *Callibaetis fluctuans* hatching in early June on waters in Maryland and Virginia, and somewhat earlier on the Nantahala watershed in North Carolina. The widely distributed species *Callibaetis ferrugineus* is commonly hatching on trout ponds and slow-moving rivers late in May, with a second brood emerging toward the third week in July.

1.   Pale Speckle-Wing Dun (*Callibaetis fluctuans*)

These little mottled mayflies hatch in May and June in our eastern coastal regions, and emergence typically takes place in late morning. The nymphs average about three-eighths inch.

Tails: Tannish with dark markings at midpoints, ⅛ inch
Body: Mottled light brown with delicate median stripe, ¼ inch
Gills: Pale yellowish brown, 1/64 inch
Thorax: Mottled light brown, 1/16 inch
Wing cases: Mottled light brown 1/16 inch
Legs: Mottled light brown, ⅛ inch
Head: Mottled light brown, 1/32 inch

Hook: Sizes 16-18 Orvis Premium 1X long
Nylon: Tan 6/0 nylon
Tails: Mottled light brown pheasant-tail fibers displaying dark brown markings
Body: Mottled light brown fur dubbing, with a yellowish cotton darning thread tied in at the tails, the thorax, and wrapped over the thorax to suggest the median stripe and secured with fine gold wire
Gills: Pale yellowish brown goose quill ribbing
Thorax: Mottled light brown dubbing
Wing cases: Mottled brown feather section tied over thorax
Legs: Light brown partridge
Head: Tan nylon

2.   Pale Speckle-Wing Olive (*Callibaetis ferrugineus*)

These handsome little speckle-winged duns are widely distributed in American waters, with specimens recorded along the eastern coastal regions from Quebec to the Carolinas, and west as far as Michigan, Wisconsin and Minnesota. The nymphs hatch sporadically through the summer cycle of their broods, and fully developed forms average three-eighths inch in length.

Tails: Medium brown with dark markings at midpoints, ⅛ inch
Body: Mottled medium brown with dark markings, ¼ inch
Gills: Pale yellowish brown, 1/64 inch
Thorax: Mottled medium brown, 1/16 inch
Wing cases: Dark brownish gray, 1/16 inch
Legs: Dark mottled brownish, ⅛ inch
Head: Dark mottled brown, 1/32 inch

Hook: Sizes 16-18 Orvis Premium 1X long
Nylon: Medium brown 6/0 nylon
Tails: Dark mottled brown pheasant-tail fibers with dark markings at midpoints
Body: Dark mottled dubbing of hare's mask
Gills: Pale yellowish brown dyed goose quill ribbing
Thorax: Dark mottled dubbing of hare's mask
Wiig cases: Dark brownish gray feather section tied down over thorax
Legs: Dark partridge hackle fibers
Head: Medium brown nylon

3.   Little Speckle-Wing Quill (*Callibaetis coloradensis*)

These darkly speckled little mayflies emerge on lakes and ponds in the Rocky Mountains in extensive numbers. My notes indicate that fly hatches of this species occurred in lakes at about six to seven thousand feet in early June. September hatches are typical on Colorado lakes and reservoirs at about nine to ten thousand feet. The nymphs average about three-eighths inch.

Tails: Olive-brown mottled with distinctly marked at midpoints, ⅛ inch
Body: Brownish olive mottled with dark markings, ¼ inch
Gills: Pale olive grayish, 1/64 inch
Thorax: Dark brownish olive darkly mottled, 1/16 inch
Wing cases: Dark olive gray, 1/16 inch
Legs: Darkly mottled olive, ⅛ inch
Head: Dark olive, 1/32 inch

Hook: Sizes 16-18 Orvis Premium 1X long
Nylon: Dark olive 6/0 nylon
Tails: Dark mottled olive with dark markings at midpoints
Body: Dark brownish olive mixed dubbing
Gills: Pale olive grayish goose quill ribbing
Thorax: Dark brownish olive mixed dubbing
Wing cases: Dark olive gray feather esction tied down over thorax
Legs: Gray partridge hackles dyed olive
Head: Dark olive nylon

4.   Medium Speckle-Wing Quill (*Callibaetis pacificus*)

This dully mottled little mayfly is recorded from trout waters as diverse as the mountain lakes in New Mexico, the famous plateau of small lakes on Grand Mesa in Colorado, the high lakes of northern Arizona, and along the Pacific Coast from the San Jacinto Mountains of southern California to the forest-rimmed lakes of Oregon and Washington. Hatches sometimes evolve four broods over a full season of fishing, and the nymphs average about three-eighths inch in length.

Tails: Pale brown with brownish markings at midpoint, 3/16 inch
Body: Pale brownish mottled with brown, ¼ inch
Gills: Pale yellowish brown, 1/64 inch
Thorax: Pale brownish mottled with brown, 1/1 6inch
Wing cases: Pale brownish mottled, 1/16 inch
Legs: Pale mottled brown, ⅛ inch
Head: Pale mottled brown, 1/16 inch

Hook: Sizes 16-18 Orvis Premium 1X long
Nylon: Light brown 6/0 nylon
Tails: Light brown pheasant-tail fibers
Body: Light brown dubbing mixed with guard hairs
Gills: Pale yellowish brown goose quill ribbing
Thorax: Light brown dubbing mixed with guard hairs
Wing cases: Light mottled brown feather section tied down over thorax
Legs: Light brown partridge hackle fibers
Head: Light brown nylon

5. Medium Speckle-Wing Dun (*Callibaetis americanus*)

These medium-sized *Callibaetis* flies are found throughout the Rocky Mountains, and specimens are also recorded from the Pacific Northwest and British Columbia. Their nymphs average seven-sixteenths inch in length.

Tails: Medium brown strongly marked at midpoints, ⅛ inch
Body: Dark mottled brownish, 5/16 inch
Gills: Medium brown, 1/32 inch
Thorax: Dark mottled brownish, ⅛ inch
Wing cases: Dark slate brown, ⅛ inch
Legs: Dark mottled brown, 3/16 inch
Head: Dark mottled brown, 1/32 inch

Hook: Sizes 14-16 Orvis Premium 1X long
Nylon: Brown 6/0 nylon
Tails: Medium brown pheasant-tail fibers
Body: Medium brown hare's ear dubbing mixed with guard hairs
Gills: Light brown goose quill ribbing
Thorax: Medium brown hare's ear dubbing mixed with guard hairs
Wing cases: Dark slate brown feather tied down over thorax
Legs: Dark brown partridge hackles
Head: Brown nylon

6. Pale Speckle-Wing Sulphur (*Callibaetis pallidus*)

This pale-yellowish species is found in ponds and sluggish streams at surprisingly high altitudes, and the first specimens in my collection were taken on Busk Creek at approximately ten thousand feet in Colorado. These headwaters of Turquoise Lake are serpentine and extremely slow-moving pools. The flies were collected in late August, indicating that the initial brood of the summer must have hatched early in the preceding month, about the time the milky high-water thaw was clearing.

Needham records specimens in his *Biology of Mayflies* from Colorado and Utah, and other hatches from Wyoming and Idaho are reported. The nymphs average approximately seven-sixteenths inch in length, and like their swimming sister species should be fished with a teasing broken-rhythm retrieve.

Tails: Pale olive distinctly marked at midpoints, 3/16 inch
Body: Pale olive distinctly mottled with brown, 5/16 inch
Gills: Pale olive yellow, 1/32 inch
Thorax: Pale olive distinctly mottled with brown, 1/16 inch
Wing cases: Pale olive, ⅛ inch
Legs: Pale olive mottled with brown, 3/16 inch
Head: Pale olive mottled with brown, 1/32 inch

Hook: Sizes 14-16 Orvis Premium 1X long
Nylon: Pale olive 6/0 nylon
Tails: Pale olive-dyed pheasant-tail fibers
Body: Pale olive and hare's ear mixed dubbing
Gills: Pale olive-dyed goose quill ribbing
Thorax: Pale olive and hare's ear mixed dubbing
Wing cases: Olive-dyed feather section tied down over thorax
Legs: Gray partridge dyed pale olive
Head: Pale olive nylon

7. Dark Speckle-Wing Quill (*Callibaetis nigritus*)

Specimens of this relatively large western species are recorded from both the Rocky Mountains and the Pacific Northwest. Emergence occurs in the middle weeks of June, early August, and a third brood sometimes appears in September. *Callibaetis nigritus* is closely related to *Callibaetis coloradensis* except for its slightly larger size and darker coloring. Its nymphal stages measure just under a half-inch at full development before a hatch.

Tails: Dark olive brown with dark markings at midpoints, ⅜ inch
Body: Dark olive brown heavily mottled, ⅜ inch
Gills: Dark olive, 1/32 inch
Thorax: Dark olive brown heavily mottled, ¼ inch
Wing cases: Dark olive brown, 3/16 inch
Legs: Dark olive brown heavily mottled, ⅜ inch
Head: Dark olive brown, 1/16 inch

Hook: Sizes 12-14 Orvis Premium 1X long
Nylon: Dark olive 6/0 nylon
Tails: Dark olive-dyed pheasant-tail fibers
Body: Dark brownish olive dubbing
Gills: Dark olive-dyed condor quill ribbing
Thorax: Dark brownish olive dubbing
Wing cases: Dark slate-gray feather iection tied down over thorax
Legs: Dark partridge dyed olive brown
Head: Dark olive nylon

The Fast-Water Swimming Isonychias

THERE WAS MIST layered over the river, and it was getting darker now. The road climbs north into the Allegheny forests. The pastoral valley of the Susquehanna dropped behind, with its red barns and silos filled with fodder, and the Big Pine flowed, smooth and whispering below the trees. It was cooler now and I stopped for gas. It was a filling station out of my boyhood, virtually unchanged by the antiseptic cacophony of modern life. The portico above the gas pumps was a steep-roofed shelter of timbers and slates. There was a semicircular tank for checking inner tubes. Jawbreakers filled the big apothecary jars behind the counter, and the penny machine was a brightly colored collection of gumballs.

Its lights reached out into the darkness, silvering the leaves and reaching the macadam road. Crickets and katydids performed their shrill chorus. It seemed that time had stopped. The ancient pump circulated the gasoline through its tall glass cylinders, its bubbles tumbling and churning as it filled the tank.

Suddenly there was something I had missed. The lights had attracted hundreds of big mayflies. They hung upside down on the timbers of the portico, the bigger, egg-laden females in the darker sheltered places. They were elegant big drakes.

Don't know what them flies are, said the owner.

The mayflies were large, their gleaming wings measuring as much as seven-eighths inch. Their bodies were a bright reddish brown, with two slender tails and pale cream legs. The forelegs were chocolate colored and the eyes were a deep rusty orange.

They're mayflies. I collected several, carefully.

Mayflies? The station-owner tested the word curiously. *What're them green-colored balls on the big ones?*

Egg sacs, I explained. *Those are the females.*

See them flies every year 'bout this same time, he continued. *Don't know where they come from.*

They hatch from the river, I said.

It had obviously been a heavy hatch of the big drakes. Their size identified them as *Isonychia sadleri,* and their numbers seemed to promise good dry-fly sport on the Big Pine and its beautiful ledgerock tributary, tumbling little Slate Run. There were good hatches the next several evenings, with big slate-colored flies all over the water, and the trout rose eagerly where the cold water of Slate Run cooled the warming midsummer currents of the Big Pine.

But there was no dry-fly fishing. The trout concentrated greedily on the nymphs, and the traditional Leadwing Coachman recommended for the *Isonychia* hatches was completely refused. It did take three or four small fish, and a stomach check confirmed their nymphing. It also confirmed the need for better nymph imitations.

These slender *Isonychia* nymphs are perhaps the most remarkable of the fast-water mayfly species. Most of these lotic swift-water forms cling or clamber among the bottom stones, but the nymphs of *Isonychia* boldly swim in the heaviest currents. They love the crevices between large rocks and boulders, holding in the rubble of the river-bed. Others prefer swift, thin-flowing currents over the ledges and bedrock bottoms, sliding currents filled with oxygen, and the sheltering edges of half-submerged stones.

The agility and precision of their swimming, darting from place to place in the current, is remarkable. Once they have a fresh feeding station, the nymphs anchor themselves with their middle and rear legs, with the current sweeping over their extended gills, bringing the oxygen they require. They are poised like an aquatic mantis, heads erect and forelegs extended in the attitude of prayer. Their fringed caudal plumes trail flat against the stones. These tails are fringed on both sides of the middle filament, while the outer tails are fringed only on the inside edges.

Most intriguing is the food-gathering equipment of the forelegs. They are fringed with two rows of stiff little hairs on their anterior sides. These bristles are set at a sharp angle, extended upstream and opening into the currents. Together they form a collecting basket, gathering the minuscule bits of food carried in the current. The head and mouth lie at the base of this collection system.

Emergence involves migration from its swift-water lies to the shallows and quieter eddies, much like the stoneflies. They are usually evening hatches, but in overcast weather they can emerge sporadically throughout the day. The facts that the nymphs have great agility, their emergence occurs away from the main fish-sheltering currents, and the subimago does not emerge below the surface film like the nymphs of the *Epeorus* flies all combine to protect these *Isonychias* from the hungry trout.

Like the stoneflies, these nymphs strangely favor certain stones and deadfalls to emerge. This puzzle may have its solution in the surface textures or current-tongues at such favored hatching places. However, several flies regularly select the same rocks for hatching, escaping their nymphal skins at precisely the same water level. Yet an adjacent stone will have no trace of nymphs. It is another of the manifold enigmas of nature, and the fish are well aware of its existence, following the migrating nymphs into their primary hatching zones.

1. Great Mahogany Drake (*Isonychia sadleri*)

This is the largest of our eastern species. Its fully grown nymphs measure about thirteen-sixteenths inch, and are a mouthful for the biggest fish. Specimens are recorded from rivers in Vermont, New York, Pennsylvania, Connecticut, New Jersey, Michigan, and Wisconsin. Its hatches have triggered some exceptional sport in recent years, and the species seems hardy enough to survive conditions that have decimated other mayflies.

The nymphs closely resemble those of *Isonychia bicolor*, a related species of our eastern rivers. However, it is somewhat larger and lacks the pale dorsal stripe singularly descriptive of the better known *bicolor* species. It is well distributed on my home beats along the Brodheads in Pennsylvania, and I described a superb hatch on the Namekagon in Wisconsin in my book *Remembrances of Rivers Past*. Heavy hatches on the White and the Otter are reported by my good friend David Ledlie, a young chemistry professor at Middlebury College. Experienced Michigan regulars also regard the *Isonychia sadleri* a major hatch on the swift-water reaches of the Au Sable and the Sturgeon. They are big insects of considerable interest to the fish.

These mayflies generally emerge toward the last ten days in June, with good hatching activity for about three weeks. They have given me exceptional fishing, both with dry flies and nymphs.

Tails: Medium olive brown with dark markings at the third point, ⅜ inch
Tergites: Dark purplish brown heavily mottled, ½ inch
Sternites: Dark purplish brown, ½ inch
Gills: Medium olive brown, 1/32 inch
Thorax: Dark purplish brown heavily mottled, 3/16 inch
Wing cases: Dark purplish brown, 3/16 inch
Legs: Light mottled olive, 5/16 inch
Head: Dark purplish brown, ⅛ inch

Hook: Sizes 10-12 Mustad 9672 3X long
Nylon: Dark brown 6/0 nylon
Tails: Darkly marked pheasant-tail fibers
Foundation: Two brass pins or pieces of wire at sides of hook
Body: Dark purplish brown dubbing mixed with hare's ear guard hairs on purple silk
Gills: Medium olive brown marabou laid at sides of body and secured with fine gold wire
Thorax: Dark purplish brown dubbing mixed with guard hairs on purple silk
Wing cases: Dark purplish brown feather section tied over thorax
Legs: Dark mottled brown partridge fibers
Head: Dark brown nylon

These nymphs are relatively flat-bodied, and therefore can benefit from the Grant body techniques of building a floss foundation over an over-body of flat nylon. For fishing deep, the tier can secure short pieces of brass wire on either side of the hook shank, and for fishing shallow during a hatch, two thick pieces of nylon will suffice. Such imitations should be fished with a rather teasing, swimming retrieve suggestive of the naturals, and a fine dressing for *Isonychia sadleri* is as indicated.

2. White-Gloved Howdy (*Isonychia albomanicata*)

This is the famous hatch first described by Charles Wetzel in his book *Practical Fly Fishing*, with his account of the immense hatches that once occurred on Big Kettle Creek in Pennsylvania. Those were the years when the little river was one of the superb brook-trout fisheries in the history of American angling. Rapacious lumbering had cleared the forests of hemlocks. The acid in their bark was needed for tanning the flood of buffalo hides coming east on the railroads. The giant pines themselves had supplied ties and trestles for those railroads, shoring and timbers for the coal mines of the Appalachians, and the explosive growth of our cities that followed the Civil War and the opening of the American frontier.

The timbering had already passed when Wetzel was fishing the Kettle in the years after the First World War. It was a time when the little river had a circle of great fly-fishermen, and their backcountry Camelot was the clapboard Trout Run Hotel, operated by John Van Horn.

Every trout stream has its vagabond poet, a skilled fly-fisher who seldom works at anything except an understanding of and affection for his river. Rube Kelley was its Villon, always in competition with his friend the hotelkeeper. Rue Wykoff was another of these bucolic experts, along with equally skilled men like Shanghai Pierce, and the old-time lumberjack Ira Weede. Ole Bull and his famous Norwegian colony lived there too. Although these *dramatis personnae* did not realize it then, the Kettle was dying.

The lumbering had already raised its midsummer temperatures, forcing the native brook trout into the springholes in June. The yellow mine wastes had already eradicated the trout from the lower mileage of the Kettle, and the loss of the coniferous tree cover was a more subtle form of pollution, since it raised the thermal character of every springhead.

Kettle Creek is now primarily a brown-trout fishery, with smallmouth bass and other warm-water species encroaching on its lower pools. There are still wild brook trout in tributaries like Trout Run, Cross Fork, and the laurel-sheltered Hammersley Fork, but the fish are small. The brook trout were slowly forced into the colder headwaters, and the once-marvelous hatches of Green Drakes and *Isonychia albomanicata* slowly declined under the impact of pollution and lumbering. Although these mayflies no longer hatch in the clouds described by Wetzel, their emergence can generate excellent fishing. The fully grown nymphs measure five-eighths inch.

Tails: Pale brown tails with markings at third points, 5/16 inch
Tergites: Mottled medium brownish, ⅜ inch
Sternites: Mottled medium brownish, ⅜ inch
Gills: Pale yellowish brown, 1/32 inch
Thorax: Mottled light brown, 5/32 inch
Wing cases: Mottled light brown, ⅛ inch
Legs: Pale mottled brownish yellow, 5/32 inch
Head: Mottled light brown, 1/16 inch

Hook: Sizes 12-14 Mustad 9672 3X long
Nylon: Tan 6/0 nylon
Tails: Pale brown pheasant-tail fibers
Foundation: Two brass pins or pieces of wire on either side of hook
Body: Medium brownish dubbing mixed with hare's ear guard hairs,
Gills: Pale yellowish brown marabou laid at sides of hook and secured with fine gold wire
Thorax: Medium brownish dubbing mixed with hare's ear
Wing cases Mottled brownish feather section tied down over thorax
Legs: Pale brown partridge hackle fibers
Head: Tan nylon

Specimens of *Isonychia albomanicata* have been recorded on many rivers from Ontario to North Carolina. There are especially fine hatches on New York and Pennsylvania rivers, some Michigan waters, and on the limestone streams of Maryland and West Virginia. Hatching normally occurs in the middle of June.

3. Medium Claret Mayfly (*Isonychia harperi*)

This is a medium-sized mayfly, somewhat paler than the related *Isonychia albomanicata,* and having full-grown nymphs measuring five-eighths inch in length. It is found in good hatches on the Au Sable in Michigan, which appear in August and September. Definitive collections include specimens from New England, New York, Michigan, and Wisconsin. It is especially common on Catskill and Adirondack rivers.

Tails: Brownish olive with dark markings at third points, 5/16 inch
Tergites: Dark blackish brown with olive markings, ⅜ inch
Sternites: Dark mottled brown, ⅜ inch
Gills: Pale grayish purple, 1/32 inch
Thorax: Dark mottled blackish brown, 5/32 inch
Wing cases: Dark slate-grayish, ⅛ inch
Legs: Pale mottled brownish, 3/16 inch
Head: Dark mottled brown, 1/16 inch

Hook: Sizes 12-14 Mustad 9672 3X long
Nylon: Dark brown 6/0 nylon
Tails: Brownish olive pheasant-tail fibers
Foundation: Two brass pins or pieces of wire on either side of hook
Body: Dark brown dubbing mixed with hare's ear guard hairs
Gills: Pale grayish purple marabou laid at sides of hook and secured with fine gold wire
Thorax: Dark brown dubbing mixed with hare's ear
Wing cases: Dark slate-grayish feather section tied down over thorax
Legs: Pale brownish partridge hackle
Head: Dark brown nylon

4. Great Leadwing Drake (*Isonychia bicolor*)

This is one of the principal fly-hatches on American waters. It was first identified in the classic *Book of Trout Flies* which the late Preston Jennings published in 1935. His studies on several eastern watersheds, from the Brodheads in northeastern Pennsylvania to the Schoharie in the upper Catskills, indicate that it emerges in that range throughout the month of June. Although not as large as the *Ephemera* drakes, which continued to hatch in profusion when Jennings was writing, it was still considered an important facet of his fly boxes.

Art Flick found it even more important in his *Streamside Guide*, which described it as a splendid mayfly. His pastoral little Schoharie still has fine hatches of the beautiful *Stenonema* flies, the Cahills and March Browns and Grey Foxes, but Flick is so fond of the Leadwings that he finds it difficult to choose a favorite summer hatch. Flick also found it a hatch quite enticing for large trout, particularly the big rainbows sometimes found in the Esopus and the Schoharie.

The rare occasions when Flick found them hatching during the daytime hours, the fish rose freely and seemed to lose their usual sense of caution. It has also been my experience with the species. Several years ago I was fishing the Dam Pool on the Henryville beats of the Brodheads with Jim Rikhoff. It was dark and a light rain occasionally misted down the stream. The *Isonychia* flies started coming off late in the morning and the fish began working immediately. There were not many, but we quickly took a half-dozen with dry flies. These were fish lying well down the tail shallows intercepting the emerging flies as they left their nymphal skins on the broken stonework of the dam. The best went only twelve inches and we released them all.

Something caught my attention in the heavy currents where the river had long ago severed the uncoursed rubble of the milldam. Few experienced anglers can explain such clues, but their senses somehow can sort the workable answers from the myriad voices of a river. I selected a big nymph from my fly book and fished it deep upstream at the footings of the masonry work. It had scarcely settled when a strong twenty-two-inch fish showered spray in a vicious roll, and the fight lasted almost thirty minutes, working deep under the dam and the brush piles before it finally surrendered.

The nymphs of *Isonychia bicolor* are almost as large as those of the largest eastern species of its genus, measuring approximately three-fourths inch in length. Its typical specimens are somewhat paler, and have a distinct dorsal stripe running their entire length, from the head to the tails.

Tails: Dark olive with brown markings at the third points, 3/8 inch
Tergites: Dark reddish brown with pale median stripe along the dorsal surfaces, 1/2 inch
Sternites: Dark reddish brown, 1/2 inch
Gills: Medium purplish gray, 1/32 inch
Thorax: Dark reddish brown, 3/16 inch
Wing cases: Dark reddish brown, 3/32 inch
Legs: Brown partridge hackle dyed olive, 1/4 inch
Head: Dark reddish brown, 3/32 inch

Hook: Sizes 10-12 Mustad 9672 3X long
Nylon: Dark brown 6/0 nylon
Tails: Dark olive pheasant-tail fibers
Foundation: Two brass pins or pieces of wire on either side of the hook
Body: Dark reddish brown dubbing with a pale stripped quill tied in at tails, laid olong dorsal median, tying off at thorax
Gills: Medium purplish gray marabou laid at sides of hook and secured with fine gold wire, seating the dorsal quill as well
Thorax: Dark reddish brown dubbing
Wing cases: Dark reddish brown feather section with a pale stripped quill tied down over the thorax
Legs: Brown mottled partridge hackle fibers
Head: Dark brown nylon

The Great Leadwing Drake Nymph that has produced consistently for me was perfected only this past season, and it took a dozen selective fish from a single pool on the Brodheads one evening.

5. Pale Western Leadwing (*Isonychia campestris*)

This is a relatively small species indigenous to the swift-flowing rivers of the northern Rocky Mountains and the Pacific Northwest, with specimens recorded from Alberta and British Columbia. Both nymphs and adults are considerably paler than most species among the *Isonychia* mayflies. The nymphs measure about a half inch.

Tails: Pale brownish with dark markings at the third points, 3/16 inch
Tergites: Pale mottled grayish with a light gray median stripe, 5/16 inch
Sternites: Pale mottled grayish, 5/16 inch
Gills: Pale bluish gray, 1/32 inch
Thorax: Pale mottled grayish, 1/8 inch
Wing cases: Pale mottled grayish, 1/8 inch
Legs: Pale mottled brown, 3/16 inch
Head: Pale mottled gray, 1/16 inch

Hook: Sizes 14-16 Mustad 9672 3X long
Nylon: Dark gray 6/0 nylon
Tails: Pale brownish pheasant fibers
Foundation: Two brass pins or short pieces of wire
Body: Pale mottled grayish dubbing mixed with hare's mask guard hairs and a gray stripped quill tied in at tails and tied off at thorax
Gills: Pale bluish gray marabou laid at the sides of the hook and secured with fine gold wire, seating the dorsal quill as well
Thorax: Pale mottled gray dubbing mixed with hare's mask
Wing cases: Dark gray feather section tied down over thorax
Legs: Pale brown partridge hackle
Head: Dark gray nylon

These nymphs are rather grayish, compared with the darker sepias and claret colorings of the other *Isonychia* species. They are typically found emerging in late summer and early fall.

6.   Great Western Leadwing (*Isonychia velma*)

This important western species is the largest of its genus endemic to American waters, its nymphs measuring almost seven-eighths inch in length. The late Don Martinez ranked it as a major fly hatch on the swift-flowing rivers of the Yellowstone country, coming off on his rivers from the third week in May until as late as the first week in July. E. H. Rosborough of Chiloquin, also rates the emergence of *Isonychia velma* as one of the high points of the Pacific Northwest season. The duns hatch on dark days, although peak emergence usually occurs just at dark on rivers like the Deschutes and MacKenzie and Metolius.

Tails: Olive brown with dark markings at the third points, ⅜ inch
Tergites: Dark rusty purple with a dull median stripe, ½ inch
Sternites: Dark rusty purple, ½ inch
Gills: Medium purplish gray, 1/32 inch
Thorax: Dark mottled dusty purple, 3/16 inch
Wing cases: Dark purplish brown, 3/16 inch
Legs: Pale mottled brown, ¼ inch
Head: Dark purplish brown, 3/32 inch

Hook: Sizes 8-10 Mustad 9672 3X long
Nylon: Dark purplish brown 6/0 nylon
Tails: Olive brown pheasant fibers
Foundation: Two brass pins or two pieces of wire set along hook shank
Body: Dark rusty purple dubbing
Gills: Medium grayish purple marabou laid at sides of hook and secured with fine gold wire
Thorax: Dark rusty purple dubbing
Wing cases: Dark purplish brown feather section tied down over thorax
Legs: Pale brown partridge hackle fibers
Head: Dark purplish brown nylon

These nymphs are not only the largest *Isonychia* species found on American waters, but their coloring is more richly claret-colored than any of the others. Their distribution ranges from the rivers of the upper Rocky Mountains to the Pacific coastal rivers from northern California to British Columbia. My dressing for the nymphs of *Isonychia velma* varies slightly from the pattern favored by Rosborough, in the sense that I favor a system of seating pale purple-dyed marabou to suggest the gills.

The Thick-Gilled Leptophlebia Nymphs

O *kra-lee-o!* The bird call echoed sweetly.

It was early in April, and the season was only a week old. The marshes that line the smooth, waist-deep currents of the river were filled with red-wing blackbirds. Winter was finished and the birds had returned north. The sunlight was weak and pale. There were bloodroot and fresh shoots of skunk cabbage in the trees. Two geese were feeding in the pondweed shallows, and the blackbirds flew restlessly back and forth across the still current. The scarlet-shouldered males filled the morning with their calling, while the females worked at nesting places in the reeds.

Okra-lee-o! the redwings cried. *Okra-lee-o!*

The current was black and smooth. It whispered almost soundlessly through the cattails and swamp willows. Phoebes waited in the branches, catching the dark-winged mayflies that were coming off above the boat landing. The flies were hatching where the current eddied in the trailing *Hygrohypnum* and eelgrass and elodea. There was the soft porpoise roll of a trout along the dense beds of pickerelweed that lined the current.

The geese rose majestically into the sun, working their slow wingbeats toward the springhole ponds in the marshes upstream. The wind was cool, riffling the still surface of the river. There were deadfalls in the river, rotting and moss-covered in the current. Its tongues were cold and surprisingly strong. The willows had a pale flush of yellow, and there were scarlet buds on the swamp maples in the bend above the boat landing. Deep in the shadows of their overhanging limbs, where the bright green moss grew lush on the bottom, another fish swirled.

Okra-lee-o! came the melody again.

It is like that along the gentle Nissequogue in April. It flows a winding course toward the sound from a series of spring-fed marshes on northern Long Island. It is a quiet little river with an old and distinguished past.

Daniel Webster once fished its Wyandanche Club, the century-old membership that controls its headwaters. Its roster has included captains of industry and shipping and finance, and its present members are no less famous. Webster dominates that history, and local legends still speak of the huge baskets of brook trout he killed on the Nissequogue.

It is a living legend in our time. Its rambling clapboard house sits high above the millpond, its sweeping porches and roof slates half hidden in the majestic elms that line the drive. The gravel is richly ornamented with the occasional Bentley or sleek Aston-Martin, gleaming Mercedes-Benz, and the odd Lamborghini. There are worn oriental carpets in the sitting rooms. The paneling is covered with paintings and prints, and a cut-glass decanter filled with a fine sherry waits on the cherry-wood sideboard.

The long dining-room table is often covered with steaming platters of trout and bacon-wrapped woodcock and venison. It is a clubhouse where time has stopped. Its silent rooms seem filled with the memories of seasons past. Tackle is shelved and stored in the mahogany lockers upstairs, each with the brass nameplate of its owner on the door. Similar engraved plates identify their personal liquor cabinets, and beyond the velvet-soft felt of the billiard table is a huge rack of fly-rods—rich with Leonards and Paynes and Garrisons gleaming with the patina of the years.

The beats are carefully marked in the woods, with duckboard walks in the marshy bottoms. The fishing is drawn on one of the six river-beats with numbers from a leather dicecup at breakfast. Beat Five is a stillwater reach of river that winds a half-mile above the boat landing used to fish the mill-pond above the dam. It is challenging water.

There are a number of fine holding-lies. Fish cruise the open currents between the docks, often lying deep along the pickerelweed. There is a second place near the upper dock, where the sliding current works along the alders, clearing the silt from the gravel. Upstream there are beds of eelgrass, where pale stones lie in the eddying currents. It is a place where I once took a fat twenty-inch rainbow on a dark little *Leptophlebia* nymph. There is a deep run under the alders in the bend above the boathouse, and trout are lying there. Thirty yards of shallow flat are next, sometimes good for a cruising fish, and then there is a fine three hundred feet of river. It has undercut roots along the willows and alders, with brushy deadfalls breaking the current. It is a deep dark-water run that has often given me brown trout between sixteen and eighteen inches.

The swamp maple lies ahead. There are always good fish in the shadows of its low, overhanging limbs. Above the maple there is a delicate limb leaning across the smooth current, and it once surrendered a richly spotted, three-pound brown that slipped from its shadows to intercept my swimming nymph.

The river loops west again, and upstream another snag maple leans out over the glassy shallows. There are always fish there, and they lie tight under the alder roots above and below the trees. It is a fine place for the upstream nymph. Two hundred feet of soft-bottomed flat lies above. It surrenders the odd trout, but the next really productive run lies around the bend, tight against the willows and sheltering trees, deep along the roots at the head of the run, where the current slides into the bend and shelves off into chest-deep water. I once took a fine rainbow of almost four pounds. The fish flashed to the nymph and there was a heavy pull. When I tightened, the trout cartwheeled upstream wildly, running the reel as it bolted across the sandy flat like a startled bonefish. It finally slipped weakly across the net-frame, and it was some time before it edged back into deep water after it had been released.

It is perfect water for the thick-gilled *Leptophlebia* nymphs, which love our sluggish eastern and midwestern rivers. The Nissequogue has excellent hatches of these agile, swimming nymphs, and their imitations are deadly there. The little river holds many memories for me, fishing in April hatches of *Leptophlebia* with my good friends Lester Brion and Tony Coe.

There are a number of eastern and midwestern rivers that are ideally suited to the big *Leptophlebia* mayflies, and the Nissequogue is perhaps one of the best. Good hatches also are found on the Schoharie, particulary below Lexington, and the headwater flats on the West Branch of the Ausable are also known for heavy hatches of this genus. The lower Beaverkill below Cook's Falls, and the stillwater reaches of the South Raritan in New Jersey are also fine habitat. Otter Creek and the headwaters of the Battenkill provide good hatches of these flies. Wetzel mentions them in *Trout Flies* as appearing in large numbers on Penn's Creek and the still flats of Big Fishing Creek in Pennsylvania, and there are fine hatches on any number of Michigan rivers. Watersheds like the Big South Pere Marquette and the lower reaches of its Little South Branch, along with the Manistee and the Au Sable, are perfect habitat.

The flies now classified in this genus were described under the genus *Blasturus* in the definitive *Biology of Mayflies* that Needham published at Cornell in 1935. The result for the American fly-fisher is a number of books which discuss these hatches, particularly the well-known eastern species *Blasturus cupidus*, under a taxonometric description no longer recognized in aquatic entomology. Jennings, Wetzel, and Flick have all used the older generic keys in their work, though all of their *Blasturus* flies are now in the *Leptophlebia* genus.

The genus has no parallel among the European mayflies. Its nymphs are distinguished by the exaggerated width of their thickly lamellate gills, and the slender emargination at their tips. The gills are double and lamelliform, spreading like tiny little leaves with apical stems, and are found on all seven abdominal segments. The species vary individually in size, coloration, depths of angulation between segments in the gills, and alignment of their spinal tips. Jay Traver made extensive studies of these flies, particularly in the monograph entitled *Observations on the Ecology of the Mayfly Blasturus cupidus*, which was published in 1925. Her studies concluded that the species was rather sluggish in character, and that although the mating swarms deposited their eggs in running currents, after eclosion from the ova the nymphs migrated into the stiller reaches of river. Her observations on their general behavior were as follows:

> These nymphs seem to depend for protection more upon coloration than upon swiftness of movement. Quiet backwaters are more favorable for their development. The nymphs will often feign death when disturbed, especially when removed from the water.

The nymphs have relatively long antennae and tails. Their antennae are longer than the head and thorax combined, and their tails are much longer than the bodies. The three tails in the nymphal stage are of about equal length, while in the adults the middle tails are rather short. The nymphs are quite common in March and April, mottled with pale markings against their overall chestnut color and exaggerated tracheal structure.

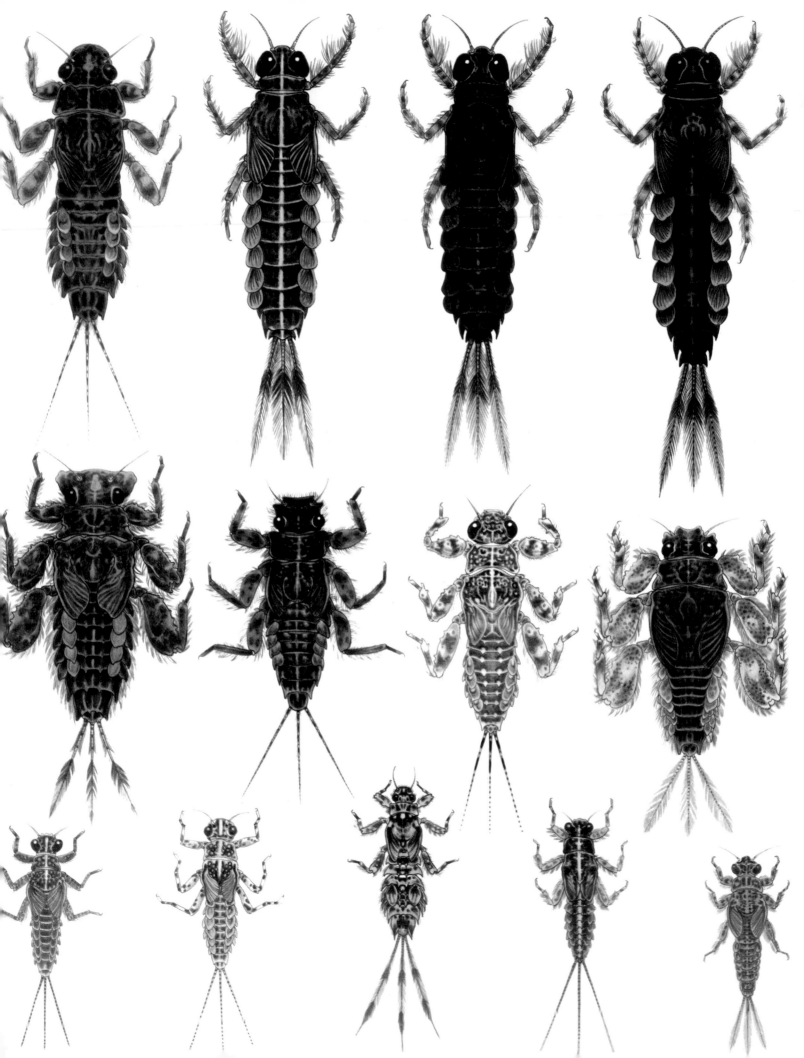

2. Early Black Quill (*Leptophlebia cupida*)

These mayflies are perhaps the best-known species of the entire *Leptophlebia* genus, since it has been exhaustively studied by biologists and has appeared in the books of fishing writers like Jennings, Wetzel, Grove, and Flick. It is also widely distributed. Its range along the eastern seaboard ranges from specimens collected in Newfoundland to the April hatches of North Carolina. Its western specimens reach past New York and Pennsylvania into the rich marl-swamp rivers and tea-colored watersheds of Michigan and Wisconsin. Specimens are also recorded from Minnesota, Ontario, and Manitoba.

The nymphs are slightly smaller and darker than those of *Leptophlebia nebulosa,* and their peak hatching occurs somewhat later. Their coloring is dark brown with olive mottlings. The nymphs are found in both lakes and streams, favoring the rotting sticks and leaf-drifts of backwaters and eddies. The adults are called Black Quills on many eastern rivers, particularly by anglers on Penns Creek and Big Fishing Creek in Pennsylvania, although their wings are actually a dark iron-blue dun. Nymphs measure a half inch in length.

Tails: Pale mottled brown, 7/16 inch
Tergites: Dark brown heavily mottled with medium brown, ¼ inch
Sternites: Paler mottled brownish, ¼ inch
Gills: Dark olive brown with delicate fringes, ⅛ inch
Thorax: Dark brown heavily mottled with medium brown, ⅛ inch
Wing cases: Medium brown, ⅛ inch
Legs: Medium olive brown, 5/16 inch
Head: Medium brown, 1/16 inch

Hook: Sizes 12-14 Mustad 9671 3X long
Nylon: Dark brown 6/0 nylon
Tails: Pale barred woodduck fibers
Body: Dark blackish brown hare's mask dubbing mixed with guard hairs, and spun on olive silk
Gills: Dark olive marabou laid thickly on either side of the body and secured with fine gold wire
Thorax: Dark blackish brown hare's mask dubbing mixed with guard hairs, and spun on olive silk
Wing cases: Medium brown feather section tied over thorax
Legs: Medium olive brown fibers
Head: Dark brown nylon

Top, left to right: *Ephemerella grandis, Isonychia bicolor, Isonychia sadleri, Isonychia velma*

Middle, left to right: *Ephemerella hecuba, Ephemerella doddsi, Ephemerella coloradensis, Ephemerella walkeri*

Bottom, left to right: *Ephemerella attenuata, Ephemerella maculata, Ephemerella doris, Ephemerella needhami, Ephemerella excrucians*

Hatching typically occurs from late morning until late afternoon, the flies coming sporadically from the nymphal schools. Peak emergence on our eastern rivers usually comes in late April, and about two weeks later on the large still-flowing rivers of Michigan and Wisconsin.

3. Western Black Quill (*Leptophlebia gravastella*)

This is a medium-sized western species quite similar to *Leptophlebia cupida* in size, although its coloring is somewhat paler. Specimens are well distributed from New Mexico to Montana, and the somewhat darker *Leptophlebia pacifica* is found from California to British Columbia. It has produced excellent fishing for me from the Cucharas and Conejos in southern Colorado to the still flats of the lower Big Hole and Yellowstone in Montana. Particularly good hatches emerge from Flat Creek in Jackson Hole, the slow-flowing Teton in Idaho, and the weedy currents of the classic Firehole below Old Faithful. The full-grown nymphs measure approximately one-half inch in length.

Tails: Pale mottled brown, 7/16 inch
Tergites: Medium brown mottled with yellowish olive, ¼ inch
Sternites: Paler mottled brownish, ¼ inch
Gills: Grayish olive with delicate fringes ⅛ inch
Thorax: Medium brown mottled with yellowish olive, ⅛ inch
Wing cases: Grayish brown, ⅛ inch
Legs: Grayish olive, ¼ inch
Head: Medium mottled brown, 1/16 inch

Hook: Sizes 12-14 Mustad 9672 3X long
Nylon: Light brown nylon
Tails: Pale barred woodduck fibers
Body: Medium grayish hare's ear dubbing mixed with guard hairs on light olive silk
Gills: Grayish olive marabou laid thickly on either side of the body and secured with fine gold wire
Thorax: Medium grayish dubbing on light olive silk
Wing cases: Grayish brown feather section tied over thorax
Legs: Grayish olive hackle fibers
Head: Light brown nylon

Hatches are sporadic throughout the daylight hours. They have given me some wonderful fishing on the slow ranch-country reaches of the Encampment in Wyoming, the still pools of the South Platte in Colorado, and the Logan in the foothill country of Utah. There have been some classic days over big cutthroats in the spring-fed channels of the Snake above Moose Crossing, and on the famous cutthroat rivers of the Yellowstone country—the remote little Bechler and the rich meadows of Slough Creek and the upper Yellowstone itself.

4. Dark-Blue Quill (*Leptophlebia johnsoni*)

This is a dark little mayfly of our eastern rivers, quite similar to the bigger *Leptophlebia cupida* species, but measuring only about three-eighths inch in length. Unlike the larger related species, these little nymphs are more widely distributed in various types of water. The flies are relatively common from New England to the mountain rivers of North Carolina. They usually live quite openly in all types of current speeds, and they thrive in smooth, gravelly riffles. Emergence typically occurs throughout May.

The imitation that I like is quite similar to the patterns we dressed many years ago on the Grundbach at Fischen-Im-Allgäu.

Tails: Pale mottled brown, ⅜ inch
Tergites: Dark blackish brown mottled with light brown markings, 3/16 inch
Sternites: Paler·mottled brownish, 3/16 inch
Gills: Dark olive with delicate fringes, ⅛ inch
Thorax: Dark blackish mottled brown, 3/32 inch
Wing cases: Dark blackish brown, 3/32 inch
Legs: Dark brownish olive, 3/16 inch
Head: Dark blackish brown, 1/16 inch

Hook: Sizes 14-16 Mustad 9672 3X long
Nylon: Dark brown 6/0 nylon
Tails: Dark barred woodduck fibers
Body: Blackish hare's mask dubbing mixed with guard hairs on olive silk
Gills: Dark olive brown marabou laid thickly on either side of the body and secured with fine gold wire
Thorax: Blackish hare's mask dubbing on olive silk
Wing cases: Dark blackish brown feather section tied over thorax
Legs: Dark brownish olive hackle fibers
Head: Dark brown nylon

This species is not recorded by Justin Leonard in his definitive little textbook *Mayflies of Michigan Trout Streams*, and it must be presumed that it is not found in those waters. However, there are a number of similar dun-colored mayflies on the rivers of Michigan and Wisconsin, and these diminutive insects are members of the closely related *Paraleptophlebia* Mayfly genus.

The Tiny Fork-Gilled Paraleptophlebia Nymphs

SEVERAL YEARS ago my good friend David Rose called me on a cold and rainy April morning. There were snowflakes in occasional flurries outside my studio, and it was not a day for fly-fishing. The trout season in New Jersey was only a few days old, and the tragicomic supermarket crowds of opening weekend were past.

Cabin fever, David explained. *I've got it bad!*

David Rose is a physician who takes a midweek break in order to have regular office hours on Saturday. We normally drive north to fish the Brodheads each week, but the Pennsylvania opening was still a few days away. Public water on most New Jersey streams is hopelessly crowded, and we seldom enjoy the elbow-to-elbow fishermen typical of its early-season weeks.

You really want to go? I laughed.

It's a terrible case of too much winter, he continued, *and I just need to get outside. Where should we go?*

Let's try the South Raritan.

There is a stretch of pretty water in the hemlock-dark valley above High Bridge that is restricted to fly-fishing. It is a memorial to the late Ken Lockwood, the famous tournament caster and fishing writer from New Jersey. It is usually crowded in April, but on a rainy day in the middle of the week there was a chance. It is good water.

Pick you up in ten minutes.

There were violets along the river, and there were still old snowbanks in the shaded ravines. It was cold and raw. We ate lunch in the car, and there was no sign of rising trout.There were a few *Paraleptophlebia* flies coming off at the tail of the big pondlike pool at the top of the Lockwood Gorge. Two bait-fishermen were sitting at the middle of the pool. It seemed warmer after lunch.

Let's try it a while, David suggested.

He chose to walk downstream and fish the pocket-water. There were still a few *Paraleptophlebia* flies in the air, and I selected a tiny nymph imitation. The current gathers and narrows in the tail shallows, and there are several big rocks under the hemlocks.

Looks good, I thought.

No fish were working visibly. It was a time for a light-tackle variation on salmon tactics. Without a sign of a rising trout, it is necessary to cover the water with a series of disciplined casts and current-swings. Each cast dropped tight against the rocks across the river, just a few inches farther downstream, working concentrically back across the current. Such tactics cover every fish in the run, making sure that any trout in the mood to rise will see the fly.

Eleven casts worked deep on the four-weight sinking line, teasing back rhythmically along the bottom with the rod tip. The next cast simply stopped at the *moment critique,* the critical three-quarter point in the fly-swing when the fly has reached maximum depth and has just begun to rise back toward the surface like a hatching nymph.

It felt like a snag on the delicate seven-foot Leonard. There was no movement for several seconds. Suddenly the fish wrenched its head angrily and writhed downstream toward the broken water there. The tiny seven-foot rod buckled wildly, almost out of control. Finally the fish stopped at the swift lip of the pool, hanging in its gathering currents like a big salmon. The tension of the current against the belly of the line nagged at the fish until it grudgingly worked back upstream into the pool, thinking the pressure came from below.

It was a long fight. The trout worked stubbornly along the bottom, trying to slip under the rocks or find a snag. But finally it surrendered and circled weakly against the 6X tippet in the shallows. David had seen the duration of the fight, and had walked back upstream to watch.

Big fish? he asked.

Pretty good, I said. *Big for this water.*

The trout threshed and threw water angrily. *It's at least a three-pounder,* David said excitedly. *What did he take?*

Paraleptophlebia nymph, I said.

It was a deep-bellied, twenty-inch brown, an impressive trout for such heavily fished public water. Although the small fork-gilled nymphs of the *Paraleptophlebia* genus are typically less than seven-sixteenths inch, they are so numerous and so widely distributed that they are an important facet of the trout diet.

The nymphs are the crawling types, their bodies slender and rounded and fringed with delicate little fork-shaped gills. They regularly inhabit lakes and streams and ponds, and they are relatively poor swimmers when compared with the other tiny mayfly nymphs, particularly the agile little nymphs of the *Baetis* and *Centroptilum.* European species typically love soft-bottom habitats like silt, detritus, gravel, sand, and moss-covered stones. The most active of the European species is perhaps the little *Paraleptophlebia cincta,* and its nymphs are rather streamlined. Their tails are slender, with delicate, ribbonlike gills. This species is prototypical of the American ecotypes, which are more current-loving than their European cousins. They live in rapid and smooth-flowing reaches among weed and trailing mosses, requiring more oxygenated water than slow-water species of the genus. The principal late-summer and early-autumn hatches on European rivers are often *Paraleptophlebia cincta,* and it was these flies that were the hatches on the little Grundbach at Fischen-im-Allgäu—the fishing described in the epilogue to the chapter on nymph-fishing tackle.

Like the *Leptophlebias* these nymphs have relatively long antennae and tails, with the antennae measuring more than head and thorax combined, and tails longer than the body. The gills on abdominal segments two through seven are double fork-shaped types, with two filamentous apical extensions of the medial trachea. The heads are rectilinear, held with the mouthparts down like the attitude of a grasshopper. The mouthparts are similar to the physiology of the *Leptophlebia* nymphs; the tinier *Paraleptophlebias* exhibit four to six pectinate spines below the crown of the maxilla. Spinules are present on the apical margins of each tergite. Lateral spines are found on segments eight and nine, although a few species exhibit such spinules only on segment nine.

The diminutive little *Paraleptophlebia* nymph is similar to its larger cousins in its habit of schooling like tiny baitfish. These schools often migrate along the river before hatching, concentrating in the quiet backwaters in huge numbers. Hatches can be heavy, resulting from such densely populated nymphal schools.

Unlike the *Leptophlebias* these streamlined little nymphs are fond of flowing water. They are most common in gravel-bottomed riffles with a depth of six inches to two feet. Like spawning fish, they seem to favor a current of one to two and a half feet per second.

1. Early Blue Quill (*Paraleptophlebia adoptiva*)

Since it was described more than twenty-five years ago in the classic books of Preston Jennings and Art Flick, this handsome little species is perhaps the best known of the American *Paraleptophlebia* flies. It produces superb fly hatches in late April and May on most eastern and northern rivers, and the fish respond to them readily. The nymphs hatch in open currents, using the surface film to split their skins.

Specimens are recorded from Quebec to Maryland along the eastern seaboard, and westerly from the gravelly shallows of Carman's River on Long Island to the rivers of Michigan and Wisconsin. *Paraleptophlebia assimilis* is a similar species indigenous to Virginia, West Virginia and North Carolina rivers.

The species is quite common on the smooth-flowing gravelly streams of Michigan and Wisconsin, and during my boyhood years we often found them hatching quite early, sometimes mixed with spring snow flurries. Memories of these hatches are clear, as I write, fishing with the bite of snowflakes in my face on rivers like the Brule and the Namekagon in Wisconsin, and along the sweeping riffles of the Pere Marquette.

Tails: Dark mottled tannish, 5/16 inch
Body: Dark grayish brown distinctly ringed, 3/16 inch
Gills: Dark grayish brown heavily fringed, 1/16 inch
Thorax: Dark grayish brown, 3/32 inch
Wing cases: Dark grayish brown, 3/32 inch
Legs: Dark grayish olive 5/32 inch
Head: Dark grayish brown, 1/16 inch

Hook: Sizes 14-16 Orvis Premium 1X long
Nylon: Dark tan 6/0 nylon
Tails: Dark barred woodduck
Body: Dark grayish brown dubbing tightly spun on brown silk
Gills: Dark grayish brown marabou secured with fine gold wire
Thorax: Dark grayish brown spun on brown silk
Wing cases: Dark grayish brown feather section tied down over thorax
Legs: Dark grayish olive hackle fibers
Head: Dark tan nylon

The dressing of marabou fibers on the imitations suggests their delicate gill structures, with a fly-dressing technique accidentally discovered years ago on the Grundbach hatches, when a tiny drowned dry fly proved more deadly than a conventionally dressed nymph once its hackle had loosened and slipped back along the body. The natural nymphs measure about three-eighths inch at maturity.

2. American Iron-Blue Dun (*Paraleptophlebia mollis*)

This fine little mayfly is the American counterpart of a British species that has appeared in the literature of fly-fishing since Richard and Charles Bowlker described both the hatch and its imitation in their classic *Art of Angling*. Their superb book had its genesis on the rivers of Shropshire, and proved so definitive that it came to dominate angling literature through the entire eighteenth century.

It is a widely distributed hatch. Its nymphs drift considerable distances in the current, and its freshly hatched subimagoes continue to ride the surface film as much as a hundred feet in rainy weather. Fully grown nymphs measure about five-sixteenths inch, and are found across the entire eastern seaboard from Quebec to North Carolina. Good populations are also recorded from coastal watersheds to Michigan and Wisconsin. Hatches occur in late May on the major eastern rivers, while peak emergence is found in early June on more northerly watersheds from Upper Michigan to Maine. Like *Paraleptophlebia adoptiva*, these little flies spend considerable time in hatching, drifting with the current just under the surface film.

Tails: Dark mottled tannish ¼ inch
Body: Dark iron-blue distinctly ringed grayish, 5/32 inch
Gills: Dark brownish heavily fringed, 1/16 inch
Thorax: Dark iron-blue grayish, 1/16 inch
Wing cases: Dark brownish, 1/16 inch
Legs: Dark olive, ⅛ inch
Head: Dark iron-blue grayish, 1/64 inch

Hook: Sizes 16-18 Orvis Premium 1X long
Nylon: Dark brown 6/0 nylon
Tails: Dark barred woodduck
Body: Dark blackish brown hare's mask dubbing tightly spun
Gills: Dark brownish marabou secured with fine gold wire
Thorax: Dark blackish brown hare's mask
Wing cases: Dark brownish feather section tied down over the thorax
Legs: Dark olive hackle fibers
Head: Dark brown nylon

The slightly smaller parallel species designated as *Paraleptophlebia swannanoa* is found in the rivers of North Carolina and Tennessee. My imitation of these little iron-blue nymphs is dressed with the indicated materials, its configuration paralleling that of the *Paraleptophlebia* species in their nymphal stages.

3. Dark Blue Quill (*Paraleptophlebia debilis*)

This superb little fly hatch is also rather widely distributed, and is a dark-winged mayfly that begins to emerge in late June. Hatches are often found steadily throughout the summer months, finally ending in the first wintry days of October. Its coloring is somewhat similar to that of the *Paraleptophlebia adoptiva* nymphs, with their mottled heads and generally dark palette. However, they have dark markings behind each lateral ocellus, and at each lateral tergite margin. The pale median stripe at the head and thorax is less apparent than with the nymphs of the slightly larger *Paraleptophlebia adoptiva*. The yellowish-olive legs are more heavily mottled than those of that sister species. Like most of the mayflies of this genus, its hatching begins in the late morning, as the river warms, and flies continue to emerge sporadically all day. The fully developed nymphs measure approximately five-sixteenths inch in length.

Tails: Dark mottled tannish, ¼ inch
Body: Dark brownish distinctly ringed, 5/32 inch
Gills: Medium olive heavily fringed, 1/16 inch
Thorax: Dark brownish, 1/16 inch
Wing cases: Dark brownish, 1/16 inch
Legs: Medium olive, ⅛ inch
Head: Dark brownish, 1/64 inch

Hook: Sizes 16-18 Orvis Premium 1X long
Nylon: Medium olive 6/0 nylon
Tails: Dark barred woodduck
Body: Dark brownish dubbing tightly spun on olive silk
Gills: Medium olive marabou secured with fine gold wire
Thorax: Dark brownish dubbing on olive silk
Wing cases: Dark brownish feather section tied down over thorax
Legs: Medium olive hackle fibers
Head: Medium olive nylon

The fork-shaped gills are quite dark and rather fully developed in these nymphs. They move with considerable agility in hatching.

4. Little Summer Blue Quill (*Paraleptophlebia praedipita*)

This delicate little olive-gilled nymph is quite widely found in large, somewhat warmer trout rivers from New Brunswick to Virginia, and west to Wisconsin and Michigan. Its rather pale nymphs measure about five-sixteenths inch at full growth, with a gill structure resembling that of *Paraleptophlebia debilis* in their configuration. Hatching occurs sporadically throughout the summer months.

Tails: Pale mottled grayish, ¼ inch
Body: Pale grayish distinctly ringed, 5/32 inch
Gills: Pale olive grayish, 1/16 inch
Thorax: Pale grayish, 1/16 inch
Wing cases: Dark grayish, 1/16 inch
Legs: Pale olive grayish, ⅛ inch
Head: Pale grayish, 1/64 inch

Hook: Sizes 16-18 Orvis Premium 1X long
Nylon: Dark gray 6/0 nylon
Tails: Grayish brown mallard fibers
Body: Pale grayish dubbing tightly spun on olive silk
Gills: Pale olive gray marabou secured with fine gold wire
Thorax: Pale grayish dubbing tightly spun on olive silk
Wing cases: Dark grayish feather section tied down over thorax
Legs: Pale grayish olive hackle
Head: Dark gray nylon

There is a similar western species, the handsome little *Paraleptophlebia pallipes* mayfly, with a coastal distribution from British Columbia to southern California. Specimens are also recorded from New Mexico to Alberta in the Rocky Mountains, with particularly fine hatches common on rivers like the South Platte in Colorado.

5. Pale Summer Quill (*Paraleptophlebia strigula*)

This is a relatively pale little mayfly which emerges throughout July and

August in its more important hatching cycles, although sporadic flights occur as late as October. Its amber-colored little nymphs measure about five-sixteenths inch at maturity.

Tails: Pale mottled brownish, ¼ inch
Body: Pale grayish amber distinctly ringed, 5/32 inch
Gills: Pale yellowish olive, 1/16 inch
Thorax: Pale grayish amber, 1/16 inch
Wing cases: Pale grayish brown, 1/16 inch
Legs: Pale yellowish olive, ⅛ inch
Head: Pale grayish amber, 1/64 inch

Hook: Sizes 16-18 Orvis Premium 1X long
Nylon: Tan 6/0 nylon
Tails: Pale barred woodduck fibers
Body: Pale grayish amber dubbing tightly spun on yellow silk
Gills: Pale yellowish olive marabou secured with fine gold wire
Thorax: Pale grayish amber dubbing on yellow silk
Wing cases: Pale grayish brown feather section tied down over thorax
Legs: Pale yellowish olive hackle
Head: Tan nylon

This mayfly is distributed from Ontario to Michigan, and hatches are recorded in the northern rivers of Pennsylvania and New Jersey.

6. Western Blue Quill (*Paraleptophlebia californica*)

This little western species measures about three-eighths inch at its full nymphal development, like the closely related *Paraleptophlebia gregalis* species, and these two little insects are found in Pacific rivers from British Columbia to California. Their early emergence occupies a similar place in the cycle of the season on Pacific rivers to the eastern hatching of *Paraleptophlebia adoptiva*. Its hatches are eagerly taken by the trout.

Both *Paraleptophlebia californica* and *Paraleptophlebia gregalis* hatch in open currents, taking considerable time to escape their nymphal skins. Their populations are particularly heavy in Washington and Oregon, where the marine climate and its rainy weather combine to keep the newly hatched flies on the surface for as much as a hundred and fifty feet. *Paraleptophlebia gregalis* is primarily a species found from northern California to Washington. Sometimes these fly hatches are also mixed with the less common *Paraleptophlebia compar*.

Tails: Dark mottled amber, 5/16 inch
Body: Dark grayish brown distinctly ringed, 3/16 inch
Gills: Pale grayish brown, 1/16 inch
Thorax: Dark grayiih brown, 3/32 inch
Wing cases: Dark grayish brown, 3/32 inch
Legs: Dark grayish brown, 5/32 inch
Head: Dark grayish brown, 1/16 inch

Hook: Sizes 14-16 Orvis Premium 1X long
Nylon: Dark tannish gray 6/0 nylon
Tails: Dark barred woodduck fibers
Body: Dark grayish brown dubbing tightly spun on brown silk
Gills: Pale grayish marabou secured with fine gold wire
Thorax: Dark grayish brown dubbing on brown silk
Wing cases: Dark grayish brown feather section tied over thorax
Legs: Dark grayish brown hackle
Head: Dark tan nylon

7. Western Blue Dun (*Paraleptophlebia packii*)

This is the largest species of this widely distributed little genus, and its unique pale-olive pincers readily identify its specimens on western rivers. Needham in his *Biology of Mayflies* records fly hatches of this species only on the rivers of Utah, but it has since been observed on both the watersheds of the Pacific coast and the Rocky Mountains. Its fully developed nymphal forms measure approximately seven-sixteenths inch in length.

Tails: Dark mottled brownish, 5/16 inch
Body: Dark purplish gray distinctly ringed, 3/16 inch
Gills: Dark olive brown, 1/16 inch
Thorax: Dark purplish gray, 3/32 inch
Wing cases: Dark purplish gray, 3/32 inch
Legs: Dark olive brown, 5/32 inch
Head: Dark purplish gray, 1/16 inch

Hook: Sizes 12-14 Orvis Premium 1X long
Nylon: Dark gray 6/0 nylon
Tails: Dark barred woodduck fibers
Body: Dark grayish dubbing tightly spun on purple silk
Gills: Dark olive brown marabou secured with fine gold wire
Thorax: Dark grayish dubbing spun on purple silk
Wing cases: Dark purplish gray feather tied down over thorax
Legs: Dark olive brown hackle
Head: Dark gray nylon

Because of the mandibles of these nymphs, as Paul Needham reports in his book *Trout Streams,* some western anglers call them tuskers. I have seen particularly good hatches on the South Platte at Deckers. The slightly smaller and closely related *Paraleptophlebia bicornuta* is generally found in the rivers from Wyoming to Alberta. These are hatches of late summer and early fall.

8.   Little Western Red Quill (*Paraleptophlebia heteronea*)

Memories of this elegant reddish-bodied little mayfly take me back to boyhood summers on the Frying Pan in Colorado. Its smooth gravel-bottom flats and elodea beds are gone now, buried forever in the icy depths of the reservoir at Ruedi, but I can remember those cool, almost cloudless September mornings as clearly as I see the shadbush blossoms in the trees outside my studio.

The nymphs begin emerging in late morning on the Colorado rivers, and hatches seem heavier with a misting rain. These *Paraleptophlebia* nymphs measure about five-sixteenths inch in full pre-hatching growth, and are found from New Mexico to Alberta.

Although the fish rise exceptionally well to the freshly hatched *Paraleptophlebia* flies, there are times when they prefer a nymph struggling just under the surface film.

Tails: Dark mottled brownish, ¼ inch
Body: Dark reddish brown distinctly ringed, 5/32 inch
Gills: Dark rusty brown, 1/16 inch
Thorax: Dark reddish brown, 1/16 inch
Wing cases: Dark chocolate brownish, 1/16 inch
Legs: Medium brownish, ⅛ inch
Head: Dark reddish brown, 1/64 inch

Hook: Sizes 16-18 Orvis Premium 1X long
Nylon: Dark brown 6/0 nylon
Tails: Dark barred woodduck fibers
Body: Dark reddish brown dubbing tightly spun on ruby silk
Gills: Dark rusty brown marabou secured with fine gold wire
Thorax: Dark reddish brown dubbing spun on ruby silk
Wing cases: Chocolate brown feather tied over thorax
Legs: Medium brownish hackle
Head: Dark brown nylon

Those stillwater shallows on the Frying Pan are gone now, but I clearly remember the frost-sharp September nights in the Cold Creek campsite with my father, and the fine hatches of *Paraleptophlebia heteronea* we witnessed during a week of fishing.

There was another early autumn weekend in the smooth pools at the bottom of the Ruedi stretch, when we stayed at the Frontier Hotel in Basalt, driving upriver through the red bluffs that sheltered the steep-walled canyon of the Frying Pan. Dexter Keezer and Jeffrey Norton had met me in Colorado Springs that September, and we drove over the foothill ranges of the mountains just after daylight. The bunchgrass basin of the South Park reached for miles at the bottom of the Wilkerson Pass, and in the distance, beyond the Buffalo Mountain and the barren Mosquito Range, were the highest mountains in the Rockies. Their summits were purplish with the first sunlight of the morning, and they towered majestically from the triple peaks of beautiful Mount Princeton to the solitary pyramid-shaped Mount Elbert farther north. Climbing steadily above Twin Lakes, their sprawling surfaces smooth in the windless autumn morning, we wound into the Clear Creek bottoms between Mount Harvard and the 14,431-foot summits of Elbert. There was fresh snow below the highest switchbacks of Independence Pass, powdering its loose gravel hairpins and grass-covered parks. Aspen lay beyond, beside the headwaters of the Roaring Fork, at the bottom of the stair-step western approaches to the pass. The Frying Pan joins the Roaring Fork at Basalt.

It was a fine weekend of cold nights and faultless, shirtsleeve days, with the frost yellowing the cottonwoods along the river, and the evening wind sailboating their leaves across its pools and flats. Our last afternoon I encountered a fine *Paraleptophlebia* hatch in the Ruedi stretch, catching and releasing a dozen browns between twelve inches and two pounds on nymphal imitations.

It was a beautiful reach of river in those days. Although it lies buried beneath the impoundment at Ruedi, its persistence in my memory tells me that nothing we remember ever really dies. Its currents still flow smoothly in the mind, riffling gently past its trailing weeds, and its trout still work softly to the tiny *Paraleptophlebias* in the tail shallows. Although its river music has now become a requiem, its magic still lives in my daydreams.

Minute Nymphal Forms of the Caenidae

Iᴛ ɪs a pastoral landscape of prosperous farms, their cornfields and rich pastures lie sheltered between the folded tree-covered ridges of the Appalachians. It is a countryside of well-filled granaries and silos. Herds of black-and-white dairy cattle graze lazily in the meadows and stare at fishermen from the sheltering buttonwoods. The whitewashed fences are as immaculate in these tailored fields as the clapboard farmhouses themselves. The barns are painted bright red, their cantilevered hay-wagon floors sheltering the cattle stalls toward the south. Their design permits the cattle to be gravity-fed from above; the stored grain and ensilage and hay above the livestock pens insulates the cattle and holds their body-heat inside the barn, and the low winter sun slants deep into their stalls. The builders mixed this primitive functionalism and climatology with witchcraft too, covering their bets both ways, with hex signs to protect the farm and its livestock and its inhabitants from evil spirits. The foundations and gable ends of the barns are examples of the magnificent amber-colored masonry work typical of the Pennsylvania Dutch.

Its trout streams are unusual too. Many emerge full-blown from limestone fissures that release the flow of vast underground caverns. Their currents are so rich with lime salts that their fertility rivals the storied chalkstreams of Europe—rivers like the Risle and Andelle in France, and the still more famous Itchen and Test in the chalk downs of southern Britain.

The limestone springs are remarkable for their volume and clarity, surrendering thousands of gallons per minute into these gentle little meadow rivers. The result is a habitat rich in fly life, currents that remain ice-free, and water temperatures so constant that the fish feed and grow steadily throughout the winter.

Their fly hatches are typically rather small. The roster of limestone waters is a roll call of pastoral little farm-country streams. The list begins with the Paulinskill and Musconetcong in western New Jersey, crossing the Delaware to include the Little Lehigh in Pennsylvania. Following the cretaceous riches of the subterranean limestone country, there are the better known Big Spring and Letort Spring Run west of Harrisburg, the home streams of superb fly-fishermen like Charles Fox and the celebrated Vincent Marinaro. The limestone region curves south, reaching into the drainage of picturesque little Falling Spring Run at Chambersburg, and finally to the Conococheaque and Antietam in Maryland.

Fishing these American chalkstreams has become perhaps a matter of pilgrimage rather than mere sport. The smooth currents are silken in the watercress and elodea, and the fish dimple almost imperceptibly to tiny flies. There are late summer hatches of the Caenidae, minute mayflies that greatly multiply the problems of selectivity and tiny flies and delicate leaders. These are hyperselective trout, and as Swisher and Richards argue in their book *Selective Trout*, when the hatch consists of minute mayflies of less than three-sixteenths inch in length, an error of a single hook size in imitation becomes a mistake of thirty-odd percent.

Caenidae are often morning flies, coming off the smooth limestone currents between daylight and nine o'clock. The peak hatches typically come between seven and eight in the morning, missed by fishermen who insist on leisurely breakfasts at a normal schedule. It is a time when these lush summer valleys still lie cool with their night temperatures, and the meadows are jeweled with dew. Fishing these tiny mayflies is a challenge. Their hatching typically begins in late June, with flies emerging throughout the summer, and some Caenidae are still coming off in October.

These are not the only rivers where these tiny mayflies, the genera *Brachycercus, Tricorythodes* and *Caenis*, are important far beyond their proportions of mere size. They have given me excellent fishing on the flats of the Battenkill and Ausable, and on all of the storied Catskill rivers. Fly-fishermen experienced with late-summer canoe floats on the Delaware have witnessed truly remarkable hatches of these tiny insects, hatches on smooth, half-mile flats so numerous that the autopsies on three-to-four-pound rainbows reveal as many as three to four thousand of these tiny nymphs in their digestive tracts after feeding on a single morning rise. There are western rivers, too, with silken flats like those on the Snake and the Yellowstone and the Henry's Fork in Idaho, where thousands of fish dimple to these midge-sized mayflies every morning for weeks. Western anglers who have evolved beyond the fish-the-water simplicities of big nymphs and hairwing dry flies are aware of these tiny flies on both their big-water flats and spring creeks, and on their lakes and impoundments. The Caenidae are important almost everywhere there is suitable habitat, and fish taking their hatching nymphs have always been part of the baffling puzzle of hundreds of rising fish that steadfastly refused dry flies. Although these hatches are distributed throughout the country, it was the limestone streams from the Musconetcong to Falling Spring Run that first taught me their importance, and those rivers are always in my mind when thoughts turn to past experiences with the tiny Caenidae.

Their nymphs are unique lenitic ecotypes, primarily found in silt-bottomed ponds and impoundments and still currents. These bottom-sprawling nymphs are rather stiff-legged and covered with delicate filamentous hairs. They have relatively thick little bodies and thinly fringed little tails. Their small size, the protective coloration they achieve when their body hairs are thick with silt, and their relatively sluggish movements all combine to protect them from the fish. Therefore, their safety depends on camouflage rather than agility of movement. When collected along with bottom silts, the Caenidae are virtually invisible in the screening until they betray themselves with movement.

The nymphs love silt and detritus and weeds. Such quiet places require gill structures that filter out turbidity, protecting them from silt that could clog them and interfere with their respiration. Therefore their gills are somewhat unique. The forward pair of gills is relatively broad and thickened into an operculate gill covering. These gill covers overlap the actual gill-systems underneath, protecting them from abrasive silts. The coverings are alternately lifted and lowered in breathing, and interlacing fringes at the margins of the underlying gills filter the water as it enters the gill system. These fringes keep the inner gill structure clean. These operculae permit the Caenidae to thrive in silty waters so turbid that they would quickly smother less hardy species, and the gill filtration structures of the *Caenis* mayflies are even more effective than those of their sister *Brachycercus* and *Tricorythodes* nymphs.

The nymphs of the *Brachycercus* mayflies differ from their sister Caenidae in the prominent tubercles on their heads, one above the root of each antenna and one over the middle ocellus. The abdominal gills of the second segment, like those of the *Caenis* nymphs, overlap slightly across the dorsal median. These gills are rounded on their outer margins. The forelegs are widely separated at the sternum, and the pronotum is considerably wider at its posterior margins.

Although *Brachycercus* prefers still waters and relatively warm temperatures, it is found in quiet streams as well as lakes. Like its sister silt-loving nymphs, *Brachycercus* is hairy and well camouflaged with detritus and minute bottom trash. The nymphs move sluggishly over the bottom, and swim so laboriously toward the surface on hatching that only a dead-drift presentation should be used to imitate them. Emergence occurs in the early morning hours, and hatches start in the middle of July, lasting about four weeks. Such hatches can be extremely heavy.

1.   Tiny White-Winged Sepia Quill (*Brachycercus lacustris*)

These minute little mayflies are recorded from Minnesota to Maine, their nymphs measuring five-sixteenths inch at full growth. The closely related species *Brachycercus prudens* is found in Rocky Mountain waters from New Mexico to British Columbia, although its nymphs are only an eighth inch when mature.

Tails: Dark amber mottled, 5/32 inch
Body: Dark brownish ringed, 5/32 inch
Gills: Two grayish operculate gills, 3/32 inch
Thorax: Dark brownish, 3/32 inch
Wing cases: Dark brownish gray, 3/32 inch
Legs: Dark brownish olive, 1/8 inch
Head: Dark brownish, 3/32 inch

Hook: Sizes 14-16 Orvis Premium 1X long
Nylon: Dark brown 6/0 nylon
Tails: Dark barred brown mallard fibers
Body: Dark brownish dubbing ribbed with oval gold tinsel
Gills: Dark grayish feather section tied down like a wing case
Thorax: Dark brownish dubbing
Wing cases: Dark brownish gray feather tied down over thorax
Legs: Dark brownish olive hackle fibers
Head: Dark brown nylon

2. Tiny White-Winged Red Quill (*Brachycercus nitidus*)

These rusty-brown little mayflies are found along our eastern watersheds from Ontario to North Carolina. Their nymphs measure approximately three-sixteenths inch at full development.

Tails: Dark brownish mottled, ⅛ inch

Body: Dark blackish brown distinctly ringed, 3/32 inch

Gills: Two dark grayish operculate gills, ⅛ inch

Thorax: Dark blackish brown, ⅛ inch

Wing cases: Dark grayish, ⅛ inch

Legs: Dark iron-bluish olive, ⅛ inch

Head: Dark brownish, ⅛ inch

Hook: Sizes 16-18 Orvis Premium 1X long

Nylon: Black 6/0 nylon

Tails: Dark brown mottled

Body: Dark blackish dubbing ribbed with oval silver tinsel

Gills: Slate-colored feather section tied down like a wing case

Thorax: Dark blackish dubbing

Wing cases: Slate-colored feather section tied down like a wing case

Legs: Dark iron-blue hackle fibers

Head: Black nylon

Tricorythodes is the second important genus of these minute early-morning mayflies. Their nymphs are quite small, ranging between an eighth and three-sixteenth inch in length. These immature forms have apical margins of the labrum rather deeply notched at the median. The mandibles are relatively wide, apically toothed or lobed. The maxilla are conical at the apex. The pronotum is rather longer than the other Caenidae, and the femora are wider in the median. No rudimentary gills are found on the first body segment. The gill covers on the second segment are elytroidal, triangular lamellae. These lamellae cover the functional gills on segments two through six. Each gill consists of two platelike divisions with entire margins, although not fimbricate in structure like its related two genera. There is a minute whorl of spines at each tail joint.

There are six American species of *Tricorythodes* having interest to the fly-fisherman. Their nymphs prefer bottoms of silt mixed with sand or very fine gravel, sometimes inhabiting algal mosses and larger weeds. The hatches occur very early in the morning, often coming not long after four o'clock, and sometimes last until almost ten-thirty. The cycle of emergence can last from late July until the last weeks of October, and hatches are so heavy that the trout seldom ignore them, in spite of their diminutive size.

1. Tiny White-Winged Brown Quill (*Tricorythodes allectus*)

These nymphs measure approximately three-sixteenths inch, and are distributed from Quebec to Maine in slow-flowing rivers and lakes. Although the adults are similar to those of the *Brachycercus* flies, the nymphs are structurally different, as well as smaller. *Tricorythodes minutus* is slightly smaller, and is found in suitable habitats in the Rocky Mountain region.

Tails: Dark brownish mottled, ⅛
  inch
Body: Dark blackish brown, ⅛ inch
Gills: Dark slate-colored operculate
  gills, ⅛ inch
Thorax: Dark blackish brown, 1/16
  inch
Wing cases: Dark slate-colored
  grayish, 1/16 inch
Legs: Dark blackish brown, ⅛ inch
Head: Dark blackish brown, 1/32
  inch

Hook: Sizes 20-22 Orvis Premium 1X
  long
Nylon: Black 6/0 nylon
Tails: Dark barred brown mallard
Body: Dark blackish brown dubbing
Gills: Dark slate-colored feather
  section tied down like a wing case
Thorax: Dark blackish brown dubbing
Wing cases: Dark slate-colored feather
  section tied down over thorax
Legs: Dark blackish brown hackle
  fibers
Head: Black nylon

2. Tiny White-Winged Black Quill (*Tricorythodes stygiatus*)

These are perhaps the best-known mayflies of this diminutive genus, since writers like Vincent Marinaro have written extensively about their hatching. Specimens are recorded from Quebec to Minnesota, and as far south as Maryland. Swisher and Richards also included the species in their book *Selective Trout*, noting that related mayflies of considerable importance existed on western waters. The nymphs of *Tricorythodes stygiatus* measure about one-eighth inch at their full development, and emerge on mornings from July to October.

Tails: Dark brownish mottled, 3/32
  inch
Body: Dark blackish, 3/32 inch
Gills: Dark brownish gray aperculate
  gills, 3/32 inch
Thorax: Dark blackish, 3/64 inch
Wing cases: Dark brownish gray,
  3/64 inch
Legs: Dark blackish brown, 3/32 inch
Head: Dark blackish, 1/64 inch

Hook: Sizes 22-24 Orvis Premium 1X
  long
Nylon: Black 6/0 nylon
Tails: Dark barred brown mallard
Body: Black dubbing
Gills: Dark brownish gray feather
  section tied down like a wing case
Thorax: Black dubbing
Wing cases: Dark brownish feather
  section tied down over thorax
Legs: Black nylon fibers
Head: Black nylon

Tricorythodes atratus is a slightly larger species of similar coloration. Its nymphs measure about three-sixteenths inch at maturity. The species is found from Labrador to New England.

3. Tiny White-Winged Claret Quill (*Tricorythodes fallax*)

This well-distributed western species is the largest of the *Tricorythodes* mayflies, its nymphs measuring five-sixteenths inch at the time of emergence. Its pale-winged little adults have purplish-brown bodies, and like the related species, they emerge in good numbers just after daylight.

Tails: Dark brownish mottled, 5/32
  inch
Body: Dark brownish claret, 5/32
  inch
Gills: Dark grayish brown operculate
  gills, ⅛ inch
Thorax: Dark brownish claret, 3/32
  inch
Wing cases: Dark grayish brown,
  3/32 inch
Legs: Dark purplish, ⅛ inch
Head: Dark brownish claret, 3/64
  inch

Hook: Sizes 18-20 Orvis Premium 1X
  long
Nylon: Dark brown 6/0 nylon
Tails: Dark barred brown mallard
Body: Dark claret-colored dubbing
Gills: Dark grayish brown feather
  tied down
Thorax: Dark claret-colored dubbing
Wing cases: Dark grayish brown
Legs: Dark purplish hackle fibers
Head: Dark brown nylon

4. Tiny White-Winged Olive Quill (*Tricorythodes texanus*)

This is a species largely found in warm-water habitats incapable of supporting trout, although it was originally found in the trout waters of Arizona, New Mexico, and southern Colorado. Ironically, it was also found in the classic smallmouth rivers of the Ozarks, rivers that have had their ecological balance radically changed by the construction of reservoirs there. The cold-water tailings of the dams have transformed these rivers into trout streams, and suddenly the tiny *Tricorythodes* flies are riding the smooth currents above an introduced population of big rainbows.

Tails: Brownish mottled, 3/32 inch
Body: Dark olive, 3/32 inch
Gills: Dark grayish operculate gills, 3/32 inch
Thorax: Dark olive, 3/64 inch
Wing cases: Dark slate-colored feather tied over thorax, 3/64 inch
Legs: Dark olive, 3/32 inch
Head: Dark olive, 1/64 inch

Hook: Sizes 22-24 Orvis Premium 1X long
Nylon: Dark olive 6/0 nylon
Tails: Dark barred brown mallard
Body: Dark olive dubbing
Gills: Dark slate-colored feather tied down like a wing case
Thorax: Dark olive dubbing
Wing cases: Dark slate-colored feather tied down over thorax
Legs: Dark olive dun hackle fibers
Head: Dark olive nylon

The adults of this species are characterized by their transformation from brownish pale-winged duns to bright olive-bodied little spinners. Fully grown nymphs measure one-eighth inch and apparently emerge from June until October. Experienced Ozark fishermen like Dave Whitlock report that these tiny little mayflies emerge in good numbers almost every morning.

Caenis is the third genus of this group of tiny mayflies, giving its taxonometric name to the entire Caenidae subfamily. The adult forms are rather small, with pale wings measuring only three-thirty-seconds to seven-thirty-seconds inch in length. Their nymphs are found in both rivers and lakes, and since such tiny flies are difficult to imitate—particularly when the rises are really to hatching nymphs—British fly-fishermen have long called them the Angler's Curses.

Their nymphs are fond of sluggish currents. Bottoms of silt mixed with sand, detritus, and fine gravel are preferred, although they also inhabit algal growth among the stones, as well as stillwater beds of weed.

Like the other members of their subfamily, *Caenis* nymphs are covered with delicate little hairs that camouflage them with layers of silt and vegetable matter. They often lie almost buried in loose detritus and mud, and their gill systems are particularly well suited to cope with such conditions. *Caenis* is therefore common in both warm- and cold-water environments, its gill systems capable of withstanding considerable silt suspended in the water. *Tricorythodes* is perhaps more common in streams.

The *Caenis* nymphs are distinguished by heads and pronota narrower than their mesonota, although their heads are still relatively wider than those of *Brachycercus*. The labrum is less broad than is found in that genus, with a slightly concave apical margin. The mandibles of *Caenis* are quite similar to those of *Tricorythodes*. Their canines are narrower than in that genus, but clearly more expansive than the canines typical of *Brachycercus*.

The maxilla is conical at its apex. The glossae and paraglossae are well differentiated in *Caenis*, rather than fused as in *Tricorythodes*. The forelegs are longer than in either *Tricorythodes* or *Brachycercus*. Their claws are slender and somewhat apically curved. There is a rudimentary gill on the first body segment. The operculate gills on the second segment are square-gilled and quadrate, the outer apical corners somewhat rounded. Each of the covered gills on segments three through six is single, and deeply fimbricate on its outer margins. The postlateral spines on the middle segments are somewhat more prominent than in *Tricorythodes*, but are not as curved and toothed as in *Brachycercus*. There are microscopic spines at each tail joint.

Caenis flies are typically found hatching from late June into September. Their duns often emerge at twilight, coming off after darkness has fallen. They molt almost immediately into their imago stage and mating, and their spinner-fall comes just at daylight the following morning.

1. Tiny Gray-Winged Blue Dun (*Caenis amica*)

These minute little mayflies are widely distributed from Quebec to Maryland along the eastern seaboard, hatching typically in midsummer. The nymphs measure one-eighth inch at full growth.

Tails: Dark brownish mottled, 1/16 inch
Body: Dark brownish gray distinctly ringed, 3/32 inch
Gills: Dark slate-gray operculate gills, 3/32 inch
Thorax: Dark brownish gray, 1/16 inch
Wing cases: Dark slate gray, 1/16 inch
Legs: Dark brownish gray, ⅛ inch
Head: Dark brownish gray, 1/32 inch

Hook: Sizes 24-26 Orvis Premium 1X long
Nylon: Dark brown 6/0 nylon
Tails: Dark barred brown mallard fibers
Body: Dark brownish gray hare's mask dubbing ribbed with fine silver wire
Gills: Dark slate-gray feather section tied down like a wing case
Thorax: Dark brownish gray hare's mask dubbing
Wing cases: Dark slate-gray feather section tied down over the thorax
Legs: Dark brownish gray hackle fibers
Head: Dark brown nylon

2. Tiny Gray-Winged Sulphur (*Caenis jocosa*)

This minute species is found from New Brunswick to Minnesota, heavily populating lakes and some quiet trout streams. Its full-grown nymphs measure one-eighth inch.

There is a slightly larger species, classified as *Caenis delicata*, which is found in New Mexico, Colorado, and the manmade rivers of the Ozarks. Its nymphs measure about five-thirty-seconds inch.

Tails: Pale brown with heavy dark markings, 1/16 inch
Body: Light brown distinctly ringed, 3/32 inch
Gills: Medium grayish brown operculate gills, 3/32 inch
Thorax: Light brownish, 1/16 inch
Wing cases: Medium grayish brown, 1/16 inch
Legs: Light brownish olive, ⅛ inch
Head: Light brown, 1/32 inch

Hook: Sizes 24-26 Orvis Premium 1X long
Nylon: Light brown 6/0 nylon
Tails: Pale barred woodduck fibers
Body: Light brown dubbing ribbed with fine silver wire
Gills: Medium grayish brown feather section tied down like a wing case
Thorax: Light brown dubbing
Wing cases: Medium grayish brown feather section tied down over thorax
Legs: Light brownish olive fibers
Head: Light brown nylon

3. Tiny White-Winged Sulphur (*Caenis simulans*)

There are four species in American waters that are quite similar in size and coloration, but *Caenis simulans* is the most widely distributed species of the entire subfamily. It is recorded in our nothern trout waters from Labrador to British Columbia, with good hatches from New England to Oregon. Its adult nymphs measure approximately five-thirty-seconds inch.

Caenis diminuta is a slightly smaller species, found in our eastern rivers from New Brunswick to North Carolina, while the closely related species *Caenis punctata* is limited in its range from Labrador to New York. Their nymphs measure one-eighth inch.

Caenis tardata is a similar White-Winged Sulphur found in our Pacific Northwest waters.

Tails: Pale brown with heavy mottling, 3/32 inch
Body: Medium brown distinctly ringed, ⅛ inch
Gills: Dark grayish brown operculate gills, ⅛ inch
Thorax: Medium brownish, 3/32 inch
Wing cases: Dark grayish brown, 3/32 inch
Legs: Medium brownish, 7/64 inch
Head: Medium brown, 3/64 inch

Hook: Sizes 22-24 Orvis Premium 1X long
Nylon: Medium brown 6/0 nylon
Tails: Medium mottled woodduck fibers
Body: Medium brown dubbing ribbed with fine gold wire
Gills: Dark grayish brown feather section tied down like a wing case
Thorax: Medium brown dubbing
Wing cases: Dark grayish brown feather section tied down over thorax
Legs: Medium brown fibers
Head: Medium brown nylon

4. Tiny Gray-Winged Rusty Dun (*Caenis latipennis*)

This minute mayfly is found from Ontario to British Columbia, and the closely related *Caenis forcipata* is distributed in our northeastern waters.

Tails: Dark browntish mottled, 3/32 inch
Body: Dark rusty brown distinctly ringed, ⅛ inch
Gills: Dark slate-colored operculate gills, ⅛ inch
Thorax: Dark rusty brownish, 3/32 inch
Wing cases: Dark slate grayish, 3/32 inch
Legs: Dark rusty brownish, 7/64 inch
Head: Dark brownish, 3/64 inch

Hook: Sizes 22-24 Orvis Premium 1X long
Nylon: Dark brown 6/0 nylon
Tails: Dark barred brown mallard fibers
Body: Dark rusty brown dubbing ribbed with fine gold wire
Gills: Dark slate-colored feather section tied down like a wing case
Thorax: Dark rusty brown dubbing
Wing cases: Dark slate-colored feather section tied down over thorax
Legs: Dark brown fibers
Head: Dark brown nylon

5. Tiny White-Winged Curse (*Caenis hilaris*)

These tiny flies are not unlike the famous British species, *Caenis macrura,* which is prototypical of the Caenidae on both continents. The species is recorded from New Jersey to Colorado, and its nymphs measure one-eighth inch.

Tails: Medium brown mottled, 1/16 inch

Body: Light tannish brown, 3/32 inch

Gills: Pale brown operculate gills, 3/32 inch

Thorax: Light tannish brown, 1/16 inch

Wing cases: Pale brownish gray, 1/16 inch

Legs: Light tannish brown, ⅛ inch

Head: Light tannish brown, 1/32 inch

Hook: Sizes 24-26 Orvis Premium 1X long

Nylon: Tan 6/0 nylon

Tails: Medium brown mottled

Body: Light tannish brown dubbing ribbed with fine gold wire

Gills: Pale brown feather section tied down like a wing case

Thorax: Light tannish brown dubbing

Wing cases: Pale brown feather section tied down like a wing case

Legs: Light tannish brown fibers

Head: Tan nylon

The Minute Cloëon, Neocloëon, and Pseudocloëon Flies

I⸙ IS A beautiful, smooth-flowing river in the dense second-growth forests of lower Michigan, and both its swift gravel-bottom riffles and its trout taught me about fishing almost thirty years ago. There are many memories of many seasons. Spring mornings were bright with cowslips and pulpit flowers and violets in the sheltered places, and the nights were cold in a sleeping bag. June was a forest thick with bright new leaves. The river flowed clear and smooth. Columbines and summer buttercups were blooming then, and August was a time of gentians and pye-weed and swamp lilies.

The history of the river is old, dating back to the time when France ruled the Michigan Territories and Father Jacques Marquette arrived in Quebec in 1666. Marquette stayed two years at the mission at Trois Rivieres, studying the languages of the aboriginal tribes in the Great Lakes country. Marquette then journeyed west to the Ottawa mission at Sault Sainte Marie, with the frontier post at Chequamegon Bay in his parish.

When clashes with the militant Sioux forced Marquette and his Chequamegon parishioners to seek refuge at Mackinac, he rebuilt the mission at Sainte Ignace, where fur traders told him stories of a gargantuan south-flowing river draining the interior of the continent. Marquette convinced Count Frontenac to dispatch him in the party of Louis Jolliet, with a mission to explore the Mississippi.

Jolliet had five experienced *voyageurs* and three freight canoes, and Marquette set out south along the west shoreline of Lake Michigan in 1673. It was still early spring, and the party followed the lake until it reached Green Bay. It journeyed inland then, following the Winnebago flowage deep into the Wisconsin wilderness. Portaging from Butte des Morts to the headwaters of the Fox, Jolliet and his men followed that stream to its junction with the Wisconsin thirty miles below its famous Dells. The party left its benchmarks in the landscape as it traveled, and contemporary names like Fond du Lac, Prairie du Sac, and Prairie du Chien are echoes of their expedition.

The explorers followed the Wisconsin to its junction with the Mississippi below Prairie du Chien, camping there to resupply before pushing south. Their expedition again left its footprints in places like Dubuque and La Grange and Cape Girardeau. Jolliet followed the Mississippi past its confluence with both the Ohio and the Missouri. When his party finally reached the mouth of the Arkansas, more than one hundred and fifty river miles below the future site of Memphis, Jolliet and Marquette were convinced that their gargantuan mystery river was the same Mississippi that ultimately reached New Orleans.

Marquette offered prayers in the wilderness, and the party began its arduous journey back to Sainte Ignace. It traveled hard upriver, leaving the Mississippi above the site of Saint Louis, and pressed northeast along the Illinois. It carried them deep into the prairies, until a short portage reached the marshy Chicago and the beaches of Lake Michigan. They had successfully traveled two unexplored water routes linking Quebec with the French capital at New Orleans. The unknown interior of America had surrendered some of its secrets, and they finally reached Mackinac in early autumn.

Marquette remained at Mackinac to recuperate from the expedition and complete his journals of its chronology. Those journals were subsequently published in the *Recueil de Voyages* assembled by Thevenot in 1681. It was fortunate that Marquette had kept his journals, since the Jolliet logs were lost in the Lachine Rapids during his return to Quebec.

The memories of the wilderness they had crossed remained stubbornly in Marquette's thoughts, and finally permission came for him to establish a mission at the mouth of the Chicago in 1675. His impatience caused him to attempt the trip early that spring, not long after ice-out. It was a bitter April, and the work of building the new mission in its raw winds proved too much. Marquette fell desperately ill. His party feared for his life, and lacking medical supplies at Chicago, they started back with Marquette along the Michigan shore of the lake.

The weather was foul and the party was often forced from the lake by the winds. It had traveled more than half the distance back to the fort at Mackinac when his health broke and Marquette died at the mouth of the classic river that bears his name—the smooth-flowing Pere Marquette.

It is born in the marl swamps of the interior. Its South Branch rises in the jackpine country above White Cloud, and the little, swift Middle Branch comes from icy springs in the marl bogs west of Reed City, and Baldwin Creek adds its currents in the first thirty miles of the river. It is a river of greatness, its currents too heavy to wade long before it reaches the Bowman Bridge. Its current is a swelling flood even in late August on the stretch at Timber Creek and Walhalla. It is a river where we camped every summer in those first years after the war, and it taught me much about selective trout before I was fifteen years old.

It was there that I tied my first Blue-Winged Olives to match a hatch of *Ephemerella* flies, when the fish refused to take the Adams that usually worked. Its swift riffles were covered with mating mayflies, the evenings filled with the hot butter-colored sparks of their egg sacs.

It also started my education in minute mayflies, and it was difficult to find hooks small enough to imitate these tiny insects. Finally I bought a tiny box of a hundred exquisite Allcock hooks in size twenty from Bill Blades, and we dressed minute imitations on them until they ran out after a year or two. The British hooks were perfect, and although the little box with the pink label has been empty for twenty years, it still has a place of honor in my fly-tying boxes.

There was a perplexing hatch of tiny gray-winged duns that came off sporadically throughout those idyllic summers on the Pere Marquette. Its minute little flies measured slightly less than three-sixteenths inch in length, much too small for my elegant little English hooks. The hatch came off in late mornings on dark overcast days, starting at about eleven o'clock and lasting until darkness covered the riffles. It was usually an evening hatch, starting about an hour before sunset and emerging until nightfall. We took fish on my oversized imitations, but lacking smaller hooks, our efforts at matching the hatch were marginal at best. The pale little duns we collected are still somewhere in my files.

What are they? my father asked.

There's nothing on them in my books. I shook my head. *They're tiny mayflies—but that's all I know.*

Try the university, he suggested.

It was a possible answer, but the university was unable to identify the pale little subimagoes too. Lacking the final adult stage, even establishing the genus was difficult, and the little hatch remained a mystery.

Several years later I had obtained a copy of *The Biology of Mayflies,* and using the Needham taxonometric keys on the imagoes we had collected since the first few duns, it seemed the tiny flies were either *Cloëon* or *Pseudocloëon.*

What do they look like? asked my father.

Look yourself. I handed him the glass. *Pseudocloëon seems close but this particular species isn't listed in the Needham keys.*

It must be a new species, he said.

Perhaps, I agreed.

During subsequent years in Michigan, stomach autopsies of the fish provided a number of tiny nymphs that seemed likely subaquatic forms of this hatch. They measured slightly less than one-quarter inch, and were a delicate pale olive with chalk-colored gills. The two fringed little tails, with a vestigial median tail, identified them definitely as nymphs of the *Pseudocloëon.* Their relatively fat little bodies and single wing cases further confirmed that identification, just as the absence of single marginal veins and rear wings clearly placed the adult specimens in that genus.

Art Neumann of Saginaw finally solved the puzzle some years later, in 1962, when a copy of *Mayflies of Michigan Trout Streams* reached me in the mails. Its pages included an enlarged drawing of a pale two-tailed nymph that caught my eye, and its caption identified it as *Pseudocloëon anoka.* The species was not listed in Needham, and the fifteen-year puzzle from the Pere Marquette was solved.

Over the past few seasons, a number of minute mayfly species have proved important on widespread American rivers. Specimens of these diminutive insects have subsequently been identified as *Cloëon, Neocloëon,* and *Pseudocloëon.* Their populations are most extensive on alkaline limestone-spring or marl-bog rivers, and on the spring creeks of the west. Optimum habitat for these genera is lime-rich water, with weeds and fine gravel in a smooth-flowing current. Their diminutive size has no relationship to their importance on rivers that support good populations.

The *Cloëon* genus consists of small mayflies with wings ranging from five thirty-seconds to five-sixteenths inch. The ventral surfaces of the male imagoes range from chalky to dull olive-brown. Pale species often have rust-colored tergite markings. Female spinners are somewhat paler than the males, and are typically yellow, yellowish-orange, and reddish-brown. The turbinate eyes of the adult males are moderate to large in size. The posterior margin of the female head is slightly immarginate. The most singular taxonometric feature is the single pair of wings, and the absence of the tiny rear pair. The marginal tiny veins of *Cloëon* occur singly rather than in pairs, and these little mayflies are quite important on the big, gravel-bottomed rivers of Michigan and Wisconsin.

Cloëon nymphs are distinguished by a three-jointed maxillary palp that is almost as long as the entire maxilla. The labial palp is also three-jointed. Its apical joint is somewhat conical in shape, its outer margin extended farther than its inner one. The canines of the mandibles are short and blunt. The claws are quite slender at the tips, and rather widened at the base. The claws are finely denticulate on their inner margins, seldom more than one-third the length of the tibia. Gills are doubled on either or all body segments, or segments one through six, depending on species. The larger division of each pair is irregularly rounded in outline, their tracheation more or less distinctly palmate. There are three tails, approximately equal in their thickness and length, with the outer pair fringed on their inside edges only, and no fringes on the first one-third of the tails.

These nymphs are of the types that ascend to the surface film in open water, splitting the nymphal skin and abandoning it in the tension of the meniscus. Various nymphal ecotypes accomplish this journey to the surface in two basic ways: through swimming voluntarily, and through the generation of gases inside the nymphal skins, which buoys them involuntarily to the surface film.

It has been argued that those which swim voluntarily to the surface are attracted to the light. The others are buoyed by the gases generated beneath their integument. There is no better example of this latter behavior than the *Cloëon* nymphs. Most of their emergence activity occurs in shallow water, ranging from six inches to approximately three feet. Before hatching the darkened wing cases of the nymphs are quite evident, and they cling to the bottom stones and vegetation. When they are dislodged from their footholds, the nymphs are buoyed directly to the surface, instead of merely swimming to a new subaquatic position. Reaching the surface meniscus, they emerge after one or two seconds. The gases generated are sufficient to carry them to the surface in spite of their efforts to reach a fresh foothold. Before these gases are fully generated, the nymphs lose their usual caution, and are found on the upper surfaces of the stones and weedbeds. They are quite restless, swimming or crawling from one foothold to another, and some make preliminary ascents to the surface.

1. Tiny Gray-Winged Red Quill *(Cloëon rubropictum)*
This diminutive little mayfly is an eastern species distributed from Quebec to Michigan, and as far south as the limestone streams of Maryland and

Pennsylvania. It hatches sporadically throughout the summer, its nymphs averaging only three-sixteenths inch in length.

Tails: Brown mottled, 3/32 inch
Body: Brownish, distinctly ringed, ⅛ inch
Gills: Brownish red, 1/64 inch
Thorax: Brownish mottled, 1/16 inch
Wing cases: Reddish brown, 1/16 inch
Legs: Brown mottled, 3/32 inch
Head: Brownish, 1/32 inch

Hook: Sizes 24-26 Orvis Premium 1X long
Nylon: Dark brown 6/0 nylon
Tails: Brown mallard fibers
Body: Dark brown rayon floss
Gills: Reddish brown goose quill ribbing
Thorax: Dark brown rayon floss
Wing cases: Dark reddish-brown feather section over thorax
Legs: Brown mallard fibers
Head: Dark brown nylon

2. Tiny Gray-Winged Sepia Quill (*Cloëon simplex*)

This little hatch is recorded from Quebec to Pennsylvania, and is similar to its closely related *Cloëon rubropictum,* except that its distinctly ringed little abdomen is more chocolate-colored than rusty brown. It is a tiny hatch, its nymphs averaging only three-sixteenths inch in length. It is a hatch of midsummer.

Tails: Medium brown, 3/32 inch
Body: Medium brown, distinctly ringed, 5/32 inch
Gills: Pale yellowish brown, 1/64 inch
Thorax: Medium mottled brown, 1/16 inch
Wing cases: Dark mottled brown, 1/16 inch
Legs: Medium mottled brown, ⅛ inch
Head: Medium brown, 1/32 inch

Hook: Sizes 22-24 Orvis Premium 1X long
Nylon: Medium brown 6/0 nylon
Tails: Medium brown fibers
Body: Medium brown rayon floss
Gills: Pale yellowish brown goose quill section
Thorax: Medium brown fibers
Wing cases: Dark brown feather section tied over thorax
Legs: Medium brown mallard fibers
Head: Medium brown nylon

3. Tiny Gray-Winged Sherry Quill (*Cloëon insignificans*)

Cloëon insignificans is a species recorded from the Great Lakes region, both in the United States from Pennsylvania to Minnesota, and in the Canadian Provinces from Ontario to Manitoba. Although similar to *Cloëon rubropictum,* its identification is possible through the absence of rust-colored spots and black stigmatic markings in the imago. There are also no fawn-colored apical sternites. It hatches in summer.

The nymphs are about one-quarter inch in length.

Tails: Pale brownish, 3/32 inch
Body: Pale brownish, ⅛ inch
Gills: Pale yellowish, 1/64 inch
Thorax: Pale brownish, 1/16 inch
Wing cases: Light mottled brown, 1/16 inch
Legs: Pale mottled brown, ⅛ inch
Head: Pale brownish, 1/64 inch

Hook: Sizes 24-26 Orvis Premium 1X long
Nylon: Tan 6/0 nylon
Tails: Pale brownish fibers
Body: Pale brownish rayon floss
Gills: Pale yellowish goose quill ribbing
Thorax: Pale brownish floss
Wing cases: Light mottled brown feather section
Legs: Barred mallard fibers dyed pale brown
Head: Tan nylon

4. Tiny Gray-Winged Olive Quill (*Cloëon implicatum*)

This rather large species, with nymphs averaging about five-sixteenths inch, is widely distributed in American waters. Specimens are recorded, between this species and the closely allied *Cloëon ingens,* from Quebec to the Rocky Mountain rivers.

Tails: Medium olive, ⅛ inch
Body: Medium olive, 3/16 inch
Gills: Pale olive, 1/64 inch
Thorax: Medium olive, 1/16 inch
Wing cases: Medium olive, 1/16 inch
Legs: Mottled olive, ⅛ inch
Head: Medium olive, 1/32 inch

Hook: Sizes 20-22 Orvis Premium 1X long
Nylon: Medium olive 6/0 nylon
Tails: Medium olive fibers
Body: Medium olive rayon floss
Gills: Pale olive goose quill fiber
Thorax: Medium olive floss
Wing cases: Medium olive feather section tied over thorax
Legs: Gray mallard dyed olive
Head: Medium olive nylon

The genus *Neocloëon* is closely allied to the better-known mayflies classified among the tiny two-winged *Cloëon* group. There is only one species in this genus. The maxillary palp of the nymphs is three-jointed. The palp is longer than the maxilla, and extends well beyond the terminus of the galea-lacinia. The labial palp is also three-jointed, with a widely separated apical dilation of the distal. This dilation on the inner margin is quite close to the nymphal forms of the *Centroptilum* mayflies. The canines of the mandibles are longer, more slender, and slightly more tapered than in *Cloëon.* The claws are very long and slender, and lacking in denticulation. They are about three-quarters the length of their tarsi. Gills are present on all six body segments, and are single on each segment. The middle gills are irregularly ovoid. The other gills are somewhat straight on their anterior margins, and lobed on their posterior margins. Tracheation is pinnate, with all of the main branches rising from the inner side. There are three tails, about equal in length and thickness.

Needham conjectures in his book *The Biology of Mayflies* that these little mayflies have clear taxonometric differences with the *Cloëon* genus, but that ultimately they may be considered merely an aberrant species of that group. The nymphs resemble *Centroptilum* more closely than the subaquatic *Cloëon* forms.

5. Tiny Gray-Winged Yellow (*Neocloëon almance*)

The nymphal forms are approximately five-sixteenths inch in length, and are found from the limestone streams of central New Jersey and Pennsylvania to the rich watersheds of North Carolina.

Tails: Medium olive, 3/16 inch
Body: Medium mottled olive, 3/16 inch
Gills: Light olive, 1/32 inch
Thorax: Medium mottled olive, 1/16 inch
Wing cases: Medium mottled olive, 1/16 inch
Legs: Medium olive, ⅛ inch
Head: Medium olive, 1/32 inch

Hook: Sizes 20-22 Orvis Premium 1X long
Nylon: Medium olive 6/0 nylon
Tails: Pheasant-tail fibers dyed medium olive
Body: Brownish olive dubbing
Gills: Light-olive-dyed condor quill ribbing
Thorax: Brownish olive dubbing
Wing cases: Olive-dyed feather section tied over thorax
Legs: Medium olive hen hackle fibers
Head: Medium olive nylon

Pseudocloëon mayflies are like the preceding closely related genera, tiny insects that are surprisingly important on rivers throughout the country in spite of their diminutive size. They typically emerge in great numbers in midsummer. The trout are quite fond of them, following the nymphs into midstream and taking them freely.

Like the preceding *Cloëon* and *Neocloëon* flies, these tiny flies are multi-brooded. This means that several cycles of emergence can occur, overlapping and mating and hatching again, through a single summer. However, there are typically two periods of peak activity. The first is usually found from the last of June until the middle weeks of July. The second commonly comes off in late September. Dark, cool days find these tiny mayflies hatching at about eleven o'clock each morning, with emergence continuing sporadically until dark. However, more typical summer weather finds the *Pseudocloëon* flies starting to hatch about one hour before sundown, and coming off steadily until nightfall.

The adults have only two wings, the rear pair typical of the mayflies being completely absent. Their marginal veinlets are present in pairs. The basal abdominal segments of the imago males range from chalky whitish to dark olive brown. They are quite small. Their wings range between one-eighth and one-quarter inch. The female imago is somewhat paler and yellowish. The ocelli of the male are turbinate and very large. Female eyes are relatively small and widely separated, and the posterior margin of the head is almost straight.

The forelegs of the male are approximately equal to the body in length. Both the forelegs and rear legs of the females are similar to the hind legs of the males. The forewings of the male imago has paired marginal intercalary veins.

The nymphs of *Pseudocloëon* are relatively streamlined, like the swimming riffle forms of the *Baetis* flies. However, they are somewhat more robust in their proportions. The thoracic structures are wider in relation to the abdominal segments, and the body swells slightly toward the fifth segment before tapering sharply to the tails. They are abundant in shallow, gravel-bottom streams.

The maxillary palps of the nymphs are short and two-jointed, extending a minimal distance beyond the galea-lacinia. The labial palp is three-jointed. The distal joint is apically rounded and exhibits short spinules. Basally, the palp is somewhat fused at its second joint, appearing in some species to have only two joints. The mandibular canines are relatively wide and stout, and somewhat even across the top. The claws are widest at the base, tapering into slender tips. Their inner margins are denticular. There are obovate gills on each segment, with tracheal pinnation. There are two fringed tails, totally lacking in filaments at their basal thirds, and an atrophied, somewhat vestigial center tail without segments.

When emergence is approaching, the maturing nymphal forms are observed crawling restlessly on the bottom gravel and submerged aquatic vegetation. Nymphal imitations fished along the bottom then, and to rising fish as the hatch actually begins, are quite effective.

6. Minute Gray-Winged Watery (*Pseudocloëon futile*)

This tiny little nymph averages only three-sixteenths inch in length, and is recorded from Colorado north along the Rocky Mountains into Alberta. It is a major hatch on our western spring creeks.

Pseudcloëon dubium is a species that is slightly smaller, and is distributed from Ontario to North Carolina. Some specimens are recorded from the Great Lakes region.

Tails: Pale watery olive, 3/32 inch
Body: Pale watery olive, 3/32 inch
Gills: Pale whitish cream, 1/64 inch
Thorax: Pale watery olive, 1/16 inch
Wing cases: Pale medium olive, 1/16 inch
Legs: Pale watery olive, 1/16 inch
Head: Pale watery olive, 1/64 inch

Hook: Sizes 24-26 Orvis Premium 1X long
Nylon: Pale olive 6/0 nylon
Tails: Pale watery olive fibers
Body: Pale watery olive cellulite floss
Gills: Pale whitish goose quill ribbing
Thorax: Pale watery olive cellulite floss
Wing cases: Pale grayish-olive feather section tied over thorax
Legs: Pale watery olive fibers
Head: Pale olive nylon

7. Minute Gray-Winged Brown (*Pseudocloëon carolina*)

These little nymphs are widely distributed from Quebec to the mountain rivers of North Carolina. Hatching typically occurs in a series of multi-brooded cycles, with peaks in late May and August. There is sometimes a third hatching peak in October that can provide autumn fishing in states with extended seasons. The nymphs average about three-sixteenths inch.

Tails: Light olive, ⅛ inch
Body: Light olive, 3/32 inch
Gills: Pale olive gray, 1/64 inch
Thorax: Light olive, 3/32 inch
Wing cases: Medium olive, 1/16 inch
Legs: Light olive, 3/32 inch
Head: Light olive, 1/32 inch

Hook: Sizes 22-24 Orvis Premium 1X long
Nylon: Light olive yellow 6/0 nylon
Tails: Light yellowish olive fibers
Body: Light yellowish olive
Gills: Pale olive grayish goose quill ribbing
Thorax: Light yellowish olive
Wing cases: Medium olive feather section tied over thorax
Legs: Light olive hackle fibers
Head: Light olive

8. Minute Gray-Winged Olive (*Pseudocloëon anoka*)

These elegant little gray-winged olives are the hatch that so frustrated me in those boyhood summers on the Pere Marquette. Their nymphs are swimming, current-loving species like the *Baetis* mayflies, but differ from that genus in their single pair of wing pads and in having two tails, and a vestigial center tail without joints. Hatching occurs from the last days of June until early October, and the species is primarily an ecotype found in the Great Lakes country.

Tails: Pale olive, ⅛ inch
Body: Pale olive green, ⅛ inch
Gills: Pale whitish olive, 1/64 inch
Thorax: Pale olive green, 1/16 inch
Wing cases: Pale olive gray, 1/16 inch
Legs: Pale olive green, 3/32 inch
Head: Pale olive, 1/32 inch

Hook: Sizes 22-24 Orvis Premium
Nylon: Pale olive green 6/0 nylon
Tails: Pale olive fibers
Body: Pale olive green rayon floss
Gills: Pale whitish olive
Thorax: Pale olive green rayon floss
Wing cases: Pale olive gray feather section tied over thorax
Legs: Pale olive green hackle fibers
Head: Pale olive green

Tiny Swimming Nymphs of the Centroptilum Hatches

THE BLACK CURRENT flowed swiftly through the bridge-cribbing where we crossed from the island into Livington. There was an old brakeman in the railroad cafe, and two cowboys came inside rubbing their hands in the cold. The cowboys stowed a weathered saddle in a corner and sat down at the counter. The old sheepdog scratched at the door, and when the cook wiped his hands and let him inside, the collie limped awkwardly toward his corner behind the potbellied stove.

It was already late September. The first hard-frost nights had colored the aspens, and the cottonwoods in the river bottoms were starting to turn. There was still mist layered in the swampy places along the backwaters, but the rain had stopped. Its overcast was burning off the barren peaks of the Gallatins, and north of the town the sun was already hot on the foothill shoulders of Crazy Mountain.

September is beautiful in Montana. The sun is deceptively warm and it softens the cool wind. The cottonwoods turn yellowish orange along the winding of the river channels. The wind rises late in the morning, scattering their bright leaves like confetti into the swift currents. The mountains are somber at daylight against the pale windless skies, and the cold nights start the pintails and greenhead mallards migrating downriver toward the silt-brown Missouri.

Yellowstone country. Joe Brooks squinted across the valley into the morning sun, his deeply tanned face wrinkling around his eyes. *It's always meant September somehow.*

The sun was warm in the pale grass. We drove down into the river bottoms where two mule deer were browsing below the cattle pens. The lane of poplars led to the ranch. The deer melted into the willows. The red corrugated roofs of the ranch house and its outbuildings stood among the sheltering cottonwoods. We parked the station wagon and rigged our gear. The path wound down into the alders and the watercress bogs toward the spring creek.

It's not much water, Joe pointed, *but its hatches are heavy with tiny sulphurs, and the fish are picky.*

Looks a little like Letort Spring Run, I said.

Exactly. He crossed the shallows.

There are many chalkstreams in Montana, and late September finds them at their peak. The watershed of the Gallatin has several, and there is a fine spring creek on the Madison outside Ennis. Lewistown has an excellent weed-filled spring creek too. There are the two best known chalkstreams near Livingston—on the Nelson and Armstrong ranches—and there are others on the Big Hole at Wise River and Twin Bridges.

These little spring creeks rise in geyser basins and limestone marl bogs and hot springs. Some gather their alkalinity from pale phosphate hills, flowing rich with weeds and fly life. They are not unlike the storied chalk-streams of Hampshire and Wiltshire, where the dry-fly method was born over a century ago.

We walked down through the hayfields, passing the freshly stacked bales below the irrigation trestle. The spring creek rises in a watercress lagoon of several acres, its currents gathering in the marl shallows to wind three quarters of a mile toward the main channel of the Yellowstone.

The first two hundred yards is a series of channels in the elodea and watercress and moss-green algae. The little stream is a shallow sixty-yard riffle over gravel the color of sweet corn where it swings past the ranch, and then it eddies deep and slow under the irrigation-ditch trestle. There is a wide lagoon below the trestle, too choked with pondweed and eelgrass that September for fishing it, and its outlet channel was deep and bluish-green between the cress.

Big fish there when the weed's still down, Brooks said in the soft accents of his tidewater Chesapeake. *We found a dead rainbow here once that went almost ten pounds.*

That is a big fish, I agreed.

The outlet channel is about forty yards of swelling silk-smooth currents, where a poplar deadfall lies covered with the trailing bright green *Dichelyma* moss. The last reach of water lies like a shallow canal, straight across the buffalo grass flats to the Big Yellowstone. There are a series of shallow pools lined with thick beds of watercress, and bright green accents of algae cling to the pale bottom.

It's about time, Brooks looked up toward the sun. *The little sulphurs should be coming.*

He was right most of the time. The little mayflies were soon riding the smooth current like tiny sulphur-colored sailboats. The trout began working softly, their bulging rises scarcely disturbing the surface film.

It was a difficult morning. The fish porpoised steadily in the shallow pools, bulged in the elodea channels, and sipped flies imperceptibly against the cress. We both took a few small fish with tiny dry-fly imitations, but the bigger rainbows ignored everything we showed them. The hatch lasts two to three hours on a typical day, and it was about finished for the afternoon when I tried a tiny nymph on a four-pound rainbow that was rising steadily—it reached him right in rhythm with his feeding, and he took it without a pause.

That's better! Joe grinned.

We released the fish and I gathered several tiny nymphal shucks from the shallows. There were already a dozen of the tiny mayflies in my collecting bottle.

What are those little sulphurs? Joe asked.

I don't know, I said, *but before we're finished with these specimens we should know more.*

It's an important hatch on the spring creeks, he said.

It was the last time we fished together, and although the little mayflies that morning were from the *Centroptilum* genus, somehow I never got around to writing him about that except in my mind.

The general form of these little nymphs is similar to the morphology of the other swimming genera. The bodies are slender and streamlined, the legs are relatively long and delicate looking, the thorax is slightly hump-backed, and the heads are small and rounded. *Centroptilum* is not a widespread genus either in American waters or on the rivers of Europe, although the writings of Skues, Dunne, Sawyer, and Harris have made them more important among British anglers in recent years. They were a group of mayflies virtually ignored in the work of Halford, although on some British and Irish rivers they form important hatches.

The American species are found in both rivers and lakes, and the riverine specimens are indigenous to a surprisingly full spectrum of current speeds. The tiny swimming nymphs are fond of sheltering weedbeds in swifter currents, although in quiet waters they forage openly.

It is interesting to discover that the European species are found in both acid and alkaline waters, but that they do not result in significant fly-hatches except in the limestone and chalkstream ecosystems, with their rich alkalinity. Similar studies have not been made with the *Centroptilum* flies in this country, but it is curious that the genus went virtually unnoticed on our major rivers over the years—and that its importance in the trout diet first became obvious on the lime-rich spring creeks of Montana.

Like the *Baetis* and *Callibaetis* mayflies, these tiny blue-winged and gray-winged sulphurs are apparently many-brooded, since hatching seems to peak in both early summer and late September. Autumn hatches are the heaviest, perhaps because the summer cycle reaches nymphal maturity under less harsh environmental conditions than the nymphs which must winter to hatch in May and June. Similar hatching behavior occurs in the United Kingdom.

The nymphs are quite small among the known American species, ranging between three-sixteenths and three-eighths inch in length at full development. Although they forage boldly, their swimming lacks the agility found in the *Baetis* and *Pseudocloëon* flies. Their gills are slender and blade-shaped, perhaps to facilitate their clambering in the weeds. Their tails are less heavily fringed than the caudal setae of other swimming species, but they still function as efficient sculling oars. Imitations should be fished with a slow, rather deliberate swimming-retrieve.

Adult *Centroptilum* mayflies have two tails, although the nymphs display three having approximately equal length and thickness. The maxillary palp of the nymph is three-jointed, fully as long as the maxilla itself, and extending slightly beyond the terminus of the galea-lacinia. The labial palp is three-jointed, its distal joint both dilated and apically truncated. The mandibles are sharp and slender in most species. Claws are long and relatively delicate, although only in *Centroptilum elsa* are these tarsi denticulate. The gills display pinnated tracheation, and exhibit single pairs on each of the first seven abdominal segments.

1. Pale Watery Dun (*Centroptilum album*)

This pale little species is distributed from New England to Michigan in our eastern waters, although it achieves importance only in rich limestone streams. It averages about one-quarter inch, and its hatching continues from late June until October.

Tails: Pale amber yellow, ⅛ inch
Body: Pale amber yellow, 5/32 inch
Gills: Pale whitish cream, 1/64 inch
Thorax: Pale amber yellow, 1/16 inch
Wing cases: Pale amber yellow, 1/16 inch
Legs: Pale mottled amber, ⅛ inch
Head: Pale amber yellow, 1/32 inch

Hook: Sizes 20-22 Orvis Premium 1X long
Nylon: Pale yellow 6/0 nylon
Tails: Pale yellowish amber fibers
Body: Pale yellowish amber rayon floss
Gills: Pale cream goose quill ribbing
Thorax: Pale yellowish amber dubbing
Wing cases: Light brown feather section tied down over thorax
Legs: Lemon woodduck fibers
Head: Pale yellow nylon

2. Pale Gray-Winged Sulphur (*Centroptilum convexum*)

This little mayfly is also found throughout the northeast, and westward into Michigan and Wisconsin. It hatches throughout the summer, and its delicate little nymphs are about one-quarter inch in length.

The nymph imitation is as follows:

Tails: Pale olive yellow, ⅛ inch
Body: Pale olive yellow, 5/32 inch
Gills: Pale whitish cream, 1/64 inch
Thorax: Pale olive yellow, 1/16 inch
Wing cases: Pale olive gray, 1/16 inch
Legs: Pale mottled olive yellow, ⅛ inch
Head: Pale olive yellow, 1/32 inch

Hook: Sizes 20-22 Orvis Premium 1X long
Nylon: Pale olive 6/0 nylon
Tails: Pale olive yellow fibers
Body: Pale olive yellow rayon floss
Gills: Pale cream goose quill ribbing
Thorax: Pale olive yellow floss
Wing cases: Pale olive-gray feather section tied over thorax
Legs: Pale olive-dyed barred mallard fibers
Head: Pale olive

3. Tiny Blue-Winged Olive (*Centroptilum bellum*)

This species is largely limited to river watersheds along the eastern seaboard, although there are similar species in the west. It is somewhat smaller than the preceding hatches, its nymphs averaging approximately three-sixteenths inch in length.

Tails: Reddish brown, ⅛ inch
Body: Reddish brown, 3/16 inch
Gills: Light ginger, 1/64 inch
Thorax: Reddish brown, 1/16 inch
Wing cases: Dark slate gray, 1/16 inch
Legs: Brown mottled, 3/32 inch
Head: Reddish brown, 1/32 inch

Hook: Sizes 22-24 Orvis Premium 1X long
Nylon: Dark brown 6/0 nylon
Tails: Dark reddish brown fibers
Body: Dark reddish brown floss
Gills: Reddish brown goose quill ribbing
Thorax: Dark reddish brown floss
Wing cases: Dark slate-colored feather section
Legs: Brown mallard fibers
Head: Dark brown nylon

4. Tiny Blue-Winged Quill (*Centroptilum simile*)

This species is also limited largely to eastern rivers, and like *Centroptilum bellum*, it measures about three-sixteenths inch in length.

Tails: Medium brown, ⅛ inch
Body: Medium brown, 5/32 inch
Gills: Light brown, 1/64 inch
Thorax: Medium brown, 1/16 inch
Wing cases: Slate-colored brown,
    1/16 inch
Legs: Medium brown, ⅛ inch
Head: Medium brown, 1/32 inch

Hook: Size 20-22 Orvis Premium 1X
    long
Nylon: Medium brown 6/0 nylon
Tails: Medium brown fibers
Body: Medium brown rayon floss
Gills: Light brown goose quill
    ribbing
Thorax: Medium brown rayon
Wing cases: Slate-colored feather
    section tied over thorax
Legs: Brown mallard fibers
Head: Medium brown nylon

Top, left to right: *Paraleptophlebia packii, Leptophlebia johnsoni, Leptophlebia cupida, Leptophlebia gravastella, Leptophlebia nebulosa*

Middle, left to right: *Paraleptophlebia adoptiva, Paraleptophlebia californica, Paraleptophlebia heteronea, Paraleptophlebia debilis, Brachycercus lacustris, Brachycercus nitidus*

Bottom, left to right: *Rhithrogena impersonata, Rhithrogena sanguinea, Rhithrogena jejuna, Rhithrogena doddsi*

5. Tiny Lead-Winged Red Quill (*Centroptilum rufostrigatum*)

This widely distributed hatch is found from the limestone streams of Pennsylvania to the spring creeks of our western mountains. It is perhaps the most common American species of this diminutive genus of flies. Its nymphs average about three-sixteenths inch in length, and it hatches from June until October.

Several times I have seen this hatch on the limestone spring creeks of Ohio, particularly the famous trout club waters at Castalia, and on the watercress headwaters of Mad River. The public trout water in Ohio has exceptionally rich limestone alkalinity, watercress, and weeds, and good fly hatches. Unfortunately, it has been poorly managed and stocked with rainbows. Their migratory tendencies cause them to work downstream along the Mad River until trapped and killed by the pollution below Urbana and Springfield. Perhaps in the future some knowledgeable trout biologist will abandon the more glamorous rainbow for the brown, and its tendencies to remain where it is stocked could turn the cavern-chilled headwaters of the Mad—and its watercress tributaries like Cedar Creek and Piatt Creek—into another of the famous eastern limestone streams.

Tails: Dark mottled brown, 3/32 inch
Body: Dark purplish rayon floss,
    5/32 inch
Gills: Rich purplish brown, 1/64 inch
Thorax: Dark purplish rayon floss,
    1/16 inch
Wing cases: Dark purplish black,
    1/16 inch
Legs: Dark purplish brown, 3/32
    inch
Head: Dark purplish brown, 1/32
    inch

Hook: Sizes 22-24 Orvis Premium 1X
    long
Nylon: Dark brown 6/0 nylon
Tails: Dark brown mallard fibers
Body: Dark purple rayon floss
Gills: Pale purple-dyed goose quill
    ribbing
Thorax: Dark purple rayon floss
Wing cases: Slate-black feather
    section tied down over thorax
Legs: Dark brown mallard fibers
Head: Dark brown nylon

6. Pale White-Winged Watery (*Centroptilum walshi*)

This little hatch is apparently limited to our trout waters of the midwestern states, and knowledgeable fishermen report its presence, or the existence of a closely allied species, on the man-made trout streams of the Ozarks. Its nymphs average one-quarter inch in length.

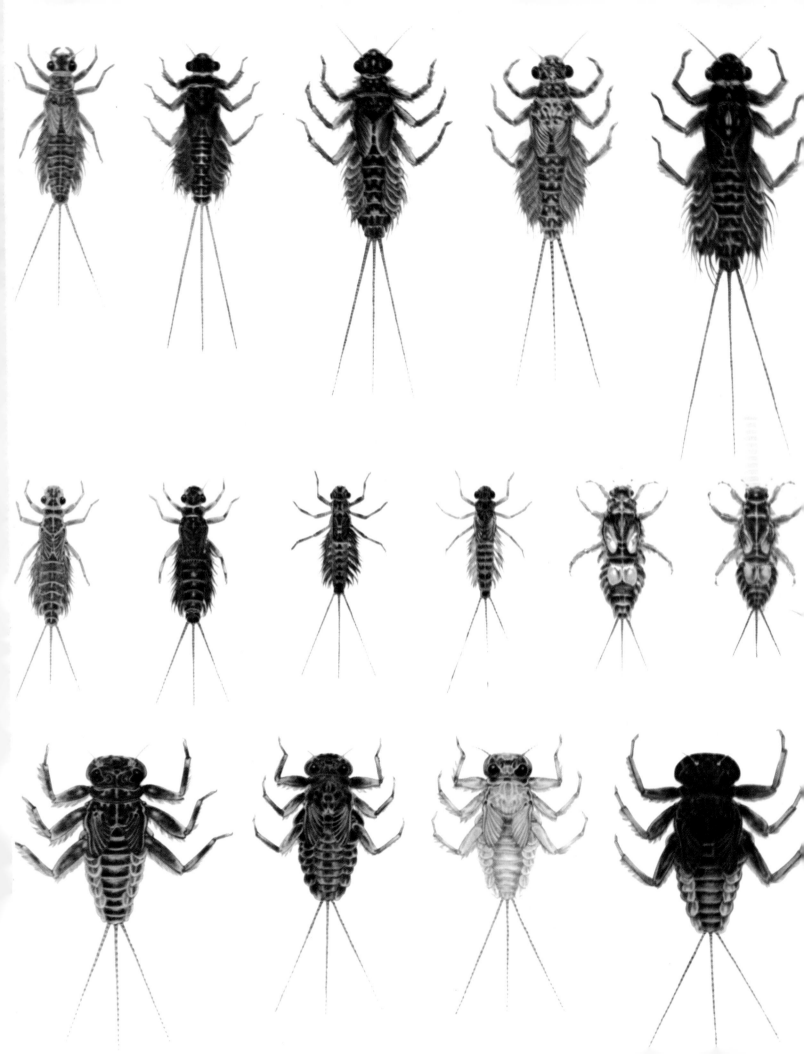

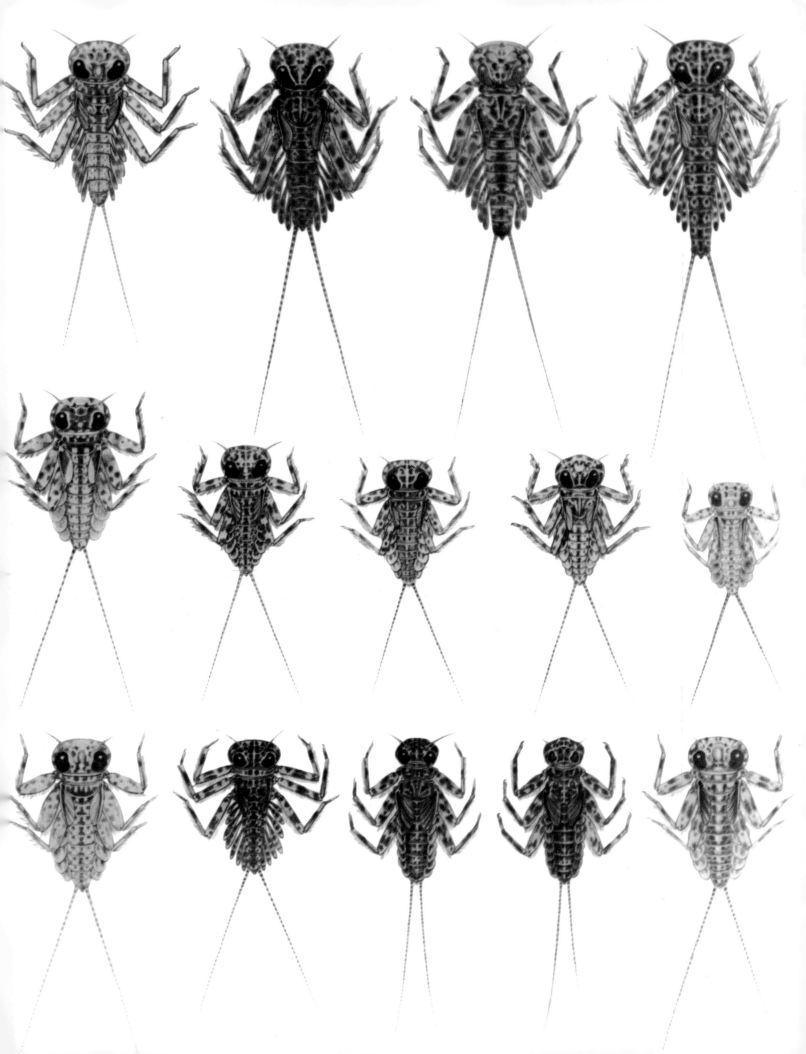

Tails: Light brown, ⅛ inch
Body: Pale yellowish brown, 5/32 inch
Gills: Pale yellowish gray, 1/64 inch
Thorax: Medium yellowish brown, 1/16 inch
Wing cases: Pale bluish gray 7/16 inch
Legs: Pale mottled amber, ⅛ inch
Head: Pale yellowish brown, 1/32 inch

Hook: Sizes 22-24 Orvis Premium 1X long
Nylon: Tan 6/0 nylon
Tails: Light brown fibers
Body: Pale yellowish tan rayon floss
Gills: Pale yellowish tan goose quill ribbing
Thorax: Pale yellowish tan floss
Wing cases: Pale bluish-gray feather sections tied down over thorax
Legs: Barred mallard dyed woodduck
Head: Tan nylon

7. Tiny Dark-Winged Olive (*Centroptilum asperatum*)

This dark little hatch is quite important on many of our western spring creeks and alkaline rivers. It hatches sporadically from June until October, and its nymphs are about three-sixteenths inch.

Tails: Mottled olive, 3/32 inch
Body: Medium olive, 5/32 inch
Gills: Pale olive, 1/64 inch
Thorax: Medium olive, 1/16 inch
Wing cases: Dark slate-colored olive, 1/16 inch
Legs: Dark mottled olive, 3/32 inch
Head: Dark olive, 1/32 inch

Hook: Sizes 22-24 Orvis Premium 1X long
Nylon: Dark olive 6/0 nylon
Tails: Barred teal fibers dyed dark olive
Body: Dark olive rayon floss
Gills: Pale olive-dyed goose quill ribbing
Thorax: Dark olive rayon floss
Wing cases: Dark slate-colored olive feather section
Legs: Barred teal fibers dyed dark olive
Head: Dark olive nylon

Top, left to right: *Epeorus hesperus, Epeorus fraudator, Epeorus pleuralis, Epeorus nitidus*
Middle, left to right: *Epeorus humeralis, Epeorus dispar, Epeorus albertae, Epeorus punctatus, Epeorus rubidus*
Bottom, left to right: *Epeorus lagunitas, Epeorus longimanus, Epeorus proprius, Epeorus vitreus, Epeorus youngi*

8. Pale White-Winged Sulphur (*Centroptilum elsa*)

This pale little species is perhaps the principal insect making up the tiny Cahill-colored hatches that western anglers have reported on such alkaline streams as Silver Creek in Idaho, Flat Creek in Jackson Hole, and the spring creeks above Livingston in the Yellowstone country. Its hatching nymphs average about five-sixteenths inch in length.

Tails: Medium olive gray, ⅛ inch
Body: Light brown, 3/16 inch
Gills: Pale olive gray, 1/64 inch
Thorax: Medium brownish, 1/16 inch
Wing cases: Medium brown, 1/16 inch
Legs: Mottled medium olive, 3/16 inch
Head: Light brown, 1/32 inch

Hook: Sizes 18-20 Orvis Premium 1X long
Nylon: Light brown 6/0 nylon
Tails: Medium olive gray fibers
Body: Light brown rayon floss
Gills: Pale olive gray goose quill ribbing
Thorax: Medium brown rayon floss
Wing cases: Medium brown feather section tied over thorax
Legs: Barred mallard fibers dyed medium olive
Head: Light brown nylon

It is late September again outside my studio, and Montana lies more than two thousand miles west across the eastern mountains and cornfields and wheat-stubble prairies of this country. The sunlight is sharp this morning, and the squirrels are busy with an unusual crop of acorns in the oaks above the house. The cool wind has a touch of fall in its breath, and the dogwoods are bright with berries.

It is a strangely sad morning. My breakfast copy of *The New York Times* has the obituary of Joe Brooks, briefly describing his career in fishing the rivers of the world, his ten books about fly-fishing, and the eight-paragraph skeleton of his life. It is unexpected, although he was seventy years old and his life was ripe with many seasons astréam. The coffee in my cup is bitter when I finish the obituary. It concludes with a simple sentence informing us that the services and burial will take place tomorrow in Livingston, but his friends know that somehow Joe Brooks is going home to sleep beside the Yellowstone, and men who loved both the river and the man are the only readers who know what that final sentence means.

Looking out through the trees, and watching the cirrus clouds against the autumn light, it seems like a morning when the tiny *Centroptilum* flies are on the spring creeks above Livingston. The timeless cycle of the little rivers, ceaselessly flowing down the riffles of their watercress shallows, can sometimes remind us of our own mortality. Their music has another truth too, and it tells us that no man as admired and loved and remembered as Joe Brooks ever really dies.

Fishing the Two-Tailed Epeorus Nymphs

THESE DELICATE little two-tailed mayflies include several of our most famous fly hatches. *Epeorus* is the generic designation currently used to describe insects that have also been classified among the *Iron* genus in past books on trout stream insects. These hatches are all grouped in the *Epeorus* genus in modern entomological taxonomy.

Perhaps the best-known hatch on our rivers consists of the celebrated Gordon Quills, hatches that are most common on the half-legendary rivers of our eastern mountains—rivers like the tumbling Beaverkill and Willowemoc and Brodheads.

Thirty-five summers ago, in his poetic little book of chalkstream studies called *A Summer on the Test,* the British writer John Waller Hills observed that anglers are equally intrigued with daydreams of remote rivers and their home rivers, particularly if those familiar waters have a sense of history. Any fly-fisherman who has traveled the world searching out rivers of greatness understands the truth of his premise.

Sometimes such home rivers dance riffle-bright through our thoughts, often in the last delicious moments before sleep, and we fish them again and again in the time-mellowed weather of the memory and the mind. It happens in our daydreams too.

Both our memories and our senses are sharper on familiar waters. Our feet know the uncertainty of their algae-smooth ledges and the security of their fine gravel bottoms. Our eyes remember the bulge of a nymphing trout in some insignificant run deep under the trailing branches. Our legs know the chill of the April currents, and the tumbling rhythms against our waders in a favorite reach of riffles. The heart knows its quickening rhythms too, when our experience and patience seek out a favorite run with building anticipation, and we find our judgement rewarded with a hatch of fluttering *Epeorus* flies.

There are remembered odors too, like the smell of varnish in our rod-cases, the musky scent of the river and the thawing earth stirring in spring-time, bug-dope and line dressing and bird sandwiches and a river-chilled Pouilly Fuissé—all mixed with the remembered harmony and counterpoint and atonality of the river, with its wind chorus in the trees.

Such experiences are layered through the years, like the slate ledges above a favorite pool. Such pools are rich with memories, and in these terms my home river is certainly the gentle little Brodheads in Pennsylvania, particularly its Henryville water. Its memories are filled with many rich afternoons of fishing the *Epeorus* flies.

Its traditions are old and rich. Its history is perhaps the wellspring of American angling, and its singular *dramatis personae* include almost all of our major fishing writers since 1845. Its past and its pervasive mood easily meet the criteria Hills established in his *Summer on the Test*—that a well-loved river should have the patina of time, its paths worn patiently under the wading brogues of generations.

The home pools of our Henryville water meet those standards, and thoughts of them are inextricably mixed with memories of their *Epeorus* hatches. They have the rich patina of time. Their character is like a favorite rod, its action sweetened in countless summers astream, like a worn Cheviot tweed with baggy knees and worn sleeves, or some delicate-looking English doublegun, its walnut like oiled velvet and its bluing paled in the wood-cock covers of a lifetime.

There are many famous pools. Jefferson's Chute marks the top of our water, the sluicelike falls that leapfrogs down a series of faults in the ledges. It is named for the actor who often fished the Brodheads with Grover Cleveland. Fishing presidents were not unusual, and Calvin Coolidge took several trout on nightcrawlers in a deep, eddying pool that the old-timers on the river called the Coolidge Hole. Pyramid is next, with its huge pyramidal boulder lying in midstream, and below is the hundred-yard ledge pool called Bryan's Deep. It is named for Charles Bryan, a wealthy brewer who was a founder of both the Brooklyn Flyfishers and the Angler's Club of New York. Some years ago I was sitting on the ledges above the pool, idly sorting flies and enjoying the spring sunshine, when I dropped a Wheatley fly box. It clattered along the ledge and stopped just above the pool. When I scrambled down to retrieve it, I found the names of Charles Bryan and his fishing friend Lodie Smith carved into the stone, with the chiselled date of 1896.

There is the Amphitheatre Pool, with its moss staircase of ledges above the river, which lies below the mouth of Cranberry Run and the simple farmhouse we rent for our headquarters. There is Charlie's Hole, down-stream, where the riffling river collides with another outcropping, gouging out a deep, turbulent chute of a pool. It is named for the late Henryville Charlie Ross, an old poacher who fished only with the fly. Ross had also guided Grover Cleveland, Theodore Roosevelt, Gifford Pinchot, and Calvin Coolidge when they fished the Brodheads. His yardstick for politicians was simple and austere, like his life on the river.

Cleveland, Roosevelt, and Pinchot could fish, Henryville Charlie laughed. *Coolidge couldn't!*

The Cave Pool is downstream, where the ledges overhang the still currents in deep, almost cavernous shadows. The Ledge Pool below is a three-part puzzle. There are its upper riffle and slate-shadowed upper run, its extremely deep and slowly eddying middle, and the tail shallows over pale gravel. Its mossy ledges and hemlocks and laurel thickets echo a primeval past, when the Brodheads flowed cathedral-dark through its forests of conifers. Its upper run is often the source of fine Gordon Quill hatches on April afternoons, and the little duns sometimes drift a gauntlet of rising fish that lasts for sixty yards. It is a pool that produced two fish over four pounds this past season, and it still holds many secrets.

Pine Tree is more a flat than a pool, with a gentle, highly productive riffle upstream. Its secrets seem uncomplicated and open to the world, its bottom gravel visible everywhere. But its open face is deceptive, and the pool holds many puzzles. Large fish are often hooked there, just at twilight or in rainy weather, and they are usually lost when the tippet is sheared on a deadfall or sheltering stone.

The large, two-part pool below the ruined mill dam has never been a favorite of mine. My reservations are perhaps esthetic, since the shattered dam is ugly and the pool below is confused and scarred by broken pilings and abutments. The pool itself is shaped like an hourglass. Its upper chamber is turbulent and deep, while its lower chamber is still and smooth-flowing under a spreading oak. It has produced some large dry-fly trout in recent years, and a half-century ago it once produced a twenty-six-inch brown on a delicate Hare's Ear.

There is a beautiful run of broken water for the next two hundred yards, riffles and boulder-strewn pocket water filled with *Epeorus* nymphs. It slides and pounds into the Twin Pools downstream.

They are a favorite reach of water. The Twin Pools tumble down the valley below Henryville House, under a steep hillside dark with conifers and rhododendron. Lower Twin has filled in badly these past few years. It no longer holds a good head of trout, its deep holding-lies tight against the tree roots across the stream. Upper Twin is still one of the best pools on the river, and it has been a favorite of mine since Henryville Charlie showed it to me on a Gordon Quill afternoon fifteen years ago. Its upper currents fight the boulders, forming both a swift run and a long backwater eddy. Their currents gather together, sliding past a large pyramid-shaped rock into the principal chest-deep channel of the pool. Its currents are broken between a stone that lies under its sliding surfaces and a larger boulder across the tongue of the pool. Good trout lie all along this current, dropping back sometimes into its shallows to take hatching nymphs.

More pocket-water lies downstream, ending in a wildly plunging corner where the main currents collide with a huge boulder. It is the beginning of the Bridge Run, its swift pockets sheltering a great many good browns, and its oxygenated currents filled with *Epeorus* mayflies. It is a superb eighty yards of water, filled with free-rising trout and frequent fly hatches to start them working.

Its smooth current slides into the Bridge Pool. Good fish always lie in its April shadows, taking the Gordon Quills that ride the main current tongue and flutter along the face of the bridge abutments. There are always fish there too, tight against the concrete, sipping the delicate subimagoes. Its dark, sheltering structure has always concealed a big brown or two, and it has surrendered several three- and four-pounders.

The Bridge Flat was formed by a recent flood which eradicated the old Hewitt Pool and transformed it into a smooth-bottomed shallow where surprisingly good fish drop back to feed. The springhole below the bridge trickles in through the willows, and the main gravelly spine of the pool flows past, waist-deep and the home of several free-rising trout. This past season I took a fine eighteen-inch brown twice during the Gordon Quill hatches, and although the fish was showing regularly in the Bridge Flat, it refused everything but an *Epeorus* nymph.

Below lies a hundred yards of broken water that ends in the Birches Pool, named for a stand of trees killed years ago in an autumn hurricane flood. The name remains because family legend at Henryville House maintained that Birches was the site of Edward Ringwood Hewitt's first attempt at fishing the dry fly. It was better before its high-water damage. Birches still produces good fish each season, but my favorite memory of the pool was several years ago, when a particularly canny brown lived at the roots of the birches. It was a selective two-pound fish that regularly busied itself with a hatch, and several times we played catch-and-release tag that season. It usually held where the current bulged and eddied at the roots of the largest tree, and it rose regularly during the two-week hatch of *Epeorus* flies. It took dry-fly imitations twice that opening week, and catching and releasing it triggered an unusual metamorphosis.

First it dropped back into a slightly different feeding position, below the roots and lying in more complicated eddies. Dry-fly presentation was virtually impossible there, but the fish did take an *Epeorus* nymph once when it was lying deeper than its surface-feeding position. Finally that no longer worked, but a nymph tied hatching-style with nylon-stocking mesh to simulate its diaphanous emerging wing structure proved workable, since the *Epeorus* nymphs begin escaping their nymphal shucks along the bottom, and all migrate toward the surface as proto-winged flies. These nylon-stocking emergers were the only thing that fooled the Birches Pool fish in the end, and after releasing it several more times, we never saw it again.

Dominie is not really a pool, but a short, thigh-deep run past the boulders that form the tail of Birches. It produces a surprising number of fish for its open character and relatively small size, although I have never taken one there above fifteen to sixteen inches. It slides over a gentle riffle of pea-gravel into one of our best holding pools.

Buttonwood is a charming sixty-yard reach of river I have loved since the first day I fished the Henryville water. The swift tail shallows of Dominie are filled with green caddis larvae and *Isonychia* nymphs and the clinging nymphs of the early-season Gordon Quills. The current gathers and slides over the pale gravel, working into a diminishing tongue against the roots of the first buttonwood tree. It is a dark run tight against the bank, shallow-looking until one tries to retrieve a fly snagged against the roots, and then the current is armpit-deep and strong enough to unseat an unsuspecting wader. It also holds a good fish each season, and this past April, fishing in the rain with David Rose and David Ledlie, I hooked a fat hen-fish there that went twenty-two inches and fought me like a salmon, rolling and showing its spade-sized tail.

The middle of the pool is thirty yards of smooth, waist-deep water under the overhanging sycamores. The trout love their leaf-flickering shadows, and they lie in the swift run and tight against the roots. There are always fish rising there, but their soft rise forms are overlooked by many fishermen. Presentation is difficult, since a cast must be placed a dozen feet under branches that almost touch the current, but a hatching *Epeorus* nymph is always good for a fish or two.

The swift thirty yards of Laurel Run lie below, filled with fast-water insects and fish. There are towering rhododendrons sheltering the run where the swift shallows end abruptly, turning against the base of the mountain into Slide Pool. The bottom shelves off deeply against the steep root-tangle slide. The shadow of the mountain reaches the pool not long after lunch, and evening comes earlier there. The spreading tail shallows are punctuated with a single willow, and the throat of the pool is a turbulent chute, its principal current tongue tight against the steep toe of the rock slide. The pool is fickle and moody, and it has never been especially kind to me. It has often been dominated by a large fish, forcing lesser trout to live in fear. Its hatches have produced several two-pound fish for me in recent summers, but its murky depths remain an enigma not quite mastered.

This is home water to the Henryville Flyfishers, two miles of classic stream half-mythic in its history, and it tumbles and dances riffle-bright in my thoughts throughout the year. Such thoughts are always mixed with the *Epeorus* hatches.

It's a happy time of year, Henryville Charlie mumured softly on the river one April afternoon. *Them flies coming off the water means our river's come back to life again from a right hard winter—it's still alive this spring, and so are we.*

The *Epeorus* flies are harbingers of springtime.

Their oxygen requirements are so high that their nymphs are found only in the swift currents, clinging to the crevices between the stones. Their ability to survive pollution has a fragile threshold, and their need for cold, extremely pure currents rivals that of the brook trout. The nymphs can readily be distinguished from their sister mayfly genera by their two tails, when all other Ephemeroptera nymphs display three, except for the minuscule flies of the *Pseudocloëon* genus.

The bodies of these nymphs are flattened ventrally, their dorsal surfaces slightly convex in cross section. Both the frontal and lateral margins of the head are wide and flaring, covering the mouthparts completely. The eyes are wholly dorsal. The proportions of the lateral and apical margins of the head, and its region of greatest dimensional width, vary considerably from species to species. The labrum is relatively small, usually about two times as wide as its length. The anterolateral margins are rounded. There is usually a small rounded depression at the median line on its anterior margin. The inner canine of the mandibular structure is half to three-quarters the length of its outer canine. Lacinia are absent, or consist only of two or three short hairs. There is no fringe of hairs along the lacinial region. There is a triad of stout spinules, each slightly incurved and bearing at its apex a slender, threadlike appendage, which lies at the inner apical margin of the galea-lacinia. Configuration of these nymphs divides them into the *Pleuralis-Longimanus* group, and the fatter *Humeralis* type of nymphs.

The triad of spinules has near its base a second group of five to seven tiny spines in the nymphs of the *Pleuralis-Longimanus* forms. These are absent in the *Humeralis* forms. There is no series of spines along the upper margin of the maxilla, however, as in most genera of the Heptageniidae family. The median portion of the hypopharynx is longer, but somewhat narrower than its lateral portions. The glossae of the labium are conoid, and are apically convergent. The lateral margins of the pronotum are somewhat dilated in its middle or anterior margins. The leg joints are fringed with delicate hairs. The apical flange of the femora is somewhat pointed in the *Humeralis* group, and more gently rounded in the other species. The claws display three to six lateral pectinations.

Each abdominal segment bears a pair of spines at its posterolateral angle. The nymphs of the *Humeralis* group display outer spines that are relatively long and slender, fully half the length of its body segment. They are three to four times as long as their own width at the base; the inner spines are approximately half the length of the outermost. Nymphs of the *Pleuralis-Longimanus* types display outer spines that are short and relatively blunt, not more than one-quarter the length of their segments. Such spines are about as long as their basal width; the inner spines are about the same length as their outer ones. The fibrillar portion of each gill appears dorsal in its position. Gills of the nymphs found in the *Pleuralis-Longimanus* group are rather slender and plumate in shape, while the gill pairs of the *Humeralis* nymphs are lamellate and rounded. However, in both groups each gill overlaps the gill behind it, and their outer margins are all pressed against the bottom stones to which the nymphs attach themselves. The anterior lobe of the lamellate portions of the first gill-pair is better developed than the others. The subaquatic function of the gills is both respiratory and to provide stability in heavy currents, forming a suction-cup system similar to that found in *Rhithrogena,* although the first and last gill pairs do not meet under the ventral surfaces in *Epeorus.*

The behavior of these nymphs has implications for imitating them in the river. The mature nymphs cling to the undersides of the stones, and in hatching do not migrate toward the surface as nymphs. These insects crawl on the upper surfaces of the bottom to split their nymphal skins and hatch there, or escape the shredding shucks within inches of the bottom, where hydraulic friction slows the swiftest currents. Wrapped in its hydrofuge of nymphal gases, the half-nymph adult is buoyed to the surface in its evolving wings and remaining subaquatic skin. The trout capture most of these insects in the intermediate depths of water, between their bottom hatching and their arrival on the surface as full-blown mayflies. Since they cannot swim, and reach the surface with self-generated nymphal gases, imitative patterns should be fished dead-drift. Such winged nymphs should perhaps be fished to rising trout. The prehatching nymphs are seldom available to the fish, except when dislodged by high water, or when they lose their footing while on the bottom waiting to emerge. Both of these instances are best imitated with a weighted nymph fished in their fast-water habitat. The hatching imitations should be dressed with wet-fly-type wings of mallard or starling, and the rolled nylon-mesh emerging wings discussed in the chapter on the *Stenonema* flies have proved extremely effective for me from the Ausable in the Adirondacks to the Frying Pan in Colorado, especially on some of the paler hatches—like *Epeorus humeralis* in the east and *Epeorus albertae* in the Rocky Mountains.

1. Little Marryat (*Epeorus humeralis*)

This hatch is prototypical of its nymphal type, and is widely distributed on our eastern rivers. Hatches have been recorded from Quebec to the swift mountain streams of Pennsylvania and New Jersey. Its nymphs average three-eighths inch in length, and emergence occurs from early May until midsummer, with the best hatches coming in late May and early June. It is principally an afternoon and evening hatch.

Tails: Pale mottled brownish, 7/16 inch

Body: Pale amber with a delicate brown median stripe and dark margins, over pale sternites, ¼ inch

Gills: Pale amber and broadly camellate, ⅛ inch

Thorax: Pale amber mottled with brown, over a pale sternum, ⅛ inch

Wing cases: Pale amber with brown outside margins, 3/32 inch

Legs: Pale amber spotted with brown, ¼ inch

Head: Pale amber mottled with brown, 3/32 inch

Hook: Sizes 14-16 Mustad 9671 2X long

Nylon: Tan 6/0 nylon

Tails: Pale barred woodduck

Body: Pale amber dubbing marked with light brown felt-tipped pen, and securing a brownish darning cotton with fine gold wire to suggest median stripe

Gills: Amber marabou fibers secured at sides with wire ribbing

Thorax: Pale amber dubbing marked with light brown

Wing cases: Light brownish feather section tied down over thorax

Legs: Pale brown partridge

Head: Tan nylon

2. Pale Evening Quill (*Epeorus punctatus*)

This diminutive little mayfly has nymphs that average approximately five-sixteenths inch in length. Its range lies from Quebec to Pennsylvania, and it is a major hatch on New England rivers. Emergence occurs in June and July, and I have seen impressive twilight hatches on the Ausable and Saranac in the Adirondacks.

Tails: Pale mottled brownish, 5/16 inch

Body: Pale grayish amber with delicate lateral spotting and dark median stripe, over pale sternites, 5/32 inch

Gills: Pale amber spotted with brown, ⅛ inch

Thorax: Pale grayish amber heavily mottled with brown, over a pale sternum, ⅛ inch

Wing cases: Heavily mottled brownish, 3/32 inch

Legs: Pale amber grayish mottled with brown, 3/16 inch

Head: Pale grayish amber mottled with brown, 3/32 inch

Hook: Sizes 16-18 Mustad 9671 2X long

Nylon: Grayish tan 6/0 nylon

Tails: Pale barred woodduck

Body: Pale grayish amber dubbing marked with brown felt-tipped pen to suggest lateral mottling and a dark brown darning cotton or crewel median stripe.

Gills: Amber marabou secured at sides with fine gold wire

Thorax: Pale grayish amber dubbing marked with brown

Wing cases: Dark mottled brown feather section tied down over thorax

Legs: Pale grayish brown partridge

Head: Grayish tan nylon with brown dorsal lacquer

3. Pale Evening Olive (*Epeorus fragilis*)

Distributed from Quebec to Pennsylvania, this hatch occurs in midsummer with some emergence as late as September on some rivers. Its nymphs are somewhat more yellowish than those of *Epeorus punctatus*, a similar mayfly occupying the same range. The nymphs average about one-quarter inch in length.

Tails: Pale mottled brownish, ⅜ inch

Body: Pale yellowish amber mottled with brown and a dark median stripe, over pale sternites, 5/32 inch

Gills: Pale yellowish amber mottled with brown, 1/32 inch

Thorax: Pale amber mottled with brown, over a pale sternum, 1/16 inch

Wing cases: Pale amber mottled with brown, ⅛ inch

Legs: Pale amber mottled with brown, 3/16 inch

Head: Pale amber mottled with brown, 1/16 inch

Hook: Sizes 16-18 Mustad 9671 2X long

Nylon: Tan 6/0 nylon

Tails: Pale barred woodduck

Body: Pale amber dubbing mottled with a brown felt-tipped pen, and with a dark median stripe of brown darning cotton or crewel

Gills: Pale yellowish gray marabou secured at sides with fine gold wire

Thorax: Pale amber dubbing marked with brown

Wing cases: Pale mottled brownish feather section tied down over thorax

Legs: Pale brown partridge

Head: Tan nylon

4. Gray-Winged Yellow Quill (*Epeorus vitreus*)

This is one of the larger pale hatches among the *Epeorus* flies, their nymphs averaging about seven-sixteenths inch. Hatching occurs from the last week in May, and lasts until the middle of July. It is apparently a species primarily found in the swift trout streams draining into the Great Lakes. It is an evening hatch except on dark afternoons.

Tails: Dark mottled brownish, 7/16 inch

Body: Dark amber heavily mottled with brown, defining a pale median stripe above pale sternites, 3/16 inch

Gills: Dark amber gills heavily mottled with brown, ⅛ inch

Thorax: Dark amber heavily mottled with brown, defining a pale median stripe above a pale sternum, 3/32 inch

Wing cases: Dark amber heavily mottled, 3/32 inch

Legs: Dark amber heavily mottled with brown, ¼ inch

Head: Dark amber mottled with brown, 1/16 inch

Hook: Sizes 14-16 Mustad 9671 2X long

Nylon: Dark amber 6/0 nylon

Tails: Dark barred lemon woodduck

Body: Dark amber mottled with brown, securing a pale quill along the darsal median

Gills: Dark amber marabou secured at sides with fine gold wire

Thorax: Dark amber mottled with brown

Wing cases: Dark mottled amber tied down over thorax, with a pale quill to simulate median stripe

Legs: Dark brownish partridge

Head: Dark amber nylon

5. Little Yellow Quill (*Epeorus dispar*)

This pale little hatch is sometimes imitated with cream-colored dry flies, dressed with bright-yellowish flicker-quill bodies on the mountain streams of North Carolina. It hatches at twilight in June and July, and its nymphs average five-sixteenths inch.

Tails: Pale mottled brownish, 5/16 inch

Body: Dark amber heavily mottled with brown, defining a strong median stripe above pale sternites, 3/16 inch

Gills: Dark amber heavily mottled with brown, ⅛ inch

Thorax: Dark amber heavily mottled with brown, and having a strong median stripe above a pale sternum, ⅛ inch

Wing cases: Dark amber heavily mottled with brown, 3/32 inch

Legs: Dark amber mottled with brown, 3/16 inch

Head: Dark amber mottled with brown, 3/32 inch

Hook: Sizes 16-18 Mustad 2X long

Nylon: Light brown 6/0 nylon

Tails: Dark barred woodduck

Body: Dark amber dubbing mottled with brown felt-pen, and a chocolate brown darning cotton to suggest median stripe

Gills: Medium brownish marabou secured at sides with fine gold wire

Thorax: Dark amber dubbing mottled with brown felt-pen

Wing cases: Mottled brown feather section tied down over thorax with a chocolate brown darning cotton

Legs: Dark brown partridge

Head: Light brown nylon

6. Dark Gray-Winged Quill (*Epeorus rubidus*)

This dark little hatch has nymphal forms that average a diminutive one-quarter inch in length. It is also a pale-ocherous nymph found in the trout streams of the Blue Ridge and the Great Smokies, hatching sporadically at twilight throughout the summer.

Tails: Pale mottled brownish, ⅜ inch

Body: Pale amber delicately mottled and spotted with brown, defining a median stripe above pale sternites, 5/32 inch

Gills: Pale amber flushed with rusty brown, 1/16 inch

Thorax: Pale amber delicately mottled with brown above a pale sternum, ⅛ inch

Wing cases: Pale amber mottled with brown, 3/32 inch

Legs: Pale amber spotted with brown, 3/16 inch

Head: Pale amber mottled with brown, 1/16 inch

Hook: Sizes 16-18 Mustad 9671 2X long

Nylon: Tan 6/0 nylon

Tails: Pale lemon woodduck

Body: Pale amber dubbing lightly mottled with brown felt-pen, and using a light brown darning-cotton median stripe

Gills: Pale rusty brown marabou secured at sides with fine gold wire

Thorax: Pale amber dubbing lightly mottled with brown

Wing cases: Light mottled brown feather section tied down over thorax with darning-cotton median

Legs: Pale brown partridge

Head: Tan nylon

7. Gray-Winged Pink Quill (*Epeorus albertae*)

This little western hatch is widely distributed, with specimens recorded from New Mexico to Montana, and I have seen especially heavy midsummer hatches on the western-slope rivers of Colorado and Wyoming. It is principally a fast-water hatch of late afternoon and evening, and its nymphs average five-sixteenths inch.

Tails: Dark mottled brownish, 5/16 inch
Body: Dark amber mottled with brown markings that define a pale median stripe, above pale sternites, 3/16 inch
Gills: Dark amber strongly marked with brown, ⅛ inch
Thorax: Dark amber mottled with brown, above a pale sternum, ⅛ inch
Wing cases: Dark amber mottled with brown, ⅛ inch
Legs: Dark amber strongly marked with brown, 3/16 inch
Head: Dark amber mottled with brown, 1/16 inch

Hook: Sizes 16-18 Mustad 9671 2X long
Nylon: Grayish tan 6/0 nylon
Tails: Dark barred lemon woodduck
Body: Dark amber dubbing spun on pink silk and mottled with brown felt-pen and using a white quill overlay to simulate the pale median stripe
Gills: Dark amber marabou secured at sides with fine gold wire
Thorax: Dark amber dubbing marked with brown
Wing cases: Dark mottled amber tied down over thorax
Legs: Medium brown partridge
Head: Grayish tan nylon

8. Little Blue Quill (*Epeorus deceptivus*)

This is a fine little hatch found in the Rocky Mountain rivers from northern New Mexico to Montana, hatching in late June and July in Colorado and Wyoming. The nymphs hatch in late morning and early afternoon, and average about five-sixteenths inch.

Tails: Dark mottled brown, ⅜ inch
Body: Dark amber heavily mottled with brown and a pale median stripe, above pale sternites, 3/16 inch
Gills: Dark amber marked with brown, 1/16 inch
Thorax: Dark amber heavily mottled with brown, defining a pale median above a pale sternum, 1/16 inch
Wing cases: Dark amber heavily mottled with brown, 3/32 inch
Legs: Dark amber heavily mottled, 3/16 inch
Head: Dark amber mottled with a pale median, 1/16 inch

Hook: Sizes 16-18 Mustad 9671 2X long
Nylon: Tannish gray 6/0 nylon
Tails: Dark barred lemon woodduck
Body: Dark amber dubbing mottled with felt-pen and using a pale quill to suggest median stripe
Gills: Dark amber secured at sides with fine gold wire
Thorax: Dark amber dubbing mottled with felt-pen
Wing cases: Dark amber mottled feather section tied down over thorax
Legs: Dark brown partridge
Head: Tannish gray nylon with brown dorsal lacquer

9. Medium-Blue Quill (*Epeorus proprius*)

These dark-winged little mayflies are found on Rocky Mountain rivers in Colorado and Wyoming. The nymphs average seven-sixteenths inch, and hatch in early summer, beginning in late morning.

Tails: Dark amber mottled, 7/16 inch
Body: Dark amber mottled with brown over pale sternites, 3/16 inch
Gills: Dark amber mottled with brown, 1/16 inch
Thorax: Dark amber mottled with brown over a pale sternum, 3/32 inch
Wing cases: Dark mottled brownish, ⅛ inch
Legs: Dark amber heavily mottled with brown, ¼ inch
Head: Dark mottled brownish, 1/16 inch

Hook: Sizes 14-16 Mustad 9671 2X long
Nylon: Tan 6/0 nylon
Tails: Dark barred lemon woodduck
Bodu: Dark amber dubbing mottled with brown felt-pen
Gills: Brownish marabou secured at sides with fine gold wire
Thorax: Dark amber dubbing mottled with brown
Wing cases: Dark mottled brown feather tied over thorax
Legs: Dark brown partridge
Head: Tan nylon with brown dorsal lacquer

10. Western Little Marryat (*Epeorus lagunitas*)

This is a medium-sized species rather closely allied to *Epeorus albertae*, but it is found in the Pacific Coast rivers of California. Its nymphs average seven-sixteenths inch, and emerge during the evenings of early summer.

Tails: Pale mottled amber, 7/16 inch
Body: Pale yellowish amber mottled dian stripe above cream sternites, with brown, defining a dark median stripe above cream sternites, 3/16 inch
Gills: Pale yellowish amber flushed with brown, 1/16 inch
Thorax: Pale yellowish amber flushed with brown, 1/16 inch
Wing cases: Pale yellowish amber, ⅛ inch
Legs: Pale yellowish amber lightly spotted with brown, ¼ inch
Head: Pale yellowish amber mottled brown, 3/32 inch

Hook: Sizes 14-16 Mustad 9671 2X long
Nylon: Yellow 6/0 nylon
Tails: Pale barred woodduck
Body: Pale yellowish dubbing spun on yellow silk, with a light brown darning-cotton median stripe
Gills: Pale amber marabou secured at sides with fine gold wire
Thorax: Pale yellowish dubbing on yellow silk
Wing cases: Pale mottled amber tied down over thorax
Legs: Gray partridge dyed yellowish
Head: Yellow nylon

11. Western Gray-Winged Yellow Quill (*Epeorus youngi*)

This August hatch of pale little *Epeorus* flies is indigenous to the swift rivers of Oregon, Idaho, Washington, and Montana. The nymphs are similar to those of the California species *Epeorus lagunitas*, and average almost seven-sixteenths inch.

Tails: Pale mottled amber, ½ inch
Body: Pale yellowish amber mottled with brown, defining a broad pale median above pale cream sternites, 3/16 inch
Gills: Pale yellowish amber spotted with brown, 1/16 inch
Legs: Pale yellowish amber mottled with brown, defining a 3/32 inch pale median stripe above a pale sternum
Wing cases: Pale brownish amber, ⅛ inch
Legs: Pale yellowish amber mottled with brown, ¼ inch
Head: Pale mottled amber, 3/32 inch

Hook: Sizes 14-16 Mustad 9671 2X long
Nylon: Yellow 6/0 nylon
Tails: Pale barred woodduck
Body: Pale yellowish dubbing spun on yellow silk and mottled with light brown felt-pen, with a white darning-cotton on crewel median stripe
Gills: Pale yellowish gray marabou secured at sides with a fine gold wire
Thorax: Pale yellowish amber dubbing on yellow silk
Wing cases: Pale mottled brown tied over thorax
Legs: Gray partridge dyed yellowish
Head: Yellow nylon

12. Pale-Winged Pink Quill (*Epeorus dulciana*)

This is an important hatch from Oregon into the tumbling rivers of British Columbia, its nymphs similar to those of *Epeorus youngi* although smaller and slightly darker. The nymphs emerge in late summer, averaging five-sixteenths inch.

Tails: Dark mottled amber, ⅜ inch
Body: Dark mottled amber with a faint median, over pale sternites, 3/16 inch
Gills: Dark mottled amber, 1/16 inch
Thorax: Dark mottled amber above a pale sternum, 1/16 inch
Wing cases: Dark mottled brownish amber, 3/32 inch
Legs: Dark mottled amber, 3/16 inch
Head: Dark mottled amber, 1/16 inch

Hook: Sizes 12-14 Mustad 9671 2x long
Nylon: Tannish gray 6/0 nylon
Tails: Dark barred woodduck
Body: Dark amber dubbing mottled with light brown felt-pen, and a silghtly darker median of darning cotton
Gills: Dark amber marabou secured at sides with fine gold wire
Thorax: Dark amber dubbing mottled with light brown
Wing cases: Dark mottled brown feather section tied over thorax
Legs: Dark brown partridge
Head: Tannish gray nylon

13. Western Gordon Quill *(Epeorus longimanus)*

This is the prototypical western species of the *Pleuralis-Longimanus* group of nymphs, and it is widely distributed from the rivers of northern New Mexico along the Rocky Mountains into Alberta. There are exceptional hatches in Colorado and Wyoming, and I have had superb midday fishing with these mayflies on the Gros Ventre in Wyoming and the swift Cache la Poudre in northern Colorado. It hatches primarily in late June and July.

Tails: Dark mottled amber
Body: Dark brownish mottled above dirty amber sternites
Gills: Dark brownish mottled
Thorax: Dark brownish mottled above a dirty amber sternum
Wing cases: Dark brownish mottled
Legs: Dark brownish mottled
Head: Dark brownish mottled

Hook: Sizes 12-14 Mustad 9672 3X long
Nylon: Tannish gray 6/0 nylon
Tails: Dark barred woodduck
Body: Dark brownish dubbing with a darker darning-cotton median
Gills: Dark brownish marabou secured at sides with fine gold wire
Thorax: Dark brownish dubbing
Wing cases: Dark mottled brown feather tied down over thorax with a darker darning-cotton median
Legs: Dark brown partridge
Head: Tannish gray nylon with brown dorsal lacquer

14. Little Yellow Mayfly *(Epeorus hesperus)*

This is a relatively large straw-colored *Epeorus* mayfly found in the rivers of Oregon, Washington, and British Columbia. Some hatches are recorded from the swift watersheds of northern California, and the pale mottled nymphs average one-half inch in length. It is undoubtedly the species imitated by the Little Yellow Mayfly Nymph developed by Polly Rosborough on the rivers of Oregon. It hatches there from late May until the first week in July.

Tails: Pale mottled amber, 7/16 inch
Body: Pale grayish mottled amber with a brownish median stripe above pale sternites, ¼ inch
Gills: Pale mottled amber, ¼ inch
Thorax: Pale grayish amber heavily mottled with brown, 3/32 inch
Wing cases: Pale brownish, 3/32 inch
Legs: Pale grayish mottled amber, ⅜ inch
Head: Pale grayish mottled amber, 3/32 inch

Hook: Sizes 14-16 Mustad 9672 3X long
Nylon: Tannish gray 6/0 nylon
Tails: Pale barred lemon woodduck
Body: Pale grayish tan dubbing with a slightly darker median stripe of darning cotton
Gills: Pale amber marabou secured with fine gold wire
Thorax: Pale grayish tan dubbing
Wing cases: Pale brownish feather section tied over thorax
Legs: Pale grayish partridge hackle
Head: Tannish gray nylon

15. Dark Slate-Winged Purple Quill (*Epeorus nitidus*)

These large, dark-winged mayflies are unique, coming off cold, high-altitude rivers in late June and early July. My first specimens came from the ten-thousand-foot headwater meadows of the Arkansas in Colorado, water that has since been ruined by the clay-lenses pierced in a mine-drainage tunnel between Leadville and Climax. The hatches usually occurred if a rain squall misted across the bottoms about noon, and the dark little subimagoes lasted about two hours. The nymphs are rather large for this genus, averaging five-eighths inch in length.

Tails: Dark mottled brownish, 9/16 inch

Body: Dark mottled blackish brown above dirty grayish sternites, with a dark median stripe, 5/16 inch

Gills: Dark mottled brownish, ⅛ inch

Thorax: Dark mottled brown with a pale median stripe, above a pale sternum, 3/32 inch

Wing cases: Dark mottled brown, ⅛ inch

Legs: Dark amber mottled with brown, ⅜ inch

Head: Dark mottled brown with a pale median stripe, ⅛ inch

Hook: Sizes 12-14 Mustad 9672 3X long

Nylon: Brown 6/0 nylon

Tails: Dark barred woodduck

Body: Dark brownish black dubbing mixed with hare's mask guard hairs on ruby silk, using a slightly darker crewel to suggest a median stripe

Gills: Dark brownish gray marabou secured at sides with fine gold wire

Thorax: Dark brownish black dubbing mixed with hare's mask

Wing cases: Dark mottled brown feather tied down over thorax with pale quill median

Legs: Dark partridge dyed brown

Head: Brown nylon

16. Light-Blue Quill (*Epeorus confusus*)

The nymphs of this eastern species are found in rivers from New England to Pennsylvania, averaging seven-sixteenths inch in length. Peak emergence occurs in early afternoon, from late April until the last week in May. The subimagoes are often mistaken for the Gordon Quill hatch.

Tails: Dark mottled brownish, 7/16 inch

Body: Dark mottled brown with a darker median stripe above pale sternites, 3/16 inch

Gills: Dark mottled brownish, 1/16 inch

Thorax: Dark mottled brownish with a pale sternum, 1/16 inch

Wing cases: Dark mottled brownish, 1/16 inch

Legs: Dark mottled brownish, ¼ inch

Head: Dark mottled brownish, 1/16 inch

Hook: Sizes 14-16 Mustad 9672 3X long

Nylon: Brown 6/0 nylon

Tails: Barred woodduck

Body: Medium grayish brown hare's mask dubbing on brown silk, with a darker crewel median stripe

Gills: Dark brownish gray marabou ribbed with fine gold wire

Thorax: Medium grayish brown dubbing

Wing Cases: Dark mottled brown feather tied down over thorax

Legs: Dark brown partridge

Head: Brown nylon

17. Dark Gordon Quill (*Epeorus fraudator*)

This species is widely distributed from Quebec to the Catskills of New York, and it is this hatch that Art Flick describes in his *Streamside Guide*. The subimago is recognizable by its ringed abdomen, both on its dark tergites and paler sternites. It is an early-season hatch which comes off the swift riffles in April, its activity commencing about half-past one in the afternoon. The best hatches occur the last ten days in April, although on Adirondack rivers they may last until the middle of May. The nymphs are about nine-sixteenths inch in length.

Tails Dark mottled brownish, 9/16 inch

Body: Dark mottled brownish with a darker median stripe above paler sternites, ¼ inch

Gills: Dark mottled brownish, ⅛ inch

Thorax: Dark mottled brownish above a paler sternum, 3/32 inch

Wing cases: Dark mottled brownish, ⅛ inch

Legs: Dark mottled brownish, ⅜ inch

Head: Dark mottled brownish, ⅛ inch

Hook: Sizes 12-14 Mustad 9672 3X long

Nylon: Dark brown 6/0 nylon

Tails: Dark barred lemon woodduck

Body: Dark brown dubbing mixed with hare's mask guard hairs, and with a darker median stripe of darning cotton or crewel

Gills: Dark brownish marabou secured at sides with fine gold wire

Thorax: Dark brown dubbing

Wing cases: Dark mottled brown feather tied down over thorax

Legs: Dark brown partridge

Head: Dark brown nylon

18. Gordon Quill (*Epeorus pleuralis*)

This is perhaps the best-known American mayfly species, since it has become associated with the dry-fly pattern created at the turn of the century by Theodore Gordon, the father of fly-fishing on the classic eastern rivers of the Catskills.

Paler than its sister hatch, the *Epeorus fraudator* flies, it is more widely distributed. Hatches are recorded from the rivers of the Catoctins in Maryland to the Adirondacks, and the forested mountains of Vermont and New Hampshire. Its sternites are paler, almost olive on some rivers like the Brodheads, where oldtimers called it the Yellow Quill. The nymphs are very much like those of *Epeorus fraudator*, and average about one-half inch in length.

Tails: Medium mottled brownish, 9/16 inch

Body: Medium mottled brown with a dark median zone above paler sternites, ¼ inch

Gills: Medium mottled brown, ⅛ inch

Thorax: Medium mottled brownish above a pale sternum, 3/32 inch

Wing cases: Medium mottled brownish, ⅛ inch

Legs: Medium mottled brownish, ⅜ inch

Head: Medium mottled brownish, ⅛ inch

Hook: Sizes 12-14 Mustad 9672 3X long

Nylon: Medium brown 6/0 nylon

Tails: Medium barred woodduck

Body: Medium brown dubbing mixed with hare's mask guard hairs, and using a slightly darker median of darning cotton or crewel

Gills: Medium brownish marabou secured at sides with fine gold wire

Thorax: Medium brown dubbing mixed with hare's mask

Wing cases: Medium brown feather tied down over thorax

Legs: Medium brown partridge

Head: Medium brown nylon

These *Epeorus* nymphs are relatively flat, and over the years I have been experimenting with weighted brass-wire and stainless music-wire outriggers to form a flat-body foundation system. It is most valuable in the hook sizes above sixteen, of course, although weighting these nymphs is most important. Since they escape their nymphal skins in the bottom currents, the trout seldom see them at intermediate depths or just under the surface film, like the other mayflies. *Epeorus* patterns are most effective when their ventral surfaces are painted with lacquer to suggest their pale coloring. Hatching patterns should always be dressed with emerging wings, either conventionally dressed to proper color like a Hare's Ear or Little Marryat, or a rolled wing of nylon stocking-mesh.

Emerging patterns are extremely important to the flyfisher in working the *Epeorus* hatches, since the naturals escape their nymphal skins at the bottom and migrate toward the surface in a proto-winged state. The stocking-mesh dressings on lightwire Orvis Premium hooks have proved themselves over the past several seasons, using these same patterns with emerging wings and outriggers of lightweight stainless to create the proper flat-bodied configuration. It is a deadly secret.

The Clinging Plate-Gilled Rhithrogenas

THE RIVER rises high in the smoke-colored ridges that shield Mount Marcy, its rolling summits reaching more than five thousand feet above the dense Adirondack forests. Its brook-trout beginnings lie in the thick stands of spruce and swamp birches and pines, in feeders that plunge wildly down the mountains with a thawing wind, fighting the polished boulders of glacier-scarred granite.

There are still bears and bald eagles and ospreys living high in these forests. Cliff-sheltered lakes and beaver ponds abound like those in the north-country watercolors of Winslow Homer, and sometimes there is the report of a mountain lion, seen with a freshly killed whitetail near the barren hiking-trail summits.

The headwaters are swampy with beaver ponds, the leachings of their stickwork dams and drowned willows turning the river dark and tea-colored. Its tumbling rapids look starkly white against its acid-brown currents, and foam gathers among the rocks.

It is difficult country and a difficult river. The acid soils made for poor farming, scarcely worth clearing the land and piling its glacier stones into fences from a rock sledge. Winters are roof-deep with snow and biting cold. Few farms survived its barren winters and thin, almost infertile topsoil, and the men who first worked in its lumber camps and farmsteads were a firm-lipped breed tempered in hard times. The upper reaches of the river lie in such an unprotected valley between Algonquin and Marcy that its winters are legendary, even in a region famous for the bitterness of its weather. Its frozen lakes and heavy snowfalls resulted in the selection of nearby Lake Placid for the Winter Olympics of 1932.

Although these headwaters may seem uncultivated and wild, the valley has a long history of settlement reaching back to the American Revolution. Its stony soil and harsh winters also tempered the colonial patriot John Brown, who abandoned the comfort of the American seaport towns after his graduation from Yale in 1771, preferring to clear a farmstead in the Adirondacks. Brown became skilled in guerrilla tactics, and played a major role with Ethan Allen in the capture of Fort Ticonderoga in 1775. John Brown was killed fighting in the Mohawk Campaign of 1780, and is buried on the headwaters of the river. It is strange that the better-known John Brown of Harper's Ferry, who was executed for leading that insurrection on the eve of the Civil War, is also buried nearby at North Elba.

The brownish currents tumble swiftly the first few miles until it reaches the flat-water meadows below Lake Placid. Here are weedy flats and willow-sheltered currents worthy of the British chalkstreams. These meadows are relatively undeveloped and wild. Below the willow-lined bends and grassy undercut banks are several miles of smooth-flowing forest water, where the quiet currents glide in the leafy shadows of giant oaks and American elms.

Below the gravel county-road mileage, the river gathers its powerful forces in a series of ledgerock chutes and granite-bottom pools. It is not water for a faint-hearted angler, and as Bergman described it in *Trout* more than thirty years ago, it is a river you like best when you are young.

It is the storied West Branch of the Ausable, the most famous of the several Adirondack rivers, and its character has held the imagination of American anglers for seventy-five years.

The valley soon narrows into a steep-walled gorge, its famous Wilmington Notch, where the current rages through the house-sized boulders and tumbling falls. Several anglers have lost their lives here.

Whiteface Mountain dominates the valley now. There are relatively open stretches of pocket-water downstream from the gorge, but it is tough wading that a man attacks easiest before he reaches forty-five. The millpond at Wilmington produces some incredible hatches of the swimming *Siphlonurus* nymphs, and some of the best big-drake mating swarms still existing on our eastern rivers. There are superb populations of fast-water nymphs on its pocket-water mileage.

Below the Wilmington Dam, the river has a varied character that ranges from the *pianissimo* moods of the Hazelton water, to the powerful crescendos downstream, with their apogee in the famous Slant Rock Pool. There have been serious pollution problems below Ausable Forks, where it joins the East Branch, draining the adjacent valley. Hopefully, the efforts of several conservation groups—particularly the Theodore Gordon Flyfishers based in midtown Manhattan—seem to hold some promise.

It was the Ausable that introduced me to the clinging plate-gilled *Rhithrogena* nymphs, just as Preston Jennings described their importance on that river in his *Book of Trout Flies* more than thirty years ago. It was a cold morning in early June, and a pale sun glittered dully on the current. While we stopped to eat lunch at streamside, a hatch of dark blue-winged little mayflies began coming off the swift-water pockets upstream. Fish began working eagerly.

It's a hatch coming! I said.

My father began repacking his lunch quickly. *Come on!* he said excitedly. *When the fish are rising it's foolish to waste time eating.*

It's a good motto, I laughed.

The flies superficially resembled the earlier Gordon Quill hatch, with their two tails and brown-mottled femora, but the *Epeorus* mayflies usually emerge on the Ausable in the beginning of May. It was two weeks into June, and the Hendricksons that typically follow the earlier Gordon Quills were virtually finished too. Jennings recommended a well-tied Gordon Quill or occasionally the Red Quill for these flies. Since they were hatching well into June, they were undoubtedly the *Rhithrogena impersonata* flies Jennings had described, but his dry-fly prescription failed completely.

Fish after fish refused our dry-fly imitations, sometimes rising so close to their lines of float that our flies were drowned in the swirls. We tried desperately, again and again. Finally I stopped casting over a good fish and just watched. Several dark little mayflies drifted through his feeding position, and the fish refused them too. The rises continued.

They're not taking these flies, I shouted.

My father was using a darkly tied Red Quill downstream. *What are they taking?* he asked.

Must be the hatching nymphs, I yelled.

We had never collected a *Rhithrogena* nymph, and since the hatching subimagoes looked like the earlier Gordon Quill flies, I tried the imitation worked out for the *Epeorus* naturals by Edward Sens. It was also a complete failure. Finally I took a foolish trout of about twelve inches on a fat, roughly dubbed Hare's Ear, fished upstream like a sunken dry fly. The hatch soon stopped.

The slender little knife sliced cleanly from the anal fin to the gill covers, and I stripped the gills and entrails free. Carefully opening the stomach, I found a small handful of extremely dark, flat-looking little nymphs.

The nymphs of *Rhithrogena* are perhaps the most unusual of the lotic swift-water mayflies. Their heads are strikingly flattened, with both antennae and eyes on the dorsal surfaces. They also have broad femora, slender tibiae, and wide, stabilizing tails. Such lotic nymphs are so closely attached to the stones in the stream bottom that they are difficult to see until the angler removes the stones, turns them into the light, and waits for the nymphs to move in their algae-covered surface film. The frightened little nymphs move about rapidly, clinging firmly to the stones. Needham observes in his *Biology of Mayflies* that these lotic ecotypes cling so efficiently to their stony havens that they seem almost encised into the rock. They cling flat-legged with their bellies and tails lying in the meniscus of water and algae growth, sliding rather than crawling as they travel the bottom. They move a single step at a time, almost simultaneously loosening and refastening their footholds, and seem equally adept at moving in any direction. They range freely over the upper surfaces of the stones on dark days, and in the twilight feeding hours they exhibit much less caution in their movements. Between the subaquatic surfaces of the stones, there are always sheltering crevices where the nymphs can hide.

However, much of this clinging ability stems from the unique gill structure of the *Rhithrogena* nymphs. The heads are also clearly demarked from the thorax. The gill plates are larger than those of any other clinging nymphal form, with each gill strongly overlapping the succeeding one. They spread laterally, forming a bladelike extension of the sternite segments. The first and last gill plates meet underneath the center of the sternum and the tails, forming an unbroken circle of suction. These lamellae press against the stones, forming a suction-type vacuum underneath its body. Using such systems, the nymphs can achieve a limpetlike grip on the smoothly polished bottom surfaces, maintaining their position when other nymphs would be washed away. The strength of their hold becomes apparent when one attempts to break their leechlike tenacity. These fast-water skills permit the nymphs to inhabit the gathering tail-shallows of a pool, holding in the swiftest currents like a fresh-run salmon.

1. Dark Red Quill (*Rhithrogena impersonata*)

This widely distributed species hatches into a slate-winged mayfly of good size, with a reddish, distinctly ringed body. It was the subimago hatching that midday on the Ausable. It typically emerges from late May until the end of June. The species is distributed from Quebec to the swift rivers of Michigan and Wisconsin, and its fully developed nymphs measure seven-sixteenths inch.

The nymphs swim clumsily, like many of the clinging ecotypes, and they migrate toward the surface as much through the gas generated to split their nymphal shucks as through their awkward wriggling. The imitations should be fished dead-drift.

Tails: Pale mottled amber, ⅜ inch
Body: Dark reddish brown distinctly ringed, ¼ inch
Gills: Grayish green, 1/32 inch
Thorax: Dark mottled reddish brown, ⅛ inch
Wing cases: Dark mottled reddish brown, ⅛ inch
Legs: Dark mottled brownish olive, 5/16 inch
Head: Dark mottled brown, 3/32 inch

Hook: Sizes 12-14 Mustad 7948A
Nylon: Dark brown 6/0 nylon
Tails: Lemon Woodduck fibers
Body: Reddish brown dubbing on flattened foundation of brass wire outriggers and plastic floss
Gills: Pale Grayish green marabou fibers densely bunched along both lateral edges of the body, and secured with fine gold wire
Thorax: Reddish brown dubbing dressed full
Wing cases: Dark brownish feather section tied over thorax
Legs: Dark partridge dyed olive
Head: Dark brown nylon

2. Dark Olive Upright (*Rhithrogena pellucida*)

This medium-sized mayfly occupies a similar position in the lexicon of American fly hatches, as the European species *Rhithrogena semicolorata* has on the British rivers. Its distribution ranges from Quebec to Minnesota, and its mature nymphs measure about three-eighths inch. Peak emergence occurs throughout July, with heavy hatches on rivers like the Pere Marquette early in that month.

These nymphs are almost black, with somber olive reflections seldom visible without a glass. They are most numerous in fast, gravelly riffles on swiftly flowing rivers, particularly rivers like the Battenkill below Arlington, and open-bottomed Michigan rivers like the Fox, Sturgeon, Pere Marquette, and the swift-flowing Pine.

Tails: Medium mottled olive brown, 5/16 inch
Body: Dark blackish olive, 3/16 inch
Gills: Dark olive gray, 1/32 inch
Thorax: Dark blackish olive, 3/32 inch
Wing cases: Dark slate-colored olive, ⅛ inch
Legs: Dark mottled olive, ¼ inch
Head: Dark blackish olive, 1/16 inch

Hook: Sizes 14-16 Mustad 7948A
Nylon: Black 6/0 nylon
Tails: Lemon Woodduck fibers dyed light olive
Body: Dark blackish olive dubbing tied on brass wire flat-foundation outriggers
Gills: Dark olive gray marabou fibers densely bunched and secured with fine gold wire
Thorax: Dark slate-colored feather section tied over thorax
Legs: Dark partridge dyed dark olive
Head: Black nylon

3. Medium Olive Upright (*Rhithrogena jejuna*)

This nymph is a medium-sized, grayish-olive species measuring above three-eighths inch in length. Its peak emergence occurs about one week ahead of *Rhithrogena impersonata*, coming off during the month of May where it is found. Some overlapping of these two species occurs. The Medium Olive Upright is found from New Brunswick to the swift rivers draining into Lake Superior.

These nymphs are well imitated by the following fly pattern, fished dead-drift in the swift riffles they inhabit.

Tails: Pale olive mottled, 5/16 inch
Body: Pale olive gray, 3/16 inch
Gills: Pale grayish white, 1/32 inch
Thorax: Pale olive gray, 3/32 inch
Wing cases: Pale olive gray, ⅛ inch
Legs: Pale olive gray, ¼ inch
Head: Pale olive gray, 1/16 inch

Hook: Sizes 14-16 Mustad 7948A
Nylon: Pale olive 6/0 nylon
Tails: Pale lemon woodduck fibers
Body: Pale olive gray cellulite floss over outrigger foundation
Gills: Pale grayish marabou secured at sides with fine gold wire
Thorax: Pale olive gray cellulite floss picked apart and dubbed
Wing cases: Pale olive gray feather section tied down over thorax
Legs: Pale olive-dyed barred mallard fibers
Head: Pale olive nylon

4. Red-Gilled Nymph (*Rhithrogena sanguinea*)

This dark reddish-brown nymph is readily identified by its bright-rust-colored gills; its femora and head are also flushed with red. Full-grown nymphs measure about three-eighths inch. Their distribution reaches from Quebec to Minnesota, with the most extensive populations found in the slightly acid rivers draining the pre-Cambrian formation of Canada and the northern United States.

These nymphs thrive on gravelly bottoms in surprisingly swift currents. Peak hatching comes throughout June and the middle of July.

Tails: Brownish mottled amber, 5/16 inch
Body: Mottled brownish distinctly ringed, 3/16 inch
Gills: Dark rusty reddish, 1/32 inch
Thorax: Mottled brownish, 3/32 inch
Wing cases: Mottled brownish, ⅛ inch
Legs: Mottled brownish, ¼ inch
Head: Mottled brownish, 1/16 inch

Hook: Sizes 14-16 Mustad 7948A
Nylon: Dark brown 6/0 nylon
Tails: Dark lemon woodduck fibers
Body: Dark reddish-brown dubbing on wire outrigger foundation to suggest flatness
Gills: Dark rusty reddish marabou bunched at sides of flat body and secured with fine gold wire
Thorax: Dark reddish brown dubbing
Wing cases: Dark mottled reddish brown feather tied over thorax
Legs: Dark mottled woodcock fibers
Head: Dark brown nylon

5. Western Red Quill (*Rhithrogena doddsi*)

The Western Red Quill is a relatively large mayfly species found extensively in our Rocky Mountain rivers, from New Mexico to Alberta. Specimens from Utah and Idaho are also recorded. Its nymphs measure slightly more than seven-sixteenths inch at full maturity, and it hatches sporadically in July and August.

Tails: Dark mottled amber, ⅜ inch
Body: Dark rusty brownish, 3/16 inch
Gills: Pale grayish purple, 1/32 inch
Thorax: Dark reddish brownish, ⅛ inch
Wing cases: Dark reddish brownish, 5/32 inch
Legs: Dark mottled reddish brown, 5/16 inch
Head: Dark reddish brown, 3/32 inch

Hook: Sizes 10-12 Mustad 7948A
Nylon: Dark brown 6/0 nylon
Tails: Dark lemon woodduck fibers
Body: Dark rusty brown dubbing over a wire-body outrigger
Gills: Pale purple marabou secured at sides with fine gold wire
Wing cases: Dark rusty brown feather section tied over thorax
Legs: Dark partridge dyed rich reddish brown
Head: Dark brown nylon

There is a slightly larger western species, *Rhithrogena virilis*, with nymphs measuring as much as nine-sixteenths inch. It is found in the northerly latitudes of the Rocky Mountains, from the rivers of Montana and Wyoming to watersheds farther north in Alberta and British Columbia. Its nymphs are somewhat darker than those of *Rhithrogena doddsi*, and the still darker *Rhithrogena robusta* is found from Colorado to Canada. Its nymphs measure a half inch at maturity.

Clinging Nymphs of the Minor Heptageniidae

There was a thin September ice-skim on the cattle tank below the cabin, and a hundred yards across the corral bottoms the Gunnison glittered in the morning sun. The horses were restless and their nervous whinnies echoed on the wind. It carried the sounds of the haying crew in the fields across the river.

The sounds of frying bacon and eggs filled the cabin, and the breakfast kindling shifted in the wood stove. The cooking and coffee smells were good, and I left a half-finished fly in the vise when the food was ready.

Think those flies will work? asked Frank Klune.

They should, I said. *It's been going on for three days now, with those little cream-colored mayflies coming off—fish start working but they pass up the floating duns.*

You really think they're nymphing? he asked.

Have to be nymphing. It was a good guess. *It has to be these darkly mottled little nymphs we found in your fish.*

Maybe so, said Klune. *More eggs?*

We finished breakfast and I tied several types of experimental nymphs while Klune cleaned up the breakfast mess. The hatch was about due on the side channels across the river, so we shouldered into our gear and hiked upstream.

The pale little mayflies started hatching, and the fish started rising on schedule. *Watch that mayfly!* I pointed to a struggling little subimago that had just popped to the surface. *Watch it reach that rising fish!*

The insect passed the trout without being taken.

You're right, Klune agreed.

He clinched one of the experimental nymphs to his tippet and soaked it in some backwater silt. When it was thoroughly wet, he cast upstream to the feeding position of the fish. The nymph settled and began to sink when the rainbow swirled and the leader twitched across the current tongue.

It worked! Klune laughed. *He took it!*

We took several good fish that morning, each repeating the same scenario. There was a steady feeding rhythm during the hatch of the pale little mayflies. The trout ignored both the naturals and our dry-fly imitations, and then the same fish fell all over themselves to intercept and take our artificial *Heptagenia* nymphs.

Our selectivity problems were solved.

It was a good lesson, and even the hatches that are considered of relatively minor importance can generate fine rises of fish at various times.

Although not as important as such related genera as the *Stenonema* and *Epeorus* and *Rhithrogena* flies, there are times when the relatively minor Heptageniidae are critical to anglers, particularly in the west. The most important minor genera are *Heptagenia* and *Cinygmula*.

The *Heptageniidae* are generally quite recognizable in their nymphal stages by their strongly flattened abdomen and thoracic structures. The heads are also dramatically flattened, and somewhat larger than those of other mayfly families. Their prominent eyes are wholly dorsal, while their mouthparts lie entirely on the ventral surfaces of the head. There are gills present on the first seven body segments, each pair consisting of a dorsal lamellate and a ventral fibrillar portion. There are three tails in the nymphs. The adults display five-jointed tarsi in the rear legs, and are distinguished by four cubital intercalary veins in the forewings. The middle tail is atrophied and vestigial in the adult flies. The eyes are large and subspherical in the male imagoes, and respond dramatically to variations in light. The ocelli are typically pale during daylight hours, and polished black at night.

The nymphs of the *Heptagenia* genus are quite distinct from the other subaquatic forms of the Heptageniidae family. The gills on segment seven of the abdomen do not resemble the threadlike seventh gills of the *Stenonema* flies, but the other six are quite similar.

Heptagenia nymphs have flat heads that are proportionally quite large. The thorax and abdominal structures are ventrally flattened and somewhat dorsally convex. The labrum has a width approximately four times its length. The inner canine of the right mandible is about three-quarters the length of the outer one. Both joints of the maxillary palp are relatively slender when compared with the related genera. There are a series of pectinate spines along the apical margin of the galea-lacinia. The glossae of the labium are strongly arched. The claws are not pectinate. There are postlateral spines on segments six through eight. The filamentous portion of the gills is well developed. The general coloring of the dorsal surfaces is darkly mottled blackish or brown. There are pale submedian markings on each tergite, which sometimes merge into a pale median stripe, although this color variation is not always evident in the species I have collected.

1.   Little Gray-Winged Olive (*Heptagenia pulla*)

This dark smoky-winged little olive is quite similar in its appearance to the famous British hatch of Blue-Winged Olives, although it has only two tails in its subimago stages and the British hatch is from another genus having three. The nymphs average one-half inch at maturity, and hatch sporadically from early June until the beginning of August.

The species is identified from New Brunswick to upper New York and the Great Lakes region. The western *Heptagenia solitaria* is quite similar. The nymphs are colored somewhat like those of *Heptagenia elegantula*, except that they are darker and more olivaceous.

Tails: Dark mottled brownish, 7/16
inch
Body: Dark mottled brownish with
pale sternites, 3/16 inch
Gills: Dark mottled brownish, 3/32
inch
Thorax: Dark mottled brownish
with pale sternum, 1/16 inch
Wing cases: Dark mottled brownish,
3/32 inch
Legs: Dark mottled brownish, ⅜
inch
Head: Dark mottled brownish, ⅛
inch

Hook: Sizes 12-14 Mustad 9671 2X
long
Nylon: Brown 6/0 nylon
Tails: Dark mottled brown mallard
Body: Dark mottled brown dubbing
mixed with hare's ear guard hairs
with light brown lacquer on ventral
surfaces
Gills: Fine oval gold tinsel divides
dubbing into segments
Thorax: Dark mottled brown dubbing
mixed with hare's ear guard hairs
and light brown lacquer on sternum
Wing cases: Dark brown feather
section tied down over thorax
Legs: Dark mottled partridge
Head: Dark brown nylon

2. Little Evening Sulphur (*Heptagenia minerva*)

These little insects are quite similar to those of the British fly hatches of the Little Yellow May or Yellow Hawk mayflies. It appears sporadically in late summer, and its nymphs average one-quarter inch in length. Specimens are recorded from Maryland to Ontario.

This species is closely allied with the *Heptagenia aphrodite* hatch recorded from North Carolina.

Tails: Pale mottled brownish ⅜
inch
Body: Pale mottled brownish with
tan sternum, 5/32 inch
Gills: Pale mottled brownish, 1/16
inch
Thorax: Pale mottled brownish with
tan sternum, 1/32 inch
Wing cases: Pale mottled brownish,
1/16 inch
Legs: Pale mottled brownish, ¼ inch
Head: Pale mottled brownish, 3/32
inch

Hook: Sizes 14-16 Mustad 9671 2X
long
Nylon: Tan 6/0 nylon
Tails: Pale mottled woodduck
Body: Pale mottled brown dubbing
mixed with hare's mask guard hairs,
and pale lacquer on sternum
Gills: Fine oval gold tinsel divides
dubbing into segments
Thorax: Pale mottled brown dubbing
mixed with hare's mask and pale
sternum lacquer
Wing cases: Pale mottled feather
section tied down over thorax
Legs: Pale mottled brownish partridge
Head: Pale brown nylon

3. Little Pale Evening Dun (*Heptagenia juno*)

This pale whitish-yellow species hatches primarily at twilight, its nymphs averaging about one-quarter inch at maturity. It is a species that hatches sporadically through the summer.

This species is recorded from Quebec to Pennsylvania and northern New Jersey rivers, and the *Heptagenia thetis* found on the rivers of Virginia and North Carolina is quite similar, as is the *Heptagenia simplicoides* indigenous to Montana, Wyoming, and the Pacific Northwest.

Tails: Pale mottled gray, ⅜ inch
Body: Pale mottled grayish with cream sternites, 5/32 inch
Gills: Pale mottled grayish, 1/16 inch
Thorax: Pale mottled grayish with cream sternum, 1/16 inch
Wing cases: Pale mottled grayish, 3/32 inch
Legs: Pale mottled grayish, 3/16 inch
Head: Pale mottled grayish, 3/32 inch

Hook: Sizes 14-16 Mustad 9671 2X long
Nylon: Tan 6/0 nylon
Tails: Pale barred mallard
Body: Pale grayish brown dubbing mixed with hare's mask guard hairs, and pale cream ventral lacquer
Gills: Fine oval gold tinsel divides dubbing into segments
Thorax: Pale grayish brown dubbing mixed with hare's mask, and pale lacquer on the sternum
Wing cases: Pale grayish brown feather tied down over thorax
Legs: Pale mottled gray partridge
Head: Pale mottled brown dubbing

4. Little Evening Yellow (*Heptagenia hebe*)

These little nymphs also average about one-quarter inch in length, and are widely distributed from Quebec to Minnesota, and south along our eastern seaboard to North Carolina and Tennessee. It hatches from early June until late August, and is quite similar in its subimago stage to the European species *Heptagenia sulphurea*, the famous yellow mayfly found on British rivers.

Tails: Pale mottled brown, 5/16 inch
Body: Pale mottled brownish with tan sternites, 5/32 inch
Gills: Pale mottled brownish, 1/16 inch
Thorax: Pale mottled brown with tan sternum, 1/16 inch
Wing cases: Pale mottled brownish, 3/32 inch
Legs: Pale mottled brown, 3/16 inch
Head: Pale mottled brown, 1/16 inch

Hook: Sizes 14-16 Mustad 9671 2X long
Nylon: Tan 6/0 nylon
Tails: Pale barred woodduck
Body: Pale brown dubbing mixed with hare's mask guard hairs, and cream lacquer sternites
Gills: Fine oval gold tinsel divides dubbing into segments
Thorax: Pale brown dubbing mixed with hare's mask, and with cream lacquer sternum
Wing cases: Pale brown feather section tied down over thorax
Legs: Pale brown partridge
Head: Pale brown nylon

5. Little Gray-Winged Dun (*Heptagenia criddlei*)

This handsome little insect is found in the rivers of the Rocky Mountains from Colorado to Montana, and northwest into Oregon, Washington, and the Canadian provinces. The other western species, *Heptagenia otiosa*, is similar, and their nymphal forms are quite dark, averaging about one-quarter inch in length. Peak emergence occurs from early June until the middle of July.

Tails: Dark mottled brown, 5/16 inch
Body: Dark mottled brown with light brown sternites, ⅛ inch
Gills: Dark mottled brown, 1/16 inch
Thorax: Dark mottled brown with light brown sternum, 3/32 inch
Wing cases: Dark mottled brownish, 3/32 inch
Legs: Dark mottled brown, 3/16 inch
Head: Dark mottled brown, 1/16 inch

Hook: Sizes 14-16 Mustad 9671 2X long
Nylon: Dark brown 6/0 nylon
Tails: Dark brown mallard fibers
Body: Dark brown dubbing mixed with guard hairs
Gills: Oval gold tinsel suggests body segments
Thorax: Dark brown dubbing mixed with guard hairs
Wing cases: Dark mottled brown feather tied down over thorax
Legs: Dark brown-dyed partridge hackle
Head: Dark brown nylon

6. Western Pale Evening Dun (*Heptagenia elegantula*)

This species was mistakenly identified during the preparation of *Matching the Hatch* as another mayfly of a related genus, when in fact it is a pale-cream-colored hatch found from New Mexico north along the Rocky Mountains into Canadian waters. It is somewhat larger than its related species, its nymphs measuring about three-eighths inch in length.

Tails: Dark brownish mottled, 7/16 inch
Body: Dark brownish distinctly ringed, and pale grayish yellow sternites, 3/16 inch
Gills: Dark brownish mottled yellow, 3/32 inch
Thorax: Dark brownish mottled yellowish, 3/32 inch
Wing cases: Dark brownish, 3/32 inch
Legs: Dark yellowish heavily mottled with brown, 5/16 inch
Head: Dark yellowish mottled with brown, 3/32 inch

Hook: Sizes 12-14 Mustad 9671 2X long
Nylon: Tan 6/0 nylon
Tails: Darkly barred lemon woodduck
Body: Dark brownish dubbing roughly mixed with guard hairs, and with creamish yellow lacquer on the sternites
Gills: Fine oval gold tinsel suggests body segments
Thorax: Dark brownish dubbing mixed with guard hairs, and with creamish yellow lacquer on sternum
Wing cases: Dark brownish feather tied over thorax
Legs: Darkly barred partridge hackle
Head: Pale brown nylon

The hatches occur primarily in August, with some emergence occurring into the following month. The species was incorrectly classified *Stenonema verticus* during preparation of my earlier book, which is apparently a non-existent taxonometric form. The insect identified as *Heptagenia elegantula* is apparently a subspecies of the *Epeorus* flies.

Some years ago, fishing friends in Colorado sent me a bottle filled with specimens of an elegant little mayfly which looked like a dark two-tailed version of the eastern *Ephemerella needhami*, the classic Little Red Quill. The Colorado specimens had hatched in late May and the first days in June, and had resulted in excellent rises of fish.

The specimens were identified as belonging to the *Cinygmula* mayflies, a genus unfamiliar in my experience at that time. However, since that summer almost twenty years ago, mayflies of this genus have appeared several times on rivers that I was fishing, and I have attempted to learn more about them.

Like the other *Heptageniidae*, these mayflies are distinguished by their strongly flattened cross section. The head, thoracic segments, legs, and abdomen are all flattened in shape. The head is somewhat disproportionately large for the size of the nymphs themselves. The prominent ocelli are wholly dorsal in their placement, and the mouthparts are visible only on the ventral surfaces. The adult mayflies are characterized, like the preceding *Heptagenias* and the other genera of this family of fast-water insects, by their five-jointed segments in the tarsi of the rear legs. There are four cubital intercalary veins in the forewings. They are handsome insects.

More specific taxonometric details find the eyes of the male imagoes moderately large and ovoid. The posterior of the female head is slightly immarginate. Forelegs of the male are longer than its body, and in the female, about the same length as its abdomen. Wing venation is typical of the *Heptageniidae* family. Distinctly tinged with grayish-olive, yellow, or amber, the male forceps are four-jointed. The apical margin of the forceps base is somewhat immarginate, although some species have a slightly rounded projection at the median. There is a blunt marginal projection on either side of the forceps. Two short spinules, slightly curved to the outside, are usually found at the apex of the inner margin. Another spinule is often apparent laterally on either lower margin. The subanal plate of the female is well developed. Its posterior structure is notched at the center of its apical margin with a V-shaped indentation.

The frontal margin of the nymphal head is immarginate at its median area, and the mouthparts are quite similar to those found in the *Rhithrogena* nymphs. The femora are somewhat depressed. The claws display three to four pectinations. Gills are found on segments one through seven. These gills have rather indistinct tracheation, with their basal filaments reduced to one or two at the anterior gills. Most of the gills, excepting those on the first body segment, are ovate in configuration. The posterolateral margins of the abdominal segments are only slightly produced, and there are three tails, held rather widely apart.

1. Little Blue-Winged Red Quill (*Cinygmula ramaleyi*)

This species is the taxonometric genotype of the *Cinygmula* flies, and the hatch was sent to me for identification years ago from Colorado. It is a handsome species, typically found hatching at about eight thousand feet in June. Its nymphs average about three-eighths inch in length. The parallel species *Cinygmula par* is found in the southern Rocky Mountains, along with the northern *Cinygmula tarda* found in Canadian waters. Another closely related hatch is the slightly smaller *Cinygmula subaequalis* recorded from North Carolina.

Tails: Pale mottled brownish, ⅜ inch
Body: Mottled grayish brown with pale tan sternites, 5/32 inch
Gills: Mottled grayish brown, 1/32 inch
Thorax: Mottled grayish brown with pale sternites, 1/16 inch
Wing cases: Mottled grayish brown, 1/16 inch
Legs: Mottled grayish brown, ¼ inch
Head: Mottled grayish brown, 1/16 inch

Hook: Sizes 14-16 Mustad 9671 2X long
Nylon: Dark tan 6/0 nylon
Tails: Dark barred lemon woodduck
Body: Dark brownish mottled fur dubbing mixed with hare's mask guard hairs with amber lacquer on belly
Gills: Fine gold oval tinsel
Thorax: Dark brownish mottled fur dubbing with amber sternum lacquer
Wing cases: Dark brownish mottled feather tied down over thorax with quill to simulate median stripe
Legs: Dark brownish mottled partridge hackle
Head: Dark tan nylon

2. Western Gray Fox (*Cinygmula mimus*)

This rather large western species is reported from the rivers of the Rocky Mountains, ranging from northern New Mexico into the high country of Glacier National Park. It is also recorded from Utah, Idaho, and the Sierras of California. Its nymphs average approximately one-half inch in length, and the adults resemble a rather dark version of the eastern *Stenonema fuscum* hatches. Hatching is sporadic and occurs primarily in July.

Cinygmula mimus has sometimes been mistaken for a species from the *Stenonema* genus.

Tails: Pale mottled brownish, 9/16 inch
Body: Dark mottled brown distinctly ringed, ¼ inch
Gills: Dark mottled brown, 1/16 inch
Thorax: Dark mottled brown with a pale median stripe, 3/32 inch
Wing cases: Dark mottled brownish, 3/32 inch
Legs: Dark mottled brownish, ⅜ inch
Head: Dark mottled brownish with a pale median, 1/16 inch

Hook: Sizes 12-14 Mustad 9671 2X long
Nylon: Tan 6/0 nylon
Tails: Light barred woodduck
Body: Pale mottled brownish mixed with hare's ear guard hairs and pale cream lacquer on belly
Gills: Fine gold oval tinsel
Thorax: Pale brownish mottled fur dubbing with pale cream lacquer on sternum
Wing cases: Pale brownish mottled feather tied down over thorax
Legs: Medium brown mottled partridge
Head: Tan nylon

Nymphs of the Swift-Water Stenonema Flies

LATE SPRING and early summer is the time of the *Stenonema* hatches, some of the most important mayflies of the entire season on our American rivers. The days following the early-season species become more pleasant with each passing week. The cowslips and dogtooth violets are gone, and in their place are the shadbush and flowering dogwood, and the choking fragrance of honeysuckle.

Our eastern rivers become watery aisles through a forest arboretum, and finally the earth seems washed clean of winter. There are bright new leaves on the elms and tulip-poplars and beeches, and the oaks are still budding. There are hemlocks and pines in the forest bottoms. There are buttercups and columbine along the river, and later there are rhododendron and laurel. The wind is soft and warm after the April weather, and the air tastes like a fine Chablis. Swallows and phoebes dart and wheel above the riffles, catching the hatching flies in midflight. The trout are fully conscious of the emerging hatches now, and the fly-fisherman has the prospect of myriad insects and heavy rises of feeding fish. It is a season when it becomes possible to take large trout on the well-fished nymph.

More than twenty years ago there was a wonderful morning in the Catskills that I described in *Matching the Hatch* in 1955. It was a raw, blustery day on the Beaverkill that produced two memories—one of a great trout that was captured, and another of an equally large fish that escaped me.

Our failures sometimes remain more stubbornly in the memory than our successes. It was that kind of morning. We were on the big water of the lower Beaverkill, its heavy currents running full after a rainy spring. The first hours had passed without a rise showing at Cairns, and I pushed upstream, taking a few small riffle rainbows from the fast water of Horse Brook Run. There were still no *Stenonemas* hatching, although the flies were long overdue. Suddenly there were occasional rises at the tail of Hendrickson's, and when I reached the pool, it was covered with fluttering duns. There was a heavy splash out along the deep-water boulders, and the cool wind carried its spray.

The big *Stenonema* drakes were everywhere now. The big fish boiled heavily every few seconds, slashing at the hatching flies. When two showy rises came simultaneously, I realized with a quickening pulse that two big trout were working.

Fluttering mayflies were skating across the current in the intermittent gusts. The slashing, spray-scattering rises were exciting, and I watched in fascination for several minutes before I realized I was not fishing.

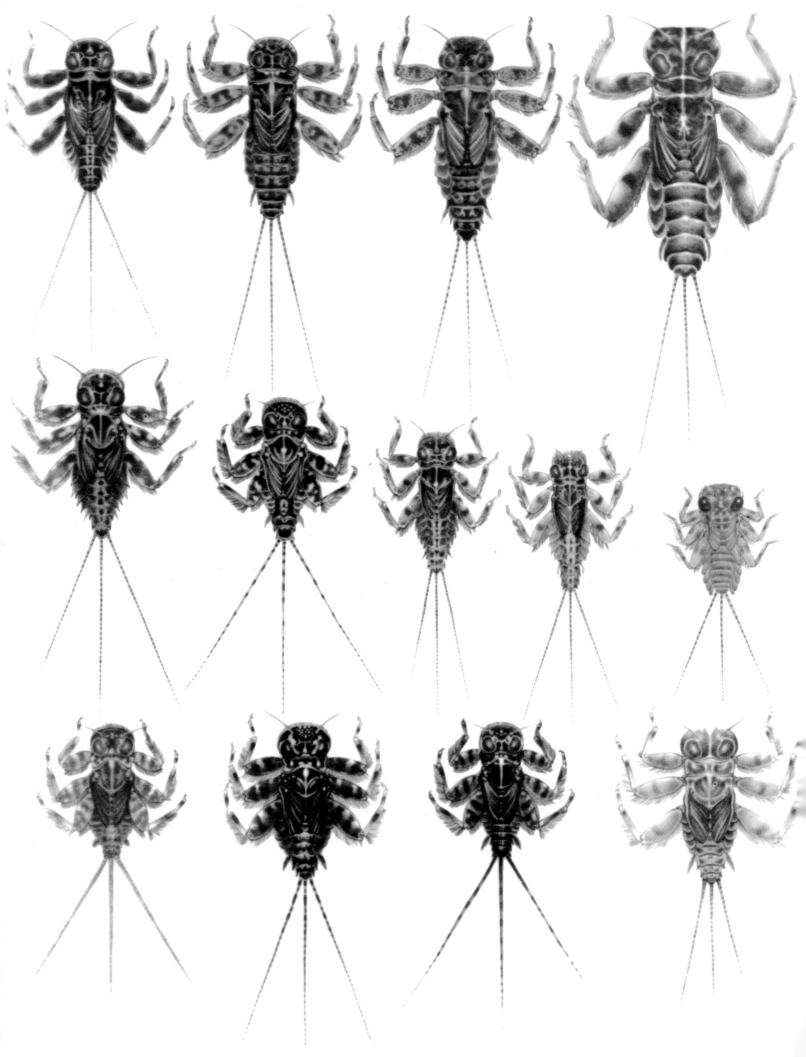

in their hatching behavior, in the sense that they spend considerable time just under the surface and pinioned in the film, escaping their nymphal skins. Most hatching occurs in relatively shallow water, and the trout follow the nymphs there. However, the twenty to forty seconds required for the nymphs to split and shuck their nymphal skins is a relatively long time. I have observed a float-distance of sixty to eighty feet in rainy weather. One of my favorite patterns in those years was an emerging March Brown, which was a *Stenonema* nymph dressed with a scraggly wing of rolled woodduck. Such a pattern is an imitation of the hatching fly about the time its wings are developed, and ready to pop through the surface.

Yet the unusually long period used by the *Stenonemas* in escaping the nymphal skin can mean that the trout may concentrate on any one of several moments in the process. The fish can remain deep, taking the nymphs as they leave the bottom stones, buoyed by the gases generated inside their nymphal skins. The next stage involves the first popping of the wings from their splitting cases, well imitated by the tuft of marabou fibers used in the patterns of E. H. Rosborough in Oregon. Such flies should be fished at moderate depths.

However, there is also a transistory stage of hatching between the first appearance of the wings and their full-blown development just before the winged state. Several years ago Ted Rogowski and I began experimenting with a new emerging nymph material.

Top, left to right: *Stenonema canadense, Stenonema ithaca, Stenonema fuscum, Stenonema vicarium*

Middle, left to right: *Stenonema frontale, Stenonema luteum, Stenonema pallidum, Stenonema proximum, Heptagenia hebe*

Bottom, left to right: *Stenonema integrum, Stenonema nepotellum, Stenonema rubrum, Stenonema carolina*

It was Rogowski who hit on the technique, and I merely suggested the insects with hatching behavior best suited to the imitation of emerging wings, along with some thoughts on proportions. Rogowski outlined the theories in his *Crackerbarrel Discourses*, which appeared in an anthology compiled by the Theodore Gordon Flyfishers in 1965. His theories involved a piece of fine-denier nylon stocking.

What are these wings? I asked at their debut. *Nylon?*

Right! Rogowski laughed and handed me several more hatching nymphs. *They come in great colors these days!*

That's a bachelor for you! growled somebody.

Crackerbarrel regulars looked up from their fly vises. *Okay, Rogowski,* somebody laughed. *How do you collect your materials?*

Martinis or chloroform? I suggested.

Sodium pentothal?

Rogowski ignored our ragging and kept experimenting with pieces of nylon stocking. We evolved several basic concepts. The nymphs were tied of natural furs or dyed polypropylene, depending on whether we wanted the nymph to fish just under the surface or right in the surface film with the high-floating synthetics. Two styles of dressing the nylon wing evolved. The first involved rolling a small rectangle of nylon stocking into a tube about one-eighth inch in diameter, and then folding the tube to tie in its open ends. The second simply tied in the rolled tube, leaving one open end trailing free. The version with both open ends tied in looks neat and professionally tied, while the open-end version looks rough and its fibers soon begin to shred apart—ragged and upkempt, but a fine simulation of the emerging wings.

It is a secret worth knowing. It produced an impressive catch for me some years ago when I fished the little Rolling Rock with my good friend Bill Oliver. The emerging little nylon wing fooled not only the freshly stocked club fish, but also a significant number of sixteen- to nineteen-inch browns that had survived both the fishing pressures of the preceding season and the rigors of winter. There are also times when I wonder how well such hatching imitations might have done on that long-ago week along the Beaverkill, when the heavy *Stenonema* hatches had even the biggest fish working to the hatching nymphs. Such conjecture fills our winters, when we are months away from fishing except in our thoughts.

The *Stenonema* genus includes the largest and most important insects of the entire Heptageniidae family. They are typical in the nymphal state of that family as a whole. Such nymphs are easily identified in their strongly flattened configuration. The heads are proportionately large to their bodies, with their eyes wholly on the dorsal surfaces. The mouthparts are entirely ventral in position.

The *Stenonemas* consist of mayflies ranging from a small five-sixteenths inch wing length to wings of three-quarter inch in the largest species of the genus. The species make up the largest single genus of the Heptageniidae family, and the nymphs are easily distinguished from the other genera of the group. *Stenonema* nymphs are easily identified by the six platelike gills on the first body segments, and the filamentous fingerlike gills on segment seven. There are three slender tails of approximately equal length, their proportions relatively delicate and longer than the nymphs themselves.

The nymphs have high oxygen requirements, and are therefore completely fast-water species. Three nymphal groups are identifiable on their structural characteristics. Each of these three groups has the six platelike gills and the threadlike spinule on segment seven of the abdomen. Most species display a single trachea without lateral branches in this gill. The front of the head is slightly immarginate. The inner canine of the mandible is approximately seven-eighths the length of the outer. Nymphs of the *Tripunctatum* group are identifiable by pectinate claws, and the lamellate portions of their gills on segments one through six are rounded at the apex. Their seventh gill is fringed with long hairs, and is structured with a single forked trachea. Posterolateral spines are present on the middle or apical abdominal segments. The upper margins of the galea-lacinia bear both hairy filaments and tiny spinules. These nymphs form the smallest subgenus, with only three species.

The *Pulchellum* group of nymphs has pectinate claws in some species, but in a few species no pectination occurs. The apical margins of the first six gills are truncate. Gill seven is laterally fringed and lacks a tracheal system. Posterolateral spinules are present on the middle abdominal segments in some species. The upper margins of the galea-lacinia are both hairy and display tiny spinules, just like the *Tripunctatum* nymphs. These large nymphs constitute the largest subgenus, with more than a dozen American species.

The third group consists of the *Interpunctatum* species. These nymphs have no pectinations on their claws. The apical margins of the gills are distinctly pointed. Gill seven can have a few delicate hairs along its margin, and is structured on an unbranched trachea. There are no lateral spines on the middle abdominal segments. The upper margins of the galea-lacinia display a row of tiny pectinate spinules. This is the second-largest group of the three subgenera.

The *Interpunctatum* subgenus includes a number of extremely important American fly hatches, with about a dozen hatches indigenous to our trout streams. Six nymphs have been identified for this chapter from this subgenus of *Interpunctatum* flies.

1. Pale Gray Fox Quill (*Stenonema heterotarsale*)

These grayish-cream mayflies are a pale species which typically hatches from the middle of June until late summer, coming off sporadically from late afternoon until nightfall. Specimens are recorded from Quebec to North Carolina, and westward to Wisconsin and Michigan. The nymphs average about one-half inch in length. The nymphs are common in moderate currents in the eddies and backwaters of larger streams.

Tails: Mottled brownish, 7/16 inch
Body: Pale olive mottled brownish at lateral margins and down dorsal median, above pale olive sternites, ¼ inch
Gills: Pale olive flushed with brownish olive, 1/16 inch
Thorax: Pale olive heavily mottled with brownish olive, defining a pale median stripe above a pale olive sternum, ⅛ inch
Wing cases: Dark brownish olive, 5/32 inch
Legs: Pale olive heavily mottled with brown, ⅜ inch
Head: Olive mottled with brown, 3/32 inch

Hook: Sizes 12-14 Orvis Premium 1X long
Nylon: Pale olive 6/0 nylon
Tails: Dark barred lemon woodduck
Body: Pale olive cream dubbing mottled brownish with a felt-tipped pen at lateral margins, and with a medium brown darning-cotton dorsal stripe above pale sternites
Gills: Pale olive brownish marabou secured with fine gold wire
Thorax: Pale olive cream dubbing
Wing cases: Dark brownish olive feather section with a pale quill tied in over thorax to suggest a pale median
Legs: Brown partridge dyed pale olive
Head: Pale olive nylon

2. Little Sulphur Cahill (*Stenonema carolina*)

This widely distributed species is reported from Quebec to North Carolina, although it is most common in our southeastern streams. Its nymphs average about three-eighths inch in length, and typical hatches emerge in June and early July.

Tails: Pale mottled brown, ⅜ inch
Body: Pale olive flushed with brown, above creamy olive sternites, 3/16 inch
Gills: Pale olive brown, 1/16 inch
Thorax: Pale olive mottled with brown defining a pale median stripe, above a creamy olive sternum, ⅛ inch
Wing cases: Pale purplish olive, 5/32 inch
Legs: Pale olive yellow lightly marked with brown, ⅜ inch
Head: Pale olive brown with a median stripe, 3/32 inch

Hook: Sizes 14-16 Orvis Premium 1X long
Nylon: Pale olive 6/0 nylon
Tails: Medium barred woodduck
Body: Pale olive dubbing mottled dorsally with a felt-tipped pen, leaving pale olive sternites
Gills: Pale olive brown marabou secured with fine gold wire
Thorax: Pale olive dubbing mottled brown dorsally
Wing cases: Pale purplish olive with a pale quill tied down over thorax to simulate median stripe
Legs: Pale brown partridge
Head: Pale olive nylon

3. Little Pale Fox (*Stenonema pallidum*)

This is a pale little hatch which appears in the summer months on trout streams from southern Pennsylvania to North Carolina. The nymphs average about five-sixteenths inch in length.

Tails: Medium mottled brown, 3/8 inch
Body: Medium brown with a dark dorsal median and brownish lateral margins above grayish olive sternites, 3/16 inch
Gills: Dark brownish olive, 1/16 inch
Thorax: Dark brownish olive with a pale dorsal median above a grayish olive sternum, 3/32 inch
Wing cases: Dark brownish olive, 3/32 inch
Legs: Medium olive mottled with dark olive markings, 3/16 inch
Head: Medium brownish olive, 1/16 inch

Hook: Sizes 16-18 Orvis Premium 1X long
Nylon: Medium brown 6/0 nylon
Tails: Barred lemon woodduck
Body: Medium brown dubbing with a dorsal median of darker darning-cotton above sternites of olive gray lacquer
Gills: Dark brownish olive marabou secured with fine gold wire
Thorax: Dark brownish olive dubbing with sternum of olive gray lacquer
Wing cases: Dark brownish olive feather section tied down over thorax with pale median quill
Legs: Dark brown partridge dyed dark olive
Head: Medium brown nylon

4. Little Yellow Fox (*Stenonema proximum*)

The nymphs of this pale little species average about five-sixteenths inch in length. It hatches sporadically from June until September, coming off primarily at twilight. The species is recorded from New England to Minnesota, although Leonard fails to include it in his book *Mayflies of Michigan Trout Streams.*

Tails: Pale mottled brown, 3/8 inch
Body: Pale olive with lateral margins flushed in brown and a dorsal stripe, with grayish sternites, 3/16 inch
Gills: Pale tannish olive, 1/16 inch
Thorax: Medium olive mottled with a grayish sternum, 1/16 inch
Wing cases: Dark purplish brown, 3/32 inch
Legs: Pale tannish olive with distinct femoral mottlings, 1/4 inch
Head: Dark olive heavily mottled in purplish brown, 1/16 inch

Hook: Sizes 16-18 Orvis Premium 1X long
Nylon: Pale olive 6/0 nylon
Tails: Pale barred lemon woodduck
Body: Pale olive dubbing with dark lateral margins and a dorsal median of darker darning-cotton, with sternites of grayish lacquer
Gills: Pale tannish olive marabou secured at sides with fine gold wire
Thorax: Medium olive dubbing with a gray-lacquer sternum
Wing cases: Dark purplish brown feather section tied down over thorax
Legs: Dark brown partridge
Head: Pale olive nylon with brown dorsal lacquer

5. Pale Olive Cahill Quill (*Stenonema frontale*)

This is an entirely northern species almost indistinguishable from *Stenonema canadense,* the well known Light Cahill hatch, in its subimago stages. Its abdominal sternites are somewhat more chalk-colored than the cream-bodied ventral surfaces of *Stenonema canadense,* requiring an extremely pale dry-fly imitation in the style of William Chandler. Its wings have a faint olive cast. This species is recorded from Massachusetts to Michigan, and emerges at twilight from the second week in June until the last week in August. The nymphs seem to prefer gravel-bottomed streams and swift-running currents.

The naturals average one-half inch in length.

Tails: Medium mottled brown, ½ inch
Body: Medium brown with darker lateral margins and a dark dorsal stripe, above pale olive sternites, ¼ inch
Gills: Dark brownish olive, 1/16 inch
Thorax: Dark brownish with a pale median stripe, above a pale olive sternum, 3/32 inch
Wing cases: Medium olive brownish, ⅛ inch
Legs: Pale amber heavily mottled with olive, 5/16 inch
Head: Light brown heavily marked with dark brown, 3/32 inch

Hook: Sizes 12-14 Orvis Premium 1X long
Nylon: Medium brown 6/0 nylon
Tails: Medium barred woodduck
Body: Medium brown dubbing with darker lateral margins and a dark dorsal stripe of darning-cotton, above sternites of pale olive lacquer
Gills: Dark brownish olive marabou secured at sides with fine gold wire
Thorax: Dark brownish dubbing with a sternum of pale olive lacquer
Wing cases: Medium brownish olive with a pale median quill tied down over thorax
Legs: Light brown partridge
Head: Medium brown nylon

6. Light Cahill (*Stenonema canadense*)

This is one of the best-known hatches among the entire *Stenonema* genus, although it was incorrectly identified in the work of some American fishing writers as *Stenonema canadensis,* a nonexistent species. It is widely distributed species, with hatches recorded from Quebec to Minnesota, and south along the coast to North Carolina. Its nymphs are slightly smaller than those of *Stenonema frontale,* averaging seven-sixteenths inch.

The nymphs are commonly found in larger streams, clinging under the stones in fairly rapid currents. The duns typically hatch from early June until late August.

Tails: Dark mottled brown, ½ inch
Body: Dark reddish brown distinctly tinged above pale tannish sternites, 3/16 inch
Gills: Pale tannish brown, 1/16 inch
Thorax: Dark reddish brown with a pale median stripe above a pale tan sternum, ⅛ inch
Wing cases: Dark purplish brown, ⅛ inch
Legs: Dark mottled reddish brown, 3/16 inch
Head: Dark mottled reddish brown, 3/32 inch

Hook: Sizes 14-16 Orvis Premium 1X long
Nylon: Brown 6/0 nylon
Tails: Dark barred woodduck
Body: Dark reddish brown dubbing with sternites of pale tan lacquer
Gills: Pale tannish brown marabou secured at sides with fine gold wire
Thorax: Dark reddish brown dubbing with a sternum of pale tan lacquer
Wing cases: Dark purplish brown with a pale quill tied down over thorax to simulate a median stripe
Legs: Dark brown partridge
Head: Brown nylon

There are only three recorded species in the *Tripunctatum* group of flies. *Stenonema birdi* has been identified from Oklahoma, while *Stenonema femoratum* is also primarily a warm-water species recorded from Ohio to Georgia and South Carolina. However, its genotype *Stenonema tripunctatum* is a trout stream organism.

7. Pale Red Fox (*Stenonema tripunctatum*)

This is primarily a northern species, with hatches recorded from Maine to Minnesota. It is probably the hatch imitated by Edward Ringwood Hewitt for his cream-colored Catskill pattern called the Red Fox. The nymphs average almost five-eighths inch in length, and hatch sporadically from the middle of May until the middle of August.

The nymphs favor moderate currents, clinging under stones or among detritus and leaf drift.

Tails: Pale mottled brown, 7/16 inch
Body: Darkly mottled brownish distinctly ringed above grayish cream sternites, ¼ inch
Gills: Pale grayish, 1/16 inch
Thorax: Dark brownish with a pale median stripe above a grayish cream sternum, ⅛ inch
Wing cases: Dark purplish brown, 5/32 inch
Legs: Amber mottled with brown, 5/16 inch
Head: Dark brownish olive, 3/32 inch

Hook: Sizes 10-12 Orvis Premium 1X long
Nylon: Brown 6/0 nylon
Tails: Pale barred lemon woodduck
Body: Dark brownish dubbing with grayish cream lacquer sternites
Gills: Pale grayish marabou secured at sides with fine oval tinsel
Thorax: Dark brownish dubbing with sternites of grayish cream lacquer
Wing cases: Dark purplish brown with a pale quill median tied down over thorax
Legs: Light brown partridge
Head: Brown nylon

Except for the celebrated *Stenonema canadense* flies, the most important mayflies of this genus are perhaps found in the *Pulchellum* group. These are the well-known *Stenonema fuscum*, called the Ginger Quill or Gray Fox hatches on various rivers, and the largest drake of the genus, the *Stenonema vicarium* or March Brown.

8. Pale Gray Fox (*Stenonema pulchellum*)

This species is archetypical of the subgenus, its nymphs measuring about seven-sixteenths inch in length. Specimens are recorded from New England to the Great Lakes region, and the hatch is locally quite abundant. The nymphs prefer larger streams, where they are found in gravel-bottomed sections. Some specimens are also found clinging in extensive colonies to submerged log jams and deadfalls. Emergence occurs sporadically from the second week in June until the third week in August, and most hatches come off at twilight.

Tails: Pale mottled brown 7/16 inch
Body: Pale brownish olive with dark lateral margins and median stripe, above pale olive gray sternites, ¼ inch
Gills: Medium olive brownish, 1/16 inch
Thorax: Dark olive brown with a pale median stripe, above a pale grayish sternum, ⅛ inch
Wing cases: Dark olive brown, 5/32 inch
Legs: Dark olive heavily mottled with brown, 5/16 inch
Head: Dark olive brownish, 3/32 inch

Hook: Sizes 12-14 Orvis Premium 1X long
Nylon: Medium olive 6/0 nylon
Tails: Pale barred lemon woodduck
Body: Pale brownish olive dubbing with margins darkened by a felt-tipped pen and a dorsal median of dark crewel wool, above sternites of olive gray lacquer
Gills: Medium olive brown marabou secured by fine gold wire
Thorax: Dark brownish olive dubbing with a sternum of olive gray lacquer
Wing cases: Dark olive feather section with a white quill median tied down over thorax
Legs: Dark partridge dyed olive
Head: Medium olive nylon

9. Little Gray Cahill (*Stenonema luteum*)

These tiny nymphs average slightly less than three-eighths inch in length, with specimens recorded in northern watersheds from Quebec to Minnesota. The nymphs are swift-water flies fond of gravel-bottom reaches of river. Hatching occurs from late June until the end of August.

Tails: Dark olive heavily mottled with brown, ½ inch
Body: Dark purplish olive distinctly ringed above grayish olive sternites, 5/32 inch
Gills: Dark purplish olive, 1/16 inch
Thorax: Dark purplish olive with a pale median stripe and grayish olive sternum, 3/32 inch
Wing cases: Dark purplish brown, ⅛ inch
Legs: Pale olive mottled with dark purplish brown, 5/16 inch
Head: Dark purplish brown, 3/32 inch

Hook: Sizes 14-16 Orvis Premium 1X long
Nylon: Dark brown 6/0 nylon
Tails: Darkly barred woodduck
Body: Dark purplish olive dubbing with sternites of grayish olive lacquer
Gills: Dark purplish olive marabou secured at sides with fine gold wire
Thorax: Dark purplish olive dubbing with a sternum of grayish olive lacquer
Wing cases: Dark purplish brown with a pale median quill tied down over thorax
Legs: Dark partridge dyed pale olive
Head: Dark brown nylon

10. Pale Olive Cahill (*Stenonema rubrum*)

The nymphs of this little species are slightly larger than three-eighths inch in length. Specimens have been collected on widespread rivers from the Great Lakes region to Quebec, and south along the eastern seaboard to North Carolina. Its nymphs are fond of the open gravel-bottomed riffles of medium-sized to large rivers, and emergence is sporadic from the second week in June until the middle of August.

Tails: Dark mottled brownish, 7/16 inch
Body: Dark purplish brown distinctly ringed, with grayish tan sternites and a touch of rusty scarlet at tails, 3/16 inch
Gills: Medium purplish gray, 1/32 inch
Thorax: Dark purplish brown with pale median stripe, above grayish tan sternum, 3/32 inch
Wing cases: Dark purplish brown, ⅛ inch
Legs: Dark olive heavily mottled with brown, ¼ inch
Head: Dark olive heavily mottled, 1/16 inch

Hook: Sizes 14-16 Orvis Premium 1X long
Nylon: Dark brown 6/0 nylon
Tails: Darkly barred lemon woodduck
Body: Dark purplish brown spun on ruby silk, allowing the scarlet to show through at tails, with grayish tan lacquer sternites
Gills: Medium purplish gray marabou secured with fine gold wire
Thorax: Dark purplish brown dubbing with a grayish tan lacquer sternum
Wing cases: Dark purplish brown feather section tied down over thorax with a white quill median
Legs: Dark partridge dyed olive
Head: Dark brown nylon

This species is quite similar in the nymphal state to *Stenonema rubromaculatum,* most certainly the insect that resulted in the Pink Lady much favored by the late George La Branche. Its imagoes have a distinct pinkish cast to their bodies.

11. Pale Cahill Quill (*Stenonema integrum*)

This hatch is found in swift little rivers from Michigan and Wisconsin south to Texas, Georgia, and North Carolina. It is found in somewhat warmer rivers than its sister species, and is quite common on the man-made Ozark trout streams. Hatching activity occurs from the middle of July until the last week in August.

This hatch is undoubtedly the prototype for the Paulinskill dry-fly pattern originated by Ray Bergman. The nymphs average about three-eighths inch in length, and the imitative pattern follows:

Tails: Dark olive mottled with
brown, ½ inch
Body: Dark olive mottled with
brown above pale olive gray
sternites, 3/16 inch
Gills: Medium brownish olive, 1/16
inch
Thorax: Medium brownish with a
pale median stripe above a pale
olive gray sternum, 3/32 inch
Wing cases: Dark brownish olive,
⅛ inch
Legs: Olive gray mottled with brown,
¼ inch
Head: Olive mottled with brown,
1/16 inch

Hook: Sizes 14-16 Orvis Premium 1X
long
Nylon: Dark brown 6/0 nylon
Tails: Darkly barred lemon
woodduck
Body: Dark olive dubbing mottled
with brown, and yith pale olive
lacquer suggesting sternites
Gills: Medium olive marabou
secured with fine gold wire
Thorax: Dark olive dubbing with a
pale olive lacquer sternum
Wing cases: Dark brownish olive
feather section tied down over
thorax
Legs: Dark partridge dyed olive
Head: Dark brown nylon

12. Olive Cahill Quill (*Stenonema nepotellum*)

This rather dark little *Stenonema* is distributed from Quebec to Minnesota and Wisconsin. Extensive populations are found in New York and Pennsylvania trout streams. The species is particularly well suited to fairly fast currents, both rapids and gravelly riffles. Hatching usually occurs just at twilight, although some flies are often observed coming off in late afternoon in rainy weather, and emergence has been recorded sporadically from late June until early October.

The nymphs are seven-sixteenths inch in length.

Tails: Dark mottled brownish, 1/16
inch
Body: Dark mottled olive brownish
above pale olive gray sternites,
3/16 inch
Gills: Dark olive brown, 1/16 inch
Thorax: Dark olive brown mottling
with a pale median stripe above
a pale olive sternum, 3/32 inch
Wing cases: Dark brownish olive,
5/32 inch
Legs: Dark olive heavily mottled
with brown, 5/16 inch
Head: Dark olive mottled with
brown, 3/32 inch

Hook: Sizes 14-16 Orvis Premium 1X
long
Nylon: Dark brown 6/0 nylon
Tails: Darkly barred woodduck
Body: Dark olive brown dubbing
with olive gray lacquer sternites
Gills: Dark olive brown marabou
secured at sides with fine gold
wire
Thorax: Dark olive brown dubbing
with olive gray sternum
Wing cases: Dark brownish olive
feather section with a white quill
tied down over thorax
Legs: Dark partridge dyed olive
Head: Dark brown nylon

13. Light Gray Fox (*Stenonema ithaca*)

The nymphs average one-half inch in length. Emergence occurs typically from the middle of July until the last week in August. Although somewhat paler than the better-known *Stenonema fuscum* mayflies, these insects are quite similar. Their importance varies considerably from river to river, since local populations are often sparse or quite extensive. Specimens are found from Quebec to North Carolina, with good populations west to Michigan and Wisconsin.

Tails: Dark mottled brownish, ½
inch
Body: Dark mottled brown distinctly
ringed, with pale grayish olive
sternites, ¼ inch
Gills: Medium brownish, 1/16 inch
Thorax: Dark mottled brown with a
pale median stripe, ⅛ inch
Wing cases: Dark purplish brown,
⅛ inch
Legs: Dark olive heavily mottled
with brown, ⅜ inch
Head: Dark olive heavily mottled,
3/32 inch

Hook: Sizes 12-14 Orvis Premium 1X
long
Nylon: Dark brown 6/0 nylon
Tails: Dark barred lemon woodduck
Body: Dark mottled brownish
dubbing, with sternites of cream
lacquer
Gills: Medium brown marabou
secured with fine gold wire
Thorax: Dark mottled brownish
dubbing, with a cream lacquer
sternum
Wing cases: Dark purplish brown
feather section tied over thorax
with a pale quill
Legs: Dark partridge dyed olive
Head: Dark brown nylon

14.   Dark Gray Fox (*Stenonema fuscum*)

This has been a familiar fly hatch to American anglers since Preston Jennings published his *Book of Trout Flies* in 1935. It has also been written about in the books of writers like Wetzel, Flick, and Grove. During cloudy weather these pale, mottled little mayflies can emerge sporadically throughout the afternoon, although hatching is usually concentrated in late afternon and lasts until nightfall.

Tails: Medium mottled brownish, ½
inch
Body: Medium brown heavily
mottled with brown and distinctly
ringed, above grayish cream
sternites, ¼ inch
Gills: Medium reddish brown, 1/16
inch
Thorax: Medium mottled brownish
with a pale median stripe above
a grayish cream sternum, 5/32
inch
Wing cases: Medium purplish olive,
5/32 inch
Legs: Medium brownish heavily
mottled with dark brown, 5/16
inch
Head: Medium brownish flecked
with pale spots, 3/32 inch

Hook: Sizes 12-14 Orvis Premium 1X
long
Nylon: Medium brown 6/0 nylon
Tails: Medium barred woodduck
fibers
Body: Medium brown dubbing
heavily mottled with darker felt
pen, and sternites of creamish
gray lacquer
Gills: Medium reddish brown
marabou secured with fine gold
wire
Thorax: Medium brown dubbing
with grayish cream sternum
Wing cases: Medium purplish olive
feather section with a white quill
median tied down over thorax
Legs: Darkly mottled partridge
Head: Medium brown nylon

The species is widely distributed, having been observed on widespread rivers from Quebec to the Middle Atlantic states, and westward to Michigan and Wisconsin. Populations are dense and indigenous to almost every suitable habitat in this range. The nymphal forms relish medium-fast currents, clinging to the dark side of their bottom stones. Specimens in my collection are nine-sixteenths inch long, rather fat and juicy, with thick, somewhat flattened femora. *Stenonema fuscum* hatches from the middle of May until the middle of July, although peak emergence comes in late May and early June. It is a major fly hatch.

15.   American March Brown (*Stenonema vicarium*)

This species is the largest drake of this rather sizable genus. Its nymphs average a robust five-eighths to three-quarters inch. Although its hatches are never as heavy as those of the *Stenonema canadense* and *fuscum* mayflies, its larger size can attract very big trout to both the nymphs and its emerging subimagoes. Sometimes there are very heavy hatches, which can lead to rises of fish like those described on the Beaverkill in the opening passages of this chapter, or the wonderful nymph feeding described by Art Flick in his *Streamside Guide*.

Like the stoneflies, these nymphs are often found under the stones in moderate to rapid currents. Some specimens cling to deadfalls and log jams, with others concealing themselves in bottom detritus and leaf drift. There is another pattern of behavior that parallels the fast-water Plecoptera flies. It is the habit of migrating into relatively shallow water before emergence, although they split the nymphal skin in the surface film rather than crawling on a stone to hatch.

Stenonema vicarium typically emerges from the first week in May until the middle of June, although some subimagoes have been observed as late as the third week in July.

Tails: Medium mottled brownish, ⅝ inch
Body: Medium brownish distinctly ringed, and with pale cream-colored sternites, 5/16 inch
Gills: Medium reddish brown, 3/32 inch
Thorax: Dark mottled brown with a pale median stripe above a cream-colored sternum, 3/16 inch
Wing cases: Dark purplish brown, 3/16 inch
Legs: Medium brown darkly mottled with brown, ½ inch
Head: Dark mottled brown with a pale median, ⅛ inch

Hook: Sizes 10-12 Orvis Premium 1X long
Nylon: Dark brown 6/0 nylon
Tails: Dark mottled woodduck
Body: Medium brownish dubbing with dark felt-pen margins and median stripe, and with creamish gray lacquer sternites
Gills: Medium reddish brown marabou secured with fine oval gold tinsel
Thorax: Dark mottled brown dubbing with a creamish gray lacquer sternum
Wing cases: Dark purplish brown with a white quill median tied down over thorax
Legs: Dark brownish partridge
Head: Dark brown nylon

These nymphal imitations of the *Stenonema* genus give us a number of prototypes for matching a subaquatic hatch. Weighted versions could be fashioned with fine brass dressmaker's pins wrapped on either side of the hook shank. This both sinks the nymph for fishing it deep in the broken water, and creates a flat core for its body and thorax suggestive of the natural insects. Lightwire hooks, pieces of heavy monofilament wrapped along the hook shank, and fur dubbing can fashion nymphs that fish quite shallow under the surface. The same hooks, and nylon flat-body foundation can also be dubbed with polypropylene, and its specific gravity and floating qualities will shape a nymph that rides virtually in the surface film. The nylon-stocking wing can be used with these last two prototypes, suggesting the wings of an emerging nymph.

Since these nymphs can occupy from fifteen to forty-five seconds, drifting in or slightly below the surface while hatching, the trout may focus on any stage of this rather lengthy process. Given these several clues, an observant fisherman should be able to discover what stage of the hatch is interesting the trout, and to dress special nymphs capable of fooling them.

The Hump-Backed Nymphs of the Baetisca Flies

T HE NEVERSINK headwaters rise in one of the last completely undeveloped valleys in the east, since its principal mileage lies in a series of country estates with histories almost a century in the past. It is all private water, and since the completion of the Neversink Reservoir, with its extremes of flow on the once-famous mileage around Bridgeville, the headwaters are really all that remains of a river that Theodore Gordon and Edward Ringwood Hewitt praised in their writings for its fine sport, cold temperatures, and remarkable clarity.

Most of the famous Hewitt water lies at the bottom of the reservoir now, but its rough camp and log-cribbing pools and the battered old limousine with its holes cut in the roof for fly rods still live in *The Fly and the Fish*, the elegant book written and illustrated by the late Jack Atherton.

The headwaters of the Neversink are surprisingly cold, since other Catskill streams usually tightrope between trout temperatures and the lukewarm preferences of bass and bluegills in midsummer. It is probably the biggest piece of eastern water south of Maine that still supports a population of wild brook trout. Several of the landowners do not stock their mileage, and there are no pools filled with foolish truck-fish like most private water in the east. Patient stream improvement and wild fish are their preferences, and the cold, incredibly clear river is its own reward. It is a result of an isolation that discouraged development, and landowners totally disinterested in profit at the expense of change that could irrevocably damage the crystalline river they have loved for generations. It is a valley where time has stopped.

There are deer in the valley that are much prized in the Catskills, big whitetails grown apple-fat on the fruit of colonial orchards long overgrown with second-growth timber. Woodcock and grouse are plentiful for men who know the covers, and pileated woodpeckers are not uncommon. Several bears are regularly seen along the river, and in recent years there was a report of a puma. Such solitude is getting scarce in the Catskills.

Leonard Wright is a skilled fly-fisherman and fly-tier who lives much of the year in the Catskills, spending many hours on the Neversink each season. His knowledge of its fish and its fly hatches is thorough and complete, and his stubborn refusal to accept angling fashion in either fly-dressing or tackle is an index of his character.

We were fishing the river late in May a few seasons ago when he asked me a startling question. *What do you know about the Baetisca flies?* he said over lunch.

The little humpbacked flies? I asked.

The nymphs are pretty ugly, Wright continued, *and the subimagoes are like a deformed March Brown.*

Don't know much about them, I admitted. *I've never seen a river where they've been important.*

You have now, he said.

We finished coffee spiced with a little cognac, slipped into our waders, and hiked down to the river. It flowed swift and cold along a fifty-yard cribbing Wright had built by himself, wrestling the logs and stones into place manually.

Wright reached into the swift riffle and extracted a pair of grapefruit-sized stones. Their undersides were thick with *Rivularia* scum and several little tent-shaped forms that did not move until most of the water had dripped from the stone. They looked like tent-shaped caddis cases, with their exaggerated dorsal carapaces. These bony wing cases covered not only the thoracic structure, but also the first body segments and gills.

Baetisca! Wright announced. *Baetisca nymphs and the river's full of them!* He dropped several into my hand.

Look at these tent-shaped backs, I said. *They're really triangular through the thorax—no wonder Hewitt wrote about filing a triangular slot in a pair of sharp-nosed pliers!*

Exactly, Wright agreed. *He did it to make a template that could shape a nymph body of fat dubbing soaked with lacquer.*

That explains his triangular nymphs! I said.

Since that spring afternoon on the Neversink, I have learned more about the *Baetisca* mayflies. There are apparently six species indigenous to American waters, and they are widely distributed in cold, relatively acid watersheds. Such preferences in habitat could explain their importance in the Upper Neversink. Both the nymphs and the adults differ strikingly in proportion to the size of their wings. Their configuration is unique.

The *Baetisca* genus is the only group found in the mayfly subfamily classified as the Baetiscinae. The rather stout-bodied nymphs are utterly unique among our American ecotypes. Their most striking feature is the exaggerated dorsal carapace, its bony, shell-like structure covering the legs, thoracic sections, the first five abdominal segments, and the tracheal gills. The dorsal surface of the sixth body segment bears a conspicuous triangular prominence which anchors the posterior margins of the carapace. The final body segments taper quickly to the three tails. These tails are nearly equal in length, and are relatively short compared with the proportions of the complete nymph. The legs are also relatively short for such a robust nymphal form; both head and carapace are marked by hornlike projections.

Taxonometric details are found in *The Biology of Mayflies,* beginning with the mesonotal shield of the carapace. This bony structure covers the dorsum of the mesothorax, metathorax, and the first five body segments. It also covers the basal half of the sixth segment. Its apical margin dovetails precisely with the pyramidal enlargement on segment six. Such an exaggerated thoracic shield is found elsewhere only in the rare *Prosopistoma* mayflies of northern Europe.

Dorsal and lateral spines are usually present, although not on every specimen. The head frequently bears more or less prominent frontal projections. There are also spiny projections from the anterior angles of the genae. The second joint of the labial palp bears a spiny projection on its inner margin, which forms a pincerlike structure with its distal joint. The posterolateral spines are more or less well developed on each of the body segments from six through nine. The three tails are fringed with delicate hairs, except at their extreme bases. They are often held erect or reflexed over the abdomen. The rather short legs consist of a femur that approximately equals the length of the tibia and tarsus combined. The claws are not denticulate, and are rather sharp and slender.

1.   Humpbacked Nymph (*Baetisca obesa*)

This species is designated the genotype typical of the *Baetisca* flies as a whole. Since the nymphal forms of the six American species are virtually indistinguishable, except for differences of geographic distribution and minor taxonometric distinctions, only one imitation in several sizes is required. The nymphs vary from about three-sixteenths to seven-sixteenths inches in length.

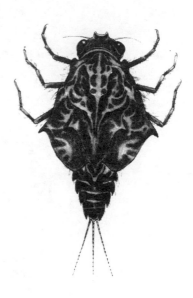

Tails: Dark mottled brown, 3/16 inch
Body: Dark grayish olive distinctly ringed with brown, 3/16 inch
Thorax: Dark grayish olive, ¼ inch
Legs: Dark brownish, 3/16 inch
Carapace: Dark brownish olive, ¼ inch
Head: Dark olive brown, 1/16 inch

Hook: Sizes 12-18 Mustad 7948A
Nylon: Dark brown 6/0 nylon
Tails: Brown mallard fibers
Body: Dark muskrat dubbed on olive silk
Ribbing: Dark rusty brown dubbing wrapped on olive silk
Thorax: Dark muskrat dubbing roughly mixed with mottled brownish guard hairs from a hare's mask
Legs: Suggested by the thorax guard hairs
Carapace: Two sections of dark brown olive-dyed goose quill sections tied on either side of the tent-shaped thorax
Head: Dark brown nylon

My technique of dressing the imitations to suggest their triangular cross section is simple. It involves tying a soft brass wire in along the top of the hook shank, its free end protruding about an inch ahead of the eye. Leaving about a thirty-second inch behind the eye, the wire is then bent back and tied down at the posterior point of the thorax. This creates an arched, airfoil-shaped outrigger above the hook shank. The wire is then used to support a body core constructed of rayon floss, winding it around both the wire ridge-beam and two tiny brass pins wound under the nylon working thread at the hook shank. With the wire securely anchored and wrapped, the resulting floss foundation becomes a roughly triangular cross section with the hook shank as its base. Then the fly is conventionally tied with well-waxed nylon on this shaped foundation.

Bastica callosa is distributed from Quebec to West Virginia, and its three-sixteenths-inch nymphs are imitated with the above pattern on size eighteen hooks. The closely related species *Baetisca carolina* is recorded

from the eastern seaboard, with particularly good populations in North Carolina. It is imitated with the Humpbacked Nymph dressed on a fourteen hook. *Baetisca lacustris* is found from New Brunswick to Minnesota, and a size twelve hook is perfect. The slightly smaller *Baetisca laurentina* is recorded from Quebec to the trout rivers of Michigan. The ecotype described above is the most widely distributed of our *Baetisca* flies, with specimens reported from New Hampshire to North Carolina. Its imitations should be dressed on size twelve. The diminutive *Baetisca rubescens* is principally recorded from New England and the Maritime Provinces of Canada.

These imitations should perhaps be weighted, using brass pins suggested for seating under the wrapped nylon working thread at either side of the hook shank. Since the *Baetisca* nymphs inhabit heavy currents and are clumsy swimmers, imitations should be fished dead-drift. Sometimes these nymphs are so covered with *Rivularia* and detritus that they literally become the color of the river bottom.

The Ubiquitous Nymphs of the Ephemerella Flies

THE MAYFLIES of the *Ephemerella* genus are the largest and most widely distributed nymphs of all the American aquatic species. They are found in virtually all types of water, from slow eddies and backwaters carpeted with leaf drift to the tiny collections of detritus between the stones in surprisingly heavy currents. The principal fly hatches on European rivers are members of this genus, like the classic *Ephemerella ignita* of the British chalkstreams of Hampshire, and they are equally important on most American waters.

Their abundance is almost legendary on rivers well suited to their requirements. Field studies revealed more than twelve hundred specimens from a single square-foot bottom sample taken at Lovells on the North Branch of the Au Sable in Michigan. My own studies on the Lower Musconetcong in New Jersey and the particularly rich Yellow Breeches in Pennsylvania reveal similar densities.

The *Ephemerella* genus includes a number of famous fly hatches in all parts of the country. There are the storied Hendricksons and Blue-Winged Olives and Sulphurs on our eastern rivers, and these hatches are important in our Great Lakes region too. There are Red Quills of several sizes. Western hatches like the Pale Morning Duns and Pale Olive Quills and Great Red Quills are *Ephemerellas* too, and the biggest Mayflies found on western rivers are probably the superb Great Lead-Wing Olive Drakes that emerge from the middle of June until early July in the Rocky Mountains—the fluttering dark-winged *Ephemerella grandis* that creates incredible rises of trout on the Madison and Yellowstone and Henry's Fork.

Every angler has a favorite hatch of flies on his home rivers, and that favorite echoes his experience in the timeless cycle of the seasons. Each river is unique, too, with its own fingerprint of fly hatches. Our favorites change with our rivers, and the layers of time that accumulate in the mind are like the tree rings in the buttonwoods above a favorite pool. My own fly-fishing life has been similar.

My book *Remembrances of Rivers Past* includes a chapter on the several Hendrickson-type hatches that occur on our rivers from Michigan to Massachusetts, and south along the seacoast into the mountains of North Carolina. These classic *Ephemerellas* are probably my favorite fly hatches across the many years.

Although I have enjoyed the Hendrickson hatches on many rivers for almost thirty years, from the gentle Nissequogue on Long Island to the swift Brule in Wisconsin, it is difficult to choose a favorite river for these mayflies. There are good hatches on Adirondack rivers like the Ausable and Saranac and Chazy, and across Lake Champlain in Vermont there are fine *Ephemerellas* on the Otter, the Battenkill, and the Lamoille. There are heavy hatches on all of the Catskill rivers, the shrines of American fly-fishing history, and on my home rivers like the Musconetcong and Brodheads these hatches are often the highlight of the entire season.

Yet when my thoughts turn to these prolific blue-winged *Ephemerella* flies, the memory invariably drifts back to the boyhood rivers of Michigan where I first fished them. There were excellent hatches then, and we fished them all over the years, from the Pere Marquette to the swift-flowing Sturgeon—but the best of those storied Michigan rivers in the time of the Hendricksons was always the beautiful Au Sable.

It is a river of many secrets, its several branches born in the cedar swamps and spring bogs of northern Michigan. Its Middle Branch rises in a series of springs east of Otsego Lake, and is joined by the tamarack-bog flowage of Bradford Creek east of the long-abandoned logging camp at Deward. The East Branch merges its marl-swamp flowage in the town of Grayling, forming the main river with its currents from the pickerelweed shallows of Loon Lake. The Main Branch is a full-blown river now, winding through the sandy moraines and second-growth forests below Grayling. Its bottom is pale, amber-colored gravel and its smooth currents are broken by deadfalls of cedar and pine. It is these tangled deadfalls that are part of its secret, since they shelter a surprisingly large population of trout, and the rest of the secret is its rich alkalinity—born in the lime-marl bogs and subterranean limestone of this sand-country forest.

Fish them sweepers! Earl Madsen used to chide my father. *Get your fly in closer to them sweepers!* He held the slender Au Sable boat steady in the current. *That's where the fish are!*

Madsen was right, and fishing tight against the deadfalls is critical on the Au Sable. *Fish them sweepers*, he repeated.

It's not so easy! My father smiled.

The main river gathers its strength slowly, flowing past the fishing camp at Wash-Ka-Da, and spreading into the wide riffles below the canoe landing at Stephan's Bridge. It is named for Henri Stephan, who emigrated to America with his family from the cathedral city of Rouen in France, and whose sons became well-known guides on the river. The river receives the flow of cedar-swamp springs below the Black Bend stretch, and Barker Creek comes in from the north above the Rainbow Camp. It is a full-blown river at Wakeley Bridge, where the half-day floats from Stephan's come out, flowing deep and strong in the twilight.

The famous South Branch is next. It rises near Roscommon and Lake Saint Helen south of Grayling, winding northeast through a surprisingly wild region. Beaver Creek comes in below Roscommon, and then the South Branch flows east into the stretch once owned by the late George Mason. It reaches the main river below Smith Bridge and the Oxbow Club. Several cold feeders come into the river there, and the fourteen-mile reach of water remains virtually unchanged since logging days, except for the storied cabin where Mason had his headquarters. Mason willed his holdings to the fly-fishermen of Michigan in 1954, with the stipulation that no roads or improvements be built into his old property. The reserve is about fourteen miles long and three miles wide, with the river as its spine, and Mason insisted in transferring title that access be restricted to either walking or float trips—and that his river be fished in perpetuity without killing its trout, and with fly-fishing only.

The North Branch is a legend in itself. The river rises in a series of springs north of Lovells, the logging camp named after a timber company surveyor, gathering the flowages of Opal and Turtle Lakes. It is already good-sized when it reaches the site of Dam Two, about ten miles north of Lovells. The dam was built by logging engineers and lumberjacks in 1869, opening up the vast timber reserves of the North Branch. Dam Three was not far above Lovells, and Dam Four was four miles downstream. Their impoundments were used to collect and float huge rafts of logs, carrying them downriver in the spring floods. The lumbering was in full swing when the Jackson, Lansing, and Saginaw pushed its trackage from Grayling across the pine flats to Lovells. Its giant sawmill was completed with the right-of-way. The railroad brought civilization and fishermen—although the North Branch must have been incredible in the quality of its sport to survive the rapacity of the timber barons.

There were a number of hotels and fishing camps built there about the turn of the century. The Douglas Hotel was the focal point of a sawmill and railroad town with more than a thousand people, and Tom Douglas was its spiritual leader. Edward Kellogg built his cabin at Kellogg's Bridge, and later contracted to build log cabins and fishing houses for sportsmen in the valley. William Mershon developed his famous place below Lovells, and in books like *The Passenger Pigeon* and *Recollections of My Fifty Years Hunting and Fishing,* Mershon recorded his concern and sorrow for the decimation of his Michigan wilderness. There were other places on the river, too, like the Kantagree Club and Halfway House and the Morley Place. Big Creek is the principal feeder of the North Branch, and its Big Creek Lodge has long been a privately held fishing reserve of some eight hundred acres. Big Creek joins the river below the Kellogg Bridge. Between its mouth, and the stretch where the North Branch joins the main Au Sable below McMasters Bridge there are a number of famous fishing camps. Scott's Lodge is a series of pleasant cabins below the mouth of Big Creek, and the old Pierce-Breakey Camp lies at Flashlight Bend. Arnold Copeland was once poet-in-residence on the river, fishing from his Brush 'n Rod not far downstream, and Hazen Miller has his fishing house nearby, with this fragment of Shakespeare above its door:

And this our life, exempt from public haunt
Finds tongues in trees and books in running brooks,
Sermons in stones, and good in everything.
I would not change it.

The main river is already powerful in the famed Stillwater below the South Branch, and it is almost too much water for fly-fishing. Downstream from the McMaster's Bridge and the mouth of the North Branch, the Au Sable is a compelling force.

It has a surprisingly long history that reaches back into centuries of tribal lore. Its utilization as a primary water route across Michigan is relatively ancient, and its currents were well traveled when the Ojibwa and Chippewa and Ottawa tribes fished and trapped and hunted its forests. French influence in Michigan began with the expedition mounted by Etienne Brulé in 1618, and the *voyageurs* trapped and traded furs and explored its wilderness in the century that followed. It was these *voyageurs* who named it the Au Sable.

Both the aboriginal tribes and the trappers used the river to cross the lower peninsula of Michigan. Leaving the wind-swept expanse of Lake Huron above Saginaw Bay, they traveled upriver more than two hundred miles on its winding, riffle-bright currents until they reached the river-bend site of modern Grayling.

The Au Sable turns north there, and the hardy *voyageurs* trekked a few miles overland to the reedy shallows of Portage Lake. Like the Indians before them, their encampments were made on the sheltered north shore, and from there it was a simple morning portage to the headwaters of the Manistee. It carried them swiftly downstream almost three hundred miles by river to Lake Michigan, in a journey that is now repeated every summer by campers in canoes.

Saginaw was established as a frontier garrison and trading outpost in 1819, and when Alexis de Tocqueville arrived there twelve years later, the Au Sable country was still unmapped wilderness. James Lanman described the country in his *History of Michigan* in 1839, referring to the heavy populations of beaver, bear, otter, wolverines, deer, panthers, elk, porcupines, and wolves that existed above Saginaw. Lanman also speculated on the worth of the vast acreage of Michigan timber.

Henry Schoolcraft had already negotiated his Treaty of Saginaw in 1836, opening the Michigan Territories to the railroads and timber barons and settlement. It was both the beginning of modern Michigan and the end of a unique wilderness frontier. Development came slowly in the marginal forest soils of the Au Sable country until the mines, and the buildings of the railroads, and the Civil War created an insatiable market for Michigan lumber. Its timber camps grew so quickly that operations were in full swing long before Appomattox Courthouse. The spring log drives used the thawing spates of late winter to carry the timber to Lake Huron, and in the thirty years that followed, more than five billion board-feet were cut from the watershed of the Au Sable. The lumberjacks cut a third of a billion board-feet in 1890 alone, and the woods were filled with the thunder of falling trees and the scream of sawmills. The spirit of these log drivers is captured in the verses that Douglas Malloch included in his book *Tote Road and Trail* in somewhat different form:

> There's folks that loves the good dry land,
>   And folks that likes the sea,
> But rock and current, shoals and sand
>   Are good enough for me!
> There's folks that loves the ocean's crests,
>   And folks that lives in town,

> But what I really loves the best is
>   When the drives goes down!
> So pole away, you river rats,
>   From the log-slides to the lake.
> There's miles o' pine to keep in line,
>   Five hundred jams to break!

The miracle of the river lies in its past ability to survive such ecological damage, at the scope of five billion board-feet in uncontrolled cut-and-slash lumbering over only thirty years. The clearing of the sweepers and log jams and deadfalls from the channels of the Au Sable watershed came first, opening the river to the log drives that followed. The sluice dams followed, with their impoundments to collect the timber on the ice, snaking the big trees out of the woods on the snow. The lumberjacks cleared the forest, taking the pines for lumber and stripping hemlock bark for the tanneries, leaving the trees to rot. There was no shade left on the rivers, the soil eroded swiftly into the watercourses and logging dams, and the roots of the coniferous trees were lost too—with their unequaled ability to entrain rainfall in the earth gone, every springhead in the region ran a few degrees warmer.

The logging-dam impoundments raised the river temperatures too, while their stillwaters erased the fast-water hatches. Silt collected behind their cribbings and settled in the quiet reaches of the river. Sawdust from the mills was added, its decay contributing to the acidity of the river, and combining with the silt to smother both riffle hatches and spawning beds. The man-made floods released from the dams did flush the silt accumulations, but they also scoured the bottom of zoöplankton, killed fish, and eradicated insect life. The log drives themselves scarred the shallows and smashed deadfall cover and uprooted cedars and willows along the banks. Between the drives, an army of fishermen killed trout and grayling in vast numbers, both for sport and for the fish markets farther south. Dozens of ice wagons took fish daily to the railhead at Grayling and Lovells, for shipment to the posh Victorian dining rooms in Detroit and Grand Rapids and Chicago. It was still a time of plenty.

The gentle Michigan grayling was already doomed to extinction. The rapacity of the lumber barons had already left the thin forest soil naked and exposed. Warming springheads had ended their ecosystem forever, without the side effects of logging dams, silt and sawdust, man-made flooding, and the log drives.

There were river men who understood the danger, but they were outcasts who worked only when it suited them, and even then they lived by guiding sportsmen or timber surveyors, jacklighting a deer in the river bottoms when they wanted meat. Such men had no political influence in the legislature or the cities.

Their names are forgotten except among those who have fished the Au Sable since boyhood. The most colorful was probably Chief Shoppenagons, the Saginaw tribal leader who lived out his years guiding hunters and fishermen along the river. There were Arthur Wakeley, whose father was a one-armed veteran of the Civil War, Ike Stillwagon, Charles Shellenbarger, Henri Stephan, Len Jewell, and Rube Babbitt on the main Au Sable. Tom Douglas, Vinegar Bill Christenson, and Ed Kellogg were early guides on the North Branch. It was Len Jewell, battle-scarred veteran of the 14th Michigan Infantry in the Civil War, who guided famous anglers like Fred Mather, Seth Green, Grover Cleveland, and Thaddeus Norris on the Au Sable.

However, it is perhaps Rube Babbitt who is best remembered on the Au Sable for his role in its history. His father had come to Grayling in 1873 with a surveying party for the Jackson, Lansing and Saginaw Line. The elder Babbitt liked the country and stayed on, settling in a frontier farmstead along the Au Sable. It should come as no surprise that his sons grew up with the rhythms of the river in their blood.

Rube Babbitt was a favorite guide of Judge Daniel Fitzhugh, and the two men often fished the Au Sable together. It was entirely a grayling river then, and apparently no one realized then that it was a unique species, endemic only to the Lower Peninsula of Michigan. Judge Fitzhugh sent specimens of the fish to Washington, where the government biologists decided they were an unclassified strain of grayling. Market fishermen continued to ship them to Chicago and Detroit restaurants at incredible prices of twenty-five cents a pound, and both fishing pressure and the logging camps had set irrevocable forces in motion. The grayling could not be saved, in spite of the efforts of Judge Fitzhugh and William Mershon. However, these anglers saw the need for a new species capable of surviving the warmer temperatures. There were apparently brook trout in the dark, tea-colored rivers further north, and rivers like the Black and Thunder Bay and Pigeon are still famous for their brook-trout fishing.

But the Michigan grayling is extinct.

It seems strange almost a century later that transplanting brook trout to the declining rivers farther south was not possible because of poor transportation, and that it was easier to ship fingerlings from the trout hatcheries at Caledonia in New York. However, that is exactly what transpired in 1870, when A. H. Mershon received a shipment of brook trout from the Caledonia hatcheries of Seth Green. These fish were successfully planted in the Tobacco watershed near Clare.

Later, Judge Daniel Fitzhugh transferred brook trout fry from the Tobacco to other rivers like the Hersey, the headwaters of the Muskegon, and the swift little Rifle. It was the beginning of a revival that continued with the emigration of both the rainbow and the European brown trout, and it was Rube Babbitt who carried them on a train in milk cans to stock them in the Au Sable. Babbitt was aware that the time of the grayling was measured, and his understanding is obvious in some words written in his final years:

> The loggers are responsible for the death of the grayling. When the pines went, the streams became impure through erosion. Soil was washed into them by the rains, and the grayling could not live in dirty water. No longer sheltered by the trees, the rivers rose in water temperature, and the grayling needed pure water almost as cold as ice.

When the logs came down the rivers they raked the spawning beds, destroying the eggs and the young fish. The others were too easy to catch. In the big jams, the bark was ground off the pines, filling the water with fine particles that sifted into the grayling's gills. I found innumerable dead fish with festered gills, and in every case, fine particles of bark were the cause.

The grayling can never return, because the character of the streams has changed. They have tried to plant Montana grayling below the Straits in recent years, but they always died. The grayling is gone forever—gone with the pines and the passenger pigeons and the Michigan that used to be.

The tragedy is two-edged. Obviously, the building of the nation required vast tonnages of lumber, and without those Michigan forests many important things in our history could not have happened as early in our development. Yet the rapacity of the timber barons combined with our ecological ignorance permitted the blind cutting of trees in mile after mile of virgin forest. There was no thought of selective or phased cutting to check erosion and reseeding of cut-over acreages. No one cared about erosion and creating another forest. When William Mershon and his friends demonstrated at their own expense that reforestation was possible, the farm-property promoters who wanted to sell the cut-over acreage to unsuspecting veterans of the Civil War fought the Mershon tree farm with political pressure and punitive taxes. Its magnificent stand of pine is now one of the most beautiful forests in all of Michigan, except for the tragically small plot of virgin timber donated to the public park system by the Hartwick family of Grayling. Its towering, two-hundred-foot pines are an eloquent testimony to the primeval Michigan forests that died with the passenger pigeon and the grayling.

The other edge of the tragedy lies in the fact that thoughtful timber harvesting could have prevented the stripping of shade from the rivers. Some concern for topography could have alleviated the erosion that silted in the rivers. Shipping the timber on the railroads would have made the sluice dams and log drives unnecessary, and although the romance of the lumber camps might have been lost to our tumultuous frontier history, all the lumberjack tales and doggerel poetry of the lumber drives cannot equal the loss of the grayling and its icy little rivers.

But intelligent planning of the timber harvest, with protection of the rivers and phased replanting of the trees, would have given us the board-footages of lumber, while replacing the tree cover and preserving the grayling. The lumber would have cost us more and some of the richest families in Michigan would have a little less money in their trust funds and tax-free bonds, but they might still be in the lumber business—certainly the anglers among them will admit that the extinction of the Michigan grayling was too high a price to pay for their present comfort.

There is a tragic lesson here.

It is a rich and sad-hearted heritage that has reached us across the years, not because it was bequeathed to our generation through the foresight and wisdom of our fathers and grandfathers. That shibboleth has the bitter taste of foolishness. The history of the Au Sable is not an isolated example of the rapacity which has truly characterized our ancestors. It is perhaps the best example of an ecosystem which was almost totally destroyed by ignorance and greed, yet had such resilience that an entirely different environment has evolved and stabilized. Coniferous forests with grayling and brook trout have been gradually replaced with second-growth hardwoods and the sophisticated brown.

We lost everything once, Art Neumann said thoughtfully one April afternoon along the Au Sable. *We can't let it happen again—there's nothing left if we ruin it for the brown trout too!*

It is a beautiful river still, winding through its chalky bluffs and sand morraines, its currents sliding through the deadfalls. Its hatches of *Ephemerella* flies in early season are probably heavier now than they were in its grayling years, since they are not common in extremely cold watersheds. It is rich in memories of Hendricksons.

Certainly my remembrances of the river are filled with thoughts of *Ephemerella subvaria* hatches at the end of April. The mind savors them in the swift runs of the upper river at Grayling, the swift gravelly riffles below Stephan's Bridge, and in the waist-deep flats below Lovells on the North Branch. It is easy to remember them over the years, coming like clockwork in the half-hearted sunlight of those April afternoons, the current literally covered with slate-colored little sailboats.

It is challenging sport. The Au Sable is lined with cedar deadfalls, the sweepers that enrich both the dialogue and the lives of its river people. Without these fallen trees and tangled log jams, the vast trout population of the river would not be possible, but fishing in this jackstraw thicket is impossible. Experienced Au Sable fishermen argue that perhaps ninety percent of the fish are concealed in these sweepers along the banks. Fishing from the Au Sable longboats is a tricky sport, perhaps best described as trapshooting from a toboggan. The slender boat slides along the current, dragging its chain-link anchor on the bottom gravel, and held occasionally with a pole in the swift places.

The fisherman has only a quick shot into the tangled logs, and then his fly is whisked away by both the currents and his boat. Wading fishermen struggle against the middle currents of the open rivers, casting into the narrow slots and overhanging branches and sand traps of the cedars projecting well into the river. It is frustrating to watch big trout working deeper in the tangle, their porposing swirls completely safe and sheltered in the brush. Such fish never even see an artificial fly in their sanctuaries, so seldom is a successful cast and float achieved.

Many times a downstream check-cast accomplishes a brief dry-fly float, but the hooking percentages are poor. You are pulling the fly away from the fish when it takes. Both the Hendrickson duns and their subsequent spinner falls are impressive on the Au Sable, and frustrating in the sweeper tangles. It took me some years to realize that a hatching nymph would often hang up on the underwater snags, but that swinging under the surface, it would also reach a lot of places impossible with a dry-fly drift.

There are clearly identifiable reasons why the nymphal stage of the *Ephemerella* hatches is important, patterns of behavior endemic to the genus. These mayflies are without question the largest and most important genus of our American Ephemeroptera, there being so many species that they are grouped in eight distinct groups or subgenera. There are seventy-odd species.

The habits of the nymphs seem designed to make them readily available to feeding trout, and large numbers are found in the alimentary tracts of the fish all year. Their sequence of behavior during emergence is also optimal in terms of their availability to the trout. The maturing nymphs first expose themselves restlessly on the bottom a few hours before hatching. Generating gases inside the nymphal skin, the nymphs are finally buoyed toward the surface, riding the eddying currents.

Such stages in the hatch are typical of flies that emerge in open river, but these *Ephemerellas* often escape their nymphal skins when still five to ten inches below the surface. Struggling free from the shuck, their hydrofuge abdominal envelopes prevent drowning in the few seconds required to reach the atmosphere. Once reaching the surface film, several seconds are also expended in unfolding the wings and drying them. The newly hatched subimago often tries its wings in a few tentative beats, settling again to the current. Like the *Stenonema* flies, several seconds and a current drift of as much as thirty feet can occur in the winged subaquatic stage, followed by another thirty to forty feet on the surface as a winged subimago. During this entire process of emergence, these hatches are remarkably vulnerable, almost as if nature had provided them for the fly-fisher.

The happy result is readily evident in my notes, from stomach autopsies over the years. The fish obviously take them in good numbers at all stages of the hatch: the nymphs at the bottom and in the intermediate depths, the winged nymphs about a foot below the surface, the adult with its relatively unformed wings some five to ten inches below the surface, and the freshly hatched duns are all eaten freely.

This means that weighted and unweighted nymph imitations are valuable in our fly books. It also means that unweighted nymphs should also be dressed with emerging wings of duck or starling wing-quill sections, dressed downwing style like a standard wet fly, but with wings only about forty percent of normal length and proportions. The use of rolled nylon-stocking sections, discussed in the chapter on the *Stenonema* nymphs, can also be an extremely effective imitation of the emerging *Ephemerellas*. Such hatching imitations are extremely important for a genus which emerges into its winged state just below the surface.

Ephemerella nymphs in general are quite variable in their overall configuration. Several lines of natural selection and ecosystemic adaptation have evolved. Some exhibit slender, highly streamlined forms; others display flattened ventral surfaces, with humpbacked thoracic structures and broad femora. Many have developed prominent dorsal tubercles or spinules on the head, thorax, abdomen, and legs. Several species are smooth, while others are covered with filamentous hair.

The mouthparts are relatively consistent throughout the entire genus, especially within the subgeneric groups. The labrum is wider than its length, and occasionally immarginate on its anterior surfaces. The attitude, size, and proportion of the mandibular canines is quite variable. Maxillae are relatively conical at their apex, with one or more spines at their terminal areas. The maxillary palp may be rudimentary in most species, and entirely lacking in some. The most-developed palp does not extend beyond the galea lacinia, and most are considerably shorter. The labial palp is also relatively short in length, along with the four apical parts of labrum. These apical parts are frequently short, conical, and equal in length. The tarsal claws are denticulate

Lateral extensions are typically present on the abdominal segments, with posterolateral spines of greater or lesser development. Paired dorsal spines are present in many species. Gill pairs are carried on segments three to seven in some nymphs, and on body segments four to seven in others. These latter species have semi-operculate or operculate gills on segment four, covering all or part of the remaining gill pairs. All species display wholly dorsal gill positions. Tails are always three in number, equal in length, and as long as or slightly shorter than the body. Some species display filamentous tails, and some have whorls of minute spinules at their joinings. Many species hold their tails almost upright or slightly arched.

The most distinct and homogeneous of the eight subgenera is perhaps the *Bicolor* group, embracing ten species. The nymphs bear a rudimentary gill on the first segment, no gill pair on the third, and the fourth gill is operculate. There are prominent dorsal spines on the tergites. The lateral margins of the abdominal segments are quite flattened and expanded, having rather prominent posterolateral spinules. The following species is typical:

1. Blue-Winged Yellow Quill (*Ephemerella doris*)

This southeastern species averages three-eighths inch in its nymphal stages, and is distributed from Maryland to Georgia. It is quite well represented in the rivers of North Carolina, and *Ephemerella lutulenta* and *Ephemerella temporalis* are slightly larger species of the same group. These related species are distributed from Quebec to North Carolina, and although their configuration parallels that of *Ephemerella doris*, their coloring is somewhat more reddish brown.

Tails: Olive with dark markings at tips and midpoints, 5/16 inch
Body: Amber strongly mottled with brown, 3/16 inch
Gills: Amber mottled with brown, one operculate, 1/16 inch
Thorax: Amber darkly mottled with brown, 5/32 inch
Wing cases: Amber darkly tinged with brown, ⅛ inch
Legs: Amber mottled with grayish brown, 3/16 inch
Head: Amber mottled with brown, 1/32 inch

Hook: Sizes 14-16 Orvis Premium 1X long
Nylon: Tan 6/0 nylon
Tails: Tan pheasant fibers mottled with brown, with sternites of creamish yellow lacquer
Body: Rough amber dubbings mottled with brown felt-tip pen
Gills: Amber marabou fibers secured with fine oval gold tinsel
Thorax: Amber dubbing with creamish yellow lacquer at the sternum
Wing cases: Amber feather section mottled with brown, tied down over the thorax
Legs: Medium brownish partridge hackle
Head: Tan nylon

The *Simplex* subgeneric group is a heterogeneous series of three species. Its adults have male penes broadened more at their apex than at the base, and having minute apical palpillae laterally displayed. The nymphs have gills on segments four through seven, with the fourth gill semi-operculate. These two species are typical.

303

2. Dark Blue-Winged Olive (*Ephemerella attenuata*)

This is a major eastern fly hatch in spite of its relatively small size, its nymphs averaging about three-eighths inch. Specimens are recorded from Quebec to North Carolina, with emergence coming in late May and June.

Tails: Dark mottled brownish, 3/16 inch
Body: Dark blackish olive distinctly ringed with bright olive green sternites, 3/16 inch
Gills: Dark blackish olive, 1/32 inch
Thorax: Dark mottled blackish olive, 3/32 inch
Wing cases: Dark olive brown, ⅛ inch
Legs: Darkly mottled olive brown, 5/32 inch
Head: Dark mottled olive, 1/32 inch

Hook: Sizes 14-16 Orvis Premium 1X long
Nylon: Black 6/0 nylon
Tails: Dark barred woodduck
Body: Dark blackish brown hare's mask underfur with a bright green lacquer on the sternites
Gills: Dark blackish brown marabou secured with a ribbing of .0041 monofilament
Thorax: Dark blackish brown hare's mask with a bright green sternum
Wing cases: Dark olive brown feather section tied down over thorax
Legs: Dark partridge dyed dark olive
Head: Black nylon

3. Dark Slate-Winged Olive (*Ephemerella simplex*)

These nymphs are distributed from Quebec to North Carolina, and average approximately three-eighths inch in length. These flattened nymphs are often found concealed on the bottom, the silt and debris clinging to their body hairs. Emergence is relatively late, coming from late June until the middle of September.

Tails: Dark mottled brownish 3/16 inch
Body: Dark mottled blackish olive, with light olive sternites, 3/16 inch
Gills: Medium olive, one operculate 1/32 inch
Thorax: Medium olive darkly mottled with brown, above a light olive sternum, ⅛ inch
Wing cases: Medium olive, 3/32 inch
Legs: Medium olive darkly mottled with brown, 3/16 inch
Head: Medium olive mottled brown 1/16 inch

Hook: Sizes 14-16 Orvis Premium 1X long
Nylon: Dark brown 6/0 nylon
Tails: Dark barred woodduck
Body: Dark blackish brown hare's poll dubbing on olive silk, with pale green lacquer sternites
Gills: Medium olive marabou secured at sides with fine gold wire
Thorax: Dark blackish brown hare's poll dubbing
Wing cases: Medium olive feather section tied down over thorax
Legs: Dark partridge dyed dark olive
Head: Dark brown nylon

The nymphs of the *Serrata* subgenus include the two species described in the following paragraphs. Species typical of the eleven species in the group, their nymphs have gill pairs on their abdominal segments three through seven. None are operculate in conformation. There are no spines on the anterior margins of the foreleg femora. The tail joints each have a minute whorl of spines, and the maxillary palp is either weak or missing entirely absent in these species.

4. Dark Iron-Blue Quill (*Ephemerella serrata*)

These nymphs are distributed from Quebec to North Carolina, and are rather small species averaging a mere one-quarter inch in length. Their hatching is sporadic from the third week in June, lasting sometimes as late as the second week in August.

Tails: Darkly mottled tannish, ¼ inch
Body: Darkly mottled brown with creamish brown sternites, and segments four through six pale olive brown, 3/16 inch
Gills: Pale olive brown, 1/32 inch
Thorax: Dark mottled brown with a pale median stripe, creamish brown on the sternum, 5/32 inch
Wing cases: Dark mottled brown with a pale median, ⅛ inch
Legs: Pale amber mottled with brown, 3/16 inch
Head: Dark mottled brownish 1/16 inch

Hook: Sizes 16-18 Orvis Premium 1X long
Nylon: Medium brown 6/0 nylon
Tails: Dark barred woodduck
Body: Dark mottled brown dubbing with pale cream lacquer sternites
Gills: Pale olive marabou fibers secured at sides with fine gold wire
Thorax: Dark mottled brown with a pale quill median tied down over thorax
Legs: Medium brown partridge
Head: Medium brown nylon

5. Dark Lead-Winged Olive (*Ephemerella deficiens*)

These tiny nymphs average five-sixteenths inch in length, and are found from Quebec to North Carolina, as well as westward to the Great Lakes country. These nymphs are fond of moderate currents in organic bottom detritus and leaf drift. Emergence occurs from the middle of June until the first week in August.

Tails: Brown darkly marked at midpoints, 3/16 inch
Body: Dark brownish olive distinctly ringed, with medium olive sternites, 3/16 inch
Gills: Pale grayish olive, 1/32 inch
Thorax: Dark brownish olive with a medium olive sternum, ⅛ inch
Wing cases: Dark brownish olive ⅛ inch
Legs: Dark amber heavily mottled with brown, ¼ inch
Head: Dark brownish olive, 1/16 inch

Hook: Sizes 16-18 Orvis Premium 1X long
Nylon: Dark olive 6/0 nylon
Tails: Brown pheasant fibers darkly marked at midpoints
Body: Dark brownish olive dubbing, with sternites of medium olive lacquer
Gills: Pale grayish olive marabou secured at sides with fine gold wire
Thorax: Dark brownish olive dubbing, with a sternum of medium olive lacquer
Wing cases: Dark brownish olive feather tied down over thorax
Legs: Dark brown partridge
Head: Dark olive nylon

Nymphs of the *Needhami* group are distinguished by gills on segments three through seven. There are nine species presently classified from our American rivers, although two have been chosen as prototypical for fly-fishing purposes. The femora display only minor and inconspicuous spinules on their margins, although none are usually present on the upper surfaces of the forelegs. Dorsal abdominal spines are often present in these species. The maxillary palp is extant, and the tails have whorls of spines at each joint in its basal half.

6. Dark Brown-Winged Olive (*Ephemerella maculata*)

The nymphs of this species average about three-eighths inch in length, and are found in rivers from Oregon to the San Gabriel Mountains of southern California. It hatches from late July until September. Its nymphs are particularly fond of swift currents which also support dense beds of subaquatic vegetation.

Tails: Pale mottled amber, 5/32 inch
Body: Pale amber mottled with light brown along a pale median stripe, above pale cream sternites, 3/16 inch
Gills: Pale amber lightly touched with olive, 1/16 inch
Thorax: Pale amber mottled with brown, defining a pale median stripe, above a cream sternum, ⅛ inch
Wing cases: Medium olive gray with a partial median stripe, ⅛ inch
Legs: Pale amber mottled with brown, 5/32 inch
Head: Pale amber mottled with brown defining a pale median stripe, 1/32 inch

Hook: Sizes 14-16 Orvis Premium 1X long
Nylon: Grayish tan 6/0 nylon
Tails: Pale barred woodduck
Body: Pale amber dubbing mottled brown with a felt-tipped pen, using a pale quill median and creamish white lacquer sternites
Gills: Pale amber marabou secured at sides with fine gold wire
Thorax: Pale amber dubbing mottled brown, with a creamish white lacquer sternum
Wing cases: Medium olive grayish feather section with a white quill median tied down over thorax
Legs: Pale brown partridge
Head: Grayish tan nylon with brown dorsal lacquer

7. Little Blue-Winged Red Quill (*Ephemerella needhami*)

These little nymphs average approximately three-eighths inch. Emergence is typically concentrated into a period of two weeks, usually occurring at the end of June. They prefer swiftly running streams, particularly those having good growths of weeds. However, the nymphs are also found clinging to deadfalls and log-jams, hiding in *Potamogeton* beds or coarse gravel, and lying in leaf-drift eddies. Their range is from Quebec to Pennsylvania, and west into the rivers of Michigan and Wisconsin.

Tails: Dark mottled amber, ¼ inch
Body: Dark brownish olive defining a strong cream colored median stripe, above olive sternites, 3/16 inch
Gills: Medium olive, 1/16 inch
Thorax: Dark brownish olive with a strong median stripe, above an olive sternum, ⅛ inch
Wing cases: Dark brownish olive, ⅛ inch
Legs: Pale mottled amber, 5/32 inch
Head: Dark brownish olive with a median stripe, 1/32 inch

Hook: Sizes 14-16 Orvis Premium 1X long
Nylon: Dark olive 6/0 nylon
Tails: Dark barred woodduck
Body: Dark brownish olive dubbing with a pale median quill, above olive lacquer sternites
Gills: Medium olive marabou secured with fine gold wire
Thorax: Dark brownish olive dubbing with an olive lacquer sternum
Wing cases: Dark brownish olive feather section with pale quill median tied down over thorax
Legs: Pale brown partridge
Head: Dark olive nylon

Ephemerella hecuba is a subgeneric group in itself. The atrophied gills of the nymph are present in the subimagoes, which occurs in some other species of the genus. The head of the nymph is uniquely shaped, and exaggerately wide at its frontal margin. Gills occur only on segments four through seven, with an operculate fourth gill pair. There are dorsal spines on tergites two through eight. The lateral margins of segments two through nine are flattened into toothlike appendages. There are sharp spines at the apical margins of the femora.

8. Great Blue-Winged Red Quill (*Ephemerella hecuba*)

This large western mayfly was incorrectly identified in my book *Matching the Hatch,* which designated these big lead-wing duns with the darkly ringed bodies as *Ephemerella grandis.* It is fortunate that the error has finally been corrected.

The nymphs are large, averaging about five-eighths to three-quarters inch. Their bodies are hairy and exaggeratedly flattened. The head is rather broad and wedge-shaped, although the thoracic structure and mid-abdominal zone are somewhat wider in many specimens. The maxillary palp is strongly developed. The heavy mandibles have well-developed canines. The pronotum is widest at its posterior margin. The legs are flattened and hairy. The claws lack pectinations. The abdomen is quite stout and flattened. Its segments have sharp posterolateral spines. Gills are present on segments four through seven, operculate in the fourth gill pair. Dorsal spines are often present on tergites four to six. There are three fringed and heavily mottled tails.

These are the nymphs of a major western hatch which emerges from the first days in July until late August, depending on latitude and altitude. Hatches are recorded from the Rocky Mountain rivers, reaching from New Mexico to Montana.

These nymphs should employ wire-outrigger tying techniques to simulate the exaggeratedly flat bodies of the naturals:

Tails: Brown heavily fringed and marked at the midpoint with brown, ¼ inch
Body: Dark brownish with a strong purplish cast, above grayish sternites with purplish markings, ⅜ inch
Gills: Dark grayish brown, ⅛ inch
Thorax: Dark mottled brownish gray, 3/16 inch
Wing cases: Dark mottled brownish gray, 3/16 inch
Legs: Dark brown-mottled grayish, 1/16 inch
Head: Dark mottled brownish, 3/32 inch

Hook: Sizes 8-10 Orvis Premium 1X long
Nylon: Dark gray 6/0 nylon
Tails: Dark brownish gray pheasant fibers with dark brown markings at the midpoints
Body: Dark brownish gray dubbing on olive silk, ribbed with reddish brown dubbing on ruby silk
Gills: Dark grayish brown marabou secured with fine gold wire
Thorax: Dark brownish gray dubbing on olive silk
Wing cases: Dark brownish gray feather tied down over thorax
Legs: Dark partridge hackle dyed olive
Head: Dark gray nylon

The mayflies of the *Fuscata* subgeneric group are the largest series of species among all of the *Ephemerella* mayflies. More than twenty American species make up this group of insects, with their corpulent and flat-looking nymphs. These nymphal forms are atypical and highly specialized in their configuration. Many of the twenty-odd species bear spines or tubercles on the anterior margins of their femora. Gills are found on segments three through seven, with a well-developed maxillary palp.

9. Medium Olive Dun (*Ephemerella allegheniensis*)
These brownish-olive little nymphs are found distributed from West Virginia and Maryland to the Adirondacks and New England. The genotypical specimens were taken on the swift-flowing Cacapon in West Virginia, and hatched in June and July.

Ephemerella tuberculata is a closely related, slightly darker species, and the nymphs average three-eighths inch:

Tails: Amber mottled, ¼ inch
Body: Medium olive distinctly ringed, with pale olive sternites, 3/16 inch
Gills: Medium olive grayish, 1/32 inch
Thorax: Medium olive darkly mottled, with a pale olive sternum, ⅛ inch
Wing cases: Medium olive grayish, ⅛ inch
Legs: Pale amber mottled with brown, ¼ inch
Head: Medium olive mottled with brown, 1/16 inch

Hook: Sizes 14-16 Orvis Premium 1X long
Nylon: Olive 6/0 nylon
Tails: Pale barred woodduck
Body: Medium olive dubbing with sternites of pale olive lacquer
Gills: Medium olive gray marabou secured at sides with fine gold wire
Thorax: Medium olive dubbing with a pale olive lacquer sternum
Wing cases: Medium olive gray feather tied down over thorax
Legs: Pale brown partridge
Head: Olive nylon

10. Dark Iron-Winged Olive (*Ephemerella cornuta*)

These little nymphs measure about one-half inch in length, and are typically hatching early in July. These nymphal forms prefer moderate to swift currents over gravel and rubble-bottomed riffles. It is a widely distributed mayfly, with specimens recorded from Quebec to North Carolina along the Atlantic Coast and into the Great Lakes region to the trout streams of Minnesota and Wisconsin.

Tails: Amber mottled, ¼ inch
Body: Dark mottled olive brown with a dull median stripe, and olive sternites, ¼ inch
Gills: Light brownish, 1/16 inch
Thorax: Dark mottled olive brown with a dull median, and an olive sternum, 5/32 inch
Wing cases: Mottled olive brown, ⅛ inch
Legs: Pale olive mottled with brown, ¼ inch
Head: Mottled olive brown, 1/16 inch

Hook: Sizes 12-14 Orvis Premium 1X long
Nylon: Medium olive 6/0 nylon
Tails: Medium barred woodduck
Body: Dark olive brown with a dull median stripe of flat monofilament, above olive lacquer sternites
Gills: Light brownish marabou secured at sides with fine gold wire
Thorax: Dark olive brown with an olive lacquer sternum
Wing cases: Mottled olive brown feather section tied over thorax
Legs: Pale brown partridge
Head: Medium olive nylon

11. Large Lead-Winged Olive Dun (*Ephemerella walkeri*)

This rather large species hatches from nymphal forms averaging about five-eighths inch in length. It is distributed from Quebec into the Great Lakes region, and south into New York and Pennsylvania. It hatches from late June until August.

The genotypical hatch of this group is a slightly darker and smaller insect designated *Ephemerella fuscata*, which measures about seven-sixteenths inch in length. It also hatches from late June until August, and is distributed from Quebec to Pennsylvania and northern New Jersey.

Tails: Fringed grayish olive, ¼ inch
Body: Dark blackish olive distinctly ringed, with pale olive grayish sternites, ¼ inch
Gills: Pale olive grayish, 1/16 inch
Thorax: Dark mottled olive brownish, ¼ inch
Wing cases: Dark mottled olive, 3/16 inch
Legs: Pale olive mottled and striped with brown, ½ inch
Head: Dark mottled olive brownish, 1/16 inch

Hook: Sizes 12-14 Orvis Premium 1X long
Nylon: Dark olive 6/0 nylon
Tails: Grayish olive pheasant fibers
Body: Dark blackish hare's mask dubbing on olive silk, with pale olive lacquer sternites
Gills: Pale olive grayish marabou secured with fine gold wire
Thorax: Dark blackish hare's mask dubbing on olive silk, with a pale olive lacquer sternum
Wing cases: Dark mottled olive feather section tied down over thorax
Legs: Pale brown partridge hackle
Head: Dark olive nylon

12. Light Blue-Winged Olive (*Ephemerella lata*)

These small nymphs emerge into an extremely important summer hatch on rivers from Quebec to North Carolina, and specimens are also recorded in Michigan and Wisconsin. The nymphs average five-sixteenths to three-eighths inch. It is an extremely important hatch in June on the classic little Brodheads.

Tails: Pale mottled amber, 3/16 inch
Body: Olive mottled with brown, with pale yellowish olive sternites, ¼ inch
Gills: Pale olive grayish, 1/16 inch
Thorax: Olive mottled with brown, and a pale yellowish olive sternum, 3/16 inch
Wing cases: Olive mottled with brown, 5/32 inch
Legs: Pale olive grayish lightly marked with brown, 5/16 inch
Head: Olive mottled with brown, 1/16 inch

Hook: Sizes 14-16 Orvis Premium 1X long
Nylon: Medium olive 6/0 nylon
Tails: Pale barred woodduck
Body: Medium olive mottled brown with a felt-tipped pen, and pale creamish gray lacquer sternites
Gills: Pale olive grayish marabou secured with fine gold wire
Thorax: Medium olive mottled brown with a felt-pen, and pale creamish gray lacquer sternum
Wing cases: Brownish olive mottled feather section tied down over thorax
Legs: Pale brown partridge dyed olive
Head: Medium olive nylon

13. Medium Slate-Winged Olive (*Ephemerella longicornis*)

These nymphs measure approximately seven-sixteenths inch. They are recorded from the limestone streams of New Jersey and Pennsylvania south into Virginia and North Carolina. They are a midsummer hatch.

Tails: Pale tannish mottled, ¼ inch
Body: Medium brown distinctly ringed, with tannish cream sternites, 3/16 inch
Gills: Pale brownish yellow, 1/32 inch
Thorax: Medium brown with a pale median stripe, above a tannish cream sternum, ⅛ inch
Wing cases: Medium brownish, ⅛ inch
Legs: Amber mottled with brown, ¼ inch
Head: Medium mottled brown, 1/16 inch

Hook: Sizes 14-16 Orvis Premium 1X long
Nylon: Medium brown 6/0 nylon
Tails: Pale barred woodduck
Body: Medium brown dubbing, with cream lacquer sternites
Gills: Pale brownish yellow marabou secured with fine gold wire
Thorax: Medium brown dubbing, with a cream lacquer sternum
Wing cases: Medium brownish feather with a pale median quill tied down over thorax
Legs: Pale brown partridge
Head: Medium brown nylon

14. Light Slate-Winged Olive (*Ephemerella coloradensis*)

These large, brown-mottled nymphs average one-half inch in length, and hatch in midsummer on our western rivers. Hatches occur from June until September, and specimens are recorded from widespread rivers. Excellent hatches are extent from New Mexico into Montana, with particularly good populations in Colorado, Wyoming, and the rivers of Idaho.

Tails: Pale tannish heavily mottled, 3/16 inch
Body: Medium brownish distinctly ringed, with pale cream sternites, ¼ inch
Gills: Medium brownish gray, 1/16 inch
Thorax: Medium brownish heavily mottled, with a pale median stripe and sternum, 3/16 inch
Wing cases: Medium brownish gray, 5/32 inch
Legs: Pale amber mottled with light brownish gray, 5/16 inch
Head: Medium mottled brown, 1/16 inch

Hook: Sizes 12-14 Orvis Premium 1X long
Nylon: Medium brown 6/0 nylon
Tails: Dark barred woodduck
Body: Medium brownish dubbing, with pale cream sternites of lacquer
Gills: Medium brownish gray marabou secured with fine gold wire
Thorax: Medium brownish dubbing with a pale cream lacquer sternum
Wing cases: Medium brownish gray with a pale median quill tied down over thorax
Legs: Pale brown partridge hackle
Head: Medium brown nylon

15. Dark Slate-Winged Olive (*Ephemerella flavilinea*)

Similar to *Ephemerella coloradensis*, these nymphs average a slightly smaller seven-sixteenths inch. Hatches emerge from the rivers of northern Colorado to the tumbling glacier-melt waters of Alberta. The species is especially important in Idaho and Wyoming. The emergence cycle begins in late June, lasting until August.

Tails: Dark mottled brownish, ¼ inch
Body: Dark mottled brown distinctly ringed, with a pale median and cream colored sternites, 3/16 inch
Gills: Medium olive brown, 1/16 inch
Thorax: Dark mottled brown with a pale median, and a creamish gray sternum, ⅛ inch
Wing cases: Dark brownish olive, ⅛ inch
Legs: Pale brown heavily mottled with darker brown, ¼ inch
Head: Dark mottled brownish, 1/16 inch

Hook: Sizes 14-16 Orvis Premium 1X long
Nylon: Dark brown 6/0 nylon
Tails: Dark barred woodduck
Body: Dark brown mottled dubbing with a pale median quill, and creamish lacquer sternites
Gills: Medium olive brown marabou secured with fine gold wire
Thorax: Dark brown mottled dubbing, with a creamish lacquer sternum
Wing cases: Dark brownish olive feather section tied down over the thorax with a median quill
Legs: Dark brown partridge
Head: Dark brown nylon

16. Dark Blue-Winged Red Quill (*Ephemerella doddsi*)

This is perhaps the most widely distributed western *Ephemerella* hatch, emerging from early July through the last week in August. Its nymphs measure approximately nine-sixteenths inch. Hatches are distributed from Colorado to Alberta in the Rocky Mountains, as well as the Pacific drainages from California to Washington. Specimens are also recorded from rivers in Idaho and Utah.

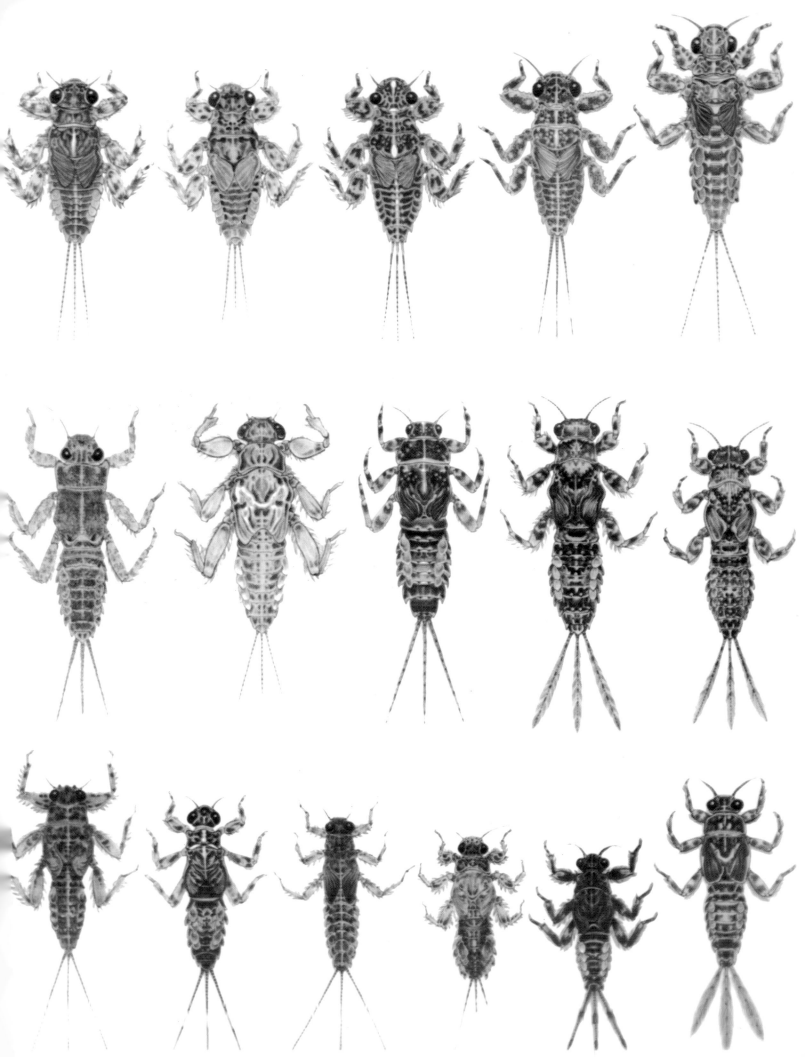

The species is found from Colorado to Montana, and particularly fine hatches occur in Utah, Wyoming, and Idaho.

Although it is not as large as the preceding subgeneric group of flies, the *Invaria* group contains many of the most famous hatches of the entire genus of *Ephemerella* mayflies. These nymphs are generally characterized by the presence of rather slender spines along the posterior margins of the femora. There are also spines on the upper margins of the forelegs, often in irregular transverse bands near the apical ends. Whorls of spines are totally absent on the tails of the nymphs.

19. Dark Blue-Winged Hendrickson (*Ephemerella invaria*)

This is a great hatch, widely distributed on American rivers and present in large numbers where it is found. Specimens are recorded from Quebec to North Carolina, on classic rivers from the Allagash and the Ausable to the Sweetbriar and the Nantahala. Its nymphs average approximately seven-sixteenths to one-half inch in length, and are found in relatively swift currents, preferring gravel-bottomed streams with good alkalinity to reach optimal populations. Emergence typically occurs from late April until the middle of July, but the best hatches are usually found at the end of April, lasting into the first weeks of May.

This species is the genotype of its subgeneric group, and its imitative nymphs are tied as follows:

Top, left to right: *Ephemerella longicornis, Ephemerella alleghensis, Ephemerella tuberculata, Ephemerella flavilinea, Ephemerella yosemite*

Middle, left to right: *Ephemerella inermis, Ephemerella lata, Ephemerella subvaria, Ephemerella invaria, Ephemerella dorothea*

Bottom, left to right: *Ephemerella cornuta, Ephemerella serrata, Ephemerella infrequens, Ephemerella simplex, Ephemerella deficiens, Ephemerella rotunda*

Tails: Fringed brownish, ¼ inch
Body: Darkly mottled brownish with yellowish spots, and pale yellowish-brown sternites, 5/16 inch
Gills: Pale yellowish brown, 1/16 inch
Thorax: Mottled dark brownish with pale yellowish anterior margins, and a pale yellowish-brown sternum, 3/16 inch
Wing cases: Mottled dark brownish, ⅛ inch
Legs: Amber darkly mottled with brown, ¼ inch
Head: Medium brownish, 1/16 inch

Hook: Sizes 12-14 Orvis Premium 1X long
Nylon: Medium brown 6/0 nylon
Tails: Medium brown pheasant fibers
Body: Darkly mottled brownish-yellow dubbing mixed with hare's mask guard hairs, and with yellowish tan lacquer sternites
Gills: Pale yellowish brown marabou secured at sides with fine gold wire
Thorax: Darkly mottled brownish-yellow dubbing mixed with hare's mask, and with a yellowish tan lacquer sternum
Wing cases: Dark mottled brownish feather section tied down over thorax
Legs: Dark brown partridge hackle
Head: Medium brown nylon

20. Little Gray-Winged Red Quill (*Ephemerella excrucians*)

This is an elegant little mayfly of the *Invaria* group, its nymphs averaging about one-quarter inch in length. They differ from the somewhat larger nymphs of *Ephemerella invaria* and *rotunda* in both coloring and the absence of paired spinules at the rear margins of their abdominal segments. Habitat consists of open gravel bottom, with shallow currents at a rather swift two to three feet per second. Emergence occurs during the last two weeks in June, and specimens are recorded from New Brunswick to Michigan and Wisconsin.

Tails: Pale grayish fringed, ⅛ inch
Body: Mottled grayish olive, with pale olive sternites, 3/16 inch
Gills: Grayish olive, 1/32 inch
Thorax: Mottled grayish olive with pale olive sternum, 3/32 inch
Wing cases: Dark grayish olive, ⅛ inch
Legs: Dark grayish olive mottled with brown, ⅛ inch
Head: Mottled grayish olive, 1/32 inch

Hook: Sizes 16-18 Orvis Premium 1X long
Nylon: Dark gray 6/0 nylon
Tails: Dark grayish pheasant fibers
Body: Mottled grayish dubbing on olive silk, with olive lacquer sternites
Gills: Grayish olive marabou fibers secured with fine gold wire
Thorax: Mottled grayish dubbing on olive silk, with olive lacquer sternum
Wing cases: Dark grayish olive feather section tied down over the thorax
Legs: Dark partridge dyed grayish olive
Head: Dark gray nylon

21. Pale Morning Dun (*Ephemerella infrequens*)

This popular name was given to this species by Doug Swisher and Carl Richards in their fine book *Selective Trout,* and it is such an appropriate description that I wish I had thought of it myself. The hatch is important on western trout streams from Colorado to Montana in the Rocky Mountains, and is also reported from Idaho to Oregon and the Sierras of California. When I first described *Ephemerella infrequens* almost twenty years ago, it was called simply a western variation of the Hendrickson, but in the future I shall always think of it as the Pale Morning Dun.

The natural nymphs average about one-half inch in length.

Tails: Pale mottled amber, ¼ inch
Body: Mottled brownish with an amber median stripe and sternites, 3/16 inch
Gills: Mottled brownish amber, 1/16 inch
Thorax: Dark mottled brownish with an amber sternum, ⅛ inch
Wing cases: Dark mottled brownish, 3/32 inch
Legs: Pale amber lightly mottled with brown, 3/16 inch
Head: Dark mottled brownish, 1/16 inch

Hook: Sizes 12-14 Orvis Premium 1X long
Nylon: Dark brown 6/0 nylon
Tails: Pale barred woodduck fibers
Body: Mottled brownish dubbing with an amber quill median, and pale amber lacquer sternites
Gills: Brownish amber marabou secured with fine gold wire
Thorax: Mottled brownish dubbing with an amber lacquer sternum
Wing cases: Dark mottled brownish feather section tied down over thorax
Legs: Pale brown partridge
Head: Dark brown nylon

22. Pale Morning Olive (*Ephemerella inermis*)

This is another superb western hatch that first appeared in *Matching the Hatch,* and in the years after the war, when I fished extensively in the Rocky Mountain region, it gave us some Olympian rises of fish on the Frying Pan stillwaters in Colorado, the spring creeks of Jackson Hole, and the Snake in its giant meadows below Henry's Lake. It is widely distributed. Specimens are reported from northern New Mexico into Colorado, Wyoming, and Montana. Utah has good hatches, and it is especially important on the stillwater spring creeks of Idaho. It is one of the principal hatches on Silver Creek at Sun Valley. Hatches are also recorded from the Yosemite rivers and Hot Creek in the Sierras, and correspondents assure me that it also occurs in heavy concentrations on such slow-flowing rivers as the Metolius in Oregon.

Peak hatching usually occurs during July, although sporadic local activity has been recorded throughout the entire summer, lasting until the end of August.

Tails: Pale mottled amber, ¼ inch
Body: Pale mottled amber distinctly ringed, with pale amber sternites, ¼ inch
Gills: Pale yellowish amber, 1/16 inch
Thorax: Pale mottled amber with pale sternum, 3/16 inch
Wing cases: Medium mottled amber, ⅛ inch
Legs: Pale mottled amber, ¼ inch
Head: Pale mottled amber, 1/16 inch

Hook: Sizes 12-14 Orvis Premium 1X long
Nylon: Tan 6/0 nylon
Tails: Pale barred woodduck
Body: Pale mottled amber dubbing spun on pale olive silk, with pale amber lacquer sternites
Gills: Pale amber marabou secured with fine gold wire
Thorax: Pale mottled amber dubbing on pale olive silk, with a pale amber lacquer sternum
Wing cases: Mottled amber feather section tied down over thorax
Legs: Pale amber partridge fibers
Head: Tan nylon

23. Pale Sulphur Dun (*Ephemerella dorothea*)

Some angling writers have called these our Pale Evening Duns, perhaps in homage to the *Ephemerella notata* on British rivers, but after many seasons on the gentle limestone rivers of Pennsylvania with Charles Fox and his circle of anglers, the hatch is firmly imprinted in my mind as the time of the Pale Sulphurs.

Tails: Pale amber fringed, ¼ inch
Body: Pale mottled brownish with pale sternites, ¼ inch
Gills: Pale amber touched with brown, 1/32 inch
Thorax: Pale mottled brownish with pale sternum, 3/16 inch
Wing cases: Medium brownish, 3/32 inch
Legs: Amber mottled with brown, ¼ inch
Head: Pale mottled brownish, 1/32 inch

Hook: Sizes 14-16 Orvis Premium 1X long
Nylon: Tan 6/0 nylon
Tails: Pale amber pheasant fibers
Body: Medium brown dubbing lightly mixed with hare's mask guard hairs on pale yellow silk, with yellowish lacquer sternites
Gills: Pale amber marabou secured with fine gold wire
Thorax: Medium brown dubbing lightly mixed with hare's mask guard hairs on pale yellow silk, with a yellowish lacquer sternum
Wing cases: Medium mottled amber feather section tied down over thorax
Legs: Light brown partridge
Head: Tan nylon

It is an unmistakable hatch, popping through the surface film and riding the currents. Its pale grayish-blue wings look straw-colored in the evening light. The fat bodies of the females are a bright yellow of intense chroma, and the males have a touch of orange in their abdominal segments, making the flies look orangish yellow in the twilight.

But the nymphs are darkly mottled with brown, averaging about three-eights inch in length. The species is widely distributed. Hatches are recorded from Quebec to North Carolina. These handsome sulphur-colored *Ephemerellas* are also important on the trout streams of Michigan, Wisconsin, and Minnesota. Populations in the swift mountain rivers of North Carolina, South Carolina, and Tennessee are equally important to fly-fishermen. The nymphs like gravelly riffles and rocky pocket-water, with a swift

314 current flowing smoothly. Emergence is sporadic, lasting from the middle of May until the beginning of July. However, the principal hatches on most rivers occur during May and early June in northern latitudes.

24. Dark Red Quill (*Ephemerella rotunda*)

Ephemerella rotunda subimagoes are quite similar to the rust-colored, blue-winged mayflies described in the writings of Art Flick, the handsome males typical of *Ephemerella subvaria* on his Schoharie riffles. Its fringed tails and habitat are both indicative of a preference for swift currents, and a requirement of highly oxygenated water.

The species is distributed from Quebec to North Carolina. Leonard describes it as a major fly hatch in *Mayflies of Michigan Trout Streams*, and it is unquestionably present in Minnesota and Wisconsin as well. Its nymphs measure about seven-sixteenths inch, and are recognizable through the small tubercles on the rear margins of their abdominal segments. Both Traver and Needham report that the nymphs of *Ephemerella rotunda* are larger than either *subvaria* or *invaria* specimens, but Leonard tells us that his specimens are intermediate in size between the big *invaria* nymphs and those of *subvaria*. His specimens were taken largely from the rich alkaline watersheds of the Au Sable and Pere Marquette. My own specimens are slightly smaller than both of its sister *Ephemerella*, being about the size of the Pale Sulphur nymphs. They emerge from the middle of May, with hatches coming off for about three weeks.

Tails: Medium brownish fringed, 3/16 inch
Body: Medium brownish mottled, distinctly ringed with paler sternites, ¼ inch
Gills: Pale brownish gray, 1/32 inch
Thorax: Medium brownish mottled, with paler sternum, 5/32 inch
Wing cases: Dark brownish gray, ⅛ inch
Legs: Dark amber mottled with brown, ¼ inch
Head: Medium mottled brownish, 1/16 inch

Hook: Sizes 12-14 Orvis Premium 1X long
Nylon: Medium brown 6/0 nylon
Tails: Medium brownish pheasant fibers
Body: Medium mottled brownish dubbing spun on yellow silk with pale amber lacquer sternites
Gills: Pale brownish gray marabou secured with fine gold wire
Thorax: Medium mottled brownish dubbing on yellow silk, with pale amber sternum lacquer
Wing cases: Dark brownish gray feather section tied down over thorax
Legs: Dark brown partridge
Head: Medium brown nylon

25. Blue-Winged Hendrickson (*Ephemerella subvaria*)

This is probably the best known of the American mayfly hatches, along with the Green Drakes and the Gordon Quills, and it was first described in the *Streamside Guide* published by Arthur Flick in 1947. It is a fly hatch on our classic eastern rivers that parallels the importance of *Ephemerella ignita* on the rivers of Hampshire and Wiltshire, the almost legendary Blue-Winged Olive deified in the books of British writers like Halford, Moseley, Skues, Mottram, and Dunne.

The species is indigenous to rivers from Quebec to North Carolina, and throughout the Great Lakes watersheds, although its heaviest populations are apparently in its northerly range. Hatching over much of its distribution occurs from the last week in April, with sporadic stragglers coming until

June. However, the best hatches emerge before the middle of May.

The nymphs vary quite widely, perhaps because of comparative water chemistry across their relatively wide range. Needham reports their average length as ten millimeters, approximately seven-sixteenths inch in length. His specimens were taken on slightly acid watersheds in New York and Quebec. Leonard describes much larger specimens in his *Mayflies of Michigan Trout Streams*, and interestingly enough, these Michigan nymphs were collected in the tea-colored rivers of the Upper Peninsula. His specimens from the rich marl-spring rivers of Crawford and Lake Counties are apparently larger, averaging as much as twelve millimeters, approximately one-half to nine-sixteenths inch. These nymphs are extremely numerous in the swift gravel-bottomed reaches of those Michigan rivers, and I have seen the April currents of the Au Sable thick with miniature regattas of hatching *Ephemerella* flies.

My favorite imitation of these nymphs varies somewhat from most commercial versions, attempting to suggest the strong pale-colored banding of their tergites and gills.

Tails: Dark mottled amber, ¼ inch
Body: Dark brownish distinctly ringed, with pale amber middle tergites and amber sternites, ¼ inch
Gills: Pale yellowish amber, 1/32 inch
Thorax: Dark mottled brownish with a pale median stripe, and an amber-colored sternum, 3/16 inch
Wing cases: Dark mottled brownish, ⅛ inch
Legs: Dark amber mottled with brown, ¼ inch
Head: Dark mottled brownish, 1/32 inch

Hook: Sizes 10-14 Orvis Premium 1X long
Nylon: Medium brown 6/0 nylon
Tails: Dark barred woodduck fibers
Body: Mottled amber dubbing on yellow silk, and mottled with dark brown felt-tipped pen to suggest markings of naturals
Gills: Pale amber marabou secured with fine gold wire
Thorax: Mottled amber dubbing on yellow silk and marked with felt-tipped pen
Wing cases: Dark mottled brownish feather section tied down over thorax
Legs: Dark brown partridge fibers
Head: Medium brown nylon

There are many memories and reasons for loving this hatch and its sister *Ephemerellas*. The trout are made fully conscious of surface food by the dark little stoneflies and mayflies that usher in the season. The Hendricksons appear when the first brave leaves are budding in the trees, their rattling branches washed with yellow and rose.

The midday sun begins to have some warmth then. There are dogtooth violets in the sheltered places. Swamp maples are budding, and the blood-root is blooming when the first *Ephemerellas* are coming on the Nissequogue. Dogwood and shadbush are in blossom when the hatch finally reaches the Neversink and the Battenkill.

Some signals are found in nature nearer home. There is our local barometer of magnolia trees. Commuters on our morning trains pass the richly flowering magnolias that shelter Blair Walk, where it leads down from the Gothic arches of the Princeton campus to the railroad station. Most passengers admire their blossoms, walking on a carpet of dollar-sized petals. But the fly-fishermen feel condemned to ride the train those mornings, hiding their disappointment in the pages of the *Journal* and the *Times*, desk-bound on a day that promises Hendricksons.

Many mayflies are temperamental, emerging sporadically or completely failing to appear when all the conditions are right. The *Ephemerellas* are usually punctual and predictable. There is nothing timid about them once hatching has started, and they often come in incredible numbers. Most emerge sporadically just before noon, continuing through lunch, but the peak of the hatch comes like clockwork with the Hendricksons. The main hatches appear about half-past two. Their hatches are still remarkably heavy, because these hardy insects are surviving the damage we are inflicting on our rivers. Perhaps such hardiness means they are likely to survive as major fly hatches, and our sons can enjoy them in the future as much as our grandfathers loved them in the past.

There is something especially civilized about fishing these *Ephemerella* hatches. Fly-fishers can rise at a leisurely hour and spend a contemplative breakfast. There is time to fuss properly over tackle and dress a few extra flies. My memory and my fishing logs are filled with notes of these hatches, particularly images of trout porpoising eagerly to their emerging nymphs, and I think of them often while the November rains trickle down the windows—and the bitter February snows are sifting through the trees.

Bibliography

Adamson, W. A. *Lake and Loch Fishing for Salmon and Sea Trout*. London: Black, 1961.

Aelianus, Claudius. "De peculiari quadam piscatu indu Macedon," in *De natura animalium*. Third century A.D.

Aldam, W. H. *A Quaint Treatise on Flees and the Art of Artyfichall Flee Making*. London: 1876.

Allee, W. C., and Stein, E. R. "Light Reactions and Metabolism in Mayfly Nymphs." *Journal of Experimental Zoology* 26:423-458 (1918).

Allen, K. R. "Some Observations on the Biology of the Trout (Salmo trutta) in Windermere." *Journal of Animal Ecology* 7:333-49 (1938).

Argo, Virgil. "The North American Species of the Genus Potamanthus, with a Description of a New Species." *New York Entomological Society* 35:319-328 (1927).

Atherton, John. *The Fly and the Fish*. New York: Macmillan, 1951.

Austin, R. S. "Dry Fly Fishing on Exe and Other North Devon Streams." Manuscript, n.d.

Bainbridge, G. C. *The Fly-Fisher's Guide*. Liverpool: 1816.

Banks, Nathan. "A List of Neuropteroid Insects from North Carolina." *Proceedings of the Entomological Society of Washington* 9:151 (1908).

———. "A Synopsis, Catalogue and Bibliography of the Neuropteroid Insects of Temperate North America." *Transactions of the American Entomological Society* 19:331-332, 345-348 (1892).

———. "New Genera and Species of Nearctic Neuropteroid Insects." *Transactions of the American Entomological Society* 26:245-251 (1900).

———. "Notes on the Eastern Species of the Mayfly Genus Heptagenia." *Canadian Entomology* 42:197-202 (1910).

Barker, F. D. *An Angler's Paradise*. London: Faber & Faber, 1929.

Barker, Thomas. *The Art of Angling*. London: 1651.

———. *Barker's Delight, or the Art of Angling*. London: 1657.

318   Bartram, J. "A Further Account of Libellae or Mayflies." *Transactions of the Royal Society of London* 10:28 (1750).

Beever, John ("Arundo"). *Practical Fly Fishing*. London: 1849.

Bengtsson, Simon. "Kritische Bemerkungen ueber einige nordische Ephemeropteren, nebst beschreibung neuer Larven." *Lund Universität Archivskrift* (Sweden). 2, Bd. 26:1-27 (1936).

———. "Umdersökningar ofver äggen hos Ephemeriderna." *Entomologiske Tidskrift* (1914).

Bergman, Ray. *Just Fishing*. New York: Knopf, 1932.

———. *Trout*. New York: Knopf, 1938.

Berners, Dame Juliana. *A Treatyse of Fysshynge wyth an Angle*, in the *Boke of St. Albans*. Westminster: 1496.

Betten, Cornelius. "The Caddis Flies or Trichoptera of New York State." *New York State Museum Bulletin* 292. Albany: 1934.

Blacker, William. *The Art of Fly-Making*. London: 1843.

Blades, William F. *Fishing Flies and Fly Tying*. Harrisburg: Stackpole, 1951.

Bogoescu, Constantin. "Contributiuni la Studiul morphologic si biologic al phanerelor larrelor de Ephemerine." *Bucharest Institute de Arte Grafice E. Marva. Mircea* 10:1-100 (1932).

Bowlker, Richard and Charles. *The Art of Angling*. Worcester: M. Olivers, n.d. (c. 1746).

Bridgett, R. C. *Loch Fishing in Theory and Practice*. London: Jenkins, 1924.

Brookes, R. *The Art of Angling*. London: 1799.

Brooks, Joe. *Trout Fishing*. New York: Harper & Row, 1972.

Bucknall, Geoffrey. *Fly-Fishing Tactics on Still Water*. London: Muller, 1966.

———. *Fly-Fishing Tactics on Rivers*. London: Muller, 1968.

Burks, B. D. "The Mayflies, or Ephemeroptera, of Illinois." *University of Illinois Natural History Survey* (1953).

Carroll, W. *The Angler's Vade Mecum*. Edinburgh: 1818.

Cartwright, Rev. W. *Rambles and Recollections of a Fly-Fisher*. 1854.

Chetham, James. *The Angler's Vade Mecum*. London: 1681.

Claassen, Peter W. *Plecoptera Nymphs of America (North of Mexico)*, Vol. III. Springfield, Ill.: Say Foundation, 1931.

Clegg, J. *The Observer's Book of Pond Life*. London: Warne, 1956.

Clemens, W. A. "Mayflies of the Siphlonurus Group." *Canadian Entomology* 47: 243-260 (1915).

———. "New Species and New Life Histories of Ephemeridae or Mayflies." *Canadian Entomology* 45:246-262 (1913).

Coe, R. L., Freeman, P. and Nuttingly, P. S. *Handbook for the Identification of British Insects*. Royal Entomological Society Part 9, 2:121-206 (1950).

Colquhoun, John. *Moor and Loch*. Edinburgh: Blackwood, 1840.

Comstock, J. H. *An Introduction to Entomology*. Ithaca: Comstock, 1925.

—— and Needham, J. G. "The Wings of Insects." *American Natural History* 33:117-126 (1898).

Cotton, Charles. *The Compleat Angler, Part 2.* London: 1676.

Cross, Ruben R. *Fur, Feathers and Steel.* New York: Dodd, Mead, 1940.

——. *The Complete Fly-Tyer.* New York: Dodd, Mead, 1950.

Cutcliffe, H. C. *Trout Fishing on Rapid Streams.* South Molton: 1863.

Davis, K. C. "Sialididae of North and South America." *New York State Museum Bulletin* 68. Albany: 1903.

Dennys, John. *The Secrets of Angling.* London: 1613.

Dewar, George A. B. *The Book of the Dry Fly.* London: Black, 1910.

Dick, St. John. *Flies and Fly Fishing.* 1873.

Dodds, G. S. "Mayflies from Colorado." *Transactions of the American Entomological Society* 49:93-114 (1923).

—— and Hisaw, F. L. "Ecological Studies of Aquatic Insects." *Ecology* 5:137-148, 262-271; 6:123-137, 380-390 (1924-1925).

Dunne, J. W. *Sunshine and the Dry Fly.* London: Black, 1924.

Eaton, A. E. "A Monograph on the Ephemeridae." *Transactions of the Entomological Society,* London 1-158 (1871).

——. "A Revisional Monograph of Recent Ephemeridae or Mayflies." *Transactions of the Limnology Society of London (Zoology)* Series 2, 3 (1871).

Edmonds, Harfield H., and Lee, Norman N. *Brook and River Trouting.* Bradford: n.d. (1916).

Edmunds, F. George Jr. "Mayflies of Utah (Ephemeroptera)." University of Massachusetts, 1952 (thesis).

Flick, Art. *Streamside Guide to Naturals and Their Imitations.* New York: Putnam, 1947; Crown, 1970.

Foster, D. *The Scientific Angler.* London: Bemrose, 1882.

Fox, Charles K. *The Wonderful World of Trout.* Harrisburg: 1963.

——. *Rising Trout.* Carlisle: Foxcrest, 1967.

Fox, H. Munro, Simmonds, B. G., and Washburn, R. "Metabolic Rates of Ephemerid Nymphs from Swiftly Flowing and from Still Waters." *Journal of Experimental Biology* 12.

Fox, H. M., Wingfield, C. A., and Simmonds, B. G. "Oxygen Consumption of Ephemerid Nymphs from Flowing and from Still Waters in Relation to the Concentration of Oxygen in the Water." *Journal of Experimental Biology* 14.

Francis, Francis. *A Book on Angling.* London: Longmans Green, 1867.

Franck, Richard. *Northern Memories.* London: 1694.

Frost, W. E. "The Fauna of the Submerged Mosses in an Acid and an Alkaline Water." River Liffey Survey III. *Proceedings of the Royal Irish Academy* 47B No. 13 (1943).

Gingrich, Arnold, editor. *American Trout Fishing.* New York: Knopf, 1966.

Goddard, John. *Trout Fly Recognition.* London: Black, 1966.

Gordon, Sid. *How to Fish from Top to Bottom.* Harrisburg: Stackpole, 1955.

Gordon, Theodore. *The Complete Fly-Fisherman: The Notes and Letters of Theodore Gordon,* John McDonald, editor. New York: Scribner, 1947.

Grant, George. *The Art of Weaving Hair Hackles for Trout Flies.* Butte: 1971.

Greendrake, Gregory. *The Angling Excursions of Gregory Greendrake in the Counties of Wicklow, Meath, Westmeath, Longford and Cavan.* Dublin: n.d.

Greene, H. P. *Where Bright Waters Meet.* London: Allan, 1934.

Grove, Alvin. *The Lure and Lore of Trout Fishing.* Harrisburg: Stackpole, 1951.

Haig-Brown, Roderick. "Izaak Walton—His Friends and His Rivers." *Field & Stream* Vol. 58 No. 1 (May 1953).

Halford, Frederic M. *Floating Flies and How to Dress Them.* London: 1886.

——. *Dry Fly Fishing in Theory and Practice.* London: 1889.

——. *Dry Fly Entomology.* London: 1897.

——. *Modern Development of the Dry Fly.* London: 1910.

Hansard, G. A. *Trout and Salmon Fishing in Wales.* London: 1834.

Harding, Colonel E. W. *The Fly-Fisher and the Trout's Point of View.* London: 1931.

Harris, J. R. *An Angler's Entomology.* South Brunswick: Barnes, 1952.

Heacox, Cecil. "The Compleat Life." *Field & Stream* Vol. 58 No. 1 (May 1953).

Henzell, H. P. *The Art and Craft of Loch Fishing.* London: Allan, 1937.

Hewitt, Edward Ringwood. *Telling on the Trout.* New York: Scribner, 1926.

——. *A Trout and Salmon Fisherman for Seventy-five Years.* New York: Scribner, 1948.

Hickin, N. E. *Caddis.* London: Methuen, 1952.

——. *Caddis Larvae.* London: Hutchinson, 1967.

Hills, Major J. W. *A History of Fly-Fishing for Trout.* London: Allan, 1921.

——. *A Summer on the Test.* London: Allan, 1924.

——. *River Keeper.* London: Bles, 1934.

Hodgson, W. Earl. *How to Fish.* London: Black, 1907.

Hoffman, C. H., and others. "Field Studies on the Effect of DDT on Aquatic Insects." *U.S. Department of Agriculture, Bureau of Entomology* E-702 (1946).

Hofland, T. C. *The British Angler's Manual.* 1839.

Hsu, Yin-Chi. "Some New Morphological Findings in Ephemeroptera." *Fifth Congress of the International Entomological Society,* 1932 (1933).

Humphries, C. F. "The Chironomid Fauna of the Grober Plöner See, the Relative Density of Its Numbers and Their Emergence Period." *Archiv für Hydrobiologie* 33 (1938).

Hynes, H. B. N. "A Key to the British Species of Plecoptera (Stoneflies)." *Sci. Pub. Freshwater Biology Assn.* No. 2 (1940).

——. "A Key to the Adults and Nymphs of British Stoneflies." *Sci. Pub. Freshwater Biology Assn.* 17:1-77 (1958).

Ide, F. P. "The Effect of Temperature on the Distribution of the Mayfly Fauna of a Stream." *Biology Series 39, Ontario Fisheries Research Laboratory* 50:9-76 (1935).

———. "The Nymph of the Mayfly Genus Cinygma Eaton." *Canadian Entomology* 62:42-45 (1930).

Imms, A. D. *Outlines of Entomology.* London: Methuen, 1942.

Ivens, T. C. *Still Water Fly-fishing.* London: Deutsch, 1961.

———. "The Wet Fly in Still Water" in *The Art of Angling* 3:194-217. London: Caxton, 1957.

Jackson, John. *The Practical Fly-Fisher.* London and Leeds, 1854–1880.

Jennings, Preston J. *A Book of Trout Flies.* New York: Derrydale, 1935; Crown, 1970.

Jensen, Steven. "Mayflies of Idaho." University of Utah (thesis).

Johannsen, O. A. "Aquatic Nematocerous Diptera." *New York State Museum Bulletin* 68. Albany: 1903.

———. "Aquatic Nematocerous Diptera II." *New York State Museum Bulletin* 86. Albany: 1905.

———. "New North American Chironomidae." *New York State Museum Bulletin* 124. Albany: 1908.

———. "Aquatic Diptera." *Cornell University, Agricultural Experiment Station Memoirs,* I (1934), II (1935), III (1937).

Joly, Emile. "Études sur l'embryogénie des Éphémères notamment chez la Palingenia virgo." *Memoirs of the Academy of Science,* Toulouse 243-254 (1876).

Jordan, David Starr, and Evermann, Barton Warren. *American Food and Game Fishes.* New York: Doubleday, 1902.

Kennedy, C. H. "The Nymph of Ephemera guttulata Pictet with Notes on the Species." *Canadian Entomology* 58:61-63 (1926).

Kimmins, D. E. "Underwater Emergence of Heptagenia lateralis." *Entomologist* 74 (1941).

———. "Keys to the British Species of Ephemeroptera with Keys to the Genera of the Nymphs." *Freshwater Biology Association* No. 7 (1942).

Kite, Major Oliver. *Nymph Fishing in Practice.* London: Jenkins, 1963.

Klapalek, F. *Ephemerida die süsswasserfauna Deutschlands.* 8 vols. Jena: Fischer, 1909.

Kloet, S., and Hincks, W. D. *A Checklist of British Insects.* Stockport: 1945.

Krogh, A., and Zeuthen, E. "The Mechanism of Flight Separation in Some Insects." *Journal of Experimental Biology* 18 (1941).

La Branche, George M. L. *The Dry Fly and Fast Water.* New York: Scribner, 1914.

Lameere, A. "Etude sur l'evolution des Éphémères." *Bulletin of the Society of Zoology,* France 42:41-59, 61-81 (1917).

Lane, Jocelyn. *Lake and Loch Fishing for Trout.* London: Seeley, Service, 1954.

Lawson, William. *The Secrets of Angling.* London: n.d.

Lawrie, W. H. *English Trout Flies.* New York: A. S. Barnes, 1969.

322

Leisenring, James E., and Hidy, Vernon S. *The Art of Tying the Wet Fly and Fishing the Flymph*. New York: Crown, 1971.

Leonard, J. Edson. *Flies*. New York: Barnes, 1950.

Leonard, Justin W. and Fannie A. *Mayflies of Michigan Trout Streams*. Bloomfield Hills: Cranbrook Institute of Science, 1962.

Lestage, J. A. "Contribution à l'étude des larves des Éphémères paléarctiques." *Annals of the Biological Society Lacustre* 8:213-456 (1917).

———. "Les Éphémères de la Belgique." *Annals of the Belgian Entomological Society* 68:251-264 (1928).

Lutz, Frank E. *Field Book of Insects*. New York: Putnam, 1948.

Macan, T. T. "The Freshwater Shrimp." *Country Sportsman* 27:67-68 (1950).

———. "A Key to the Nymphs of the British Ephemeroptera." *Salmon & Trout Magazine* 143:59-70 (1955).

———, with Frost, W. E. "Corixidae as Food of Fish." *Journal of Animal Ecology* 17: 2: 174-179 (1948).

Mackintosh, Alexander. *The Driffield Angler*. 1806.

Magan, T. T. and Z. "Preliminary Notes on the Ephemeroptera and Plecoptera of the Hampshire Avon and Its Tributaries." *Journal of the Society of British Entomology* 2 (1940).

Marinaro, Vincent. *A Modern Dry-Fly Code*. New York: Putnam, 1950; Crown, 1970.

Markham, Gervase. *A Discourse of the Generall Art of Fishing with the Angle*. London: 1614.

Marston, R. B. *Walton and Some Earlier Writers on Fish and Fishing*. London: Stock, 1894.

Mascall, Leonard. *A Booke of Fishing with Hooke and Line*. London: 1590.

McClane, A. J. *The Practical Fly Fisherman*. New York: Prentice-Hall, 1953.

McDonald, John. *The Origins of Angling*. New York: Doubleday, 1963.

McDunnough, J. "New Canadian Ephemeridae with Notes." *Canadian Entomology* 55:39-50 (1923).

———. "New Ephemeridae from New England." *Boston Society of Natural History* 5:73-76 (1924).

———. "New North American Ephemeridae." *Canadian Entomology* 56:221-226 (1924).

———. "New Ephemerella Species (Ephemeroptera)." *Canadian Entomology* 57:41-43 (1925).

———. "The Bicolor Group of the Genus Ephemerella with Particular Reference to the Nymphal Stages (Ephemeroptera)." *Canadian Entomology* 63:30-42 (1931).

———. "The Genus Isonychia (Ephemeroptera)." *Canadian Entomology* 63-157-163 (1931).

———. "The Eastern North American Species of the Genus Ephemerella and Their Nymphs (Ephemeroptera)." *Canadian Entomology* 63:187-197 (1931).

Mellanby, H. *Animal Life in Fresh Water*. London: Methuen, 1938; 1963.

Miall, L. C. *Natural History of Aquatic Insects*. New York: Macmillan, 1912.

Michael, William W. *Dry-Fly Trout Fishing*. New York: McGraw Hill, 1951.

Miller, Hazen L. *The Old Au Sable*. Grand Rapids: 1963.

Milne, L. J. *Studies in North American Trichoptera*. Cambridge: 1934.

Morgan, Ann Haven. *Field Book of Ponds and Streams*. New York: Putnam, 1930.

—— and Grierson, Margaret C. "The Functions of the Gills in Burrowing May-flies (Hexagenia recurvata)." *Physiology and Zoology* 5:230-245 (1932).

Mosely, M. E. *The Dry-Fly Fisherman's Entomology*. London: Routledge, 1921.

——. *The British Caddis Flies*. London: Routledge, 1939.

Mottram, J. C. *Fly-Fishing: Some New Arts and Mysteries*. London: Field & Queen, 1915.

Murphy, E. "Notes on the Biology of Our North American Species of Mayflies." *Lloyd Library Series Bulletin, Entomology Series* No. 2. Cincinnati: 1921.

Murphy, Helen E. "Notes on the Biology of Some of Our North American Species of Mayflies." *Lloyd Library Series Bulletin, Entomology Series* No. 2: 1-46 (1922).

Neave, Ferris. "Migratory Habits of the Mayfly Blasturus cupidus." *Ecology* 11:568-576 (1930).

Needham, James G. "Ephemeridae." *New York State Museum Bulletin* 86. Albany: 1905.

——. "Plecoptera"; "Ephemerida"; "Neuroptera"; in "Aquatic Insects in the Adirondacks." *New York State Museum Bulletin* 47. Albany: 1901.

——. "Burrowing Mayflies of Our Larger Lakes and Streams." *Bureau of Fisheries Bulletin Vol. 36* (1920).

——. "Ephemeridae," in "Aquatic Insects in New York State." *New York State Museum Bulletin* 68. Albany: 1903.

——. "A New Mayfly, Caenis, from Oneida Lake, New York." *New York State College of Forestry, Technical Publication* 9 (1918).

——. "The Life History and Habits of the Mayfly from Utah." *Canadian Entomology* 59 (1927).

——. "The Rocky Mountain Species of the Mayfly Genus Ephemerella." *Annals of the Entomological Society of America* 20 (1927).

—— and Lloyd, J. T. *Life of Inland Waters*. Ithaca: Comstock, 1916.

—— and Needham, Paul R. *A Guide to the Study of Fresh-Water Biology*. New York: 1927.

——, Traver, J. R., and Hsu, Yin Chi. *Biology of Mayflies*. Ithaca: Comstock, 1935.

Needham, Paul R. *Trout Streams*. New York: Winchester Press, 1970.

——. "The Mortality of Trout." *Scientific American*, Vol. 188 No. 5 (May 1953).

Oatts, H. A. *Loch Trout*. London: Jenkins, 1948.

Ogden, James. *On Fly-Tying*. Cheltenham: 1879.

Ovington, Ray. *How to Take Trout on Wet Flies and Nymphs*. Boston: Little, Brown, 1951.

Percival, E., and Whitehead, H. "Observations on the Biology of the Mayfly Ephemera danica Mull." *Proceedings of the Leeds Philosophical Society* I (1926).

Phillips, Ernest. *Trout in Lakes and Reservoirs*. London: Longmans, Green, 1914.

Pictet, F. J. *Histoire naturelle, général, et particulière des Insectes Neuroptères, Famille des Éphémèrines*. Geneva and Paris: 1843.

Platts, W. C. *Modern Trout Fishing*. London: Black, 1938.

Pritt, T. E. *Yorkshire Trout Flies*. Leeds: Goodall & Suddick, 1885.

———. *North-Country Flies*. London: Low, 1886.

Pulman, G. P. R. *Vade Mecum of Fly-Fishing for Trout*. London and Axminster: 1841.

Quick, Jim. *Fishing the Nymph*. New York: Ronald, 1960.

Radcliffe, William. *Fishing from the Earliest Times*. London: Murray, 1921.

Rawlinson, R. "Studies on the Life History and Breeding of Ecydonurus venosus (Ephemeroptera)." *Proceedings of the Zoological Society*. London (1939).

Rhead, Louis. *American Trout Stream Insects*. New York: Stakes, 1916.

Ritz, Charles. *A Fly Fisher's Life*. New York: Winchester Press, 1969.

Ronalds, A. *The Fly-Fisher's Entomology*. London: 1836.

Rosborough, E. H. *Tying and Fishing the Fuzzy Nymphs*. Manchester: Orvis, 1969.

Rousseau, E. *Les larves et nymphes aquatiques des insectes d'Europe*. Brussels: Lebègue, 1921.

Salter, Robert. *The Modern Angler*. 1811.

Sawyer, Frank. "Two British Spurwings." *Salmon & Trout* No. 114 (1945).

———. *Keeper of the Stream*. London: Adam & Charles, 1952.

———. *Nymphs and the Trout*. London: Stanley Paul, 1958.

Schaldach, William J. *Currents and Eddies*. New York: Barnes, 1944.

Schoenemund, E. *Eintagsfliegen oder Ephemeroptera. Die Tierwelt Deutschlands und der angrenzenden Meeresteile*. Jena: Fischer, 1930.

Schwiebert, Ernest. *Matching the Hatch*. New York: Macmillan, 1955.

———. *Remembrances of Rivers Past*. New York: Macmillan, 1972.

Scotcher, George. *The Fly-Fisher's Legacy*. Chepstow: n.d.

Seeman, Theresa M. "Dragonflies, Stoneflies, and Mayflies of Southern California." *Journal of Entomology and Zoology* 19:40-51 (1927).

Shepherd, David. "Ephemerella hecuba Eaton; Description of Various Stages (Ephemerida, Baetidae)." *Canadian Entomology* 61:260-264 (1929).

Skues, G. E. M. *Minor Tactics of the Chalk Stream*. London: Black, 1910.

———. *The Way of a Trout with a Fly*. London: Black, 1921.

———. *Sidelines, Sidelights and Reflections*. London: Seeley Service, 1932.

———. *Nymph Fishing for Chalk Stream Trout*. London: Black, 1939.

———. *Silk, Fur and Feather*. London: 1950.

Smart, J. "The British Simuliidae, with Keys to the Species in the Adult, Pupal and Larval Stages." *Sci. Pub. Freshwater Biology Association* No. 9 (1944).

Smedley, Harold Hinsdill. *Fly Patterns and Their Origins*. Muskegon: 1944.

Spencer, Sidney. *The Art of Lake Fishing with Sunk Fly*. London: Witherby, 1934.

Steel, Frank R. *Fly Fishing*. Chicago: Paul, Richmond, 1946.

Steger, A. Louise. "Some Preliminary Notes on the Genus Ephemerella." *Psyche* 38:27-35 (1931).

Stewart, H. *Loch and Loch Fishing*. London: Chapman & Hall, 1899.

Stewart, W. C. *The Practical Angler*. Edinburgh: 1857.

Stoddart, Thomas. *The Art of Angling as Practised in Scotland*. Edinburgh: 1835.

Sule, K., and Javrel, L. "Ueber epoikische und parasitische Chironomid Larven." *Acta. Soc. Sci. Nat. Moravicae* 1:383-391 (1924).

Swain, Ralph B. *The Insect Guide*. New York: Doubleday, 1948.

Swammerdam, Jan. "Ephemera," in *Biblia naturae; sive Historia insectorum*, Vols. I and II. 1737.

Swisher, Doug, and Richards, Carl. *Selective Trout*. New York: Crown, 1971.

Taverner, Eric. *Trout Fishing from All Angles*. London: Seeley Service, 1929.

Taverner, John. *Certaine Experiments Concerning Fish and Fruite*. London: 1600.

Taylor, Samuel. *Angling in All Its Branches*. London: 1809.

Theakston, Michael. *British Angling Flies*. Ripon: Low, 1883.

Thompson, Leslie P. *Fishing in New England*. New York: Van Nostrand, 1955.

Tillyard, R. J. "The Wing-Venation of the Order Plectoptera or Mayflies." *J. Linn. Soc. London* (Zool.) 35:143-162 (1923).

Timmins, D. E. "A Revised Key to the Adults of the British Species of Ephemeroptera." *Sci. Pub. of the Freshwater Biology Assn.* 15:1-68 (1954).

Traver, J. R. "Observations on the Ecology of the Mayfly Blasturus cupidus." *Canadian Entomology* 57:211-218 (1925).

———. "Seven New Southern Species of the Mayfly Genus Hexagenia, with Notes on the Genus." *Annals of the Entomological Society of America* 24:59-1620 (1931).

———. "The Ephemerid Genus Baetisca." *Journal of the New York Entomological Society* 39:45-66 (1931).

———. "Mayflies of North Carolina." *J. Elisha Mitchell Scientific Society* 47:85-236 (1932).

Turton, John. *The Angler's Manual*. 1836.

Ulmer, G. "Eintagsfliegen (Ephemeroptera)" in Brohmer, Ehrmann, and Ulmer, *Die Tierwelt Mitteleuropas*, Vol. lv. Leipzig: 1929.

———. "Uebersicht ueber die Gattungen der Ephemeropteren, nebst Bemerkungen ueber einzelne Arten." *Stettin Entomologische Zeitschrift* 81:97-144 (1920).

Usinger, Robert L. *Aquatic Insects of California*. Berkeley and Los Angeles: University of California, 1918.

Vavon, Antoine. *La truite et ses moeurs et l'art de sa pécher*. 1927.

Vayssière, Albert. "Recherches sur l'organisation des larves des Éphémèrines." *Ann. Sci. Nat. Zool.* (10) 17:381-406 (1882).

Venables, Robert. *The Experienced Angler*. London: 1662.

Wade, Henry. *Halcyon*. London: 1861.

326

Walker, C. F. *Lake Flies and Their Imitations*. London: Jenkins, 1960.

Walley, G. S. "Review of Ephemerella Nymphs of Western North America (Ephemeroptera)." *Canadian Entomology* 62:12-20.

Walls, G. L. *The Vertebrate Eye, and Its Adaptive Radiation*. Michigan: Cranbrook Institute of Science, 1942.

Walton, Izaak. *The Compleat Angler*. London: Rich, Marriot, 1653.

Ward, H. B., and Whipple, G. C. *Fresh Water Biology*. New York: Wiley, 1918.

Webster, David. *The Angler and the Loop Rod*. Edinburgh: Blackwood, 1885.

Welch, P. S. *Limnology*. New York: McGraw-Hill, 1935.

West, Leonard. *The Natural Trout Fly and Its Imitation*. Liverpool: Potter, 1921.

Westwood, J. O. "Ephemeridae" in *An Introduction to the Modern Classification of Insects*. London: n.d.

Wetzel, Charles M. *Practical Fly-Fishing*. Boston: Christopher, 1943.

———. *Trout Flies*. Harrisburg: Stackpole, 1955.

Wheatley, Hewett. *The Rod and Line*. London: 1849.

Whitney, R. J. "Thermal Resistance of Mayfly Nymphs from Ponds and Streams." *Journal of Experimental Biology* 16 (1939).

Wigglesworth, V. B. *Insect Physiology*. London: Methuen, 1934.

Wingfield, C. A. "Function of Gills of Mayfly Nymphs." *Journal of Experimental Biology* 16 (1939).

Younger, John. *On River Angling for Salmon and Trout*. Edinburgh: 1840.

Zim, Herbert S., and Cottam, Clarence. *Insects*. New York: Simon and Schuster, 1956.

Zimmerman, O. "Ueber eine eigentümliche Bildung der Ruckengefässes bei enigen Ephemeriden Larven." *Zeitung für zoologische Wissenschaft* 34:404-406.

Index

sanguinea, 268
semicolorata, 267
Rhode Island, 214
Rhyacophila basalis, 83-84, 93
  bifila, 81, 93
  coloradensis, 81-82, 93
  fenestra, 83
  grandis, 81, 93
  hyalinata, 81
  lobifera, 83-84, 93
  pacifica, 81, 93
  wyaynata, 93
Rice, James, 68
Richards, Carl, 14, 24, 186, 226, 229, 312
Riffle-Burrowing Dragonfly Nymph, 151
Riffle Crane Fly Larva, 103
Riffle Dragonfly Nymph, 150
Riffle Smuts, 108
Rifle River, Michigan, 296
Rikhoff, James, 65-67, 208
Ritz, Charles, 15, 28, 35
Rio Grande River, Colorado, 45
River Angling (Younger), 8
Roaring Fork River, Colorado, 37, 93, 111, 224
Rock Creek, Colorado, 120
Rocky Mountains, 40, 46, 49, 53, 60, 63-64,
  74-75, 77, 79-81, 102, 112, 133, 138, 156-
  157, 159, 161, 166, 194, 199, 201-203,
  209, 214, 221, 223-224, 227, 229, 239,
  241, 254, 258, 260, 273, 276, 293, 306,
  309, 312
Rogowski, Ted, 24, 279
Rolling Rock, 280
Ronalds, Alfred, 8, 10, 17, 21, 110
Roosevelt, Theodore, 250
Rosborough, E. H., 24, 46, 64, 190, 210, 260,
  279
Rose, David, 217-218, 252
Ross, Charlie, 250-251, 253
Rouen, France, 292
Ruby River, Montana, 37
Ruedi, Colorado, 48, 166, 223

Saginaw Bay, Michigan, 296
Saint Helen, Lake, Michigan, 294
Sainte Ignace, Michigan, 234-235
Saint Louis, Missouri, 235
Salisbury, Wiltshire, England, 11, 15, 28
Salisbury Cathedral, 11
Salvelinus fontinalis, 28, 192
Sand Gnats, 107
Sangre de Cristo Mountains, Colorado, 153
San Gabriel Mountains, California, 304
San Jacinto Mountains, California, 201
Saranac River, New York, 165, 255, 294
Sault Sainte Marie, Michigan, 234
Sausalito, California, 183
Savannah, Georgia, 178
Sawkill River, Pennsylvania, 82
Sawyer, Frank, 15-16, 18, 28, 244
Sayre, R. J., 68
Scaly Mountain, North Carolina, 178
Schmidsmühlen, Germany, 1-2
Schoharie River, New York, 21-22, 51, 64, 66,
  164, 179, 208, 213, 314
Schoolcraft, Henry, 294
Scientific Anglers System 8 (reel), 33
Scotcher, George, 7
Scotland, 110
Scott's Lodge, North Branch of the Au Sable,
  Michigan, 295
Scrope, William, 73
Secrets of Angling (Dennys), 5

Selective Trout (Swisher and Richards), 14,
  24-25, 186, 226, 229, 312
Sens, Edward, 23-24, 75, 266
Sepia Damselfly Nymph, 157
Seven Castles Pool, Frying Pan River, Colo-
  rado, 82
Shakespeare, William, 295
Shellenbarger, Charles, 298
Shinhopple, New York, 179
Shooting Creek, North Carolina, 178
Shoppenagons, David, Chief of the Saginaw
  Indians, 297
Shropshire, England, 5-6, 13, 60, 220
Shushan, New York, 52
Sialis infumata, 143
Sidelines, Sidelights and Reflections (Skues),
  15
Sierra Nevada Mountains, California, 77
Silk, Fur and Feathers (Skues), 15
Silvercliff, Colorado, 153
Silver Creek, Idaho, 133, 247, 312
Simulium arcticus, 108
  hirtipes, 108
  piperi, 108
  tuberosum, 108
Siphlonurus alternatus, 185
  barbarus, 186
  mirus, 186
  occidentalis, 187
  phyllis, 188
  quebecensis, 188
  rapidus, 189
  spectabilis, 189
Siphloplecton basale, 190-191
  signatum, 190
Skues, George Edward Mackenzie, 9-28, 106,
  183, 244, 314
Slant Rock Pool, Ausable River, New York,
  265
Slate Run, Pennsylvania, 204
Slide Pool, Brodheads Creek, Pennsylvania,
  253
Slough Creek, Yellowstone Park, 216
Small Spotted Sedge, 77
Smith Bridge, South Branch of the Au Sable,
  Michigan, 294
Smith, Lodie, 68, 250
Smoky Mountains, North Carolina, 52, 167,
  172-173, 178, 257
Snake River, Wyoming, 216, 226, 293, 310
Snedecor, Abraham, 68
Snedecor, J. L., 68
Snipe and Yellow, 96
Snipe Fly Larva, 104
Soldier Fly Larva, 104
South Carolina, 101, 200, 283, 313-314
South Park, Colorado, 99, 224
South Platte River, Colorado, 53, 64, 99-100,
  112, 133, 187, 216, 221, 223
Sparse Grey Hackle, 68
Speckled Olive Damselfly Nymph, 158
Speckled Peter, 76
Spencer, Sidney, 16
Spring Creek, Bellefonte, Pennsylvania, 163-
  164, 188
Springfield, Ohio, 246
Spruce Cabin Inn, Brodheads Creek, Pennsyl-
  vania, 23
Spruce Creek, Pennsylvania, 164, 189
Starling and Brown, 8
Starling Spider, 8
Stauffenburg, Count Klaus von, 161
Stauffer, Chip, 21-23